PEARL HARBOR:

The Verdict of History

ALSO BY GORDON W. PRANGE

AT DAWN WE SLEPT
with Donald M. Goldstein and Katherine V. Dillon
MIRACLE AT MIDWAY
with Donald M. Goldstein and Katherine V. Dillon
TARGET TOKYO
with Donald M. Goldstein and Katherine V. Dillon

PEARL HARBOR:

The Verdict of History

GORDON W. PRANGE
WITH
Donald M. Goldstein
and Katherine V. Dillon

McGraw-Hill Book Company

New York   St. Louis   San Francisco   Bogotá   Guatemala
Hamburg   Lisbon   Madrid   Mexico   Montreal   Panama   Paris
San Juan   São Paulo   Tokyo   Toronto

1 2 3 4 5 6 7 8 9 D O C D O C 8 7 6 5

ISBN 0-07-050668-X

LIBRARY OF CONGRESS CATALOGING IN PUBLICATION DATA

Prange, Gordon William, 1910–1980
Pearl Harbor : the verdict of history.
Bibliography: p.
Includes index.
1. Pearl Harbor (Hawaii), Attack on, 1941.
I. Goldstein, Donald M.   II. Dillon, Katherine V.
III. Title.
D767.92.P722   94 54'26   85-13961
ISBN 0-07-050668-X

CONTENTS

Part III: FIELD COMMANDERS AND OPERATORS

Part IV: THE VIEW FROM THE CROW'S NEST

Appendices

INTRODUCTION

This volume is the story not of Pearl Harbor but of the responsibility for Pearl Harbor. It deals not with action but with reaction. No book on this subject has ever given such complete coverage to the acts, failures to act, and the mental attitudes that made the Japanese attack on Pearl Harbor possible and successful.

Gordon Prange considered this book the most highly personal of his work. In his other volumes, the chronology and momentum of events assisted him; here he relied largely upon his own thoughts and analyses. The undersigned have participated in this project more directly than in its three predecessors, however.

Prange intended this book to be the fourth of a projected tetralogy about the Pearl Harbor attack. When his massive study was condensed into a single volume (*At Dawn We Slept*), space permitted use of only a very few items extracted from Prange's original Volume IV. The basic manuscript presupposed that the reader would be fully aware of the actions and backgrounds. In order that this book might stand on its own, we had to make certain insertions in the text to explain the meaning of terms and references, and to introduce key personnel.

To determine whether or not Prange's concepts were still valid, in view of much heralded "new material," we examined thousands of Magic diplomatic messages in the National Archives, declassified and released in 1978. We found that none of these "new" documents added anything substantial on the subject of Pearl Harbor, cast any shadow upon the logic of Prange's conclusions, or caused us to revise any of his findings. In fact, the most significant of these messages have been available for years, having been reproduced in the records of the joint congressional committee that met in 1945–46. In addition, the Department of Defense published them in 1977 in a series of volumes entitled *The Magic Background of Pearl Harbor*. In footnoting these messages we have used the published source rather than the National Archives citations, both because those sources are readily available to interested scholars who might not be able to visit the National Archives, and because we do not wish to convey the impression that these are new discoveries when they have long been in the public domain.

Certain references throughout the volume to works published since Prange's death, such as John Toland's *Infamy*, are of course our work. We believe ourselves justified in making these insertions, because (1) if Prange were living, he certainly would have done so, and (2) it helps to bring the book up to date.

The Prologue is ours, and serves as a very brief reminder of what happened at Pearl Harbor—after four and a half decades a surprising number of people need the reminder—and of the many questions the attack raised and which this book addresses.

We have also inserted a chapter that was largely Prange's work, but which was not originally in his Volume IV. This discusses the events of December 8, 1941 (local time) in the Philippines. Hawaii's was not the only military establishment taken by surprise. Although MacArthur's headquarters had been notified of the attack on Pearl Harbor, the Japanese caught the American planes on the ground at Clark Field just as they did on Oahu.

We wrote the chapter on the "Winds" controversy. Prange decided, after meticulous checking, that this whole subject was irrelevant, and that receipt or nonreceipt of a "winds execute" message would not have affected the issue at Pearl Harbor one way or the other. Therefore, he did not want to devote precious time and space to an unprofitable subject. We agree with his judgment, but in view of the clouds of rumor, misunderstanding, and controversy that still surround this subject, we felt obligated to deal with it.

A related subject is the revisionist anti-Roosevelt thesis. *At Dawn We Slept* covered this subject briefly; however, the keen interest demonstrated in it whenever Goldstein participated in a talk show or open-end radio program revealed that the question is far from resolved in the public mind. Indeed, opinions were about evenly divided between pro and con. So we decided to retain Prange's chapters on revisionism and to expand them to include consideration of such recent works as *Infamy*.

Although the book is divided as indicated below, we have dealt with individual subjects on a chapter-by-chapter basis. Thus the reader of specialized interest need not necessarily read the whole book, although of course such a perusal would give an overview of the entire matter of Pearl Harbor. But anyone who is primarily interested in a single topic, or who becomes intrigued with any of the provocative questions contained in the Prologue—"winds," radar, revisionism, diplomacy, the War and Navy departments, the military establishment on Oahu, etc.—can readily find what we had to say on that subject centralized in the appropriate chapter or chapters. To assist the reader, we have headed each chapter with a brief summation of its contents.

Verdict of History is divided into four parts. Part I, "The Base and the Summit," touches upon the American people as a whole— their attitude between wars, their reluctance to admit that the Axis nations posed any danger to the United States. It proceeds to the role of the Congress, which had the power of authorization and to act without presidential consent. This section considers the issue of isolationism and America First, whose most prominent advocate was Charles A. Lindbergh. Many members of Congress were isolationists, and this played a part in the legislative problems of 1941.

At the White House level, the book deals with the revisionist school of historians whose position is that Roosevelt knew the Japanese were headed for Pearl Harbor and deliberately withheld information from the Army and Navy on Oahu to ensure the attack would come in unopposed. Prange could not credit this thesis, and in this volume took pains to refute it on the basis of solid scholarship. By the same token, he did not assume that Roosevelt was beyond criticism; hence this portion of the book presents instances where the President might have been ill-advised, and where more dynamic leadership on his part might have been desirable.

Part II, "Advisers, Planners, and Chiefs," considers first the role of the cabinet, particularly the three members most involved, namely, Secretary of State Cordell Hull, Secretary of War Henry L. Stimson, and Secretary of the Navy Frank Knox. In dealing with Hull, the book discusses the most controversial incidents in the diplomatic conversations with Japan during 1941—the economic embargo of the summer, the so-called modus vivendi, and the Hull Note, all in the context of the talks under way and Japan's actions taking place at the same time.

This section also devotes careful consideration to the Washington level immediately below the cabinet secretaries—the Chief of Staff of the Army, General George C. Marshall; the Chief of Naval Operations, Admiral Harold R. Stark; and their staffs, with special reference to their respective war plans officers, Brigadier General Leonard T. Gerow and Rear Admiral Richmond Kelly Turner. Here the book touches upon the controversy surrounding the director of the FBI, J. Edgar Hoover. This section ends with a chapter concerning the famous "winds" code and whether or not a "winds execute" message was ever received in Washington.

Part III, "Field Commanders and Operators," covers the responsibilities of the military establishment on Oahu. This section devotes three chapters to Lieutenant General Walter C. Short, who as commanding general, Hawaiian Department, was charged with the primary mission of protecting the U.S. Pacific Fleet at moorings in Pearl Harbor. Two chapters break fresh ground in analyzing the position of Rear Admiral Claude C. Bloch, whom most studies of Pearl Harbor barely mention. Yet he was on the same command level as Short, and was responsible for implementing the Navy's plans for the defense of Oahu. Finally, this section covers Admiral Husband E. Kimmel, Commander in Chief, United States Fleet, who as senior naval officer present drew much of the lightning of criticism.

Part IV, "The View from the Crow's Nest," begins with a brief consideration of events in the Philippines on the first day of combat. This section also stresses that, regardless of American major and minor mistakes, the Japanese owed their success at Pearl Harbor to their own exhaustive tactical plans, preparations, training, technological breakthroughs, and a large portion of luck. However, their overall strategy was considerably less admirable and led to their ultimate defeat.

Chapter 31 deals with what Prange considered the root of the problem in the United States—the failure of all concerned to believe that a Japanese attack on Pearl Harbor was possible, much less that it could succeed.

Pearl Harbor had results both immediate and far-reaching, and the next chapter considers how its reverberations still sound in modern ears, while cautioning against considering Pearl Harbor the cause of every international development from December 1941 onwards. The book closes with a chapter expounding the lessons the United States learned—or *should* have learned—at Pearl Harbor. Prange admired the analysis of those lessons which Edward P. Morgan worked out for the congressional committee which investigated Pearl Harbor, and used Morgan's categories as an outline which he filled in with his own ideas. Prange devoted much time and thought to this chapter, for he believed that the lessons of Pearl Harbor were universal and timeless, and therefore to be remembered and acted upon.

Many writers have treated the military aspects of the Pearl Harbor story as almost extraneous. Prange recognized that, on the contrary, Pearl Harbor was a military problem. The Hawaiian Department, the Fourteenth Naval District, and the U.S. Pacific Fleet were obligated to be alert in their own areas, regardless of the diplomatic situation in Washington. And no amount of political maneuvering in either Washington or Tokyo could have made the attack a success; that depended upon the Japanese Navy.

Over the years, many Americans have seemed less interested in asking themselves "How could Pearl Harbor have been prevented? What mistakes were made and how can we avoid them in the future?" than in finding out "Whom can we hang?" What a relief it would be if one individual, or two, could take the rap so that everyone else could relax in the comfortable consciousness of "no fault"!

Very shortly after beginning to delve into the American side of Pearl Harbor, Prange found that the question was not that simple. After dozens of interviews with Pearl Harbor survivors and others who had been in positions of responsibility at the time, plus many years of documentary research, he reached two conclusions: There were no Pearl Harbor villains; there were no Pearl Harbor scapegoats. No one directly concerned was without blame, from Roosevelt on down the line. They all made mistakes.

In some ways this was not an easy position for Prange to take, because a number of those concerned had given him interviews, and he liked them personally. But the subject was too important for him to allow personalities to affect his judgment. He believed most firmly that those errors should be analyzed and remembered, so that future generations might ponder them and learn from them. And that was his purpose in writing his book.

DONALD M. GOLDSTEIN, PH. D.
*Associate Professor of Public
    and International Affairs
University of Pittsburgh
Pittsburgh, Pennsylvania*

KATHERINE V. DILLON
CWO, USAF (Ret.)
Arlington, Virginia

In the perspective of history, the span of forty-five years is only a flash. But it is a long time in the life of an individual. Those who today "remember Pearl Harbor" as a direct experience have attained "senior citizen" status. Yet the subject continues to fascinate. Why?

No doubt one reason is the irrational but undeniable glamour of defeat. Americans like to win, but they remember and sympathize with their losers. There is no Northern counterpart of *Gone with the Wind*. Another factor that keeps Pearl Harbor a living issue is the puzzle factor. The merciful years have erased much of the pain and anger, but the puzzle remains, an eternal doublecrostic where the clues help fill in the story and the story helps provide the clues.

Instead of clarifying the subject, the years have compounded the problem. It is difficult for a member of the post–World War II generations to visualize a world in which Japan was not an industrial giant, a world where the Japanese challenged the West, not as today with automobiles, television sets, and computers, but with tanks, guns, and warships. It is equally difficult to realize that in 1941 the United States armed forces were little more than a cadre to be fleshed out by draftees, if war came. And in the summer of 1941, with a world war raging, the Congress came within one vote of scuttling the draft.

To understand Pearl Harbor even partially, and to evaluate intelligently the mistakes and misapprehensions on the American side which so unwittingly and ironically contributed to the Japanese victory and achievement of surprise, one should consider the event in the context of the society, technology, ideas, and leadership of the day in both the United States and Japan. Following are a few points to keep in mind which the reader may find helpful:

Japan was a racially homogeneous society which only recently had been what today would be called an "emerging nation." A provision of law which made mandatory that the ministers of war and the navy be flag officers on active duty gave the military a stranglehold on the national government. As a result, the armed forces called the tune, and enormous prestige clung to the military. The highest honor to which a young Japanese male could aspire was selection to the Army or Naval Academy. The soldier was the public ideal of patriotism, of honor, of machismo. The individual civilian counted for little. The system conceived of the people as existing to support the state. They were expected to endure any privation necessary to achieve the national expansionist aims about which they had no say.

In contrast, the United States was a racially mixed society with a thriving economy and a bone-deep belief in the supremacy of the civil arm over the military. From its founding, the United States feared the idea of a professional military class, and put its trust in the "civilian soldier." The regular army and navy were tolerated rather than honored. With a few notable exceptions, "the best and the brightest" went into business, the sciences, and the professions rather than into the armed forces. In 1941, as now, the very root of United States society was the concept of the state as the servant of the people.

At the time of the Pearl Harbor attack, to many Americans the label "Made in Japan" was almost a guarantee of shoddiness. But Japan cared little about consumer goods; much of the national treasure and expertise went into war matériel. It lacked such refinements as the Norden bombsight and had not developed radar. But Japan's torpedoes worked, and its warships were comparable to foreign vessels of their class. Combat aircraft were flimsy by Western standards, lacking armor and self-sealing fuel tanks designed to protect the crews. This was because, in Japanese eyes, men were readily expendable; speed and maneuverability were not. In research and procurement, money was no object; what the military wanted, the military got. Technologically speaking, Japan's soft spot was the lack of raw materials to manufacture armaments and of the oil to keep them running.

In this same period, American military equipment would have been a national scandal had the people really cared. The beginning of World War II found the U.S. Army seventeenth in the world in terms of strength. All too often, maneuvers found the troops drilling with broomsticks, the mechanical cavalry using jeeps marked "tank." If a torpedo exploded on contact, this was considered a real feat. The armed forces had to wring the last minute of life out of obsolescent ships, planes, and ordnance, because for years appropriations had been frustratingly sparse. The United States' strength was in the area of Japan's weakness—plentiful raw materials and oil, or ready access to them.

Japan was somewhat paranoid in this period. Spy-consciousness was almost a mania, and security-consciousness virtually an article of faith. The seas around the home islands gave the Japanese a sense of claustrophobia, and they considered themselves surrounded by menacing enemies, not the least of which was the United States. The necessity to break out of this imaginary circle, the need for raw materials, and a high birth rate—which Japan deliberately encouraged as did the Nazis—formed the rationale for an expansionist program. The Japanese honestly believed themselves divinely appointed to rule all Asia. Their navy was still a battleship navy, and Yamamoto was a battleship admiral, but he was sufficiently flexible to authorize the formation of the First Air Fleet, the carrier force around which the Pearl Harbor attack force would be built.

Far from being expansionists, most Americans asked for nothing but to be left alone within their own borders. Instead of feeling boxed in by the Atlantic and Pacific, many Americans considered those oceans protective barriers. They had no mystic sense of inherent mission, but they had a very good opinion of themselves. The United States was the biggest and the best and the richest and the toughest, so Japan would never dare strike it, and a Japanese spy was a comic notion. In some respects, the military was overenthusiastic—they expected miracles of the B-17 four-engine bomber—but all too often resisted new ideas. The misuse of radar on Oahu was a case in point. Moreover, the aircraft carrier did not really come into its own until after the battles of the Coral Sea and Midway in 1942. Thus the idea set forth by some of Roosevelt's critics—that he had ordered the carriers out of Pearl Harbor to save them from the Japanese attack he wanted and expected—is based upon twin misconceptions. Few outside of the naval air arm itself realized the potential of this weapon, and the carrier missions in question were fully under the control of

the Commander in Chief, U.S. Pacific Fleet, who established the
sailing dates and could have canceled the missions had he so desired.

Japan had some good men in high positions in her Navy—Yamamoto was possibly the most charismatic, daring admiral afloat in
1941—and would have had more of them except for a strange tradition
which held that after an officer reached a certain position, he exercised
less of his responsibilities and his subordinates took over. In the case
of Operation Hawaii, the original idea was Yamamoto's, but the creative mind behind it was that of a commander, Minoru Genda. In
the development of great military leaders, Japan was handicapped
not for lack of material, but by a national tendency to value conformity
over originality.

In the United States, almost never has the general or the admiral
who was expected to lead in battle actually done so. The leader has
emerged under the pressure of combat, and sometimes he has been
a most unlikely prospect. Fortunately, in the services as elsewhere,
there has been nothing to prevent anyone from rising by his boot-
straps, and so the United States was able to take advantage of these
bonuses of fate. At times, however, channels have been unyielding,
and the junior with ideas has found it difficult to catch the ear of his
seniors. Pearl Harbor demonstrated both the favorable and unfavorable aspects of the American armed forces. The Hawaiian Department, in particular, did not seem to encourage its young men to
question the judgment of their superiors, while the actual combat
conditions brought out many an example of initiative and bravery.

Thus, while Pearl Harbor was not in itself the cradle of great
leaders, it did create the climate that sped the search for new men
in top positions, and hence indirectly gave the United States such
stars as Admirals Chester W. Nimitz, Raymond A. Spruance, and
William F. Halsey.

Here, then, in very sketchy outline, were the antagonists who
faced each other across the Pacific in 1941.

During his quest to understand the Japanese aspects of all his
projects, including his Pearl Harbor study, Prange turned many times
to one particular Japanese. In what turned out to be Prange's last
address to his fellow members of the University of Maryland, he paid
tribute to this man who had been "like a brother' to him over the
years. We have met this gentleman, who is one of the leading Japanese
authorities, if not *the* leading one, on the Pacific war, and we un-

derstand why Prange thought so highly of him. We are sure that, if Prange were here to do so, he would dedicate this book, in gratitude and affection, to Masataka Chihaya, scholar, gentleman, officer, and loyal friend.

LIST OF MAJOR
PERSONNEL

Name	Position
Arnold, Maj. Gen. Henry H.	Commanding general, Army Air Forces
Barnes, Harry Elmer	Historian
Bellinger, RADM. Patrick N. L.	Commander, Patrol Wing Two
Bloch, RADM. Claude C.	Commandant, Fourteenth Naval District
Bratton, Col. Rufus S.	Chief, Far Eastern Section, G-2
Brewster, Owen	Senator from Maine; member, joint congressional committee
Chamberlin, William Henry	Historian
Churchill, Winston S.	Prime Minister, Great Britain
Clausen, Lt. Col. Henry C.	Assistant recorder, Army board; conducted follow-up inquiry
Davis, Cmdr. Arthur C.	Aviation officer, U.S. Pacific Fleet
Dunlop, Col. Robert H.	Adjutant general, Hawaiian Department
Farthing, Col. William E.	Commanding officer, Fifth Bomb Group
Ferguson, Homer	Senator from Michigan; member, joint congressional committee
Fielder, Lt. Col. Kendall J.	G-2, Hawaiian Department
Flynn, John T.	Historian
Forrestal, James V.	Secretary of the Navy, May 1944–September 1947
Frank, Maj. Gen. Walter H.	Member, Army Board
Fuchida, Cmdr. Mitsuo	Leader, air attack on Pearl Harbor
Fukudome, VADM. Shigeru	Chief of staff, Combined Fleet, November 1939–April 10, 1941; then Chief, First Bureau, Naval General Staff.

Furlong, RADM. William R. Commander, Minecraft, Battle Force, U.S. Pacific Fleet

Gearhart, Bertrand W. Congressman from California; member, joint congressional committee

Genda, Cmdr. Minoru Air staff officer, First Air Fleet

Gerow, Brig. Gen. Leonard T. Chief, War Plans Division, War Department

Greaves, Percy L., Jr. Historian

Grew, Joseph C. U.S. ambassador to Japan

Grunert, Lt. Gen. George Chairman, Army Board

Halsey, VADM. William F. Commander, Aircraft, Battle Force

Hart, Adm. Thomas C. Commander in Chief, U.S. Asiatic Fleet; conducted inquiry

Herron, Lt. Gen. Charles D. Commanding general, Hawaiian Department, 1940

Hewitt, VADM. H. Kent Conducted follow-up inquiry

Hitler, Adolf Führer of Germany

Hoover, J. Edgar Director, Federal Bureau of Investigation

Hornbeck, Dr. Stanley K. Far Eastern expert, State Department

Hull, Cordell Secretary of state

Ickes, Harold L. Secretary of the interior

Ingersoll, RADM. Royal E. Assistant Chief of Naval Operations

Keefe, Frank B. Congressman from Wisconsin; member, joint congressional committee

Kimmel, Adm. Husband E. Commander in Chief, U.S. Pacific Fleet

King, Adm. Ernest J. Commander in Chief, U.S. Atlantic Fleet; later Commander in Chief, United States Fleet

Knox, Frank Secretary of the navy

Konoye, Prince Fumimaro Premier of Japan, July 1940–October 1941

Kramer, Lt. Cmdr. Alwin D. On loan from Far Eastern Section, ONI, to Translation Section, Communications Division, Navy Department

Kurusu, Saburo Special envoy to Washington

Kusaka, RADM. Ryunosuke Chief of staff, First Air Fleet

Layton, Lt. Cmdr. Edwin T. Intelligence officer, U.S. Pacific Fleet

Lucas, Scott W. Senator from Illinois; member, joint congressional committee

MacArthur, Maj. Gen. Douglas Commanding general, U.S. Army Forces Far East

Marshall, General George C. Chief of Staff, U.S. Army

Martin, Maj. Gen. Frederick L.	Commanding general, Hawaiian Air Force
McCollum, Cmdr. Arthur H.	Chief, Far Eastern Section, ONI
Miles, Brig. Gen. Sherman	Acting ACS/Intelligence, War Department
Mollison, Brig. Gen. James A.	Chief of staff, Hawaiian Air Force
Morgan, Edward P.	Assistant counsel, joint congressional committee
Morgenstern, George	Historian
Morgenthau, Henry, Jr.	Secretary of the treasury
Murphy, John W.	Congressman from Pennsylvania; member, joint congressional committee
Nagano, Adm. Osami	Chief, Naval General Staff
Nagumo, VADM. Chuichi	Commander in Chief, First Air Fleet
Nimitz, Adm. Chester W.	Commander in Chief, U.S. Pacific Fleet (from December 31, 1941)
Nomura, Adm. Kichisaburo	Ambassador to the United States
Noyes, RADM. Leigh H.	Chief, Communications Division, Navy Department
Phillips, Lt. Col. Walter C.	Chief of staff, Hawaiian Department
Pogue, Forrest C.	Historian
Poindexter, Joseph B.	Governor, Territory of Hawaii
Pratt, Adm. William V.	Former Chief of Naval Operations
Pye, VADM. William S.	Commander, Battle Force, U.S. Pacific Fleet
Ramsey, Lt. Cmdr. Logan C.	Operations officer under Bellinger
Richardson, Adm. James O.	Commander in Chief, U.S. Fleet, 1940
Roberts, Owen J.	Associate Justice, U.S. Supreme Court; chairman, Roberts Commission
Rochefort, Cmdr. Joseph J.	Chief, Communications Intelligence Unit, Fourteenth Naval District
Roosevelt, Franklin D.	President of the United States
Rudolph, Brig. Gen. Jacob H.	Commanding General, Eighteenth Bombardment Wing
Russell, Maj. Gen. Henry D.	Member, Army board
Sadtler, Col. Otis K.	Chief, Military Branch, Signal Corps
Safford, Cmdr. Laurence F.	Chief, Security Section, Communications Division, Navy Department
Short, Lt. Gen. Walter C.	Commanding general, Hawaiian Department
Smith, Capt. William Ward	Chief of staff, U.S. Pacific Fleet
Spruance, RADM. Raymond A.	Commander, Fifth Cruiser Division, December 1941
Stark, Adm. Harold R.	Chief of Naval Operations
Stimson, Henry L.	Secretary of war

Theobald, RADM. Robert A.	Assisted Kimmel at Roberts inquiry
Toland, John	Historian
Turner, RADM. Richmond Kelly	Chief, War Plans Division, Navy Department
Welles, Sumner	Undersecretary of state
Wilkinson, Capt. Theodore S.	Director of Naval Intelligence
Yamamoto, Admiral Isoroku	Commander in chief, Combined Fleet
Yoshikawa, Takeo	Chancellor, Honolulu consulate

ABBREVIATIONS

AA	Antiaircraft
ABC 1	American-British-Canadian military agreement of March 1941
ABCD powers	American-British-Chinese-Dutch
Abwehr	German Military Intelligence
AC/S	Assistant Chief of Staff
ADB	American-Dutch-British proposed agreement of April 1941
AWS	Aircraft Warning Service
BuDocks	Bureau of Yards and Docks
BuNav	Bureau of Navigation
CinCAF	Commander in Chief, Asiatic Fleet
CinCLANT	Commander in Chief, Atlantic Fleet
CinCPAC	Commander in Chief, Pacific Fleet
CinCUS	Commander in Chief, United States Fleet
CNO	Chief of Naval Operations
Com 14	Commandant, Fourteenth Naval District
CPO	Chief Petty Officer
DIO	District Intelligence Office
DIP	Diplomatic
FBI	Federal Bureau of Investigations
FCC	Federal Communications Commission
G-1	Personnel
G-2	Intelligence
G-3	Operations
G-4	Supply
GMT	Greenwich Mean Time
JAG	Judge Advocate General
JCD-42	Joint Coastal Frontier Defense Plan
JD 19	A Japanese diplomatic code
LA	A Japanese diplomatic code
MS	Monitoring Station

NA	National Archives
OIC	Officer in Charge
ONI	Office of Naval Intelligence
OPNAV	Naval Operations
Op-20-G	Security Section, Naval Communications
PA-K2	A Japanese diplomatic code
Reurad	Reference your radio
RG	Record Group
SIS	Signal Intelligence Service
USAFFE	United States Army Forces in the Far East
WAC	Women's Army Corps
WPL-46	The U.S. Navy's current war plan (Rainbow Five)
WPPac-46	The U.S. Pacific Fleet's current war plan

SIMPLIFIED CHART OF EXECUTIVE BRANCH

As of December 7, 1941

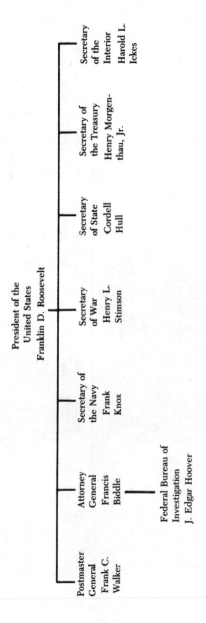

President of the
United States
Franklin D. Roosevelt

Postmaster
General
Frank C.
Walker

Attorney
General
Francis
Biddle

Federal Bureau of
Investigation
J. Edgar Hoover

Secretary of
the Navy
Frank
Knox

Secretary
of War
Henry L.
Stimson

Secretary
of State
Cordell
Hull

Secretary of
the Treasury
Henry Morgen-
thau, Jr.

Secretary
of the
Interior
Harold L.
Ickes

SIMPLIFIED CHART OF NAVY DEPARTMENT

As of December 7, 1941

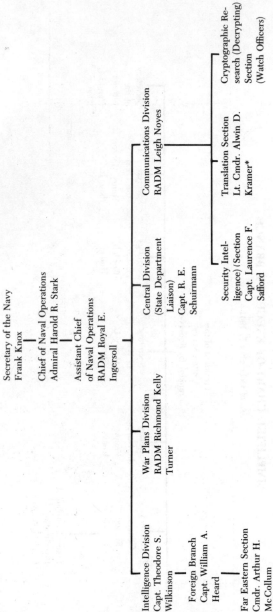

Secretary of the Navy
Frank Knox

Chief of Naval Operations
Admiral Harold R. Stark

Assistant Chief
of Naval Operations
RADM Royal E.
Ingersoll

Intelligence Division
Capt. Theodore S.
Wilkinson

Foreign Branch
Capt. William A.
Heard

Far Eastern Section
Cmdr. Arthur H.
McCollum

War Plans Division
RADM Richmond Kelly
Turner

Central Division
(State Department
Liaison)
Capt. R. E.
Schuirmann

Communications Division
RADM Leigh Noyes

Security Intel-
ligence) (Section
Capt. Laurence F.
Safford

Translation Section
Lt. Cmdr. Alwin D.
Kramer*

Cryptographic Re-
search (Decrypting)
Section
(Watch Officers)

*On loan from Far Eastern Section, Intellligence Division

SIMPLIFIED CHART OF WAR DEPARTMENT

As of December 7, 1941

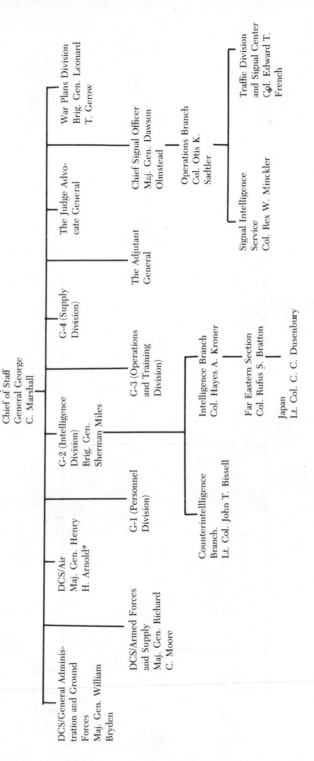

*Also Commanding General, Army Air Forces

SIMPLIFIED CHART OF HAWAIIAN DEPARTMENT

As of December 7, 1941

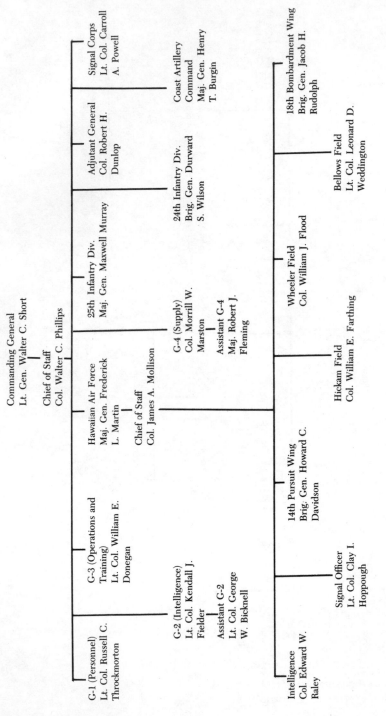

Commanding General
Lt. Gen. Walter C. Short

Chief of Staff
Col. Walter C. Phillips

G-1 (Personnel)
Lt. Col. Russell C. Throckmorton

G-2 (Intelligence)
Lt. Col. Kendall J. Fielder

Assistant G-2
Lt. Col. George W. Bicknell

G-3 (Operations and Training)
Lt. Col. William E. Donegan

G-4 (Supply)
Col. Morrill W. Marston

Assistant G-4
Maj. Robert J. Fleming

Adjutant General
Col. Robert H. Dunlop

Signal Corps
Lt. Col. Carroll A. Powell

Hawaiian Air Force
Maj. Gen. Frederick L. Martin

Chief of Staff
Col. James A. Mollison

25th Infantry Div.
Maj. Gen. Maxwell Murray

24th Infantry Div.
Brig. Gen. Durward S. Wilson

Coast Artillery Command
Maj. Gen. Henry T. Burgin

Intelligence
Col. Edward W. Raley

Signal Officer
Lt. Col. Clay I. Hoppough

14th Pursuit Wing
Brig. Gen. Howard C. Davidson

Hickam Field
Col. William E. Farthing

Wheeler Field
Col. William J. Flood

Bellows Field
Lt. Col. Leonard D. Weddington

18th Bombardment Wing
Brig. Gen. Jacob H. Rudolph

SIMPLIFIED CHART OF 14TH NAVAL DISTRICT
As of December 7, 1941

Commandant
RADM Claude C. Bloch

Chief of Staff
Capt. J. B. Earle

Intelligence Officer
Capt. I. H. Mayfield

Communications Security
(Intelligence) Unit
Cmdr. J. J. Rochefort

As commandant, 14th Naval District, Bloch was directly under the Navy Department. He was commander, Hawaiian Naval Coastal Sea Frontier, and commandant, Pearl Harbor Navy Yard. He was also an officer of the Fleet and under CinCPAC as commander, Task Force Four, and as commander, Naval Base Defense Forces. In the latter capacity, he had administrative control over

RADM PATRICK N. L. BELLINGER
who held down four positions:

1. Commander, Hawaiian Based Patrol Wing, and Commander, Patrol Wing Two.
2. Commander, Task Force Nine (Patrol Wings One and Two with attending surface craft).
3. Liaison with commandant, Fourteenth Naval District.
4. Commander, Naval Base Defense Air Force.

Theoretically, Bellinger was responsible to five superiors:

1. Commander, Aircraft Scouting Force (type command for patrol wings), based at San Diego.
2. Commander, Scouting Force, of which Patrol Wings One and Two were a part.
3. CinCPAC when commanding Task Force Nine.
4. Commanders of Task Forces One, Two, and Three for patrol planes assigned those forces.
5. Commandant, Fourteenth Naval District, in Bloch's capacity as Commander, Naval Base Defense Force, when Bellinger was performing duties as commander, Naval Base Defense Air Force.

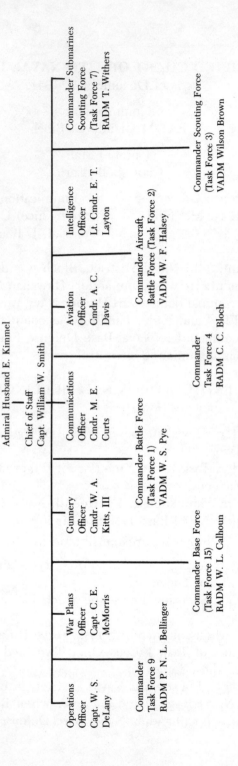

SIMPLIFIED CHART OF U.S. PACIFIC FLEET

As of December 7, 1941

Commander in Chief
Admiral Husband E. Kimmel

Chief of Staff
Capt. William W. Smith

Operations
Officer
Capt. W. S.
DeLany

Commander
Task Force 9
RADM P. N. L. Bellinger

War Plans
Officer
Capt. C. E.
McMorris

Commander Base Force
(Task Force 15)
RADM W. L. Calhoun

Gunnery
Officer
Cmdr. W. A.
Kitts, III

Commander Battle Force
(Task Force 1)
VADM W. S. Pye

Communications
Officer
Cmdr. M. E.
Curts

Commander
Task Force 4
RADM C. C. Bloch

Aviation
Officer
Cmdr. A. C.
Davis

Commander Aircraft,
Battle Force (Task Force 2)
VADM W. F. Halsey

Intelligence
Officer
Lt. Cmdr. E. T.
Layton

Commander Scouting Force
(Task Force 3)
VADM Wilson Brown

Commander Submarines
Scouting Force
(Task Force 7)
RADM T. Withers

PROLOGUE

In the predawn hours of Sunday, December 7, 1941, a Japanese task force under the command of Vice Admiral Chuichi Nagumo bore down upon Oahu. His formidable armada centered around six aircraft carriers. Upon reaching a point some 220 miles north of the island, they launched two successive waves totaling 350 aircraft—40 torpedo bombers, 78 fighter aircraft, 103 high-level bombers, and 129 dive bombers.

Their targets were the ships of Admiral Husband E. Kimmel's U.S. Pacific Fleet at moorings in Pearl Harbor. The Japanese also concentrated heavily upon American airpower located at army airfields and naval air stations throughout the island—Hickam, Wheeler, Ford Island, Kaneohe, and Ewa. Before a single shot had been fired, Commander Mitsuo Fuchida, leader of the air strike, knew that the Japanese had achieved surprise, and so advised the flagship, *Akagi*, by the code word *Tora! Tora! Tora!* ("Tiger! Tiger! Tiger!").

At 0750 Fuchida signaled for the general attack. Approximately four hours later, his aircraft, the last to leave the scene, touched down on *Akagi*'s flight deck. He and his men left behind them a devastating sight. They had sunk, capsized, or damaged in varying degrees a total of eighteen warships—eight battleships, three light cruisers, three destroyers, and four auxiliary craft. The U.S. Navy's air arm had lost eighty-seven aircraft of all types.

The Japanese also destroyed 77 aircraft of Major General Frederick L. Martin's Hawaiian Air Force, which was under Lieutenant General Walter C. Short's Hawaiian Department of the U.S. Army. An additional 128 aircraft had been damaged; however, 80 percent of these were later salvaged. Worst of all, 2,403 personnel of the Army, Navy, Marine Corps, and civilians had been killed, were listed as missing, or died later of wounds, while those wounded but not killed totaled 1,178.

In sharp contrast, the Japanese had lost twenty-nine aircraft, one large submarine, and five midget undersea craft. The Nagumo force sailed triumphantly out of the area unseen, its ships untouched.

How could the unthinkable have happened? How could a large Japanese fleet enter Hawaiian waters undetected? How could their aircraft have evaded the impersonal, all-seeing radarscope? How could an enemy pounce upon Pearl Harbor, widely believed to be impregnable? How could they successfully launch aerial torpedoes in its shallow waters? Where was American aerial reconnaissance? Why were the Hawaiian Air Force's planes lined up in plain sight on the aprons, perfect targets for Japanese bombing and strafing? How could officers of the stature of Kimmel and Short be caught by surprise?

Had United States intelligence services fallen flat on their faces, or had someone mishandled the available intelligence? Had information been available in the War and Navy departments that did not reach Short and Kimmel, respectively, and if so, whose fault was it?

It was no secret in 1941 that the Japanese had embarked upon a course of aggression and that Japanese-American relations were "friendly" only in the official sense of still maintaining diplomatic contacts. But could the whole tragedy have been avoided by a more creative, more flexible posture on the part of the U.S. State Department? Had American embargoes placed Japan in such a bind that it had no choice but to fight for its life? Did it really matter to the United States that Japan was a member of the Berlin-Rome-Tokyo Axis, that it was waging a bloody but undeclared war in China, that it obviously had designs upon French, Dutch, British, and perhaps American possessions in Southeast Asia? Had Secretary of State Cordell Hull offered Japan only terms so harsh that no sovereign nation could accept them?

Was Washington too preoccupied with the war in Europe and in the Atlantic? Had the transfer of a portion of Kimmel's ships to the Atlantic in the spring of 1941 so weakened the Pacific Fleet that Admiral Isoroku Yamamoto, Commander in Chief of Japan's Combined Fleet, dared to plan the Pearl Harbor attack and insist that it be carried out? Had Great Britain received matériel which should have remained in American arsenals? Had Hitler's attack on the Soviet

Union further distracted American attention from the Japanese? For that matter, had the decision that the Philippines might, after all, be defensible, resulted in a denuding of the military forces in the Hawaiian Islands?

Had Congress fulfilled all its obligations? Could larger appropriations have been translated into a stronger defense in time to affect the issue? Should Congress have insisted upon investigating Japanese espionage in the United States? Would such an investigation have resulted in a recommendation to close the Japanese consulates, as the German had been closed, and would this measure have tightened security? And, as the American people elected their representatives to Congress, should the entire adult populace examine its individual and collective conscience?

Most disturbing of all, how much did the White House know about all this? Could it be possible that President Franklin D. Roosevelt, with his outspoken sympathy for embattled Britain, had a commitment to the British to go to war on their behalf? As no incident of sufficient importance to warrant a declaration of war on Germany had happened in the Atlantic, had Roosevelt egged on the Japanese to attack the United States? Did he know about the Pearl Harbor attack in advance and withhold information from Oahu's defenders to ensure that the Japanese would not abort the mission?

These and many other questions have plagued the American public from December 7, 1941, until this very day. Eight official investigations,* culminating in an eight-month-long inquiry by a joint congressional committee, produced reams of testimony and documentation but could not come up with the clear-cut, foolproof answers that would have satisfied the American people. Nor could the investigators settle upon any single individual as solely responsible for the American debacle; therefore the public never had the satisfaction of being able to vent its wrath upon a readily identifiable villain. Too many strands were twisted into the cord of responsibility for any such happy ending. Today the story of American unreadiness at Pearl Harbor remains a puzzle with no single answer, a drama with no individual villain.

---

*The fact-finding trip which Secretary of the Navy Frank Knox made to Oahu shortly after the attack was not an official investigation. For a list of the investigations and their personnel, see Appendix 1.

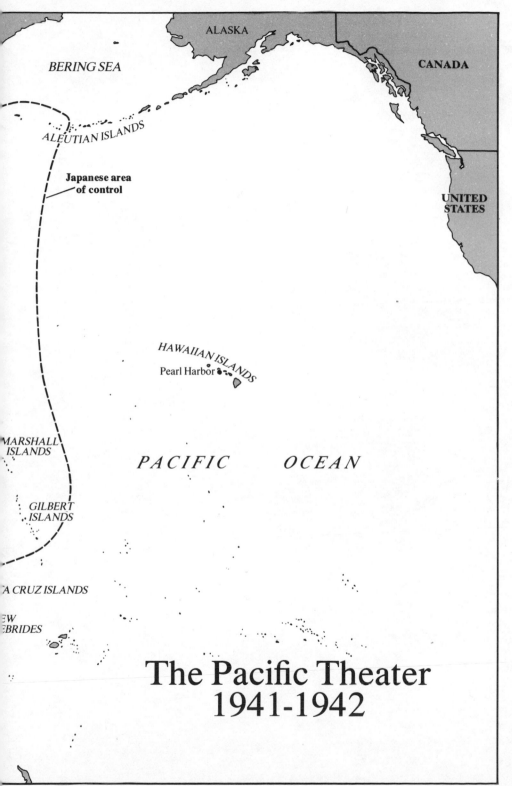

ALASKA

BERING SEA

CANADA

ALEUTIAN ISLANDS

Japanese area
of control

UNITED
STATES

HAWAIIAN ISLANDS
Pearl Harbor

MARSHALL
ISLANDS

PACIFIC   OCEAN

GILBERT
ISLANDS

A CRUZ ISLANDS

EW
EBRIDES

The Pacific Theater
1941-1942

Paul J. Pugliese

PART I

THE BASE
AND THE SUMMIT

CHAPTER 1

"We Were All Out There"

Were the American people primarily responsible?—
The role of the press—Post–World War I disillusion-
ment—"Merchants of Death"—Reluctance to increase
armed forces—Assurance of U.S. safety—Postevent
press charges—Isolationism

Almost before the echoes of Japanese engines had
died away, some individuals in the United States declared that the
American people must accept a portion of the blame for Pearl Harbor,
because of "our blindness, our provincialism, our complacency, even
our ignorance as a people."[1] Seldom if ever has the nation indulged
its propensity for self-chastisement and breast-beating more thoroughly than in relation to Pearl Harbor. Each investigation, each
development, brought a fresh outburst, culminating on August 30,
1945, when President Harry S. Truman pronounced: ". . .the country
as a whole is basically responsible in that the people were unwilling
to take adequate measures to defense [sic] until it was too late to
repair the consequences of their failure to do so."[2]

Was this a valid judgment? Did Truman's remark spring from a
profound search for the root of the matter, or had he spread the
responsibility so thinly that no one could carry more than a token
share?

Certainly, responsibility for the American aspects of what happened on December 7, 1941, was too widely diffused to pin exclusively on any one man, or even any two men. Newspaper editor
William Allen White warned against passing the buck too far, however, although he added courageously, ". . .the writer of these lines
is by no means innocent."[3]

This admission made White a rare bird among journalists. Yet the
American press had been the prime medium of popularizing and
perpetuating myths of Japanese inferiority, of American superiority,
of the country's security from Axis attack. For example, an editorial

3

in the Chicago *Tribune* on Navy Day, 1941, ridiculed the idea of war with Japan:

> She cannot attack us. That is a military impossibility. Even our base at Hawaii is beyond the effective striking power of her Fleet. She may threaten the Philippines but the Philippines are of so little vital interest to this country that we have already arranged to give them their independence within five years.
>
> And what has Japan that we want? Nothing.[4]

Thus the *Tribune* bestowed its prestige upon two dangerous fallacies: First, the United States held in its own hands the choice of peace or war; second, Hawaii was out of reach of the Japanese Navy. Moreover, the *Tribune* callously suggested that the United States should toss the Philippines to the wolves because its "vital interests" were not directly involved, although in 1941 those islands were under American protection.

Possibly the Honolulu *Advertiser* tacitly included the press when it admitted that the errors in judgment involved at Pearl Harbor "belonged to all America, and, thus all America must share in the national complacency that found us unprepared."[5]

The reasoning of those who blamed the people split into two streams. The first took an almost mystical attitude of *mea culpa*. The people of the United States had sinned, so the Lord punished them with Japanese bombs and torpedoes as the modern equivalent of fire and brimstone. Henry R. Luce spoke for this school of thought: "The disaster . . . was a sign of all the weakness and wrongness of American life in recent years."[6] Following publication of the report of the tragedy that Secretary of the Navy Frank Knox made shortly after the event, the blunt-penned Dorothy Thompson poured an avalanche of scorn over her countrymen:

> And I will tell you where the ultimate responsibilities lies, for Hawaii and for everything else. It lies with us. . . .
>
> For a whole generation the American idea has been to get as much as it could for as little effort. For a whole generation the American motto has been, "I guess it's good enough."
>
> I accuse us. I accuse the twentieth-century American. I accuse me. . . .[7]

Walter Lippmann carried this reasoning another decimal point or two: ". . . what happened at Pearl Harbor is the very pattern and image of the deadly illusions and the moral failings which have prevailed among us since the other war . . ."[8]

Others took a more practical view of why the American people were culpable. The Meridian (Mississippi) *Star* crisply expressed this rationale: "For years and years we refused to face facts and demand from our congressmen an army, navy and air corps big enough and strong enough to hold its own against all comers. . . . The result? A nation that was unprepared. . . ."[9]

The Charleston (West Virginia) *Gazette* attributed this torpor to the fact that some "honestly thought we could build a wall of steel around ourselves and retire within it in complete safety, there to remain isolated until the storm passed."[10]

This withdrawal did not result from a heartless disregard for the rest of humanity. No natural disaster could occur in so remote a corner that Americans would not reach into their hearts and pockets to help alleviate suffering. But to involve themselves again in the Old World's man-made holocausts was something else.

The United States had entered World War I in a spirit of high sacrifice. Uncle Sam and his noble allies would fight the war to end all wars, would make the world safe for democracy, a world fit for heroes to live in. After they came out of the ether, American survivors looked around and what did they see? In Germany an iron-fisted, sadistic regime which made Kaiser Bill's "huns" look like Boy Scouts by comparison; Benito Mussolini, trying to remodel the genial Italians into scowling Roman warriors, had hooked them ignominiously to Adolf Hitler's tailboard; Russia was proving that if you scratched a commissar you drew Romanov blood; Japan had run amok.

Instead of war being at an end, the nations of Europe and Asia were arming to the back teeth; the world had never been less safe for democracy; it was not a suitable abode for everyday, peace-loving human beings, let alone heroes. An indignant public concluded that Uncle Sam had been played for a sucker.

Popular imagination seized upon "merchants of death," a catchphrase of the 1930s, publicized by a number of books on the manufacture and sale of armaments.[11] This concept culminated in the Senate investigations of the munitions industry held between 1934 and 1936, presided over by Senator Gerald P. Nye of North Dakota. Nye's committee found:

While the evidence . . . does not show that wars have been started
solely because of the activities of munitions makers and their agents,
it is also true that wars rarely have one single cause, and the committee finds it to be against the peace of the world for selfishly
interested organizations to be left free to goad and frighten nations
into military activity.[12]

It was not a pretty picture that the Nye Committee held up to
the eyes of a disgusted nation. Not the least disquieting aspect of the
inquiry was the revelation of the close relationship between the armed
forces and the munitions industry. Naturally, the Army and Navy
wanted the United States to have a strong capacity to produce armament, but in some cases they went over the line. Perhaps most
damaging from the standpoint of the American people, testimony
concerning the munitions industry's publicity campaigns cast doubt
upon the credibility of the press in crisis reporting. Nye remarked
to a witness that he had noted over a period of nine years

> that just preceding the advent of each naval appropriation bill we
> have had a great deal in the papers about trouble with Japan. How
> much of these annual scares are occasioned by what was strictly
> propaganda, having your own personal interests at stake? How many
> of these annual scares of trouble with Japan have you and others
> interested in the munitions game played up?[13]

Yet the years of the Nye Committee—1934 to 1936—covered a
period of acute need for close, objective reporting and a well-informed
public. Japan had given notice that it would abandon the Washington
Naval Treaty and had withdrawn from the second London Conference. Germany had repudiated the arms limitations sections of the
Versailles Treaty, denounced the Locarno Pact, and sent troops into
the Rhineland. All the iniquities of the arms trade could not nullify
these iron facts.

There was definite appeal in the naïve concept that the basic cause
of war was the "merchants of death" drumming up trade: It absolved
of war guilt all except an infinitesimal, sinister minority; it relieved
the average citizen of the humiliating conviction that he had been a
gullible rube; it reduced war to a simple matter of dollars and cents,
which most people could understand.

Of course, the theory was entirely too pat, too neat, and ignored
the whole sweep of man's life on earth. War was a long-lived, wide-

spread phenomenon whose roots struck much deeper than a munitions maker's profit-and-loss statement. This thesis helped drive the United States still further into its self-imposed "ivory tower" mentality. The nation had already achieved something of a record in inconsistency. By standing aloof from the League of Nations it had rejected collective security, yet it had refused to provide for itself an adequate unilateral national defense system.

As a result of the Washington Naval Conference of 1922, the United States scrapped twenty-eight vessels, including eleven capital ships in various stages of completion, and converted two battle cruisers, *Lexington* and *Saratoga*, to aircraft carriers, then considered to be instruments of defense rather than offense. Moreover, the United States pledged itself not to increase existing fortifications of Guam, Tutuila, the Aleutians, and the Philippines.[14] In effect, this left American outlying possessions in the Pacific at the mercy of Japan and removed the means of enforcing American foreign policy in the Far East.

The Navy did not even build up to treaty limits during the administrations of Calvin Coolidge and Herbert Hoover. Matters began to look up when Roosevelt became President. He took a personal interest in the sea service; nevertheless, he did not press for a big Navy. Always a master of the possible, he tacked to catch the prevailing winds. And the little breezes of public opinion did not yet blow in that direction. But the little scraps Roosevelt gave the Navy were an improvement over the nothing bestowed by the two previous administrations.[15]

The Army was in no better shape. The Versailles Treaty had limited Germany to an army of 100,000 men, deemed the absolute minimum required to preserve national order while rendering Germany harmless to the rest of the world. Yet when the Preparatory Committee for the Geneva Conference first met on May 18, 1926, the United States had reduced its own land forces to 118,000.[16] Considering the relative size of the two countries, the United States had voluntarily denuded itself far beyond what even Germany's late enemies believed essential to declaw the double eagle.

In 1932 the U.S. Regular Army, with not quite 120,000 active-duty enlisted men, ranked seventeenth among the world's armies. When General George C. Marshall became Chief of Staff in September 1939, the Army and its Air Corps combined had less than 200,000 men.[17] As late as April 1941, in a magazine article urging reorganization of the air forces, one finds this suggestion for financial savings:

> The planes which have been built and those to be built can be reduced in productive cost by eliminating the idea that the airplane should be built like the automobile—to last for four or five years. Careful study of the records of this modern air warfare reveals that the average pilot's life is between thirty and fifty hours in the air. Therefore, why build the airplanes to last longer than the pilots who fly them?[18]

One would give much to have heard the reaction in General H.H. "Hap" Arnold's staff to the idea of no-deposit no-return aircraft.

Authority for a 20-percent increase in the Navy finally became law on May 17, 1938, "after strenuous debate." It called for forty-six combatant ships and twenty-six auxiliaries. "Opponents of the expansion dubbed it 'monstrous' and 'indefensible,' and tagged it a 'super-Navy bill.' "[19]

A peculiar aspect of American thinking in this period was preoccupation with beating the corpse of World War I. Some Americans decried the alleged sins of their former Allies while ignoring the rearming and the frankly expressed aggressive intentions of the Axis. In a radio address on January 28, 1938, Representative Herbert S. Bigelow of Ohio urged against passage of the "super-Navy" bill. He "put no trust in the governments of Europe. They roped us in once, but I say never again. . . . Let us not be a Nation of old maids looking under the bed every night for Germans or Japs."[20]

Representative Thomas O'Malley of Wisconsin spoke like an irreconcilable Irishman: "God grant we may not be led into another [war] by that wily little island in the Atlantic. . . ." If the United States needed to defend itself, why not spend the money on coastal defenses, antiaircraft guns and other protective measures, instead of "$75,000,000 apiece for battleships that can be destroyed by $350,000 bombing planes? . . ."[21]

Nye, too, was unhappy about the expanded Navy. He thought it would be too big for defense, not big enough to attack Japan, and too late "to stop Japan in China." He favored a Navy "strong enough to defend this nation." But he was dead set against anything that might be "part of an adventurous gamble on a foreign war."[22]

The ever eloquent Representative Hamilton Fish of New York

announced his readiness "to vote millions for defense" but did not propose "to vote one single dollar for purposes of offenses and aggression." He laid the whole problem upon the Administration rather than on the Axis, and accused Roosevelt of trying to build a navy "not merely for defense but for aggression, to enable him to quarantine and police the world."[23]

The United States did not really waken to a sense of peril until the Germans had conquered Poland, invaded Denmark and Norway, smashed Holland, Belgium, and France, and were racing headlong for the channel ports. On June 14, 1940, Congress passed an 11-percent naval expansion bill, and one for 70 percent on July 19, 1940. Nevertheless, not until 1944 did the U.S. Navy reach the strength authorized in 1934.[24]

In the weeks between release of the Knox report and that of the committee chaired by Associate Justice of the Supreme Court Owen J. Roberts,* the press continued to slug at John Q. Public. "Our army and navy personnel were not the only people not on the alert," avowed newsman Quincy Howe. "It was a case of the whole nation being asleep at the switch."[25] Exactly one year later, columnist Barnet Nover termed Pearl Harbor

> the tragic epitome of an entire era in our foreign relations, an era whose dominant characteristic was a mood of well-nigh indestructible unreality. . . .
>
> . . . The policy pursued by the nations and particularly by the United States during that decade [1931–1940] was, in effect, one of every one for himself and the devil take the hindmost. . . .[26]

It was less a case of "every one for himself"—which implies a readiness to enter the race with the will to win—than of the "well-nigh indestructible unreality." A large segment of the public had yet to learn that the United States was no longer invulnerable geographically. Modern shipping, the submarine, the aircraft carrier, and the transoceanic airplane had made this planet a very small world indeed.

The American people did not seem to understand that the seas had no intrinsic protective quality. And, like all the forces of nature, the oceans played no favorites. Whether they were bulwarks or causeways, well disposed or inimical, depended upon who controlled them.

---

*See Appendix 1.

As author Leonard Baker noted in later years, the Atlantic was a protection for the United States solely because the British Navy patrolled it. The case would be far otherwise if British ships fell into German hands.[27]

By the same token, the waters that laved the American West Coast were friendly or hostile depending upon how far the U.S. Navy yielded control of the Pacific to Yamamoto's Combined Fleet.

Many also failed to understand the threat of ideological warfare, the insidious campaign of words to sap the morale, cloud the reason, and weaken the will to the point where physical defense became meaningless.

Most isolationists were patriotic Americans, and they were not all of one stamp. As Wayne S. Cole stated in his admirable study, *America First,* both interventionism and isolationism "were composed of extremely heterogeneous elements. Each group drew support from all regions of the country; from different age, ethnic, and social groups; and from persons holding widely diverse economic and political views."[28]

Few of the isolationists were pacifists. The majority heartily joined with the interventionists in advocating armed forces strong enough to defend the United States. The question over which they parted company was: How much was enough? Many isolationists also took the position that the United States should remain aloof from the Old World and its age-old quarrels. One of the sincerest of them was Charles A. Lindbergh, who believed that global war would mean the end of present civilization. Their big mistake lay in believing that this country could remain cloistered if it wished to.

Isolationism involved a certain amount of defeatism. Note the revealing title of a little book by Anne Morrow Lindbergh: *The Wave of the Future.* This became virtually required reading in isolationist circles. Her message came across loud and clear: For all the barbarism, what was happening in Europe was the wave of the future, so one had better scramble onto one's surfboard and ride with it. Her husband told an America First rally in New York City:

> By 1938, I had come to the conclusion that if a war occurred between Germany on one side, and England and France on the other, it would result either in a German victory, or in a prostrate and devastated Europe. I therefore advocated that England and France build their military forces with the utmost rapidity, but that they permit Germany to expand eastward without declaring war.[29]

Here was defeatism allied with a cold-bloodedness toward the peoples of Eastern Europe startling in a man as sensitive as Lindbergh. And one wonders how he could have advocated a course that might well result in Hitler's not only absorbing the Poles and other intervening nations of Eastern Europe, but in conquering European Russia. That in turn would mean German industrial skill and military efficiency allied to Russian manpower and resources, with Western Europe at Hitler's mercy.

No wonder that some believed Lindbergh to be not merely simplistic, but actively pro-Hitler. "If I should die tomorrow, I want you to know this," said Roosevelt to Secretary of the Treasury Henry Morgenthau, Jr., at lunch on May 20, 1940. "I am absolutely convinced that Lindbergh is a Nazi."[30]

Responsible isolationist groups tried officially to keep their skirts clear of Nazism, anti-Semitism, and communism. Nevertheless, isolationism could not help but further the Axis cause. There being no possibility whatever of the United States joining the war in the Axis corner, the most Hitler could hope for was to keep the Americans from joining the British. Nevertheless, the whole isolationist movement paid so little attention to Japan that it is reasonable to conclude that the noninterventionists contributed in no small measure to diverting public attention from the Asiatic menace.

According to Cole, Lindbergh did not think that Orientals had the natural talents for aviation and air power that Americans and Europeans had. And Lindbergh insisted that geography and the oceans enhanced America's defense relative to "warring armies of Europe and Asia." Lindbergh wrote, "The air defense of America is as simple as the attack is difficult." What is more, he believed it "obvious . . . that air power made it costly, if not impossible, for naval forces to operate within the effective bombing range of an enemy coast adequately protected by aircraft."[31]

A theory also existed that modern weapons had developed so monstrously that any nation that set these horrors in motion would become automatically an outcast people. No war prize would be worth such a cost. Observed the noted journalist William Allen White:

> The American people generally were sure that we were approaching a degree of civilization where men on the whole were decent, were honorable and reliable. We were under the vast delusion that human

nature was going through an evolutionary process which would make it easy to be generous, profitable to be kind, and worth while to be sincerely, practicably neighborly.[32]

Thus White voiced another opinion as to why and how the American people had been guilty: They had erred through their virtues as well as their vices.

Like the English up to the last minute, the Americans did not understand the nature of the forces opposing them. They did not comprehend a life-style that glorified belligerence, deliberately reverted to the barbarism which always lurks dangerously near the surface of civilization, and did not give a plugged nickel for world opinion.

As the fate of those under the Axis heel became impossible to ignore, events awakened an almost atavistic dread in the United States—that of loss of freedom. The instinct of the American people to shut their eyes to evil collided with the instinctive knowledge that to condone it would both countenance slavery for the conquered and risk it for themselves. The conflict between the drive to freedom and the recoil from direct involvement produced heavy stresses and apparent inconsistencies. Some resolved the conflict by flight into unreality. "Let's ignore it and maybe it will go away" might have been the motto of those who convinced themselves that Old World catastrophes could not strike the New.

One of the prime press reactions to the Roberts report had been agreement that, while Kimmel and Short were guilty as charged, the entire nation shared their culpability. "In a sense we were all out there," the Milwaukee *Journal* stated in a challenging editorial.

We were all . . . substituting our "beliefs" for factual information available. The Axis had shown that it was out to conquer the world. A good many people did not want to believe that, so they didn't. Axis powers had demonstrated that they would strike friend or foe without warning. That was not a comfortable thought, so discard it. The time was short—too short—but if we adopted that idea we should have to pursue a course which would interfere with "life as usual." So we pushed aside the disagreeable warnings. . . .
. . . We thought we could pursue our peaceful, often lax, always controversial way and be safe from a nation that had determined to challenge us in the Pacific, and prepared for 10 years to do this, and had behind it years of military training. . . .[33]

The Roberts report provoked journalist Dorothy Thompson to another outburst. Again she saw the guilt of the American people as fundamentally a moral and intellectual failure.

> The complacency rose out of conviction that we could adequately defend Pearl Harbor and that the enemy must know this—therefore, wouldn't act. But the Japanese knew something else, something more important than the defenses—the attitude of our mind—therefore, did act. . . .
>
> There are no miracles in history. The fall of France was no miracle; the resistance of Britain none; the comeback of Russia none; the blitz of the Japanese none. There is such a thing as morale and efficiency, and there is such a thing as the lack of them, and national characteristics always show in a crisis. . . .[34]

The passage of two years did not make the press any easier on the American people. On April 24, 1944, the New York *Sun* commented on the annual report of Commander in Chief Admiral Ernest J. King to the secretary of the navy. In the *Sun's* view this document demonstrated that

> the attack on Pearl Harbor merely crippled still further a naval force that was already inadequate for its job; a force that had been weakened through those long, snail-like years when virtually the only increase in our naval strength was the annual addition of another year to the age of obsolescent vessels.

In his endorsement to the Navy Court of Inquiry's report, King observed, "It is true that the country as a whole is basically responsible in that the people were unwilling to support an adequate army and navy until it was too late to repair the consequences of past neglect in time to deal effectively with the attack that ushered in the war." But he did not blame the American people exclusively. In his opinion, the Army and Navy had certain responsibilities which they could not disregard.[35]

With the release of the Army and Navy reports in August 1945, the press fired another volley at its countrymen. The Honolulu *Advertiser* lamented:

> The shame of Pearl Harbor was not a one-man shame. . . . The tragedy of the American attitude was the product of towns and villages, of big cities and big factories, of oil, copper, cotton and scrap iron that flowed to potential enemies, of "America First-ism," the

corn and hog farmer and of the slushy societies that were sure that love and understanding were all that a sick world needed.[36]

During the investigation conducted by a joint congressional committee in 1945–46,* the nation broke out in another rash of self-accusation. The *Christian Science Monitor* hinted that the United States had more or less invited attack by projecting the image of a country "too flabby and sleepy to see what was going on in the world." It further declared, "No amount of physical power, without the will to use it rightly, can spell security for a nation."[37]

Reminding its readers of Marshall's testimony that his attempts to beef up the Hawaiian Air Force had virtually denuded the mainland units, the Milwaukee *Journal* asked sharply:

> Whose fault was that? That was America's fault and we cannot escape responsibility for it. Few of us would listen to the warnings, and those who are now trying to pin responsibility for the attack at Pearl Harbor on this country were the loudest in shouting "warmonger" every time President Roosevelt urged the country to strengthen its defenses.[38]

Yet precisely how does one measure the responsibility or the guilt of a whole people? Writer-politician David Lawrence, for one, wanted no part of the collective guilt theory, which he termed a "new alibi for incompetence and neglect of duty" and "a plea in avoidance."[39]

The people of the United States were not directly to blame for the military and naval failure at Pearl Harbor. Their part was more subtle. "A nation's armed forces are a cross section of the nation itself," declared the Chicago *Sun*. "The mentality that prevailed at Pearl Harbor . . . was the mentality that prevailed at home. . . ."[40]

Kimmel, Short, and their superiors in Washington were part of the American people and shared the national attitudes. Those beliefs and hopes, those prides and prejudices, those blind spots and those clear visions, formed the soil from which the men of the armed forces drew their strengths and their weaknesses. But the American people could not send up Kimmel's air reconnaissance for him, or force Short to change his alert status from antisabotage to all-out.

---

*See Appendix 1.

CHAPTER 2

"Slow in Waking Up"

Did Congress share responsibility?—Isolationism—
Appropriations—Authority to wiretap—Oil and scrap
iron for Japan—Concentration on Europe—Draft almost repealed—Disbelief in danger to the United States

The American people did not and could not operate the national government directly, so as an inevitable accompaniment to their thunders against the citizenry, many newspapers apportioned to Congress part of the blame for Pearl Harbor.

Lawmakers, however, tended to be highly circumspect in suggesting that they might share in the onus. If one can take the *Congressional Record* at face value—and in this instance one probably can—no member of the Senate or House rose up to echo Dorothy Thompson's uncompromising "I accuse me."* Indeed, in the immediate post–Pearl Harbor period, some seized upon the occasion to hand bouquets to themselves and toss brickbats at their opponents. Representative Jed Johnson of Oklahoma reminded his colleagues pointedly,

> those Members of Congress who consistently and persistently opposed a two-ocean navy, also the Fortification of Hawaii, Guam, the Philippine Islands, and other American possessions, on the flimsy excuse that we could not afford to offend Japan, or upon the repeated assurance by them that there was not the remotest possibility of America ever being dragged into war on the Pacific, must also now realize that their advice and council [*sic*], if followed, would have meant total disaster, humiliation, and defeat for the United States.[1]

Senator Joseph C. O'Mahoney of Wyoming observed that the sinking of the British warships *Prince of Wales* and *Repulse* convinced him "that the fault at Pearl Harbor lay not with the personnel upon any of our naval vessels but to the fact that the new weapon of warfare,

*See Chapter 1.

the air force, . . . has not been sufficiently developed in this Nation."
And he conceded, "We in Congress must accept some blame for our
lack of preparation."[2]

Such unspecific self-deprecation lends force to a cartoon in the
Washington *Post* of February 5, 1942, that pictured a potbellied, top-
hatted figure labeled "Congress" pointing to its reflection in a mirror
and remarking smugly, "Everybody's Guilty But You." That image
did not apply to Senator George W. Norris of Nebraska. "Congress
cannot escape its part of the blame for this thing," he told newsmen
following release of the Roberts report. "Long ago it should have
streamlined our military organization."[3]

Senator Alben W. Barkley of Kentucky admitted, "All of us must
take more or less responsibility for Pearl Harbor—everybody in the
United States and every Member of Congress. We might go back a
number of years from now and recite what might have been done in
the Pacific that was not done that would have averted the disaster."

But hen pressed by Senator David I. Walsh of Massachusetts,
Barkley backed down a bit, assuring him that he meant Congress
shared "the general smugness of the American people," not that Congress had neglected "to take any action that might have changed the
situation." Walsh wanted to make clear that he could not accept on
behalf of his fellow legislators any direct part in the tragedy of December 7. "The operations at Pearl Harbor were an executive function, and responsibility for them was lodged in the departments. Congress
has no direction or control of operations of the Navy or Army, and
should not be expected to have." This was undeniably true.

Walsh also pointed out that the initiative for the two-ocean navy
came largely from Congress. Barkley agreed "that if all of us had had
enough foresight years ago, we would have had a two-ocean navy
when this war started." He preferred to blame American virtues
rather than American faults:

> We wanted to believe that mankind desired peace . . . it is one of
> the weaknesses of human nature that if people want to believe a
> certain thing will not happen, they govern themselves according to
> that belief; and I think the peace-loving nations and the peaceful
> people of the world were slow in waking up to what was really in
> store for them.[4]

This was not a bad description of some isolationist attitudes. Congress contained a powerful isolationist bloc whose members the St.

Louis *Star-Times* called "the men who did their best to make a Pearl Harbor of the entire United States."[5] The isolationist lawmakers had fought to the last ditch against lend-lease and repeal of the Neutrality Act. Nye had opposed special naval appropriations tooth and nail. "We do have an adequate national defense," he proclaimed in 1938. "Anyone lying awake at night worrying about an attack on the United States is wasting a lot of energy that might be expended in more useful ways."[6] Wrote the well-known journalist Ernest K. Lindley, "It is noteworthy that some of the Senators and Representatives who are calling for the heads of higher-ups were previously conspicuous for their belittling of the danger confronting the United States. Any just purge from office of incompetents who were asleep at the switch would begin with them."[7]

As did a number of newspapers, the Emporia *Gazette* gave the isolationist members of Congress a drubbing:

> The recent congressional votes of congressmen who registered disapproval of arming our ships, leaders who would tear down our national guard army in the face of the enemy, gave Japan the idea that this country was divided. Under that delusion Japan dared to strike. Those who cast those appeasing Quisling votes are more directly responsible for this war today than any other one force in American politics. . . .[8]

After Senator Robert A. Taft of Ohio called for an investigation of Hull and Knox, the Indianapolis *Star* observed sourly, "When Senator Taft makes such a demand he should not resent a survey of his own record dealing with the nation's Pacific policy. By speeches in the Senate and elsewhere, and by his votes, the senator opposed the increased fortifications of Pacific outposts."[9]

The *Daily Worker*, mouthpiece of American communists, had found itself in some rather incongruous company since June 22, 1941, when Germany invaded the Soviet Union. Upon publication of the Roberts report, it declared the prewar conviction "that Japan had no intention of making any such raid" to be

> the fruit of the propaganda of the appeasers, of the America First Committee,* of people like Charles Lindbergh and Norman Thomas, of papers like the New York Daily News and the Chicago Tribune,

---

*The America First Committee, under General Leonard Wood, was a group of isolationists very prominent in the early days of World War II.

of political figures like Senators [Burton K.] Wheeler [of Montana] and Nye. For did not these appeasers day in and day out sing their treasonous refrain of "Japan is our friend; Japan wants peace; Japan has no designs on the United States"?[10]

In San Francisco, the *People's Daily World* likewise jumped on this element:

> As the President gradually tightened restrictions against Japan, the appeasement clique led by America First, its shouters in Congress and the Hearst newspapers, with the Scripps-Howard press trailing along, grew even more vocal in its protest and to justify appeasement insisted that, as [William Randolph] Hearst in person wrote on December 3: "Japan is not threatening the United States, the United States is threatening Japan."
>
> Anyone who absorbed such an atmosphere was bound to ignore national security; and it is notable that the same Congressmen who were most active in creating this atmosphere, are now trying to decry the Administration and howling loudest for the blood of those who learned their dereliction of duty from them.[11]

Comedian Zero Mostel turned upon the isolationists in Congress the most potent weapon of all—ridicule. Throughout the war he delighted nightclub audiences with his imitation of an isolationist senator, fulminating, "What was Hawaii doing out there in the middle of the Pacific anyway?"[12]

Yet it would be unjust to leave the impression that Roosevelt was a consistent, valiant fighter for a strong army and navy, hamstrung by a recalcitrant, tightfisted Congress. Consider military and naval appropriations for the fiscal years 1937 through 1941. In every year, the Bureau of the Budget whacked off huge slices of the armed forces' requests before passing them on to Capitol Hill. In 1941, Congress restored a large portion of the Navy's cut. In other years, Congress made further cuts, which with one exception were comparatively minor. The exception was 1938, when the lawmakers sliced off a second sum larger than the Bureau had already chopped.[13] The Army fared better. For each of the sample years except 1940, Congress appropriated more than the Bureau had approved.[14]

The isolationists were not the only lawmakers who could have extracted a little humility from the remembrance of past actions and of comments made a few days before Pearl Harbor. Senator Tom Connally of Texas, who had chewed out Knox at a White House conference the evening of December 7, had boasted on December 2 at Coral Gables, Florida, "If Japan wants war and must have a fight, she will find that we have a navy in the Pacific that can shoot straight. Let me say to the Japanese premier that we have rights and are not afraid to fight for them."[15]

On December 5, Representative Andrew J. May, Chairman of the House Military Affairs Committee, blustered that if he were secretary of state he would tell Japan "to take our terms or take what follows." When asked whether "what follows" would mean a declaration of war, the congressman answered, "Well, yes—unless we won't bother with it and just steam our navy right in there and blow the hell out of Tokyo."[16]

Such remarks from supposedly reliable, knowledgeable sources could not help but give Americans an inflated idea of their navy's strength.

Watching the verbal smoke and flame emerging from the Capitol in the days immediately following the strike, newsman Walter Locke pronounced that if certain congressmen felt the need to investigate anybody, "let it be an investigation of congress itself."[17] Although no congressman suggested such action, several criticized their colleagues. Said Representative Adolph J. Sabath of Illinois:

> Some Members of Congress and certain sections of the press have permitted themselves to be influenced or blinded, and have refused to see clearly the danger which was confronting our country. Only the shock of an actual attack by these little yellow rats has finally opened their eyes. . . .[18]

Representative Charles A. Plumley of Vermont admitted, "The complacent state of mind of the people has been reflected in the attitude of many Members of Congress, as a result of which, we have found ourselves unprepared. . . ."[19]

As the "day of wrath" drew nearer, increasingly the isolationists in Congress appeared to oppose Roosevelt himself rather than just his foreign policy. "Nobody is worrying about Japan coming over here and attacking us," asserted Representative William P. Lambertson of Kansas on December 4, 1941. "No man is getting more fun out of dictatorship than Franklin Roosevelt. He shows from way back that he likes war."[20]

One cannot pin solely on the isolationist solons the entire blame for congressional sins of omission and commission in relation to national defense for a very important reason: They were in the minority. They raised their voices loud and long—reasonable voices, foolish voices, respected voices, despised voices, voices to be agreed with or argued with—but they were only voices. Power lay with the majority.

By the autumn of 1941, the America First movement had lost much of its edge. On September 11, Lindbergh made an unfortunate speech at Des Moines, Iowa, one with anti-Semitic overtones. This speech, however, was only one sign of the times, and intelligent members of Congress could read them clearly. Representative Everett M. Dirksen of Illinois had made a name for himself as an isolationist, having opposed lend-lease and extension of the draft. But in September 1941 a recess of Congress gave Dirksen the opportunity to test the public temperature. As a result, he reversed his field and became a supporter of Roosevelt's foreign policy. Nor did the Republicans drum him out of the regiment. Many of his fellow minority congressmen applauded him heartily. From that time, Dirksen's star began to rise.[21]

In the thrashing about to determine who was responsible for the Hawaiian disaster, some shrewd blows landed, but many swings went wild. Among the latter were at least two charges against Congress much discussed at the time.

The first was the so-called refusal to fortify Guam. This question haunted the elections of 1944. In a speech at Bremerton, Washington, in August of that year, Roosevelt declared, "We were not allowed to fortify Guam. . . ." In his report on the progress of the war dated April 23, 1944, Admiral King also wrote, "Proposal was made to proceed with the fortification of Guam, but after considerable debate in Congress it was rejected."[22] These statements reflect no credit upon these two men. Congress had not refused permission to fortify Guam, because the administration never asked for it. Representative George J. Bates of Massachusetts, a member of the Naval Affairs Committee, told the House on September 7, 1944:

> The only thing that we ever had before the committee was the bill calling for the dredging of the harbor and the striking off of the coral reefs, the building of a breakwater, and improving the seaplane take-off area so that the commercial planes and perhaps some Navy planes on their way to the Philippines could find safe refuge in the harbor of Guam.[23]

In the Naval Expansion Act of May 17, 1938, Congress, entirely on its own, directed the Navy "to set up a board to determine the need for additional bases." This board recommended, among other items, "fortification of Guam at a cost of $80,000,000." The bill that Roosevelt and the Bureau of the Budget ultimately sent to Congress pruned this to $5,000,000 for harbor improvement.[24]

On January 21, 1939, Representative E. E. Cox of Georgia introduced a bill for $52,000,000 to cover "12 aviation developments." The only controversial part concerned Guam. He quoted the testimony of Admiral William D. Leahy, Chief of Naval Operations, before the Naval Affairs Committee: "The authorization in the bill . . . does not provide for the development of a base at Guam." He added, however:

> The establishment of a base for submarines and aircraft on the island of Guam would be extremely valuable in augmenting the defensive power of the American Fleet because no foreign power would like to project an advance in force across the Pacific without first reducing such a base.[25]

But Leahy would not recommend such a buildup. One can readily understand why. A glance at the map of the Pacific in the 1930s shows that, no matter what Guam's defenses or lack of them, the island was hostage to Japanese good will. Rear Admiral Arthur B. Cook, Chief of the Bureau of Aeronautics, told the Naval Affairs Committee that even if the air and submarine base went through, an enemy could reduce it in thirty days. As it stood, he estimated one day would suffice. (Events made him a prophet; Guam fell on December 12, 1941, precisely one day after the Japanese attacked it in force.)[26]

For three days, the House argued about improving Guam's facilities. Congressman Fish argued against the proposal on the grounds that an airbase on Guam would be "a dagger at the throat of Japan and an arrow aimed at the heart of its communications and its trade. . . . There is no country that has the ability or capacity to attack us if they wanted to do so."[27]

Among the fifteen Republicans who supported the bill was Representative Melvin J. Maas of Minnesota. Although he thought the House was "making an awful, awful fuss about nothing," he warned his colleagues solemnly:

> if you Members of Congress today vote to prevent the dredging of a harbor . . . for our scouting planes so that they may know of the

possibility of an enemy movement toward us, you are going to take a terrible responsibility upon yourselves, perhaps that of the loss of millions of American lives . . . our Navy may be caught in a most unfavorable situation for defense against an attacking fleet; and our Navy under such circumstances may suffer defeat, even annihilation . . . the mere presence of American naval scouting planes in Guam will tend to reduce to the minimum even the danger of hostile activities upon the part of Japan . . . by destroying the chance for a surprise naval attack.[28]

Later each political party tried to saddle the other with defeating the Guam bill. Actually, both were at fault. The Republicans registered a firm 138 to 15 against it; the Democrats voted in favor 153 to 64—not enough for passage.[29] One factor in its defeat was hesitancy to offend the Japanese. "Spent the entire forenoon testifying before the Senate Naval Committee," Leahy wrote in his diary on March 6, 1939:

The principal objection by members of the Committee was to a request for authority to improve the harbor of Guam with the purpose of facilitating the handling of seaplanes at that place. There appeared to be apprehension on the part of some members of the Committee that this development constitutes a threat to Japan.[30]

At that time Japan was seeing or pretending to see enemies behind every cherry tree. But it was absurd of knowledgeable Americans to pander to these fantasies. Guam presented no threat to Japan. Not until February 1941 did Congress vote $4,700,000 for harbor improvements at Guam. Then the proposal sailed through without opposition. The work was just beginning when Japan struck.[31]

What did Guam have to do with Pearl Harbor? Actually, little or nothing, although some claimed a connection. "The whole point, of course, is that if we'd had a base for scouting planes at Guam in 1941, it would have been completely impossible for the Japs to have surprised our Navy at Pearl Harbor," observed writers Charles Van Devander and William O. Player, Jr., in August 1944.[32] They were badly mistaken, for it is virtually impossible that a scout based on Guam could have spotted Nagumo's task force on its cruise. For that matter, Maas was equally mistaken in postulating that the mere presence of U.S. scouting planes would be any guarantee against surprise, as events on Oahu so painfully proved.

Any effect the neglect of Guam had upon events at Pearl Harbor was tangential. It may have bolstered two of Japan's erroneous beliefs: that isolationism ruled the American roost, and that Washington would back down rather than risk offending Tokyo. But even this is problematical.

The second action for which Congress drew unfair criticism was the matter of wiretapping suspected spies. Upon release of the Roberts report, the Washington *Star* stated that in the summer of 1941 the House had passed a bill that would have enabled the FBI and armed forces intelligence officers "to listen in on the wire and wireless messages of spies and saboteurs and to use the information thus obtained as evidence in court. . . ." The *Star* claimed that Wheeler, then chairman of the Senate Interstate Commerce Committee, pigeonholed the bill and allowed it to die a natural death. The House later defeated similar legislation "by a close vote after opponents had raised the old cry against 'invading the privacy of the home.' " The *Star* pointed out that as a result, "fantastic as it may seem, our counterespionage agents in Hawaii were compelled by law to stand by helplessly while known spies were using the wires and radio to plot our destruction. . . ."[33]

This article brought then Senator Truman to his feet a few days later. He told his colleagues:

It has been charged that the senior Senator from Montana . . . has prevented enactment of a law to authorize the tapping of the wires of spies, and that if he had not done so the Japanese could not have surprised our forces at Pearl Harbor on December 7, 1941. A perusal of the official records will show that the charge is not tenable. . . . The facts will also show that the surprise attack on Hawaii was in no respect due to the unwillingness of Congress to pass a law authorizing wire tapping. . . .[34]

Truman explained what had happened. After the defeat on June 30, 1941, of a House bill to authorize wiretapping, he presented a resolution that "an appropriate standing committee of the Senate should be directed" to study the subject. This resolution went to the Interstate Commerce Committee. Wheeler appointed a seven-member subcommittee to tackle it.

This body, of which Truman was chairman, gave a representative of the Department of Justice "the fullest opportunity for a complete exposition of the subject of wire tapping, and of his reasons in support of a wire-tapping bill." They also heard some of the House testimony "that wire tapping might endanger national defense, might hurt workers' morale, and thus interfere with maximum production." Organized labor "asserted that such a power would be used more against labor than spies." Further testimony indicated that wiretapping was inefficient as well as undesirable. Of course, "there was much testimony on the other side of the question." Truman insisted that Wheeler never pressured any member of the subcommittee one way or the other.[35]

Truman told the Senate that some wires were tapped in Hawaii. The law as it stood did not prohibit the practice. The offense under current statutes was to intercept any communication and "divulge and publish" same. Truman explained that it was also "entirely lawful for the Government to subpoena copies of telegrams in the files of cable and telegraph companies." So the law did not prevent securing copies of the messages "sent by Japanese spies over the commercial lines between Hawaii and Japan in the weeks and months preceding the attack on Pearl Harbor."

Truman concluded that "the absence of a wire-tapping law had nothing whatever to do with the failure to detect in advance the surprise attack. . . ." What is more, "If any Government department deemed it necessary to have such a bill rushed through, that department would say so, plainly, clearly, unmistakably. No Government department has said so."[36]

Wiretapping in Honolulu could not have revealed the Pearl Harbor secret, because no known telephone conversations discussed Yamamoto's plan. But if wiretapping was legal provided one did not "divulge and publish" the findings, and if proper authorities could have subpoenaed copies of messages, why all the mental anguish during 1941 on the part of American counterintelligence agencies on Oahu in regard to the Japanese consular messages and the telephone tap on the Honolulu consulate?[37] Of course, a definitive interpretation of "divulge and publish" posed the sort of problem that can occupy lawyers for days on end. Then, too, American authorities would never grant such a power casually. One becomes involved in the eternal dilemma of democracy: How far can a nation go in defending liberty before liberty itself becomes a license to kill for those who would murder liberty? In any case, one cannot lay blame in respect to wiretaps on the doorstep of Congress.

Nevertheless, the protests of the lawmakers that they did not take certain actions because the administration did not ask for them are not convincing. If Congress believed that certain courses were for the good of the nation, it would have overridden the White House or taken the lead. The Congress of the United States was a very different proposition from the German Reichstag, Hitler's dependable mass echo.

Some lawmakers kept an alert eye on developments vis-à-vis Japan. For example, to an intelligent observer, activities on the financial front could be just as significant as troop movements. That is why Senator Alexander Wiley of Wisconsin became suspicious when he learned "that in January and February [1941] the Japanese government and Japanese businessmen, instead of depositing credits in the New York banks to meet their obligations there, were withdrawing money."

So on February 14 he offered a resolution calling for a closed executive session with Hull and his undersecretaries "to discuss the eastern situation and other related matters." Wiley wanted to find out if the U.S. Pacific Fleet "was like the Russian Fleet was in the Japanese war." He also hoped to determine "whether our fleet had a coordinating air arm such as the war had recently demonstrated every fleet should have." Likewise he "wanted to know our military position and our condition in the Philippines, and whether we had sufficient airplanes, and whether we were ready for any eventuality." But "no attention was paid" to his resolution.[38] Just what material results might have emerged from such an inquiry is anybody's guess. But one thing is certain: Wiley was right on target.

Another financial area was much more obvious and of more direct interest. After Pearl Harbor, the American public had been particularly angry when they reflected upon the policy of shipping scrap iron and other strategic materials to Japan. Even in 1941, when Congress's interest in foreign affairs was almost wholly centered in Europe, certain lawmakers urged a stop to this practice as both morally indefensible and politically shortsighted. In a radio address over station WINX in the nation's capital in March 1941, Representative John B. Coffee of Washington stated: "By arming Japan the United States has become a partner in Japan's acts of aggression. For this crime we, as well as Japan, will have to answer before the international bar of justice. History will not acquit us. Our punishment may come soon."[39]

The next month found Senator Arthur Capper of Kansas on the air at the same station to stress the folly of "promoting Japanese imperialism" in this manner. "With the Philippines, Alaska, and Hawaii vulnerable, it is possible we might ourselves become embroiled in a war with Japan and have the armaments which we have furnished her used against us."[40]

In May 1941, Representative H. Carl Andersen of Minnesota noted that while selling scrap iron had been stopped, oil was still going to Japan. "Surely we all know that the chances are at least 50–50 that our own fleet may be engaged in deadly combat with that of Japan. It may be fighting against ships constructed from our scrap iron imported from our Nation and whose engines feed on our oil."[47]

In the election campaign of 1944, some Republicans in Congress blamed the administration for having pursued this policy. Senator Henrik Shipstead of Minnesota claimed that the United States not only furnished Japan scrap metal and oil but the money to pay for them:

> The United States adopted in 1933 a policy of revaluation which . . . involved the purchase of gold and of silver at prices substantially above those in effect when Mr. Roosevelt took office.
> . . . The Treasury paid an inflated price for the gold stolen from Chinese Manchuria, and for the silver they [the Japanese] smuggled out of China. And we shoveled out military and industrial equipment to them in ever greater quantities. Japan could not have paid for it. We paid for it by financing, and by bonuses in the sale of stolen metals, and of course, by buying heavily of her commodities to give her more exchange.[42]

During the congressional inquiry this matter was still a surefire subject of editorials. The St. Louis *South Side Journal* proclaimed:

> The American businessmen who sold Japan scrap iron and airplanes, well-knowing the uses to which these items could and probably would be put, should be in the dock. . . . The same businessmen whose shipments of scrap iron were piled up on west coast docks on December 7, 1941, ready for shipment to Japan, knew they weren't shipping this metal to be used in the manufacture of skillets and teakettles for resale in America.[43]

These dealers were less than selfless patriots, and the policy was a prime error, but it was not illegal. If Congress so desired, it could have legislated against this trade long before it did.

One reason the policy lasted so long may have been ignorance of and indifference to what was going on in Asia. For if anything jumps off the pages of the *Congressional Record* for 1941 it is the almost total absence of debate or comment about the Far East. Page after page slips by without so much as mention of the word Japan. In the foreign policy field, these lawmakers were obsessively preoccupied with Hitler and the war in Europe. A few quotations concerning Japan, such as those cited herein, rise out of the sea of discussions about Europe like lonely rocks in the South Atlantic. Rare indeed was the speaker who devoted any significant time to the ominous events in Asia. One such was Senator Claude Pepper of Florida. Yet his recognition that Japan presented a threat was tied to its relationship with Germany. In a long speech on the floor of Congress on May 6, 1941, Pepper proclaimed:

> . . . there is enough evidence to convince any observer that there has been a solemn compact between Japan and Germany, and that, for the first time, the occidental and the oriental conquerors have covenanted to meet in India and bring into cohesion their old worldwide conquest.
>
> . . . They [the Japanese] say, of course, that our own defenses must be weakened; that we must reduce Hawaii to a naval base of relative impotence. . . .
>
> With Japan on the other side, the vast pincer movement begins to crush us between its two jaws. Of course, Japan started off first, as he [Hitler] taught her to start, by taking a bit of territory, pinching it off and assimilating it. . . .

Pepper thought it high time for the United States "to get tough on the foreign front" and warned that Japan was awaiting her opportunity to strike. The United States should "demand and receive certain safeguards against this assassin lurking behind the door to stick a stiletto in our backs as soon as we become more engaged in the Atlantic. Like another Mussolini with his dagger poised on France . . . stands Japan ready to assassinate us at the first possible opportunity."

So Pepper urged modifying the current laws about volunteering so that Chiang Kai-shek might "have the advantage of some gallant American boys at the controls of some first-class American bombing planes, fifty of them, in my opinion, can make a shambles of Tokyo."[44] Thus Pepper's thesis was not exactly a model of realism. According to him, Japan was acting under Hitler's instructions and, while it would like to stick a knife into American ribs, fifty American volunteers with the Chinese could handle the situation. This was part and parcel of the underestimation of Japan prevalent in the United States throughout 1941.

Some congressmen spoke and acted to the point when the occasion demanded. At times they had taken the bit in their teeth when they disagreed with Roosevelt. For example, in May 1940, on the eve of Hitler's conquest of France, the President asked for $1 billion for defense—a ridiculously inadequate sum. When Congress authorized the appropriation, Roosevelt said they "might as well go home." But they "stayed on the job and voted $7,000,000,000 more." On May 28, 1940, the President "told the press he had no thought of asking for the draft. Congress voted it."[45]

These independent, farsighted actions in 1940 made all the more peculiar the recalcitrance of Congress during the summer of 1941. On July 16, the House walloped by 199 to 96 a routine bill to bring the United States Corps of Cadets at West Point up to authorized strength. According to Leonard Baker, "The result was a shock to the War Department, and officials there quickly and properly read it as a sign that any move to extend the induction period for draftees would be opposed most strenuously. The members of Congress were going on record against militarism."[46]

The War Department, and subsequently Baker, may have given the House undue credit. A reading of the debate concerning the strength of the military academy leaves the impression that the lawmakers were much less concerned with abstract concepts than with what a number saw as a possible threat to their individual prerogatives to appoint cadets. The only tinge of antimilitarism was a fear some expressed that the proposed method for filling the vacancies might result in too many appointments going to the sons of Army officers.[47]

But a possible administration defeat concerning the draft extension was a matter for genuine concern. Retention of trained selectees was essential for an effective Army. With the prospect of all he had sought to accomplish tumbling about his ears, Marshall arranged with Representative James W. Wadsworth of New York to round up about forty Republicans. Since becoming Chief of Staff, Marshall had dealt with Congress with a combination of honesty and deference that had won him trust and respect. So some of the minority lawmakers might at least listen to him.

For five hours he explained, appealed, and batted arguments to and fro. One isolationist told him, "You put the case very well, but I will be damned if I am going along with Mr. Roosevelt." Shocked, for once Marshall spoke to a congressman with anger in his voice: "You are going to let plain hatred of the personality dictate to you to do something that you realize is very harmful to the interest of the country." On the other hand, he was touched when a few of those present assured him that they would uphold the bill although to do so would lose them their seats.[48]

The fight was worth every bit of Marshall's experience and skill, for the opposition was determined and eloquent. Many argued that to extend the period of service would be a breach of faith with the draftees. This line of argument was more sentimental than logical, because the original selective service act of September 16, 1940, had modified the one-year term of service by the words "except that whenever the Congress has declared that the national interest is imperiled, such 12-month period may be extended by the President to such time as may be necessary in the interest of national defense."[49] This is why Representative Plumley was on fairly firm ground when he told Vermont's American Legion convention on July 25, "All this talk about a broken contract is a red herring drawn across the trail by those who do not or will not realize that we are preparing for a defensive war and every minute counts."[50]

Those opposed argued that the legislation was unnecessary. War conditions had improved for the free world. Britain had held off Hitler's threatened invasion and the Nazi army was locked in mortal combat with the Russians. Senator Arthur H. Vandenberg of Michigan declared, "My opinion is that the situation today, at least from a layman's standpoint, looks infinitely safer. . . . I simply cannot understand the statement by anybody that the situation is more perilous today than it was a year ago. . . ."[51]

His opponents could and did. Senator Josh Lee of Oklahoma heaped on a shovelful of current history. In September 1940 "Japan was . . . on the fence, and both Finland and Turkey were friendly to Great Britain. Today Turkey is neutralized, while both Finland and Japan are active Allies of Hitler." The French government was under Hitler's control; Spain's General Francisco Franco was strongly pro-Nazi. The Mediterranean had become almost a German lake. Hitler had a strong military footing in North Africa. He had taken control of Roumania,

Belgium, Yugoslavia, Greece, Crete, and the Baltic states. Allied shipping losses were estimated at 100,000 tons a week. So far Germany was winning the war in Russia. The prospect filled Lee with gloom: "If this be true, then it will be only a matter of time until large bodies of seasoned German troops can be withdrawn from the eastern front ready for an attempted invasion of the British Islands. . . . If Hitler conquers Russia, he will then be in control of the Siberian territory, and almost within shouting distance of Alaska." In view of all this, how "could anyone doubt that greater danger threatens America today than threatened us in September 1940"?[52]

Antiadministration forces countered with a figurative "So what?" Nobody wanted to attack the United States, nor could if they so wished. Therefore, why keep the men in service longer than one year? The United States would need a mass army only if it entered the war, and that could only happen on Washington's initiative. "Events indicate very clearly that Japan has no desire for war with the United States. . . . If we get into war, it will not be because Hitler wishes it, or Mussolini, or Japan wishes it," asserted Senator Alva B. Adams of Colorado. "I say that neither Germany, Italy nor Japan could bring to our shores at one time 250 airplanes of a fighting or bombing character."[53]

Senator Wiley also belittled any direct danger to the United States: "It is conceded that no successful attack could be made on this country without landing armed forces, and a thousand miles from shore we could put out of business any fleet assembled by a combination of all the powers on earth, for the reason that they could not bring along with them the air arm with which to protect their fleet."[54]

Thus Wiley furthered the delusion that the U.S. Navy would fight off any Japanese attack force far out in the Pacific before it could reach striking distance of American territory. This position included the deadly assumption that the U.S. armed forces would have advance notice of the enemy's approach and thus be able to deal with him decisively before he could execute a surprise attack.

This simplistic concept shadowed much military and naval thinking in 1941. And one wonders whether these lawmakers honestly believed it or were simply pushing their cause with a good head of rhetorical steam. One wonders, too, to what extent these members of Congress contributed to the illusion of American invincibility.

The opposition to the amendment demonstrated unquestioning

faith in the U.S. Navy. "Our first line of defense is alert, ready, and able," said Congressman Young. "Our Navy is the most powerful in the world; our naval aviation is superb."[55] Representative William J. Ditter of Pennsylvania, a member of the Naval Affairs Committee, was even more convinced that the nation could depend upon the sea service:

> I heartily believe . . . that when the hearings before the Military Affairs Committee on this conscription bill disclosed this utter lack of readiness on the part of the responsible heads of the Army, the people of the United States reverently thanked God that at least they had a Navy—a Navy which had not been asleep—a Navy which then was and now is, and which always will be, the best, the most modern, and the most powerful in the world—a Navy which is always fully manned, fully trained, and completely prepared to fight whenever and wherever the occasion may demand it. . . .[56]

In short, one could sum up the anti-administration position in the crisp words of Representative Usher L. Burdick of North Dakota: "The only way we can get into this war is to butt into it."[57]

To the proposition that nobody wanted to fight the United States there was a logical answer, which Senate Majority Leader Alben Barkley expressed with a characteristic touch of humor. Hitler "did not want war with Austria; he just wanted Austria." And so on down the line of all the countries Germany had conquered.[58] Armed combat had been Hitler's court of last resort.

The other part of the argument was less easy to counter, because the debate revealed that none of those participating truly believed in a direct, imminent military threat to the United States. Once again, references to Japan were few and far between. And many of those were tempered by three concepts: first, that Japan threatened American interests, not United States' soil (except perhaps the Philippines); second, that Germany was behind Japan's unfriendly moves toward the United States; and third, that the initiative for peace or war between Japan and the United States lay with Washington.

Representative Dow W. Harter of Ohio warned that Japan was "on the move," and that many foreign relations experts considered Japan more of a threat to the United States' security and possible involvement in the war than anything else. "We have seen her move her troops . . . into territory in Indochina, outflanking the Philippines, getting ready perhaps to move into the Netherlands East Indies and to attack Singapore. I do not think the United States is going to stand idly by if she makes an ultimate move in that direction."[59]

Representative Wadsworth asked of his colleagues, "Against whom was the alliance between Japan and the Axis primarily directed? Against the United States; have no doubt about it. . . . See what the Japanese are doing. Every sensible man knows that our vital interests are menaced. . . ."[60]

Representative Bertrand W. Gearhart of California usually voted with the Republicans, and was destined to be an active minority member of the joint congressional committee to investigate Pearl Harbor. But in this case he sided with the Administration and saw Japan as menacing the Philippines: "Their battleships patrol the waters of our Philippines, their bomb-laden airplanes threaten and menace Manila as we frantically muster against the anticipated raids upon our territory by a hostile army that has spent years in preparing for the assault."[61]

House Majority Leader John W. McCormack of Massachusetts agreed "that Japan is moving." But he added, "We know that Japan would never move of itself against the United States." Tokyo must choose between the friendship of Berlin and that of Washington.[62]

Extension of the draft squeaked through the House by a single vote—203 yeas, 202 nays, 27 not voting. Historian Forrest C. Pogue was undoubtedly correct in crediting "Marshall's firmness and personal standing" with the cliff-hanger victory.[63]

Seldom in American history has there been a less propitious moment for flirting with unilateral disarmament. Considering the climate of the times, the anti-Army vote smacked of the blind panic that prompts a drowning man to try to fight off a lifeguard. It also reflected the ingrained habit of opposing administration legislation, especially if it seemed by any stretch of the imagination to bring the United States closer to war. In many instances before 1940, passage of defense legislation, even if successful, had been like uprooting crabgrass.

In the years immediately preceding Pearl Harbor, Congress was ambivalent. It had acted wisely and foolishly, it had run ahead of the White House and dragged its feet, it had been clear-sighted and blind. In short, the lawmakers were no better and no worse than the voters who sent them to Washington and whom they had to satisfy.

Moreover, Congress could have passed enabling legislation every hour on the hour, and appropriated all the gold at Fort Knox, without making an iota of difference at Pearl Harbor so long as Hawaii's defenders and their superiors in Washington were not on the qui vive. Lawmakers cannot legislate an awareness of danger. Money cannot buy alertness. But the indifference of the Congress to the Far Eastern situation as compared to its preoccupation with the war in Europe may well have contributed to the lack of awareness, the lack of alertness that prevailed on Oahu.

CHAPTER 3

"Too Deeply to Bury Their Hate"

Executive responsibility—Principle of civil dominance—The anti-Roosevelt position—Lyttelton incident—Three revisionist theories—Revisionist
charges—Dangers and fallacies

Despite the thunderclouds of criticism that loomed
over the American people and Capitol Hill, the White House drew
the lightning. The initial censure did not arise from any idea that the
President and his cabinet had engaged in chicanery; the cause was
the American principle of civil dominance. In Japan, the Army and
Navy decided on their aims and capabilities, then so informed the
cabinet, which tailored its policies accordingly. In the United States,
the government established the policy, and the armed forces had to
cut their cloth to fit the pattern.*

In retrospect, Captain Joseph K. Taussig, Jr., who as a young
ensign was seriously wounded aboard *Nevada* during the Pearl Harbor
attack, saw the governmental set-up as the basic cause of Japan's initial
success:

> . . . The Constitution places the authority as Commander-in-Chief
> directly on the shoulders of the President. . . . Through an obscure,
> though nonetheless actual, process of reasoning, statute, and tradi-
> tion, the "authority" chain of command is, and was, understood to
> flow to the Secretaries of the services. . . .
> . . . In fact, the entire premise of "civilian control" is based on
> the theory that the military officer should stick to his profession, and
> merely carry out the policies and orders of his civilian peers. . . .[1]

Soon this realization that the White House could not escape some
blame by the very nature of the American system burst the bounds
of reason. The Emporia (Kansas) *Gazette* predicted on December 15,

*See page xxv for Chart of Executive Branch.

1941, that it would take "about two weeks for this lovey-dovey business about the President to wear out. . . . The fellows who hated Roosevelt last week, hated him too deeply to bury their hate. Soon they will remember how they hate him. . . ." The *Gazette* anticipated that the "same old Quislings and appeasers" would soon be "trying to get a knife under the President's political ribs."

This cynical prophecy proved all too accurate. The faction accustomed to blaming Roosevelt for everything from rising taxes to a rained-out ball game was soon in full cry. The legend began that the disaster was Roosevelt's fault. If one sought an American target—soothing to the ego, for otherwise one must admit that the United States had not held the reins in dealing with Japan—who could fill the bill better than "That Man in the White House"?

To a degree this reaction was natural. As the war dragged on, and the initial surge of crusading spirit simmered down into a grim day-in, day-out struggle, Roosevelt's political enemies had time to remember their old antagonism. Somehow or other, they reasoned, the United States' participation in this dreadful conflict must be Roosevelt's fault, either through stupidity or malice.

Unwittingly, the British added to the controversy. Departing from a prepared speech to the American Chamber of Commerce in London on June 20, 1944, Minister of Production Oliver Lyttelton stated, "Japan was provoked into attacking the Americans at Pearl Harbor. It is a travesty on history ever to say that America was forced into the war. Everyone knows where American sympathies were. It is incorrect to say that America was ever truly neutral even before America came into the war on an all-out fighting basis."[2]

Almost before Lyttelton had closed his mouth, the fat was sizzling in the fire. Comments in the United States ran the gamut from insinuating agreement to vigorous outrage. Upset by these reactions, Lyttelton explained:

> I wished to make the point that the Americans did not wait until they entered the war before showing where their sympathies lay, and that the aid which they gave to Britain will always be remembered with the liveliest sense of gratitude. This aid was, of course, directed to the war against Germany, and could not have been regarded as a provocation of a peace-minded Japan. But the Japanese aggressor chose to regard it as a provocation, and made the unjustified and treacherous attack at Pearl Harbor.[3]

So Lyttelton, who naturally saw the war from the British perspective, had meant only to compliment the United States for having been all along on the side of the angels. He misunderstood the motivation behind Japan's attack on Pearl Harbor, and out of his ignorance put his foot right through a hornet's nest. Human nature being what it is, Lyttelton's explanation did not have the impact of his original statement. Of such bits and pieces are legends constructed. No dyed-in-the-wool revisionist work is complete without reference to Lyttelton's unhappy expression, usually out of context and with the implicit or stated conclusion that he was absolutely right.[4]

This leads to the consideration of the revisionist school of historians, their theories and techniques.[5] Nothing is wrong with revisionism per se. On the contrary, for generally accepted standards and concepts to come up for periodic review is healthy. Anyone who can prove, on the basis of sound research and scholarship, that a misconception exists which can and should be corrected has performed a useful historical service.

Some revisionists were reputable, experienced scholars whose views deserve open-minded, careful consideration. However, it is precisely after such an examination that serious misgivings arise as to their objectivity.

The revisionist school was divided roughly into three camps. The first one claimed that Roosevelt's foreign policy was mistaken, because American participation in the war ultimately worked to the benefit of the Soviet Union. This thesis, adopted by William S. Neumann and William Henry Chamberlin,[6] ignored the fact that the United States had to deal with an immediate danger, the Berlin-Rome-Tokyo Axis, and could not operate on the basis of what was then a problematical future menace.

Possibly the ablest advocate of the second revisionist camp was Charles A. Beard, who amassed an awesome reputation as a historian. Beard believed that Roosevelt maneuvered the United States into the war. But he merely insinuated rather than stated outright that Roosevelt knew about the Pearl Harbor attack in advance and deliberately permitted it to come unopposed.[7]

Spearhead of the third revisionist school, with which we shall deal in detail, was sociologist and historian Harry Elmer Barnes. None of Beard's cautious insinuations for Barnes! He believed that, to get around Roosevelt's campaign promise that he would not lead the

United States into war unless attacked, the President and most of his top military and political advisers schemed to maneuver Japan into striking. To ensure that event, Barnes postulated, Pearl Harbor must not be alerted, hence Roosevelt and Marshall, acting alone, arranged that such warning be withheld. And finally, many of Roosevelt's advisers joined with him in a massive cover-up.[8]

Among those who, like Barnes, could accept Roosevelt's guilt was the President's former son-in-law, Curtis B. Dall. His book is loaded with suggestions that Roosevelt was the tool of so-called "Advisors," unnamed but sinister to the last degree:

> For the Advisors, however, it was a matter of managed news and correct timing. . . . Their managed news repeatedly pointed to political pie-in-the-sky. . . .
>
> The "pie" was in the sky, for sure, and the crusts of dereliction of duty manifestly in Washington. By dint of the devious maneuvering of some leading American and British politicians and others, the "pie" was rained down from the sky directly upon the unsuspecting heads of thousands of our loyal, unalerted American troops at Pearl Harbor one December morning. Over 3,800 of them died! What treason! . . .
>
> I have often wondered if, as part of a long-range plan, FDR deliberately ignored the possibility and danger of an attack on Pearl Harbor by the approaching massive Japanese Task Force, an attack made on us almost by engraved invitation. He must have! Then, if such were the case, he must have wanted it. Who told him to "want" it? . . .
>
> *Who told FDR* that a "Pearl Harbor" was necessary? Did he fall for the one-world-despot theory? [Dall's italics][9]

Many naval personnel interviewed in connection with Pearl Harbor, especially those who had been enlisted men or junior officers at the time, believed the Roosevelt-as-villain thesis. Chief John Crawford of *Vestal* declared, "FDR was a dirty so-and-so!"[10] Lieutenant Commander Harley F. Smart, also of *Vestal*, believed that "Roosevelt knew about Pearl Harbor all along."[11] CPO Thomas E. Forrow, who was stationed on Ford Island in December 1941, reflected, "It just doesn't add up, and the man is dead who controlled it all—Roosevelt."[12]

Historian Leonard Baker also noted this phenomenon:

Kimmel claimed the surprise at Pearl Harbor was not due to any lack of responsible action on his part. Rather, he charged, the Roosevelt administration withheld information from him. The charge has been investigated dozens of times by friends of Kimmel and remains without any proof. The Navy, not officially but certainly informally, still will not accept that one of its best men could have done less than expected of him. To so acknowledge means acknowledging that the system by which the Navy produces officers is at fault. Kimmel's story is widely believed among career men in the Navy.[13]

Yet that same system produced brilliant leaders who piloted the U.S. Navy to resounding victory in World War II. For that matter, until December 7, 1941, Kimmel had racked up an impeccable record. Nevertheless, there was evidence that the Navy unofficially identified with Kimmel. Rear Admiral Dundas P. Tucker wrote to Lieutenant Commander Charles C. Hiles on June 2, 1968, "I am glad to learn you are going ahead on Kimmel because you will be clearing not only him, but the professional Navy as a whole. . . ."[14]

A number of nonprofessional historians of the revisionist school were either ex-Navy or strongly pro-Navy. These people could not concede that the U.S. Pacific Fleet had been so appallingly surprised and defeated unless treachery had been involved. Underestimating to the bitter end Japan's determination, aggressiveness, and ability, they believed that Japan would never have attacked the United States if not provoked beyond endurance.

Some revisionist writers were good craftsmen and could readily beguile anyone unfamiliar with the Pearl Harbor documentation. Their published works revealed a tendency toward presenting opinions and generalities as proved facts, and a cavalier attitude toward solid evidence. They also adopt the position that they alone were the guardians of the truth about Pearl Harbor. This insistence upon infallible purity can be hypnotic, and a surprising number of people still believe the anti-Roosevelt thesis, or at least have an uneasy feeling that there may be something in it.

The more vociferous revisionists made statements concerning the thoughts of others, thereby reaching conclusions with no visible means of support. In particular, they did not doubt their ability to read Roosevelt's mind at any given moment—a feat far beyond the closest of his friends and advisers. For example, Rear Admiral Kemp Tolley wrote that the President "sweated out that last week in an agony of apprehension that the Japanese would bypass the Americans for the time being. . . ." A little later in his story, Tolley wrote concerning the so-called "commitment" to Britain by Rainbow Five, the U.S. Navy's basic war plan, "Which would come first? The execution or the legitimization? The President prayed it would be the latter."[15] Tolley could not possibly have direct knowledge of Roosevelt's state of mind or the context of his prayers.

John Toland, most recent recruit to revisionism, also adopted this regrettable habit of claiming to be able to read minds: "Roosevelt must have felt somewhat like a pawn in the hands of his belligerent Cabinet."[16] If ever a President dominated his cabinet, it was Roosevelt. In one instance, Toland even presumed to quote an individual's thoughts directly; "Kimmel was thinking: 'They all know where to get it . . . every Goddamn one of them.' "[17] Perhaps Kimmel did think that, but Toland's footnotes showed no source for this quotation.

A number of revisionists have been careless about readily ascertainable facts. For example, in discussing Kimmel's visit to Washington when he was CinCUS, Dall claimed to have asked, "Admiral, on that June trip, did you try to see FDR?" According to Dall, Kimmel answered, "Yes, I tried, but Roosevelt did not wish to see me."[18] It is incredible that Kimmel, a man of honor, made such a statement, for he did visit with Roosevelt on June 9, 1941, and wrote a memorandum of their conversation.[19]

Some or all of such misinterpretations might have been due to misunderstanding or ignorance, but anyone examining the extreme revisionist position should proceed with due caution. We would not devote so much space to it except for two frightening aspects. First, such disregard for the laws of evidence undermines the structure of Occidental justice, so laboriously erected over the centuries. If contemporary documents and sworn testimony can be disregarded in favor of unsupported charges and personal venom, no citizen is safe. Second, the reluctance to admit that the U.S. Army and Navy had left themselves wide open for defeat on Oahu implies a refusal to profit by experience. It also recalls uncomfortably the notion so widespread among the Germans after World War I, and such a favorite thesis with Hitler, that Germany did not really suffer military defeat, but had been stabbed in the back by politicians on the home front.

One relying entirely upon revisionist works in an attempt to understand Pearl Harbor might assume that the United States military and naval field forces in 1941 were manned solely by Beetle Baileys, too lethargic or too stupid to think and act intelligently unless Washington told them in words of one syllable exactly what to expect and what to do. This refusal or inability to realize that the question of why Oahu's defenders were surprised on December 7, 1941, is fundamentally a military, not a political, question, is a major weakness of the revisionist position.

An equally shaky foundation stone in their edifice was their tendency to regard the Japanese as mindless pawns for Roosevelt and his advisers to push around at will. Inevitably this led to the attitude that those pawns were not only maneuverable but innocent. Barnes lamented, ". . . Japan veritably crawled on its diplomatic belly from the end of August 1941, until the middle of November of that year in an attempt to reach some workable understanding with the United States. . . ."[20]

Throughout his book, Toland took the attitude that the Japanese sincerely tried to avoid war with the United States, and negotiated in good faith. Of course, the Japanese did not want to fight the Americans if they could attain their goals without cost. But nothing in the available evidence, written or oral, indicates that they ever planned to move one inch out of their appointed path, whatever the United States did about it. In fact, all the evidence points to the contrary.

Suppose, for example, that Washington had agreed to Japan's proposals of November 20, 1941,* although knowing from Magic† that this was Japan's final offer? Such action would have done nothing toward a lasting peace; it would merely have postponed the inevitable crisis. If the lessons painfully learned throughout history have any validity, one can say with confidence that the Japanese would have considered the Americans so contemptibly weak that in the future they could demand more and more for less and less, as is the nature of dictatorships and aggressor nations. Rudyard Kipling said it best:

> . . . we've proved it again and again,
> That if once you have paid him the Dane-geld
> You never get rid of the Dane.[21]

---

*See Appendix 2.
†Magic was the name given to the process whereby the Americans intercepted and decrypted Japan's diplomatic codes.

Some Japanese, writing in the postwar years, would have been very happy to "verify that the war was not caused by Japan's own aggression but was imposed upon her," in the hope that thus "the spot left upon the morality of the nation's history will be removed and the honor of our nation will be restored."[22] But the many Japanese interviewed for this study who either helped plan, participated in, or made a special study of Japan's military moves during World War II, especially the Pearl Harbor attack, deprecated this attitude. They believed that, in the context of the time, their country did what it had to do and was the pilot of its own ship of state. They felt no pangs of conscience over their role.[23]

The revisionists seemed to think that the Pearl Harbor strike was a simple exercise that could have been whipped up at the last minute. They had no conception of the meticulous planning and Spartan training involved, of the long struggle necessary to win the Naval General Staff's acceptance of Yamamoto's plan, of the last-minute mechanical breakthroughs that preceded the sortie of the task force. They treated the entire subject as almost irrelevant, and certainly had no understanding of the strategic purpose of the attack.

The extreme revisionists reasoned that, in Toland's words, "An attack conceived in such secrecy would necessarily depend on complete surprise for success, and once discovered out of range of its target, *Kido Butai** would have turned back."[24]

The Japanese hoped for surprise and took every possible precaution to ensure it; but they did not really expect it, and were astonished and gratified when they achieved it. In his farewell address to the task force officers, Yamamoto himself had warned them, ". . . you must take into careful consideration the possibility that the attack may not be a surprise after all. You may have to fight your way in to the target."[25] Nagumo was so sure that total surprise was unattainable that he argued for a southern route to Hawaii, to take advantage of good weather and smooth seas, in preference to the less frequented northern route.[26]

Maximum damage, not surprise in itself, was the Japanese objective in the attack on Oahu. Surprise would aid considerably in achieving that goal, but the loss of surprise would not be sufficient reason to abort Operation Hawaii. No officer worth his commission would

---

*The Nagumo task force.

plan and embark upon such an operation without being ready for all-out battle. One of the reasons Vice Admiral Gunichi Mikawa, who commanded Nagumo's support force, wanted four battleships instead of two was because he anticipated a possible slugging match at sea.[27] Yamamoto wanted to destroy Kimmel's ships, not to hit Pearl Harbor as such. As he told his chief of staff, Rear Admiral Shigeru Fukudome, in the spring of 1940, his target was the U.S. Pacific Fleet "wherever it might be found in the Pacific."[28] In view of Yamamoto's objective, one can only assume that, if the task force had encountered any part of Kimmel's ships heading out to meet it, Nagumo would have attacked at once.

Some of the Japanese planners and participants in the Pearl Harbor attack stated that if the Washington discussions had resolved matters to Japan's satisfaction, the task force was under orders to turn back. But a number of them agree that after a point this would have been like asking them to put toothpaste back into a tube. Lieutenant Commander Chuichi Yoshioka, assistant to Cmdr. Minoru Genda, Nagumo's air officer, believed that once the task force rendezvoused at Hitokappu Bay "the die was virtually cast and Nagumo settled down somewhat because he knew this operation would have to be carried out."[29] Fuchida stated that when the task force left Hitokappu Bay, the staff officers "fully expected that hostilities might break out at any time."[30]

That the Navy-minded Roosevelt would have staked out the U.S. Pacific Fleet as a lure for the Japanese is such an incongruous idea that even some of his most implacable enemies did not accept it. John T. Flynn, whose pamphlet, *The Truth about Pearl Harbor,* first presented the revisionist position, charged Roosevelt with "appalling negligence, ineptitude and ignorance." Flynn believed that the President "wanted to provoke Japan to attack. But he utterly and pitifully misunderstood the variety of attacks to which he exposed the country. He certainly never looked for an attack which would kill 3,000 Americans and knock the American Navy and Army out of the war in a day. . . ."[31] In a later article, Flynn stressed this idea that Roosevelt had snared himself through ignorance: "He was completely sure the Japs would not strike at Pearl Harbor. . . . Thus he completely miscalculated. . . . When the attack came he was appalled and frightened. . . ."[32]

Others were not so logical. According to one story, around the

1st of December, 1941, Roosevelt is supposed to have shown Curtis Dall a Naval Intelligence report containing an intercept from the "Commander of the Japanese Navy to the effect that the Japanese Fleet is going to attack the United States. . . . Roosevelt said that the prospective attack would cause some damage to our Fleet, but (rubbing his hands together) that it would get us into the war."[33] This sensational incident was deflated almost nine years after its reported occurrence. Dall told Percy L. Greaves, Jr., that he "couldn't explain how the story got so twisted but admitted it was a good one and he wished it were so."[34]

Toland suggested that Roosevelt let the attack proceed because he expected that "the Pacific Fleet would not only stem any Japanese attack with little loss to U.S. shipping but deal a crushing blow to *Kido Butai* itself."[35] With this remark Toland stripped the gears of his own principal thesis, for how could Roosevelt expect the Pacific Fleet to deal a "crushing blow" to the Nagumo task force if he did not ensure that Kimmel and Short were fully alert? An American victory at Pearl Harbor would have served his alleged purpose just as well as a shattering defeat.

On September 24, 1945 the St. Louis *Star-Times* stressed this aspect in a blistering indictment of the isolationist arguments against Roosevelt. If the President "wanted to precipitate us into the war . . . that could have been accomplished just as readily if the Japanese had attacked us at Pearl Harbor and we had been ready for them as it was when they attacked us in a state of unpreparedness."[36]

William F. Friedman, the renowned cryptologist who played a key role in breaking the Japanese Purple code, pounced on this weakness in the revisionist position:

> If all that Roosevelt thought necessary for his purposes, if all that he was seeking, was "to maneuver the Japanese into firing the first shot," . . . would it not have been possible . . . to accomplish his purpose without such terrible loss of American lives and, without loss of any of the ships that constituted the apple of the President's eye, the Navy's big battleships?

If the Americans caught the Japanese near Hawaii, "nobody could possibly claim they were on a simple, harmless reconnaissance mission. . . ." So why would Roosevelt not inform Kimmel and Short and put them in a position to intercept Nagumo?[37]

Why not, indeed? Neumann, himself a revisionist of the milder variety, wrote to Barnes on August 15, 1962: "Any attack on Pearl Harbor would have brought Congressional action on war, he [Roosevelt] didn't *have to have* the fleet sunk and handicap him for the first year or more of the war. This would have meant that he was clinically 'mad' and I can't buy that argument . . ." (Neumann's italics).[38]

In fact, any maneuvering at Pearl Harbor such as the revisionists postulated was unnecessary. Whether or not the Japanese attacked there, war was coming. Whether or not the Nagumo force attacked as planned, and whether it won or lost the engagement, Japan was going forward with the rest of its expansive war plans. Pearl Harbor was not the sole or even the primary operation. It is unrealistic to imagine that the United States could have avoided war in the Pacific after the Japanese attacked Guam, Wake, and the Philippines—all under the American flag—without tacitly withdrawing from the world scene into the status of a third-rate power at the mercy of the Axis.[39]

CHAPTER 4

"Bait for a Japanese Attack"

"Three little ships"—Did the Japanese break radio silence?—Evidence to the contrary—*Lurline* incident—Seaman Z—*I-23* incident—Alleged sightings off Dutch Harbor—Ranneft incident—Ramifications of alleged cover-up

In support of their theories concerning Roosevelt's villainy, revisionists have presented a number of incidents, enough to fill a full book. A careful scrutiny of these reveals one characteristic in common, namely, a complete lack of proof of Roosevelt's evil intentions or, in many cases, that he was involved at all. The evidence against the President lies in the judgment of the writers submitting them, not in the incidents themselves.

An example was the saga of the "three little ships." According to anti-Roosevelt dogma, the President planned this as a decoy operation because he wanted the Japanese to sink an American naval vessel, thus providing him with the excuse to ask Congress to declare war.

One of the first to accept this concept was Frederic R. Sanborn, who wrote, "On December 1, 1941, Mr. Roosevelt very secretly issued the needless order to send the Cockleshell Warships to their appointed positions of destruction."[1] Harry Elmer Barnes took the position that the small craft "could move out into the path of the Japanese task forces going southward and draw fire from Japanese planes or ships, thus giving Roosevelt his all-important and indispensable attack, and one that was on an American ship."[2] Latest to join the chorus has been John Costello, who headed his brief account of the incident "Roosevelt's Trip Wire."[3]

A close look at the documents and testimony reveals nothing worse than a rather irritating busybodyism on Roosevelt's part. Admiral Harold R. "Betty" Stark, Chief of Naval Operations, had been speculating with the President as to the ultimate target of the Japanese

45

expedition headed south. Roosevelt opted for the Kra Peninsula, and
Stark agreed. But the Philippines and the East Indies were also possibilities.* To assist in reaching a definite conclusion, the President
directed that a special mission of three small vessels be dispatched
toward the Indochina coast as pickets.[4]

On December 2, 1941 the Navy Department sent this message
to Admiral Thomas C. Hart, Commander in Chief, Asiatic Fleet:

> President directs that the following be done as soon as possible and
> within two days if possible after receipt of this despatch. Charter 3
> small vessels to form a "defensive information patrol". Minimum
> requirements to establish identity as U.S. men-of-war are command
> by a naval officer and to mount a small gun and 1 machine gun would
> suffice. Filipino crews may be employed with minimum number
> naval ratings to accomplish purpose which is to observe and report
> by radio Japanese movements in west China Sea and Gulf of Siam.
> One vessel to be stationed between Hainan and Hue one vessel off
> the Indo-China Coast between Camranh Bay and Cape St. Jacques
> and one vessel off Pointe de Camau. Use of Isabel authorized by
> president as one of the three but not other naval vessels. Report
> measures taken to carry out presidents views. At same time inform
> me what reconnaissance measures are being regularly performed at
> sea by both army and navy whether by air surface vessels or sub-
> marines and your opinion as to the effectiveness of these latter meas-
> ures.[5]

Stark explained to the congressional committee, "Well, if you have
fairly well in mind the points where the vessels were you will see
where the President put them they were well placed to get information either positive or negative . . ."

Roosevelt gave Stark no indication of any reason for the mission
"other than the general desire to have information concerning Japanese movements." Stark testified, "We were scouting by air, and I
simply think that he thought that was additional precautions. He
was intensely interested in every move at that time, as we all
were."[6] Revisionist George Morgenstern later ridiculed Stark's testimony:

> Admiral Stark put on a deadpan display before the congressional
> committee four years later, saying that the dispatch read that the

---

*See Chapter 8.

"patrol" was to be sent out for information; so that was its sole purpose. Adults will persist in the belief that Roosevelt was attempting to rig a lynching which would relieve him of his embarrassments by putting this sacrifice force in the path of the Japanese fleet, where it would be run down or shot up.[7]

Morgenstern's use of the word "adults" implied that anyone who did not swallow this cynical line was immature. One would hope, instead, that "adults will persist in the belief" that solid evidence and sworn testimony outrank unsupported speculation.

Rear Admiral Roland M. Brainard, director of Ship Movements Division, drafted the message in question. His office was primarily a record-keeping and information center concerning ship locations; Brainard "was not in on questions of broad general policy."[8]

Rear Admiral Royal E. Ingersoll, Assistant CNO, also "had a large part" in preparing the dispatch. But his testimony revealed clearly that he disapproved of the mission. Asked why the Navy wanted the three vessels in such positions, he replied, "The reason that we wanted them there is because it says in the beginning of the dispatch the 'President directs that the following be done as soon as possible.' That was our reason for doing it. Admiral Stark was told by the President to do it." Ingersoll was "sure Admiral Stark would not have done this unless he had been told." He further emphasized, "We did not initiate this movement, sir, and we were getting, I think, so far as Admiral Stark was concerned, sufficient information from Admiral Hart by the searches which his planes were making."[9]

Although not consulted, Rear Admiral Richmond Kelly Turner, chief of the War Plans Division, knew of the project. He "never would have sent or requested" that these ships be dispatched because Hart "was competent to take care of the situation so far as possible with the forces at his disposal." But Turner reminded the congressional committee that the Navy Department had suggested to Kimmel that when necessary he employ "small craft out there as lookouts on three different occasions."[10]

Senator Homer Ferguson of Michigan asked Ingersoll, "Would that have been an overt act if one of these small boats had been fired on?" The admiral replied, "It would have been." He went further: "It would have been an incident on which we could have declared war had we wished to." However, he pointed out, "Of course, our

men-of-war had been fired upon before, like the Panay incident,*
and we did not go to war."[11]

The records do not indicate whether or not the Navy informed
the Army of this mission. Marshall testified that he had no recollection
of the OPNAV message to Hart which established the project.[12] Brigadier General Sherman Miles, acting assistant chief of staff, Intelligence (G-2), knew nothing about it. "To the best of my knowledge
and belief, this is the first time I have ever seen that message," he
told the congressional committee. Ferguson prodded him persistently
in an obvious attempt to secure an admission that if Miles had seen
the message at the time, it would have conveyed some special meaning to him. Miles refused to rise to the bait.[13] Brigadier General
Leonard T. Gerow, as chief of the War Plans Division, did not know
about this operation until the story came out before the congressional
committee.[14]

Although the President had directed that the mission be carried
out "as soon as possible," no one seemed to feel any great sense of
urgency. Hart's reply to the Navy Department on December 2 revealed that he was less than enthusiastic about the instructions:

> Am recalling Isabel from current mission and sending toward Pa-
> daran. She is too short radius to accomplish much and since we have
> few fast ships her loss would be serious. Therefore have to recom-
> mend against carrying out Isabel's movement though it is improbable
> that can start any chartered craft within two days. . . . Am searching
> for vessels for charter that are suitable but cannot yet estimate time
> required to obtain and equip with radio.[15]

Nor was that Hart's only problem. Aerial reconnaissance gave him
difficulties, too. "It was the northeast monsoon season. That whole
area is filled with rain squalls," he explained to the congressional
committee. Even so, he did not fulfill the President's orders. "Time
did not serve. One ship . . . the *Isabel* was dispatched in consequence
of this instruction and was nearing her station when the Japanese
attack occurred. The second one to be made ready was on the point
of sailing and the third was not yet ready."[16] According to Barnes:

> Hart realized that on this assignment the *Isabel* was to be bait for a
> Japanese attack, which displeased him since the vessel was very

---

*Japanese military planes attacked and sank the American gunboat *Panay* in the Yangstze river
in December 1937.

useful to the fleet. Yet he did not wish to seem to be defying the President's wishes. He sensibly solved his dilemma by sending the *Isabel* out as directed but under instructions which rendered it as unlikely as possible to be attacked and sunk by the Japanese. These instructions were directly contrary to Roosevelt's plans and intentions, and Hart knew they were.[17]

If Hart knew "Roosevelt's plans and intentions," he must have added telepathy to his other accomplishments. No doubt the instructions from Stark upset and displeased him. Tolley quoted a letter that Hart wrote on May 5, 1952, to Director of Naval History Rear Admiral John Heffernan:

> It was a definite and flat order, so worded as to bear the highest priority. We received it with consternation. Carrying out the order consumed effort we could ill spare from more valuable objectives. As a war measure the project was very ill-advised. Pickets in such locations could not be useful because the Japanese were bound to have them marked down—the order was to place them close to the Indo-China coast—which would mean no chance to let them see anything of value. Therefore, to no commensurate end, we were to risk ships and valuable personnel.[18]

These comments offer a sound, commonsense assessment of the project's weaknesses. Whatever his private thoughts, Hart took elaborate precautions and thoroughly briefed *Isabel*'s skipper, Lieutenant John Walker Payne, Jr., as was natural in view of the current military and political situation.

Isabel got under way at 1447 on December 3, Payne in command. On December 5 a Japanese aircraft, number Z126, circled the ship and Payne ordered battle stations. But the Japanese only took pictures, and *Isabel* returned the compliment. At 1910 the ship sighted the coast of Indochina twenty-two miles away. Ten minutes later, she received a message from CinCAF to return immediately to Manila. So Payne reversed course and arrived at Manila at 0822 on December 8.[19]

Giving his imagination a free rein, Barnes claimed, "If the *Isabel* episode had been handled in the manner that Roosevelt wished and provided the maximum provocation to trigger-happy Japanese pilots or gunners there might not have been any attack on Pearl Harbor and the fleet could have been saved."[20] This suggestion that Yamamoto would have aborted Operation Hawaii had some "trigger-happy" Japanese sunk what was little more than an American yacht in Southeast Asian waters is too absurd for serious consideration. The mission of the Nagumo task force was to immobilize the U.S. Pacific Fleet for a minimum of six months, not to provide Roosevelt with an excuse to declare war.

The second little ship, *Lanikai,* was a two-master of about 150 tons, with top speed of seven knots, "a fine little sea boat."[21] She was commissioned on December 5, at Cavite Navy Yard, and remained there all the next day. On December 7 she got under way "in accordance with CinCAF confidential despatch orders" at 1415. At 1545 she dropped anchor six and a half miles from Corregidor light. The next day she was anchored two and a half miles from Corregidor light when at 0300 she

> received radio information that the Japanese had attacked United States forces through the Pacific area. Ordered to return to Manila. Noted with satisfaction that a delay of several days would have meant the sure loss of the ship, in view of the nature of its mission to scout off French Indo China in the vicinity of CAMRANH BAY.
>
> At 0615 got under way in accordance with orders to return to MANILA, feeling very glad to be alive. [Capitals in original][22]

Tolley became firmly convinced that *Lanikai* had been intended as bait for the Japanese. He even suggested that the Filipino crew members had been ordered aboard to make sure the Philippines would demand war also.[23] Tolley further claimed that many years later Hart declared that he thought the "three little ships" were "set up to bait an incident," and could prove it. But he would not do so, and cautioned Tolley not to try.[24]

Hart did indeed think "that Roosevelt wanted Japan to attack us."[25] But if he really believed that the "three little ships" mission had been a deliberate trap, why did he not so testify to the congressional committee? Tolley informed Lt. Cmdr. Charles C. Hiles, USN (Ret), who devoted considerable study to Pearl Harbor, that Hart once told him if its members "had been cleverer and had delved further into the thing, 'then the fat would have been in the fire,' as he would have had to say what he knew."[26]

Yet Ferguson had put this direct question to Hart: "Will you give us the purpose, if you know, that was to be served by these three small men-of-war?" How much deeper could Ferguson have probed?

If Hart had any startling revelations to make, here was his opportunity. But he replied merely, "I know nothing, Senator, that is not contained in the dispatch. . . ."[27]

No solid evidence exists that Roosevelt ordered out the small craft to stir up a war in the Far East for which the United States was ill prepared and which it did not want. Moreover, it is ridiculous to postulate that the United States would have considered the loss of one of these tiny vessels a reason to declare war on Japan when it had overlooked the loss of much more valuable ships in the Atlantic.

The only evidence of Roosevelt's intentions available to date was contained in the message initiating the mission. His track record in relation to the Navy showed a firm belief in the efficacy of small craft.[28] It was characteristic that he should want to use the "three little ships" for scouting even though Hart was already covering the job by aerial reconnaissance.

Nor was it surprising that Roosevelt should have dabbled his fingers in the tactical details of a relatively minor operation instead of simply ordering it done and leaving the nuts and bolts to the Navy. Admiral Ben Moreell, who had been chief of the Bureau of Yards and Docks (BuDocks) from December 1937 to November 1945, pointed out to Greaves that Roosevelt "had obsessions on some things one day and forgot them the next." The President "apparently developed intense interest in certain things and then his mind flitted on to others and he never got back to his original interest." Ingersoll also told Greaves that "FDR often concentrated on details, particularly when it concerned his pet projects."[29]

Instead of Roosevelt's ordering the vessels militarized in the hope that a sinking would provide an excuse to go to war, it is far more likely that this was, as General Miles suggested, "for the protection . . . of the personnel, had they been captured by an enemy." In that case, in Ferguson's words, "they could not be treated as spies. . . . They would have to be treated as prisoners of war. . . ."[30]

Air Chief Marshal Sir Robert Brooke-Popham, British Commander in Chief in the Far East, had asked Major General Douglas MacArthur, in command of U.S. Army Forces in the Far East, to send a B-17 on a photographic reconnaissance over the area in question—Camranh Bay. MacArthur refused on the grounds that "orders from Washington" prevented him from doing so.* Roosevelt may have

---

*See Chapter 5.

directed the mission of the "three little ships" to supply the intelligence the British had requested in a less, rather than a more, provocative manner than by overflying the area. However, this is speculative.

In all the Pearl Harbor investigations, no one but Ferguson seemed to think that a sinister motive might lurk behind Roosevelt's action. He questioned Kimmel on the subject, but, although the admiral was exceedingly bitter, his native honesty brought this sensible reply: "That was a perfectly natural thing for us to do on the basis that we wanted to know what the Japanese were doing; we wanted to know whether they would have come to the Philippines or not."[31]

Even the congressional committee's minority report, so critical of the administration, cited the case only as an occasion when "the obligation of an officer was weakened by intermeddling of superiors" and specifically by Roosevelt's directing "detailed operations for which field commanders were responsible."[32] That seems to be a reasonable assessment. The evidence showed an ill-conceived operation dreamed up by a politician who considered himself an expert on naval matters. But stupidity is not yet prima facie evidence of villainy.

Toland's *Infamy* is replete with somewhat lurid accounts which do not stand up very well under close scrutiny. Prange was well aware of most of the incidents that Toland took up, such as those involving Kilsoo Haan and Major Warren J. Clear, and the *Lurline* incident discussed below. On the basis of interviews and other research, Prange concluded that no solid evidence existed to support them.

Here we should like to consider four of Toland's cases which have a major point in common—the presumption that the Nagumo task force broke radio silence. One of the most intriguing of these stories is that of the Matson liner *Lurline*, one of whose assistant radio operators, Leslie C. Grogan, claimed to be picking up signals in a Japanese code from several stations in Yokohama, using the lower marine radio frequency, all controlled from some central point, probably Tokyo. Grogan claimed "that signals were being repeated back" from Japanese ships in an area north and west of Honolulu. When the liner docked at Honolulu, Grogan and the chief radio operator allegedly took their findings to Lieutenant Commander George Warren Pease of the Fourteenth Naval District office. He promised to forward the information to his superiors but, according to Toland, there is no record of his having sent it either to Captain Irving Mayfield, head of the district's Intelligence Office, or to Washington. Then, when *Lurline* docked at San Francisco on December 10, 1941, a naval officer supposedly came aboard and asked for the log which was given him, along with notes for the period November 30 to December 7. Once again: "There is no record in the Navy files of these documents or the incidents that took place."[33]

Prange was well aware of Grogan's story and could not credit it, because the evidence that the Japanese maintained strict radio silence is overwhelming, based upon the statements of actual members of the task force, plus diaries and official records. For example, the diary of the Third Battleship Division related, "The absolute radio silence of the Task Force did not leak anything. The precise broadcast from the Tokyo Signal Corps contributed to swift communications of important telegrams."

The diary of the First Destroyer Division reproduced copies of important messages received during the voyage. Nagumo sent a number of messages to his force, but all were by signal (by flag during the day; by blinker at night), not radio. In his personal diary, Rear Admiral Sadao Chigusa, who at the time was executive officer of the destroyer *Akigumo*, also mentioned "signals," but never radio traffic. It is fairly certain that he would have recorded any violation of radio silence, because he noted everything else newsworthy, even what food his crew ate.

In the summer of 1942 the Yokosuka Naval Air Corps, Air Branch Committee, Battle-Lessons Investigating Committee, compiled an official study of lessons of "the Sea Battle Off Hawaii." It attributed the Japanese success to a number of factors, among them:

> Strictest radio silence.
> In order to keep strict radio silence, thorough steps such as taking off fuses in the circuit, holding and sealing the keys were taken. During the operation, the strictest radio silence was perfectly carried out.[34]

Mitsuo Fuchida, who led the air attack, wrote, "The Force maintained the strictest radio silence throughout the cruise."[35] Genda stressed that radio silence was so important that the pilots agreed not to go on the air, even if their lives depended upon it.[36] And Rear Admiral Ryunosuke Kusaka, who as Nagumo's chief of staff certainly knew what was going on, wrote as follows:

Each vessel was kept on the alert position. . . . All transmitters were sealed, and all hands were ordered to be kept away from any key of the machine. . . .

Since skippers and crews of oilers were veterans who had grown up at sea for many years they were able to master refueling works and others in comparatively short period of trainings, but a difficult problem to them was to maintain a formation at night without any lamps. Vessels which had been in a formation in the evening often became lost of sight in the following morning. In peacetime they could be gotten in touch with by wireless, but that method could not be utilized because of the radio silence.[37]

In an attempt to pin this down even further, we wrote to Prange's friend and representative, Masataka Chihaya, formerly of the Imperial Japanese Navy, and found that he was a step ahead of us already. *Bungei Shunju* had run a long extract of Toland's book, and Chihaya was preparing to refute the article. He replied:

Regarding Toland's claim that the U.S. picked up radio signals of the Nagumo Force on Dec. 2, I made a double check with Genda and [Susumu] Ishiguro, then communication staff officer of the 2nd Carrier Div. Both of them claim that there couldn't be absolutely any such case, since they made utmost care of keeping radio silence even by sealing transmitter keys. . . .[38]

It is possible that someone aboard *Lurline* or elsewhere may have picked up the broadcasts from Japan which went out quite regularly. Every message was repeated several times to make sure that Nagumo received them, and special coded messages were sent every odd-numbered hour throughout the day until superseded. The reason for this arrangement was to avoid the very type of feedback which Toland's source claimed to have picked up.[39]

Incidentally, there was nothing unique about the treatment of the *Lurline*'s log. "As in the case of all ships at sea on December 7, the log of the Lurline was taken over by the Office of Naval Intelligence when the Lurline slipped into San Francisco on December 10 after a race for her life," wrote Alf Pratte in the Honolulu *Star-Bulletin* on the twenty-fifth anniversary of Pearl Harbor.[40]

Toland's attitude in this matter was puzzling, in view of his thesis, which was that the Japanese task force had to be permitted to come in and hit Pearl Harbor, because if the slightest hint that they had been discovered leaked out, the Japanese would have turned tail and scuttled back to Japan.[41] Yet he could accept without question this picture of the Nagumo force chit-chatting its way across the Pacific for any American ears to pick up.

This leads us to the story of "Seaman Z," a twenty-year-old electronics expert of the Twelfth Naval District in San Francisco in 1941. According to Toland, "Z's task was to collate reports from commercial ships in the Pacific as well as the four wire services" in an attempt to find the Japanese carriers. On December 2, Z took cross-bearings and informed his chief, Lieutenant Ellsworth A. Hosner, that some "queer signals" they had been receiving "could possibly be the missing carriers." Hosner told the chief of Intelligence, Captain Richard T. McCollough. "Hosner felt assured that not only O.N.I. but the President would be promptly informed. It was common knowledge in the office that McCollough was Roosevelt's personal friend and had access to him through Harry Hopkins' telephone in the White House."[42]

The next day, Hosner and Z allegedly "had tracked the Japanese carrier force to a position northwest of Hawaii." Again they informed McCollough and assumed that he passed the word to Washington, including Roosevelt.[43] And to cap the climax, on December 6 they "had tracked *Kido Butai* to a position approximately four hundred miles north-northwest of Oahu. There was now no doubt at all. Pearl Harbor was going to be raided the next morning. After passing on their calculations to Captain McCollough the two men had a private celebration. Tomorrow the Japanese were going to get the surprise of their lives."[44]

Toland seemed to have entertained no doubt that Roosevelt knew of these alleged transmissions,[45] though by his own account Hosner and Z only assumed that McCollough had informed Washington.

Even before the identity of Seaman Z was revealed and further details produced, this story raised questions. If one could grant—which we cannot—that the task force broke radio silence, it would be interesting to know how the Twelfth Naval District in San Francisco could pick up information that the Fourteenth Naval District, much nearer the action, missed. The Japanese changed call signals on December 1,[46] and on December 2 the Fourteenth Naval District's Communications Intelligence Summary remarked:

Almost a complete blank of information on the Carriers today. Lack of identifications has somewhat promoted this lack of information.

However, since over two hundred service calls have been partially identified since the change on the first of December and not one carrier call has been recovered, it is evident that carrier traffic is at a low ebb.

The next day, according to the Fourteenth Naval District, there was "No information on submarines or Carriers." Their report for December 5 remarked, "No traffic from the Commander Carriers or Submarine Force has been seen either."[47]

A memorandum from the office of Commander Arthur H. McCollum, chief of the Far Eastern Section, ONI, concerning Japanese fleet locations as of December 1, 1941, placed *Akagi* and *Kaga* in southern Kyushu; *Soryu, Hiryu, Zuikaku*, and *Shokaku* in Kure.[48]

Chihaya dealt at length with this question of possible interception of radio traffic from the task force:

Even if the Nagumo Force used radio signals in the worst case, though it was not the case at all, picking them up far from San Francisco is, from the technical viewpoint, impossible. In such a worst case, VHF (very high frequency) waves were usually used, which is considered not to reach beyond visibility. Moreover, the Nagumo Force passed through the northern Pacific routes, where the sun is so low in the winter time that VHF waves may not be bounced back by an ionization layer at all to reach beyond visibility. Even by the today's high standard technologies, it is utterly inconceivable to pick up VHF waves some 4,000 miles away at San Francisco, said an expert on radio direction finding of a certain leading maker of such items here, whom I sought his view on it. [sic]

One more important point is that the Nagumo Force was passing a point some 4,000 miles away from San Francisco, when Toland claims the U.S. picked up radio signals. A difference of one degree direction means at such a long distance some 70 miles. Since radio direction finding can not be determined by a sharp point but by a very low curve, it is very usual that radio direction finding involves several degrees error at least. In a worst case, radio signals sent from the northern part of Japan Proper might be mistaken as signals from the moving force by such a away [sic] position as San Francisco. As a matter of fact, the Japanese Navy had some radio stations and ships staying in the homeland send radio signals by using code signals of the Nagumo Force in order to conceal its whereabouts. Toland claims that the U.S. traced the Japanese attack force after Dec. 2, [sic] is almost nonsense since the Japanese force steamed almost east toward

San Francisco and it was impossible to determine its position, unless some cross bearings were made by Wake or Midway, even if the Nagumo Force did send radio signals.[49]

In 1983, the identity of Seaman Z was established as Robert D. Ogg, a retired California businessman, and he participated in an oral history review conducted by Commander I. G. Newman, USN. A careful reading of the transcript of this interview rather drastically modifies Toland's version. Ogg's job under Hosmer* was wiretapping and "bugging suspected Japanese spy meeting places." He was also involved in "monitoring of Trans-Pacific telephone cables."[50] He had not been collating reports, nor had he been involved in actually "picking up the Japanese transmissions, but getting the recordings of them, or ultimately tracking—or plotting the DF [direction finder] positions . . . that Hosmer brought to me those first days of December."[51] Ogg was unaware of the monitoring by the four wire services. Every day he carried dictaphone records for Hosmer from the Twelfth Naval District, but he was not involved in translating them. Newman asked him: "You're assuming now that there was . . . Japanese Fleet transmissions on these recordings because Hosmer told you there were. Is that correct?"

"That would be correct," replied Ogg. "I would have had no reason to question that they were anything but that."[52]

Ogg recalled Hosmer coming to him on December 2 or 3, "extremely interested and excited" over transmissions on a megacycle range "not before known to be with the Jap ships." Hosmer asked him to plot these on a great circle chart "and the initial ones were North of Hawaii, a long way West, just East of the International Date Line." Newman queried, "How were these transmissions being identified as being of Japanese origin?" Ogg answered, "I never questioned that at the time. They just said these were Japanese and I presumed either the language or the—and I presume these were in language, but I'm not sure of that either." He thought Hosmer got his data "solely from commercial sources." He did not recall whether or not Hosmer had obtained additional information from the Twelfth Naval District. Both of the bearings came from points in California, one in San Francisco, the other, to the best of Ogg's recollection, from

---

*Toland gave the name as Hosner; it appears in the Ogg interview transcript as Hosmer, so henceforth we will use the latter spelling.

somewhere on the southern coast. He had no more than two bearings on each day in question.[53]

Ogg flatly contradicted Toland's statement that he, Ogg, had told Hosmer that this could be the missing carrier force:

> I never made such a mention to Hosmer whatsoever. I just knew that there were some form of Jap transmission that was on these odd frequencies in that area East of the International Date Line. Certainly no reference that it was a carrier force rather than it was a fishing force.[54]

There is no suggestion in the Ogg interview of any such scene of gloating on December 6 as Toland portrayed. On the contrary, Ogg "certainly had no feeling that an entire Jap fleet . . . was involved." Not until December 7 did he equate the signals with the force that hit Pearl Harbor.[55]

He was quite convinced that the Japanese did break radio silence, but not to the extent of "any great activity." He thought that some of the ships "in that storm situation had to of [sic] violated radio silence."[56] Ogg did not clarify what he meant by "that storm situation." Available information about the Japanese voyage from Hitokappu Bay to Hawaii indicates that the weather was unusually good, considering the route the task force was following and the time of year. It encountered some fog, high seas, winds, and occasional light rain, but nothing in the nature of a major storm.[57]

In brief, nothing in Ogg's account gives any real reason to override the solid Japanese testimony and the tactical necessity to maintain radio silence.

Nor does the incident of a disappearing submarine, cited in the postscript to the paperback edition of Toland's book, add support to his thesis. Toland claimed that Tsutomu Kenno, researching for a Japanese TV special on the Pearl Harbor attack, discovered in the official history, *Hawai Sakusen (Operation Hawaii)*,

> that one of the two submarines accompanying *Kido Butai*, the *I-23*, reported it was having engine trouble on November 30, 1941 (Tokyo time), and maximum speed was reduced to 80 percent efficiency. The submarine fell behind, soon dropping out of range of flag or light signals. There is no further record of *I-23* in *Operation Hawaii* until December 6 (Tokyo time) when it was noted that "*I-23* has finally rejoined the main body after emergency repairs." There is no

record of how this submarine, which was not equipped with a direction finder, managed to relocate the carrier force.

Mr. Toland suggested that further research into this case could be fruitful.[58]

The Prange files shed some light in this area. In the first place, not two but three submarines (*I-19*, *I-21*, and *I-23*) were attached to the task force. Originally these submarines were scheduled to precede the main body, but the task force leaders decided to keep them on the flank lest the submarines' poor visibility and poor communications result in loss of contact in the fog and overcast which had developed. Captain Kijiro Imaizumi, the veteran submariner who commanded the three undersea craft, stated that "nothing in particular took place during the cruise."[59] Presumably the loss of one of his charges for approximately five days would have qualified as a noteworthy event.

Two extracts from the diary of the First Destroyer Division, both dated December 2, 1941, dealt with *I-23*'s troubles. At 0500, Nagumo signaled the entire task force: "*I-23* submarine seems to drop out of formation and to be following up the force from the rear. Take care of lookout." At 0855, he signaled the Eighteenth Destroyer Division: "Bring up *I-23* which is seen in the direction of 170 degrees." In other words, apparently *I-23* fell behind for a mere four hours, give or take five minutes, then she was sighted and a destroyer was ordered to round her up.

In the Postscript of the paperback edition of *Infamy*, Toland quoted a message from Alaska Defense Command to Headquarters Thirty-seventh Infantry received at 0105 December 6, 1941:

> RADIO REPORT
> NAVY REPORTS
> JAP SHIPS 270 MILES
> SOUTHEAST OF DUTCH
> HARBOR.[60]

This would have placed the sighting at about 48° north latitude, 165° west longitude. Whatever ships may or may not have been at that position at 0105 on December 6, 1941, they were not the Japanese task force headed for Pearl Harbor, for it was considerably farther than 270 miles southeast of Dutch Harbor.

As the *pièce de résistance* of his buffet of tip-offs, Toland claimed that Captain Johan E. M. Ranneft, naval attaché of the Netherlands in Washington, visited the Office of Naval Intelligence (ONI) and was shown on a wall map "the Japanese Task Force proceeding east." The position was halfway between Japan and Hawaii. This was on December 2. Ranneft cabled the headquarters of his navy in the exile capital at London and reported in person to his minister in Washington, Alexander Loudon. Then he wrote in his official diary, "Conference at Navy Department, O.N.I. They show me on the map the position of two Japanese carriers. They left Japan on easterly course."

According to Toland, ONI took Ranneft into its confidence because the Navy owed him a favor. Sometime before, without consulting his government, he had secured from Batavia blueprints of the Dutch Bofors AA guns and turned them over to the U.S. chief of naval ordnance. Bofors was a Swedish firm, and Swedish as well as Dutch patents were involved. When the Swedish naval attaché protested, "Ranneft assured him that the decision had been made by the Dutch government in London and any complaints should be lodged there."[61]

Considering how much reliance Toland placed upon Ranneft, one must ask how reliable Ranneft was as an individual and an officer. This incident raises serious doubts. Here was the naval attaché turning over one of his homeland's prime weapons to a foreign nation without the knowledge and consent of his own government and in violation of patent rights. Men have been cashiered for much less. What is more, he did not have the strength of character to take the responsibility when his Swedish colleague protested. Instead, he lied that the Dutch government had made the decision.

There was more to Toland's story: That same night, December 2, Barnet Nover, associate editor of the Washington *Post*,

> was wakened by a telephone call from a British official who begged him to come at once to his room. Once Nover arrived the official, in great agitation, explained that a Dutch officer had told him two Japanese carriers had been discovered north of the Marshalls and were bound either for the Dutch Indies or Pearl Harbor. The Briton confessed he could not sleep since he was certain the carriers' destination was Pearl Harbor.

In a footnote, Toland advised the reader that Ranneft denied being the Dutch official mentioned, and Toland suggested it may have been the military attaché, Colonel F. G. L. Weijerman.[62]

This strange tale raises many questions. The insistence upon *two* Japanese carriers is puzzling. The task force included six carriers plus their escort vessels. What had happened to the rest of Nagumo's fleet? And why should this type of information be given to a foreign officer who had no need to know, who could be depended upon to pass the information to his immediate superior, to his government, and quite possibly to others in his ministry, who in turn were fairly certain to spread the word? According to Toland, that was exactly what did happen, for in the course of one day the story seemed to have gone from ONI to Ranneft to Weijerman to a British official to Nover. One would certainly suppose that the destination of these carriers would be determined before breaching security so majestically. A ship headed for the Netherlands East Indies could not possibly be headed for Pearl Harbor, and vice versa. Indeed, it would have been quite appropriate to give Ranneft the latest word on the Japanese fleet steaming toward Dutch territory.

As noted, the Japanese had changed the fleet's code signals on December 1, and on December 2 the Fourteenth Naval District reported, "Almost a complete blank of information on the Carriers today."[63] And just to make matters more interesting, there was indeed a carrier task force "north of the Marshalls" on December 2 (December 3 in its time zone, the ships in question having crossed the International Date Line). This was Vice Admiral William F. Halsey's Task Force Eight, centered around *Enterprise* and headed for Wake Island.[64]

The next chapter in the saga of Ranneft took place on December 6, when once again he visited ONI and asked about the two Japanese carriers:

> Someone put a finger on the wall chart four hundred miles or so north of Honolulu. "What the devil are they doing there?" asked the amazed Ranneft. Someone said vaguely that the Japanese were perhaps interested in "eventual American intentions." This made little sense to Ranneft but he said nothing. And no one mentioned anything about a possible attack on Pearl Harbor.[65]

If the Americans actually saw two Japanese carriers in that position, the objective was obvious. Having gone so far with Ranneft, why not go the whole hog? And again, why *two* carriers? If ONI knew the whole story, why deceive Ranneft?

Nowhere in Toland's book did he cite any document, interview, or anecdote which proved or even attempted to prove any connection of the White House with any of the incidents he brought forth as evidence of the President's villainy. Toland may have genuinely believed that these tip-offs were passed on to Roosevelt, but such assumptions are not evidence.

To point out the weaknesses and illogic in all the tales that revisionists cite in support of their anti-Roosevelt thesis would be far beyond the scope of this study. But before leaving the subject, we would like to make a few suggestions.

The ramifications of such a presidential plot would be almost endless, and the whole business virtually impossible to keep quiet. Nover—the very journalist in whom the British official was supposed to have confided—challenged his readers on the eve of the congressional investigation: "If Roosevelt is to be accused—directly or by implication—of advance knowledge of Japan's Pearl Harbor attack and of taking only indifferent measures to avert it his attitude must have been part of a general conspiracy. Does anybody believe that?"[66]

Toward the end of his life, Barnes recognized that the "general conspiracy" thesis would not hold water. He informed Prange that the idea held by Morgenstern and Rear Admiral Robert A. "Fuzzy" Theobald

> to the effect that all the top authorities in Washington knew about the attack but were held back by Roosevelt's order in the matter of refraining from warning Short and Kimmel is no longer tenable. It is now obvious that all the top civilian and military authorities in Washington, save for Roosevelt, Marshall and Harry Hopkins were absolutely certain that the Japanese were going to attack in the Southwest Pacific and not at Pearl Harbor.[67]

Unfortunately, Barnes's jetburst of common sense did not propel him beyond the gravity pull of his anti-Roosevelt bias; it only carried him to the point where his logic itself was illogical, for a three-man conspiracy is even less credible than a widespread one.

To begin with, Roosevelt's associates in the White House, especially his military and naval aides, would have to have known what was happening, if only to keep them from inadvertent indiscretion. The idea of good-natured, kindly Major General Edwin M. "Pa" Watson going along with such villainy staggers the imagination. Even more fantastic is the picture of Captain John R. Beardall acquiescing in a scheme that could well mean the deaths of his own son and all his son's shipmates aboard the light cruiser *Raleigh*, then in Pearl Harbor.

Hull and many others in the State Department would have to have known, and there is no evidence that they did.* Granted Hull's entire life and character, few circumstances are less likely. Moreover, the position in the Pacific during the autumn of 1941 was so delicate that war could break out at any minute without any maneuvering on Roosevelt's part.

Henry L. Stimson and Frank Knox, respectively secretaries of war and the navy, would have to have known, as well as key members of their departments. While Stimson and Knox were not exactly cooing doves, neither were they braying jackasses. None realized better than they the importance of keeping in the clear militarily in Asia until the United States could handle a two-front war. Stimson went on record as opposing the war-by-incident approach when on May 24, 1941, he gently chided Roosevelt for lack of resolution:

> The American people should not be asked to make the momentous decision of opposing forcefully . . . the evil leaders of the other half of the world possibly because by some accident or mistake American ships and men have been fired upon by soldiers of the other camp. They must be brought to that momentous resolution by your leadership in explaining why any other course than such forceful resistance would be forever hopeless and abhorrent to every honored principle of American independence and democracy.[68]

Stimson therefore wanted the United States to share the burden of the fight. But he believed war should come by act of reason, not by the emotion of a moment.

Knox had supported Stimson in cabinet discussions; nevertheless, if human psychology has any validity, one can say confidently that he never would have countenanced using his beloved ships and sailors as cheese in a mousetrap for Japan.

Stimson and Knox could not have performed the war and navy departments' share in a Rooseveltian conspiracy single-handedly. Marshall and Stark would have to have been aware, as would various

---

*Subsequent chapters will deal with the roles of Roosevelt's cabinet members close to the problem, and with their staffs.

members of their staffs. Documentary evidence is overwhelming that Marshall and Stark understood the current weakness of their respective branches and repeatedly begged for time to prepare for a two-ocean war. With all these chiefs, many "Indians" would have to have been involved, such as secretaries, typists, file clerks, and message center personnel.

To accept the revisionist position, one must assume that almost every one of those individuals, from the President on down, was a traitor. Somewhere along the line someone would have recalled his solemn oath to defend the United States against all enemies, foreign and domestic, and have blown the whistle. It is also difficult to visualize such a plot under way in the Washington area without the ladies and gentlemen of the press finding out.

One must also consider Roosevelt's own character and background. As a statesman, he realized that the ultimate defeat of Hitler would necessitate active American participation in the war. Possibly he felt a certain relief, as many did, when the Japanese took the situation out of his hands. Further, he was a consummate politician adept at bending circumstances to his will. However, nothing in his history suggests that this man could plot to sink American ships and kill thousands of American soldiers and sailors.

A type of mentality exists that would weigh all the factors dispassionately and then coldly, deliberately move toward the goal, counting the cost well spent. Roosevelt was not such a man. To picture him steadily advancing on his target with all the skill, patience, and single-mindedness of an Indian brave stalking a covered-wagon train is not even a caricature. The caricaturist, however biased, sticks closely enough to reality that the sketch is recognizable.

Consistency never bothered Roosevelt. He had few political principles that he could not jettison if expediency demanded. There was some undeniable truth in Clare Booth Luce's remark, "All famous men have their characteristic gestures. Churchill has his V sign, Hitler his upraised arm, and Roosevelt . . ." Whereupon she moistened her index finger and held it aloft to test the wind.[69]

In Roosevelt's complex, pragmatic character, at least one aspect remained steadfast. Even his enemies conceded that he loved the sea service and felt a personal affinity with it. Roosevelt made no secret of his bias. On one occasion, Marshall begged him good-naturedly, "At least, Mr. President, stop speaking of the Army as 'they' and the Navy as 'we.' "[70]

Evidence of Roosevelt's love for the sea and seamen confronts the visitor to the Franklin D. Roosevelt museum and library at Hyde Park. Wandering among the exquisite ship models, the fine old nautical prints, and other memorabilia, one appreciates the incongruity of ascribing a plot against the Fleet to such a man as Roosevelt.

A thoughtful reading of the facts about him discloses neither a blameless hero nor a villainous plotter. One sees rather a man with the best interests of the free world at heart, a man who loved the Navy, a man in whom the practical, at times devious, politician was inextricably tangled with the statesman.

Elting E. Morison, Stimson's biographer, noted the sequence of snafus at Pearl Harbor. "Not even a system schemed out in total depravity to produce all the wrong things at all the wrong times could have organized such compounding error and misfortune," he wrote.[71] How very true! Anyone who could have stage-managed that tragic concatenation of mistakes and bad luck would have possessed superhuman powers. And Roosevelt was very much of this earth.

CHAPTER 5

"To Avoid War with Japan"

British-U.S. relations—Keep Japan out of the war—
Lend-lease—ABC-1—ADB—Transfer of ships to Atlantic—Atlantic Charter meeting—Matador—Japanese moving out—Pledge of U.S. support—Creighton
message—Merle-Smith message—Tokyo-Budapest
Message

The keystone of the thesis that Roosevelt pulled the
United States into World War II by the back door was the belief that
he had made a secret agreement with Prime Minister Winston S.
Churchill to join the conflict if Japan struck British territory. Revisionists clung stubbornly to this conviction, and for good reason, from
their point of view: if the keystone were knocked out, the structure
would tumble down. If Roosevelt had no such agreement with Churchill, he had no reason to bait Japan.

Contemporary documentation buttresses sworn testimony that the
alleged Roosevelt-Churchill agreement never existed. Churchill most
earnestly desired the United States as an active ally in Europe and
on the Atlantic. But the last thing he wanted was war with Japan
while Hitler's Germany was giving the British all they could handle.
London's Asian policy aimed at keeping the Japanese out of the conflict as long as possible lest they cut the British lifeline in the Indian
Ocean. And the British believed that the best way to rein in Japan
would be a firm commitment from the United States concerning the
Far East.[1]

Much as Churchill hoped for eventual American participation in
the European war, he had no delusions about the magnitude of the
task facing him as wartime Prime Minister, and he was far too realistic
to expect the Americans to come charging across the Atlantic to his
immediate rescue. "If necessary, we shall continue the war alone and
we are not afraid of that," he telegraphed Roosevelt on May 15, 1940.

". . . All I ask now is that you would help us with everything short of actually engaging armed forces."

Then he listed Britain's "immediate needs," ending, "Sixthly, I am looking to you to keep that Japanese dog quiet in the Pacific, using Singapore in any way convenient."[2]

Exactly one month later, Churchill sent a second telegram to the President, having heard that France's decision "to continue the war from overseas" depended upon Roosevelt's assurance that the United States would enter the war shortly. "I am afraid there is no getting away from the fact that this is the choice before us now," Churchill added. He continued by way of explanation: "When I speak of the United States entering the war I am, of course, not thinking in terms of an expeditionary force, which I know is out of the question. What I have in mind is the tremendous moral effect that such an American decision would produce."[3]

British Permanent Under-Secretary of State for Foreign Affairs Sir Alexander Cadogan placed no dependence upon the Americans. "We'll all fight like cats—or die rather than submit to Hitler," he wrote on June 15, 1940, in his somewhat dyspeptic diary, into which he poured all of his irritations and frustrations. "U.S. look pretty useless. Well, we must die without them."[4]

With so much weighing upon him during this tense period, Churchill wanted to avoid any further trouble, and under Japanese pressure he agreed to close the Burma Road, China's sole lifeline to the outside world. Cadogan considered this "a capital mistake" and doubted very much that Japan would have taken drastic action if the British had refused.[5]

By October 1940 matters in the Far East had cooled sufficiently for Churchill to decide upon reopening the Burma Road. He asked Roosevelt whether he could send a large American squadron "to pay a friendly visit to Singapore." Churchill explained: "Anything in this direction would have a marked effect upon a Japanese declaration of war upon us over the Burma Road opening. I should be very grateful if you would consider action along these lines as it might play an important part in preventing the spreading of the war."[6]

As 1940 moved toward its end, Churchill estimated that, while the danger of Britain's "being destroyed by a swift overwhelming blow" had receded, in its place had come "a long, gradually maturing danger. . . . This mortal danger is the steady and increasing diminution of sea tonnage." If this threat to Britain's lifeline could not be met, the nation might yet "fall by the way and the time needed by the United States to complete her defensive preparations may not be forthcoming."

The Far East posed another danger. "Here it seems clear that the Japanese are thrusting Southward. . . . We have today no forces in the Far East capable of dealing with this situation should it develop."[7]

On December 31, 1940, the State Department prepared a personal letter for Roosevelt to send to Francis B. Sayre, high commissioner of the Philippines. Its phraseology indicates that Roosevelt shared Churchill's concern about an extension of the war to the Far East. "We of course do not want to be drawn into a war with Japan— we do not want to be drawn into any war anywhere," stated the draft emphatically. But it pointed out the close connection between the hostilities in the Far East and the War in Europe.

If Japan gained possession of the Netherlands East Indies and Malaysia, "would not the chances of Germany's defeating Great Britain be increased . . . ?" The draft added, "I share your view that our strategy should be to render every assistance possible to Great Britain without ourselves entering the war." Britain depended, however, not only upon the United Kingdom's "strong local defenses" but also upon its ability to draw on the resources of the Empire. Therefore, United States strategy "must envisage both sending of supplies to England and helping to prevent a closing of channels of communication to and from various parts of the world." The draft observed sharply: "We have no intention of being 'sucked into' a war with Japan any more than we have of being 'sucked into' a war with Germany." But it added an uncomfortable truth: "Whether there will come to us war with either or both of those countries will depend far more upon what they do than upon what we deliberately refrain from doing."[8]

Churchill believed that Japan would shrink from war with the United States; he realized, however, that a formal British-American alliance against Japan would entail the risk that Japan might opt for war rather than abandon her program of expansion. Nor did he minimize the problems that war with Japan would pose. But if the United States did join the conflict, that would outweigh all other evils.[9] So Churchill, that positive thinker, was prepared to look on the bright side regardless of what developed.

There is no question that most Americans sympathized with Britain and understood that the national interests of the United States were bound up with those of the free world. And Roosevelt, backed by a majority in Congress, had compromised American neutrality. John T. Flynn had a point when he wrote of the lend-lease arrangement: "This was not a declaration of war. But to say it was not making war on Germany is to juggle words. It is possible to say that the country was doing the right thing in this action, but it is not possible to say that it was not war."[10] On the other hand, for all practical purposes the status before lend-lease was just as unneutral. Having planned and prepared for war, Germany had a plentiful stockpile of weapons and resources, and exploited as it conquered. Therefore American neutrality did not affect Germany one way or the other. But England and France, caught up in post–World War I recoil, had hoped for and expected peace. So they were not prepared for war and urgently needed American help. Under the circumstances, to withhold aid from the Allies would be of distinct advantage to Hitler.[11]

Certainly, Washington preferred to concentrate upon the Atlantic theater and avoid a confrontation with Japan. Stark's famous Plan Dog* which formed the basis of American strategy, expressed the situation crisply: "Any strength that we might send to the Far East would, by just so much, reduce the force of our blows against Germany and Italy."[12] This was because the United States armed forces were not yet prepared to handle more than one front.

Defying this logic, Percy L. Greaves, Jr., asserted, "Early in 1941 administration officials reached a secret agreement with British and Dutch officials which committed us to go to war against Japan if Japanese forces crossed a certain line."[13] Actually, what happened was this: Representatives of the American and British army and navy staffs held discussions in Washington from January 29 to March 27, 1941. These meetings culminated in a secret military agreement (ABC-1 of March 1941).[14] Although Roosevelt did not approve ABC-1, the United States later amended Rainbow Five to fit this strategy. Then in April 1941, at Singapore, attempts were made to work out an American-Dutch-British operating plan for the Pacific. This proposed agreement (ADB) set forth certain Japanese actions which would place

---

*In the phonetic alphabet of the day, *Dog* stood for the letter *D*, and this concept was stated in paragraph D of the plan, hence "Plan Dog."

the signatories at a military disadvantage if they failed to counteract them. These limits were:

   (a) A direct act of war by Japanese armed forces against the Territory or Mandated Territory of any of the Associated Powers. . . .

   (b) The movement of the Japanese forces into any part of Thailand to the West of 100° East or to the South of 10° North.

   (c) The movement of a large number of Japanese warships, or of a convoy of merchant ships escorted by Japanese warships, which from its position and course was clearly directed upon the Philippine Islands, the East coast of the Isthmus of Kra or the East coast of Malaya, or had crossed the parallel of 6° North between Malaya and the Philippines, a line from the Gulf of Davao to Waigeo Island, or the Equator East of Waigeo.

   (d) The movement of Japanese forces into Portuguese Timor.

   (e) The movement of Japanese forces into New Caledonia or the Loyalty Islands.[15]

Doubtless this was the "secret agreement" to which Greaves referred. But no "administration officials" committed the United States to anything at the Singapore conference. In the first place, the highest ranking American participant was Captain W. R. Purnell, chief of staff of the Asiatic Fleet. In the second place, Marshall and Stark withheld their approval because, among other reasons, ADB contained "political matter" and the proposals set forth therein did not constitute "a practical operating plan."[16]

These plans and discussions did not commit the United States to go to war with Japan and Germany, or with either one; they outlined the military strategy to be followed if the U.S. joined the conflict. One might suggest, as did Herbert Feis, that these strategic plans "conveyed responsibility of a moral sort." In his opinion, they obligated the administration to ask Congress and the American people "to play the part designed in the joint plans if Japanese assaults crossed the land and sea boundaries of resistance that were defined at these staff conferences."[17]

Ingersoll succinctly explained to the congressional committee why the United States had engaged in military planning with the British:

> . . . everybody knew . . . that sooner or later we were all going to be involved in a war in the Pacific which would include the Dutch, the Chinese possibly, the Russians, the British, and ourselves, and we had to make preliminary arrangements to explore what could be

done to arrange for a means of communicating with each other, for establishing liaison, intelligence, and other things, so if war did come, we would not be floundering around for months until we got together.

To Ingersoll's mind, not to have taken such action "would have been indefensible."[18]

The U.S.-British discussions were initiated neither by Churchill nor Roosevelt but by Stark. He did not ask permission to hold these talks from either Roosevelt or Knox. When he informed the President of the arrival of the British mission, Stark "told him that I would prefer to be panned for being ready than being reproved when the time came and I was not ready, and he let it go at that." The reasoning behind Stark's arranging for these discussions was characteristically simple and logical: no one could deny the possibility, however remote, that the United States might be drawn into the war, and there was no possibility whatsoever of its fighting on the side of the Axis. So Stark would have been "utterly derelict" in his duty had he not done his best to ensure that "if and when war did eventuate . . . there would be ample working plans, so far as possible, to dovetail and coordinate our effort."[19] However, in Stark's "initial orders regarding those plans" he "stated specifically that no political commitment could be made."[20] On the Army side, Gerow, who as chief of the War Plans Division took part in these talks, likewise testified that the participants had no authority to commit the United States to war: "Those were purely staff discussions."[21]

The British wanted a definite political commitment, but Roosevelt remained elusive. He instructed the U.S. naval observer in London, Rear Admiral Robert L. Ghormley, "not to, by any possible chance, make any commitment or say or do anything that would lead the British to think we were going into the war."[22]

On February 6, 1941, Cadogan learned of some "more very bad-looking Japanese telephone conversations, from which it appears they decided to attack us." Accordingly, he instructed the British ambassador in Washington, Lord Halifax, "to pass on to U.S. government our information about the machinations of these beastly little monkeys."[23]

Two days later, Foreign Minister Sir Anthony Eden received "a broad hint" from Roosevelt's confidant Harry Hopkins, who was in Britain, as to "what the President would do if Hong Kong were attacked." Yet Eden wrote Churchill that day that he "saw no hope for a joint declaration by the United States and the British Empire, such as the Chiefs of Staff looked for, that any attack on the Netherlands East Indies, or on British possessions in the Far East would involve Japan in immediate war with all the powers concerned."[24]

On February 8, too, Roosevelt told Halifax that his country "would declare war on Japan if the latter attacked American possessions." He thought, however, that "public opinion would be unlikely to approve of a declaration of war if the Japanese attack were directed only against British or Dutch territories." Then the President came to the heart of the matter:"if the United States were involved in war with Japan, an active campaign in the Pacific would be a dangerous diversion of forces and of material from the main theater of operations, i.e., the Atlantic and Great Britain."[25]

The British Foreign Office sent two telegrams to its embassy in Washington on February 11. The first outlined how current Japanese movements would "weaken the strategic position of the British Empire in the Far East." The Foreign Office "felt certain that the Japanese are acting with the encouragement of Germany and that they are planning more vigorous aggressive measures in direct agreement with the German Government. For these measures to help Germany, they must directly affect British interests and are therefore probably designed to force Great Britain into war with Japan." Spelling out the baneful consequences of such an eventuality, the Foreign Office stressed, "It is essential, therefore, in the interests not only of the British Empire but of the United States, to take steps which will prevent the Japanese from taking the plunge."[26]

The second telegram boiled down the problem and expressed the British attitude in the clearest terms:

> The important point to emphasize is that the initiative lies with Japan. If Japan is bent on war in combination with Germany, mere attempts on our part to avoid the issue are unlikely to be successful. The only thing likely to avert war is to make it clear to Japan that further aggression will meet with the opposition both of the United States and of ourselves.
>
> A joint declaration . . . that any attack on the Netherlands East Indies or on British possessions in the Far East would involve Japan in war immediately and irreparably with both the United States and the British Empire is obviously the course most likely to achieve

this end. It is realized, however, that such a proposal may present certain difficulties from the point of view of the United States.[27]

Churchill took up the discussion in a telegram to Roosevelt on February 15: "Many drifting straws seem to indicate Japanese intentions to make war on them in the next few weeks or months." These "straws," of course, might be "a war of nerves." Still, "The weight of the Japanese Navy, if thrown against us, would confront us with situations beyond the scope of our naval resources." Churchill could visualize the dangers all too clearly, and he set them forth starkly, evidently sure that one student of the sea would understand the other:

> The attack which I fear the most would be by raiders including possibly battle-cruisers upon our trade routes and communications across the Pacific and Indian Oceans. We could by courting disaster elsewhere send a few strong ships into these vast waters, but all trade would have to go into convoy and escorts would be few and far between. Not only would this be a most grievous additional restriction and derangement of our whole war economy, but it would bring altogether to an end all reinforcements of the armies we had planned to build up in the Middle East from Australasian and Indian resources. Any threat of a major invasion of Australia or New Zealand would of course force us to withdraw our fleet from the Eastern Mediterranean with disastrous military possibilities there. . . . You will therefore see, Mr. President, the awful enfeeblement of our war effort that would result merely from the sending out by Japan of her battle-cruiser and her twelve eight-inch-gun cruisers into the Eastern oceans, and still more from any serious invasion threat against the two Australasian democracies into the Southern Pacific.

Again Churchill urged that the United States stand firm to give Japan pause: "Everything that you can do to inspire the Japanese with fear of a double war may avert the danger. If however they come in against us and we are alone, the grave character of the consequences cannot easily be overstated."[28]

In pursuance of the European orientation, Roosevelt transferred ships from the Pacific to the Atlantic and instituted patrols in the Atlantic. Revisionists such as Flynn later pointed out that scouting for the British Navy placed the United States in a war situation vis-à-vis Germany.[29] They were not alone in this opinion. Roosevelt's failure or refusal to face this fact troubled Stimson. At a conference on April 24, 1941, Roosevelt "kept reverting to the fact that the force in the Atlantic was merely going to be a patrol to watch for any aggressor and to report that to America." Stimson interrupted, smiling, "But you are not going to report the presence of the German Fleet to the Americas. You are going to report it to the British Fleet." Despite his show of good nature, Stimson was disappointed in the President. "I wanted him to be honest with himself. To me it seems a clearly hostile act to the Germans and I am prepared to take the responsibility of it. He seems to be trying to hide it into the character of a purely reconnaissance action which it really is not."[30]

Still, all such support of Britain was no substitute, in British eyes, for a formal alliance. Roosevelt could have halted or curtailed any of these measures if he had deemed it expedient to do so. Lacking a firm commitment, the British were somewhat nervous when the United States contemplated embargoing Japan in July 1941. Cadogan noted on July 21 that Churchill "digs his toes in against any assurance to the Dutch. He's frightened of nothing but Japan." Three days later Cadogan recorded disdainfully, "These stupid Dominions of course get cold feet, and don't want to freeze Japanese assets without an assurance of support from U.S. They *must* know that they can't *get* this" (Cadogan's italics).[31]

The Foreign Office understood that Roosevelt could not officially commit the United States even if he wished. "The constitutional position of the United States made it impossible for the President to give a definite assurance of support, and anything less than a clear promise would have been more embarrassing than helpful," wrote Sir Llewellyn Woodward.[32]

The famous Roosevelt-Churchill meeting in Argentia Bay is a favorite subject with revisionists. Tolley's book contains a picture of the two leaders seated together. Under it appears, "Well might Winston Churchill look smug at Argentia, Newfoundland, August 1941. President Roosevelt . . . had just promised him American aid in the Far East in the event of a Japanese attack on the British. . . ."[33] Admiral Theobald also declared that Roosevelt "made mutual commitments with the British Prime Minister at Newfoundland in August, 1941, which promised mutual support in the event that the United States, Great Britain, or a third country not then at war were attacked by Japan in the Pacific."[34] Barnes firmly believed that at Argentia Roosevelt and Churchill "arranged the details of entering the Second World War through the backdoor of a war with Japan."[35]

Totally misreading the situation, Chamberlin wrote, "From his [Churchill's] standpoint it would be just as well if America got into the war in the Pacific as in the Atlantic."[36] However, Churchill's prime consideration in the Pacific was not to spread the war but to contain it. "Drafted scheme of 'parallel' declarations by U.S., selves and Dutch, designed to restrain Japanese from further devilry and to provide mutual aid," noted Cadogan aboard *Prince of Wales* on August 10.[37]

Churchill stated his views in the clearest possible terms to Welles when the latter was leaving *Prince of Wales* on that day. According to Welles's memorandum of this conversation, the Prime Minister impressed upon him "his belief that some declaration of the kind he had drafted with respect to Japan was in his opinion in the highest degree important." He "did not think that there was much hope left unless the United States made such a clear-cut declaration of preventing Japan from expanding further to the south, in which event the prevention of war between Great Britain and Japan appeared to be hopeless." Churchill

> said in the most emphatic manner that if war did break out between Great Britain and Japan, Japan immediately would be in a position through the use of her large number of cruisers to seize or to destroy all of the Pacific merchant shipping in the Indian Ocean and in the Pacific, and to cut the lifelines between the British Dominions and the British Isles unless the United States herself entered the war. He pled with me that a declaration of this character participated in by the United States, Great Britain, the Dominions, the Netherlands and possibly the Soviet Union would definitely restrain Japan. If this were not done, the blow to the British Government might be almost decisive.[38]

However deeply the Americans sympathized with Churchill's plight, in August 1941 the United States was in no position to challenge Japan for the sake of the British. The armed forces were in poor shape and might well be in worse when, in a few days, the House of Representatives would vote on the proposed extension of the draft. Congress showed every evidence of laying back its ears. If it voted down the draft, the United States would not be able to defend itself, let alone help another nation.

So instead of the joint commitment the British wanted, on August 17 Roosevelt presented a note to Japanese Ambassador Admiral Kishisaburo Nomura, after Hull had toned it down. It ended:

. . . if the Japanese Government takes any further steps in pursuance
of a policy or program of military domination by force or threat of
force in neighboring countries, the Government of the United States
will be compelled to take immediately any and all steps which it
may deem necessary toward safeguarding the legitimate rights and
interests of the United States and American nationals and toward
insuring the safety and security of the United States.[39]

This note named no nations except Japan and the United States,
and did not threaten the Japanese with armed force. Boiled down to
its essence, it simply stated that if Japan extended its aggression the
United States would protect its citizens and its interests, which is the
right and duty of any government.

So the British Foreign Office was far from "smug" over the Tokyo-
Washington aspects of the Atlantic Conference. In fact, in Halifax's
words, it "thought the situation was unfavourable to Great Britain in
the sense that the President's warning was not in itself a guarantee
of American help in the event of a Japanese attack on British or Dutch
territory in the Far East."[40]

Despite this setback, Churchill entertained no doubt that Roosevelt really longed to join the fray, and he continued to hope that
Roosevelt would move to keep Japan at bay. He wrote to him on
October 20, 1941: "I still think . . . that the stronger the action of
the United States toward Japan, the greater the chance of preserving
peace."[41]

Great Britain was not seeking trouble with Japan. Churchill stressed
this when he wrote to Eden on November 23: "Our major interest
is: no further encroachments and no war, as we have enough of this
latter." The British could trust the United States "not to throw over
the Chinese cause," and he was sure Washington would not agree to
any arrangements that left Japan free to attack Russia. "Subject to
the above, it would be worth while to ease up upon Japan economically
sufficiently for them to live from hand to mouth—even if we only got
another three months," wrote Churchill. "I must say I would feel
pleased if I read that an American-Japanese agreement had been made
by which we were to be no worse off three months hence in the Far
East than we are now."[42]

There was nothing reprehensible about Churchill's efforts to secure an alliance with the United States for war in the West and to
contain Japan in the East. As prime minister, naturally and properly

he put the interests of the British Empire above all else. As for Roosevelt, probably, like so many of his countrymen, he believed that war with Germany must come eventually. But, in the meantime, the last thing he wanted or needed was war in the Pacific, which would drain off manpower, matériel, and energy needed to support the British in Europe and on the Atlantic.

Meanwhile, according to Tolley, Brooke-Popham "had made several visits to Manila during 1941 for some fruitless conferences with Hart and MacArthur that had done more harm than good." Tolley thought that "Brooke-Popham's noisy flamboyance around town . . . had widely advertised to the Japanese the probability of joint Anglo-American planning."[43] The Japanese no more needed Brooke-Popham to tell them that the British and Americans probably would plan jointly than they needed his help to notice that the sun rose in the east.

Since appointed on October 17, 1940, the air chief marshal's prime guideline had been "that it is the policy of His Majesty's Government to avoid war with Japan." To the end of November 1941 the British in Singapore believed, for seemingly logical diplomatic, strategic, and meteorological reasons, "that the Japanese did not intend immediate hostilities."[44]

Soon after formation of British General Headquarters Far East on November 18, 1941, a plan was developed to "hold a position North of Haad Yai Junction," a short distance southwest of Singora. This would enable the British to maintain control of the southern end of the Kra Isthmus, especially the Singora region. To this end, they prepared a detailed plan code-named "Matador." If they hoped to forestall Japan, they would need at least twenty-four hours notice before the Japanese landed.[45]

During late November and early December, Brooke-Popham and his advisers "felt great need of aircraft capable of doing high-altitude photographic reconnaissance," especially over Camranh Bay. On that area they had "no information whatever." Nor did they possess aircraft suitable for scouting. "It seemed highly undesirable to aggravate a strained situation by sending over an aeroplane which would in all probability have been intercepted and definitely identified as British," Brooke-Popham later reported to London. "I asked General MacArthur to carry out a photographic reconnaissance from Manila with one of his Boeing Fortresses, which had the necessary speed and ceiling, but he replied that orders from Washington prevented him from carrying out my request."[46] MacArthur referred to the famous War Department message of November 27, which cautioned against action that Japan might construe as overt.*

In Washington, Hull met with Halifax on November 25. The former "repeated that he was being strongly pressed by his technical advisers to gain time, since the whole defensive situation of the United States in the Pacific depended on delay." Halifax was still up in the air. He told Hull

> that, while the Staffs could discuss hypothetical developments, it would be necessary, before any general action, for the two Governments to be "absolutely together" on policy. . . .
>
> Lord Halifax thought that the only way to make progress in coordinating policy would be for the Foreign Office to tell him exactly what we were prepared to do, and instruct him to put precise questions to the United States Government.[47]

Matters speeded up on December 1 when Roosevelt met with Halifax and Hopkins. He explained that, Hull being ill, he, Roosevelt, was going to have Welles present a note to the Japanese asking about their troop movements. Naturally Halifax wondered what the next step would be, "since the Japanese reply would be either evasive or a lie." Roosevelt thought the time had come for London and Washington to "settle what they would do in the various situations which might arise." If Japan attacked the British or Dutch, they "should obviously be all together." But he wanted Halifax to ask for his government's policies in various "less plain" eventualities.

Halifax already was under instructions to tell the United States government that the British expected the Japanese to hit Thailand. Such an attack probably would include "a seaborne expedition to seize strategic points in the Kra Isthmus." He also explained that the British "proposed to counter this plan—as soon as we had evidence that escorted Japanese ships were approaching Thailand—by a rapid move by sea into the Isthmus to hold a line just north of Sengora [sic]." But because of the obvious political disadvantages should the Japanese forestall the British, London "wanted to know urgently what view the United States Government would take of this plan, since it was most important for us to be sure of American support in the event of war."

---

*See Appendix 3.

Therefore Halifax posed the key question: What about American support if the British carried out their plan? Roosevelt assured him that Britain "could certainly count on American support, though it might take a few days before it was given." He suggested that the British might guarantee the Thai government its future "full sovereignty and independence" if Thailand resisted the Japanese. As President of the United States, he could not make such a guarantee, but if the British did so, they could be sure of "full American support."[48]

Not yet aware of this development, Churchill met with his cabinet on December 1, and the next day he informed Eden by memorandum:

> Our settled policy is not to take forward action in advance of the United States. Except in the case of a Japanese attempt to seize the Kra Isthmus there will be time for the United States to be squarely confronted with a new act of Japanese aggression. If they move, we will move immediately in support. If they do not move, we must consider our position afresh. . . .
>
> A Japanese attack on the Dutch possessions may be made at any time. This would be a direct affront to the United States, following upon their negotiations with Japan. We should tell the Dutch that we should do nothing to prevent the full impact of this Japanese aggression presenting itself to the United States as a direct issue between them and Japan. If the United States declares war on Japan, we follow within the hour. If, after a reasonable interval, the United States is found to be incapable of taking any decisive action, even with our immediate support, we will, nevertheless, although alone, make common cause with the Dutch.
>
> Any attack on British possessions carries with it war with Great Britain as a matter of course.[49]

Thus Churchill unequivocally pledged support to the United States. But he and his government could not be certain that "full American support" in Southeast Asia would mean American entry into the European war. If Hitler exercised a little patience, Great Britain might be at war with Japan with no assurance of American belligerency, and with the United States still uncommitted to war in Europe.

The President and the ambassador returned to their discussion on the evening of December 3. At that time Roosevelt told Halifax that the British could count on "armed support." But the British understood that the President still hoped to avoid war with Japan, however temporarily, through a personal approach to the Emperor.

As late as December 5, he asked Halifax that London hold up its assurance to the Thais until he had decided about his letter to Hirohito.[50]

So finally, on December 1, Roosevelt promised Churchill support in the Far East, and on December 3 armed support. Events had overtaken the policy of restraining the Japanese, who were already on the move. The only remaining question was where they would strike first. Of course, Roosevelt could not commit the United States to war with Japan on anyone's behalf without congressional authority. Moreover, "armed support" for Britain did not necessarily mean becoming an active belligerent; the United States had been giving Britain "armed support" against Hitler for months while remaining technically neutral.

But within these limits, the British were pleased. "Things look critical, but the American attitude seems firm and sound," noted Cadogan on December 3.[51] Eden wrote in his journal on December 4, "A good message from Roosevelt about the Far East. To my intense relief was able to induce Winston to agree to full assurance to Dutch on the strength of it." And on December 5, Halifax telegraphed London that Roosevelt had "agreed to warn Japan against any attack on Thailand, Malaya or the Netherlands East Indies." Roosevelt had suggested that the United States, Britain, and the Netherlands issue independent warnings, with Washington taking first place, "so that it should not appear that he was following our lead."[52]

Roosevelt seemed to have made these important pledges without consulting his chief advisers. Possibly he did not consider his promises to Halifax major departures in policy, merely an extension to the Pacific of that already in effect in the Atlantic.

In any case, on December 1 Hopkins phoned Stimson that the President "was all right. He had not himself weakened at all." But if Hopkins gave the secretary of war chapter and verse, the latter did not record them in his voluminous diary. Instead, Stimson complained because Roosevelt was "so irregular in his habits of consultations." The President had five official advisers—Hull, Stimson, Knox, Marshall, and Stark—"and here he is going along with them and suddenly he stops and makes his decisive decision without calling us into conference again."[53] Possibly, indeed almost certainly, the "decisive decision" referred to Roosevelt's pledge to Halifax of support for Britain.

While these discussions were under way in the first week of December 1941, the U.S. Navy had been holding back the Dutch by the coattails. On December 2, Ghormley informed Stark from London that the Dutch had learned that the Japanese were concentrating an expeditionary force in the Palaus. If it crossed the Davao-Waigeo-Equator line, the Dutch "were inclined to regard such a movement as a direct threat to the territories and interests of Great Britain and the United States, which should immediately be countered by force." But before "making up their minds" the Dutch wanted the CNO's views.

Stark doubted that the Japanese were assembling in the Palaus. In any case, he could not give political advice. The Dutch had taken up this subject with the British as well. Ghormley suggested to the Admiralty that the Dutch might declare the area south of the Davao-Waigeo-Equator line "an area dangerous to shipping." The British thought it would be less provocative to designate it "as a defense zone rather than as a dangerous zone."[54]

Dutch Foreign Minister E. N. van Kleffens made a proposal to Eden that "invited a joint declaration of a defense zone by the United States or Great Britain." After checking with the Admiralty, Eden replied:

> . . . (A) That during the continuance of the present negotiations between Japan and the United States, it was undesirable that any declaration be made unless there was the plainest evidence that the Japanese were preparing an expedition against the Netherlands territory, and that until more definite evidence becomes available that Japanese concentrations are threatening Dutch territory no declaration should be made. (B) That Great Britain recognizes the military value the declaration of a defense zone would have, but that it considers it would be less provocative to Japan and less prejudicial to the Washington negotiations if it were confined to a unilateral declaration by the Netherlands East Indies of a zone manifestly designed as a defense measure for their own shores.[55]

On December 5, Stark reiterated that he considered the Palaus rumor unfounded. Even so, he could not rule out the possibility of a Japanese attack on the Philippines or the Netherlands East Indies. He pointed out the disadvantages of a defensive zone: it would cripple British and American naval shipping as well as Japan's, and cause excessive delays in U.S. reinforcements to the Philippines and to all U.S. shipping through the Torres Strait. Such action might "create a precedent for Japan to close the Okhotsk Sea, Sea of Japan, the western part of the South China Sea, and the Gulf of Siam. If the United States acquiesced in the Dutch declaration, it would be difficult to object to similar declarations by the Japanese." Such a Japanese defensive zone would knock out American aid to the USSR via the Okhotsk Sea and the Sea of Japan. Therefore, the proposed Dutch defensive zone "would be prejudicial to the naval and military interests of all three powers."[56]

Stark did not recall whether he consulted with Roosevelt about this matter. He assumed, however, that he would have taken up any such dispatch with Knox and have cleared it with the State Department.[57] Yet State did not appear to have been on top of events in this sensitive field. On December 6, U.S. Ambassador to Great Britain John G. Winant informed Hull of an Admiralty conference which Cadogan attended. His message contained this paragraph: "British feel pressed for time in relation to guaranteeing support Thailand fearing Japan might force them to invite invasion on pretext protection before British have opportunity to guarantee support but wanting to carry out President's wishes in message transmitted by Welles to Halifax."[58]

During the congressional investigation, the staff tried unsuccessfully to find the cited message pertaining to the "President's wishes." Welles could recall only a personal letter he wrote Halifax on December 2, forwarding copies of the Hull Note of November 26,* along with a document that Welles handed Nomura on the morning of December 2. That was a statement from Roosevelt citing recent Japanese troop movements into southern Indochina and in effect asking their intentions.[59]

Another Winant dispatch interested the congressional committee. This one had been received in Washington at 1040 on December 6, and told about two Japanese forces seen off Cambodia Point. Senator Ferguson asked Welles why Hull and Roosevelt had been notified concerning these ships "if he did not have some agreement in relation to their movement?"

Welles replied, "Because the information given in this telegram . . . was a clear indication that the Japanese were already . . . proceeding further on their course of domination of the

---

*See Chapter 11 and Appendix 6.

Southwest Pacific region." He thought this "gave a clear indication that the Japanese were disregarding what we had asserted to be our legitimate rights and our security." He referred to the memorandum of August 17, 1941.[60]

Japan was no longer a candidate for British or American restraint, if indeed it ever had been. A State Department Memorandum for the Record reveals that on December 5, Halifax brought to Hull at his apartment a message from Eden containing the British view that the time had come "for immediate cooperation with the Dutch East Indies by mutual understanding." Hull expressed his "appreciation."[61]

"What else did you express, good, grey, Secretary Hull?" insinuated Tolley. "Whatever it was, it apparently was sufficient to warrant Halifax's flashing the promise to London, then to Singapore, where it dovetails with Phillips'* and Captain Creighton's disclosures to an astonished Hart that he and the British were now Allies in fact."[62]

There is no reason to suppose that Hull expressed anything more than appreciation of the British view.[63] Roosevelt, not Hull, gave the pledges of support for Britain in the Far East directly to Halifax. And, of course, the Americans and the British were not yet "Allies in fact."

Tolley's remarks quoted above lead the story to a controversial incident. It began when Captain John M. Creighton, the U.S. Naval Observer at Singapore, sent the following message to Hart on December 6 at 1526 Greenwich Time.† Manila received it on the 7th:

> Brooke Popham received Saturday from War Department London Quote "We have now received assurance of American armed support in cases as follows: Afirm we are obliged execute our plans to forestall Japs landing Isthmus of Kra or take action in reply to Nips invasion any other part of Siam XX Baker if Dutch Indies are attacked and we go to their defense XX Cast if Japs attack us the British XX Therefore without reference to London put plan in action if first you have good info Jap expedition advancing with the apparent intention of landing in Kra second if the Nips violate any part of Thailand Para

---

*Admiral Sir Tom Phillips, commander of the Far East British Fleet, arrived at Singapore with *Prince of Wales* and *Repulse* on December 2, 1941. On December 5 he flew to Manila to confer with Hart, returning to Singapore on December 7 (*Grand Alliance*, pp. 590, 616).

†Creighton testified that as there was no other time indication it was probably GMT (*PHA*, Part 10, p. 5082). This would have been 2326 Manila-Singapore time on the 7th, and 1026 on the 7th in Washington.

If NEI are attacked put into operation plans agreed upon between British and Dutch" Unquote.[64]

The passage of time had erased this message from Creighton's memory. When he read of it in newspaper accounts of Hart's testimony before the congressional committee, he could remember nothing about it. So he called Hart, who authorized him to obtain a copy from his office. After reading it, Creighton was none the wiser.[65]

At the time Creighton sent his dispatch, he had received no word of what U.S. policy would be other than what was contained in the cited message. This he admitted was itself "a matter of hearsay." He "never knew Brooke-Popham intimately enough to have received from him directly such information as this." When Creighton testified to the congressional committee, he had not "the faintest idea" who "had told him of those things."[66]

Creighton thought that his "housemate," U.S. Army Colonel Francis G. Brink, the liaison officer with Brooke-Popham, could have obtained it from the latter. Creighton's British contact, Admiral Geoffrey Layton, did not give it to Creighton. The latter did not recall who did so, and he did not know "how many hands it had gone through" before it reached him. By that time, "it was really nothing more than rumor."

Creighton notified Hart because he had served in the admiral's flagship for about six weeks, during which time he received the impression that Hart "felt he was constantly suffering from lack of information from home." Creighton considered he had a duty "to try to give him any current informantion or reports." He realized "that a policy involving whether we were going to assist Britain in a contingency had to come from Washington," not London. He had no way of knowing how reliable the information was, or for that matter if Brooke-Popham had actually said it.[67]

Creighton's most likely source, Brink, knew Brooke-Popham. But he claimed that he never talked with him about "what our policy would be should the Japanese attack the British or Dutch." He did not know of the contents of the message, nor did Brooke-Popham give that information to him.[68]

Hart did not recall Phillips's mentioning the subject during their conferences.[69] And Creighton's dispatch did not tell him that he and the British were "now Allies in fact"; it told him that the United States had promised "armed support" to Britain under certain conditions. That is precisely what Hart understood, according to a message he sent to OPNAV with an information copy to CinCPAC on December 7 at 0645 GMT:* "Learn from Singapore we have assured British armed support under three or four eventualities. Have received no corresponding instructions from you."[70] Therein lay the problem. However Creighton received the word, it was accurate, and had Washington been as prompt to clue in its armed forces as London had been, much confusion at the time and more postwar suspicion could have been avoided.

Churchill later explained:

> A series of lengthy telegrams passed between us and our Commander-in-Chief in the Far East, and also with the Australian and American Governments, about whether we should take forestalling action to protect the Kra Isthmus. It was rightly decided, both on military and political grounds, that we should not complicate the course of events by striking first in a secondary theatre.[71]

In his history of Britain's war in the Far East, S. Woodburn Kirby wrote: "On the 5th, the Chiefs of Staff informed Sir Robert that American assurance of armed support had at last been vouchsafed, conditional on the Japanese attacking British territory, or the Netherlands East Indies, or on 'Matador' being undertaken either to forestall a Japanese landing on the Isthmus of Kra or as a reply to a violation of any other part of Siamese territory." Therefore, London authorized Brooke-Popham to order Matador "without reference to London."[72]

Brooke-Popham's report clarified his own situation. Curiously, he did not mention a commitment by the United States:

> Up to the 5th December, Matador was not to be carried out without reference to the War Cabinet, but on that date a telegram was to the effect that I could order it without reference to London in either of the following contingencies:—
> (a) If I had information that the Japanese expedition was advancing with the apparent intention of landing on the Kra Isthmus; or
> (b) If the Japanese violated any other part of Thailand (Siam).

---

*This would have been 1455 December 7 Manila time, 0145 December 7 in Washington. Hart thought the time not too reliable, but did not explain why. (*PHA*, Part 10, p. 4803).

A few days earlier it had been impressed on me that carrying out
Matador if the Japanese intended to make a landing in Southern
Siam would almost certainly mean war with Japan, and in view of
this I considered it my duty to be scrupulously careful in acting on
the telegram of the 5th December.

As of December 6, Brooke-Popham received word of the two
Japanese convoys steaming toward Southeast Asia. Even so, he reacted cautiously, as he reported to the British chiefs of staff: "Bearing
in mind the policy of avoiding war with Japan if possible—a policy
which had been reaffirmed by the Chief of Staff as recently as the
29th November and the situation in the United States with the Kurusu
talks still going on in Washington, I decided that I would not be
justified in ordering 'Matador' on this information." But he ordered
an alert and a watch kept on the convoys. "It is pertinent to record
that, until the Japanese had committed some definite act of hostility
against the United States, the Dutch or ourselves, permission had
not been given to attack a Japanese expedition at sea."[73]

So, American support or not, the British were still trying to avoid
hostilities in Asia if at all possible. And the United States was not
formally allied to Great Britain until Congress so declared. But revisionists today continue to assert that, in Barnes's words, "Roosevelt
knew by the forenoon of the 6th, if not on the 5th, that the United
States was already at war with Japan due to our commitments to the
British and Dutch under ABCD and Rainbow 5."[74]

Barnes thought he had found support for that thesis in the testimony of Lieutenant Robert H. O'Dell, formerly assistant military
attaché in Australia, who appeared before the Army and Clarke inquiries.* O'Dell and his immediate superior, Military Attaché Colonel
Van S. Merle-Smith, attended a conference in Melbourne on Thursday afternoon, December 4. Among those present were Air Chief
Marshal Sir Charles Burnett, chief of staff of the Royal Australian Air
Force, and a naval liaison officer from the Netherlands East Indies.
This conference "principally concerned itself with the movement of
a Jap Task Force in the South China Sea."

About an hour after the two Americans arrived, some additional
information came in, "the exact nature of which" O'Dell "wasn't told
at the time." But when they left the meeting, Merle-Smith instructed

---

*This was an inquiry which Colonel Carter W. Clarke of G-2 conducted in regard to the manner
in which certain "Magic" messages had been handled. See Appendix 1.

him to prepare a cable, the principal part of which, "other than the movement of this convoy was that the Dutch had ordered the execution of the Rainbow Plan, A-2." O'Dell remembered that A-2 "was a part of the joint ABducan plan only to be taken in the event of war."

He considered the Dutch action significant, because "the plan called for joint operations" on the part of the Australians, the Dutch, and, to the best of his knowledge, the U.S. Navy as well. "That was to go into effect only in case of war and here the Dutch had ordered it." This caused "a bit of flurried excitement," O'Dell testified. Burnett asked Merle-Smith to hold up the cable so that Burnett could first report the information at a meeting of the War Cabinet scheduled for that evening. Merle-Smith, "although impatient" to send the message, agreed to wait twelve hours.

Meanwhile, O'Dell coded the cable, preparing one for MacArthur and another in a different code for Short, with the request that Short repeat the dispatch to Washington. The attachés did not notify G-2 in Washington directly because of the time factor.[75] A little confusion exists as to the time of dispatch. O'Dell told the Clarke inquiry they sent it on the morning of December 5 local time. At the Army board hearings, Major General Henry D. Russell pointed out that it was dated December 6. That, O'Dell explained, was local time, which would be December 5 Hawaiian time.[76]

An exact copy of the message reads as follows:

> Based on Dutch intelligence report unconfirmed here of Naval movements from Pelau [Palau] objective Manado and or Ambon, Dutch ordered execution plan A-2 and suggested RAAF reciprocal movement be directed Laha Ambon and Keopang. So ordered pm yesterday including flight Catalina to Rabaul task reconnaissance Buka and northwest passage Australian army reinforcements Ambon Keopang subject to request Dutch East Indies. This message held 17 hours by . . . [sic] government eight am Dutch reported advancing planes to be on Keopang not now considered necessary. Eleven am chief of air corps desired proceed with all aircraft forward movements Manilla [sic] informed.[77]*

Another reason beyond "the urgency of the time factor" impelled Merle-Smith to contact Short directly. O'Dell explained somewhat incoherently:

---

*Manado is located on Celebes; Ambon was the Dutch naval base in the Moluccas; Keopang on Timor, Rabaul in the Bismarcks, and Buka in the Solomons.

. . . I don't know enough about it to say much, but it is my under-standing that A-2 fell into the Rainbow Plan and that certain action was called for by the American Navy under Plan A-2; and, therefore, if the Dutch had ordered the execution of Plan A-2, some reciprocal action was required on the part of the American Navy, and that they in Pearl Harbor—that is, that the Commanding General, Hawaiian Department, would naturally inform the Navy of the fact. . . .[78]

The Army attachés believed that the Hawaiian Department knew about the plan in question. "That point came up . . . because of Pearl Harbor being the Naval Headquarters and the Plan A-2 being for U.S. participation mostly in a naval manner. We certainly assumed that if anybody knew A-2, Pearl Harbor did know it." If Merle-Smith believed this to be a matter primarily involving the U.S. Navy, it seems strange that he did not turn it over to his naval colleague, Captain Charles A. Coursey. O'Dell testified: ". . . we informed him of that and curiously enough Captain Coursey did not send any message like that. I do not believe he did. I'm not qualified to say for certain, but he was not in the same state that we were about it."[79]

Perhaps Coursey failed to share their agitation because the Navy was already in close touch with the British and Dutch about the Japanese ship movements in question. In any case, it is most unlikely that Kimmel would have ordered his fleet to war on the basis of fifth-hand information. At the very least he would have sought confirmation from his superiors in the Navy Department. The problem did not arise, because the Hawaiian Department did not decode the message; it sent it on to the War Department to be decoded and repeated.[80]

When Barnes discovered this message he was sure he had a scoop. Morgenstern, Greaves, and later Ladislas Farago had mentioned the subject, but "did not develop its full significance." Unwilling or unable to understand the difference between a war plan and a duly ratified treaty or pact, Barnes proclaimed that "the United States had been put into war with Japan by the action of the Dutch authorities at Batavia, approved by the Dutch government, on December 3rd, Washington time."

Predictably, Barnes decided that the authorities in Washington had deliberately withheld another warning from Short. "At any rate, nothing in the Merle-Smith message was sent back to Short after being decoded and read by the Signal Corps in Washington," Barnes wrote. "Had it been sent back to Short in full immediately after it should have been received and processed, it could have produced a full alert at Hawaii on the morning of the 5th, Washington time. It certainly could have been sent back to Short in time to produce an alert during the 5th, Washington time, and averted the Japanese attack on Pearl Harbor."[81]

Barnes's timing did not coincide with the official receipt time of "7:58 P.M." on December 7 recorded on the message itself.[82] This was about five hours after the attack had begun. But that did not break Barnes's stride. That "alleged late arrival," he claimed, was "most probably a fraudulent evasion." He concluded also that the transmission date recorded on December 6 was "phony."[83] In short, the document was doctored.

All of which was irrelevant because Rainbow Five was not an instrument to declare war; it was a plan for conducting the war once it started. Moreover, the Netherlands East Indies could not commit the United States to war, regardless of what actions the Dutch took or recommended for their own protection.

By a curious coincidence, another message helped convince Theobald, for one, that war with Japan had already been planned. This dispatch went from Budapest to Tokyo on December 7, 1941: "On the 6th, the American Minister presented to the Government of this country a British Government communique to the effect that a state of war would break out on the 7th."[84] Theobald jumped to this conclusion: "Everyone in Washington and London, acquainted with Magic, was convinced that Japan would initiate war with the Anglo-Saxon nations that day. The British Government had so informed the Hungarian Government the day before."[85]

Others who should have known better fell into this same trap. At the Navy Court of Inquiry, that body's judge advocate showed the message in question to Captain Roscoe E. "Pinky" Schuirmann, the Navy liaison officer with the State Department in 1941. "How would the American minister on the 6th of December know about war breaking out?" he asked. Schuirmann answered, "I have no idea how he would know that war was going to break out on the 7th. If I were evaluating the report, I would evaluate it as a guess by the man reporting. I haven't the faintest idea how he would get such information." Schuirmann knew of no "direct dispatch" to Washington from the U.S. minister in Budapest.[86]

In fact, this message did not apply to Japan and the United States.

On December 6, Great Britain had notified the Hungarians, as well as the Finns and Roumanians, that if they did not agree to cease fighting the Soviet Union, London would declare war on them. This action would have little or no effect on the British war effort, but would range these satellite countries with the Axis in postwar peace talks. Anyone could have determined the meaning of the Budapest-Tokyo message by checking the American newspapers for December 6, 1941. Most of them carried the story on the front page.[87]

In short, the notion that Roosevelt schemed to enter the war by way of Japan because of a commitment to Great Britain is without foundation in fact. The President did not promise the British "armed support" in the Far East until December 3, 1941, and London did not so advise Singapore until December 5. Roosevelt's somewhat equivocal commitment came much too late to have any relationship to the Pearl Harbor attack. By December 5, Nagumo had already received orders to "climb Mount Niitaka,"* hence was irrevocably committed. Vice Admiral Mitsumi Shimizu's submarines were lurking in Hawaiian waters. Throughout 1941, the Japanese planned and trained for the operation, and the many factors Yamamoto and the Naval General Staff took into account did not include Roosevelt's preferences. They based their strategy upon the foreign policy of one nation, and that nation was Japan.

---

*By this message, Tokyo established the fact that Japan had decided upon war with the United States, effective December 8, 1941, Japan time.

CHAPTER 6

"He Had Supreme Responsibility"

Kimmel's appointment—"Foreign wars"—Willkie—
Public-opinion polls—Calls for firm leadership—"First
shot" controversy—Roosevelt's policy vis-à-vis Japan

The pall of smoke that hung over Pearl Harbor had scarcely dissipated when Roosevelt drew a crossfire of blame, from one side for doing too much, from the other for doing too little. Certain newsmen, without bothering to learn the facts, spread the rumor that Kimmel owed Roosevelt his appointment as CinCUS because of personal friendship.

On January 28, 1942, Representative Earle Wilson of Indiana introduced into the *Congressional Record* an editorial from the Madison Indiana *Courier* of January 26, 1942, which remarked, ". . . Kimmel is a personal friend and former associate of the President, jumped over other officers by him, and his appointment is felt to have been occasioned by the President's inclination to place his family and friends in choice assignments." This editorial called for a "further investigation which would show whether Short and Kimmel held their posts by Presidential favoritism."[1]

Columnist Ray Tucker helped circulate the myth that Kimmel had been "a long-time White House favorite . . . F.D.R.'s aide in World War days."[2] The St. Louis *Post-Dispatch* praised the Roberts Commission because it had not hesitated to indict Kimmel and Short although the admiral was "an intimate friend of the President."[3]

The fact is, Roosevelt and Kimmel were never more than the most casual of acquaintances. In 1915, Roosevelt, then assistant secretary of the navy, had accompanied the Vice President to California "to open the San Francisco and San Diego expositions which were in celebration of the opening of the Panama Canal." At that time, Kimmel had served as Roosevelt's aide for a ten-day period. They had run into one another not more than four or five times during World War I. From 1918 until June 1941, when Kimmel conferred briefly with the President,* he had no further contact with Roosevelt beyond passing by him once or twice in a White House receiving line.[4]

Others recalled bitterly the President's famous promise of October 30, 1940: "Your boys are not going to be sent into any foreign wars." Presidential adviser Samuel Rosenman had recommended that he add the words, "except in case of attack." But Roosevelt rejected the suggestion, saying, "Of course we'll fight if we're attacked. If somebody attacks us, then it isn't a foreign war, is it?"[5]

This was logical, but perhaps too subtle. It is never safe to assume that others will understand one's meaning unless one spells it out beyond all ambiguity. Oddly enough, Roosevelt personally added that same phrase—"except in case of attack"—to the Democratic campaign platform of 1940, which took its stand against participation in "foreign wars." Still, no one could justly claim that this promise kept Roosevelt in the White House, for on that score the voters had little choice. Republican candidate Wendell L. Willkie, speaking at St. Louis on October 16, 1940, declared, "We do not want to send our boys over there again." And he promised, "If you elect me President, they will not be sent."[6]

Nevertheless, Roosevelt's statement handed the isolationists a heavy club with which to belabor him. "It is a feeling of the man in the street that he tricked us into this war," wrote Alfred M. Landon, who had run against Roosevelt in 1936. "I heard it in New York, I heard it on the way home, and it is being repeated here. 'He promised never to send our boys to fight on foreign soil.' And I repeat, this is coming from those who heretofore trusted him."[7]

The attitude Landon cited rose from the ingenuous belief that at all times and under all circumstances the United States had absolute control of events. Neither Roosevelt nor Willkie should have made a flat pledge that they might well be unable to keep. By the autumn of 1940, it had become obvious to every thinking man and woman that, in Leonard Baker's felicitous words, "The price of freedom is the risk of death, and the price must be paid."[8]

Some averred that if the President "had the guts and the ability to be a real leader," he would have put politics aside and cracked

---

*See Chapter 3.

down on organized labor, which had indulged in a number of costly strikes in 1941. If he had done so, "it might be a different story."[9]

On December 24, 1941, commenting upon the meeting of Roosevelt and Churchill at the White House, the Chicago *Tribune* remarked:

> We have suffered a great defeat at Pearl Harbor as the result of overconfidence, carelessness, and stubborn unwillingness to learn and the responsibility for the defeat lies as much in Washington as in Hawaii. . . .
>
> The careers of both Churchill and Roosevelt are studded with evidence of recklessness. It is to be hoped that by this time the leaders of our two countries have chosen discreet and competent military advisers and are in a mood to accept their guidance. We can afford no more errors of judgment, no more disposition of our forces by amateur strategists. . . .

Most contemporary criticism of the President, however, blamed him for having been overly patient with the Japanese, and for the administration's policy of selling the tools of war to Japan for so long. On December 16, 1941, William Allen White recalled that his old Dodge car literally "went west" some years before. "Indeed it would not be surprising if one of the big whams which broke a hole in the big battleships in Pearl Harbor the other night was not that same old Dodge—God forgive us!"[10]

Public opinion polls of the day indicate that a majority of the American people marched ahead of the President in their willingness to fight, both to defeat the Axis in Europe and to contain Japan in Asia. The course of European events in 1940, in particular the stunning fall of France followed by the noble stand of Britain, deeply stirred the American people. In July 1940 the polls had showed 59 percent opposing aid to England at the risk of war, 36 percent in favor. In October, those figures were exactly reversed—36 percent opposed, 59 percent in favor. Significantly, the Republicans had nominated Willkie for President. He was a man of considerable personal magnetism but a political novice. Although, like Roosevelt, he was hamstrung to a degree by the isolationists in his party, Willkie was an internationalist. In bypassing such able party stalwarts as Senators Vandenberg and Taft, the Republican bigwigs demonstrated that they knew most citizens were satisfied with Roosevelt's foreign policy. By

January 1941 the percentage favoring aid to Britain had increased to 68. And the Lend-Lease Act sailed triumphantly through the House of Representatives by 317 to 71 and the Senate by 60 to 31.[11]

Public opinion sampling on a related subject—Was it more important to defeat Germany than to keep out of war?—showed a 62 percent positive answer in May 1941, while by December this had climbed to 68 percent. If anything, the nation was less divided on taking a firm stand toward Japan than on how best to assist the Allies in Europe. In September 1940, 59 percent approved the embargoing of scrap iron. One year later, those agreeing that the United States should take measures to check Japan even at the risk of war stood at 70 percent. Thus Roosevelt was following the popular mandate.[12] Lord Halifax noted particularly "that Japan was more strongly disliked and distrusted by Americans than any other nation in the world." As early as February "it seemed to him that the administration underrated the popular willingness to stand up to her."[13]

On November 17, a constituent of Vice President Henry A. Wallace protested against securing "ONLY a promise from a gangster of peace for ourselves by throwing some innocent third party to these wolves. . . . In the end that method must fail if only [because] the supply of innocent third parties is limited, and the appetite of wolves is not. . . ."[14]

This same individual, however, thought that the Japanese would back down if Roosevelt exercised strong leadership. "And I say to hell with the Japs, I believe they will lay down cold with their tails between their legs if F.D.R. would say, 'I'll fix your damn clock inside of two weeks unless you sit down and behave yourself.' "[15]

From November 21 through November 25, 1941, the State Department worked on a possible modus vivendi with Japan.*[16] One of the suggestions that Hull considered originated with Harry Dexter White of the Treasury Department. But Morgenthau opposed accommodation with the Japanese. In a letter to Roosevelt, which Morgenthau did not send, he wrote, "I cannot but be deeply alarmed by the hints that have come to me of the direction of the negotiations." He begged for "iron firmness" in dealing with Japan:

> No settlement with Japan that in any way seems to the American people, or to the rest of the world, to be a retreat, no matter how temporary, from our increasingly clear policy of opposition to ag-

---

*See Appendix 4.

gressors, will be viewed as consistent with the position of our Government. . . . The parallel with Munich is inescapable.[17]

On December 2, Walter Lippmann wrote in his column "Today and Tomorrow":

If the negotiations fail, we shall not declare war upon Japan and attack Japan, but Japan may start a war in which we shall have to fight back. The country realizes this, and that is why there is no such division of opinion as there has been over our Atlantic policy. The country understands that if war is to be avoided, it can only be by making it perfectly clear to Japan that we can retreat no further.[18]

Two days later, the ever-readable Emporia *Gazette* observed, "We cannot change our policy of opposition to aggression even when Japan, backed by Germany, threatens to pursue her greedy policy in Asia. . . . If this means war, it will have to mean war. Uncle Sam may well raise his hand and cry: 'God helping me, I can do no other.' "

Throughout 1941 and much of 1940, Stimson complained in his diary about the President's failure to seize the reins the people held out to him. So did Secretary of the Interior Harold L. Ickes, as well as Morgenthau. Instead, for most of 1941 the Executive Branch handled the Japanese with kid gloves. Chief of the Bureau of Ordnance before his transfer to Oahu in 1941 as commander, Minecraft, Battle Force, Rear Admiral William R. Furlong remembered that Knox always called in his bureau chiefs following any conference with Roosevelt. More than once Knox asserted to his assembled chiefs that both he and Roosevelt were determined that the Navy should take no action that would provoke Japan.[19]

In pursuance of this policy, the United States did the following: kept open the Japanese consulates although closing the German and Italian, which permitted such spies as Takeo Yoshikawa, titular chancellor of Japan's consulate in Honolulu, a free hand; as a favor to Nomura, allowed Japanese agent Lieutenant Commander Itaru Tachibana to return to his homeland, which thus reaped the benefit of his considerable experience in America and his intelligence knowhow; left the Japanese consular agents (*toritsuginin*) in Hawaii at liberty; and squelched the efforts of Senator Guy M. Gillette of Iowa and Representative Martin Dies of Texas to dig into Japanese espionage.[20]

Action to cork these holes in American security was long overdue. In its analysis of the Roberts report and the tragedy at Pearl Harbor, the *Daily Worker* hinted that the FBI was too busy "persecuting" Harry Bridges, labor, communists, "and other loyal supporters of the country and the war" to deal with the Hawaiian "fifth column" and Japanese espionage.[21]

Passing over the "loyalty" of American communists, still one might contrast the attitude of the United States toward Tachibana with that of Japan toward the Soviet spy Richard Sorge. Japanese-Russian relations were delicate, to say the least, in the autumn of 1941, yet Tokyo did not hesitate to jail Sorge and ultimately hang him. And Moscow did not lift a finger.[22]

Not until Japan entered southern Indochina did Roosevelt slap embargoes on high-octane gasoline and crude oil, although for months irritated taxpayers had wondered aloud why they were being asked to curtail their own use of gasoline while the United States government continued to fuel Japan's war machine.

At cabinet level, Morgenthau had long protested about valuable resources "slipping through our fingers every day" instead of being preserved for the defense of the United States. He believed that sanctions would weaken Japan militarily and serve notice on Tokyo that the United States intended to resist aggression in the Orient. The State Department, which opposed sanctions lest an acute shortage of oil drive Japan to invade the Netherlands East Indies, "just drives me crazy," Morgenthau wrote.[23]

He had a bold ally in Stimson, who believed that one had to deal with Japan "with firm actions and firm language, as being the only things she understands." As he stated, "Japan has historically shown that she can misinterpret a pacifistic policy of the United States for weakness."[24]

It is an open question whether Roosevelt could have appeased Japan by any measure short of capitulation. As early as October 2, 1940, Ernest K. Lindley replied to the suggestion "that the Roosevelt Administration created this two-ocean threat [the Tripartite Pact] by an unsympathetic attitude toward Japan":

> Could anyone except a gullible believer in bedtime stories believe that Japan promulgated these imperial ambitions because of anything we said? They promulgated them and are carrying them out in spite of everything we, and others have said. Like other expanding imperial powers, they will not be checked until they are checked by force.[25]

The notion that Japan took the road to conquest and war because it was forced to by the United States and, by extension, the entire Western world, has enjoyed a long shelf life. It was offered for sale as late as 1982 in *Infamy*:

> But the United States did not fully understand that this course of aggression had been the inevitable result of the West's attempts to eliminate Japan as an economic rival after World War I, the Great Depression, her population explosion, and the necessity to find new resources and markets to continue as a first-rate power. How could the United States, rich in resources and land, free from fear of attack, understand the position of a tiny, crowded island empire with almost no natural resources, which was constantly in danger of assault from a ruthless neighbor, the Soviet Union?[26]

This was the classic *"Lebensraum"* rationale which Japan as well as Nazi Germany used to justify their aggression. It did not take into account the fact that Japan's "population explosion" was largely the result of a deliberate campaign to encourage families to produce more and more children, just as in Nazi Germany. The argument that Japan had to steal its neighbors' territory and resources because it had so few of its own falls down before the example of Japan itself. Today Japan has less territory and less resources than when it embarked upon its expansionist career, yet it is "a first-rate power" because it has turned its people's energies into productive channels.

Hull for one understood that the very nature of a government bent on conquest "required increasing momentum, further seizure and subjugation of peoples, further glories for their armies." Totalitarian regimes thrive on crises. They need violence, threats of "encirclement," and the like to keep a stranglehold on their nations. Hence it was incongruous to deal with Japan on the premise that it wanted peace and "normalcy." With these come a weakening of centralized power, just as conversely in wartime a democracy must grant the national government unusual emergency authority. Japan was convinced of its right to a place in the sun and, like other empire builders throughout history, seized the day and exploited its circumstances. The United States had to deal with this reality unless it preferred to watch Japan swallow one target after another, in Hull's words, "like a boa constrictor swallowing a squirrel."[27]

Roosevelt was walking a tightrope, trying to balance the desirable against the possible, granted current American military means. Sumner Welles explained, ". . . you could not divorce what was done in the military field from what was done in the diplomatic field, or vice versa. . . . In other words . . . the military was not being made subservient to the diplomatic nor the diplomatic subservient to the military; . . . the policy was being worked out along parallel roads."[28]

Roosevelt had to recognize an incongruous situation, as expressed by Ralph Ingersoll, publisher of the New York *PM:*

> *The outstanding fact about the present position of the democracies vis-à-vis the Axis is the paradoxical fact that it's the poor Axis that's rich and the rich democracies that are poor.* For the coinage of the world is no longer either men, raw materials or money. *The coinage of the world is finished weapons in working condition, on the scene of battle, along with the trained men to operate them.* [Ingersoll's italics.]

Ingersoll believed that the Allies should follow the general procedure by which Hitler had jockeyed Germany into a position of mastery: "Hitler never went to a party that was beyond his means. Small as these means were in the beginning, he invariably sought and found some sector where his opponents were still weaker." Ingersoll considered Japan to be one such vulnerable area:

> In Japan we have a "dagger in the back" type of enemy, waiting and anxious only for the place and moment when it can sink that dagger to best advantage. In this showdown war, reasons multiply for annihilating this kind of enemy. Japan comes under the head of being a soft spot because, unlike Germany, its position has long since been extended, and it has had armies beaten—in Siberia by the Russians and, on occasions, by the Chinese despite their inferior equipment.[29]

But holding a firm line diplomatically and economically was one thing; overt action against Japan was quite another. For this Roosevelt was not prepared. Nor was he entirely without fault for the dilemma in which he found himself—trying to keep Japan in check without a navy powerful enough to permit him to deal from strength.

Roosevelt's bias toward the Navy is so well known that one might easily believe the President and the sea service lived in a state of happy symbiosis. In fact, Roosevelt did not have quite the grasp on naval affairs that he believed he did. Admiral James O. Richardson, Kimmel's predecessor as CinCUS, who while chief of the Bureau of

Navigation in 1938–39 had become very close to Roosevelt, later wrote that the President "had a considerable knowledge of its [the Navy's] problems and credited himself with a complete knowledge of these problems."[30]

Yet his interest and knowledge did not always resolve themselves into concrete terms. His Bureau of the Budget frequently cut naval funding requests mercilessly. As late as July 1, 1939, the Navy had "only two transports, three cargo ships, three oilers and one ammunition ship in commission."[31] These statistics provide convincing evidence that the U.S. Navy had neither aggressive intentions nor the means to carry them out if it had.

During the pre-election skirmishing in 1944, Representative Daniel A. Reed of New York reminded his colleagues of "the ridicule which the President heaped upon those who prior to Pearl Harbor urged a two-ocean Navy."[32] Less than a month later, Representative August H. Andreson of Minnesota also recalled to the House "that President Roosevelt opposed the building of a two-ocean Navy, authorized by Congress, which I and a majority supported." He backed up his assertion by quoting *The New York Times* of May 15, 1940:

> Mr. Roosevelt brushed aside as utterly stupid suggestions that developments in the European struggle and their implications in the Pacific strengthened the arguments for a two-ocean American Navy. If it ever had any merit, that theory became outmoded in the acquisition of California in 1847, he said. Such a conception of the Nation's floating defense was just plain dumb, he added.[33]

In 1941, Roosevelt was still resisting Stark's requests for personnel. "I am struggling, and I use the term advisedly, every time I get to the White House, which is rather frequent, for additional men," the CNO wrote to Kimmel on February 10 of that year. "It should not be necessary and while I have made the case just as obvious as I possible [*sic*] could, the President just has his own ideas about men. . . . I feel that I could go up on the Hill this minute and get all the men I want if I could just get the green light from the White House."[34]

In view of the conditions of the times, Roosevelt's policy toward Japan was wise and logical in its broad aspects. Nonetheless, it was both unwise and illogical to oppose Japanese aggression vigorously while at the same time bending over backwards to avoid annoying

Japan, especially when such misguided delicacy could harm the defensive position of the United States. Roosevelt and the State Department knew from Magic that unless they accepted *in toto* Japan's proposals of November 20, 1941, appeasement was a lost cause. Yet the kid-glove treatment continued.

Perhaps, with his master politician's flair for the art of the possible, Roosevelt did not quite understand just how far Japan would go. As late as December 3, he misread the situation. He told Morgenthau that "he had the Japanese running around like a lot of wet hens after he asked them the question as to why they were sending so many military, naval and air forces into Indo-China." Special Envoy Saburo Kurusu had asked to see a number of people, including Bernard Baruch, "to try to bring influence to bear on the President." Roosevelt added, "I think the Japanese are doing everything they can to stall until they are ready." Meanwhile, he was "talking with the English about war plans as to when and where the U.S.A. and Great Britain should strike." Morgenthau, who did not have access to Magic, thought the Japanese in Washington had "instructions to do everything possible to keep the United States from getting in at this time or at least until such time as the Japanese can get their troops into whatever position they want."[35]

So, with Pearl Harbor only four days in the future, old illusions were still entrenched in the executive branch: Japan was stalling; the United States and Great Britain held the initiative and could strike if and when they wanted.

Until almost the last minute, Roosevelt's don't-rock-the-boat policy forbade Kimmel to act against suspected submarine contacts in United States waters. It entered into Kimmel's hesitancy to activate the Joint Coastal Frontier Defense Plan (JCD-42).[36] "It might have been considered by the Japanese an overt act. It would have tended to upset the Japanese-American relations, which we had been enjoined to maintain in status quo," he explained to the Army Board.[37] This was overreaction on Kimmel's part or possibly self-justification after the fact. There was no logical reason why the United States should not act as it saw fit in its own territory and local waters.

The Army, too, carried this reluctance to irritate Japan to absurd lengths. On the morning of December 7, one reason why Marshall did not telephone Short was because "it could be construed as an overt act involving an immediate act of war against Japan."[38] With such fantastic conclusions influencing the War Department, no wonder the Japanese believed the Americans lacked the will and the courage to wage all-out war.

The United States was not alone in its attempts to "reason together" with the dictatorships and to ignore danger until it battered down the door. Most of Europe had made the same mistake in regard to Germany, even though Hitler had spelled out his intentions in *Mein Kampf* and in fire-eating speeches before 1933 just as unmistakably as Japan asserted its aims in its government-controlled press.

The overconcern of the United States with Japan's easily bruised feelings—Tokyo showed no such delicacy about stamping on American toes—helped yield the political initiative to the Japanese and left Roosevelt in an equivocal position. In the words of the congressional committee's minority report, "having resolved that he would avoid even the appearance of an overt act against Japan, the President chose the alternative of waiting for an overt act by Japan." Therefore, "he had supreme responsibility for making sure that the measures, plans, orders and dispositions necessary" to meet and counter such an attack were taken.[39] But this he did not do.

Both a close correlation and a profound difference existed between Washington's gingerly attitude toward the Japanese and its desire that, if war must come, it should be by Japanese initiative. The "first shot" question* was based upon practical considerations. During Marshall's appearance before the congressional committee, his questioners dealt exhaustively with the reasons why the caution about wishing Japan to fire the first shot had been incorporated into the Army's warning message of November 27. Marshall's testimony, although slightly incoherent, set forth the logic of the problem:

> . . . it was the strong desire of, I will say, the War Cabinet, certainly of the Army and Navy officials and I am quite certain of the President of the United States, that the Japanese be given no opportunity whatever to claim that we had taken some overt act which forced a state of war upon them.
>
> The feeling was . . . at that time that if the Japanese could have created a situation, however unjustified, however illogical, in which they could have led at least a portion of the people to believe that our overt action had forced them into an act of war and we would

---

*See Chapter 12.

have had a divided country, which would have been a terrible tragedy in a war situation.

Therefore, each move we made had to be taken carefully into account to avoid the possibility that the Japanese would instantly make a claim that we had forced the issue, that we had really made the overt act and they were forced to fight us.[40]

In view of the situation existing the last week of November 1941, it is difficult to see what viable alternative Roosevelt and his advisers could have adopted. The choice lay between the admitted risk of conceding the "first shot" to Japan, capitulation to Tokyo's demands, or a preemptive strike. The American public would not have tolerated either of the latter two actions.

But the overly placating attitude toward Japan that Roosevelt espoused was another matter, and may well be judged a major error. For if anything should have been clear from experience with the totalitarian nations, it was this: The still, small voice of reason sounded in their ears as the whimpering of weakness. Washington's policy in this matter could not help but reinforce one of Japan's prime psychological errors: Tokyo's image of the United States as basically soft.

In fairness, one must remember that Roosevelt was not merely trying to keep Japan quiet; he had to contend with the isolationists at home. Speaking against lend-lease, Representative George H. Tinkham of Massachusetts did not hesitate to accuse the President of treason:

> I oppose the carefully planned involvement of the United States in war, the cynical flouting of international law on the plea of expediency, and the totalitarian dictatorship bill just proposed to Congress by President Roosevelt and Secretary of State Hull.
>
> The whole conduct is reprehensible. I charge that President Roosevelt and Secretary of State Hull have betrayed the American people and have been disloyal and traitorous to the United States, its integrity, its Constitution, its institutions, its traditions and its safety. . . .[41]

Yet after Pearl Harbor no element was more vociferous in its complaints than these isolationists. "The tragic fact at this moment is that most of the criticism leveled at the Administration comes from those least qualified and with the least right to speak," charged writer Freda Kirchwey. "One can listen with respect to the criticisms and proposals of Wendell Willkie. But the Wheelers and Vandenbergs, who opposed even the inadequate steps taken before Pearl Harbor, who did their best to hamstring defense and promote appeasement— let these men be silent today. Every word they speak is suspect."[42]

In June 1944, Norman Thomas, perennial Socialist candidate for the Presidency, publicly asked Hull, "Even if there had been no . . . attack upon us, was the Administration planning a military offensive against Japan at a time of its own choice?" We have found no record of a Hull reply. However, in his *Memoirs*, he listed a preemptive strike as an action not to be taken.[43] The Washington *Post* frankly regretted having to answer Thomas in the negative. It believed that such an offensive might have saved "a great many million human lives":

> But the Administration was so beset by men like Norman Thomas, who wrote books and made speeches to prove that the events in Asia and Europe were none of our concern, that it was slow in planning even an adequate defense. When it advocated even the most elementary measures of security, Mr. Thomas accused it of war-mongering.
>
> No, the Administration, so far from planning an attack on Japan, was appeasing that country and allowing its aggression in China to go unchecked until dangerously late in the day.[44]

Few world leaders have ever been in a more uncomfortable situation than Roosevelt was in attempting to deal with the Japanese. This he and his State Department knew well: "If a firm stand may lead to war, it must be remembered that appeasement also may lead to war, but war on Japan's terms and with Japan holding the initiative."[45] Europe's recent history had demonstrated the harsh truth which the President's isolationist opponents refused to learn: An aggressor could not be satisfied unless he had the will to be satisfied. England had tried to appease Hitler; it had not worked. France had hoped that if it ignored the danger it would go away; it had not worked. Holland, Luxembourg, Belgium, Norway, and Denmark had tended to their own business and harmed no one; it had not worked. The USSR had tried a nonaggression pact and had supplied Germany with matériel the Russians sorely needed themselves; it had not worked. Italy had followed the path of complete cooperation; it had not worked. Mussolini was no longer Hitler's partner but his dependent and an object of the world's contempt.

Roosevelt was like a ship's captain who saw a typhoon roaring down on him and knew that unless it changed course it would engulf his vessel. The captain could react in several ways. He could turn tail and run (the way of appeasement). He could go about his normal business and pretend the danger did not exist (the way of isolationism). He could steer straight for the storm in the hope of either breaking through or at least going down fighting (the way of interventionism). Or he could face the gale bravely but cautiously, try to steer out of its path, and meanwhile batten down the hatches and prepare to ride it out. Basically, this is what Roosevelt and his State Department did.

CHAPTER 7

"On Lines of National Policy"

Transfer of ships from Pacific to Atlantic—Safety vs.
availability—Two-ocean navy not ready—Pacific Fleet
not a deterrent—Disadvantages of Pearl Harbor

The dynamics of Japan's expansionist policy; the momentum generated since the Manchurian Incident of 1931; the drive to secure raw materials in Southeast Asia; the almost mystical belief of the Japanese people in their right and duty to rule East Asia; the conviction that destiny beckoned—all of these factors gave Japan the political and strategic initiative in the Far East, and forced the United States into a defensive position. These circumstances formed virtually impassible obstacles to a mutually satisfactory accommodation between Washington and Hitler's Axis partner.

It is most unlikely that anything Roosevelt attempted could have changed the direction of Japanese plans and programs. He had, however, at least three opportunities in 1941 to reassess American policy in the Pacific and the Far East which might or might not have had an effect on Japanese strategy and timing, with what result who can say? Each of these far-reaching developments called for serious rethinking of the American posture. In considering Roosevelt's role in the Pearl Harbor drama, one must examine such lost opportunities for creative leadership, rather than imaginary conspiracies. The first of these chances came in the spring, when he ordered a number of Kimmel's ships transferred to the Atlantic Fleet. These moved in increments and totaled forty-one vessels—three battleships, one carrier, four light cruisers, seventeen destroyers, three oilers, three transports, and ten auxiliaries.[1]

The President did not sufficiently co-ordinate diplomacy with available military strength. To a degree, he could not do otherwise. Since the end of World War I, the United States had tried to play the part of a first-class power with third-class armed forces. With "Prussianism" soundly defeated in 1918, Americans hoped that the world had evolved to the point where international relations could be based upon mutual respect. They pointed with pride to the border with Canada, undefended since 1818. The United States and its northern neighbor had had their squabbles, probably always would have them, but both nations had reached a level where settling disputes by force seemed grotesque.

Granted equal goodwill throughout the world, this ideal might have succeeded. But this was the age of the Axis. Roosevelt had to deal with hard facts. He could admit that the United States did not have the clout to play in the big leagues and therefore must abandon the field, or he could try to hold the line until the United States developed power to match its position. The latter was the only real choice. That is why Marshall and Stark consistently sounded the note of caution throughout 1941. Nevertheless, Roosevelt had to consider other points of view besides the military one.

As was its duty, the State Department made its recommendations from the standpoint of diplomacy. Dr. Stanley K. Hornbeck, adviser to the State Department for Far Eastern affairs, compared the relationship of the Navy *vis-à-vis* the State Department to "the guard arm of a boxer. . . . If the guarding arm is not in position, the punching arm is rendered impotent."

Hornbeck had definite ideas concerning the basing of the Fleet and was not a bit shy about expounding them. For example, in 1940 he reacted vigorously to the suggestion that it be withdrawn from Hawaii for sixty days to engage in maneuvers southward from San Diego:

> I have contended constantly and consistently during recent months that, the situation in the Far East having been and being what it is, the most advantageous point at which to hold our Fleet is Pearl Harbor. I believe that the presence of the Fleet at that point has rendered the Fleet more useful than would have been its presence at any other point, so long as disposal of the Fleet is simply for guard duty and general defense. I do not today share the view . . . that the presence of the Fleet at Honolulu no longer exercises any restraining influence as regards the situation in the Far East. I believe that withdrawal of the Fleet eastward would diminish our diplomatic influence as regards that situation even though it be announced that the withdrawal is only temporary. . . .[2]

Sumner Welles strongly supported the Fleet's retention at Pearl Harbor. In his opinion, "if the Fleet had been withdrawn from Hawaii the Japanese military lords would have unquestionably interpreted that withdrawal as an indication that the United States was acquiescing in the spreading domination of the entire Pacific and Asiatic region by Japan and would have begun an increasing encroachment upon the legitimate rights of this country."[3]

To Welles's testimony columnist George Dixon took emphatic exception: "I will admit there is practically no one, short of a mongoloid idiot, who knows less about naval strategy than I do, but I can't go for that one." United States naval experts had been "overruled by our nonseagoing wizards of ooze." Dixon added sourly, "Here we were . . . getting increasingly tough with Japan, but with a fleet which was in no condition to fight. So—if we accept Welles' argument— the thing to do was put this unfit fleet out in front where it could be flattened with one surprise Sunday punch."[4]

But the Lewiston (Maine) *Evening Journal* had other ideas: "The State Department, however, hardly can be blamed because our Pacific fleet was caught at anchor in Pearl Harbor. The State Department favored its remaining in Hawaiian waters, but obviously did not urge that it set itself up as easy target for enemy attack."[5]

To the day he wrote his autobiography, Hornbeck believed that the place for the Fleet was Pearl Harbor. However, he made it plain that he and Hull were only two among many advisers to Roosevelt. The President had the final say. "Whether that decision was or was not wise was and is a matter of opinion," he noted. "The fact that ultimately on the morning of December 7, 1941, a considerable part of that fleet, lying at anchor in Pearl Harbor, was attacked and destroyed there by the Japanese in no way proves that that decision was strategically unwise. . . ."

Hornbeck emphasized an important aspect of the problem: "the disposal of the units of the fleet was a matter of naval operations. Neither Roosevelt nor Hull nor Hornbeck had anything to do with or was in any way responsible for the particular fact that on the morning of Sunday, December 7, many of the ships were together, within the confines of Pearl Harbor. . . ."[6]

Weighing the technical considerations against the diplomatic urgencies, Roosevelt based the Fleet in Hawaii "on lines of national policy rather than Naval policy."[7] The two are not, or should not be, mutually exclusive. The only excuse for a navy's existence is to further the overall national interests. Roosevelt had every right to use the U.S. Pacific Fleet wherever in American waters he thought best for the nation's good. If that disposition involved an element of danger, such was the nature of the Navy's business. The Pacific Fleet did not exist to be safe; it existed to fight if war came. The Honolulu *Star-Bulletin* considered the suggestion that the Fleet would have been safer on the Pacific coast to be "plain silly. What is a fleet for, if not to face danger?"[8] As RADM Richmond Kelly Turner, Chief of War Plans Division, explained to the congressional committee:

> The reason for the fleet's being in Hawaii was not for its own safety or its own security. The reason was for the security of Hawaii and the security of the United States. Hawaii was, under war conditions, a dangerous place. . . . The fleet would have been more safe if it had been on the Pacific coast or if it had been in the Atlantic, but it was out there for the purpose of engaging in a fight with the Japanese and winning the fight.[9]

From the standpoint of strategical logic, Turner was correct. Unfortunately, in terms of practical logistics, Kimmel was in no position to challenge Yamamoto, much less defeat him. It behooved the President to remember the homely saying, "Don't cloud up unless you can rain." The United States was not prepared to rain in both oceans at once, a fact which the War and Navy departments fully appreciated. The U.S. Pacific Fleet had a limited readiness and mission. "It was ready for war in accordance with the war plans," said Stark. "It was not ready for an advance into the western Pacific, which would have required a large train and which we did not have."[10] RADM Royal E. Ingersoll, Assistant CNO, testified that Kimmel "did not have a sufficient train, nor transports, nor troops to proceed across the Pacific and establish bases and establish the fleet in the Pacific."[11]

This was no part of Kimmel's mission at the time. The sparseness of the Pacific Fleet's support vessels and manpower demonstrates clearly that the United States did not expect to rush southwestward to "deter" Yamamoto's ships from embarking on the Southern Operation. "The primary mission assigned the Pacific Fleet under existing Navy War Plans was the making of raids on the Marshalls. These were to divert Japanese strength from the so-called Malay barrier," wrote Representative Frank B. Keefe of Wisconsin, a minority member of the congressional committee. "No existing War

Plan of the United States in 1941 contemplated that the Pacific Fleet would go to the rescue of the Philippines or resist Japanese naval forces attacking the Philippines. The Pacific Fleet was so inferior to the Japanese Navy in every category of fighting ship that such a mission was considered too suicidal to attempt."[12]

Therefore, when Stimson urged the transfer of the main strength of the Pacific Fleet to the Atlantic in the spring and summer of 1941, he put his finger on the basic weakness of Roosevelt's position: The President was keeping the Fleet at Pearl Harbor as the ostensible instrument of an action the United States had no intention of taking.[13]

Thus Stimson believed, and argued forcefully, that the ships should be in the Atlantic. The United States should throw all its naval strength into keeping open the sea lanes of the Allies, in accordance with the primary objective of defeating Hitler.[14] Although this would give Japan a free hand for a while, when Germany fell Japan would have to face the undivided might of the ABCD powers. Then that imaginary wolf "Encirclement," long the pet of Japanese propagandists, would really be crouching on Japan's doorstep, licking its chops. Under those circumstances, Tokyo might have been willing to negotiate realistically with Washington.

Some believed that the Fleet at Hawaii served British interests better than it would in the Atlantic. This appraisal entailed some underestimation of Japan's potential. Journalist William Howard Gardiner wrote that "the United States capital fleet, based on the Hawaiian archipelago, has long been playing a very important role in the present defense of the British Isles." Describing the strategic picture, he stated that Japan had aimed "for decades" to control Eastern and Southeast Asia as well as the Pacific islands. But the British could be of good cheer. "For the incomparable United States capital fleet, now based on Hawaii and its auxiliaries . . . are now fully ready to drive the Japanese fleet and merchant shipping into their home waters. That doing so would not involve us in as difficult a war as might be thought follows from the Japanese now being critically overstrained. . ."[15]

The plain fact is, the U.S. Pacific Fleet was in no condition to drive the Combined Fleet anywhere. True, once the Japanese launched their massive Southern Operation, they would be overextended. But they proved much better able to handle the problem than many Americans had believed possible. Gardiner continued optimistically:

It should be realized that the United States Fleet on the Pacific is now performing its primary proper function; namely, that of being so manifestly able to enforce respect for American policies that it will not have to fight for them . . . as things stand, the United States Fleet on the Pacific is keeping the Japanese from attacking the British lines of communication on the Indian ocean. . . .[16]

Some difference of opinion seems to have existed in the Navy as to just how much of a rein on Japan the Fleet actually represented. During the congressional inquiry, Ferguson asked Stark, "Admiral, wasn't the only deterrent in the Pacific as far as Japan was concerned the fleet at Hawaii?" Stark replied judiciously, "Yes, I think that is a fair statement." But he emphasized that the U.S. Fleet merely roosting in Hawaiian waters posed little threat to Japan. What the Japanese feared was Kimmel's ships as a potential danger to the flank of their own fleet operations in the south.[17]

Stark believed, however, that ultimately the Japanese "would have to lick the fleet or be licked by the fleet."[18] He did not hesitate to station the ships in Hawaii, danger or no danger, because "it was the furthest point westward that we could approach at that time." He stressed, "The fleet was never secure in the possibility of war, unless it was back in the navy yards somewhere on the home coast."[19] By the time Kimmel assumed command, the Navy Department "no longer considered and talked about bringing the fleet back."[20]

Kimmel's attitude toward his ships as a deterrent was rather inconsistent. "The strength of the fleet in the Pacific was what governed Japan," he told Representative John W. Murphy of Pennsylvania at the congressional inquiry. "After the fleet had been in Hawaii for over a year it might well have been interpreted as a sign of weakness if they had brought it back to the coast." But he added, "That, however, I very much doubt."[21]

Naturally, Kimmel was convinced that matters would have been different had Washington not transferred any of his ships to the Atlantic. "I felt that the way to keep Japan out of the war was to have a fleet out there which would deter them from doing anything," he explained to Seth Richardson, counsel of the joint congressional committee.[22] Later he replied to a query by Congressman Bertrand W. Gearhart of California, "I think it would have been much more of a deterrent had they retained those ships in the Pacific."[23]

Apparently Kimmel never understood that it was his potential strength, not his weakness, that drew Yamamoto's eyes toward Pearl

Harbor. The Japanese began planning their audacious attack when the U.S. Pacific Fleet was at its peak of prewar strength in the Hawaiian area. The stronger it was, the more reason Yamamoto believed he had to strike it.

When Ferguson postulated to Ingersoll that Kimmel's ships were "the only deterrent in the Pacific" to Japan's move south, the admiral could not go along with him because, realistic as always, he considered the Fleet no deterrent at all. "The Pacific Fleet had no train, it had no transports, it did not have sufficient oilers to leave the Hawaiian Islands on an offensive campaign and Japan knew it just as well as we did," he stated bluntly, "and she knew that she could make an attack in the area in which she did, that is, Southeast Asia and the Philippines, with impunity."[24]

Nevertheless, Ingersoll had no quarrel with basing the Fleet at Pearl Harbor. "You can't defend the Western Hemisphere, that is our west coast, from a position on the coast," he said. "You can only defend it from an advanced position, which was the Hawaiian Islands. That was the best central location from which the fleet could cover the Pacific coast, Alaska, and the Panama Canal." He did not believe Kimmel's ships "in a position of peril" in Pearl Harbor. "If all of the measures for the defense of Hawaii were operating . . . the fleet was safer in Pearl Harbor than it would have been at sea."[25] Of course, matters did not turn out that way.

The Japanese had a vested interest in keeping the United States as weak as possible in the Pacific, and made little effort at subtlety in that direction. For example, on October 21, 1938, the Tokyo *Asahi*'s New York correspondent personally visited Admiral Leahy to request that he "help to allay the fears of the Japanese people by not advocating the building up of America's naval strength."[26]

The United States had more concrete criteria for its naval policy than the chronic, unfounded "fears of the Japanese people." Japan's naval leaders knew this well, so the transfer of the Fleet to Hawaii did not surprise them. Admiral Koshiro Oikawa, navy minister in the second cabinet of Prince Fumimaro Konoye, said that the Japanese expected that if the United States moved its fleet to the Pacific it would base at Pearl Harbor, the only suitable location. The Philippines were too far from the mainland. The policy had its good and bad features, he thought; nonetheless, the Japanese Navy considered it a step along the road to war.[27]

Yamamoto's favorite staff officer, Captain Yasuji Watanabe, believed that basing the Fleet at Pearl Harbor was an error, because it gave the Japanese an accurately defined target. In time of emergency, the Fleet's base should be a secret, and at Pearl Harbor the United States exposed its position.[28] Watanabe was more than optimistic if he thought the principal base of a major fleet could be kept secret in an open society.

Admiral Fukudome wrote in effect that this action speeded up Japan's naval program. Its "Great All-Out" strategy of luring the U.S. Pacific Fleet westward into Japanese-controlled waters depended upon the enemy's seizing the initiative, and time favored the American buildup.

> The Japanese Navy was accordingly compelled to find some means for assuring an early decisive engagement. Now, with the U.S. Fleet already advanced to its Hawaiian base, it could readily advance to the Western Pacific, thus creating a definite threat to Japan. As long as it remained at its Hawaiian base, it created a strategical situation incomparably more tense and threatening to the Japanese than had existed when it was based on the Pacific coast . . .[29]

The position of all these gentlemen as dedicated officers of the Imperial Navy considerably colored their opinions. It is possible that, at this truculent stage of their history, very few Japanese could quite understand how a "have" nation could maintain a strong navy without planning to turn it loose on its "have-not" neighbors at the earliest possible moment. Themselves aggressors, the Japanese fully expected to become aggressees if and when a more powerful candidate disputed the pecking order.

However, the American attitude was the precise opposite. "Very definitely it [the U.S. Pacific Fleet] was not there as a threat to Japan because we had no idea of offense," Grew explained to the congressional committee. "Our whole policy was one of defense and nothing else."[30]

Stark testified before the Senate Naval Affairs Committee in April 1940 concerning the Navy's position in regard to a possible war with Japan or anyone else. "If we can get peace on earth and good will to men we are all for it. The Naval officers are not in favor of war. If there is any officer in existence who wants war I would like to find him," said Stark, with unusual force. "Our recommendations are solely with the view of the peaceful interests of this country in mind. If anything happens we have got to bear the brunt of it. Our job is taking care of you people." At the congressional investigation, Stark repeated that he certainly did not want war with Japan. But he knew that Germany presented a special case. He testified:

> I spent many hours speculating myself as to what was the best course for this nation to pursue. Every thinking man of responsibility did. I had seen Hitler's game of one at a time. I felt that without our help England might fail. . . .
>
> That was also paralleled by the possibility of a war in Asia. And the combination might have worked a squeeze play on us which would have been a terrible thing for this country. . . .
>
> However, I did have this background, that Congress, through lend-lease, and the knowledge of what we were doing, had, in my opinion, taken the position and the country was committed to seeing that Hitler should not win, and on that basis I felt we might wait too late. . . .

Stark emphasized, too, that neither Knox, Stimson, Hull, nor Roosevelt wanted war with Japan. "To the best of my knowledge and belief all were in sympathy from the military standpoint to avoid that war if we could do it without walking back on our principles."[31]

Thus Washington writhed in a forked stick, on the one hand wanting to defeat Hitler, on the other to restrain Japan. Hence Roosevelt divided his naval strength. Nevertheless, while he based the Fleet at Hawaii as a matter of foreign policy, the decision to use Pearl Harbor as its anchorage was that of Admiral James O. Richardson, Kimmel's predecessor.

Richardson strongly disapproved of moving the Fleet from the West Coast to Hawaii, for logistical reasons rather than strategic or political ones.[32] With the move, the Battle Force based primarily at Lahaina Roads, but near the end of 1940 Richardson decided "not to permit any of the heavy ships to anchor outside of Pearl Harbor." While Pearl Harbor was not absolutely safe, it was safer than Lahaina.[33]

As Kimmel explained, Lahaina was "absolutely open." Then, too, "There are very swift currents over there, and it was finally decided that if we put mines in the number necessary to protect that harbor there was an enormous area to mine, and that we would destroy more of our own ships than we did of the enemy, due to mines breaking loose in those swift currents."[34]

Pearl Harbor was easier to defend than Lahaina, being almost surrounded by Army forts and air bases, while enemy standard-sized submarines could not operate in its shallow waters. Nonetheless, its configuration caused problems once the ships had steamed inside. The possibility of a vessel foundering in the narrow channel and bottling a large part of the Fleet either in or out gave the Navy recurring nightmares. Even under the best of conditions, sortie was a major operation, requiring time, skill, and caution.

Kimmel "accepted the hazard" of the Fleet's basing in Pearl Harbor, although he reminded both Stark and Roosevelt of "the vulnerability of Pearl Harbor as a base."[35] As he remarked to the Navy Court, "These were factors which were well known both to the President and the Chief of Naval Operations, prior to any statement by me."[36]

The War Department apparently had no qualms about basing the Fleet at that anchorage. "We had assumed that in Pearl Harbor we had a reasonably secure base for the fleet," Marshall testified.[37] The Navy Department knew that Pearl Harbor was less than ideal. One of the reasons Stark had sent "the so-called Hawaiian Detachment" there in October 1939 had been his hope "that basing such a detachment at Pearl Harbor would demonstrate the weakness of that most important base and that the remedies for those weaknesses would thereby be facilitated."[38]

But the fact remained: "the fleet was moved out there before Pearl Harbor had been completed and was ready to receive and to protect the fleet."[39] Congressman Keefe outlined the situation with merciless clarity:

Under these circumstances, the position of the Fleet in the Hawaiian area was inherently untenable and dangerous. The Fleet would sacrifice its preparations for war, and its potential mobility for war, if it concentrated its resources on the defense of its base. Moreover, with only four tankers suitable for fueling ships at sea, ships of the Fleet had to come into Pearl Harbor for refueling, to say nothing of maintenance and repair, and the necessary rest and relaxation of crews. Once the ships were in Pearl Harbor, with its single channel, they were a target for any successfully launched air attack from carrier-borne planes. The severity of the attack might be mitigated, but damage to the ships found in port was inevitable. To prevent a hostile carrier from successfully launching planes required that it be first discovered and attacked. Discovery, other than by lucky accident, required air reconnaissance of the perimeter of a circle of 800-mile radius from Oahu. The Fleet did not at any time have patrol planes sufficient in number to carry out such reconnaissance. . . . An engagement at sea would have found the preponderant strength with Japan.[40]

Regardless of the disadvantages, the Hawaiian Islands offered no safer location for the Fleet. The damage Kimmel's ships sustained there could not compare to what they would have suffered had the Japanese caught them at Lahaina, where the deep waters would have swallowed beyond salvage any sunken vessel.

Basing the Fleet at Pearl Harbor presented the Japanese with an espionage bonus. With its polyglot population, Honolulu was an Oriental spy's dream location. Any competent Japanese agent could move about without attracting a second glance. Then, too, the geography of the Pearl Harbor area greatly eased the task of scouting the Fleet.

Oahu's defenders knew all too well this major, unavoidable weakness. Lieutenant General Charles D. Herron, who preceded Short in command of the Hawaiian Department, testified, "Hawaii, or Pearl Harbor, is a gold-fish bowl. We assumed that the only thing the Japanese did not know was how we would use our troops in the event of attack."[41] Kimmel told the congressional committee, "You must remember that these Japs could go up in the hills and look down in the daytime and see everything."[42]

The Japanese reaped another benefit from the location of Pearl Harbor. The concentration upon one relatively small island of so much airpower, intended as a protection, actually gave the attackers another cohesive, valuable target. With his gift for propagandizing disguised as questioning, Gearhart asked Captain Ellis M. Zacharias, a long-time Naval Intelligence officer:

> Now, by concentrating our fleet in this limited area around the Hawaiian Islands and in that one harbor that they have over there that is at all important, did we not offer the Japs a temptation to come there and with one fell swoop to immobilize our whole fleet and accomplish something which would have been difficult to accomplish if the fleet had been scattered along the Pacific coast as advocated by others and naval strategists?

Zacharias deftly closed this invitingly open gate. "Well, that is a matter of policy, undoubtedly, based on information which was not at my disposal. I prefer not to comment on that." But a little later in their exchange this clever if controversial officer added:

> I think the important consideration is this: If the fleet had been at some point on the west coast, the Japanese would not have been in a position to immobilize the aircraft at our disposal, which would have resulted in a very sizable aircraft force being sent out against the forces which had come in to make this attack. . . . In addition to that they [the Japanese] would have had to travel 2,500 miles further than Hawaii, which would have put them in a position strategically vulnerable because of the location of the air forces at Hawaii and Dutch Harbor to the northward.[43]

One could argue that events gave Zacharias's thesis a validity it would not otherwise have possessed. Had Oahu's defenders been on the alert, Nagumo might have found his carriers shuddering under aerial bombardment while his airmen encountered in full force the sort of resistance that two intrepid fighter pilots, Lieutenants George S. Welch and Kenneth Taylor, gave the second attack wave.[44] In that case, students of military history could tsk-tsk over the folly of attacking a site swarming with hostile aircraft.

Kimmel and his staff were acutely alive to the inconsistency of placing the Fleet at Pearl Harbor ostensibly as a deterrent to Japan, then using it as a mine of manpower and ships for the Atlantic.[45] The problem of how much belonged in each ocean was far from simple to solve. In January 1941, Rear Admiral Yates Stirling, Jr., urged concentration in the Atlantic to convoy war materials to Great Britain. "A defensive attitude with a smaller fleet against Japan seems mandatory in order that the Atlantic fleet can be built up for such a mission," he wrote. "The defeat of Hitler must be our first objective. If we become too involved now in the Pacific we shall be playing into the hands of Hitler with Japan." Then he added, "Anything Japan takes now can be retaken if England wins."[46]

Against this policy stood those who called for a two-ocean defense. They based some of their arguments in large part upon the twin illusions of American superiority and Japanese inferiority, especially in the area of naval aviation. Wrote journalist Charles G. Ross shortly after the first transfer of Kimmel's ships to the Atlantic:

> . . . There is no disposition here to make light of the Japanese fleet; it is recognized as a strong fighting force; but the aviation experts

tell you that after two or three weeks of battle with the American Navy, it would have to fight, thanks to our naval aviation, without eyes.[47]

Those closer to the scene were unhappy about the weakening of the Pacific Fleet. The movement of ships to the Atlantic "considerably alarmed" Hawaii's Governor Joseph B. Poindexter. In Washington during August 1941 he complained to Secretary Ickes about the removal of naval strength, leaving the islands "possibly defenseless in the event of an attack."

Poindexter recalled that Ickes replied in effect, "Oh, you people need not be alarmed whatever. There is going to be no attack on Hawaii. It is too far away." Time blurred the governor's recollection of all of Ickes's exact words. But this sentence stuck sharply in his memory: "The battle is on the Atlantic."[48]

Not even Republican Senators Brewster and Ferguson disputed the wisdom of the decision to make the Atlantic theater primary. Yet in their minority report they pointed out "that such decision resulted in the failure of the military authorities in Washington to supply the Pearl Harbor base with the military defense equipment which everyone agreed was essential." Therefore they concluded that the administration should have brought the Fleet back to the mainland.[49]

With his customary attitude of making do with the realities of the moment, Admiral Raymond A. Spruance agreed that the Fleet should have been stationed on the West Coast until after war began. This would have afforded greater protection because of the distance from Japan. After the conflict exploded, the ships could sail to Hawaii. With Japan and the United States at war, the element of surprise would have been largely eliminated, and Pearl Harbor's defenders alert to expect anything.[50]

But former CNO Admiral William V. Pratt had no patience with those who argued that the Fleet should have been based on the West Coast. "To those naval men who remain obsessed with preparation and training for war, even in the face of imminent danger, the answer might have been West Coast ports," he wrote. "But to those men . . . who place morale and the fighting heart even ahead of preparation in time of danger, the answer should have been—station the fleet in the Hawaiian Islands."

Then Pratt made a pertinent point: "a fleet that is always preparing to fight is never quite ready to fight when the time comes." He next delved into the more nebulous area of the spirit. To move back to the mainland

> would have been a slap in the face of naval morale. Jap morale would have been raised over and above anything they could have hoped to gain in battle. We would have been the laughing stock of every great sea power in the world. The entire Hawaiian Islands would have been open and ripe for invasion.
>
> In the meantime, the Japs, counting our withdrawal as a great naval victory, which in fact it would have been, would have been given ample time to entrench themselves in the Far East and Southwest Pacific. . . .

Thereupon Pratt delivered another of his thrusts to the center: "Once a retiring defensive policy is taken, it is with the greatest difficulty that the offensive can be resumed."[51]

Admiral Furlong took a position somewhere between Spruance and Pratt. "You cannot operate in the Pacific unless you have a base," he said. "The object of a base is to protect ships and to service them. If we were going to fight Japan we needed Pearl Harbor. The business of keeping our Fleet on the West Coast was OK in case we did not go to war. But if we fought Japan we had to go to Hawaii. There was no other way."[52]

One high-ranking officer who disagreed with the transfer of substantial units to the Atlantic was Hart, whose little Asiatic Fleet would be right in the path of Japan's Southern Operation. He let the Navy Department know unofficially his "total disagreement in not keeping almost all of our force in the Pacific waters during those times." But he conceded that he "did not have very good knowledge of what the requirements and responsibilities were in the Atlantic."[53]

In view of those "requirements and responsibilities," one may well argue that the main strength of the Navy belonged neither in Hawaiian waters nor on the West Coast but in the Atlantic. Of all the advice Roosevelt received concerning the use of the Pacific Fleet, Stimson's was probably the most realistic as well as the boldest and most original in the context of the time. On the Pacific coast, Kimmel's ships might have been safer and certainly would have enjoyed many logistical benefits, but they would have been relatively useless to the cause of the free world, in effect awaiting Japan's pleasure.

To the Japanese, it mattered little where in the Pacific the United States based its ships: Japan was going ahead in any case. Events proved that stationing the Fleet in Hawaii did not deter Japan in the least. In fact, as Japan became more and more obviously set on its course, the U.S. Pacific Fleet became proportionately less and less a "deterrent." For this reason, Kimmel's ships might have been better employed against the number one enemy in the Atlantic.

Perhaps more thought should have been devoted to the type of ships to be transferred to that theater. Ingersoll suggested to Greaves that the United States did not need Kimmel's battleships in the Atlantic; it needed destroyers and antisubmarine craft. It is true that the naval situation in the two oceans presented very different problems. In the Atlantic, Hitler was fighting primarily a war of attrition. His most potent naval weapon was the U-boat, against which battleships were useless. In contrast, if an old-style surface slugging match developed with the Axis, it was much more likely to be with Japan's Combined Fleet in the Pacific. Retrospectively, however, Ingersoll thought the transfer turned out for the best. Otherwise more ships might have been trapped at Pearl Harbor.[54] In any case, the original decision to base at Pearl Harbor should have come up for recurrent review as the international situation changed.

Before the event, Richardson had observed to Roosevelt that the U.S. Pacific Fleet might deter a civilian government, but the Japanese, being military, knew too much about its real strength to be impressed.[55] Nonetheless, the cold historical fact remains that, weak as it was, the U.S. Pacific Fleet impressed Yamamoto sufficiently to impel him to risk sending the bulk of his naval air power all the way to Hawaii to knock Kimmel's ships out of action.

John T. Flynn completely misread the situation when he scored Roosevelt for transferring sea power to the Atlantic: "The President literally opened the doors to the attacks on the Philippines and Hawaii by sending half of the Pacific fleet out of the Pacific into the Atlantic."[56] Later Flynn went even further: "The stripping of the naval and airplane and military defenses of Hawaii—particularly the naval defenses—was the second great cause of the disaster at Pearl Harbor."[57]

It is idle to claim that if Roosevelt had left the Fleet intact the Japanese would not have struck at Pearl Harbor. Yamamoto had conceived his idea, Rear Admiral Takijiro Onishi and Commander Minoru Genda had worked out their initial draft, the First Air Fleet had been organized, and staff work on the plan had been started when the Pacific Fleet was at the height of its strength.[58] The potential danger it posed, not its weakness, brought about Yamamoto's concept. Therefore, one may well argue that the American error lay not in moving certain ships to the Atlantic, but in leaving the bulk of the Pacific Fleet in Pearl Harbor.

During the congressional hearings, the Honolulu *Star-Bulletin* threw cold water over the question of basing the Fleet. This newspaper considered the argument "over where the fleet should have been based in late 1941" irrelevant to the subject of the inquiry. "The key to the Pearl Harbor disaster was lack of alertness on the part of the local commands, and nothing will ever change this."[59]

Assistant Counsel Edward P. Morgan came to the same conclusion when he prepared his draft report for submission to the congressional committee. He believed that the decision to base the Fleet in the Hawaiian Islands had "no proximate or reasonable bearing on the causative factors of the disaster." He pointed out the absurdity of the "ifs, ands, and buts" approach:

> To say that the debacle of December 7 was occasioned because of the decision to base the fleet at Pearl Harbor in May of 1940 is like saying that the commanding officers would not have been embarrassed by the attack if they had not been made commander in chief of the Pacific Fleet and commanding general of the Hawaiian Department early in 1941 or, going back still further, if they had never entered the Army and Navy.[60]

That was the crux of the matter. Once the political and strategical decision had been made, the protection of the Fleet at its home base and the readiness of the Fleet for action became the responsibility of the commanders on the spot.

CHAPTER 8

"Looking in the Wrong Direction"

Russo-German war—Pessimism about Russian chances—Would Japan attack the Soviet Union?— Decision to defend Philippines—Dependence on B-17—Concentration on Southeast Asia.

The second point at which Roosevelt should have reviewed the United States naval policy was when the tensions of the European-Atlantic theater, already the prime focus of American attention, escalated on June 22, 1941: when Germany attacked the Soviet Union. Some Americans saw this turn of events as a special dispensation of Providence. Left to themselves, Hitler and the Soviet dictator, Josef Stalin, might remain at each other's throats until both their nations were too exhausted to menace anyone else for at least a generation. From the vantage point of 1962, Ingersoll insisted that aiding the Soviet Union was one of the United States' primary mistakes. He would have preferred that Washington stand aside while the Russians and Germans fought it out. "It would have kept the Germans busy pushing the Russians back to the coast."[1]

Hitler's thus dividing Germany's strength gave the British a chance to catch their second wind. To many Americans, the time seemed ripe to exert all possible pressure on the Atlantic front. On the morning of June 23, Stimson discussed the situation with Marshall and members of the War Plans Division. As Stimson wrote to Roosevelt that day:

> They were unanimously of the belief that this precious and unforeseen period of respite should be used to push with the utmost vigor our movements in the Atlantic theater of operations. They were unanimously of the feeling that such pressure on our part was the right way to help Britain, to discourage Germany, and to strengthen our own position of defense against our most imminent danger.

Stimson considered the matter so urgent that he personally hand-carried this letter to the President. Speed was of the essence, because "Germany will be thoroughly occupied in beating Russia for a minimum of one month and a possible maximum of three months."[2]

Knox, too, was enthusiastically in favor of "immediate use of the Navy to clear the North Atlantic" in view of this "God-given chance now that Hitler's back was turned in Russia."[3] With the secretary's blessing, on June 24 Stark pleaded with Roosevelt to initiate convoying in the Atlantic, even at the risk of war, while Hitler fought the Russians. Stark believed that further delay in joining the conflict "might be fatal to Britain's survival," and that "only a war psychology" could step up American production to the necessary peak.[4]

To understand this pressure for speed, one must recall that in 1941 the Soviet Union was not yet a superpower. Many American experts fully expected the Germans to defeat the Russians in a few weeks, then return to the western front enormously strengthened by access to such vital resources as Ukrainian grain, oil from the Caucasus, and unlimited Russian manpower. Marshall's G-2 was far from sanguine about the Soviet Union's chances, estimating that the Germans could finish the job in six weeks. Marshall himself was not quite that pessimistic.[5] Nor was Hull, although he was aware that estimates both in the United States and abroad gave the Soviet Union only a few weeks.[6]

But Roosevelt did not panic, nor, significantly, did he plunge immediately into the war through the "front door" thus invitingly held open for him. Instead, he temporized to a degree that irritated Ickes, who was impatient with Roosevelt for failing to make a prompt, decisive statement of immediate support for the Soviet Union. He contrasted the President's vacillation with "the vigorous statesmanship of Churchill" who, although a staunch anticommunist, "did not lose sight of the fact that it is Hitler who is the main threat to the civilization of the world and that our primary purpose must be to defeat him." Ickes added, "It was extremely fortunate for us that Churchill stepped forward in this forthright manner because there was not a word from the President. . . . It would be just like him to wait for some expression of public opinion instead of giving direction to that public opinion."[7]

By invading the Soviet Union, Hitler drastically modified the situation in Asia as well as in Europe. He put the Japanese in an embarrassing spot. "Japan is in a quandary as a result of the German-Soviet war; she is pledged to the Axis and also pledged to neutrality vis-à-vis Soviet Russia; what policy will she now follow?" Joseph C. Grew, U.S. Ambassador to Japan, asked his diary on June 23.[8]

For a while it appeared that Japan might decide to strike the Soviet Union, both to rid itself of a threat which far preceded the communist takeover of Russia and to secure some mainland territory as a cushion against too much "togetherness" with either the Russians or the Germans. For the early German successes against the Soviet Union disturbed certain intelligent Japanese, who did not care in the least for the idea of the swastika flying over Vladivostok. An alliance with Hitler was at its best when operated by remote control—the more remote the better. For example, in a conversation with Joseph W. Ballantine of the State Department, Colonel Hideo Iwakuro* observed "that even though we could not profitably pursue conversations at the present time an opportunity might arise again in the future, perhaps if Germany should vanquish Russia and move over to the Far East. He thought that under such circumstances the basis for our conversations might by different."[9]

On the other side of the Pacific, Lieutenant Colonel Harry I. T. Creswell, the U.S. military attaché in Tokyo, reported:

> Although it appears that the Japanese would prefer, and, as a matter of fact expect, a German victory, it is plain that the degree of the victory they both expect and desire is a matter of no small concern. They obviously do not relish a Soviet which can prove itself strong enough to neutralize, if not defeat the German attacks, nor, on the other hand, are they enthusiastic over so complete a German victory as would place the Germans in control of the Soviet and thereby a neighbor of Japan along the Manchukuo and Korean borders and on the west shores of the Japan sea.

Creswell pointed out that most of Japan's newly mobilized strength had been sent to Manchuria. Then he added, "The local conclusion . . . is that, in the event of a Russian collapse, the Japanese will solve the above problem by moving against the Maritime Provinces and other areas either with or without German consent and thus insure at one stroke that Germany will not become too close a neigh-

---

*Iwakuro was an assistant military attaché in the Japanese Embassy in Washington, and worked closely with the so-called "John Doe" group. See Chapter 9.

bor and that the Soviet threat to Japan via Vladivostok is disposed of."[10]

Nomura, too, worried because "Japan now found herself isolated." While "the Trans-Siberian railroad remained open there was at least the possibility that Germany would give assistance to Japan, but . . . now with the Trans-Siberian railroad closed for a period no one could predict, Japan could get no assistance that way."[11]

Thus one can readily understand the widely held, persistent belief among Americans that Japan would seize this opportunity to attack the hard-beset Russians instead of moving south, which almost inevitably would risk war with the United States. On August 6, 1941, Major F. P. Munson, assistant military attaché in China, estimated as follows:

> While it is impossible to evaluate with any degree of accuracy the conflicting reports concerning Japan's next move, the preponderance of opinion seems to point that it is toward Siberia. Not only have troops and military supplies of all kinds been pouring into Manchukuo during the last month, but large stocks of rails, machinery and rolling stock have been removed from North China yards and sent east through Tientsin toward Mukden. Another plausible reason for Japanese action in Siberia lies in the fact that if the Germans can crumble Soviet resistance in the west, there is no telling how far east the German army may move and it would behoove the Japanese to annex as much territory as possible if only to protect themselves from this new menace. It is also possible that the occupation of Indo-China may act as a check to the British in Malaya and keep them from attempting any operation designed to help the Soviets, if attacked by the Japanese.[12]

In mid-September Colonel Francis G. Brink, the U.S. Army liaison officer in Singapore, reported that the British had concluded that they had "at least four months in which to improve their own strategic position, and to contain and coerce the Japanese to make them realize that the only hope for them is to abandon their pro-Axis policy and cooperate with the U.S., China and Great Britain." One reason for this optimism was their belief that the Japanese "have set up their forces for a northern offensive and they cannot switch rapidly to the south."[13]

On October 17, Washington received a jittery message from its representatives in Chungking: "Early Japanese attack in Siberia probably a matter of days predicted by Chinese Army leaders. If Russia collapses or weakens Siberia garrison as reported, Japanese will consider time for invasion opportune." Four days later, citing as the source the chief of British Far East Intelligence, London estimated:

1. It is thought that Japan will not advance southward, except possibly into Thailand, because of the danger of becoming embroiled with the United States and Britain. . . .

2. . . . The new Premier is wholly pro-German. It is believed that the Japs will advance on Vladivostok and the Maritime Provinces the minute Soviet disintegration appears imminent. . . . The Russians are still believed stronger in Siberia in spite of possible transfer of troops to the other theaters, but the Maritimes and Vladivostok unquestionably could be captured by the Japs.[14]

In view of such information from the sources closest to the problem, it is not surprising that certain of Roosevelt's advisers expected the Japanese to strike north and west rather than south and east. On July 3, Stark sent Kimmel, among other addressees, a Top Secret estimate of Japanese intentions in which he stated, "The neutrality pact with Russia will be abrogated and major military effort will be against their maritime provinces which will probably be toward the end of July."[15] That same month, Miles's G-2 estimated that within a year Germany would have defeated the USSR and occupied the country "to Lake Baikal and possibly to the Pacific." Japan might have occupied the Maritime Provinces.[16]

Yet these assessments were based almost entirely upon the activities of the Japanese Army and its support units. There seemed little appreciation of the fact that however much the Japanese Army, traditionally Russian-oriented, might long for the opportunity to clip a few miles off the Soviet borders, their ability to do so would depend in large measure upon a continuous flow of raw materials unobtainable on the northern front.

The key to Japan's imperial dream lay southward, and only its Navy could open the golden door. Nomura had remarked to Welles that with the Trans-Siberian Railroad closed, "the chief responsibility for the future of Japan rested upon the Japanese Navy."[17] This comment raised a very important point: in effect, when Hitler attacked the Soviet Union, he unleashed the tiger of Japanese sea power. From the minute the Germans struck, thus isolating Japan from her tenuous overland connection with her Tripartite partners, the United States should have directed all possible efforts to determining the plans and preparations of the Japanese Navy. That navy was one of the best in the world, with a superior air arm, and headed by an admiral who was a born leader of men. Yet obviously Yamamoto's Combined Fleet would be of little use against the Soviet Union's Siberian mass. Therefore, the United States could expect the Japanese—now temporarily freed from their perennial fear that Russia would strike them—to center their aggression on areas where their fleet could wield power. This was doubly true because those areas—in Southeast Asia—coincided with the sources of raw materials that Japan sorely needed. So it behooved the political and naval leaders of the United States to increase their watch over the one instrument in Japan's military arsenal that could move either southward to Japan's El Dorado or eastward to attack United States forces on Oahu or wherever they might be found in the Pacific.

There was another element for the Americans to ponder: Once again the world had received an object lesson in the futility of relying on conventional diplomacy in dealing with the Tripartite powers. Stalin had gone much further with Hitler than any American but the most hard-shelled isolationist would be prepared to go with Japan. Yet this had not saved the Soviet Union once Hitler decided to attack. Obviously the niceties of international relationships and the sanctity of treaties meant nothing to the Axis. One principle alone guided them: self-aggrandizement. Where they saw prospective profit, they would strike ruthlessly.

But instead of causing the United States to keep an ever sharper eye out for possible Axis surprise attacks anywhere, the Russo-German war only distracted American attention. As late as October 15, 1941, Roosevelt wrote in a brief note to Churchill, "I think they [the Japanese] are headed North."[18]

Nevertheless, the United States by no means ignored Japan's openly stated greed for southern treasure. Washington hoped to block Japanese aggression in Southeast Asia by building up strength in the Philippines. This was a major revision of defense policy. "There had always been a feeling that we couldn't hold the Philippines, that we would have to abandon them," said Stark.[19] Actually, this was much more than a "feeling"; it was a realistic if regrettable acknowledgment of reality.

In Appendix A of a study dated December 2, 1935, Brigadier General Stanley D. Embick, at that time chief of War Plans, declared, "In the event of an Orange* war under existing conditions, the early dispatch of our fleet to Philippine waters would be literally an act of madness." In the summary section of his disconcerting paper, Embick made it clear that the Army would be in no less of a bind:

1. The maintenance in the Philippine Islands of military forces adequate to defend a base is wholly impracticable. . . . It would be lost immediately after the opening of hostilities.

2. Unless we are to jeopardize our vital interests, we can confront Japan with decisive armed forces in the Far East only after the progressive conquest of the Mandated Islands. This means that:

a. We can not move to the early relief of a Philippine base.

b. We can not protect the Philippine Islands against invasion and occupation.[20]

The situation had not improved by the summer of 1940, when Stimson turned down a proposal to double the number of Philippine Scouts. "We already have about 5,000 white troops and 6,000 Philippine Scouts out there to fall into the hands of Japan if she chooses to attack the Islands, and I don't think there is any reason for adding to them. The forces, even if augmented, would be far too small to make any difference in the situation." [21]

Few American leaders in 1941 believed that the United States as yet had reached the point where it could hold the Philippines against a determined Japanese campaign. Current war plans conceded this unhappy state of affairs. An extract from WPL-46 made it obvious that American naval planners anticipated loss of the islands:

b. TASK

SUPPORT THE LAND AND AIR FORCES IN THE DEFENSE OF THE TERRITORIES OF THE ASSOCIATED POWERS. (THE RESPONSIBILITY OF THE COMMANDER IN CHIEF, UNITED STATES ASIATIC FLEET, FOR SUPPORTING THE DEFENSE OF THE PHILIPPINES REMAINS SO LONG AS THAT DE-FENSE CONTINUES.) . . .[22]

That defense would not last long if the Army's strength in the Philippines remained what it was on May 1, 1941: A total ground

---

*Japan was designated "Orange" in war plans.

force of about 20,000 men, an air force consisting of "three pursuit squadrons, one observation squadron and one medium bombardment squadron. None of the planes were modern types."[23]

Then, in the summer of 1941, the picture changed. On July 26, Roosevelt issued the necessary orders to incorporate the armed forces of the Philippines into those of the United States. The War Department established a new command, U.S. Army Forces in the Far East (USAFFE) and recalled Douglas MacArthur to active duty with rank of Major General to assume command thereof.[24]

This move in itself signaled a hopeful attitude on the part of Washington. MacArthur brought to his post a military record brilliant enough to satisfy even himself. He possessed a total, almost mystic self-confidence. Moreover, he was proud of his Filipino troops and displayed an exuberant optimism about their ability to defend the islands.[25]

The Navy, too, was "delighted with the Army move putting the Filipinos in harness; we recommended this," as Stark wrote to Captain Charles M. "Savvy" Cooke, Jr., with a copy to Kimmel, on July 31, 1941.[26]

But what had convinced Washington that the Philippines might, after all, be defensible was neither the availability of the Philippine Army nor the ability and personality of MacArthur; it was the belief of the Air Staff that a force of B-17 long-range bombers based in the Philippines would change the entire strategic scene.[27]

The Flying Fortress was a fine aircraft in its day, one that engendered something of the love a true sailor feels for his ship. No one who saw a B-17 in flight could ever forget the impression it conveyed of power and grace. During World War II, performing the mission for which it was designed, and in the hands of crews who understood it, the Flying Fortress proved its worth many times over. But in 1941 the War Department expected much more of it than it could give. The top brass not only expected the B-17 to defend the Philippines but to deter the Japanese from attacking in that area and even to keep them out of the war. In his memorandum of October 8, Gerow spelled out the thinking for Stimson:

> Strategic considerations demand that Japan continue to remain in the status of a non-belligerent, thus permitting the bulk of the military resources of the Associated Powers to be employed in the

principal theater—the Atlantic and Europe. Should Japan actively assist the Axis Powers, the supply of materiel to Britain and Russia would be immeasurably more difficult. Shipping losses would increase and the vital line of supply to Russia through Vladivostok would be closed. This latter factor is of the utmost importance—the Vladivostok route can handle some 3,000 tons of supplies a day as against 270 tons via the Persian Gulf route which soon may be cut.

Gerow explained the problems facing Japan as he saw them: Attempts to bypass the Philippines would leave Japan's forces vulnerable to air and naval attack, while "removal of the Philippines as an obstacle to her advance south, would be a hazardous military operation, if opposed by strong aviation forces. . . . The cost of this operation would be so great that Japan will hesitate to make the effort except as a last resort." Listing the current and planned forces in the Philippines, Gerow concluded that

the air and ground units now available or scheduled for dispatch to the Philippine Islands in the immediate future have changed the entire picture in the Asiatic area. The action taken by the War Department may well be the determining factor in Japan's eventual decision and, consequently, have a vital bearing on the course of the war as a whole.[28]

No one was a more enthusiastic booster of the B-17 than the recipient of that memorandum. Having been High Commissioner of the Philippines, Stimson had a special interest in the islands, and he had no doubt of the efficacy of the Flying Fortress. The safe arrival of nine of these aircraft at Manila on the morning of September 12 delighted him. "Just at this timely moment when our State Department is trying to hold back the Japanese from going down into Indo China and Siam, this demonstration of our power to place planes which in the narrow seas can completely damage her line of ship connections with her expeditionary force is a most powerful factor."[29]

He even told T. V. Soong, Chiang Kai-shek's brother-in-law, who was in the United States on a financial mission, that "we were doing something in the Philippines that I thought was even more important in the interests of China than any aid that could go over the Burma Road just at present."[30] Stimson also informed the Netherlands East Indies' military attaché, who was "evidently itching" for some B-17s, "how we were going to use them in the Philippines and how when they were there they could cooperate with the whole scheme of defense."[31]

On October 21, in response to a query from Roosevelt about "proper strategic distribution" of the B-17s, Stimson mentioned the "melancholy list of casualties which have recently occurred to our planes in the hands of British pilots" and stressed the importance of the southwestern Pacific:

> From being impotent to influence events in that area, we suddenly find ourselves vested with the possibility of great effective power. . . .
> We are rushing planes and other preparations to the Philippines from a base in the United States which has not yet in existence the number of the planes necessary for our immediate minimum requirements in that southwestern Pacific theatre. This is the result of our deferments to the British last year. . . . Yet even this imperfect threat, if not promptly called by the Japanese, bids fair to stop Japan's march to the south and secure the safety of Singapore. . . . As you well know, however, the final success of the operation lies on the knees of the gods and we cannot tell what explosion may momentarily come from Japan. . . .[32]

Right then and there Roosevelt had the opportunity to insist upon a realistic reassessment of the whole strategy. Stimson's letter, enthusiastic as it was, had raised two disquieting points: The United States did not have in its current inventory sufficient B-17s for the "immediate minimum requirements" in the southwest Pacific, and the Japanese might act before the Americans could complete their buildup.

As of October 8, only nine B-17s had reached the Philippines; in other words, almost a month had gone by since the shipment of September 12 without a single Flying Fortress being added to USAFFE's strength. Of course, future figures on paper looked impressive: "Starting with 1942, the aviation strength will be raised to a total of 170 heavy bombers, 86 light bombers, and 195 pursuit."[33] But suppose the Japanese did not stand back waiting for the Americans to complete their preparations? Granted that the Japanese had no inhibitions about launching a preemptive strike, military strategy and common sense dictated that they attack before the Americans were ready to receive them.

The B-17 strategy was fundamentally shaky, being based upon an untested premise, namely, that a bomber designed to operate against land targets would be equally efficacious against targets at sea. Within a year, the battles of Midway and the Bismarck Sea would prove that land bombers, including the B-17, were useless against maneuvering ships. Of course, War Plans did not include crystal gazing among its talents; still, it is surprising that Roosevelt, such a devoted buff of sea power, did not raise this question with his military and naval advisers.[34]

Another practical problem cried aloud for close consideration: B-17s used aviation gasoline—and plenty of it. To keep flying aircraft based in an archipelago that produced no oil required command of the seas surrounding those islands, a friendly source of oil, and sufficient tankers to transport the oil. The War Department had already run into trouble in this regard: "Twenty-six of our big bombers are held up in this country because we have been unable to get a ship to carry the oil to be deposited at one of their stopping places on the way over," wrote Stimson on October 9.[35]

This fact applied to the Hawaiian Islands even more strongly than it did to the Philippines, and should have led to serious reconsideration of current policies and strategy for the Hawaiian area. For the decision to give the Philippines priority in assigning B-17s to the Pacific shot down the Army's thesis that the Pacific Fleet could spare ships for the Atlantic because the Hawaiian Air Force, equipped, among other items, with "35 of our most modern flying fortresses," could protect Hawaii. Marshall and his advisers had also assumed that other B-17s could be dispatched to Hawaii "immediately if the situation grew critical."[36]

The new Philippines-oriented policy superimposed upon Short's primary mission of protecting the Fleet and his secondary mission of defending Hawaii a third function—that of operating a staging post for the big bombers. Thus saddled with the job of preparing crews and planes for their next long transocean hop, Short became more firmly fixed in his preoccupation with training.

Short also convinced himself that his command had moved into a back seat and was no longer a top danger zone in Washington's eyes. He explained to the congressional committee how his strength in Flying Fortresses had dwindled. "We had 21 B-17s at one time, and 9 of those were sent to the Philippines and we were down to 12, and had to rob 6 of those planes to keep the others going through." Ferguson asked him, "Did that impress you with the fact that there was more thought to an attack in the Philippines than there was in your territory?" To this Short replied firmly, "No question about it. They were ferrying in the last few months everything to the Philippines they could."[37]

Thus not only did Washington give the Hawaiian Air Force no more B-17s, it took away most of those already on Oahu. This policy extracted the backbone from Short's means of aerial defense and of assisting the Navy in long-range aerial reconnaissance. Short was now responsible for defending Hawaii and the Fleet in Pearl Harbor with inadequate means. So the Navy would have to take up the slack. Kimmel and his staff fully appreciated that, when the chips were down, such defense would fall in part upon the Navy, even though protection of the Hawaiian Islands and the Fleet in harbor was the Army's responsibility.[38]

Washington's decision to defend the Philippines did not so much present Hawaii's defenders with a new dilemma as intensify existing ones. Kimmel still had the problem of whether to give priority to defending his ships in harbor or to getting them in tiptop operating condition for war. If his men maintained a full alert while in port, they would have no opportunity to rest or to replenish and refurbish the ships. Soon both men and ships would be too exhausted for combat readiness. Short had to figure out how to defend the Fleet and the islands and at the same time run a way station.

It is tempting to say that Washington should have assigned priorities among the tasks. But the situation was not that simple. The United States was on the defensive, so policies and priorities would shift with the actions, actual or anticipated, of the Axis powers. Moreover, in those days of military buildup, Kimmel and Short were by no means the only American commanders faced with the necessity of performing a secular miracle of the loaves and fishes. In fact, they were in better shape to do so than most.

Washington did have two major options. In the spring of 1941 the administration had decided that it could safely take some vessels from Kimmel to bolster the Atlantic Fleet because, with proposed strengthening, the Hawaiian Air Force could carry out Hawaii's defense mission. Therefore, the removal of most of the Flying Fortresses to the Philippines called for reassessing Hawaii's entire defensive position. Here was another occasion when it might have been wise to remove the bulk of the Fleet to the Atlantic or to the West Coast. Such action would have relieved Kimmel's ships of the incongruous necessity of defending themselves in port, and would have left Short with the more clear-cut, practical tasks of protecting the Islands and processing B-17s.

The War and Navy departments should have consulted with Short and Kimmel, respectively, to determine how best they could assist the local commanders in meeting this new situation. At the very least, Washington should have taken another close look at Hawaii's intelligence requirements. With so little heavy airpower remaining, Hawaii's defenders needed every scrap of information to utilize their available forces to the best advantage. Kimmel and Short should have received frequent reports about the diplomatic situation between Japan and the United States, about Japan's actions in the Far East, and in particular about the extent of Japan's spyingon Hawaii's installations and the ships of the Pacific Fleet.

By another of those strange coincidences that crop up so frequently in the Pearl Harbor story, it was on September 24, 1941, while the War Department was in full swing of preparing to implement its new Philippine policy, that Tokyo dispatched to Honolulu the first of its famous "bomb plot" series of messages.* Even if Washington thought that Kimmel and Short were reading these and other consular messages, it should have called them to their attention in the context of the overall Japanese-American situation.

But Washington neither adjusted the missions of the Fleet and the Hawaiian Department nor changed its overly secretive policy concerning dissemination of information. Obsession with the Philippines left Hawaii and its needs on the back burner. This was a very serious error.

The Philippines continued to dominate thinking in the autumn of 1941. On October 28, Hull asked Stimson if he favored immediate declaration of war against Japan. The secretary of war replied with a prompt and forceful "NO" (Stimson's capitals). He explained that he wanted "to take advantage of this wonderful opportunity of strengthening our position in the Philippines by air and to use it as a means of strengthening his diplomatic arm by forcing the Japanese to keep

---

*See Appendix 5. The "bomb plot" divided Pearl Harbor into specific areas to facilitate reporting by the Japanese consulate of the berthing positions of U.S. ships at moorings. *Plot* in this context did not mean a conspiracy.

away from Singapore and perhaps, if we are in good luck, to shake the Japanese out of the Axis."[39]

A month later, when the decision was reached to send "war warning" messages to Hawaii, the Canal Zone, the West Coast, and the Philippines, Stimson did not even mention in his diary the three other commands involved; he was totally preoccupied with USAFFE:

> The main question has been over the message that we shall send to MacArthur. We have already sent him a quasi alert, or the first signal for an alert, and now, on talking with the President this morning over the telephone, I suggested and he approved the idea that we should send the final alert; namely, that he should be on the qui vive for any attack and telling him how the situation was. So Gerow and Stark and I went over the proposed message to him from Marshall very carefully; finally got it in shape and with the help of a telephone talk I had with Hull, I got the exact statement from him of what the situation was.[40]

Between October 28, when Stimson had confidently hoped that the threat of the dread B-17 would "shake the Japanese out of the Axis," and November 27, when he helped prepare a warning for MacArthur that "hostile action" with Japan was "possible at any moment,"[41] much had happened. Quite aside from the fact that in this interim the First Air Fleet completed its rehearsals and preparations for the Pearl Harbor attack, rendezvoused at Hitokappu Bay, and sortied on its voyage to Hawaii—events of which the United States naturally knew nothing—many developments of which Washington did know hinted all too broadly that American policy to restrain Japan was having rather less than no effect on the Japanese.

On November 3, Grew warned the State Department that "Japan's resort to measures which might make war with Japan inevitable may come with dramatic and dangerous suddenness."[42] One day later, the U.S. Navy reported to Kimmel, among others, that Japan seemed to be withdrawing all its merchant shipping from the Western Hemisphere.[43]

Throughout November, Tokyo's instructions to its embassy in Washington stressed the urgency of obtaining Uncle Sam's signature on the dotted line without delay, culminating in the extension of its original deadline of November 25 to November 29, after which "things are automatically going to happen."[44]

Other Magic intercepts hinted strongly at an anticipated break in communications. On November 15, Tokyo sent to its Washington embassy detailed instructions for the destruction of code machines in an emergency.[45] Four days later, Tokyo established the "hidden word" code to be used when diplomatic relations became "dangerous."[46] The famous "winds" code, which would signal "danger of cutting off our diplomatic relations," for use if international communications should be severed, was set up that same day but was not translated until November 28.[47]*

On November 23, the Fourteenth Naval District's Communications Intelligence Summary observed, "Nothing was seen to contradict impressions gathered during the past few days and summarized previously, that movement of forces is either imminent or actually underway, at least in part, to the southward" on the part of the Japanese.[48]

Against this background, the State Department continued its discussions with Nomura and, from November 17, with Kurusu. An important point under discussion had been the presence of Japanese troops in Indochina.[49] The Japanese-proposed modus vivendi of November 20 contained important proposals concerning Indochina:

> 1. Both the Governments of Japan and the United States undertake not to make any armed advancement into any of the regions in the Southeastern Asia and the Southern Pacific area excepting the part of French Indo-China where the Japanese troops are stationed at present.
>
> 2. The Japanese Government undertakes to withdraw its troops now stationed in French Indo-China upon either the restoration of peace between Japan and China or the establishment of an equitable peace in the Pacific area.
>
> In the meantime the Government of Japan declares that it is prepared to remove its troops now stationed in the southern part of French Indo-China to the northern part of the said territory upon the conclusion of the present arrangement which shall later be embodied in the final agreement.[50]

Regardless of how ridiculous these specious proposals might seem to the Americans, British, and Dutch—not to mention the unfortunate French—Tokyo had submitted them formally as part of a suggested modus vivendi, so Washington had to assume that the Japanese

---

*See Chapter 19.

honestly considered that here was a possible area of agreement. Therefore it was only natural that Roosevelt "fairly blew up" when Stimson advised him of a large Japanese expedition that had been sighted south of Formosa. Roosevelt remarked that "that changed the whole situation because it was evidence of bad faith on the part of the Japanese that while they were negotiating for an entire truce— an entire withdrawal—they would be sending this expedition down there to Indo-China."[51]

Stimson's follow-through memorandum for Roosevelt opened as follows: "About a month and a half ago we learned through Magic that the Japanese Government informed the Vichy Government that they proposed to move approximately 50,000 troops into Indo-China in addition to the 40,000 already there by previous agreement." After describing the nature and extent of the convoy, Stimson continued, "The officers concerned, in the Military Intelligence Division, feel that unless we receive other information, this is more or less a normal movement, that is, a logical follow-up of their previous notification to the Vichy Government."[52]

Based in the main upon the two paragraphs cited above, a recent writer on the Pacific war decided that this revelation was less a "bombshell" than "a damp squib," and built up an edifice of conjecture that the United States must have received some other warning that upset the urbane Roosevelt and caused abandonment of the modus vivendi.[53]

No such speculation was necessary. In the context of the negotiations, Roosevelt's reaction was natural. And this incident was not the only reason for failing to agree to the modus vivendi, which was obviously unacceptable in any case.* Nor was the matter solely one of Japanese "bad faith." There were serious strategic implications involved. Roosevelt with Hull, Stimson, Knox, Marshall, and Stark thrashed out the matter on November 28:

> It was the consensus that the present move—that there was an Expeditionary Force on the sea of about 25,000 Japanese troops aimed for a landing somewhere—completely changed the situation when we last discussed whether or not we could address an ultimatum to Japan about moving the troops which she already had on land in Indo-China. It was now the opinion of everyone that if this

*See Chapter 11.

expedition was allowed to get around the southern point of Indo-China and to get off and land in the Gulf of Siam, either at Bangkok or further west, it would be a terrific blow at all of the three Powers, Britain at Singapore, the Netherlands, and ourselves in the Philippines. It was the consensus of everybody that this must not be allowed.[54]

As for Japan's diplomats in Washington, in a telephone conversation on November 27 with Kumaichi Yamamoto, director of the Bureau of American Affairs at the Foreign Ministry in Tokyo, Kurusu acknowledged, "As before,* that southern matter . . . was the monkey wrench."[55]

In accordance with these events, the War and Navy departments issued their famous warnings of November 27. Although Hawaii continued to receive significant information from Washington, there is no doubt that in both Hawaii and Washington attention continued to center on Southeast Asia in general and the Philippines in particular. When informed of the attack, Knox exclaimed incredulously, "My God, this can't be true, this must mean the Philippines."[56] And in Hawaii, when headquarters telephoned the news to Kimmel's Fleet Intelligence Officer, Lieutenant Commander Edwin T. Layton, he burst out, "Jesus, we were sure looking in the wrong direction!"[57]

---

*Japan's invasion of Indochina in July 1941 had resulted in the United States declaring an economic freeze. See Chapter 9.

President Roosevelt celebrates Thanksgiving at Warm Springs, 1941. After hearing a report the night before of the "vengeance" speech delivered by Premier Tojo of Japan, he prepared to cut short his visit and return to Washington (UPI).

Admiral Harold R. Stark, Chief of Naval Operations. He never quite recovered from the taint of Pearl Harbor (U.S. Navy).

Admiral Husband E. Kimmel, Commander in Chief, U.S. Pacific Fleet. Some feel he was derelict in his plans for the defense of Pearl Harbor (U.S. Naval Historical Center).

Admiral Chester Nimitz, Commander in Chief, U.S. Pacific Fleet, who relieved Admiral Kimmel (U.S. Navy Department).

From left to right, Admiral Harry E. Yarnell, Admiral Harold R. Stark, Admiral James O. Richardson and Secretary of the Navy Frank Knox in 1940, a year before Pearl Harbor.

RADM Richmond Kelly Turner, Chief, War Plans Division, Navy Department (Official U.S. Navy Photo).

General George C. Marshall, Chief of Staff, U.S. Army. Revisionists believe he knew the Japanese were going to hit Pearl Harbor and let them do it.

Frank Knox, Republican Secretary of the Navy in a Democratic Administration. On the eve of Pearl Harbor, he stated that the U.S. Navy was second to none.

Henry L. Stimson, Republican Secretary of War in a Democratic Administration.

Cordell Hull, Secretary of State. Revisionists believe he forced the Japanese to attack the U.S. because of his ultimatum.

Commander Alwin D. Kramer.

Lieutenant General Walter C. Short, Commanding General, Hawaiian Department. Was he guilty of sins of omission? (UPI)

Captain Laurence F. Safford.

Emperor Hirohito. Was he responsible for Pearl Harbor? Hirohito is still emperor to this day.

Admiral Isoroku Yamamoto, Commander in Chief, Combined Fleet.

Premier Hideki Tojo, leader of the Japanese War Party in 1941.

PART II

ADVISERS, PLANNERS, AND CHIEFS

CHAPTER 9

"With Knives and Hatchets"

State Department accused of appeasement—Roosevelt's favoritism—Embargo on oil for Japan—Did embargo make war inevitable?—"John Doe" mission

Roosevelt had had numerous opportunities to assemble his cabinet, shuffle it, and reshuffle it. Many secretaries came and went, leaving little or no impression on the national consciousness. Some, however, became public characters in their own right, and shared in the praise and blame heaped on him over the years.

Among these durable individuals, Secretary of State Cordell Hull stood out. Born in the Cumberland foothills of Tennessee, Hull had pursued a career which was virtually a distillation of the "American dream"—from log cabin to law school, from circuit judgeship to Spanish-American War volunteer, from congressman to senator. In 1941, at the age of seventy, he had been Roosevelt's secretary of state since 1933.[1] In general, he was popular and trusted, for there was something reassuring about this tall, silver-haired backwoodsman-turned-statesman.

Immediately after Pearl Harbor, however, he and his department came under heavy fire for "appeasement." For example, journalist Freda Kirchwey termed Pearl Harbor "the fruit of appeasement." Shortly after the attack, she claimed that the Far East war could have been avoided had the United States cracked down "from the first hour of Japan's invasion of Manchukuo" and refused to sell Japan the "oil and machines and metals and planes with which it extended its conquests year by year."[2] Two weeks later she let fly again: "The men in the State Department who engineered the policy of appeasement, which for the past four years has assured both Japan and the United States that this country would permit one aggression after another rather than risk trouble, are full partners in the guilt of Pearl Harbor."[3]

141

When publication of the Roberts report dumped more dry wood on the fire, the *Daily Worker* took up the refrain: "The State Department too must come in for its share of the blame. There can be little doubt that the State Department's long years of appeasement of Japan through the shipping of scrap iron, oil and munitions, helped strengthen the illusion that still another deal was in the offing."[4]

Author Robert Bendiner wrote a long diatribe against the prewar policies of the State Department. He charged that appeasement

> runs like a scarlet thread through the intricacies of our foreign relations. . . . And it gave a berserk Japan the ingredients that were to make a shambles of Pearl Harbor. The continued assumption that appeasement could bring any degree of success is the measure of the State Department's failure to appreciate the nature either of National Socialism or of Japan's boundless imperialism, its failure to grasp even faintly the scope of German and Japanese ambitions.[5]

In developing his thesis, Bendiner scored a more important point when he added,

> appeasement, once started, not only is extremely difficult to stop but may be logically defended at almost any given point. Appeasement makes the aggressor strong, and the stronger he gets, the more appeasement he can command. When he is finally in a position to demand more than can possibly be granted he is already swollen with his gains and fully prepared to fight. . . . But during the process, before the aggressor's demands have reached the ultimate stage, there is always the thought that he can be bought off with just a little more, indeed, that he must be bought off—or at least diverted.
>
> Appeasement thus tends to become a vested interest and those who are engaged in the appeasing naturally resent any interference that would threaten to irritate the potential enemy. For let the potentiality turn into fact and their whole policy stands pragmatically condemned as a ghastly blunder.[6]

This helps to explain why the revisionist school of historians, born of isolationism, turned on Hull savagely. They could not forgive him because, at very long last, he took a firm stand in dealing with Japan. They had too large a mental, political, and moral "vested interest" in appeasement to concede its failure. On the contrary, they reasoned, just a little more appeasement might have succeeded.

The charge of appeasement against Hull was not entirely ex post facto. All during 1941 he dodged complaints that he was being too easy on the Japanese. On December 5, 1941, in one of Alan Barth's periodic reports to his superiors in the Treasury Department, he quoted the St. Paul *Pioneer Press:*

> There have been unconfirmed rumors that the State Department is trying to make a deal with Japan by which the United States would throw over China, resuming trade in war materials to Japan if the latter will only take its troops out of Indo-China. . . . If the State Department should have any such thing in mind, the public outcry at the attempt will make the British revulsion against Sir Samuel Hoare for his Ethiopian deal with Pierre Laval look weak by comparison.

Barth also quoted the Nashville *Tennessean*'s dim view of any possible "appeasement" at the expense of China. "We cannot abandon one enemy of totalitarianism without sowing the seed of doubt in the minds of all who are ranged against the Axis. Our own face, as well as our own welfare, is vitally involved."[7]

But if Hull was ever an appeaser, he had passed that stage in 1941. He knew that there are many points of possible negotiation between nations, and within those areas Hull worked hard to gain for the United States the time it so sorely needed to be able to meet a two-front war. Nevertheless, he also knew that beyond the boundaries of diplomacy lies the hard core of a nation, the solid substance that is not for sale or trade.

"He is a great figure. At any time but this he would have been a great Secretary of State," conceded the *New Republic*. But it called for his dismissal. "In our time every one of his policies, save for the good-neighbor policy, has either been ineffective, or a grim failure. For lack of proper advice and support, his own high morality has been turned to amoral ends. Under Secretary Hull the Department has been an inchoate mass, moving from blunder to blunder." However, the magazine expressed doubt that this was Hull's doing. Nor was the *New Republic* satisfied with Welles as a possible replacement. Somewhat lamely it suggested Willkie or Stimson—the latter of whom the same article claimed was too old to be secretary of war.[8]

Nor was Hull exempt from the grindings of the rumor mill. Shortly after the attack, a story made the rounds that the State Department had "prevailed upon the Navy to suspend patrols around Hawaii and other American islands in the Pacific." Allegedly this was upon the request of the Japanese envoys, who had asked for "the suspension with the argument that the patrols were creating bad feeling in Japan."

Hull wrathfully denied that there was "one shred of truth, either expressed or implied," in this charge. "The secretary's rage was regarded in Washington as conclusive confirmation of the report that the state department had warned high officials that an attack was in the making," remarked the Chicago *Tribune*.[9]

To a degree this was true. More than once Hull had warned his associates that the United States should be prepared for surprise at Japanese hands. Marshall recalled that Hull said "with considerable emphasis" during the last days of the crisis, "These fellows mean to fight and you will have to watch out."[10] But no evidence has surfaced to indicate that Hull declared that the Japanese would hit Pearl Harbor.

A similar story came up in August 1944. At that time, Representative Warren G. Magnuson of Washington told the Seattle *Post-Intelligencer* that, according to reports in Washington and on the West Coast, "the Japs made a 'Patsy' out of the State Department contriving to have our fleet bottled up in Pearl Harbor where it could easily be dealt a death blow." This yarn claimed that Kurusu had protested to Hull "that American Naval Operations in the Pacific were giving militarists in Japan reason for blocking Kurusu's peace efforts."[11] Magnuson asserted:

> The report on the West Coast, and I've heard it in Washington, too, is that Admiral Husband E. Kimmel was instructed to draw in the fleet, curtail air patrols and do everything else possible to dispel the notion that America was about to attack Japan. The report is that Admiral Kimmel was instructed to take all measures necessary to insure that the Japanese consulate at Honolulu would report to the Japanese government that the fleet did not contemplate any immediate action, which is—so the story goes—why some shore leaves were granted.

Magnuson suggested that if this was true, "some of the heat" should be taken off Kimmel and Short.[12] The State Department countered with a prompt denial of the story.[13]

The isolationist press appeared unwilling to abandon this rumor of State Department interference with Oahu's defense measures. In one of a series of articles entitled "The Road to Tokyo," James R. Young wrote:

> Capt. Fuchida* says that his carriers . . . sailed from their bases November 26, 1941, en route to a point 200 miles from Pearl Harbor.
> Why the 200 mile point?
> The congressional committee . . . could discover that our planes were restricted to this area because, I am informed, of instructions from high placed persons who wanted no sign of belligerency displayed toward the Japs during the "peace" negotiations. . . . [14]

The interesting aspect of this type of rumor is that it could be so widespread and long-lived, and be taken seriously enough to warrant official denial.

Hull had no illusions about Japan's intention to dominate Asia and he cast upon Tokyo a realistic, not to say a pessimistic, eye. The record justified his misgivings. Since the initiation at Japan's request of the conversations between Hull and Nomura, Japan had consolidated its relationship with Hitler; conducted a huge mobilization; persisted in the China war and, incidentally, harassed U.S. citizens who had legitimate business in China; bombed the U.S. gunboat *Tutuila;* occupied southern French Indochina; and replaced Prime Minister Konoye (who at least made peaceful sounds at intervals) with General Hideki Tojo, thus putting the Army publicly in the saddle—all to a constant barrage of anti-American vituperation in the government-controlled press.

By no means "hell-bent for war," as Charles Tansill charged,[15] Hull would have been delighted to reach an equitable agreement with the Japanese and rid himself of the explosive Pacific situation. This event would so strengthen his own position that, as he told Willkie, "it would make a noise that could be heard on the northeast corner of the moon."[16] In fact, he had planned to retire from public life in January 1941 had not the war in Europe stirred up such a critical situation.[17]

It was not the first time Hull had contemplated resignation. Roosevelt had displayed favoritism toward Welles and permitted others among his cronies to dabble their fingers in State Department busi-

*Captain (then Commander) Mitsuo Fuchida led the air attack against Pearl Harbor. The Japanese decided upon the 200-mile limit because it was within the range of their aircraft, yet gave a measure of security to their carriers.

ness. These matters inevitably weakened Hull's grip on his department and were annoying thorns in the secretary's tough old hide.

In November 1940, Assistant Secretary of State Adolf A. Berle, Jr., pleaded with Hull not to resign. The secretary replied "that he did not want to run out; but that he had been constantly affronted and made unhappy by having Morgenthau or somebody else spring a fast diversion in foreign policy over his head, and finding that the President stood by some favorite."[18]

Among these Presidential favorites was a close group whom Berle frankly categorized as "a highly intelligent crew—and, except for Sam Rosenman, as unscrupulous a crew as ever put together. Rosenman is square.* Harry Hopkins is nice and likeable, but would commit murder for the President. The rest of the bunch would commit murder on general principles, either for the President or for themselves."[19]

That Roosevelt could permit this sabotage of his secretary of state and support such cronies while downgrading a man of Hull's caliber was a measure of the streak of pettiness that was one aspect of Roosevelt's complex character. And that Hull endured this belittling treatment despite periodic grousing, because he believed he had a job to do for his country, was a gauge of his fundamental bigness.

In the week before Pearl Harbor, Berle discovered his chief "alone and unhappy" because "everybody was trying to run foreign policy." That included Stimson, Knox, "and pretty much everyone else." Complained the secretary, "They all come at me with knives and hatchets."[20] All of which pointed up the validity of Drew Pearson's contention that the United States needed "a strong, homogeneous state department to set foreign policy and then to force all other branches of the government to stick to it.[21]

By stretching the term *appeasement*, one must agree that in one area Hull was guilty as charged. The State Department erred markedly when it blocked efforts to expose Japanese espionage, as recommended by Senator Gillette and Congressman Dies, who by the late summer of 1941 had gathered enough evidence to convince them that Japanese propaganda and espionage in the United States represented a real threat to American security.[22] This action on the part of the State Department frustrated efforts to bring to light Japanese intelligence activities in the United States, and permitted the Japa-

---

*In those days "square" was a complimentary term.

nese consulates to flourish while those of Germany and Italy were closed.

It may well be true that one reason was the valuable information being fed clandestinely from the Japanese consulate in New York.[23] But if one weighs such data against the favorable results of closing the Honolulu consulate, center of Japanese espionage on Oahu, the scales dip sharply toward the latter. Shutting off this conduit might even have persuaded Yamamoto to call off Operation Hawaii, which depended strongly upon up-to-date information from Yoshikawa, Japan's chief agent on Oahu, and his colleagues in Honolulu. Certainly Japan's "sleeper" spy on the spot, the German Otto Kuehn, could not have filled the bill nearly as effectively as Yoshikawa had the consulate closed its doors.[24]

Possibly underestimation entered the picture. Had Hull realized the full scope and value of the intelligence being funneled to Tokyo, undoubtedly he would have jettisoned his scruples about the possible repercussions on the current talks.[25] Perhaps Hull and his advisers did not believe that Japan's agents could damage the United States to any appreciable extent. To the average American in 1941, the words "German spy" conjured up a menacing, trench-coated figure, intelligent, fanatical, backed by a worldwide organization of awesome efficiency. In contrast, "Japanese spy" brought to mind something like the "Honorable Spy" of Lichty's humorous drawings—a small, bespectacled, apologetic type who might be interested in purchasing the Brooklyn Bridge for scrap iron; he was not portrayed as a serious threat to American security. Whether or not the State Department thought along such lines, it prevented the one action—short of capitulation to Japan's demands—that might have spared the United States the disaster at Oahu.

Washington did not lift a finger against Tokyo from the start of the Hull-Nomura talks until the embargo of July 1941. For one thing, the United States lacked the necessary military power in the Pacific to enforce its will. Hull knew that as well as anyone in the country. Later he explained to the congressional committee with characteristic directness, "when a nation is dealing with lawless nations and governments, with every kind of dishonest and dishonorable and ulterior purposes in view, . . . the diplomatic influence is not much stronger than the military organization behind it."[26]

That is why Stark opposed the embargo. His thinking was based upon "the seriousness that such an embargo would have or might have on our relations with the Japanese. When you throttle a nation's economic life she has got to do something if she thinks she can, particularly with regard to oil." The CNO knew that the United States was not then "ready to go all out and finish the thing up" if Japan reacted with war. He thought that the United States "had the military might to implement the war plan" and "to hold until we could go all out and win." But he acknowledged that the decision involved a "political significance" outside his province.[27]

For some time, Hull had been "under severe criticism" for not having cut off shipments of petroleum products to Japan. But he, as well as Roosevelt, had resisted the pressure, fearing that Tokyo might use such a cutoff as a rationale for invading the Netherlands East Indies.[28]

This attitude irritated Morgenthau, an early and strong advocate of embargoes against Japan. Not only did he hate to see valuable resources lost to the United States, he believed that sanctions would weaken Japan militarily and serve notice on Tokyo that Washington intended to resist aggression in the Orient.[29]

He found a bold ally in Stimson, who had long believed that one must deal with Japan "with firm actions and firm language, as being the only things she understands." As he stated, "Japan has historically shown that she can misinterpret a pacifistic policy of the United States for weakness."[30] Nor did he think it would necessarily be a tragedy if Japan did strike the Netherlands East Indies. This would dangerously extend Japan's lifeline and leave the Japanese vulnerable to the U.S. Navy and to Great Britain.[31]

The third cabinet member advocating a hard line against Japan was Ickes. "For several years now we have refrained from placing an embargo on scrap iron and oil to Japan, waiting for something to happen, and all that has happened has been continued and further aggressions by Japan," he recorded in his diary on September 22, 1940. "In other words, we have made it possible for Japan to continue its career of aggression, whereas if we had embargoed these products at the beginning, the situation in the Far East might be entirely different and far less favorable to Japan than it is today."[32]

At a cabinet meeting on July 18, 1941, he pointed out that he planned to ask the Atlantic coast states to reduce their gas consumption voluntarily by one-third. So, if the government would announce at the same time "a cessation of, or even a substantial reduction in, the amount of gasoline going to Japan" it would soften the political impact considerably.[33] So he was delighted to receive word on August 1 that Roosevelt had embargoed "all high octane gasoline . . . as well as crude oil from which high octane gasoline could be made." Such actions would be "laying a heavy hand upon the whole Japanese economy."[34]

The embargo did indeed put Japan in a bind, for the nation could not meet its oil needs through its own resources or even by purchases from Iran or Peru. Indeed, it is difficult for the average American, who learned the magical incantation "Fill 'er up" shortly after mastering the alphabet, to comprehend the seriousness of the oil problem that faced Japan in the summer of 1941. Her experts estimated that her Navy would be beached in two years and major industries shut down in less than half that time.[35] No wonder that throughout Japan the government-controlled press sounded the cry that the nation would rather fight than give up for lack of oil.[36] Some Japanese quite sincerely believed that the United States had the duty to supply Japan. Major General Akira Muto, chief of the Military Affairs Bureau of the Army General Staff, testified after the war:

> The only place where Japan could continue to get oil and other raw materials had to be from the United States. If this failed, Japan, as a nation, could not survive, especially the industries and the navy. The only way Japan would remain as a world power at this stage was to negotiate with the United States to acquire oil and other raw materials. . . . Japan felt that the United States was under obligation to furnish oil and raw materials as it meant the future existence of Japan.[37]

Of course the United States could not go along with this prime example of Japanese arrogance. Washington had no obligation to supply Japan with the wherewithal to carry out its expansionist policy, dubbed the Greater East Asia Co-Prosperity Sphere. Yet sanctions against Japan were serious steps, and the State Department did not undertake them lightly. Nor could they have come as a genuine surprise to Tokyo. "I think the Japs expected us to go to almost any lengths economically when they took this big stride in Indochina," Hull told Welles. "We could have gone further, in my opinion . . . there is naturally going to continue to be an element of risk and danger in our course, if it is sufficiently firm and extensive to checkmate them."[38]

Hull knew the futility of trying to read the Japanese mind on the subject of the embargo. "There is just as much warrant for believing that our Government's action in freezing Japan's assets retarded Japan's action as for believing that it hastened it," he wrote. "Japan was moving ahead on the fixed principle of grabbing while the grabbing is good. If we had withheld action, Japan would have been likely to have interpreted our nonaction as weakness which might have prompted her to move at an earlier date in the conviction that caution was unnecessary."[39]

The problem was more complicated than a straightforward jockeying for position on the part of the two major Pacific powers. Japan's thrust south opened global prospects which the State Department had to consider. In July 1941 the German army was rolling over the Soviet Union with alarming rapidity. To Berle, the fall of Moscow seemed "certain within a matter of weeks."[40] The picture of a triumphant Hitler joining hands with an expansionist Japan on the shores of the Pacific was enough to raise every scalp in the State Department. What could one expect of the Soviet Union if Hitler imposed a Nazi peace upon it? A totalitarian state, it had been Germany's noncombatant ally and supplier until very recently, and was fighting the invaders from sheer necessity. The U.S.S.R. had no ideological ties to the democracies and no tradition of individual freedom. The possibility had to be faced that Russia would revert to the Axis. To American eyes it appeared quite obvious who would dominate a German-Japanese coalition in Asia. Therefore, in the context of the time, any Japanese strike southward would trigger an American countermove to "embargo shipments, freeze funds and generally stiffen things up all along the line." Berle considered such action "obvious common sense; for a Japan which had occupied Indo-China and then fallen under the sway of a victorious Germany via Vladivostok would put us in a pretty bad position in the Pacific."[41]

Then, too, the United States had to consider its own oil needs, especially if the country went to war in the near future. Washington also had to weigh the fuel requirements of potential allies, not just for 1941 but for years thereafter. This is one reason why the embargo was popular in the United States. For it marked the end of an incongruous situation whereby the country was in effect fueling Japan's war machine at the expense of itself and its friends.

The policy also provided a clear signal that Washington was turning away from a path which had brought only disaster in the past. The memory of Munich still haunted the free world's consciousness. For several years, England and France had stood in a state verging on hypnosis while Hitler went from strength to strength until time almost ran out for them. Indeed, in the summer of 1941 the issue did not yet appear definitely settled. Was the terrible pattern— aggression, appeasement, more aggression, more appeasement—to repeat itself in Asia? Little wonder that the American people approved the sanctions.[42] In fact, at the time and long thereafter the principal criticism of the cutoff was that Washington had delayed it unwisely. Bendiner wrote:

> An embargo invoked against Japan in 1933 . . . might well have changed the course of history. Certainly it is inconceivable that without the vast stores of war materials accumulated in the nine years leading up to Pearl Harbor, without the naval strength that followed Japan's denunciation of the Washington Naval Treaty, without the long stretch of conquered Chinese coastline, without the strategic advantage of having most of the British Navy engaged in a death grapple elsewhere in the world—it is inconceivable that without any of these monumental factors in its favor Japan would, in 1933, have declared war on the United States over the imposition of an embargo.[43]

Instead, the United States continued to supply Japan with the wherewithal to continue the conflict in China and "to store up strength for the ultimate showdown with the United States." As Bendiner saw it, "The theory was that an embargo meant war. As time went on, and Japan became stronger and stronger, the argument gained a validity it did not originally have, until in the end, when an embargo had become desperately necessary, the enemy, with all the gains it had achieved through our assistance, was in reality in a position to retaliate."[44]

In retrospect, one wonders why Japan did not choose to moderate its foreign policy in exchange for a lifting of the embargo. As Hull remarked to Welles, "if an agreement were reached between our two countries, it would safeguard Japan far more securely than taking over Indochina."[45] This was undoubtedly true.

Unfortunately, in 1941 the Japanese were not erecting their policies upon a basis of logic. In their irrational fear of "encirclement," they had convinced themselves that the only way to avoid national strangulation was to continue expanding. Hence, any concession, however small, to relax American economic sanctions would eventually result in Japan's becoming an American satellite. "There was a certain amount of national danger in dealing with the United States," explained Captain Sutegiro Onoda.* "If Japan went too far in this direction, she would become too dependent on the United States. In time the Americans would have us securely in hand and then Japan would have to do exactly as Washington dictated."[46]

The Japanese feared also that not only would capitulation mean losing all the gains they hoped to make in the future, it might well mean pulling back from those already in hand. In particular, the prospect of abandoning the projected conquest of China was abhorrent. As chief of Japan's Naval General Staff, Admiral Osami Nagano later told then Captain Sadatoshi Tomioka, chief of his Operations Section, the average Japanese had been led to believe that Japan was "marching to victory in China," and to withdraw Japanese troops would be interpreted "as a Chinese victory." This in turn might have led to the eventual loss of Manchuria, "because China would come back and demand it, backed by both the United States and Great Britain." Nagano also believed that national bankruptcy might have resulted if Japan did not go to war, because "her world economy was built on it."[47] This was truly a sad commentary on the ruling elements of Japan in that period.

Sir George Sansom, the famous British expert on Japan, wrote that in any case it was too late for Japan to change direction, because "the power of the final decision had already passed into the hands of the extremists." These could not permit "any effective concessions" to the United States, because "this would be to admit that the whole of Japanese policy since 1931 had been a blunder, for which the military party and its civilian allies were responsible. The Army's prestige would never recover from such a blow. War was inevitable." Sir George further pointed out that the economic sanctions imposed upon Japan in 1941 were such as to make the war appear a reasonable, if dangerous, alternative."[48]

Certain revisionist historians went much further, insisting that the embargo pushed Japan into a fight for her life, and implying that this

---

*In 1941, then Commander Onoda was liaison officer for the Naval General Staff with the Navy Ministry and Army General Staff.

constituted a sort of economic Pearl Harbor.[49] Yet in actual fact, the Japanese neither used the sanctions as an excuse to declare war nor did they sever diplomatic relations. On the contrary, the Hull-Nomura talks, which Hull had broken off on July 23,[50] were resumed at Nomura's request on August 6,[51] and continued right up to December 7, 1941. Nor is there any evidence that Japan would have altered its expansionist policy in the slightest, embargo or no embargo. As for the Pearl Harbor operation, the prospect of less and less oil caused the Naval General Staff to consider Yamamoto's scheme anew. No longer could a decision be postponed until 1942.[52] Nevertheless, the Naval General Staff did not flash the green light until mid-October, and then only under pressure from Yamamoto, who threatened to resign with all his staff unless his Pearl Harbor project was made part of Japan's overall war plan.[53]

So the final break in Japanese-American relations cannot be laid upon the sanctions of the summer of 1941. Hull had displayed great patience in dealing with the Japanese who "persistently asked for a 'hunting license'—and supplies" to pursue a policy which "added up to threats to the freedom of various peoples, to the independence of various countries, and to the security of the United States." This was the opinion of Stanley Hornbeck, who continued:

> The men who were charting Japan's course, in the name of the Emperor and with the approval, by and large, of his people, had decided that their country had a date with Destiny, that it needed to expand, that it was their function to make secure its actual domain and enlarge the area of its jurisdiction, and that this they would do— by diplomatic processes if possible but if those did not suffice by use of whatever weapons, strategies and tactics they might be able to bring to bear.
>
> The American spokesmen were on the defensive. They were thinking and they argued in terms of principles. They were in effect saying to the Japanese that what had been, presumably, good for the United States would be good for Japan—and for each and all lands.[54]

The problem went much deeper than mutual obstinacy or even a conflict of interests. The United States and Japan in effect were traveling on different time tracks. The Japanese railed against Western imperialism, yet they were exploiting their fellow Asians and had a reverence for the military. Washington did not stand solely on principle, as Hornbeck's comments might indicate. The United States had found that colonialism did not work nearly as well as the mutual nourishing of trade between friends—or at least respectful acquaintances. Hull argued from experience as well as idealism. But it was like a modern American businessman trying to reach a meeting of the minds with a Spanish conquistador.

This lack of a firm foundation helps explain why Roosevelt and his State Department permitted the "John Doe Associates" to obtain a foothold in the diplomatic arena.[55] "John Doe Associates" was the State Department's term for an unofficial group consisting of Bishop James E. Walsh, Father James M. Drought, Takeo Paul Wikawa, and Colonel Hideo Iwakuro, who attempted unofficially to bring about a Japanese-American rapprochement. Briefly, the story is this: In late 1940, Father Drought of the Maryknoll Missions, who was in Japan, came up with what purported to be a blueprint for peace in the Pacific. He secured the cooperation of his superior, Bishop Walsh. They worked with Wikawa, a Japanese businessman who was a Christian and married to an American. Neither of these individuals had any official standing whatever. Later, Colonel Iwakuro joined the original group, and was accorded diplomatic status as an assistant military attaché.[56]

Of the four, Drought was the moving spirit, and it is the measure of the desperation of Roosevelt and his State Department that they were willing to meet with him. Drought had never concealed his animosity toward Roosevelt's regime. He had been very active in the Republican campaign of 1936 and had worked hard for Willkie in 1940.[57]

Drought's dabbling in partisan politics was entirely his own business. Less easy to overlook was his pro-Japanese leaning which inclined well beyond the degree of objectivity. Both White House and State Department had reason to know his bias. In 1934, Drought believed the time ripe for "a secret nonaggression pact with Japan and a commercial reciprocity agreement." While that year's London Naval Conference was in progress, Drought suggested to the President's secretary, Stephen Early, that the American delegation offer Japan parity. Furthermore, at the State Department he "stressed his belief that the American delegation in London should negotiate with the Japanese behind the backs of the British." When in 1936 Senator Key Pittman of Nevada made a rather harsh anti-Japanese speech,

Drought spearheaded an official cable with twenty-seven signers, expressing "goodwill" to the Japanese premier.[58] On the basis of Drought's past performances, Washington had no reason to consider him the ideal mediator between the United States and Japan.

Possibly the American officials believed that Drought's superior general, Walsh, would take charge. But in this particular chess game, the bishop was obviously a pawn. Accustomed to leaning upon the dynamic Drought in Maryknoll's affairs, he did so in the wider field of do-it-yourself diplomacy. In fact, Walsh did not seem to have realized to what extent the project was Drought's brainchild, and his alone.[59]

Once the two clerics reached Japan in late 1940, Drought produced a draft which no one unfamiliar with the situation could ever believe came from an American. He phrased it as if he were a son of *Dai Nippon,* using the personal pronoun "we" to mean the Japanese. A thoughtful reading of this document casts serious doubt upon Drought's motivation. Perhaps he meant well—to create a Japanese-American rapprochement, a bulwark against communism, and a climate wherein his fellow missionaries could flourish in Asia. But a memorandum that he wrote to Wikawa on March 27, 1941, smacks of the Machiavellian if not the outright treasonous. In his excellent study, R. J. C. Butow dealt with this document at length:

> According to Drought, the eleven "rules for Nations" that he had laid down in the "Preliminary Draft" were "deliberately intended to compel from the Americans a fundamental admission of the propriety and justice of the Japanese position." A careful reading, with this in mind, would lead to the conclusion that these "Rules" constituted "a real, substantial element of a complete Japanese victory in diplomacy." . . .
>
> . . . As soon as they were accepted and promulgated, they would "establish Japan's political . . . hegemony over the Far East." They have been "very carefully designed," Drought wrote, "to accomplish this purpose and have, accordingly, been put in language that would be attractive to the Americans and to the American public, who would not, of course, realize the full meaning and the inevitable consequence that I have described above. . . . From the viewpoint of diplomacy and [the] fundamental realities of Japan's own case, I am convinced that *these "Rules" now favor Japan in every way* but

serve to put the United States diplomatically on the defensive."
[Butow's italics.][60]

Such was the man whom Roosevelt and Hull, with incredible folly,
permitted to play a leading, if offstage, role in Japanese-American
relations. Nomura was equally misguided in allowing the "John
Doe" team virtually to take over his own mission. Nomura's action is
fairly understandable, however. A man of genuine humility, acutely
conscious of his lack of expertise in diplomacy, he was not above
accepting help wherever he found it. And the "go-between" was a
time-honored feature of Japanese culture.

No one in authority on either side of the Pacific seemed to have
understood the fact that this group of nondiplomats had no official
status. Yet mature reflection should have warned all concerned away
from Drought and his colleagues. Without the mutual desire of Washington and Tokyo for accommodation, the out-of-channels effort could
not succeed. And had such a desire existed, the amateurs would have
been unnecessary. If Foreign Minister Yosuke Matsuoka, who met
with Walsh and Drought in late 1940, had a genuine proposal to offer
Washington, there was no reason why he should not have entrusted
it to Nomura. Butow speculated: ". . . was Matsuoka simply taking
advantage of the Walsh-Drought visit to Japan to blow the pipes of
peace without having to dance to the tune?"[61] That would be like
Matsuoka, who knew very well that the military controlled Japan and
would veto any proposed Japanese-American agreement that did not
have the approval of the Army and Navy.

Washington erred fundamentally in this regard, in being unprepared to seize the diplomatic initiative. The State Department should
have anticipated that Nomura might bring with him nothing but his
personal goodwill and should have been ready to put forward its own
intentions and suggestions. At least both governments would have
known where they stood. Instead, the whole story of Japanese-
American relations during 1941 is one of Japanese action, American
reaction. This hesitancy on the part of the United States permitted
the "John Doe" team to come onto the field and mix up the signals
in both Tokyo and Washington. Butow summarized the dismaying
truth of that ill-conceived venture:

From start to finish the prolonged search for peace in Washington
and all corresponding contacts in Tokyo were consistently under the

pernicious influence of the misbegotten actions of the John Doe Associates operating behind the scenes. . . .

The Japanese-American quest for peace was entirely at the mercy of these three individuals—each a self-appointed diplomatic "Mr. Fix-it." The erroneous conclusions that sprang from the words and deeds of the John Doe Associates, working singly and in concert, exerted a most harmful effect, especially on the Japanese side. The confusion the Associates spread over the issues they sought to clarify was compounded with the passage of time, thus further snarling an already tangled situation. [62]

While there can be no doubt that Drought and his colleagues exercised a most "pernicious influence" upon a situation which was already horrendous enough without their ministrations, it is extremely doubtful whether they were responsible for the ultimate result. Japan's armed forces wanted the whole hog, not just a slice of bacon or even a good half of the animal. And Washington could go just so far in placating Tokyo. Had there been any action resembling a true rapprochement with the ally of Hitler, or any condonement of Japanese aggression, public opinion would have figuratively raised the Capitol dome. A workable, lasting agreement between the United States and Japan was as nearly impossible as anything in the unpredictable human equation could ever be.

CHAPTER 10

"Unsurmountable Obstacles"

The "China Incident"—Tripartite Pact—Japan's invasion of southern French Indochina—Proposal for a Roosevelt-Konoye meeting

In Nomura's attempts to bring about an amicable settlement of the differences between Japan and the United States, he recognized three "unsurmountable obstacles": the "China Incident," the Tripartite Pact, and the dispatch of Japanese troops to southern French Indochina.[1] All of these roadblocks were of Japanese making.

Foremost among them by seniority and longevity was the "China Incident," which Stark described as "a stumbling block we could not get around until either Japan backed or we backed."[2] Historian Dexter Perkins agreed that China was the "impassable barrier in our negotiations with Japan." In fact, he used Stark's exact expression: "it was the Chinese question which was the great and central stumbling block in the long negotiations that took place in 1941."[3]

The Japanese never understood why the United States supported China so stubbornly. Taking a strictly pragmatic view, they could not see why the Americans should care who ruled the Chinese, a nation with which they had no racial, cultural, religious, or political ties. Hence the Japanese imagined that the American attitude was less pro-Chinese than anti-Japanese, part of a plot to whittle their empire down to size and to deny Japan its (to them) rightful and heaven-blessed position as ruler of Asia.

Had Washington's China policy in this period indeed been governed primarily by malevolence toward Japan, Japanese evacuation of China would not have been a cornerstone of the basis for negotiations. From the purely military point of view, American self-interest dictated egging on the Japanese, or at least noninterference with the status quo. On October 2, 1941, Colonel Hayes A. Kroner, acting for

158

Brig. Gen. Sherman Miles, the G-2, explained this aspect in a memorandum for Marshall:

> at this stage in the execution of our national strategic plan, a cessation of hostilities in China followed by the withdrawal of twenty-one Japanese divisions, 20 independent brigades, and 1,000 aircraft therefrom would be highly detrimental to our interests. Such a force if returned to Japan would be potentially of such an explosive nature that only a military oligarchy could control it. These militarists would submerge or destroy the moderate element in Japan replacing it with a restless Chauvinistic element possessing neither the ability nor the inclination to continue diplomatic relations with any of the Democratic Powers.
>
> If the Japanese force in China were transferred to Indo-China or Manchukuo it would undoubtedly overflow into adjacent regions and our interests would be even further jeopardized.

Kroner also pointed out that if all or part of these troops should augment the Kwantung Army, Konoye's government would be helpless, because since 1932 the Kwantung Army had been "completely independent of the various cabinets appointed in Tokyo." Therefore, he recommended: "From the foregoing it seems imperative, for the present at least, to keep as much of the Japanese Army as possible pinned down in China. In other words we must cease at once our attempts to bring about the withdrawal of Japanese armed forces from China."

Kroner would continue all possible aid to China, and he acknowledged that the policy he recommended would be hard on the Chinese. But he asked that it be considered "in the light of cold reason." The United States must do everything possible to aid Russia against Hitler. "Any action on our part, therefore, which would liberate Japanese (pro-Axis) forces for action against Russia's rear in Siberia would be foolhardy."[4]

The United States did not adopt this policy, however strategically logical it might have been. Public opinion would never have tolerated thus tossing the hard-pressed Chinese to the wolves. Abandonment of China would have placed the United States in the inconsistent position of opposing Hitler's conquests in Europe while flashing the green light to Japanese aggression in Asia. This would have engendered widespread and justified hatred among all Asians.

Moreover, contrary to current Japanese neurotic fears, the United

States had no desire to see Japan reduced to a state of permanent weakness. American statesmen understood the importance to the world of a strong Japan, and wished to see that strength poured into constructive channels. One cannot read the full State Department Memoranda of Conversations covering the Japanese-American talks of 1941 without noting the theme of genuine concern for Japan. Indeed, in Hull's words, the United States had been "urging the Japanese to consider their own future from the standpoint of political, economic and social aspects . . . Japan, if it should conquer China, would keep China bled white and would not have the capital to aid in restoring purchasing power and social welfare."[5] In his "Plan Dog" memorandum of November 12, 1940,* Stark postulated, "It is doubtful, however, that it would be in our interest to reduce Japan to the status of an inferior military and economic power. A balance of power in the Far East is to our interests as much as is the balance of power in Europe."[6]

Looking at the global scene, Hull feared that Axis expansionism would turn the whole earth into one vast slum. He believed that world conquest by Japan and Germany, "with the methods of government which were being applied to conquered peoples, all bankrupt, would mean to set not only the world but those very conquering countries back to impossible levels of existence; that the conquering countries themselves would be the losers to an unthinkable extent."[7]

Hull spoke to Nomura of the United States' sorry experience in Latin America as proof that stability and goodwill were impossible as long as a nation kept troops on foreign soil. If Japan would pull her forces out of China, Hull "felt that, even though some losses and sacrifices might have to be faced at the outset, in the long run the gains would justify them." Personally, Nomura agreed with him.[8]

American concern for China was based only in very small part on the United States' rather slim economic interests there. The American people sympathized because the Chinese, traditionally a peaceful people, were defending their soil from invasion. By extension, China took on impressive symbolism; it represented international law in the Far East versus the law of the jungle, hence world resistance to rampant militarism. On the practical side, China had a long history

---

*This plan enunciated the "Hitler first" strategy and was perhaps Stark's most significant action as CNO.

of survival. Some writers, such as Morgenstern, bought the Japanese line that Japan's takeover of China might be in the interests of America.[9] But for the United States to write off that teeming, resilient people would have been the height of folly. As Berle noted, "the effect of sacrificing China would be to make permanent enemies of that whole population, which was there before the Japanese came and will be there after they go."[10]

The Tripartite Pact had aligned China with the democracies by elimination. What matter that Chiang Kai-shek's regime was not precisely a showcase of democracy in action? The Axis presented a clear issue: Whoever was not with them was against them. The free world had its back to the wall, and could not afford to demand that any helping hand be washed, manicured, and perfumed before grasping it.

Nevertheless, there is much truth in John T. Flynn's crusty assertion that before the outbreak of war in Europe the United States "did nothing to aid China. On the contrary it pursued a policy of aid to Japan." Flynn discounted the claim that Roosevelt did not invoke the neutrality act in the "China Incident" because had he done so he could not have assisted the Chinese.

> Actually we were giving far more aid to Japan than to China. In 1939 we sent China goods to the value of $55,600,000 while we exported to Japan goods valued at $232,000,000. We did practically the same in 1940. We sold Japan the immense quantities of iron and scrap and oil and other materials with which she carried on the war in China and prepared herself for war with us. The government sent its sympathy to China and its scrap iron to Japan. It was not until China and Japan became inextricably entangled in the European war that our government manifested its dynamic interest in China's "democracy."[11]

After World War II began in Europe, the United States had an excellent reason for trying to block Japan in China as elsewhere: to keep Britain, France, and the Netherlands from being squeezed to death between Germany and Japan. China was the fulcrum of the free world to pry apart these Axis powers. When Hitler struck the Soviet Union, China became more valuable than ever to the Allies as one means of keeping Japan from striking the Russians in the rear. Even if Germany conquered Russia, with or without Japanese help,

China would remain the one obstacle to keep a Japanese-German-Russian combination from devouring all Asia and then turning upon Europe.

Strategic considerations aside, American public opinion supported the Chinese with as near unanimity as that intangible but potent political factor ever attains. Congressman Gearhart of California, later to serve on the congressional committee that investigated Pearl Harbor, tongue-lashed the Japanese in a radio address on November 23, 1941. At the time, Gearhart, a Republican, had received the Democratic as well as the Republican renomination to Congress and had been elected four times without major opposition. So he spoke for a wide spectrum of opinion when he excoriated the Japanese as "these accursed invaders" of Chinese soil, which was "running red with the blood of her martyrs." He declared:

> The awfulness of Japan's crime against China and the Chinese people will find no counterpart in the bloody annals of man's rascality. The screams of men stricken down, the wails of widows newly made, the cries of helpless children, dying, will be heard long after the last Japanese gun is silenced by an outraged humanity, aroused at last to the challenge this evil, oriental power has flung at the world.
>
> Japan's ruthlessness makes her not only an enemy of China, but also a common foe of all nations, the United States no less than all of the others. . . .

In an outburst of indignation, Gearhart asked, "What moral right have we to barter away the territory of China, assign areas of influence within its boundaries to a nation that has invaded her soil?"[12] Allowing for the grandiloquence expected of a Congressman in 1941, Gearhart had a point.

So for many reasons the United States could not and would not abandon China to Japan's far from tender mercies. Nevertheless, Nomura was probably right in believing that had Japan kept the Open Door in China and proceeded slowly, the American people would not have fought Japan for China's sake unless provoked by an overt act.[13]

Nomura saw that as a result of failure to bring about a local settlement in China, "the Military Command became more and more dominant over the Civil Administration." But he recognized that "there was a definite limit in the scope of the actions taken by the

Military Command, so the Konoye cabinet can not be absolved from the responsibility of bringing the situation to the ultimate crisis regardless of their laying it at the door of the arbitrariness of the Military Command."[14]

That same unfortunate combination—a powerful military plus a compliant Konoye—erected the second of Nomura's "unsurmountable obstacles," the Tripartite Pact. When Konoye formed his second cabinet in July of 1940, Matsuoka asked Nomura to be ambassador to Washington. But during their talk Nomura "became acquainted with this intention of strengthening the relations of Japan with Germany." So Nomura refused the offer, recognizing "that this intention and the idea of improving the U.S.-Japanese relations would be incompatible." That others could not comprehend this simple fact surprised Nomura:

> Both Konoye and Matsuoka entertained the fallacy that by means of the Tripartite Alliance Japan would be able to extricate herself from her state of isolation and yet at the same time reach an understanding with America. It is quite astonishing that they should show such a lack of understanding of the mentality of the American people. Oikawa . . . also desired to avoid a U.S.-Japanese war, yet nevertheless supported the Tripartite Alliance. Konoye . . . did not have the perception to discern the sheer difficulty in obtaining the two incompatible things, the Tripartite Alliance and the U.S.-Japanese understanding, just as the maxim puts it, "No man can wear two pairs of shoes at the same time." This was a shortsighted blunder on the part of Japan. . . .[15]

According to Toshikazu Kase, the Foreign Ministry's director of American affairs in the Tojo Cabinet, "Nothing . . . was further removed from Konoye's mind than to engage upon war with the British Empire or the United States. On the contrary he was anxious to improve relations with them. It was his plan to use this alliance as a means of improving Japan's diplomatic position vis-á-vis the democratic powers."[16] Of this Morgenstern observed, "But such subtleties of purpose were lost upon Washington."[17] And with good reason. Perhaps Konoye had some nebulous hope that by joining the Axis Japan could coax the United States to eat out of its hand. But far from bluffing Washington into letting Tokyo have its way unchided and unhindered, the Pact irrevocably placed Japan beyond the reach of

American friendship, at least until the European war should have spent itself.

It is difficult to believe that either Matsuoka or Konoye truly expected the Pact not to alienate the United States. If its purpose was not abundantly clear it was not the fault of the Japanese press, which had preceded the Pact by "hitting every gong in the octave," in Berle's expressive phrase.[18] Certainly the bluster with which Japan's newspapers greeted the signing removed all doubt as to which way the wind blew.

Despite sundry official disclaimers that the pact pointed at any particular nation, the press frankly stated that the United States was the target. "While no specific 'Power' is mentioned in the text, it is obvious that the pact is directed mainly against the United States," remarked the *Japan Advertiser,* "for the Soviet Union is exempted from its application. . . . It signifies that if the United States should enter the European war it must be prepared to face war in two oceans simultaneously."[19]

Nichi Nichi agreed in even stronger terms. "The three-Power pact was the means through which the United States is being made to realize that it cannot enter either the European war or the China incident without running the danger of having its fingers burned."[20]

Nobody had to draw a map for the American press, either. "It puts into cold print for every American to see the fact that the dominant power in Asia and the new masters of the European continent are joined in a pact aimed at the United States."[21] The St. Louis *Post-Dispatch* sounded a note of warning:

> The three nations joining in this pact are nations armed to the teeth, headed by ambitious and desperate men. These leaders are not in the habit of making threats which they cannot back up. Many of the countries whose chiefs thought the Axis leaders were bluffing have disappeared from the map. There can be no mistake about it, this new pact is laid down with a cold and calculating menace directed against any interventionist action by the United States. . . .[22]

Throughout an interesting study, historian Paul W. Schroeder took the position that the Tripartite Pact was not really an important factor in the final break between the United States and Japan.[23] On the contrary, it was an integral part of the Japanese-American problem, as inescapable as the weather. When Germany, Italy, and Japan signed the alliance in September 1940, only two major neutral powers existed capable of attacking either or all of the signatories and thus activating the Pact: the United States and the Soviet Union. And, at the time, the latter had a nonaggression pact with Hitler, was furnishing him with supplies, and seemed to be teetering on the verge of full partnership with the other predatory powers. Naturally the Americans resented and distrusted an alliance so blatantly aimed at them.

What annoyed the United States about Japan's joining the Axis was not the added danger, for in those days most Americans were somewhat contemptuous of Japan as a potential combatant; they felt bone-deep repugnance at Japan's clasping hands with Hitler. Among other things, this action meant that Japan associated itself with proven liars who would tear up any "scrap of paper" if it suited their purpose to do so. Therefore, the Japanese had no legitimate cause for complaint if the rest of the world, especially the United States, judged them by the standards of their associates and demanded concrete proof of good faith rather than unsubstantiated promises.

This alliance between three aggressors on the make was an unnatural one and obviously would have been signed only if each thought it stood to gain by the action. Schroeder stressed the fact that Japan would not have fought for the sake of Germany, which is very true, as Nomura emphasized in the Washington talks. But Japan was prepared to fight shoulder to shoulder with Germany if it believed this would be to its own advantage.

Japan had to have artificial allies, otherwise it would have none at all. It had with no nation such close ties as linked the United States with Great Britain and to a lesser extent with the other free nations. What is more, Japan had deliberately accentuated its isolation by an attitude of being the chosen race, unique and self-sufficient. The Japanese had gone out of their way to antagonize their obvious potential allies, the Chinese, by this racial pride and by the brutal nature of the China war.

Japan did share with Germany and Italy the same type of aims, as the Tripartite Pact openly acknowledged. Americans could laugh at Mussolini and pity the assortment of lesser satellites that perforce joined the Nazi camp; they paid Japan the compliment of anger. For the United States not to take the Pact seriously would have been most unrealistic.

Roosevelt and Hull urged Nomura that Japan break with Germany in its own best interests. While it was also to the benefit of the United States that the Tripartite Pact die on the vine, the President and his secretary of state had no desire to see Japan become a poor relation at Hitler's table. On March 14, 1941, Roosevelt told Nomura "that from every viewpoint this action was contrary to the interests of Japan; that Hitler would rule over every country if once given the opportunity, just as he is today ruling over Italy and the other countries which had trusted him."[24] As late as November 27, the President warned Nomura and Kurusu, "If, however, Japan should unfortunately decide to follow Hitlerism and courses of aggression, we are convinced beyond any shadow of doubt that Japan will be the ultimate loser."[25]

Roosevelt was preaching to the choir. Nomura was no supporter of the Tripartite Pact, as he admitted on October 28.[26] Later he "dwelt at some length upon the point that Japan was getting nothing out of the Tripartite Pact except American resentment."[27] Nor did Kurusu trust the Nazis. On December 6 he told his old friend Ferdinand L. Mayer that he, Kurusu, and "the thinking people" of Japan realized that German victory might be more dangerous for Japan than for the United States. "Germany had no intention of assisting or even permitting Japan to retain any benefits that she might derive from her Axis victory."[28]

A belief that Japan was under Hitler's thumb and operating in accordance with a worldwide Axis strategy played its part in Allied thinking. On June 5, 1941, the U.S. military observer at Singapore, Lt. Col. Francis G. Brink, discussed the realistic objections to a Japanese attack on Malaya or the Netherlands East Indies. He took into consideration, among other factors, the U.S. Pacific Fleet based in Hawaii which forced Japan "to keep the bulk of her navy close to the Japanese mainland." Brink speculated:

> Of course such an attack may be part of the AXIS agreement. It appears quite possible that Japan, however, may be carrying out her portion of the AXIS agreement now by threatening Malaya, N.E.I.* and the Philippines, thereby requiring Britain to maintain large army and air forces, badly needed in the Middle East, in Malaya; forcing N.E.I. to expend millions of dollars for defense which might oth-

*Netherlands East Indies.

erwise be used for ALLIED effort elsewhere, and finally, to hold the U.S. Pacific Fleet near Eastern waters, thereby preventing its participation in the Battle of the Atlantic.[29]

When Japan signed the pact, it had already begun to line up its sights on French Indochina and the Netherlands East Indies, thereby leading to the third of Nomura's "unsurmountable obstacles." Japanese apologists like to credit the lapse of the Japanese-American commercial treaty on January 26, 1940, with sending Japan on its search for other sources of the materials it had been importing from the United States. "Consequently," wrote Chihiro Hosoya, "the region of natural resources to the south came to loom ever larger in the eyes of Japan's political leaders." Nevertheless, Hosoya admitted that "new developments on the European scene" were "the decisive factor in provoking Japan's southern advance," because Holland and France "were now under the control of the German Army." In other words, this rich territory was up for grabs. Hosoya observed, "Needless to say, the best southern policy for Japan was the one in which Japan could establish its control over Indo-China and the Dutch Indies so firmly as to insure the obtaining of essential products, without resorting to the use of force and thereby minimizing United States opposition."

So Japan began to turn the diplomatic screws. When everything had not been settled to its liking by the fall of 1940, the armed forces demanded a time limit. "Finally, on September 10, . . . the Army and Navy came to an agreement on a plan to issue an ultimatum and, regardless of the result of the negotiations, to advance into Indo-China after September 22." Hosoya added, "The enforcement of U.S. economic sanctions thus turned out to stiffen the attitude of the middle echelon officers* and provoked them to execute the plan for a southern advance."[30]

This interpretation would be more convincing if Hosoya had not just conceded that it was less American sanctions, real or potential, than French and Dutch helplessness that sent Japan on the treasure hunt southward. In this respect, the Japanese revealed a double standard: It was not "force" for them to head south and make the Dutch and French give them what they wanted, but it was "force" when

---

*Probably what the United States Army called "field grade officers," i.e., colonels, lieutenant colonels, and majors. This class was Hosoya's favorite whipping boy.

the United States made diplomatic-economic moves against Japan—moves, incidentally, which took nothing from Japan that belonged to it. And the amazing postwar development of the Japanese proves that they could have realized their national potential without resort to aggression. Japan was a "have" nation in the resource that really mattered—an intelligent, industrious, and ingenious people.

While Nomura was conducting his discussions with Hull, he knew only as much of what was going on in Tokyo as the Foreign Ministry chose to tell him, which was by no means the full story. Years later, he saw the sequence of events:

> At the Imperial Conference held on July 2, 1941, it was decided that in order to establish the Greater East Asia Co-Prosperity Sphere preparation should be made for war with Great Britain and the United States. Hence the advance of troops into southern French Indo-China was planned by the second Konoye cabinet and was put into execution by the third Konoye cabinet, so that Konoye's purpose in reorganizing his cabinet was discarded immediately, and by himself.

Nomura emphasized, "Nevertheless, the new cabinet carried out immediately the dispatch of troops to southern French Indo-China as had been planned, thereby inviting the U.S. severance of economic relations with Japan."[31] For there was a distinct difference in the implications of Japan's move into southern Indochina in July 1941 as contrasted with its takeover of the north. Dexter Perkins neatly compressed the problem into two sentences: "The occupation of *northern* Indo-China made some sense from the point of view of blocking the supply route to the Chinese Nationalists. The occupation of *southern* Indo-China made no sense, except as the prelude to further acts of aggression" (Perkins's italics).[32]

The United States had to react, and react in a way that would give Japan a real jolt. So far, American economic and diplomatic sanctions had served only to irritate Japan while doing no ascertainable good. Measures short of full embargo had proved ineffective. Now the United States had to go the whole way or tacitly concede that Japan had won a bloodless war and stood as the undisputed master of Asia. Even during 1941, Nomura admitted to Hull that "the Japanese move into south Indo-China . . . had precipitated our freezing measures which in turn had reacted in Japan to increase the tension."[33]

Thus Nomura, as patriotic a Japanese as ever lived, saw the midsummer freeze as a response, not a challenge.

All three of those actions, which made impossible any genuine rapport between Japan and the United States—the attempt to take over China, the joining with Hitler and Mussolini to form the Berlin-Rome-Tokyo Axis, and the invasion of French Indochina—took place under the premiership, and with the approval of, Prince Fumimaro Konoye. So it is more than a little ironic to find revisionists dwelling retrospectively upon the might-have-been's of a Roosevelt-Konoye meeting, scoring the President and especially Hull for not bringing it to fruition.[34] Tansill even invoked that much-abused word "ultimatum," wailing, "The rejection of the Konoye-Roosevelt meeting was a real ultimatum to Japan."[35] Chamberlin blamed Hull for the failure to take place of "the proposed meeting, which might have staved off the Pacific war."[36] Their arguments reflect failure to realize the limitations of the presidency, and especially misunderstanding of the nature of the Japanese system. Even Perkins, no revisionist, wondered why

> the experiment should not have been tried. Secretary Hull brought to this problem, as it seems to me, a rigidity of mind which may properly be criticized. In insisting on a previous definition of the issues before the meeting was held, he was instrumental in preventing it. While we cannot know what the result of such a meeting would have been, we are entitled, I think, to wish that it had been held. All the more is this true since it would appear likely that Prince Konoye was sincere in the effort which he made to avoid war.

But Perkins conceded that this particular picture had its reverse image. "We cannot be absolutely sure about Konoye's good faith. We can be still less sure of the willingness of the Tokyo militarists to support him in the far-reaching concessions that would have been necessary. And in the final analysis we cannot be sure of the ability of the American government to make concessions on its own part."[37]

Grew was "both disappointed and greatly vexed" when the proposed summit meeting fizzled out. He made quite an issue of it after his return to the United States.[38] He had "warmly recommended" the idea. As he saw it, the senior members of the American Embassy in Tokyo "believed it was a good gamble; that Konoe [sic] had come to a position where he realized the dangerous situation in which his country had got itself, and he was trying to find a way out."[39] More-over, Grew feared that failure to hold such a conference would result in "formation of a military dictatorship which will lack either the disposition or the temperament to avoid colliding head-on with the United States," as he told the congressional committee.

Senator Ferguson suggested that was another way of saying "war," and Grew agreed that was a "fair deduction." Ferguson pressed him to state that he believed "if the meeting did not take place and the Cabinet fell, and you were of the opinion that it would fall, it meant war with the United States?" But Grew demurred. "No, sir; I did not go as far as that. No, indeed." He as well as those in Washington were continuing to work for peace. "I do not think at any time it could be said any particular step or lack of step definitely meant war."[40]

Nevertheless, a meeting between Roosevelt and Konoye was a project very dear to Grew's heart, and it is easy to see why. Over thirty years in the diplomatic service had not tarnished with cynicism his curious blend of realism and idealism. Konoye had taken elaborate precautions before meeting with Grew in the summer of 1941 because of the danger of assassination by Japanese radicals if it should get about that he had been talking with the American ambassador.[41] Yet Grew saw no incongruity in the premier's proposal to get together with the President of the United States and kick Japan's armed forces in the teeth. The ambassador knew that Konoye was "saddled with the responsibility for some of the worst acts of banditry on the part of Japan which have been recorded in international history."[42] Still, Grew could believe in the prince's reformation.

No doubt Grew felt something of the evangelist's solemn joy at the prospect of leading a repentant sinner to the mourner's bench. The possibility of a Japanese-American war horrified him, so he seized upon any slender chance of averting it. If he could bring off this coup, what a glowing crown to his honorable career! Possibly he was overly inclined to accept his Japanese associates at their own evaluation; he may well have overestimated his expertise about the Japanese scene. Certainly he was not as important as his position might lead one to believe. Washington did not rely solely upon its embassy for infor-mation concerning Tokyo's psychology and intentions. Quite aside from the ever-unfolding drama of the Magic intercepts, Japan's own official press gave a very clear picture of the nature of the Japanese government. Grew's reports and opinions were only one factor, not the weightiest one at that, in the relationship between Washington and Tokyo.

Then, too, like Nomura in Washington, the American ambassador in Tokyo knew considerably less about the U.S.-Japanese situation than did certain key officials in his government. Grew did not have access to the Magic messages. Nor did he consider that his superiors kept him adequately posted. He resented this deprivation, and in postwar days identified himself with Kimmel. After reading the admiral's book, Grew wrote to him with "great respect and admiration":

> You and I encountered somewhat similar frustrations in our dealings with Washington. In fact, I often used to learn what our Government was thinking and planning, indirectly through my British colleague in Tokyo who received from London copies of Lord Halifax's reports of his talks with the President and Mr. Hull. . . . Like you, I was never informed of the Japanese intercepted telegrams.
>
> Although you and I may never have met, I have been a firm supporter of yours ever since Pearl Harbor, always looking forward to the day when your full story could be told. It has given me profound satisfaction to read every page of your recent book. History has at long last been served and you will go down to posterity as a modern martyr and a devoted servant of the American people.[43]

On the basis of his own character and knowledge, Grew, something of the romantic and entirely the cultivated aristocrat, could visualize only beneficial results flowing from a conference between the scion of Japanese nobility and the squire of Hyde Park. Somewhere in the rosy clouds Grew lost sight of the deflating fact that both Roosevelt and Konoye were prisoners of their respective systems. They were not dictators who could meet as did Hitler and Mussolini to shape national policy to their liking.

Konoye was premier of Japan by grace of the armed forces, and he had never shown any disposition to flout them. Nor had he noticeably plucked up courage by late summer of 1941. The Japanese government had gone into a virtual tailspin when on August 28 Nomura let slip to the Washington press that Konoye had sent a personal message to Roosevelt. Grew became so upset over this leak that in his opinion Nomura would be to blame had Konoye been assassinated.[44] The panic on the part of Grew and the Foreign Ministry reveals that both knew that the civil arm in Tokyo stood on very shaky ground, fearful of its own military. Under the circumstances, it is difficult to see how Grew could have expected anything constructive to come from a conference so controversial that even a hint of it might have resulted in Konoye's murder.

In December 1945 Konoye committed suicide, leaving behind hm an apologia in which, as *The New York Times* remarked, he "put the blame for the Pacific war and the disaster of his country upon everybody except himself." The *Times* pointed out that "the Premier who presided over the start of Japan's war against China, as the joint creator with Matsuoka of the fascist alliance with Germany and Italy, and as the author of the 'Greater East Asia Co-Prosperity Sphere,' Konoye was in no position effectively to oppose" the Army. The *Times* added:

> . . . in a more candid moment right after Japan's surrender, Konoye frankly admitted that the Japanese Government had long been "a two-headed dragon with the regular Government promising to do one thing and the other separate head, the military, ordering another." . . . It is to Mr. Hull's credit that he was fully aware of all this, and that he therefore demanded that Japan must change her policy before a meeting between President Roosevelt and Konoye could be of real use. For otherwise that meeting would have merely resulted in what Konoye himself expected of it in case of failure—a strengthening of Japan's will to war, and a "softening" of world opinion toward Japan.[45]

On the American side of the picture, Roosevelt was President by grace of the electorate and had to rely upon Congress to fund his projects. No one was ever more sensitive than Roosevelt to the ebb and flow of public opinion. His concern over the isolationist minority had weakened this leadership throughout 1940–41; he would never dream of flying in the face of the majority, which would have thundered in protest had he presented them with a rapprochement with Japan, partner in crime of the diabolical Hitler and unabashed aggressor in its own right.

As might be expected in a man of such supreme self-confidence and sense of theater, Roosevelt initially liked the idea of meeting with Konoye and made tentative suggestions as to a time and place.[46] But Hull shied away from the notion. He had ample reasons for skepticism, and outlined them for the benefit of the congressional committee.

"We asked ourselves whether the military element in Japan would permit the civilian element, even if so disposed, to stop Japan's course of expansion by force and to revert to peaceful courses. Time and again the civilian leaders gave assurances; time and again the military took aggressive action in direct violation of those assurances." Then, too, "Japan's formal partnership with Nazi Germany in the Tripartite Alliance was a hard and inescapable fact." Nor could the State Department ignore the "critically discouraging effect" such a meeting would have upon the Chinese.

Suppose the meeting took place and merely endorsed "general principles." Past performance suggested that the Japanese would interpret those principles to suit themselves. And if the meeting produced no agreement, Japan's military leaders would be in a position to blame the United States for the conference's failure.[47]

Hull proceeded with a roll call of Japan's actions during the three Konoye regimes which the State Department could not overlook: Konoye had headed the government when Japan attacked China; he was prime minister when Japanese forces attacked the *U.S.S. Panay* on the Yangtze River on December 12, 1937; he was prime minister at the time of the "notorious outrages in Nanking in 1937"; as prime minister, he had proclaimed in 1938 the conditions for peace in China which "would have enabled Japan to retain a permanent strangle hold on China"; he as prime minister had concluded a treaty with the puppet Wang Ching-wei regime at Nanking; he had headed the Japanese government when it signed the Tripartite Pact.

Therefore, when, over a period of months, the Japanese showed no inclination to abandon their policy of conquest, the State Department became convinced that a Roosevelt-Konoye meeting "could only result either in another Munich or in nothing at all, unless Japan was ready to give some clear evidence of a purpose to move in a peaceful direction." Neither Konoye nor any of his spokesmen came through with "anything tangible" along those lines.[48]

The wonder is not that the State Department was cool to the idea, but that it did not squelch it at the initial mention. Actually, the United States never definitely rejected the proposal; the idea died with the demise of the third Konoye cabinet.

Konoye's fall did not represent such a drastic change as the complaints of Roosevelt's detractors imply. Upon Tojo's accession to the premiership, Grew's military attaché, Lt. Col. Harry I. T. Creswell, reported from Tokyo:

When it is considered that the new Premier is known as a man who has been in sympathy with many of the ideas entertained by his predecessor while acting as Minister of War in his Cabinet, and inasmuch as four other members of the former Cabinet who were likewise thought to have been sympathetic toward its leader have continued in office, it is felt that the new Cabinet does not of necessity imply any radical, or any swift changes in policy. . . .[49]

Still, there is no reason to assume that Konoye was not sincere in attempting to arrange a summit conference with Roosevelt. Nomura had a rather poor opinion of Konoye. He thought him "weak and inexperienced, that he had made many mistakes, that he was grass-green in diplomacy, and that he was not a first-rate statesman." Nevertheless, he credited him with being "in dead earnest" about meeting with Roosevelt. Nomura believed that Konoye had become "frightened of the entire situation and wanted to do something, anything, to settle the problem and prevent war."[50]

Surely Konoye longed to pull himself out of the pit which he had helped to dig with such an enthusiastic spade. He would have winced at the prospect of being remembered as the premier who had permitted Japan to embark upon the "China Incident," from which it had achieved nothing but an ocean of squandered time, a mountain of wasted supplies, an endless harvest of dead and maimed young men, and a Great Wall of international ill will. Nor can he have relished the picture of future Japanese pointing to him as the man who had hung the albatross of the Tripartite Pact around Japanese necks, then exacerbated the situation by invading French Indochina. And unless he took drastic action, he stood on the brink of being the statesman under whose leadership Japan deliberately chose to fight the United States and the British Commonwealth as well as sundry Allied powers. No wonder he was almost frantic to reverse the tide toward war and leave to posterity a favorable image of himself.

A measure of the length to which Konoye went was his promise to Grew that when he reached an agreement with Roosevelt, he would radio Tokyo, whereupon the Emperor would "immediately issue a rescript ordering the suspension forthwith of all hostile operations." Grew did not feel able to "express any intelligent opinion" to Washington as to whether or not Konoye could have persuaded Hirohito thus to intervene.[51] But it appears extremely unlikely that Konoye would have dared thus to commit the Emperor without first receiving sanction. The fact that Baron Yoshimichi Hara, at the Imperial Conference of September 6, 1941, had expressed pleasure at Konoye's willingness to meet with Roosevelt in person[52] indicated that the Emperor approved the venture, for Hara as president of the Privy Council frequently acted as Hirohito's spokesman.

However gratifying the assurance of imperial approval, it was intangible, while accompanying Konoye on his trip would be a phalanx of top brass in the solid flesh, several of whom knew about the Pearl Harbor plan. The Navy's chief representative was scheduled to be Admiral Zengo Yoshida, former Commander in Chief of the Combined Fleet, ex-navy minister, close friend of Yamamoto, and privy to his secret plot since August 10, 1941.[53] Yoshida would take with him Vice Admiral Seiichi Ito, vice chief of the Naval General Staff. He had been Yamamoto's chief of staff from April to August 1941, and as such had been intimately connected with the Combined Fleet's planning for the attack.[54] Among the Army's nominees was Lieutenant General Osamu Tsukada, vice war minister. The Army considered Tsukada its best strategist, and he belonged to a select group of top-echelon Army officers who knew about the Pearl Harbor plan.[55]

The Army also planned to send along Major General Akira Muto, chief of the War Ministry's military affairs bureau, also privy to the plan.[56] Muto was a very important individual, for government agencies having business with the Army had to channel through him. And as a member of the liaison conference he had participated in all that conference's discussions through 1941.[57]

Another selectee was the almost legendary Lieutenant General Kenji Doihara, inspector general of Army Aviation.[58] This plump little man had been chief of the spy machine covering China. Sometimes spoken of romantically as the "Lawrence of Manchuria," he was generally conceded to be one of the brains behind the "Manchurian Incident." He had excellent German connections, being quite close to Ambassador Eugen Ott. Major General Hiroshi Oshima, Japan's ambassador to Germany, had served under Doihara as a colonel. Doihara spoke eight European languages along with several Asiatic.[59] He was the last man on earth U.S. Intelligence would care to have on the prowl in American territory, especially peering over Konoye's shoulder.

With or without imperial sanction, and regardless of who else might be included in Konoye's party, the presence of these last-named two generals would suffice to make Konoye the prisoner of the Army. Flanked by Muto and Doihara, he would have had precious little freedom of action. If he could not persuade Roosevelt to grant everything the Japanese armed forces wanted, his term of office would last about as long as it took the Army and/or Navy to reassign its cabinet minister and refuse to appoint a successor.

A Roosevelt-Konoye meeting was one of those lofty-seeming concepts which, like the ghost of Hamlet's father, fade upon the crowing of the cock. Whatever errors may be charged to Roosevelt and Hull, in fairness they should not be considered responsible for the failure of the proposed conference. As Hull testified to the congressional committee, "Our Government earnestly desired peace. It could not brush away the realities of the situation."[60]

CHAPTER 11

"Crimination and Recrimination"

Proposal B—Modus vivendi—Hull Note of November
26, 1941—Was it an "ultimatum"?

N o crisis in Japanese-American relations prior to the
Pearl Harbor attack is more closely identified with Hull than a series
of events that took place over a roughly ten-day period in the latter
half of November.

On the seventeenth, Nomura escorted Kurusu for introductory
interviews with Hull and Roosevelt, and that evening he took the
special envoy to visit Postmaster General Frank C. Walker. Normally
Walker's orbit would not touch upon diplomacy, but he was a prominent Catholic layman and had introduced the "John Doe" group to
Roosevelt. So he took a keen if unofficial interest in the proceedings.

In reporting to the Foreign Ministry, Nomura always protected
Walker's identity. He quoted "a certain cabinet member" as saying:

> The President is very desirous of an understanding between Japan
> and the United States. . . . If Japan would now do something real,
> such as evacuating French Indo-China, showing her peaceful inten-
> tions, the way would be open for us to furnish you with oil and it
> would probably lead to the reestablishment of normal trade relations.
> The Secretary of State cannot bring public opinion in line so long as
> you do not take some real and definite steps to reassure the Amer-
> icans.[1]

Quick to seize the hint, Nomura with Kurusu visited Hull at 10:30
the next morning for a three-hour conference. After some discussion,
Nomura suggested restoration of the status existing before Japan went
into southern Indochina and the United States slapped on the economic freeze. Although careful not to jump at the proposal, Hull
promised to discuss it with the British and Dutch.[2]

This unexpectedly amicable proposition probably did not surprise Hull, because Walker had spoken to him over the White House switchboard on November 17 at 6:25 P.M.—well before the postmaster general's meeting with the two Japanese diplomats.[3]

Nomura's idea had much to recommend it, but Tokyo—not Washington—promptly turned it down. Instead, on November 19, Foreign Minister Shigenori Togo advised Kurusu:

> the internal situation in our country is such that it would be difficult for us to handle if we withdraw from Southern French Indo-China merely on assurances that conditions prior to this freezing act will be restored. . . . The Ambassador did not arrange this with us beforehand . . . this can only result in delay and failure in the negotiations. The Ambassador, therefore, . . . will please present our B proposal of the Imperial Government, and no further concessions can be made.[4]

In accordance with these instructions, on November 20 Nomura and Kurusu presented Hull with Proposal B.[5]* Critics of Hull either ignore Proposal B or slip over it as smoothly as possible. Typical is the treatment of this subject by Morgenstern, who listed the provisions in his book but made no attempt to analyze them.[6] In an essay, he again cited the provisions, then affirmed, "The merit of these proposals could be established only by reference to utilitarian and empirical tests. . . . It is possible on all of these counts to contend that the United States would have lost nothing and stood to gain much by use of the Japanese paper as a basis for possible adjustment."[7]

But in Edward P. Morgan's draft majority report for the congressional committee, he wrote emphatically, "To have acceded to the Japanese ultimatum of November 20 would have been at once the most despicable and craven act in our Nation's history." The report as published cut off Morgan at the word "been," substituting for the balance of the sentence the single word "indefensible."[8] This cooled Morgan's blistering phraseology while retaining the general sense.

Close scrutiny of this brief proposal certainly supports the Morgan rather than the Morgenstern view. Indeed, it is difficult to see where Morgenstern got the idea that the United States "would have lost nothing and stood to gain much" by accepting the Japanese outline. Seldom has any nation not actually at a conqueror's feet been offered

---

*See Appendix 2.

so little in exchange for so much. After surveying this document with the skeptical eye of a seasoned diplomat, Hornbeck summarized its inner meaning as being Japan's asking

> that the United States agree to cease giving aid to China; that the U.S. desist from augmenting its military force in the western Pacific; that the United States help Japan obtain products of the Netherlands East Indies; that the United States undertake to resume commercial relations with Japan; that the United States undertake to supply to Japan "a required quantity of oil"; while Japan on her part would be free to continue her military operation in and against China and to keep her troops in Indochina and to attack the Soviet Union, would have her funds unfrozen, would be able to buy with comparative freedom from the United States, would be assured adequate supplies of oil, and would be under no obligation to remove her troops from Indochina until she should have completed her conquest of China or there had been established "in the Pacific area" conditions of peace satisfactory to her.[9]

The British Foreign Office devoted considerable attention to this note, which it believed "merely confirmed the view that they [the Japanese] wanted the speedy removal of economic pressure but not the speedy settlement of anything else." The Foreign Office had a few cogent analyses of its own:

> clause (i) related only to "armed" advances and would leave the Japanese free to carry on infiltration. The Japanese might also interpret the clause as precluding further strengthening of the Philippines and other outposts of the democratic Powers. Clause (iii) suggested that the Netherlands East Indies would be looked on merely as a storehouse without much reference to Dutch sovereignty. Clause (iv) put special emphasis on oil, of which Japan had no shortages except for war purposes. The Japanese proposals amounted not only to the withdrawal of the freezing measures but to the provision of positive assistance to Japan to acquire certain commodities, while assistance of this kind would cease to be given to China. The only offer made by Japan was to move her troops from one part of Indo-China to another.[10]

In Hull's pungent testimony to the congressional committee on this subject, he pointed out that by these proposals Japan "did not agree to abandon her policy of military conquest and aggression except in certain local areas." And the Japanese "hung on to the Germans . . ." so "all the fruits of the agreement would go to Hitler as well as to themselves." They also wanted the United States "to furnish them with all the oil that they would need to fight us as well as others." Hull added dryly, "and for some reason we declined to do it."[11]

Praising Hull's testimony, *The New York Times* remarked:

> Mr. Hull makes it plain that the Japanese war lords had confronted the United States with the alternative of either bowing to their very real ultimatum of November 20, 1941, which would have made the United States an ally of Japan at the price of surrender of American principles as abject as Munich, or facing the risk of Japanese attack.[12]

The use of the word "Munich" is significant. In 1941 that name had already entered the English language as a synonym for spineless toadying to a bully. The cold-blooded readiness of the Chamberlain government to buy off Hitler at the expense of a valiant friend had thoroughly disgusted many Americans. Japan's proposals called for the United States to make a batch of Czechoslovakias out of friends in Asia. The American people would not have tolerated it. The executive branch could lead the people or follow them, but any attempt to force them into a path inherently repugnant could only result in disaster for the administration so foolish as to try it. And few administrations have kept such sensitive, exploring fingers on the American pulse as that of Franklin D. Roosevelt.

To Sumner Welles, Japan's note seemed "an ultimatum which this Government couldn't possibly accept in its own self-defense and protection."[13] Hornbeck recalled that both Nomura and Kurusu "intimated vigorously that this was Japan's last word, that if an agreement along those lines was not quickly concluded, ensuing developments might be most unfortunate."[14] Even more significant, on November 20 the State Department had available the intercept of Togo's direction to Kurusu that "no further concessions can be made."[15]

But was the Japanese note an ultimatum? Captain Theodore S. "Ping" Wilkinson, former director of Naval Intelligence, told the congressional committee that he would not have so considered this note "because one does not reply to an ultimatum. I would have considered their message, and I do consider it, as a step in the negotiations."[16]

According to the *Random House Dictionary of the English Lan-*

guage, the word *ultimatum* means "a final, uncompromising demand or set of terms issued by a party to a dispute, the rejection of which may lead to a severance of relations or to the use of force." By that definition, Proposal B does not qualify. Its terms were unacceptable, even preposterous; however, the note contained nothing coercive. In an admirable essay, Norman Hill devoted considerable attention to this instrument. "While the Japanese note of November 20 meets most of the requirements of an ultimatum," Hill decided, "it lacked one—the intention of apprising the United States of its ultimate character, so that our government might choose between acceptance of their terms or war." Hill continued,

> While the Japanese were determined to treat the document as though it were an ultimatum, they intended to present it to us only as a strong representation in order that their attack might come with the utmost surprise to us. A note of this character does not qualify as a *bona fide* ultimatum, for it is not the intention to present that respondent with the alternatives of acceptance or war. To say that because our government discovered Japanese secrets which gave the note a more serious meaning so that it carried the implications of an ultimatum cannot alter its original purpose or the intentions of the Japanese Government.[17]

Hornbeck observed that the U.S. government "fully realized on November 20 that the chances of reaching an agreement and of dissuading Japan from her program of conquest were small indeed if existent at all." Therefore, he suggested, "If any date other than December 7, 1941 . . . is to be considered as the date when, in effect, war between Japan and the United States began, first place might well be given to November 20, 1941, the day on which the Japanese delivered their 'last word' proposal."[18]

In point of fact, however, Hull did not reject Proposal B outright. From November 21 through 25, the State Department worked hard on a counterproposal which might keep the talks going a little longer.[19] Morgenthau sent a draft from the Treasury Department, and while Hull did not appreciate Morgenthau's "persistent inclination to serve as a second Secretary of State," he found some of the suggestions worth using.[20]

While the Army and Navy were not too happy with some of the provisions, they agreed to go along with the modus vivendi, which was to remain in effect for three months, in view of the importance to the war in Europe of a reprieve from trouble with Japan.[21] Hull was too much the realist to place any bets on the possibility of Tokyo's accepting any terms but its own. But he considered that making the offer would demonstrate Washington's desire to work for peace as long as possible. If Tokyo refused, it must stand revealed as determined upon war. And if by some chance Japan agreed, so much the better. War would have been postponed for three months, and the U.S. armed forces would be that much better prepared for whatever might eventuate.[22]*

However, Hull's scheme came to nothing because of the vigorous protests from the Chinese, seconded by Churchill.[23] There was little doubt that Hull abandoned the modus vivendi reluctantly. "I remember very clearly how upset Mr. Hull was," Stark told the congressional committee, "of his telling me how the Hill was crying appeasement, that the Chinese themselves should have supported him, because he was doing this in their behalf, and that previously they didn't understand it. Also . . . [Hull] pointed out that the British, he thought, were only half-way supporting it."[24]

As a result, on November 26 Hull offered the Japanese the ten-point proposal originally intended to be attached to the modus vivendi as subjects for a general settlement if the temporary arrangement had been accepted.[25]†

The next day, Hornbeck wrote Hull congratulating him on his presentation. "The document which you presented to the Japanese representatives squares one hundred percent with the principles which you have repeatedly declared and for which you have consistently contended. . . . I believe that it cannot be assailed from any point of view with any appearance of warranty or with any argument of weight."[26]

So far so good! But Hornbeck speculated whether or not "an agreement providing on its face for a period of standstill and containing the elements of a 'trade' might have been politically advantageous." Then he answered himself:

> Nevertheless, the simple fact is that the chance that the terms which we had formulated for a *modus vivendi* would be accepted by the Japanese was small indeed; the chance that such a *modus vivendi*,

---

*See Appendix 4 for terms of the modus vivendi.
†See Appendix 6 for terms of the Hull Note.

if agreed upon, would have achieved the objective which was ours
was even smaller; and the chance that the whole transaction would
be subjected to terrific criticism by huge groups of people in many
countries, including this country, was not only great but was an
absolute certainty. . . .[27]

Thus far Hornbeck still remained in safe territory. But he moved
into sensitive terrain.

It was not, in its essential character, a completely honest doc-
cument; for, whereas its ostensible objective was to contribute toward promotion and maintenance of peace in the Pacific, all that we
really expected of it was that it would give us more time to prepare
our weapons of defense; we hoped by it to gain an advantage over
the Japanese; had we presented it to them and had they accepted
it, their acceptance of it would have been based on a hope on their
part that it would give them an advantage over us. . . .

Hornbeck then returned to his point of departure—praise of Hull's
note of November 26: "The action which you took yesterday constitutes a new entry in the record which admits of no questioning and
no reproach. And, from the point of view of practical effects, my
feeling is that it was a contribution toward rather than away from
peace."[28]

The intellectual snobbery, the holier-than-thou attitude, the patronizing tone of this effusion would have ignited even a far more
stolid man than Hull. He had entertained genuine if cautious hopes
for the modus vivendi, and only with reluctance had he recommended
to Roosevelt on November 26 that it be withheld.

No nation is so foolish as to propose a diplomatic arrangement
hostile to its own interests, so the modus vivendi offered certain
benefits to the United States. As Hull told the congressional committee, "it contained only a little chicken feed in the shape of some
cotton, oil and a few other commodities in very limited quantities as
compared with the unlimited quantities the Japanese were demanding." Still, he hoped that "if by any hook or crook it should prove
possible for the Japanese to decide that they would be willing to wait
a month or two it would be a fine thing for us."[29]

In any case, conniving at dishonesty was the last accusation a
subordinate could make safely to Cordell Hull. On November 28, he
dispatched a lengthy rebuttal of Hornbeck's letter, detailing the back-

ground and reasons for formulating the abortive modus vivendi. He assured Hornbeck "that the benefits to this Government, if the chance for an agreement had been realized—and, of course, it was only a chance—would alone have more than justified the concessions offered to Japan for ninety days."

Obviously the subject was a sore one with Hull. "It is no answer to the question of whether this proposal is sound and desirable at this most critical period to say that it probably would not have been accepted by Japan in any event; nor to say that I would have been widely criticized on the astounding theory of selling China down the river or of appeasement." He ended his letter with a snap: "If that far-fetched demagogic stuff could be rung into this sort of understanding, then there could never be a settlement between countries except at the point of a sword."[30]

This exchange was of historical importance, because it made clear that Hull would have been more than willing to offer Japan a modus vivendi instead of his celebrated note of November 26.

Hull never intended his Ten-Point Note as an "ultimatum," as first the Japanese and later certain American critics termed it. In a lengthy statement recapitulating for the congressional committee the course of Japanese-American relations during 1941, Hull wrote, "The document handed the Japanese on November 26 was essentially a restatement of principles which have long been basic in this country's history."[31]

An evaluation of the State Department's role—and of Hull's in particular—in the immediate prewar period would not be complete without discussing this document, which Hull divided into two sections. The first presented certain principles governing the conduct of nations. It included a joint promise not to use "military force aggressively against any neighboring nation." This would have kept war from Southeast Asia and guaranteed the Soviet Union against a samurai sword in its back. It also committed the United States rather heavily to a purely defensive posture in the Pacific. Section I likewise contained provisions toward "nondiscrimination in international commercial relations" which would have been very much to Japan's benefit. Section II consisted of the famous Ten Points:

Number One called for "a multilateral nonaggression pact among the British Empire, China, Japan, the Netherlands, the Soviet Union, Thailand and the United States." Such a treaty would have offered Japan greater advantages than the Tripartite Pact.

Number Two covered an attempt by both nations to neutralize Indochina. This would have given Japan an equal chance to acquire the resources of that area in a peaceful manner.

Numbers Three and Four—withdrawal of troops from China and Indochina and recognition of the Chiang regime—were strong medicine for Japan to swallow, particularly at such a late date. But they were not new provisions, and Japan could not reasonably have expected the United States to abandon them.

Number Five called for both nations to "give up all extraterritorial rights in China" and to "endeavor to obtain the agreement of the British and other governments" to do the same. Japanese propaganda had been preaching for years that their incursions into the mainland were to free the Asiatics from European imperialism. With this provision, the United States offered to get out and to persuade the other powers to go along. But, in turn, Hull asked that the Japanese also abandon their own brand of imperialism.

Number Six proposed a Japanese-American "trade agreement, based upon reciprocal most-favored nation treatment." Japan's anguished howls over the embargo proved that it had by far the more to gain from such an agreement. In fact, implementation of Number Six would lift the embargo.

Number Seven provided for mutual unfreezing of funds, a measure greatly to Japan's benefit. American money tied up in Japan caused a mere annoyance compared to Japanese distress over the congealed yen in the United States.

Number Eight called for the "stabilization of the dollar-yen rate"— a measure necessary for smooth trade between the two countries.

Number Nine stated that no agreement with "any third power or powers" should "conflict with the fundamental purposes of this agreement, the establishment and preservation of peace throughout the Pacific area." This insured that Japan would not use the Tripartite Pact as a loophole. Indeed, this provision was almost redundant, because had Japan accepted the other points, its Axis membership would have become a dead letter.

Number Ten summoned both nations to "use their influence to cause other governments to adhere to and to give practical application to the basic political and economic principles set forth in this agreement." This placed a heavier burden on the United States than on Japan, which at the time had much less influence to exert.[32]

Release of this document to the press elicited favorable reactions.

Barth's summary of November 28 concluded that many commentators had feared that the United States might retreat at the expense of China. "Hull's declaration of American principles quieted most of these fears. Every sign that there will be no yielding on this side is warmly welcomed."[33]

Events took a strange turn when the revisionists seized upon Hull's note and by christening it an "ultimatum" made it one of their articles of faith. So, ironically, Hull was criticized in 1941 for "appeasing" the Japanese, then later was charged with pushing them into war.

It is difficult to recognize in the Hull Note "The American ultimatum of November twenty-sixth, which ended all possibility of peaceful negotiation with Japan," as *The Saturday Evening Post* characterized it.[34] Or what Barnes called "Hull's ultimatum of November 26 which made imminent war inevitable."[35]

On November 6, 1945, Gearhart called this document "the ultimatum which the Japanese considered so harsh and humiliating that nothing but a resort to war remained."[36] He had no business making a public judgment without examining the evidence, but he did so on the floor of the House of Representatives before the congressional committee had opened its hearings. During the investigation, more than once he tried to beguile a witness into agreeing that the note was an "ultimatum," even going so far as to pretend admiration for it.[37]

Commenting later upon Gearhart's attitude, the Philadelphia *Record* took sharp exception:

> if Hull's note *was* an "ultimatum," then the obvious conclusion is that war-mongering United States started the war, forced poor, little innocent Japan into it when she was trying her best to preserve the peace of the world.
>
> We didn't think even the most purblind Republican, the most vindictive hater of Roosevelt, actually believed such rubbish. . . .
>
> Particularly after we learned, from Jap military records, that the Pearl Harbor "sneak attack" was organized long before Hull sent his note. [*Record*'s italics][38]

The *Record* referred to documents salvaged when a sunken Japanese heavy cruiser, *Nachi*, had been raised earlier that autumn— documents which revealed that the Pearl Harbor attack had been under preparation long before Hull presented his Ten Points. James M. Byrnes, who succeeded Hull as secretary of state, hoped that this discovery might "forever dispose of the claims of the Army Board that the so-called ultimatum of Secretary Hull started the Japanese war."[39] Byrnes was overly optimistic.

Rear Admiral Theobald, who had assisted Kimmel before the Roberts Commission, declared that Hull's note "gave Japan no choice but surrender or war." By this train of reasoning, it became part of Roosevelt's "plot" to bring the United States into the conflict by the "back door." Lamented Theobald:

> President Roosevelt, by the note of November 26, definitely and deliberately brought war to the United States. He had flung the gauntlet into Japan's face. The latter's attempt to break the encirclement had failed. She must now surrender or fight, and there was no question what her answer would be.[40]

On the contrary, the Hull document was no more and no less than a clear-cut recapitulation of the American position, offered not as the "last word" but as the basis for continuing discussion. As Hull explained, the talks had gone on for so long that the American "statement of principles . . . had almost been lost track of, and there was serious need to . . . bring them up to date."[41]

Chamberlin figuratively wrung his hands over the Hull Note, which he claimed "amounted to a demand for unconditional surrender." He continued:

> There was a suggestion for a multilateral nonaggression pact among the governments principally concerned in the Pacific. Only on those terms, which amounted to relinquishment by Japan of everything it had gained on the mainland during the preceding ten years, would the United States consent to restore normal economic relations. . . .
>
> Technically Hull's ten points did not constitute an ultimatum. . . . But when one considers the circumstances under which they were presented, and their completely uncompromising character, one may feel that the Army Board which investigated the Pearl Harbor attack was justified in describing Hull's communication as "the document that touched the button that started the war."[42]

This exposition overlooked some obvious facts. In the first place, Japan's gain "on the mainland" had come at the expense of a sovereign nation, and no more represented legitimate expansion than did Hitler's conquest of France. Moreover, the note, although firm and fundamental, was far from an iron "or else" document. It posed no threats, established no deadlines. It was not even totally one-sided, offering as it did several options distinctly beneficial to Japan, not the least of which would have been restoration of "normal economic relations" with the United States.

Berle characterized it simply as "a rather general plan for peace in the Pacific."[43] On November 8, 1942 *The New York Times* called the Ten Points "an outline for peace in the Pacific which will stand forever as a testimonial to American sincerity."

About a month later, Hornbeck emphasized that the explanatory statement covering the Ten Points specifically affirmed that they constituted an example for consideration as "a basis for *further discussion*" (Hornbeck's italics). He added:

> Only if, in replying to demands of a blackmailer, a proposal that there be further discussion, constitutes an ultimatum, could the American Government's communication of November 26, 1941 with any warrant be described as an 'ultimatum.'[44]

It is unfortunate and ironic that a misinterpretation of Grew's testimony before the Army Board either started the "ultimatum" ball rolling in the United States or gave it a swift kick forward.[45] In fact, Grew was much pleased with Hull's note. In his diary entry for November 29, 1941, he termed it a "broad-gauge, objective and statesmanlike document, offering to Japan practically everything she has ostensibly been fighting for if she will simply stop her aggressive policy." Instead of inviting inevitable defeat at the hands of the ABCD (American-British-Chinese-Dutch) combination, Japan could "obtain without further fighting all of the desiderata for which she allegedly started fighting—strategic, economic, financial and social security."[46] But Grew soon found that Tokyo portrayed the note as an ultimatum, and took care that the actual terms were not made public until after the war started. And then the Japanese government confiscated the offending newspaper.[47]

Yet, despite the evidence presented by the note itself and Grew's very clear testimony, the Army Board decided that Hull had "touched the button."[48]

Stimson rapped the Board's knuckles sharply for its adverse remarks about Hull as "uncalled for and not within the scope of their proper inquiry."[49] If indeed that body chose to make a side excursion into diplomatic territory, they owed it to the War Department and to the American people to be sure that their report accurately reflected the weight of the evidence.

No wonder that when the Board's report appeared in the press, *The New York Times* exploded: "In the light of all this, a visitor from Mars might be forgiven if he drew the conclusion that the Government of the United States had deliberately provoked Japan into war with a high-handed and arbitrary challenge, and that Japan had made the only possible answer to this 'ultimatum' by hitting us at Pearl Harbor." The editorial expressed a vigorous opinion that, on the contrary, in his document Hull

> did what any self-respecting American would have done. He refused to be bullied into the abject humiliation of his country and the complete betrayal of its ally, China. . . . But he did not slam the door on future discussion. He did not threaten the Japanese with war. He did not threaten them with anything save the further loss of American respect and friendship if they persisted in the bare-faced aggression on which they had embarked. And as a means of keeping alive at least some hope of a peaceful settlement, he offered the Japanese a program which contained a restatement of principles, which had long been basic in this country's foreign policies. . . .[50]

On September 4, 1945, just three days after this editorial appeared, Hull discussed his note with his special assistant, Breckenridge Long. "He could not accept their [the Japanese] proposal of a few days earlier," Long recorded in his diary. "Being unable to accept it, he had to propose something else or end the talks. He did not want to end the talks so he presented to them a set of principles which if observed would carry along to a peaceful world." Hull foresaw "much more crimination and recrimination on the subject." Long agreed; the congressional investigation was forthcoming, "and party politics will insure that Hull is painted in the devil's likeness by some."[50] In this both men unfortunately were correct.

The eminent historian Herbert Feis held the opinion that "the memo of November 26 was not in any usual sense of the word an ultimatum. It did not threaten the Japanese with war or any other form of forceful punishment if our terms were not accepted." Feis underscored the important point that Japan's note delivered on December 7, 1941, did not accuse Washington of having confronted Tokyo with an ultimatum, "but only of thwarting the larger Japanese aims."[52]

One might argue that the very fact of controversy over the Hull Note proves that it was not an ultimatum, since to qualify as such a message must be unequivocal. In his scholarly essay on this subject, Hill concluded:

> the purpose of an ultimatum is to give the respondent a final opportunity to accept stated terms or face coercion, a purpose that would be quite unattainable unless both of the parties had the same understanding of the diplomatic situation and were aware that a communication had been submitted with the intention of providing such an alternative.
> . . . It may be . . . that the Japanese regarded Mr. Hull's note as an ultimatum. . . . There is, of course, little to prevent a government from construing a note which it has received in any way that it pleases. But it could not be admitted that a note is an ultimatum simply because the respondent chooses to call it one. Often an attitude of this sort may be assumed only to place the blame for war on an adversary, or as justification for a sudden attack.

Like Feis, Hill pointed out that after Hull presented his Ten Points, "no official statement emanated from the Japanese Government to the effect that an ultimatum had been received by them."[53] Indeed, it was significant and characteristic of the Tojo regime of 1941 that it inflamed the Japanese people with cries of "ultimatum" while carefully avoiding any such reference in its formal closing of the Washington talks.

One reading newspaper comments about the proceedings of the congressional committee can conclude that the attitude of the press toward the Hull Note depended less upon the evidence than upon predetermined political positions. The Washington *Times-Herald* complained that Hull took the "appeasement" out of his note because of the attitude of Britain, China, and Holland. Thus ". . . what was left was so stiff a communication that the Japanese took it for an ultimatum—and it certainly reads like one today."[54]

On the other hand, the Washington *Star* agreed with Hull that his note was not an ultimatum, and pointed out:

By November 26, 1941, war in the Pacific was inevitable. It is conceivable that a policy of total appeasement might have postponed the war. But it could not have prevented it, for by that time the fatal collision of national interests could not be averted, and the Japanese thought that they were strong enough, and that we were weak enough, to risk the challenge. . . .[55]

After carefully considering the legal implications, Hill concluded that during November 1941 Washington and Tokyo had reached "a diplomatic *impasse* . . . but neither dispatched a *bona fide* ultimatum."[56] What really mattered, however, was the "impasse," not the legalisms of the situation. Moreover, those who blame Roosevelt and Hull for issuing the Ten-Point Note ignore the series of events, declarations, messages, and Japanese press releases which reveal unmistakably that Japan's idea of a satisfactory settlement with the United States meant capitulation to Tokyo's position. Furthermore, by November 26 Japan had already moved to implement her war plan.[57] Therefore, any suggestion that Hull "touched the button" on November 26 is ridiculous.

The New York Times appreciated that point. On November 19, 1945, it noted that the Nagumo force planned, trained, prepared for the Pearl Harbor attack, and sortied before the Hull Note had been delivered.

During the war, Tokyo fostered the impression that Hull's Ten-Point Note had been an ultimatum, acceptance of which would have plunged Japan into the depths of degradation. But objective Japanese rejected this easy way out. Both Nomura and Kurusu disdained to push blame for the final break on Hull. Nomura termed the Secretary "a man of great integrity, who would not sacrifice the fundamental national policy of America to compromise with Japan."[58] Interviewed in Tokyo upon publication of the congressional committee reports, Nomura declared that he did not consider Hull's proposal an ultimatum, but "some Japanese officials may have taken that view of it."[59]

Kurusu waxed reflective on the subject during his internment before repatriation:

> That old man . . . had no wish to go to war with Japan. He did his utmost to preserve peace. The trouble is, both the United States and Japan were just like two children. Diplomatically they were not mature. The United States has always had a theoretical and academic

approach, and Japan knows nothing of diplomacy. Japan's diplomats
have never been allowed free exercise of their own judgment. . . ."[60]

During the congressional hearings, Kurusu told the press that "he
was convinced that both President Roosevelt and Hull sincerely attempted to prevent, or at least postpone, war with Japan, knowing
that the United States was militarily unprepared for such a struggle."

"I am sorry to read reports that Hull is being criticized as negligent," Kurusu said. "He certainly wasn't."[61]

On December 8, 1945 *Mainichi Shimbun* published an article
about Japan's decision for war which stated, "The public thinks that
JAPAN finally made up her mind to fight because of AMERICA's
'ultimatum' . . . on 26 November . . . but it was on 20 November
that our Government and General headquarters determined to open
hostilities."[62]

In Kimmel's introduction to Theobald's book, he states that Hull's
note "effectually ended the possibility of further negotiations and thus
made the Pacific war inevitable."[63] Yet the conversations continued
right up to December 7. In fact, Kimmel himself specifically pointed
out in his defense before the congressional committee that the discussions, which the "war warning" message of November 27 had
indicated had been terminated for all practical purposes, actually did
go on.[64]

Hull told Nomura on December 1, 1941, "The United States
would be glad to give Japan all she wants in the way of materials if
Japan's military leaders will only show that Japan intends to pursue
a peaceful course."[65] The Japanese had used their need for materials
to rationalize their aggression. Again, as the United States had done
throughout the year, it offered Japan solid benefits in exchange for
the dream of ruling Asia. Unfortunately, the Japanese wanted both.

Hull wrote in his *Memoirs*, "Even though I realized at the very
outset that the chances for such an agreement were no bigger than
a gnat, I still felt we had to make the effort." He did not regret his
course. Looking back, he believed that there had been only three
ways to face the danger Japan posed: a preventive attack, capitulation,
or "simply to continue discussions with Japan, . . . to lay before her
proposal after proposal which in the long run would have given her
in peace the prosperity her military leaders were seeking in conquest." The State Department adopted this third alternative—"the
only American method."[66]

Another odd little tessera helps fill out the mosaic: No one had arranged before the war began for some neutral power to represent American interests in Japan. Berle called this "a bad slip-up on the part of the Far Eastern people." This is true. But such an omission could scarcely have occurred if the State Department expected immediate war with Japan, let alone hoped or planned for it.[67]

After Pearl Harbor, Roosevelt pushed Hull somewhat into the background. But the secretary of state continued to serve faithfully and well until a long illness forced his reluctant resignation on November 21, effective November 30, 1944. At Roosevelt's urgent request, he had withheld formal resignation until after the election.[68]

To many of his fellow countrymen, Hull's withdrawal from civic life seemed the end of an era. Few men had better exemplified the total American. Hull combined the courtliness of his native South with Yankee shrewdness, Eastern sophistication with Western vigor. And he had a contempt for pretense at all levels.

A story going the rounds early in 1946 illustrates Hull's basic character. There had been considerable criticism in Washington about poker playing in high places, and some were quite sensitive about it. For instance, when a writer mentioned in a proposed article that Thomas E. Dewey liked to relax over a Saturday-night poker game, Dewey is said to have asked that "poker" be changed to "bridge." Hull was not so touchy. Writing about Hull for *The New York Times*, Colonel Harold Hinton related that in Hull's Spanish-American War days, he played poker so well "that he kept his company continually out of funds." When Hull received the article for approval, he firmly crossed out the word "company" and substituted "regiment."[69]

No pussyfooting for Cordell Hull! He could lick any man in his regiment at poker, and if the game was not elegant enough for some people, that was no concern of his. If there is any validity in character and psychology, it seems quite certain that if such a man intended a document to be an ultimatum, he would have said so in presenting it, and would have scorned to deny it later.

This integrity is the core of the Hull legacy. More than any reasoned argument, it makes grotesque the claims of skulduggery on his part. On the bases of historical facts and of character, the rickety thesis of Hull-as-villain in the Pearl Harbor story is long overdue for the scrap heap of history.

CHAPTER 12

"To Help and Serve"

Secretaries Stimson and Knox—Postattack criticisms—Knox's appointment—His belief in and service to the Navy—Stimson as secretary of war—The "first shot" controversy—War should be by act of reason—Errors at secretarial level

Two members of Roosevelt's cabinet were much more directly involved with Pearl Harbor than was Hull: Secretary of War Henry L. Stimson and Secretary of the Navy Frank Knox. Not only were they responsible respectively for administering the Army and Navy, they were closely associated with aiding the Allies. This program came under fire as the isolationist press and solons of the day predictably if somewhat incongruously castigated the Administration for failing to foresee and stop the very event whose possibility the isolationists themselves had ridiculed—an Axis attack on the United States.[1]

Stimson and Knox, especially the latter, were thoroughly splashed by what the St. Louis *Post-Dispatch* called "the mounting wave of criticism that is rolling up as a result of what happened." As early as December 9, 1941, Senator Bennett Champ Clark of Missouri called for Knox's resignation, claiming that at least twenty other senators agreed with him. "It is difficult to believe," Clark said sarcastically, "that Col. Knox could be such an efficient administrator that he could spend most of his time making speeches throughout the country telling the people that we could lick Japan with one hand tied behind our backs." He added ominously, "I don't want to seem to be making a snap judgment. But in the light of what we know already, I think it is time to consider drastic changes."[2]

The Atlanta *Constitution* retorted that Clark, who had led the fight against the so-called fortification of Guam, was "the last man who should raise his voice in any sort of statement. . . . If Bennett

194

Clark had any intellectual honesty, he would resign from the United States Senate. His handiwork in the Pacific is apparent. No man has done the military strength of his country more harm than this smug, often-wrong, but never in doubt Senator from Missouri."[3]

The colorful, popular Knox had his supporters among the general public as well as among newsmen. One reader of the St. Louis *Post-Dispatch* wrote to the editor indignantly: "It is true that Knox may have talked too much, but he did not join an organization and stump the country against preparations for our defense nor did he ever tell the people that this country was in no danger of attack from the other side of the ocean." Another citizen suggested that "to a greater degree than we suspect, Senator Clark and other members of Congress who persistently fought the foreign policy of the United States encouraged the Japanese to declare war on us in the belief that our nation was hopelessly divided."[4]

The Chicago *Tribune* keelhauled the entire Navy Department. It declared "that the outstanding lesson of the disaster for us is the fact that the battleship is obsolete and that the men in charge of the Navy didn't know it." This steaming editorial added, "What the nation, therefore, wants to hear . . . is that the stupid, ageing burocrats [*sic*] in the navy department had been cleaned out." The "navy at the top" had revealed itself to be "without imagination and without a true conception" of modern warfare. Despite all the lessons which the European war presented, the U.S. Navy "had been putting its money into battleships and had allowed Japan to take the lead in aircraft carriers." This led to the *Tribune's* harsh judgment: "The men responsible for our present plight have been utterly discredited, but, more important than that, they have revealed a degree of incapacity which cannot be tolerated. They must go."[5]

In those early days this newspaper showed little sympathy toward Kimmel and Short. It linked them to its diatribe against the two secretaries: "The disgraceful laxness among the leaders at Hawaii, leading as it did to the worst naval catastrophe in our history, demonstrates that strong men must be put at the head of the top service departments if we are to recover from that disaster and defend America successfully."

The only charge which the *Tribune* could bring against Stimson was that he had reached the age of seventy-three and therefore suffered "the disabilities of that age, if not mentally, most certainly physically."[6] Within three days the *Tribune* temporarily abandoned him and concentrated its fire upon the secretary of the navy. An editorial headed WHY KNOX MUST GO declared, "The case for removal of Secretary Knox is the obvious one that he has failed again." It charged that evidently Knox had not learned the lessons of the "revolutionary changes" which had taken place in sea warfare during his tenure. What is more, "He had ample opportunity in his two years to become acquainted with the higher officers in the navy but gave the command to one who, when the test came at Pearl Harbor, proved himself unfit."

The *Tribune* reminded the public of Knox's annual report for 1941 in which he claimed that the U.S. Navy was "alert and ready." The newspaper conceded, "No doubt Mr. Knox thought he was telling the truth." But his words were "the measure of his incompetence for the position he holds."[7]

Apparently some Chicagoans shared the editor's views and even went beyond them. To one irate citizen, Kimmel, Short, and Maj. Gen. Frederick L. Martin, Commanding General, Hawaiian Air Force, seemed to be "the unfortunate victims of Secretary Knox's and Stimson's face saving show. These three competent and highly trained men have been made the fall guys for a couple of politicians," he wrote to the editor. "Secretaries Knox and Stimson were in a much better position to have anticipated the Japanese attack than the Pacific commanders because of their high position in the government."[8]

Following publication of the Roberts report, Senator Wayland Brooks of Illinois demanded an investigation of Knox and Stimson to "determine their responsibility for policies and dispositions of our armed forces' military equipment that caused their contribution to the disaster." He wanted to know why the United States had sent military and naval equipment to other countries; who was responsible for concentrating the Fleet at Pearl Harbor; what private enterprise they engaged in that diverted their attention from their cabinet jobs; how they determined the knowledge or ability of the officers assigned in protecting outposts; and what favors they did in granting commissions. Brooks thus cast aspersions upon Stimson's and Knox's honesty as well as their ability.[9]

On January 24, 1941, Knox had sent Stimson a letter discussing "the inherent possibilities of a major disaster to the fleet" or to Pearl Harbor, and suggesting certain measures the Army should consider to protect the ships and the harbor.[10] Stimson replied on February 7, concurring in "the importance of this matter" and spelling out what the War Department had done or proposed doing to fulfill the Hawaiian Department's responsibility to protect the fleet in harbor.[11] Revelation of this exchange roused Senator Walsh of Massachusetts to ask what steps had been taken to strengthen the armed forces in Hawaii and the Pacific after that date.

"Is it a fact that the opposite course was taken and ships were actually moved from the Pacific to the Atlantic and that practically no increases were made in the army and air corps defenses?" he prodded. Walsh added, "if the army and navy had been materially strengthened during this time, it might not necessarily have prevented the dereliction of duty that the board finds, but it would have given notice to the army and navy that the government at Washington was preparing a strong, determined fighting defense."[12]

Representative Clare E. Hoffman of Michigan could not believe "that the commanders on the island should be held entirely responsible. . . . Surely, a major portion of the blame should be placed on the shoulders of the occupant of the White House as commander in chief of the armed forces . . . and those directly responsible to him." Hoffman wanted to know why Knox and Stimson did not require specific reports "as to exactly what was done to protect American soil from an invader." He found the Roberts report good as far as it went but that it did not go far enough "in dealing out the blame to officials responsible to the American people for the security of the nation."[13]

Representative Paul Shafer, also of Michigan, was equally blunt in his criticism of the service Secretaries. "Why the island commanders were not held to a more strict accounting of their actions in response to orders from Washington before it was too late is a question the committee has not answered." Representative Maas of Minnesota claimed that "the Japanese would never have attacked Pearl Harbor if we had not split our fleet." Representative Fish thought the report fine to a point, but "woefully weak in explaining the failure of the war and navy departments to make clear to the officers on the islands the exact situation with regard to Japan."[14]

It is unfortunate that all of these complainants except Walsh were Republicans because they, as well as such newspapers as the Chicago *Tribune*, raised some valid questions which deserved nonpartisan presentation and answers. But certain journals had no patience with these questionings. The San Francisco *Chronicle* deplored "the demagogic yelps, emanating from some politicians and from the more malicious of the opposition press calling for the investigation of Secretaries Knox and Stimson."[15]

In contrast, some six weeks later the *New Republic* criticized key cabinet members in an article which for sheer ambivalence would be difficult to beat: "Of course Secretary Knox should go. Upon his shoulders falls the weight of the disasters in the Pacific . . . these disasters may be traced to the inherent weaknesses within the Navy Department." And there were many: "its backwardness in technical development, its inferior procurement, its paucity of strategy, its overcaution in action, its poor intelligence work, its abominable economic and statistical staff work. For all this Secretary Knox must be held to blame."

Having made that bald statement, the magazine about-faced and asked, "Yet is Secretary Knox to blame? Ever since his appointment he has been held prisoner within the Navy Department. The naval officers despise him and men such as Admiral King . . . are openly scornful of him." Nor did the *New Republic* have any intelligent suggestion to make concerning a replacement for Knox.[16]

The implication that all naval officers despised Knox is certainly exaggerated. Nevertheless, several of those consulted for this study believed the real brain of the Navy Department was James V. Forrestal, Knox's assistant secretary, who succeeded him upon his death. "If you wanted something done, you went to Forrestal," said RADM William R. Furlong, who in 1941 was Commander, Minecraft, Battle Force, U.S. Pacific Fleet. "Knox was purely a political appointee. Forrestal did the work; he was cooperative and considerate."[17]

There is some truth in the charge that Knox spoke and wrote too often, sometimes with too little thought. Nor can one be sure that he always understood all he learned about the Navy or that he absorbed enough of the facts. His natural enthusiasm, fervent patriotism, and devotion to the Navy led him into overblown claims for its prowess. It is never easy to acknowledge the faults of those one loves, and Knox loved the Navy.

His association with the sea service had come late in life; his own experience in uniform had been in the Army. He had served in Cuba as one of Theodore Roosevelt's Rough Riders and in World War I had volunteered as a private. He rose to the rank of major, but oddly enough thenceforth was called "Colonel." Turning to journalism after the armistice, by 1930 he was ready for his own newspaper, the Chicago *Daily News*. A longtime Republican, he had been Alf Landon's running mate in 1936. This was a curious background for a member of Roosevelt's official family, but in the crisis year of 1940, the President wanted to make at least a gesture toward a nonpartisan cabinet, and Knox enjoyed a challenge.

He had encountered some flak when he joined the cabinet, but the chance to play a part in the Navy's buildup far outbalanced such criticism. In reply to a note venomously attacking Roosevelt and Stimson, he wrote:

> I am personally obsessed with the magnificence of the present opportunity to provide this country with the kind of a fleet it must have if it is going to be safe in a world such as we live in. Time is of the very essence. If things should quiet down in Europe and Hitler begins to express pacific intentions, the American people characteristically will go to sleep again and probably hamstring any effort to bring the fleet up and maintain it. Consequently, I feel under tremendous pressure to get the fleet into being as rapidly as possible. If we can once establish definite superiority on the surface of the seas and in the air, we can live our own lives after our own fashion and tell the rest of the world "to go to hell."[18]

A visit to Pearl Harbor in September 1940 transmuted this enthusiastic sense of duty into genuine affection for the sea service, which the Fleet reciprocated. It was impossible not to like this exuberant secretary who participated in maneuvers at sea, flew off a carrier, and dived in a submarine, all with the frank gusto of a small boy.[19] Richardson reported to Stark that Knox "made a most favorable impression upon the officers and men of the Fleet."[20] And Rear Admiral Claude C. Bloch, commandant of the Fourteenth Naval District, wrote to Stark, "The Secretary is a grand gentleman, and although I never knew him before, when he left here he carried my very great affection."[21]

The secretary was equally warm in his praise of the Navy. "I found the fleet as I expected to find it, the greatest, most powerful, and most efficient fleet on the high seas anywhere in the world," he told reporters.[22]

Knox's boasting about the Navy was not just a public relations gambit; he believed what he said. On April 15, 1941, he told Stimson and Hopkins "that if the Navy were turned loose they could clean up the North Atlantic situation in thirty days." By autumn he had to admit "that his Navy was up against it in the Atlantic and had been a bit too brash in their over-confidence that they could do the job quickly."[23] The Nazi wolf-pack technique was proving "pretty hard to handle," and Stimson gained the impression from Knox that "the Navy was thoroughly scared about their inability to stamp out the submarine menace."[24]

Evidently Knox's pride and confidence were restored fairly soon, for on the morning of December 7, 1941, a page-one headline in *The New York Times* announced: NAVY IS SUPERIOR TO ANY, SAYS KNOX . . . SECRETARY'S ANNUAL REPORT CITES COMMISSIONING OF 325 NEW SHIPS, 2059 PLANES. In its story, which was datelined Washington, December 6, the *Times* reported:

> The United States Navy, now in the midst of a record expansion program and recently placed on a war footing with full personnel manning the ships of three fleets has at this time no superior in the world, Secretary Knox stated tonight in rendering the annual report of the Navy Department. . . .
>
> "I am proud to report," Secretary Knox wrote, "that the American people may feel fully confident in their Navy. In my opinion, the loyalty, morale and technical ability of the personnel are without superior. On any comparable basis, the United States Navy is second to none."

If this boastful report had seen the light on any other day, probably it would not have been nearly so controversial. No one in his right mind could ask the secretary of the navy to spell out the exact truth about his forces in that time of "unlimited national emergency." This was one of the cases where the "right of the people to know" must bow to the right of the government to keep the nation's potential enemies guessing.

The exaggerations in Knox's annual report probably rose less from any deliberate misrepresentation on his part than from his ebullient, affectionate faith in the Navy. In effect, he was its super press agent. Not the least of his wartime contributions was his acting as a bridge between the sea service and the people.

Nevertheless, he did not have the full power that one might expect of his position. Roosevelt kept a particularly firm hand on the Navy

Department. Not only did he fancy himself as an expert on naval affairs, he was out of the habit of relying upon the secretary.[25] The then Secretary of the Navy Claude Swanson had spent all of 1936 in a naval hospital and was virtually invalided from a stroke. When his assistant secretary died in early 1936, Roosevelt appointed no successor. Admiral William H. Standley, destined to be a member of the Roberts Commission, functioned as acting secretary of the navy as well as Chief of Naval Operations for the rest of his tenure.

But Roosevelt kept Swanson in office. Standley attributed this to the President's "intense loyalty and his inability to fire anyone he really liked." Then, too, Roosevelt knew "that Swanson had absolutely no resources aside from his salary." Standley added on a less kindly note, "Furthermore, the President had an inflated opinion of his own knowledge of naval strategy and tactics and he much preferred to be his own Secretary of the Navy. With no Assistant Secretary of the Navy and Swanson so ill, FDR could run the Navy just about as he pleased."[26]

When Swanson died, Acting Secretary Charles A. Edison moved up. But he was rather deaf and Roosevelt had some difficulty in communicating with him. Moreover, the President considered Edison too readily influenced by his subordinates.[27] Thus, between circumstances, habit, and preference, to all intents and purposes Roosevelt had been his own secretary of the navy for years. A remark he made to Morgenthau on April 17, 1940, gave some idea of what the President expected of his appointee in that position. He was considering U.S. Ambassador to France William C. Bullitt "for Secretary of the Navy because he will do just what I tell him to."[28]

Knox accepted his second-fiddle role with complete good nature. He developed a warm admiration for Roosevelt and was proud to be in the cabinet. He wrote to the President:

> It is the finest thing that life has brought me—to help and serve you in this momentous crisis.
> With a full emergency decreed we can do those things that need to be done to bring a victory to the right.
> God bless you.[29]

Two circumstances make impossible as clear a view of Knox as is available of Stimson. To the best of our knowledge, he kept no diary, as did the secretary of war, and he died before the Army, Navy, and congressional inquiries were conducted. Nor was he called as a formal witness before the Roberts Commission. So no verbatim, official testimony is available from Knox in relation to Pearl Harbor.

His own investigation was more a one-man survey than a formal inquiry.[30] Since many in and out of the Navy genuinely feared a Japanese return engagement, it took courage to head for Pearl Harbor, as Knox did, on December 9, 1941. "Everyone admired Knox for coming out to Hawaii so soon after the attack," said Commander Harold M. "Beauty" Martin, who commanded Kaneohe Naval Air Station. "It was risky but the smart thing to do, to get first-hand information."[31]

The nation awaited his report impatiently, in the hope that it might "facilitate the publication of a more complete account of the losses suffered." The New York *Herald Tribune* hinted that the tide of opinion might have turned in Knox's favor:

> Considerable cloakroom talk has been heard of "heads falling" in high naval circles as a result of the Hawaiian raid. . . . Earlier the thought was freely expressed that Mr. Knox might be forced to resign. Today, however, a high official spokesman said that he did not think it at all likely that Mr. Knox's resignation would be forthcoming or asked for. . . .[32]

The Atlanta *Constitution* praised Knox's effort as "one of the finest pieces of reporting the war has produced since its beginning in 1939."[33] And indeed, considering the information available and the restrictions of wartime security, it was honest and surprisingly factual. It is the measure of Knox's integrity that despite his affinity for the sea service he made no attempt at whitewash.[34] Even Kimmel, almost neurotically suspicious of the Washington establishment, conceded, "Knox was not a professional Navy man but he was basically honest."[35]

Knox was neither a strategist nor a naval technician and never claimed to be. He once confided to a friend "that his conception of the job was to find out what the top admirals wanted 'and then to do my best to see that the job gets done as economically and efficiently as possible.' "[36] To a certain extent, that was not a bad summation of his duties, but Stimson for one believed that he carried the attitude to extremes. "Poor Knox is having a hard time with his admirals," he noted in June 1941.[37] During the autumn of 1942, the secretary of war fretted over Knox's "letting these damned admirals control his action."[38] On at least one occasion even Roosevelt, so biased in favor of the sea service, became, according to Hopkins, "quite out of patience with the Navy and out of patience with Knox for not controlling them better."[39]

Knox may have deferred too much to the admirals, and he may have overrated the Navy, but he never underrated the peril to the nation that the Axis presented. Addressing the Naval War College graduating class in Newport, Rhode Island, on May 16, 1941, he warned that "it is utterly impossible to exaggerate the mortal danger of our country in this moment of history."[40] And by the war's end the Navy had more than justified the most optimistic of his claims. He steered the U.S. Navy through exceedingly choppy seas before Midway to the very shores of success. It is one of the war's cruelties that he did not live to be figuratively or literally "on deck" when *Missouri* steamed triumphantly into Tokyo Bay. He suffered two heart attacks in April 1944, and died on the 28th.[41]

Stimson received much less public criticism than Knox in the period immediately following Pearl Harbor, although the Army on Oahu had been caught just as flatfooted as the Navy. Complaints against him usually were linked with those against Knox, almost as if Stimson-and-Knox were one composite entity. For example, the Denver *Post* editorialized:

> Why didn't Secretary of War Stimson and Secretary of the Navy Knox check up on Pearl Harbor defenses and find out whether their warnings had been heeded? Why didn't they ask Short and Kimmel to report on the precautionary steps taken to guard this outpost against attack? WHY DIDN'T THEY KNOW WHETHER THEY HAD ABLE AND EFFICIENT COMMANDERS IN CHARGE THERE? There must be some generals in the army and some admirals in the navy who haven't forgotten how to think and how to act.[42]

In its wholesale blast, the *New Republic* called for Stimson's dismissal only because "the tasks of the Secretary of War are exhausting and demand a tough, young man." Yet the magazine conceded, "Within the limits of his physical strength, he has done a wonderful job."[43] In fact, Stimson's most valuable assets as secretary of war were his long, varied experience in his country's service and his ripe judgment of men and affairs. These qualities are not the attributes of youth, however "tough"; they are gifts of the years.

When Roosevelt selected him as the second Republican member

of his cabinet, Stimson was already a hardy perennial in the garden of American statecraft. If he ever cherished ambitions of elective office, he had long since left them behind, but this scion of an old, well-to-do New York family had a strong sense of noblesse oblige. He had filled a number of high-level appointive posts, among them secretary of war for William Howard Taft, high commissioner of the Philippines for Calvin Coolidge, and secretary of state for Herbert Hoover. His excellent brain, sense of duty, and a world view much similar to Roosevelt's made him an inspired choice for secretary of war.

Nevertheless, although to a lesser extent than Knox, Stimson felt the impact of Roosevelt's interest in his domain. The President not only firmly believed in the principle of civilian control over the armed forces, he as assistant secretary of the navy had had his troubles with the Navy brass. So he wanted to keep a personal hand on the armed forces. Therefore, explained Elting E. Morison, one of Stimson's biographers, Roosevelt "would survey with special care the activities of the civilian Secretaries and . . . would make certain that no centers of real power developed within the two Departments that did not derive their strength directly from him."[44]

Stimson's chief complaint about Roosevelt was not his meddling but his invincible administrative sloppiness. He termed Roosevelt "the poorest administrator I have ever worked under in respect to the orderly procedure and routine of his performance."[45] He noted that Roosevelt's mind "does not follow easily a consecutive chain of thought . . . it is very much like chasing a vagrant beam of sunshine around a vacant room."[46] And Stimson had no use for "the group of cherubs that infest the White House"—the unofficial presidential favorites.[47]

On the other hand, at times Stimson rubbed Roosevelt the wrong way, particularly in the earlier days of his secretaryship. Berle recorded in his diary on September 19, 1940, that he had heard indirectly that Roosevelt had "expressed his terrific irritation with Henry Stimson. He asked Rex [Tugwell] to tell [Fiorello H.] La Guardia that shortly after January first he would make La Guardia Secretary of War."

About a month later, Louis Johnson, former assistant secretary of war, also told Berle of "rumors that Stimson is not going to last very long and that he is to be Secretary of War; but he has his fingers crossed." Berle considered Stimson's retirement "not improbable," but thought that La Guardia would receive the nod.[48]

The prospect of the "Little Flower," effervescent mayor of New York City, as head of the War Department, is intriguing to say the least. However, if Roosevelt ever seriously considered swapping Stimson for La Guardia it is less eloquent of any weakness of Stimson's than of Roosevelt's inner conflict—the calculating politician battling with the statesman of broad vision. As time went on, Roosevelt and Stimson developed mutual respect.

On October 27, 1940, Stimson summed up his position in his diary, and his definition would be difficult to better: "—a Republican doing non-partisan work for a Democratic President because it related to international affairs in which I agreed and sympathized with his position."

One reason why Stimson enjoyed a greater degree of administrative control than Knox was the relationship between him, the President, and Marshall. Stimson and his Chief of Staff worked in close harmony and mutual regard. A stronger character than his Navy opposite, Stark, Marshall was able to maintain his distance from Roosevelt and did not let their inevitable professional contacts ripen into anything like intimacy.*

Stimson assembled a remarkable group of colleagues: Assistant Secretaries Robert Patterson and John J. McCloy, and Assistant Secretary of War for Air Robert A. Lovett. These were men of high intelligence, experience, and vision. Then there was Harvey Bundy, a brainy man who "became the moving spirit in the development of scientific information in the Department and in the coordination of matters connected with the atom bomb." These officials understood their chief, placidly ignoring occasional ferocious outbursts of temper. The example of teamwork at high levels lifted War Department morale which had sunk into the cellar during the feud between Stimson's predecessor, Harry Woodring, and Woodring's assistant secretary, Louis Johnson.[49]

No matter who disliked Stimson, his judgment, or his policies, no one who knew him seriously questioned his probity and devotion to the public good as he saw it. He never wavered from his conviction that the earth had to be cleansed of the evils of Hitler and his Axis.

---

*For a discussion of the relationship between Roosevelt and Marshall see Chapter 14.

If the task ultimately required American participation in the war, so be it. "I think we've got pretty near the fork in the road where we shall have to consider something more than assistance to Great Britain short of war," he confided to his diary on January 21, 1941.[50]

Morgenstern claimed that Stimson and Knox "were war hawks who were brought by Roosevelt into his cabinet for no other purpose than to help him procure his incident."[51] In general, however, revisionists have been much kinder to Knox than to Stimson. Some of them would have one believe that Stimson was a co-conspirator with Roosevelt to hustle the United States into the war "through the back door." In particular, they have dragged Stimson over the coals for his diary item of November 25, 1941, wherein, recording a meeting of the War Council that day, he wrote, "The question was how we should maneuver them [the Japanese] into the position of firing the first shot without allowing too much danger to ourselves."[52]

Stimson's phraseology was sufficiently vague to leave the entry open to whatever meaning one wishes to ascribe to it. Thus the interpretations ran quite a gamut. At one end stood Morgenstern, who presented the picture of Roosevelt and his advisers, forked tails lashing, pitchforks at the ready. "They reckoned with cold detachment the risk of manipulating a delegated enemy into firing the first shot, and they forced 3,000 unsuspecting men at Pearl Harbor to accept that risk."[53]

In contrast, "The Secretary's language was, I think, hurried and elliptic," wrote Feis. "The Japanese force was the attacking force. If left to choose the place and time for the first encounter, the defense might suffer. But if any of the defenders fired the first shot, they might be regarded as attackers. The problem of keeping the roles straight—without paying heavily for it—was far from easy."[54]

To Richard N. Current, this "appeared to say, but surely did not mean, that if the *defense* were left to choose the place and time, the defense might suffer!" (Current's italics).[55] Obviously Feis meant that if the Japanese were able to do so, "the defense might suffer"—which was true, and which was what Roosevelt, Stimson, et al. wished to avoid.

In cases where a brief extract arouses controversy, it is well to pause and consider the context. On October 16, Stimson wrote much the same thing in his diary, but in that case his meaning was unmistakable:

The Japanese Cabinet has fallen and a new Cabinet will probably be chosen which will be much more anti-American. The Japanese Navy is beginning to talk almost as radically as the Japanese Army, and so we face the delicate question of the diplomatic fencing to be done so as to make sure that Japan was put into the wrong and made the first bad move—overt move.[56]

On November 6, Stimson recorded that Roosevelt "was trying to think of something which would give us further time."[57] But by November 25, the situation had changed for the worse, and not at American hands. The anti-Roosevelt position implied that had the United States not "maneuvered" the Japanese into firing the first shot, that shot would not have been fired at all. This flies in the face of the evidence. In fact, Hull, not Roosevelt or Stimson, spoke the key sentence of that conference of November 25: "The Japanese are in control of the situation, we are not. . . ."[58]

Japan's intention to fight to secure Southeast Asia was abundantly clear from Magic, from communications intelligence, and from the pronouncements of Japan's leaders and its press. Massive Japanese forces were already on the move. The alternative was no longer peace or war. The question was this: Would Japan fire the actual first shot and thus stand forth in its true role as the aggressor, or would the Allies, through mistaken policy, overzealousness, or accident of timing, allow themselves to be maneuvered into firing the first shot?

In any case, the discussion that took place at noon of November 25 was more interesting as an example of the American psychology of the time than for any major historical significance. There sat the President, his secretaries of state, war, and the navy, his Chief of Staff, and Chief of Naval Operations, all worrying over what was basically a question of public image. No such delicacy bothered the Japanese. They were out to take what they wanted, by diplomacy if possible, otherwise by force of arms. If world opinion did not like it, the world knew where it could go and take its opinion with it.

The "first shot" psychology was already under open discussion in regard to the Atlantic. According to Barth's public opinion report of November 27, 1941, the press appeared to acknowledge that "a state of war" existed in the Atlantic and reflected "a rather sharp impatience with Administration anxiety to prove the Nazis guilty of the first overt blow." He quoted the Lynchburg *News:* "Who fired the first shot that started this inevitable war? Who cares except it be the ever hopeful propagandists? The responsible nation is the nation that first threatened the security of the others."[59] That may well remain as a summation of the "first shot" situation in Asia as well as in Europe.

Stimson wanted his country to stand up and be counted, not to be booted into the conflict willy-nilly through the "back door." The United States could not "permanently be in a position of toolmakers for other nations to fight." He did not doubt that when the young men of the new generation understood the issues, they would answer the call to arms.[60] Along with this sense of duty, Stimson reasoned along practical lines: only a total commitment would rouse the nation to take its role seriously. As he explained to Roosevelt, "the frank position of war would help production very much and would help the psychology of the people."[61]

Another reason why Stimson believed the United States had to join the battle line was distrust of British military ability and fear of their overconfidence. He was far from happy to see American weapons doled out indiscriminately overseas. October 15, 1941, found him "rather discouraged" by a letter from Roosevelt asking for more four-engine bombers for Britain. "He is entirely in the hands of people who see only their side of the other nations and who are wedded to the idea that with our weapons they can win the war," Stimson burst out in his diary. "I am perfectly certain that they cannot, and perfectly certain that eventually we will have to fight and that this method of nibbling away at our store of weapons is reducing our weapons down to what I fear is a dangerous thing."

Marshall stressed to the congressional committee the difference between his own point of view and Stimson's:

> He was very much afraid . . . that we would find ourselves involved in the developing situation where our disadvantages would be so great that it would be quite fatal for us when the Japanese actually broke peace.
>
> He also felt keenly . . . that we must not go so far in delaying actions of a diplomatic nature as to sacrifice the honor of the country. He was deeply concerned about that. . . .
>
> So it was a question of resolving his views . . . and mine, which . . . were much more materialistic, . . . that we would get as much time as we could in order to make good the terrible deficiencies in our defensive arrangements.[62]

Current took Stimson to task for his attitude during the inquiries into the disaster. Although an investigation is not a prosecution, he termed Stimson "the combined prosecutor and witness," and criticized "his refusal to own up to a share of responsibility, his insistence on passing the buck to a subordinate in the field."[63]

This assessment ignored the nature of the secretaryship and that of command. The secretary was an administrative official, not a commander. If it were otherwise, the secretary would be merely a duplicatory, useless step between the President as Commander in Chief and the Chief of Staff.

Stimson was not "passing the buck"; he was acknowledging the realities of military life. Furthermore, he was much more concerned with protecting Marshall than himself. Even so, he had urged revelation of the Army Board's findings in the belief that eventually the truth would come out. What is more, convinced though he was of Short's primary responsibility, he wanted the general and Kimmel to be granted due process of court-martial as soon as the military situation permitted.[64]

Neither Stimson nor Knox can be blamed for the attack on Pearl Harbor or for the events leading up to it. They did not formulate foreign policy, nor were they experts in the military and naval fields respectively. For that matter, very few of their predecessors or successors could make the latter claim. And Stimson and Knox were far from incompetent, as their previous careers and wartime handling of their departments attests.

The War and Navy departments made mistakes in connection with Pearl Harbor, some of which will be discussed later. Stimson and Knox neglected to ride herd on Marshall and Stark, respectively, following dispatch of the warning messages of November 27.* They should have insisted upon receiving daily or at least very frequent periodic follow-ups on the situation from all addressees. Such reports would have revealed quickly the disastrous inconsistencies between what Washington had intended be done in the Hawaiian area and what Kimmel and Short actually did. The importance of Hawaii and the U.S. Pacific Fleet called for serious, judicious, and unremitting attention at the highest level.

Stimson could have come to the rescue when he read Short's ambiguous reply to the alerting message of November 27: "Report department alerted to prevent sabotage. Liaison with Navy reurad†

---

*See Appendix 3.

†The military abbreviation for "reference your radio."

four seven two twenty-seventh."[65] But Stimson testified that despite his "keen interest in the situation," Short's answer gave him "no intimation that the alert order against an enemy attack was not being carried out." He "had no idea that being 'alerted to prevent sabotage' was in any way an express or an implied denial of being alert against an attack by Japan's armed forces. The very purpose of a fortress such as Hawaii is to repel such an attack and Short was the commander of that fortress."

Furthermore, to Stimson, Short's statement of liaison with the Navy, "coupled with the fact that our message of November 27 had specifically directed reconnaissance, naturally gave the impression that the various reconnaissance and other defensive measures in which the cooperation of the Army and the Navy is necessary, were under way, and a proper alert was in effect."[66] What is more, Stimson told the Army Board that had it not been for his initials on Short's message he no longer would have "any memory of it at all."[67]

Knox could have made an invaluable contribution had he insisted that Kimmel be briefed on the Japanese situation as revealed by Magic and the Honolulu consular traffic when the admiral visited Washington in June 1941.[68] What this would have done for Kimmel and his command one can only guess. Perhaps it might have averted disaster, perhaps not. But the fact that the highest echelon in Washington allowed such a splendid opportunity to slip by must be regarded as a serious mistake.

Had the Navy Department provided Kimmel with a look at Magic and the messages from the Honolulu consulate revealing its reports on U.S. warships in harbor, Knox and Stimson could have arranged for Kimmel and Short to return to the capital in the autumn for similar briefings. Such periodic consultations in Washington for all major Army and Navy field commanders should have been standard procedure in those troubled days. Certainly both Kimmel and Short, or qualified representatives of their intelligence offices, should have been summoned to examine the intelligence files about Japan's espionage in Hawaii, and their opinions and suggestions solicited. Or couriers could have been dispatched periodically to Oahu with copies of the pertinent intercepts. These measures would have uncovered the fact that neither the Pacific Fleet nor the Hawaiian Department knew what was going on in that highly important field.

Stimson's diary and his testimony give no clue as to whether he did or did not believe that Hawaii had access to Magic. But the evidence indicates that Knox thought so. Stark certainly did,[69] and there is no reason to believe that Knox had any source of information that could override his CNO. Knox appreciated the importance of Kimmel's being in the know. A month before the attack, at the secretary's behest, Captain Frank E. Beatty, Knox's aide, asked Admiral Turner, director of War Plans, "Is Admiral Kimmel getting these 'magic' messages?" Turner replied warmly, "Beatty, of course he is. He has the same 'magic' setup we have here."[70] But Turner was dead wrong.

Altogether too many people in high places, both in Washington and Hawaii, took too much for granted in 1941. They made assumptions without going directly to the source. In the intricate web of verbosity spun around Pearl Harbor in 1941, nothing did more damage than the attitude behind the word *assume*. But Stimson and Knox were not the only assumers, and none of their mistakes relating to Pearl Harbor, which were errors of omission, can be considered as having a direct, crucial effect upon what happened at Hawaii on that dreadful Sunday.

CHAPTER 13

"Faults of Omission"

Role of Stark as CNO—Character and methods—Dependence upon Turner—Belief that Kimmel had Magic—Stark's letters to Kimmel—Danger of declaring mobilization—Warnings—Failure to act independently on December 7—Discontinuance of air reconnaissance in 1940—Relief as CNO

If Stimson and Knox had searched through the entire roster of officers of both services, they could not have found two more congenial teammates than the two they inherited from their predecessors. Stimson and Marshall had a natural affinity, as did Knox and Stark.*

The latter lacked Knox's dynamic qualities, but he had an equally attractive personality and was equally devoted to the Navy. Although not brilliant, Stark was a solid professional who understood the implications of the global issues facing the United States. He was firmly committed to the strategy that gave first priority to the defeat of Germany, and hence he hoped to ward off conflict with Japan as long as possible.

As CNO, he worked on a warm, friendly basis with his staff and the subordinate commanders. He wrote stacks of long, chatty letters to Kimmel and others in the field, usually addressing them by their first names or nicknames. Invariably he ended on a pleasant note, a favorite being "Keep cheerful." These letters, as well as his testimony before the various investigating bodies, project an image of outgoing humanity, of a man affectionate toward and touchingly loyal to his friends.

Admiral Richardson, who knew Stark well, described him as "very capable, hard working and one of the best-intentioned officers in the Navy, as well as one of the most likable." Nevertheless, he believed that Stark's capacities, "although marked, were not equal to those

*See page xxvi for simplified chart of Navy Department.

required by the Chief of Naval Operations billet, under conditions then existing."[1]

Undoubtedly Stark made certain errors of omission of an amazingly basic nature. As the Washington *Star* remarked upon publication of the Army and Navy reports, "the aspect of the Pearl Harbor disaster which is really surprising is that so many people failed to do either the obvious or the sensible things."[2]

It was no part of Stark's duties to spell out chapter and verse to Kimmel. "I would not have presumed, sitting at a desk in Washington, to tell him what to do with his fleet," Stark told the congressional committee. "There were many factors involved, of which he was the only person who had the knowledge, and once I had started . . . to give him directives, I would have been handling the fleet. That was not my job."[3]

Stark's job, as set forth in article 392 of Navy regulations, charged him, under the secretary of the navy, "with the operations of the fleet, with the preparation and readiness of plans for its use in war, and with the coordination of the functions of the Naval Establishment afloat, together with the determination of priorities relating to repair and overhaul of ships in commission or about to be commissioned."[4]

This totaled to a staggering responsibility, and the fact that Stark held the position speaks volumes for his record. But he did not exercise the firm leadership which his country had the right to expect of a CNO. Stimson considered Stark "a timid and ineffective man to be in the post he holds," "a weathercock," "a little bit cautious when it comes to a real crisis," and the weakest of Roosevelt's advisers.[5] On February 16, 1942, he wrote in his diary of his discouragement with the Navy's "lack of aggressiveness" and "the whole strategy of defense which has pervaded it." Later in the war, he noted "the harsh rule of discipline which the Navy imposes on its officers and which, in my opinion, where it deals with loss of ships, had tended to produce a good deal of cowardice in naval commanders and make them prefer safety in respect to their ships rather than to daring tactics."[6]

In plain terms, this meant, "If you lose your ship, you sink too, so don't risk it." Did Stark help instill this attitude in the Navy Department? Did Stark absorb a part of his caution from the atmosphere around him? Or did he become CNO because, among other reasons, he exemplified the spirit of the Navy in prewar days, at least on the top administrative level?

Whatever the verdict, one thing is obvious: Stark seemed to forget

that the operative word in his title was *chief*, while a "staff" is precisely
what the name implies—a means of support. A chief should be able
to rely upon his staff for factual data, informed and unbiased opinions
and estimates. The power to decide and to lead must remain in his
own hands. If he permits himself to fall under the domination of one
of his titular subordinates, he puts both himself and his subordinate
in a false position. There seems little doubt that Stark had come under
Admiral Turner's influence to a dangerous degree.

Stark's loyalty to Turner extended well beyond their term of service together. On October 15, 1962, revisional historian Harry Elmer
Barnes wrote to Stark concerning the arrangements for an interview
with historian Percy L. Greaves, Jr., and Admiral Moreell. Barnes
praised Admiral Ingersoll, who had been Stark's Assistant CNO, adding:

> I am firmly convinced that if he had been Director of War Plans
> instead of Admiral Turner, there would have been no surprise attack
> on Pearl Harbor. I am aware that this office carried no direct re-
> sponsibility for dealing with Naval Communications or Intelligence,
> but Admiral Turner entered into these areas in an aggressive and
> dominant manner and prevented Admiral [Leigh] Noyes* from tak-
> ing to you crucial messages dealing with the prospect of a Japanese
> surprise attack and killed really adequate warnings. . . . There is no
> doubt that had Kimmel received these warnings, he would have
> taken steps that would have "scared" the Japanese task force back
> to the Kuriles. This leads me to believe that Admiral Turner was
> actually more responsible than anyone else (surely in the Navy) for
> the Japanese surprise attack.[7]

Barnes may have believed precisely what he wrote, but if he also
hoped to gain Stark's favor and confidence by providing him with a
convenient whipping boy, he badly mistook his man. During his
interview with Greaves, Stark leaped to Turner's defense. Turner was
"one of the best men ever. . . . He knew the Japanese, had spent
time there. He knew Nomura and was invaluable. There were not
enough superlatives in the dictionary for Turner. He worked well
with the British." And Stark wanted to know where Barnes got his
ideas. Stark "admitted Turner was wrong on Russia and on knowing

---

*Director of Naval Communications.

that Kimmel had magic but the latter probably was not his fault." Ingersoll, too, "had a high opinion of Turner."[8]

Nonetheless, Stark's reliance upon Turner in a matter outside the province of War Plans resulted in one of the most deadly of all the many assumptions that clouded the Pearl Harbor picture—that Pearl Harbor had "Magic," the means to decrypt "Purple" and other codes in use in Japan's diplomatic system of communications.* In the words of the congressional committee, "No justification for this impression existed in fact apart from the failure of these officers to inform themselves adequately concerning Navy establishments."[9]

Stark had only to consult his own Magic decrypting and decoding personnel to determine whether or not Kimmel had the same facilities. A few moments' chat with Ingersoll could have cleared up Stark's misconception, because "Ingersoll always understood P.H. could not decode Purple."[10] Instead, as Stark testified, "Well, when Admiral Turner told me he [Kimmel] could do it I did not consider it necessary to go further."[11] So Stark accepted Turner's word instead of going to the source—Noyes, the Director of Communications.

The congressional committee jumped on both Stark and Turner for failing to ascertain the truth. It accused the Navy Department officials, among others, of being "so obsessed by an executive complex that they could not besmirch their dignities by 'stooping' to determine what was going on, or more especially what was not going on, in their organizations." The committee pointed out specifically that "in a period of over 6 months, with relations between the United States and Japan mounting in tenseness and approaching a crisis, neither of these ranking officers determined for a fact whether the fleet was receiving this [Magic] information."[12]

This incident illustrates Stark's undue dependence upon Turner, as well as his failure to demand and enforce proper coordination between his staff officers.† Had he done so, "you would not have the ludicrous situation of Admiral Turner saying that he thought Hawaii was getting this stuff based on what Admiral Noyes told him. What a silly thing that is!" exclaimed Lieutenant Colonel Henry C. Clausen,

---

*"Purple" was the name given to Japan's top diplomatic code. "Magic" referred to the means whereby the United States decoded Purple and other Japanese diplomatic codes. Frequently the messages thus decoded were referred to as "Magic."
†For further discussion of Turner's role, see Chapters 16 and 17.

who conducted the Army's follow-up investigation of Pearl Harbor. Well might he ask, as he did, "What kind of a set-up is that?"[13]

This misunderstanding, along with an overriding desire to conceal the breaking of Japan's diplomatic code, led to the failure to send Kimmel information gleaned through that source except in isolated occasions. In later years, Richardson was very severe toward Stark in this regard. Pointing out that the CNO had assured both himself when CinCUS and his successor Kimmel that they would be kept posted on all pertinent matters, Richardson wrote, "I consider 'Betty' Stark, in failure to ensure that Kimmel was furnished with all the information available from the breaking of Japanese despatches, to have been to a marked degree professionally negligent in carrying out his duties as Chief of Naval Operations."[14]

Kimmel understood that the Navy Department had to balance "security as against getting the information where it will do the most good." But he believed that "information should be used, taking all the precautions." No sensible individual can quarrel with that, nor with Kimmel's inability to see why Washington could not have sent him the appropriate material by courier.[15] At the very least, Stark could have written one of his "Dear Mustapha"* letters or sent Kimmel an official dispatch, saying, "Let me have your comments on message Number so-and-so" (reference by number alone was permissible from the standpoint of security). Such a step might have rung a bell in Kimmel's mind and eventually clarified Stark's misunderstanding concerning his supposed access to Magic.

"It is a prime obligation of Command to keep subordinate commanders, particularly those in distant areas, constantly supplied with information," stated the Navy Court of Inquiry unequivocally.[16] Regardless of Stark's belief that Kimmel had his own sources of Magic intercepts, they were sufficiently important to warrant sending certain key messages to Hawaii with an inquiry as to what the man on the spot thought of them. Had Stark's headquarters done so, the first such exchange would have brought to light the fact that this information was news to Kimmel. Admiral Ernest J. King, Commander in Chief, United States Fleet, conceded that there was some merit in Stark's contention "that he considered it undesirable to send Ad-

---

*Stark often addressed Kimmel as "Mustapha," a pun on the names of Kimmel and Mustapha Kemal, the Turkish leader.

miral Kimmel these despatches" because of security. Still, "it was equally his responsibility to give Admiral Kimmel a general picture of the information contained in these messages."[17]

The long personal friendship and fine professional relationship between Kimmel and Stark foundered on the rock of this misunderstanding. Stark told Donald G. Brownlow, "I never knew why except that I think somebody got him to believe, and that is totally wrong, that the President had given me orders not to send things." Evidently Kimmel reached the conclusion, during a visit with Stark in April 1942, that the latter "was holding something out" on him. Perhaps on that occasion Stark had indeed kept back one thing—his belief that Kimmel had erred in at least one vital respect. Later Stark told Brownlow "that Hawaii was the only area where the [war warning] message did not have the right effect."[18] Being so kindhearted, and knowing Kimmel so well, probably he would not have pointed this out to his old friend, then suffering acutely. One fears that Kimmel was already allowing hatred, bitterness, and self-pity—however understandable—to distort his judgment.

In later years, Stark continued to support the claim that the intercepts gave no positive clue to the attack. "I have explored this question in my mind hundreds of times," he told a reporter. And he concluded that he had sent Kimmel all he needed to keep him as well informed "as we were in Washington."[19] Stark also emphasized to the congressional committee that his belief that "Kimmel could read certain dispatches . . . did not influence me in the slightest regarding what I sent."[20] Many years later, Stark insisted to Greaves that "he distilled his thoughts and sent the information just as he would have done if he had not thought Kimmel was reading it."[21]

Obviously, however, an officer writing to a subordinate whom he believes to be familiar with the material will select and phrase differently from one who thinks his correspondent is uninformed. Stark's statement that he had clued in Kimmel adequately was largely true in relation to the Purple traffic. It was not true of the consular exchanges, particularly the "bomb plot" series, which divided Pearl Harbor into specific areas for reporting purposes, and which contained data of direct concern to Kimmel.

The CinCUS knew that the Japanese consulate was spying on his ships. But he did not know the extent and gravity of this espionage, especially the tactical type revealed by the "bomb plot" exchanges.

However, it would be grossly unfair to blame Stark for the failure to send Kimmel this information. The fault lay with his staff members who worked directly with the material and failed to recognize its meaning and importance.* In fact, Stark told the congressional committee that he had "no recollection of having seen those particular messages." He might have seen them, but he believed he had not.[22]

In a closely related area, Stark erred when he succumbed to Turner's pressure and permitted War Plans to take over the evaluation of intelligence.[23] Whether retention of this important function in Naval Intelligence would have had any appreciable effect upon the situation on December 7, 1941, must remain speculative. In view of Turner's firm conviction that Japan was going to strike the Soviet Union, his personal estimate, at least, shot wide of the mark. One thing is about as certain as anything can be: Had War Plans added up the information from Intelligence and deduced an attack on the Fleet at Pearl Harbor, this would have come to light during the investigations. Of course, in the War Department evaluation remained in G-2 (Intelligence) which did not make the correct deduction from the information either. But the situation was not quite analogous, because the men serving under General Miles in G-2 were not naval officers thoroughly conversant with the language, organization, personalities, and psychology of the Japanese Navy.

In justice to Stark, one must point out that he was constantly hacking his way through the paper jungle of officialdom. For, as Forrestal observed in regard to the Navy Court of Inquiry:

> Within the Navy itself, the organization was such as to submerge the Chief of Naval Operations in a multiplicity of detail pertaining to the procurement and material programs incidental to the rapid expansion of the Navy. This precluded him from giving to war plans and operations the undivided and continued attention which experience has shown they require, and tended to dull his perception of the critical significance of events.[24]

Under the circumstances, it would be natural for Stark to view the War Plans–Intelligence feud as just another headquarters power struggle to be settled as quickly as possible. Whoever did the job, it was, so to speak, all in the family.

Stark's preoccupations may help account for certain discrepancies.

---

*For further discussion of this important subject, see Chapter 16.

Knox's letter of January 24, 1941, prepared in War Plans, warned that if war came Japan might initiate hostilities with an attack on the Fleet or the base at Pearl Harbor. Six days later, another Navy Department letter followed—this one prepared in Intelligence—placing "no credence" in rumors of just such an attack.[25] The congressional committee gave the Navy the benefit of the doubt in this instance, because the former missive related to possible future conflict, while the latter estimated a rumor "based on the then present disposition and employment of forces."[26]

Stark was as well-meaning and hard-working in his way as Kimmel himself. Sundays found him sending off his long letters to Kimmel. One of these may have contributed to Kimmel's state of mind which led to his failure to act promptly upon the "war warning" of November 27.* On October 16, 1941, Stark's office officially informed Kimmel, King, and Admiral Thomas C. Hart, Commander in Chief, U.S. Asiatic Fleet, that the Konoye Cabinet had resigned and that Japan might hit both the United States and Britain. But the next day, in a personal letter to Kimmel, Stark cited his dispatch, then added, "Personally I do not believe the Japs are going to sail into us and the message I sent you merely stated the 'possibility.' "[27]

Another letter of Stark's helped lull Vice Admiral William S. Pye, Kimmel's commander of battleships, for one, into a sense of false security. This was Stark's missive to Kimmel of November 25, which was not received until some days after the "war warning." In his letter, Stark admitted that he did not know what the United States planned to do—it might be "nothing" or "anything."[28] This impressed Pye and "probably those others who saw it, that the option was going to rest with us."[29] Thus Stark helped foster the illusion that Uncle Sam was in the driver's seat long after the Japanese had seized the initiative.

The congressional committee "regarded as an extremely dangerous practice for the Chief of Naval Operations to express an opinion on a personal basis to an outpost commander which has the inevitable effect of tempering the import of an official dispatch." But they let Stark down softly because "some of the most vital intelligence and orders relating to Japan were supplied Hawaii during November and December of 1941."[30]

King hinted that Stark suffered from misdirection, pointing out

*See Appendix 3.

that "the most important United States possessions in the Pacific were the Philippine Islands and the Hawaiian Islands." So Stark's attention "should have been centered on those two places, as the Pacific situation became more acute."[31] To prove that he had given plenty of attention to those locations, Stark could have flourished virtual reams of his correspondence with Kimmel and Hart. He also could have stressed, as he did to the congressional committee,

> we had long and often thought of an attack on Pearl Harbor as a possibility and something which might some day be pulled. Our fleet exercises always contained an exercise of an attack in which . . . the attacking force wanted to get in, if it could, and the defending force, of course, would first want to get the attacking forces carriers. I mean, it has been much discussed.[32]

Senator Walter F. George of Georgia asked Stark if there had been any "lapse of interest" in "the possibility and strong, maybe, probability of an air attack on Pearl Harbor" after 1940 and early 1941. "I wouldn't say there was a lapse of interest," replied Stark. "We initially pointed out what we thought was necessary and we took steps to correct the deficiencies as far as we could." Moreover, "the war plans covered what we had to give them" and the matériel was "made available substantially as the war plans stated." He added, "We had received and O.K.'d what we thought was a very splendid arrangement out there for meeting the situation and from then on, except to follow up on matériel, there was no particular mention, as I recall about the continued danger. We had set it forth."[33]

Nor did he think Kimmel had relaxed his vigilance. "I had no reason to believe . . . that the concern shown by the responsible officers there over a possible air attack on Pearl Harbor had diminished in any respect during 1941. I am certain that my concern had not."[34]

Admiral Richardson faulted Stark rather than Kimmel for the Pacific Fleet's lack of alertness.

> The Navy had been expecting and planning for a Japanese surprise attack for many years. However, the subordinates in a military organization can not stand with their arms raised in protective alertness forever. Some superior has to ring a bell that moves the subordinate members of the organization, trained, ready, and expecting a fight,

but in the corners of their fighting ring, out to the center of the ring. That bell was never rung by Kimmel's superiors in Washington.[35]

Richardson's last sentence is questionable, to say the least. If a message from the top echelon beginning, "This despatch is to be considered a war warning" did not qualify as an alarm bell, it is difficult to imagine what would have brought Oahu's defenders out of their corners. Moreover, the whole thesis that the Commander in Chief of the nation's forces afloat needed a push from Washington to read the signs of the times and be ready for trouble is an insult to the Navy's intelligence.

The idea also implied an isolation which did not exist. Kimmel and his advisers, located in a sophisticated community at an important crossroads of communications, were excellently placed to do a little evaluating of their own. Far from depending solely upon Washington to explain the Far Eastern situation, the Navy on Oahu furnished valuable raw data upon which Stark's staff relied in making estimates. For example, the information from Commander Joseph J. Rochefort's Combat Intelligence Unit was invaluable in keeping tabs on the location of Japanese ships.[36]

Stark believed that, as of early December, Washington could do no more to alert the U.S. Fleet. "In the few days immediately preceding 7 December, Admiral Ingersoll . . . , Admiral Turner . . . and I went over the information we had sent to the fleet commanders," he testified. "We were all of the opinion that everything we could do had been done to get them ready for war, and that we had sent them sufficient information and directives."[37] One notes the absence of Wilkinson, director of Naval Intelligence, from the top consultants.

Later the suggestion arose that the Navy should have clarified the situation by ordering mobilization. "If Washington didn't see fit to proclaim a mobilization, the officers naturally believed the situation could not be as serious as represented," wrote David Lawrence. "It is not the business of the commander in chief of the Pacific Fleet to mobilize. These are orders which Washington is expected to send out."[38]

Rear Admiral Claude C. Bloch, who in 1941 was Commandant, Fourteenth Naval District, cited in his own defense the fact that the Navy Department had not designated M-Day. Thus he suggested that the Navy should have ordered full fleet mobilization if it wanted an all-out alert.[39]* But the warning messages of November 27 had been intended to put the Pacific Fleet as well as the Hawaiian Department on full alert. Ingersoll explained to the Navy Court that one reason why mobilization was not ordered before December 7 was because "the Fleet was mobilized as much as it could be."[40] Stark testified to the same inquiry that he "considered the Navy at that time practically mobilized."[41]

Furthermore, an overt, saber-rattling mobilization was exactly what Washington wished to avoid. The United States was taking every precaution lest the Japanese seize upon just such an act as an excuse to declare war. Not without cause, for, in Ingersoll's words, "mobilization has always been recognized as one of the steps preliminary to war."[42] While the conciliatory policy toward Japan handicapped the armed forces, under the circumstances mobilization would have been going too far. If the commanders on Oahu had been sufficiently keyed to the urgencies of the moment, such a drastic measure should not have been necessary.

One cannot accuse the Navy Department of improper attention in the preparation of the "war warning" of November 27. Few naval dispatches received such careful consideration at such high level. But somehow the message did not convey its intended meaning to the Navy on Oahu. Perhaps, paradoxically, its authors had been on too high a plateau, too close to the problem, too steeped in the varied aspects of what was happening on the diplomatic and military fronts. To its dispatchers, the message was clear and precise; they forgot that its recipients would read it in the context of their local situation.

Stark had an opportunity to rectify the error on the morning of December 7, following receipt of the "one o'clock" message—the intercept of Tokyo's orders to the Japanese Embassy to present Japan's final note at one o'clock Washington time on December 7. A gaudy account of Stark's actions on that morning appeared in a letter from Lieutenant Commander Charles C. Hiles to Barnes. Hiles stated that "the originator must not be mentioned by name"; however, he credited "LFS"—which stood for Laurence F. Safford, who was chief of the Security Section of Naval Communications in 1941. According to this story, at a party held on "the first anniversary of Pearl Harbor,"

*See Chapter 24.

Commander McCollum, who had been chief of the Far Eastern Section of Naval Intelligence, at the time of the attack, told this tale to a number of his colleagues:

> Mac was chased out of Stark's office twice. The first time he merely recommended a war warning be sent but the second time he brought in a written message that required only Stark's initials. Wilkinson stood by like a dummy.
>
> "You get out of my office, young man, and don't you dare to come back with any more *fantastic* messages like this for me to sign," shouted Stark. But Mac had the last word, according to Rochefort: Mac said "aye aye, Sir!" as he went out the door.
>
> . . . Mac got highly indignant when his audience told him he was suffering from "Potomac Fever." "God damn it, I am telling you exactly what happened—and you people won't believe me. That's why the Pacific Fleet was taken by surprise. *Stark refused to send any warning. [Italics in original.]*

Safford had not been present, but he claimed to have heard the story from three eyewitnesses.[43] Despite Safford's genius in his own line, cryptology, he was not the world's most reliable witness when he stepped out of his area of direct knowledge. In this instance, his story conflicted with McCollum's sworn testimony. In the first place, McCollum told the congressional committee that he had not discussed the incident of the proposed warning "since October or November of 1942," which seems to rule out December of that year. McCollum and Wilkinson did go to Stark's office on the morning of December 7, 1941, but far from standing by "like a dummy," Wilkinson was the one who proposed sending a warning message.[44]

If Safford's story had any validity, McCollum had an excellent opportunity to place it on the record when he appeared before the investigation conducted by Vice Admiral H. Kent Hewitt as a follow-up to the Navy Court of Inquiry. One reason for that investigation had been to secure McCollum's evidence, and he testified before Hewitt for the entire session of May 15, 1945. At that time he placed the discussion between Stark and Marshall of their proposed warning message somewhat earlier in the day than was the consensus. "Admiral Stark talked over the telephone, I think, with the Chief of Staff of the Army, who presently came over with Colonel Bratton," stated McCollum; ". . . by 10 o'clock that morning we were given to understand that a warning message had been sent to the Commander-in-Chief, Pacific Fleet, via Army channels."[45]

McCollum amended this during the congressional inquiry, when Senator Ferguson took him over the Hewitt transcript of this incident line by line. To Ferguson, McCollum said that he had been mistaken both as to Marshall's presence and the time. Marshall had visited Stark in the afternoon, not the morning, of December 7. Moreover, McCollum's timing was "off by as much as an hour." He believed the messages went out "sometime between 11 and noon." He had not had the opportunity to read his testimony before Hewitt and correct it at the time.[46]

To neither investigation did McCollum so much as hint that he had been kicked out of Stark's office. If he had hesitated to testify against Stark to a fellow admiral, no such consideration could have inhibited him at the congressional hearings. He was on the stand for a full day's session on January 30, 1946, and Ferguson for one gave him every opportunity to sound off about the morning of December 7.

The picture of Stark chasing a well-meaning junior out of his office with shouts is unbelievable. Such action would be totally out of character. Yet the story has a hauntingly familiar look, like a well-known face glimpsed through rippling water. It harked back, not to the events of December 7, but to those of about two days earlier. At that time McCollum had prepared a warning message for the Pacific Fleet, but Turner blocked it, believing that enough warnings had already gone out.[47]

Stark made a bad enough mistake on the morning of December 7 without being cast as the subject of myths. Marshall phoned Stark, suggesting that Stark join him in his message to the Hawaiian Department about the delivery of the Japanese note to Hull at 1300. But Stark thought that he had sent so many warnings he hesitated to add another. Moreover, he believed that Kimmel already had the decrypted Japanese message. Within minutes Stark changed his mind, but instead of sending his own independent dispatch he called Marshall back with the request that he include a request to inform the Navy in his message to Short, which Marshall did.[48]

The message read: "Japanese are presenting at one pm eastern standard time today what amounts to an ultimatum also they are under orders to destroy their code machine immediately. Just what significance the hour set may have we do not know but be on alert accordingly. Inform naval authorities of this communication. Marshall."[49]

For a routine message applicable to both services, this procedure would have been commendable economy. But in such a grave matter, Stark should have sent a Navy message to duplicate and thereby to stress Marshall's dispatch. Better yet, he could have telephoned Kimmel personally. Admiral Dyer emphasized that the CNO should have called Kimmel on the spot and said to him, "This is the information that I have and you can interpret it as you like." Dyer considered Stark's failure to do so a major error.[50] Certainly Stark should not have depended on Marshall to do his work for him. In fact, Stark movingly testified to the Navy Court about his self-examination to determine whether he might have been "derelict" or "might have omitted something." The only such incident he could recall was his not having paralleled the Marshall message.[51]

Forrestal did not accept protection of "Magic" as a valid explanation for the Navy Department's "failure to transmit to Admiral Kimmel information which would have created in him the sense of tension and awareness indicated by the sequence of information available to the Navy Department." In particular Forrestal did not consider this security "an adequate explanation for failure to use the most obvious and quickest method" of warning Pearl Harbor on December 6 and 7, namely, the telephone. He believed the latter failure "a reflection on the mental habit of both the Army and the Navy rather than the necessity for security."[52] He made this opinion official in his Fourth Endorsement of August 13, 1945, to the Navy and Hewitt reports: "An acute sensitivity to the tautness of the situation would have dictated at least a plain language telephone communication to Admiral Kimmel, which might have provided a warning sufficient to bring about some material reduction in damage inflicted by the Japanese attack."[53]

All in all, Richardson believed that Stark's errors of omission "were far more important derelictions than those of any of his subordinates." This harsh judgment stranded Richardson high and dry on an uncomfortable spot. He had known Stark well for years and held him "in high esteem." So he could not conceive "how he could have treated Kimmel as he did, unless he was acting under the mistaken impression that he owed no loyalty except upward, or what I think is more likely, his failure to obey his natural impulse was due to influences or possibly direct orders from above."

With this conclusion Richardson sought refuge in the anti-Roosevelt theory. "I am impelled to believe that sometime prior to December 7 the President had directed that only Marshall could send any warning message to the Hawaiian area. I do not know this to be a fact and I cannot prove it."[54] Nor can anyone else.

How Richardson could read Stark's testimony with an open mind and doubt the CNO's loyalty to his subordinates is difficult to see. But Richardson's memoirs reveal two major biases: a pervasive, arrogant pride in the Navy, and a bitter resentment toward Roosevelt for having dared to relieve him as CinCUS.[55] So the idea of Stark hamstrung by the President and the Army's Chief of Staff relieved Richardson from the necessity of assigning to a fellow admiral more than token blame for the errors contributing to the disaster at Pearl Harbor. It did not seem to occur to him, or to the others who accepted that thesis, that this attitude did Stark no favor. If he failed to phone Kimmel through an honest error of judgment, Stark was merely a man who made a regrettable mistake. But if, as they postulated, he did not phone because he supinely yielded to an unlawful order, he would be beneath contempt.

Actually, a combination of circumstances, including atmospheric conditions, conspired to delay Marshall's warning to Short. Had Stark sent off his own by Navy communications channels, or had he telephoned Kimmel, the information might have arrived in Hawaii before the attack. But whether such a message from Stark would have made any appreciable difference no one can say. Stark and Marshall could not warn of what they did not expect, hence the Marshall dispatch did not state or even imply that the Japanese would attack Pearl Harbor at or near 1300 EST. Nevertheless, had the information reached Oahu in good time, some intelligence officer there might have worked out a time schedule that would have shown that 1300 EST would be 0730 local time, and drawn the correct conclusion therefrom. In that case, receipt of the message might have saved many lives, not to mention ships, aircraft, and other property. At the very least, its arrival at headquarters of the Hawaiian Department and of the U.S. Pacific Fleet before the attack would have cleared Washington of any possible charge of duplicity on this point, and spared Stark and Marshall many unpleasant accusations. However, this chain of possible events must remain in the realm of speculation.

The Hewitt inquiry had its own ideas of what such an advance tip-off, "even as little as one half hour," might have accomplished:

(a) Ships' anti-aircraft batteries would have been fully manned and ready. It is to be noted that the anti-aircraft fire was more effective against the subsequent attacks than the initial air strike.

(b) Enemy character of the approaching planes would have been immediately appreciated and they would have been engaged at once.

(c) The maximum condition of damage control readiness would have been set, thus facilitating the isolation of damage received.

(d) Many planes could have been in the air, in readiness.

(e) Ground dispersal of planes could have been improved.[56]

Hewitt may have been entirely correct, but like all of history's might-have-beens, his were possible but unprovable.

Richardson had another complaint against Stark. Throughout 1940, the CinCUS carried out long-range air reconnaissance against pressure from Washington. According to Richardson, the Navy Department "continued to accentuate the overriding nature of the flight training requirements and to deprecate war-training tasks involving security of the Fleet and the fighting efficiency of the aircraft in Fleet air units." Again, in December 1940, Richardson learned from his war plans officer, Commander Vincent Murphy, who was in Washington at the time, that Stark had said that "wartime measures of security" were not as yet required and that "continuous air patrols" were not necessary. So the requirement for long-range patrol was removed from Richardson's security plan. Richardson conceded, however, that "with the very modest naval long-range patrol aircraft resources available, it was obviously onlypartially effective."[57]

Richardson stated that, as a result of Stark's attitude, "some of the responsibility for the failure to have daily long-range air reconnaissance as part of the daily routine in 1941 at Pearl Harbor lies directly on the doorstep of the CNO. Having been told by the Commander-in-Chief that daily long-range reconnaissance would be carried out, he said it 'was not yet necessary.' "[58]

Nevertheless, Stark only advised—he did not order discontinuance of all aerial reconnaissance. What is more to the point, the fact that the Fleet halted long-range reconnaissance in December 1940 is no reason why Kimmel could not have reinstituted such measures in late November and early December 1941 when Japanese-American relations had deteriorated to the point where he received a "war warning."

In general, Stark escaped the more venomous attentions of the revisionists. Still, he was not universally admired. Rear Admiral James H. Shoemaker declared, "The general opinion in the Navy was that Stark was a weak sister."[59] Captain Walter J. East recalled hearing criticism of Stark in Hawaii after the disaster, and East did not think much of the admiral: "Stark just stayed alive and kept his nose clean."[60] Safford held an even more devastating opinion. He termed Stark "the poorest excuse for an admiral ever to attain that rank."[61]

Personal bias considerably colored these judgments. In the cases of Shoemaker and East, one finds the inclination of those stationed on Oahu to blame Washington for their troubles, and on Safford's part, his conviction that the top brass had deliberately withheld pertinent information from Kimmel and Short.*

But two admirals who worked closely with Stark gave a totally different assessment. "I knew him well, I was completely devoted to him," wrote Vice Admiral Charles Wellborn, Jr., who had been Stark's administrative aide.

> He was a thorough gentleman of the highest standards, completely devoted and dedicated to his country and his service. He came as close as anyone I ever knew to being the ideal Naval Officer. . . .
>
> He was rarely critical of others and used the carrot rather than the stick most of the time. He used to tell me, "You catch more bees with honey than you do with vinegar." This was combined, however, with great strength of character and determination that was not as outwardly apparent as was his velvet glove.[62]

Vice Admiral W. R. Smedberg III, Stark's former flag secretary, stressed that Stark was not a yes-man. He cited the occasion when Rear Admiral Joseph K. Taussig's testimony on April 22, 1940, before the Senate Naval Affairs Committee created a sensation. "I cannot see how we can ultimately prevent being drawn into war on account of the Far Eastern situation," said Taussig. "We need be under no delusions as to the aims and policies of Japan."[63]

Taussig's frankness upset the President, who demanded that Stark require him "to turn in his suit." But Stark fought for Taussig at the risk of his own job, and eventually Roosevelt cooled off.[64]

---

*See Chapter 19.

In March 1942, Roosevelt transferred Stark to London as commander of U.S. Naval Forces in Europe. King later claimed the transfer puzzled him:

> As Chief of Naval Operations, Stark's position in relation to the Pearl Harbor attack was less responsible than that of General Marshall as Chief of Staff of the Army. . . . The failure of the Army, and especially of the Air Corps, to discharge their responsibilities was—to King's disgust—carefully glossed over during the investigation. King has never been able to reconcile the difference in the President's treatment of Admiral Stark and General Marshall in regard to Pearl Harbor. . . .[65]

It was not true that the Roberts Commission had "glossed over" the Army's part in the tragedy. That body acknowledged the Army's responsibility to defend Hawaii and the Fleet in harbor. It charged Short, no less than Kimmel, with "dereliction of duty." The Hawaiian Air Force came under Short, and the commission dealt with it in that light.

If King's memoirs accurately describe his attitude at the time of the Roberts report in January 1942, and of Stark's subsequent transfer, it was in direct contrast to his thoughts concerning Stark when the Navy Court submitted its report in October 1944. King endorsed it in part:

> 6. The derelictions on the part of Admiral Stark and Admiral Kimmel were faults of omission rather than faults of commission. In the case in question, they indicate lack of the superior judgment necessary for exercising command commensurate with their rank and their assigned duties, rather than culpable inefficiency.
>
> 7. Since trial by general court martial is not warranted by the evidence adduced, appropriate administration action would appear to be the relegation of both of these officers to positions in which lack of superior judgment may not result in future errors.[66]

In Forrestal's Fourth Endorsement to the Navy and Hewitt reports, August 13, 1945, he directed:

> Both of these officers [Stark and Kimmel] having been retired, appropriate action should be taken to insure that neither of them will be recalled to active duty in the future for any position in which the exercise of superior judgment may be necessary. . . .
>
> . . . Admiral Harold R. Stark, USN (Retired) shall not hold any

position in the United States Navy which requires the exercise of superior judgment.[67]

According to King's memoirs, he relieved Stark of his European command only at Forrestal's insistence, and softened the blow by recommending Stark for the Distinguished Service Medal.[68] On the other hand, Stimson gained the impression from Forrestal on November 23, 1944, that "apparently Admiral King has been the one who has been standing for stiff treatment."[69] A clue to these discrepancies may rest in an interview Stark had with Greaves in the winter of 1962. At that time, Stark said that King had told him "he has signed the NCI endorsement without reading it."[70] If true, this speaks ill for King's own judgment. To complicate the picture further, on July 14, 1948, King wrote to John L. Sullivan, then secretary of the navy:

> Considering that Admiral Stark had occupied the most important post in European waters, by order of President Roosevelt, for the better part of three years immediately preceding the date of the endorsement, that he remained in that post during the entire war . . . and that his performance of duty in high office during that period was in all respects outstanding, the suggestion that he be relegated to a subordinate position in which superior judgment would not be required seems to me now to have been singularly inappropriate. . . .

King asked permission to change the record to reflect a more accurate opinion:

> 6. The derelictions on the part of Admiral Stark and Admiral Kimmel were those of omission rather than of commission—errors of judgment as distinguished from culpable inefficiency.
> 7. Since the evidence adduced warrants neither trail [sic] by general court martial nor punishment in any form, but since their usefulness in the billets assigned was impaired by the course of events, I am of the opinion that their assignment to other duties, then and now, represents appropriate administrative action.[71]

Two points leap from the pages of this letter. First, King's revision of the two paragraphs in question seemed to reflect a belief that if Kimmel had received another chance, as did Stark, he could have distinguished himself likewise. Second, King's wording hints that Stark's change of duty was "administrative action" taken because of his part in the events of December 7. Yet it is far from certain that

Pearl Harbor was the sole or even a principal factor in Roosevelt's sending Stark to London. Altogether, King's role in *l'affaire* Stark is ambiguous.

Stark's transfer was only one top-level adjustment in the Navy at the time. Following the Pearl Harbor tragedy, the Navy separated the two functions of Commander in Chief, United States Fleet, and Commander in Chief, U.S. Pacific Fleet, both of which Kimmel had carried. On December 17, 1941, Admiral Chester W. Nimitz became CinCPAC, and three days later King became CinCUS. As such, King was directly responsible to the President, with his office in Washington. Roosevelt may have realized that the combination of King and Nimitz might be able to prosecute the naval war in the Pacific more vigorously if Stark were out of the picture. *Time* also noted that certain elements had been dissatisfied with Stark:

> Most young "war-hawk" naval officers, especially aviators, were sure Stark was not their man. Flying men called him a "battleship Admiral," had bitter words to say about the need for offensive spirit where Navy plans were made. "Betty" Stark also sat as Chief of the Army-Navy Joint Board [of strategy], and some Army men were not too happy about that.[72]

Whatever circumstances demanded a new hand at the Navy's helm, the shift was hard on Stark, who in many ways had been an excellent CNO. As Robert E. Sherwood so truly wrote, "his contribution to the formation of grand strategy was immeasurable."[73] Louis Morton called Stark's Plan Dog "perhaps the most important single document in the development of World War II strategy.[74]*

Stark was a firm supporter of the "Germany First" policy, and of the thesis that the United States would have to fight its battles outside the Western Hemisphere instead of waiting until the Axis was battering down the gates. The general attitude of the Navy Department in 1941 was summed up in Wellborn's words, "the war might quickly and irretrievably be lost in the Atlantic, whereas initial reverses in the Pacific might later be retrievable."[75]

One might wonder with King why, if Stark's mistakes merited his removal from the top job, the same did not apply to Marshall, who made his share of errors as well. But Roosevelt needed Marshall

---

*See Chapter 10.

imperatively. The President had no one of comparable skill and strength who was not needed more urgently in a combat command. His actions were logical, set in the landscape of the times. Yet they resulted in a double standard on the military heights: for Stark, a demotion that hustled him overseas; for Marshall, retention as Chief of Staff with ever-increasing prestige and power.

CHAPTER 14

"Outside of Effective Contact"

Marshall as Chief of Staff—Character and testimony—"One o'clock" message—Events of December 7 in Washington—Notification to Hawaii—Should have telephoned—Whereabouts on evening of December 6—Accusations of revisionists—Too tight a rein on staff—Relationship with Roosevelt

Stark's opposite number, the Army's Chief of Staff, General George C. Marshall, was, like Stark, a professional of vast experience and dedication. But his personality was much more forceful and his mind more incisive. Many thought him a cold-blooded man who always exercised supreme self-control. His wife, however, described his temper as "like a bolt of lightning."[1] According to one Army legend, a young lieutenant summoned into his presence suffered a heart attack. His cold blue eyes could terrify junior officers.[2] He possessed an icy disdain for incompetence and drove his subordinates and himself in his quest for the absolute. For him, the peak was the normal level of operation.*

He kept George C. Marshall the man severely segregated from General George C. Marshall, Chief of Staff. He ran the Army on a strictly impersonal basis. "I cannot afford the luxury of sentiment, mine must be cold logic," he said. "Sentiment is for others."[3] Thus he handled all official correspondence, even to such longtime acquaintances as Short, on formal lines. He sent no personal letters to Short or any other subordinate commander. In fact, he rarely wrote at all to any theater commander, to avoid possible confusion between such letters and war plans. He testified that this policy had "rather given offense."[4]

Such was Marshall's dignity and reserve that, according to General Albert C. Wedemeyer, no one but General "Vinegar Joe" Stilwell

*See page xxvii for simplified chart of War Department.

ever called him "George."[5] That is not quite the case; others did, but only a few.[6]

The role of this awesome figure in the Pearl Harbor drama requires close scrutiny. In the first place, the Army was responsible for the protection of that installation and its ships, hence the question of why the Army failed so signally needs careful examination of all levels of command. In the second place, some revisionists have seized upon Marshall as a target of abuse second only to Roosevelt.

Some personal antipathy may be involved. Like all men of such powerful personality, Marshall aroused either steadfast devotion or sharp aversion. For example, Rochefort stated frankly that he would like to blame Marshall for Pearl Harbor, but admitted that this was due to his personal dislike of the general.[7]

Another reason for suspicion of Marshall might be his style in testifying. The appropriate transcripts suggest that the general's many gifts did not include the ability to speak extemporaneously in a clear, concise manner. Expressions such as "I do not recall" and "I have no recollection" occur frequently. But, of course, "the gift of the gab" is no guarantee of honesty or good faith.

It is important to recall that Marshall viewed Pearl Harbor from a much broader perspective than did those who questioned him or probed the record. At least for the time necessary to investigate or write, the inquirers and the authors were absorbed with one area only—Pearl Harbor. They have saturated themselves in it; they had facts, questions, speculations at their fingertips. They could not remember that for others Pearl Harbor was not the most important, absorbing question in the world.

To a certain extent, Kimmel and Short were in this position. Pearl Harbor was the Great Divide of their lives, thus every aspect of the event was thoroughly programmed into their minds. Then, too, each of them came to the inquiries prepared with statements, documents, aides-mémoire, and personnel to help them. In contrast, Marshall came to the hearings almost cold. So it was not too surprising that at times his testimony was rather fuzzy.

Pearl Harbor was a long way from being the center of his existence. Between the event and the inquiries lay the progress of World War II, through which he brilliantly led the U.S. Army and to which he gave his undivided attention. He reminded the congressional committee on December 12, 1945, that they were "bringing up things to me that have been, to a large extent, rubbed out by 4 years of global war. I have not investigated these things to refresh my memory until the past few days, and so I think it is not unduly remarkable that I would not remember the detailed conversations and the frequency of conferences."[8]

Marshall was not the type of man to brood over the dead past. Pearl Harbor had been a tragedy, but it was over. He could not waste time looking back, distracting his mind and sapping his mental and moral strength with vain regrets over what might have been. So he rang down the curtain upon Pearl Harbor. "That was water over the dam," he told the Navy Court of Inquiry.[9]

Perhaps he was not entirely candid. Marshall was a reticent man. "In all my contacts with him in the War Department . . . ," wrote Wedemeyer, "Marshall always seemed preoccupied. There was a reserve or hint of some mysterious, unseen but always present, force which had first call on his deeper thoughts." Again, Wedemeyer reminisced, "I know of many acts of kindness and thoughtfulness on his part . . . but he kept everyone at arm's length."[10]

Wedemeyer may have put his finger on the root of the seizure upon Marshall as a possible co-villain of the piece. Self-containment and that disturbing projection of an inner force are not popular qualities. Yet few people would care to have their every word, thought, and deed of a specific period dissected under the spotlight of publicity. In such circumstances only a class A saint could afford the truth, the whole truth, and nothing but the truth. The reservation may not cover guilty knowledge; most likely it represents a threat to the self-image—a mistaken judgment, an ill-considered word, a foolish action—which the witness hugs to himself. These little withholdings, obvious to a sensitive observer, clutter up every investigation.

To reject the Marshall-as-black-hat thesis is not necessarily to imply that he is beyond criticism. Like most of the brass involved with the American side of the Pearl Harbor attack, he made his share of mistakes, at least one of which was potentially serious. This was his handling of the famous "one o'clock" message from Foreign Minister Togo to Nomura, establishing an exact hour for delivery of Japan's formal reply to the Hull Note.

As soon as Marshall read this intercept, he prepared a message to the four Army commands in the Pacific area: the Philippines, the West Coast, Panama, and Hawaii. He instructed that these be dispatched "at once by the fastest safe means."[11] Normally, the Signal Center could have handled the assignment swiftly, but on that particular morning, by the fate that seemed to hover over the United States on December 7, atmospheric conditions cut off communications with Hawaii. So the chief of the Signal Center, Lieutenant Colonel Edward F. French—not Marshall—decided to send the message by Western Union to San Francisco, where it would be transferred to RCA for delivery to Honolulu.[12]

French considered using the Navy channels. But, he explained, the dispatch "would have to be delivered from Pearl Harbor to Fort Shafter, and knowing the Navy condition is the same as ours, my judgment was the fastest delivery for that message was by the commercial means."[13] It so happened that events in Hawaii delayed delivery until after the attack. By some oversight, the message was not marked priority. It reached the RCA office in Honolulu at 0733 local time—already three minutes past the Japanese deadline of 1300 EST. Approximately half an hour later the Japanese struck, and between the ensuing confusion, roadblocks, and massive traffic jams, the delivery boy—who happened to be a Japanese-American—did not reach Fort Shafter until 1145.[14]

The holdup at both ends was beyond Marshall's control; however, one must question his judgment in using the Signal Center at all, except as a means of confirmation. The unique nature of Japan's "one o'clock" message dictated the utmost speed in notifying the Pacific commands—and that meant by telephone.

If Colonel French had informed Marshall of the radio difficulties being encountered that morning, the Chief of Staff might have decided to risk the scrambler telephone. He told the congressional committee that he regarded the "one o'clock" message "as of great significance." He added, "It was therefore my responsibility, in my opinion, to get that out to all the various commanders in the Pacific as quickly as possible."[15] On the other hand, he still might have decided to use the tried-and-true telegraph facilities. In those days, transocean phone calls could take "quite a long time" to complete the connection.[16] But he stated that even if he had phoned, he would have called the Philippines first and the Panama Canal second, those being the most vulnerable areas.[17]

Then, too, Marshall did not trust the security of the scrambler phone. However, he indicated to the congressional committee that this did not necessarily affect his decision not to use it on December 7. At the time of his questioning, he could not "determine definitely what was going on in my head at that particular moment."[18] He said that, in military terminology, the transocean phone was "private and not secret. A casual person listening in would not know what we were talking about. The person intent and with the facilities for breaking through in your communications can do it. It was long after we were in the war before we were able to install a scrambler system . . . that was felt to be secret."[19]

So Marshall reasoned thus: "I felt if they [the Japanese] knew exactly what we were doing, which they would have ascertained from the telephone message, that there were two factors involved: One was the explanation of why we took that action, which was the receipt of a magic message, the only way we could obtain that, and the other was the fact that we were alerting the garrisons which they could construe as a hostile act."[20]

This second reason was a sad commentary on how far the United States authorities were prepared to go in order to avoid stepping on Japanese toes. Tokyo could have no valid objection to whatever action Washington might take on American soil to defend American interests.

Toland implied that Marshall's first reason was spurious: "Seven months earlier a dozen intercepted messages had revealed that the Japanese feared their top code had been broken by the United States."[21] The implication was that the breaking of Purple was no longer a secret, so Marshall could not legitimately cite the security of Magic as a reason for not using the telephone. Some messages had been exchanged between the Foreign Ministry and Nomura in May 1941 concerning possible compromise of their diplomatic code, but the flurry faded away without result. The Japanese continued to use their Purple code without alteration, and did so not only up to Pearl Harbor day but throughout the war.[22]

Curtis B. Dall, the President's son-in-law, implied that Marshall's failure to telephone the Hawaiian Department was deliberate. He claimed that the Chief of Staff's "slothful warning messages, sent over slow channels, were merely a ghastly gesture, timed to arrive after the 'surprise' attack, as a face-saving device."[23] But Theobald conceded that even if Marshall had phoned, he arrived in his office too late for the information to be of much use to Oahu.[24]

Nor did Colonel Robert H. Dunlop, Short's adjutant general, think that such a call would have changed history. For he believed that the Army on Oahu lacked sufficient matériel and "was not adequately prepared for war."[25] True, Hawaii did not have all the anti-aircraft guns and other supplies Short had requested. In fact, rare indeed is the commander who ever admits he has enough matériel. As Hart acknowledged to the congressional committee, "I think I had the common failing of all commanders in chief. You always want more."[26]

But the crucial point is this: What Short did have was not ready when the attack came. His testimony as to what prompt delivery of Marshall's message would have meant to him is rather ambivalent. He told the Roberts Commission:

> The thing that would have affected me more than the other matter was the fact that they had ordered their code machines destroyed, because to us that means just one thing: that they are going into an entirely new phase and that they want to be perfectly sure that the code will not be broken for a minimum time, say of three or four days. That would have been extremely significant to me, the code machine, much more significant than just the ultimatum.

He insisted that if he had received this message some three hours before the attack, he would have gone on "at least an alert against an air attack" and probably "against a complete attack."[27]

With the passage of time, Short became more specific. He told the congressional committee that two items—the "bomb plot" and the Marshall message—were "the really definite things that pointed to Pearl Harbor." He also claimed that the latter dispatch contained an additional indication: "the fact that the delivery of the message was at 1 P.M., Washington time, which would be shortly after dawn in Honolulu."[28]

These assessments smacked strongly of hindsight. Short did not draw any conclusion concerning the timing in his testimony to the Roberts Commission. Moreover, he had read only a threat of sabotage into the much more specific warning of November 27.* So one can only speculate as to how much effect early delivery would have had upon the Hawaiian Department's readiness. But what if any action Short took would have been his responsibility. The fact that Marshall

---

*See Chapter 21.

did not telephone him left the ball in Marshall's court, and also left the Chief of Staff vulnerable to adverse speculation.

In any case, Marshall would have been well advised to have reported to his office earlier than he did on that historic Sunday. In December, because of the "short days and cold," he arrived at the War Department on week days at about 0730, leaving between 1630 and 1700. He rode in the evenings before dinner. On Sundays his habit was "to have breakfast about 8 and then ride after that and then go to the War Department."[29] Congressman Keefe of the congressional committee pointed out that the so-called "pilot message," alerting the Japanese Embassy that the fourteen-part dispatch would be forthcoming, was available to Marshall on Saturday, December 6:

> This placed on him an obligation to make sure he would promptly receive the subsequent information which the Pilot message indicated would be soon forthcoming. He did not do so. In placing himself outside of effective contact with his subordinates for several hours on Sunday morning, he failed to exercise the care and diligence which his position required.[30]

But Marshall testified that he went to bed on December 6 and arose the next morning "without any knowledge that the Japs were sending in any reply at all." His subordinates were not blameless in this connection. The Chief of Staff explained to the congressional committee, "The orders then—and that continued throughout the war—were if anything came up at night . . . on which it was necessary I should act that night, it should be brought to my attention immediately."[31] Thus, anyone who thought the Japanese message of sufficient importance could have called Marshall's quarters, insisted that the Chief of Staff be awakened, then brought him the thirteen parts available at that time. Colonel Rufus S. Bratton, chief of the Far East Section of G-2, who carried the messages to those on the Army's Magic list, blamed himself for the mistake.[32] Not only did Marshall not see the thirteen parts on December 6, he did not realize until after the event that the "larger portion" of this message had come through that night.[33]

An even more compelling reason should have brought Marshall to his desk at or near his normal duty time that Sunday: The Japanese were destroying their codes. This act was "considered to be the immediate preliminary to war" and Marshall "so considered it."[34] So did everyone else of any importance in the Washington scheme of things. For example, Welles testified that, to him, the order from Tokyo to the Washington embassy ordering the destruction of codes signified "that the last stage had been reached." He believed that this action meant "a rupture of diplomatic relations at the very least and under the circumstances then existing the probability of war."[35] Under such conditions, Marshall belonged in his office or in the closest possible touch with it.

The Chief of Staff's inability to prove his whereabouts on the night of December 6 aroused the darkest suspicion in certain quarters. During the congressional hearings, Gearhart kept insisting that where Marshall and Stark were on the night of the sixth was "the greatest mystery of all."[36]

Certain parties attempted to charge Marshall with discreditable activities the night before Pearl Harbor. One rumor which Barnes claimed came to him "gratuitously and presumably on good authority" was this: "According to this yarn, Marshall spent that Saturday night in a hotel with a WAC . . . a very prominent Wac at that!"[37] To accomplish that feat, Marshall would have had to transport himself into the future. The bill authorizing the WAAC, forerunner of the WAC (Women's Army Corps), did not become law until May 14, 1942.

Safford's version was less lurid. "General Marshall was guest of honor at the military reunion of WWI Veterans held at the University Club at 16th & M Sts NW and was toasted as 'the next president of the US.' "[38] Safford was not there, so could not speak from personal knowledge. He based his premise upon a brief item in the Washington *Times-Herald* headed "Marshall Goes to Vet Reunion." This article told of a get-together of veterans of the First Infantry Company, ROTC, which included dinner at the University Club which Marshall "attended and [where he] was given a vote of confidence."[39]

It seems clear that Marshall did not attend the reunion in question. No other Washington paper carried the story. Marshall himself was fairly certain that he had spent that evening at home. He and his wife "were leading a rather monastic life."[40] Mrs. Marshall was convalescing from several broken ribs, and the Chief of Staff "had no dinner engagements of any kind between the 1st of November and the 7th of December, except one family dinner." He explained meticulously to the congressional committee, "So, all the evidence, in my own mind, short of absolute knowledge of the matter, is that I was home, as was customary."

Of one thing he was sure: The President did not telephone him on December 6 as he had Stark. "That is a positive answer." Marshall was also "absolutely certain" that he did not attend any meeting at the White House that night.[41] In fact, he had "no recollection of any contact" with Roosevelt on the sixth, or of talking with him on the morning of December 7 before the attack.[42]

Unfortunately, one cannot produce the firm corroboration of Marshall's account needed to nail down his schedule of the morning of December 7 once and for all. "I went to bed early Saturday night," he later told his goddaughter. "I was very tired. It had been a strenuous week. I slept through the night, and when I woke up, I was thankful that no news had come in that was sufficiently urgent to call me to the office in the middle of the night." He presumed that he arose about 0800, breakfasted, and "probably looked at the Sunday papers" before beginning his ride. But he did not recall precisely when he mounted and took off.[43]

If Marshall's original timetable of his activities on the morning of December 7 could be accepted as gospel, one would find him commencing his ride at 0830, galloping along his usual route for fifty minutes, then taking ten minutes to shower and dress. This quick change would make him ready to leave within five or ten minutes after he finished dressing for the brief spin by car to the War Department—a process involving not more than another quarter hour. Thus he should have arrived at his office at 1000 at the latest.[44] However, Marshall later told the congressional committee, "Discussions with the orderlies and also evidence that I had seen of other individuals leads me purely by induction and not by definite memory to think that I must have ridden later."[45] This throws the timetable askew. It is fairly certain that Marshall did not reach his office before 11:25. Bratton saw him as soon as he arrived, and specifically noted the time.[46]

Legends sprang up as to the general's whereabouts that morning. One story with an appealing Cincinnatus touch relates that Marshall was sawing a limb from a tree. This incident actually took place at his home at Leesburg, Virginia, "one Saturday early in September." According to another tale, Marshall was one of a party at National

Airport welcoming the new Russian ambassador, Maxim Litvinov. A check of newspaper accounts and pictures of this ceremony reveals no trace of Marshall.[47]

One cannot logically blame Marshall for being vague about his activities on December 6–7 without pointing out that Stark was no less so as to the morning of December 7 and more so concerning the night of December 6. About the latter, Stark had no independent recollection and had to rely on the memory of a friend.[48]* He thought he might have reached his office on December 7 at about 1030 because that was his usual time of arrival on Sundays. Others stated that he was at the Navy Department before that time. His "only really outstanding recollection" was the discussion of the "one o'clock" message, because "thinking the whole thing over afterwards that message is the only thing of that morning that stands out like a beacon of light."[49]

It is unfortunate that the Roberts Commission did not pin down the activities of Stark and Marshall on those critical days while events were still fresh in their memories and, if necessary, compare notes with Roosevelt himself. But no one could have foreseen the web of suspicion and slander that Roosevelt's political enemies would weave from the natural failure of two exceedingly busy men to recall their every move on those two specific days.

Marshall was by no means blameless in this matter of his whereabouts during the morning hours of December 7, 1941. There was no reason why he should have foregone his customary Sunday horseback ride, but in view of the tense international situation, he could have ridden earlier, to allow time for a full, or nearly full, day at his office. Moreover, he should have left strict instructions with his orderly that he was to be summoned immediately for any official phone call. He should have been easily located because he customarily took "the only available loop to ride in" for a canter of about fifty minutes' duration.[50]

More important, Marshall's absence from his office should not have made so much difference. One of the touchstones of a first-class chief is how well his organization functions in his absence. When it falls apart or halts pending his return, something is seriously wrong. Whereas Stark did not keep his staff under sufficiently close control, Marshall erred in the other direction. The Army Board noted that

---

*The congressional inquiry determined that he had been at the National Theater.

none of his three deputies* "was given the secret information concerning the known Jap intentions." What is more:

> Complete authority to act in General Marshall's absence does not seem to have been given to any one subordinate. Had there been an officer either with authority or with courage to act on the information that was in the War Department on the evening of December 6, and had he sent a message to Short, Hawaii should have been fully alerted.[51]

Marshall's reluctance to delegate authority was an administrative weakness. The general's tight hand on the reins resulted in most unfortunate delays on December 6 and 7, especially in sending the warning message to the four Pacific commands, including Hawaii. One of Marshall's biographers, Forrest C. Pogue, attempted to blame Marshall's subordinates, pointing out that the "war warning" of November 27 went out in Marshall's absence.

> Now, with the exception of General Marshall, every individual in Washington on the distribution list for MAGIC intercepts had seen the fourteen-part message and was in his office thirty minutes or more before the Chief of Staff arrived. It is absurd to suggest that history had to stand still until he turned his horse's head back to Fort Myer or took a quick shower.[52]

A number of things were wrong with this reasoning. In the first place, Stimson was actively involved in the "war warning" incident, and the secretary of war did not require the Chief of Staff's approval to go ahead. In the second, Marshall was on maneuvers in North Carolina on that occasion, while on December 7 he was within a short drive of his office and expected momentarily. In the third, it was not the fourteen-part message that triggered the agitation on that Saturday morning, but the "one o'clock" message. The fault was with Marshall, not his staff, that he had created a climate wherein they did not feel free to act without his approval while he was in the metropolitan Washington area.

Once Marshall reached his office on December 7, however, "he worked feverishly" to get out the last-minute warning. Despite the

---

*Marshall's three deputy chiefs of staff were Major Generals William Bryden, general administration and ground forces; Richard C. Moore, armed forces and supply; Henry H. Arnold, air.

gravity of the hour, he "did not call the President." Nevertheless, he was "greatly disturbed."[53]

No doubt he would have been even more disturbed had he known what some future writers would make of his absence from his office during those morning hours of December 7:

> The facts, as far as they have been uncovered in years of search, lead to this conclusion [wrote Barnes]: Marshall's primary interest and responsibility from Saturday afternoon until noon on Sunday . . . was to prevent any warning information about the imminent attack from being sent to Short and Kimmel. There is no reasonable doubt that he kept in contact with Roosevelt to get advice and directions as to how to handle matters. . . . Whether he did this by telephone or by going to the White House is not known. . . .
>
> [Marshall] knew he had all possible army sources well bottled up, but he could not be absolutely sure about the navy . . . there was real danger that Stark's natural impulse to do the decent thing for his country and Kimmel might overcome the restraint put on him by Roosevelt's order to Marshall that the navy send nothing to Pearl Harbor without Marshall's approval. . . .
>
> Hence, on Sunday morning, Marshall, naturally, would first go right to Stark's office at once to restrain any of Stark's humane and patriotic personal impulses. . . .

After painting this sickening picture, Barnes reminded his readers "that these apparently devious blackout operations of Marshall and Stark were wholly due to Roosevelt's orders, and the responsibility for them is entirely his."[54]

Why should the President have issued any such directive? According to the revisionist thesis, Roosevelt knew that the Japanese task force was headed for Hawaii, and wanted to ensure that the attack took place, to provide Roosevelt with the key to the "back door" to World War II. Therefore, Theobald insisted, "the possibility of causing the cancellation of the surprise attack must have been the sole reason for not sending word to Hawaii on that Sunday morning."[55]*

All the revisionist highways, however misty and convoluted, led to Public Demon Number One in the White House. Theobald assured

---

*Theobald had served under Kimmel, admired him, and assisted him before the Roberts Commission.

his readers, "Free to act, it is an absolute certainty that both Admiral Stark and General Marshall would have done everything in their power to prevent such an attack." He added unctuously, "It may surprise the reader to be told that none of this reasoning is intended as criticism of the principal actors." Then he launched into a beguiling explanation of how they could be accessories before the fact to mass murder without incurring any criticism:

> General Marshall and Admiral Stark, as heads of the Army and Navy, could do nothing throughout but obey the orders of the Nation's Commander-in-Chief, unless they preferred to ask to be relieved from their posts of duty. In that case, it would have devolved upon their successors to carry out the orders. In this connection, it must be understood that officers of the Army and Navy are trained throughout their professional lives to obey implicitly every lawful order, no matter how distasteful it may be to them. Rigid adherence to this maxim is vital to that cohesion of action which is the primary requisite of the military art.[56]

The sophistry, "I might as well do it because if I don't somebody else will," is a moss-covered refuge of moral cowardice. And the question of how far a member of the military was obligated in carrying out a lawful order was one which has plagued mankind's conscience since the beginning of recorded history. But such an order as Theobald postulated would not in fact be "lawful." And nothing whatsoever in military law or tradition obligates an officer to obey an unlawful order.

Safford, no admirer of either Marshall or Stark, confirmed this fact, and reminded Hiles, "*If* FDR had given last minute instructions to withhold warnings to P.H. and Manilla [*sic*], it would have been an unlawful order; in that case GCM and HRS would have obeyed this order at their own risk, and with full responsibility for their own actions" (Safford's italics).[57] Had the President directed Marshall and Stark thus to connive at wholesale murder and destruction, they would have been perfectly justified in telling Roosevelt where he could go.

Moreover, there was an alternative between request for relief from duty and obedience to orders—resignation from the service. As a civilian, Marshall would have been free to warn Hawaii and air the alleged conspiracy.

Granted that the President could not command Marshall's cooperation in an illegal action, what other levers might Roosevelt have pressed? An appeal to Marshall's strategic sense? Hardly! The Chief of Staff had consistently pleaded for time to build up his Army to fighting strength. "I know that we, meaning Admiral Stark and myself, made it very clear, I think, to the Secretary of State, that it was of the utmost importance to utilize every resource to delay so long as possible any outbreak in the Pacific," he testified.[58] On December 7, 1941, the U.S. Army was not ready to tackle the combined Axis powers, and no one knew it better than Marshall.

The promise of power and position? Marshall already held the Army's top job. A promotion? He wore four stars, and could achieve nothing further along that line, for the five-star rank had not yet been created. Moreover, when it was proposed to establish the ranks of Field Marshal and Admiral of the Fleet for Marshall and King, respectively, the general "was dead against any such promotion. He said it would destroy all his influence both with the Congress and with the people, and he said that it really all came about from the lower Admirals of the Navy Department forcing this upon King and Knox and upon the President."[59]

Nor would Marshall have joined Roosevelt in a plot against Pearl Harbor out of friendship or partisanship. He had never been one of the President's intimates, and avoided party politics so sedulously that he did not even vote.[60] There existed between Roosevelt and his Chief of Staff what another Marshall biographer, Leonard Mosley, called "a curiously cool relationship which would thaw slowly as the years went by and take a long time to grow warm."[61]

This aloofness emanated principally from Marshall. Possibly the general's instinct for self-preservation kept him from being swept into the vortex of Roosevelt's charm and becoming, in the process, less than himself. Perhaps he recoiled from the air of condescension which lay beneath the President's affability and which so irritated former Secretary of State Dean Acheson: "Many reveled in apparent admission to an inner circle. I did not; and General Marshall did not, the General for more worthy reasons than I. He objected, as he said, because it gave a false impression of his intimacy with the President. To me it was patronizing and humiliating."[62]

James M. Burns has written of Marshall: "Toward the President he was reserved even to the point of not laughing at his jokes; his passion for prudent planning and administrative order . . . ran counter to Roosevelt's ways, but the two men got along well in their work, partly because of Hopkins's mediation."[63]

In his three-volume biography of Marshall, Pogue expanded the theme:

> [Marshall] . . . felt that he had to hold the President at a calculated distance in order to keep his own freedom of action. For instance, he always refused to go to see Roosevelt at Warm Springs or Hyde Park for private conversations. "I found informal conversations with the President would get you into trouble," he said later. "He would talk over something informally at the dinner table and you had trouble disagreeing without creating embarrassment. So I never went. I was in Hyde Park for the first time at his funeral."[64]

Obviously Marshall took it upon himself to set the pace in his relations with his Commander in Chief. One senses the distance in their correspondence on file in the Roosevelt Library at Hyde Park. Occasionally a Presidential letter addressed Marshall as "George," but the Chief of Staff meticulously signed the most informal memorandum with his full signature, its small, left-slanted letters telling their own story of a basically private personality. In contrast, Stark signed himself "Betty" in his big, right-leaning, extroverted hand.[64] That Marshall held off the President speaks more for his ego than for his sense of protocol. For it was not a modest man who kept the President of the United States at arm's length. All told, if any man in the country was invulnerable to pressure from Roosevelt, that man was George C. Marshall.

CHAPTER 15

"A Finger of Blame"

Marshall (continued) . . . Army Board criticisms—JAG's refutations—"War warning" should have been sufficient—Failure to follow up on warnings—Short's reply—Focus on Southeast Asia—Overreliance on B-17—Misconception regarding intelligence available to Hawaiian Department—Misinterpretation of "bomb plot" series—Legends of destruction of documents and cover-up.

Criticism of Marshall was not confined to those who hoped to see Roosevelt firmly established as responsible for the tragedy of December 7, 1941. Unfavorable comments which had to be taken seriously came from the Army's own board of inquiry. Marshall had given instructions that no friend of his be appointed to this board, and evidently his orders were honored.[1] Henry C. Clausen, who served as the board's assistant recorder, noted that all three members had some reason to dislike the Chief of Staff.[2] In their report, they divided blame between Short, Marshall, and Brigadier General Leonard T. Gerow, chief of Marshall's War Plans Division. Short fared better than Marshall, Gerow worse.*

Specifically, the Army Board charged Marshall with a number of mistakes, aside from his overall responsibility as Chief of Staff:

a. Failure to advise his Deputy Chiefs of Staff . . . of the critical situation in the Pacific so that they might act intelligently for him in his absence.

b. Failure to keep General Short fully informed as to the international situation and the probable outbreak of war at any time.

c. The delay in getting to General Short the important information reaching Washington on the evening of December 6 and the morning of December 7.

---

*For a discussion of Gerow's place in the Pearl Harbor story, see Chapter 18.

d. Noting without taking action the sabotage message of Short which presumptively was on his desk on the morning of November 28, 1941.

e. His admitted lack of knowledge of the condition of readiness of the Hawaiian Command during the period of November 8 to December 7, 1941.[3]

When informed of the Board's report, Marshall said to Stimson "that he thought his usefulness to the Army had been destroyed." But Stimson "told him that was nonsense, to forget it." The secretary of war charged up Marshall's reaction to modesty,[4] but who can doubt that wounded pride was another factor in this plunge in the general's morale?

Marshall lacked the theatrical self-assurance of MacArthur, who saw himself always as the star of a majestic drama, or the mystical self-centeredness of Major General George S. Patton, who could picture himself reincarnated age upon age, each time as a warrior. Nevertheless, one cannot reach the top rung of a major nation's military ladder without a healthy streak of ego. Throughout World War II, Marshall guided the U.S. Army through the most massive conflict in its history, which by the time the Army Board met seemed well on the way to victory, at least in Europe. Year by year Marshall's reputation grew until it attained towering status.

He inspired awe, as witness the affectionate respect, almost hero worship, which Stimson accorded his Chief of Staff: "Marshall towers above everybody else in the strength of his character and in the wisdom and tactfulness of his handling of himself and handling of his plans. He is by far the biggest man that I have met in Washington."[5]

Congress, including the "loyal opposition," trusted Marshall to an unusual degree. For example, when he was being considered as Supreme Allied Commander in Europe, the ranking Republican members of the Military Affairs Committee descended upon Stimson to protest the general's removal from Washington. Not only did they rely upon him themselves, but "they were able to carry controversial matters through with their colleagues if they could say that the measure in question had the approval of Marshall."[6]

It was scarcely surprising that such a man as Marshall should rather resent the necessity to explain himself to an Army board composed of his juniors, let alone swallow its criticism.

When the board's report was made public in August 1945, Stimson backed up his Chief of Staff loyally, calling the board's criticisms of him "entirely unjustified," a judgment in which President Truman concurred "wholeheartedly."[7] Later Stimson expressed outrage over these strictures: "The Army's own Pearl Harbor Board so far misconceived the nature of military responsibility that it pointed a finger of blame at General Marshall himself, on the curious theory that the Chief of Staff is directly at fault whenever one of his subordinate staff officers fails to do a thorough job."[8]

Yet such is the very essence of the military command and staff establishment. The Washington *Evening Star* was nearer the truth when it wrote upon publication of the Army and Navy reports, "these criticisms are trivial when balanced against the enormity of the tasks and responsibilities which had devolved upon General Marshall in the summer and fall of 1941. At the same time, it is difficult to agree that they are 'entirely unjustified.' "[9]

Mosley took Marshall sharply to task for his actions shortly before Pearl Harbor:

> Yet if ever negligence was displayed by a senior officer, surely General Marshall showed it during the ten days before America's descent into World War II. From the beginning of the crisis to its climax, he was guilty of failure: failure to send a competent commander to Hawaii; failure to check that the islands' defenses were in order; failure to make sure that his warning messages had got through. What sort of picker of men was he that all along the line senior members of his staff let him down?[10]

To his credit, Marshall acknowledged that he "was responsible for the actions of the General Staff throughout on large matters and on small matters." But he added in extenuation that it was very difficult "to take each thing in its turn and give it exactly the attention that it had merited."[11] And this was most certainly true, considering the enormous responsibility on his shoulders in 1941.

In a memorandum for Stimson commenting upon the Army Board's report, Major General Myron C. Cramer, The Judge Advocate General, declared that in his opinion "none of the Board's conclusions as to General Marshall are justified."[12] But in his explanatory comments he did not touch upon the first of the board's strictures, confining himself to those pertaining directly to Marshall's actions vis-à-vis Short. Actually, the board made a valid point in its first instance.

On firmer ground, Cramer refuted the charge that Marshall had failed to keep Short informed as to the status of Japanese-American relations and the probable impending outbreak of war. He pointed out that the board's statement overlooked the fact that the War Department's warning of November 27 "pictured the Japanese–United States situation accurately as it appeared from the information available to the War Department at that time and up until 7 December."[13] He wrote with remorseless logic:

> Short as a military commander was required to take the information contained in this radio from his Chief of Staff as true and not in the critical spirit of awaiting further information or proof of what he was told. General Marshall was not in the position of carrying on a negotiation with a foreign plenipotentiary but was telling a subordinate what the situation was for his guidance.

Cramer also believed that the message of November 27 should be considered in the light of other dispatches, including those from the Navy Department, to which Short had access. "Thus, Short was fully advised of the tenseness of the Japanese situation, of the requirement that he act in accordance with the clear instructions from the Chief of Staff to prepare for both threats from within and from without, and for eventualities which could be momentarily expected."[14]

Marshall admitted to the Army Board that "to have sent the substance of this secret information" to Short "by courier or otherwise" would have been "both practical and feasible," but he "felt then that it was unwise." He tacitly conceded that this was a mistake when he added that, in view of what happened, "the situation might well have been helped by translating that information to them." Nevertheless, he believed that the alerting message of November 27 should have sufficed "for any Commander with a great responsibility." He also stressed the steady stream of men and matériel being rushed through Hawaii to the Philippines:

> Nobody could look at that without realizing that something very critical was in the wind. . . .
>
> Only the most critical necessities would have involved us in taking over all that commercial shipping, in pushing these troop movements, in pushing the cargo shipments, in taxing the Pacific Fleet's resources in providing convoys.[15]

Like Stark, Marshall could not accept the theory that in the latter months of 1941 Washington had relaxed its vigilance toward Hawaii. He insisted that "the fear of an air attack, as far as the War Department was concerned, had not faded away." He explained that reconnaissance, Magic, and other sources pointed to Japanese designs on Southeast Asia. If the War Department could build up the Philippine defenses, this might give Japan second thoughts about entering the war. And he declared that Hawaii had received as much equipment as possible and all necessary instructions.

Therefore, from late August 1941 on, Marshall and his staff "were working in the Far East" rather than continuing "discussions of one kind or another and of matériel items to the Hawaiian garrison."[16] Later he implied that any fading of concern had been in Hawaii rather than Washington:

> I never could grasp what had happened between the period when so much was said about air attack, the necessity for anti-aircraft, the necessity for planes, for reconnaissance, the necessity for attack planes for defense and the other requirements which anticipated very definitely and affirmatively an air attack. I could never understand why suddenly it became apparently a side issue.[17]

A brief recollection of the situation in the Hawaiian Department might resolve this question that puzzled Marshall. For Short, the prime issue had become sabotage. The Hawaiian Department and the Fourteenth Naval District, in cooperation with the FBI and local law enforcement agencies, had enough resources to deal with that problem.* Thus Short need not go to Marshall with his sabotage troubles, as he did for matériel.

Marshall also entertained views similar to Stark's in regard to the warning messages of November 27. Although Marshall had not shared in completing the War Department's dispatch of that date, being out of Washington at the time, he saw it the next day and had no doubt that it gave "adequate warning."[18] In his opinion, Hawaii had sufficient forces and equipment to defend itself. After that, he recalled "nothing coming in from the Hawaiian Department or any other matter which required an additional dispatch." He explained, "It is very important that you do not confuse a command direction. . . . Once the com-

---

*For further discussion of Short's fixation on sabotage, see Chapter 21.

mander is alerted, . . . the command direction stood unless you dared [*sic*] to amend it, or what would be a better procedure, completely cancel it and issue a new directive."[19] In other words, to Marshall an alert, once given, remained in effect until canceled or superseded. This attitude was reasonable and consistent with normal military procedure. But in this particular instance, the Hawaiian Department had not grasped the true meaning of the message of November 27, hence had not complied with it.

Cramer made short work of the board's charge that Marshall delayed sending Short "on the evening of 6 December or the early morning of 7 December the critical information indicating an almost immediate break with Japan." Cramer stated, "the record makes entirely clear that General Marshall personally did not receive this information until late in the morning of 7 December and that he did his best to get it to Short immediately but failed because of circumstances beyond his control."[20] There is something to be said on both sides. Certainly Marshall could not have sent out on December 6 information which he had not yet received; on the other hand, he could have acted more expeditiously on the morning of December 7, as discussed in the preceding chapter.

Cramer doubted that Marshall really had the responsibility to determine the Hawaiian Department's state of readiness between November 27 and December 7; "the record is silent as to whether this was the personal duty of the Chief of Staff." In his opinion, Marshall "was entitled to rely upon his subordinates, including Short," and to believe that the plans for the defense of Hawaii "would be carried out by a theater commander in accordance with the traditional American military policy."[21]

The congressional committee delved into this area. "Would it have been possible to send somebody out there to see that this great bastion of ours was ready for this war?" asked Keefe. "Yes, sir; somebody could have been sent out there," Marshall conceded. But he added, "The same thing would have applied to Panama, Alaska, the West Coast, and the Philippines. General Short was a lieutenant general, he was an officer of distinction and reputation and he was in command out there."[22]

To a large extent, Marshall's attitude toward Short in this respect—identical with Stark's toward Kimmel—was logical and correct. In most cases, Washington should have kept hands off the field commands, subject of course to periodic inspector general check-ups. But this was the exceptional case, so serious that Marshall and Stark should have been willing figuratively to invade Short's and Kimmel's territory if necessary to be absolutely sure that everything in the Hawaiian area was under control, and that the local commanders understood exactly what the War and Navy departments expected of them. Both Stark and Marshall definitely erred in not doing so.

Cramer did not agree with the Army Board that Marshall was to blame for the failure to follow through on Short's unsatisfactory reply to the War Department warning of November 27, which read: "Report department alerted to prevent sabotage. Liaison with Navy reurad four seven two twenty-seventh."[23] Cramer observed, "It would be a most anomalous situation if a theater commander could be heard to say that because he received warnings from the Chief of Staff and had replied with a fragmentary report that ipso facto he was relieved of his responsibilities and that these responsibilities were then fastened upon the Chief of Staff." Cramer also reminded Stimson that

> the functions of the Chief of Staff did not include the duty of personally directing and supervising the detailed administration of the various sections of the Office of the Chief of Staff. His primary duty was to advise the Secretary of War and the President, to plan and supervise the organization, equipment and training of the Army, to make decisions and give advice concerning the over-all and vital problems of military strategy. . . . The very nature of an over-all supervision in preparation for a global war makes mandatory that the Chief of Staff be divorced from administrative details.[24]

Primary responsibility for this lack of follow-through in this particular case belonged to the War Plans Division.* For that reason, Gerow did not believe either Marshall or Stimson had the responsibility to check up on Short's report. "I was a staff adviser to the Chief of Staff, and I had a group of 48 officers to assist me," he said. "It was my responsibility to see that those messages were checked, and if an inquiry was necessary, the War Plans Division should have drafted such an inquiry and presented it to the Chief of Staff for approval. . . . I was chief of that division, and it was my responsibility."[25]

Like Gerow, Marshall did not try to dodge his share of blame.

---

*See Chapter 18.

Although he did not initial the Short reply, which would have proved conclusively that he had seen it, other documents in the same batch which crossed his desk bore his initials. MacArthur's answer and Short's came to him "fastened with one of those staples that go through." He initialed the message from the Philippines, "which was on top."[26] Therefore, he thought that he must have read Short's answer; however, this was a "mere assumption," because he did not definitely recall the message.[27]

Yet his testimony to the Roberts Commission gives the impression that he had indeed seen this dispatch. For instance, Roberts asked him, ". . . you understood from the reply that these two commanders had gotten together to determine what measures they ought to take in view of the warning you had sent them?" And Marshall replied, "That was my assumption, yes."[28] In any case, he acknowledged to the congressional committee, "that was my opportunity to intervene and I did not do it."[29] It certainly would appear that, the message of November 27 having been deemed of sufficient importance to warrant dispatch in the name of the Chief of Staff, the answers thereto deserved his careful attention.

Marshall conjectured to the congressional committee that the word "sabotage" in Short's reply "did not register" because "merely expecting an alert direction for sabotage was not in anybody's mind at all." Moreover, the reference to liaison with the Navy did register "as to the assumption that the reconnaissance was on."[30] Here is another example of Marshall's ambiguity. The scouting setup in Hawaii did not meet with universal approval of the high command. The "Air Corps officials in Washington" opposed Short's arrangement but Marshall thought it "a wise one under the circumstances and therefore did not accept the local War Department Air Corps officials' protest as sound."[31]

Pogue wrote concerning the incident of Short's reply:

General Marshall's direct responsibility in November 1941 for the failure to follow up on his orders stemmed from his neglect to reorganize the War Department staff in 1940–1941. He had attempted to hold too many threads of operations in his hands and had spread himself so thin between administering the War Department staff, overseeing training, appearing before Congress, selecting officers, dealing with soldier morale, and puzzling over the demands of Lend-Lease operations, that he could not closely follow the day-by-day reports of his intelligence officers or check adequately on the response of his various commanders to orders. It was not that he was unwilling to delegate authority. Over a period of years his habit had been to give his subordinates full powers and allow them to find their way. But as the War Department was then organized he found it difficult to divest himself of authority.[32]

This paragraph is self-contradictory, because the first sentences give a very concise picture of a man who did not in fact "delegate authority." The suggestion that this situation rose from the organization of the War Department staff echoes the perpetual American quest for a perfect "system," a magic formula that in itself will dispel all the problems inherent in running a large organization. But experience proves that virtually any administrative system is as good or as bad as the people who operate it. Obviously Marshall found it more convenient to use the existing setup than to change it. System or no system, "The job of an administrator," said the congressional committee's majority report, "is only half completed upon the issuance of an order; it is discharged when he determines the order has been executed."[33] Furthermore, the Chief of Staff was more than a glorified office manager; he was also commanding general of the field forces.[34]

Marshall's touch faltered in other areas of the Pearl Harbor landscape. Take, for instance, the revealing undated aide-mémoire which he signed and which Stimson left with Roosevelt in late April or early May 1941 in support of his contention that moving ships to the Atlantic would not leave Hawaii defenseless. The document demonstrated that Marshall was certain the Japanese could not attack Hawaii because the heavy bombers and pursuit planes on Oahu lent such potency to the local defenses. This same memorandum also underlined Marshall's concern with sabotage by local Japanese in the Hawaiian Islands.[35]

This attitude on Marshall's part was especially unfortunate. The Chief of Staff's deep-seated worry over the dread possibility of fifth column activity in Hawaii may or may not have contributed to Short's fears; certainly it did nothing to allay them. That an officer of Marshall's caliber shared this obsession to the full indicates that it was no mere personal aberration of Short's but an integral part of the psychology of the time.

The evidence indicates that Marshall did not expect Hawaii to be the target of Japan's initial thrust. He told the Army board:

> The War Department had no information that an attack would be taken against the fleet at Pearl Harbor. There were many evidences of possible hostile intentions in the Far East and peculiar circumstances regarding the Japanese merchant shipping to pass through the Panama Canal. . . .
>
> Prudence dictated that warnings be sent by the War Department to those officers responsible for the defense of all our areas within reach of Japanese action.[36]

Hawaii stood well down on his list of possibilities. Of course he realized that the presence of the Fleet in Pearl Harbor necessarily made it a potential target. "Out in Hawaii the Fleet is anchored but they have to be prepared against any surprise attack," he remarked during a General Council meeting on February 17, 1941. "I don't say any probable attack but they have to be prepared against a surprise attack from a trick ship or torpedo planes. Our whole Navy power in general is concentrated there; they can't cruise for the next six months."[37]

Nevertheless, by late autumn of 1941 Marshall, like most in responsible staff positions in Washington, expeced the Japanese to strike Southeast Asia. He also assumed they would capture Guam and probably Wake as well, although the latter would be more difficult as long as the U.S. Fleet "was still in full being."

> We had in mind the possibility of an effort on the Panama Canal. We had in mind the possibility of an effort to strike a blow at our air plants in Seattle, at our air plants in San Diego, and we had in mind the possibility of a blow in the Central Pacific, in the Hawaiian district.
>
> We thought the latter was the most improbable.[38]

In brief, Marshall thought the Japanese more likely to hit the Panama Canal, Seattle, or San Diego sooner than Hawaii. A member of the Navy Court asked Marshall if he had considered before December 1941 "that the Japanese might make a surprise attack on United States territory without a prior declaration of war?" To this Marshall replied, "I was always in fear of that." Once again he stressed "that the probabilities pointed to the Panama Canal and to the Philippines before Hawaii."[39]

Indicative of how deeply convinced was Marshall that the Philippines held the key to a United States–Japanese war was an astounding secret conference he held at the War Department on November

15, 1941, for seven major Washington newsmen. This briefing also demonstrated that he extended to the Philippines his belief that B-17s constituted protection against attack. It also illuminated his amazing underestimation of Japan's naval air power and his equally surprising overestimation of Stalin's possible cooperation with the United States.

He opened by offering "anyone who did not care to share secrets" the opportunity to leave before he began to talk. "But there were some things he had to tell the key press correspondents in order that their interpretation of current and forthcoming events did not upset key military strategy of the United States."[40]

Holding this conference may seem a strange, even a foolhardy move for Marshall to make. But it followed the pattern of dealing with a potential problem which he had demonstrated before and would again: when he spotted possible danger, he made a prompt preemptive strike.

He stressed to the assembled newsmen that the United States was "on the brink of war with the Japanese. . . . Our position is highly favorable in this respect: We have access to a leak in all the information they are receiving concerning our military preparations, especially in the Philippines. In other words, we know what they know about us and they dont [sic] know that we know it." Obviously Marshall referred to the interception of messages between Japanese consulates and Tokyo.

He informed his listeners that "in great secrecy" the United States was "building up its strength in the Philippines to a level far higher than the Japanese imagine." He stressed that the United States was "preparing for an offensive war against Japan, whereas the Japs believe we are preparing only to defend the Philippines." Already thirty-five B-17s were in position, with twenty more to be added in December and sixty more in January. Large stocks of other war matériel were also pouring into the Philippines.

Marshall wanted this information "to leak privately, from the White House or the State Department directly to Japanese officials—presumably Kurusu." A public leak might place

the Army fanatics in Japan . . . in a position to demand war immediately, before we were better fortified. But if the leak is confined to Japanese officials, these officials can say to the cabinet: "Look here. These people really mean to bomb our cities, and they have

the equipment with which to do it. We'd better go slow." In that
way, no public face-saving would be necessary, and war might be
averted. The last thing the U.S. wants is a war with Japan which
would divide our strength.[41]

Nevertheless, if war came, the United States would "fight mercilessly. Flying fortresses will be dispatched immediately to set the
paper cities of Japan on fire." The B-17s could not quite make the
round trip from the Philippines, but arrangements were being made
"to provide landing fields for flying fortresses in Vladivostok."

Then Marshall launched into an exposition of grand strategy for
the Pacific. Most astonishing was his assurance that this did not include "the use of much naval force." He thought the bombers could
"do the trick against Japanese Naval strength and against Japanese
cities 'without the use of our shipping.' "

He emphasized that no word about preparations for an offensive
war must leak to Japan. "Nothing that I am telling you today is
publishable even in hinted form." Then he took the newsmen further
into his confidence. The National Guard would be "sent home," to
be "replaced gradually by new divisions of selectees." Marshall feared
that this news, when broken, might convey the idea that the Army's
strength was being depleted. "The effect of that might be disastrous
in the delicate Japanese situation. We want to put up a big front to
the Japanese, without forcing them into face-saving war measures."[42]

An account of the interview, which Ernest K. Lindley of *Newsweek*
prepared, noted that the United States had established fuel depots
on the B-17 route to the Philippines and was "making arrangements
at the Dutch airfields in the East Indies." He added an unrealistic
touch: "Our aim is to blanket the whole area with air power. Our
own fleet, meanwhile, will remain out of range of Japanese air power,
at Hawaii.[43]

This incident demonstrated that, while the U.S. Navy had sorely
underestimated the capabilities of Japanese naval air power, the U.S.
Army had erred by as wide a margin on the side of overenthusiasm
about its own air arm. Marshall and his advisers made the same error
in regard to the Philippines that they had made concerning Hawaii—
the belief that a concentration of B-17s constituted sufficient protection against attack.*

Even more surprising, Marshall seemed to be thinking in terms

---

*See Chapter 8.

of striking from Japanese skies as soon as war came. He based this strategy upon an exceedingly naïve political premise—that Stalin, perennially suspicious of the capitalist nations, would permit American military aircraft to use landing facilities at Vladivostok.

The whole psychology revealed at the press conference was so out of character for the down-to-earth Marshall that Pogue may have been correct when he wrote of this incident:

> Perhaps in his efforts to emphasize the importance of secrecy about the air build-up, he exaggerated what he expected of the B-17s. Only ten days earlier he had stated that "the main involvement in the Far East would be naval," and his current directives for air action envisaged no strikes against the civilian population of Japan. . . . Not by threatening to burn Japan's cities but through menacing Japanese expeditions that must pass near the Philippines on their way south did he expect to exert pressure on Japan.

But Pogue conceded, "In whatever hopes he held for the Far East Forces in November 1941, he was deceived. The new B-17, much improved as it was, still could not perform the major miracles that he expected of it."[44] This much was clear: In late 1941 Marshall was basing some of his prime strategic planning upon a surprisingly shaky foundation.

He likewise apparently suffered from misconceptions concerning what information was available to the Hawaiian Department. Whether he thought that Short had access to Magic is not certain. Marshall's evidence on this point is nebulous and somewhat contradictory. He informed the Navy Court of Inquiry, "I thought at the time that the commander in the Philippines and the Commander in Hawaii got part of the information because the monitoring stations are there."[45] Those installations could not read what they picked up; they served only as relay points. Then, in an affidavit submitted to the Clausen investigation, Marshall testified, "it was my understanding in the period preceding 7 December 1941 that the Commanding General of the Hawaiian Department was aware of and was receiving some of this information from facilities available in his command."[46]

The two preceding paragraphs of Marshall's affidavit dealt with his discussions of Magic with the Army Board, so the obvious conclusion is that he meant Magic. But this he denied to the congressional committee, stating that his affidavit to Clausen contained a confusion. . . . They were receiving information as to intercepts, as to the location of Japanese vessels at sea and their movement and the headquarters that were concerned in this.

The actual translation, that is, the deciphering, translation, and transmission of the magic, as such, clearly was not intended to be implied in this.[47]

Such intention was by no means clear from the content of his affidavit. Evidently Marshall was trying to convey to the committee that he had not meant to imply that Short had access to Magic. So one is left with a nagging doubt concerning Marshall's understanding of what types of intelligence were available to Short. His very vagueness opened Marshall to censure for failing to make sure of his ground in such a vital matter.

Colonel Moses Pettigrew, who had been Bratton's assistant from November 1939 until August 1941 when he became the G-2 executive officer, believed

that the Hawaiian Department was in possession of the same information he had received in Washington; that he reached this conclusion by statements . . . of Naval personnel . . . to the effect that Hawaii had everything in the way of information that Washington had; and, that the Navy had a crypto-analytic unit in Hawaii under Commander Rochefort which was monitoring and receiving these intercepts and breaking and translating the codes, as well as Washington, in the interest of saving time, utilizing personnel there available, and a subsequent exchange of intercept translations as a check one against the another [sic].[48]

This and other statements make obvious that one source of this misunderstanding was confusion in Washington as to Rochefort's mission. His task, along with radio intelligence, was to concentrate on the Japanese naval codes, especially the flag officers' codes. Apparently some officials in Washington thought that he also decrypted Magic. Rochefort never saw Purple, and he received his first consular intercepts when an agreement went into effect on December 1, 1941, which Brigadier General David Sarnoff, president of RCA, made with Captain Mayfield, the Fourteenth Naval District's intelligence officer, whereby the latter had access "in a roundabout way" to "certain information" from RCA files.[49]

The Army's Monitor Station 5, located at Fort Shafter, was "intercepting traffic between Japan, Asia and Europe"—and, obviously, Hawaii. But MS5 was strictly a relay point, forwarding its pickups in the raw to Washington, and doing no decrypting.[50]

A certain ambiguity likewise existed in Marshall's attitude toward the "bomb plot" series. He stated that he could not recall having seen those messages until he was preparing to testify before the congressional committee.[51] Later, however, he backed down somewhat from that statement. "I testified that I did not have a definite recollection of these particular messages. I must assume that I saw them."[52] In either case, he could scarcely have evaluated them carefully against those from consulates other than Honolulu. Yet he averred, "When you consider the messages came from all portions of the world, relating to naval shipping, it is a question of how much involves a check on where our ships are, and how much involves a plan for a specific operation at a certain place. That is a matter of opinion."[53] Thus Marshall voiced the standard alibi for failure to appreciate the significance of the "bomb plot" series.

Under further prodding, Marshall conceded that the information would have been of interest to Kimmel and Short. Still, he took the position that transmittal to them of these dispatches might not have affected their actions. The Japanese consular exchanges pertaining to other areas were not sent the commands in question, yet upon receipt of the War Department warning of November 27, these commands reacted properly.[54] So, like most of the Army and Navy staff officers concerned, Marshall either did not see or would not admit the difference between the Tokyo-Honolulu traffic and that between Japan and its other consulates.

While Marshall was not free from fault, Stimson refused to concede that his Chief of Staff had made any errors at all. In his official report, "Regarding the Pearl Harbor Disaster," Stimson wrote of Marshall, "throughout this matter I believe that he acted with his usual great skill, energy, and efficiency."[55] Stimson obviously was prejudiced in favor of Marshall, but the Army Board just as obviously was biased against him. The truth appears to lie between the two extremes.

Revisionists sniped at Marshall, not only for his actual and imaginary missteps before Pearl Harbor, but for allegedly conducting a cover-up following the tragedy. Toland quoted "an officer close to Marshall" that the Chief of Staff "ordered a lid put on" the Pearl

Harbor affair a few days after the event. "Gentlemen, this goes to the grave with us," Marshall was supposed to have told some of his officers.[56] The identity of this unnamed source is not secret to anyone who has researched in the extensive "revisionist" archives at the University of Wyoming, where considerable correspondence on this subject is located. So it is somewhat surprising that Toland did not mention that this officer—he was Brigadier General Carter W. Clarke— stated to Greaves "not once but several times that the oath that GCM extracted had had nothing to do with PH. . . . He refused politely but firmly to say what it had to do with."[57]

Clarke's disclaimer carried weight, because no one could reasonably accuse him of trying to protect Marshall. He made no secret of his intense dislike of the former Chief of Staff. "He [Clarke] is certain—as you yourself are—that Marshall was the evil Rasputin of the White House," the writer A. A. Hoehling informed Barnes, "but cannot produce the needed letter or even witness who overheard even one wilful conversation between 'catfish mouth' Marshall (as Clarke calls him) and FDR."[58]

One of the more persistent rumors about Marshall has been that a "winds execute" message* arrived in Washington and that, after the attack, Marshall ordered its destruction. This story offers a classic case in the evolution of a rumor and the dangers of loose talk.

The curtain rose upon a campsite at Fort Jackson, South Carolina, during the summer of 1943. Brigadier General Isaac Spalding and Colonel John T. Bissell sat "under the trees" talking shop. Bissell had been chief of the Military Intelligence Service in December 1941, while Spalding had been chief of the Officers Branch of G-1 until December 4 of that year, when he became chief of the Army Exchange Service. Spalding took a rather boyish interest in Bissell's former counterintelligence work. He "had always wanted to be a sleuth" and "was always curious concerning detective stories."[59]

They discussed Pearl Harbor and Spalding's "failure to understand how Sherman Miles and the Navy could fail to discover that those Japanese vessels had left home ports." They also talked about "the information which we must have had and which the Navy must have had and our failure to give some kind of a better warning to Gen. Short." According to Spalding,

---

*See Chapter 19.

Bissell said that certain messages had been received and were in the files of G-2 and he deemed it most necessary to destroy them. I got the impression that these messages were derogatory to the War Department and that he (Bissell) on his own responsibility destroyed them. I had the impression that they were secret information which it was most desirable that the President, Congress, the public, Mr. Stimson and Gen. Marshall not know about. . . .[60]

Bissell did not tell Spalding the source of these papers, but the general testified that they "were so hot that if Gen. Marshall had known about them it would have been very disagreeable for Gen. Marshall." Spalding added that he would not want anything he said "to transgress the integrity of Mr. Stimson or George Marshall. They are two of the finest men in the world and they would hew to the line I know."[61]

Questioned about this story, Bissell flatly denied having either destroyed such records or having told Spalding "anything from which he might infer such." In fact, his work had been strictly in counter-intelligence and had "nothing whatsoever to do with signal intelligence" until after Pearl Harbor.[62]

The scene shifted to Fort Bragg, North Carolina, some time during 1943. Spalding told Colonel Otis K. Sadtler, who in 1941 had been head of the Military Branch of the Signal Corps, "something to the effect that . . . everything pertaining to Pearl Harbor was being destroyed or had been destroyed."[63] Note that Spalding not only misquoted or misunderstood Bissell, but "certain messages" had ballooned to "everything pertaining to Pearl Harbor."

Scene three took place in Washington, where Sadtler had returned to duty. There Sadtler told his old friend, former Lieutenant Colonel William F. Friedman of the Signal Intelligence Service, "some very startling things" concerning Pearl Harbor. These left Friedman "more or less breathless." According to Friedman, Sadtler appeared positive that a Navy source had intercepted a "winds execute" message. He told Friedman in substance of the incident of a dispatch pertaining to a break in relations between Japan and Great Britain.[64]*

Friedman was already "winds"-conscious because he had been chatting with Safford. The latter "was very firm in his conviction that there had been a Winds execute message and moreover that he himself had had it in his hands. . . . And he felt that there was some very excellent reason why no copies of this message could be found,

---

*For a detailed discussion of the "winds" controversy, see Chapter 19.

and of course it left a number of questions and inferences in his mind which he naturally transferred" to Friedman's mind.[65]

So Friedman asked Sadtler, "What do you suppose happened to the Winds execute which we believe so firmly was intercepted?" Sadtler answered that "they were ordered destroyed." Taken aback, Friedman asked, "By whom?" To this Sadtler replied, "By Gen. Marshall." Friedman "just couldn't believe, swallow, or give credence" to this, and he expressed his disbelief. But Sadtler "was pretty firm in his statement and there was no checking him in that."[66]

Friedman testified that this conversation also touched upon two other messages. The first was from the War Department to Lieutenant Colonel Carroll A. Powell, Short's signal officer, asking him if the radar had been operating on December 7. The second was Powell's affirmative reply. According to Friedman, either both messages or at least Powell's answer had also been destroyed.[67]

By now "everything pertaining to Pearl Harbor" had crystallized into two specific subjects: a "winds execute" message and an exchange about radar. Moreover, the story had made a complete about-face. From Spalding's original tale that Bissell had destroyed some papers lest Marshall, Roosevelt, and others find out about them, Friedman's testimony had twisted it so that Marshall ordered the destruction. Marshall testified that there was no basis for the statement that he had ordered records destroyed and he had no knowledge of such an order.[68] What is more, he knew nothing of a "winds execute" message.[69]

Sadtler told a diametrically opposite story from Friedman's. He testified that he never saw a "winds execute" message: "I will make an absolute flat denial of that statement made by Mr. Friedman because as far as I know, that message was never in the War Department and I never made any statement that Gen. Marshall ordered it destroyed." Furthermore, Sadtler stated that, far from directing the destruction of the radar message, Marshall through the acting chief signal officer ordered all copies "collected and held intact . . . inasmuch as radar and the damage done at Pearl Harbor [were] secret at the time, the information was not to be disclosed."[70]

Friedman stressed that Sadtler's story about the destruction of these messages came at second hand. Friedman

> regarded this as merely hearsay evidence and nothing more than that; highly inconceivable that such a thing could happen. And when

I talked over the Pearl Harbor story with Captain Safford, I probably just passed that out as one of those crazy things that get started. I shouldn't have done it. I certainly had no idea that he would repeat it.[71]

But Safford not only repeated the story, he believed it, although he conceded that it was "very third-hand." He testified, "The information that I got was that written copies of the 'winds' message had been destroyed in the War Department by then Colonel Bissell on the direct orders of General Marshall."[72] That was Safford's story, and, true to his intense nature, he stuck to it tenaciously.

There was no logical reason why Marshall or anyone else should have ordered a "winds execute" destroyed. After the attack, such a message, if it ever existed, would have had only a mild historical interest. No stretch of the imagination could have twisted it into a hint that the Japanese were going to attack Pearl Harbor.

With the passage of years, one can attempt to achieve a balance between the near adulation of Marshall which existed during and after World War II and the venom of the Army Board and of his critics. Marshall was neither above making a mistake nor below the level of normal humanity. Pearl Harbor was so much the tragedy of an entire nation that no American in a position of responsibility whose orbit even tangentially touched upon the problem could escape unscathed—not even George C. Marshall.

"Primarily a Failure of Men"

Errors at General Staff level—Nature and duties—
Failure to understand Japanese psychology and to
anticipate Japanese strategy—No need for Purple machine on Oahu—Withholding of the "bomb plot" messages—Their nature and importance

Shortly after Marshall became Chief of Staff, General
Hugh Johnson described the functions of a general staff: "It never
does things itself. It only plans and watches and supervises the doing
of things by others. . . . They are there to keep the commander from
blundering, to inform his action, and to enable him to do that which,
without such service, no human being could hope to do."[1]

On the basis of these criteria, the staffs in Washington failed
signally. They planned well, but they neither watched nor supervised
adequately; they did not prevent Kimmel and Short from blundering,
nor did they keep them properly informed.

One reason why most Americans did not anticipate such an attack
as the Japanese made at Pearl Harbor was their assumption that the
Army and Navy knew their business and would ward off or at least
sight danger. Had this not been so, there would not have been such
a stinging backlash of fury and bewilderment after the event, especially following publication of the Roberts report. "Our people know
that the defense of Pearl Harbor was a military responsibility and that
the military bungled the job," wrote Senator Wiley of Wisconsin
about two weeks following release of the Army and Navy reports.[2]

One cannot understand the defeat which the United States suffered on December 7, 1941, by attempting to analyze it in terms of
economics, sociology, technology, or any other of history's neat pi-
geonholes. It arose from the nature of the men involved. Ferguson
and his fellow Republican member of the congressional committee,
Senator Owen Brewster of Maine, recognized this in their minority

report: "In our opinion, the evidence before this committee indicates that the tragedy at Pearl Harbor was primarily a failure of men and not of laws or powers to do the necessary things, and carry out the vested responsibilities."[3]

The safety of Hawaii and of the U.S. Pacific Fleet when in Pearl Harbor rested upon twin responsibilities. Washington was responsible "in respect to its intimate knowledge of diplomatic negotiations, widespread intelligence information, direction of affairs and constitutional duty to plan the defense of the United States."[4] The commanders on Oahu were responsible for carrying out their assigned missions with every means at their disposal. These bilateral responsibilities demanded of both Washington and Oahu the highest level of alertness, and a complete mutual interchange of pertinent information.

Washington had a special duty in this regard because an "inferior Fleet, under enemy surveillance in an exposed naval base without resources to protect it could only avert disaster by receiving the best possible evidence of the intentions of its potential enemy."[5] But the War and Navy departments "were not on their toes to the extent that they grasped the urgency of the situation, the fact that the minutes were ticking by which could not be recalled, which might lead to disaster unless something was done quickly."[6] Neither were the defenders of Oahu.

Top officers of the armed forces shared the general American misinterpretation of Japanese psychology and strategy. Washington had expected the main Japanese thrust to come in Southeast Asia, and it did, for, contrary to popular belief, Pearl Harbor was a secondary operation. But, explained journalist Walter Lippmann, Washington believed also that Japan would not challenge the United States directly, either in the Philippines or Hawaii, "at least until she had made the easier conquests which were open to her." It boiled down to "the elementary military principle that you must not go forward leaving a powerful military force on your flank. The question then is why the American high command, which was thoroughly schooled in orthodox strategy, did not take seriously enough the likelihood of Japan's doing the orthodox thing."[7]

However, there were two ways to implement that "orthodox strategy": by not going forward, or by attempting to eliminate the force on the flank. Japan chose the second alternative. One can understand why American strategists expected it to choose the first. "It was surprising enough that a war-weary and impoverished Japan might accept the risk of engaging a formidable combination of powers by invasion of Thailand, Burma, or Russia," commented the Springfield (Massachusetts) *Union*. "A deliberate assault on the United States seems like the superlative in incredibilities."[8]

General Miles testified that he and his colleagues on the War Department General Staff "never lost sight of the fact that Japan, if engaged in war with us, might attack Hawaii." But he amplified:

> We did grant the Japanese the best of good sense. We did very much question whether they would attack Hawaii, because such an attack must result in two separate decisions on the part of the Japanese, one to make war against the United States, which we thought in the long run would be suicidal . . . and, too, to attack a great fortress and fleet, risking certain ships that they could not replace.[9]

Had the Americans believed in the genuine possibility of an aerial attack on Oahu before the war began officially, no doubt Washington would have kept Hawaii much better posted, and the U.S. Pacific Fleet and the Hawaiian Department would have been in a far better position to repel the enemy. Many individuals, among them Lieutenant Commander Layton, Kimmel's intelligence officer, believed that the Navy Department's failure to keep the CinCPAC adequately informed lay at the root of the tragedy. "If Kimmel had known what Washington knew all along he and his staff might very well have created such a fuss as to dislodge Washington from those fixations," he said, referring to the Atlantic front and the Japanese drive south.[10]

Yet those preoccupations were sound. "Hitler first" was one of the best decisions Roosevelt ever made, and no one could ignore Japan's obvious plans for Southeast Asia. Washington erred, not in its grand strategy, but in failing to take Kimmel and Short into full confidence. This is not to suggest that the Navy and War departments should have funneled indiscriminately to their top men on Oahu all the information available in Washington concerning the Japanese. To do so would have dumped upon the Pacific Fleet and the Hawaiian Department far more paperwork than they were equipped to handle. Washington had difficulty enough in that respect. Marshall testified that for him to read all the Magic material "was an absolutely impractical proposition." He stated flatly, "if I had complete responsibility for reading all the magic I would have had to cease to function as Chief of Staff, except in that one particular division."[11]

Certainly neither Kimmel nor Short could have digested every Magic intercept and had any time remaining for his other important duties. Moreover, to send all the raw intercepts to the field would have negated one of Washington's prime functions—evaluation. Then, too, the United States armed forces did not have sufficient means to justify such an unwarranted duplication of effort. Even Kimmel did not claim that his superiors should have assigned him a Purple machine. If Washington supplied him with pertinent information, "that was a solution to the problem."[12]

Boiled down to essentials, those in Washington most concerned with the intelligence angle of the tragedy at Pearl Harbor had three primary duties: to examine the facts; to make logical evaluations thereof; and to disseminate the appropriate information and deductions to the field commands. In this respect, the War and Navy departments' General Staffs seriously mishandled a significant segment of the treasure pouring out of the intelligence cornucopia.

In 1941 no individual or agency concerned could do its job with all possible efficiency lacking Magic information pertinent to its mission. But, in the words of the congressional committee's majority report:

> so closely held and top secret was this intelligence that it appears the *fact* the Japanese codes had been broken was regarded as of more importance than the *information* obtained from decoded traffic. The result of this rather specious premise was to leave large numbers of policy-making and enforcement officials in Washington completely oblivious of the most pertinent information concerning Japan. [Italics in original]

For example, the FBI, "charged with combating espionage, sabotage, and un-American activities within the United States," never received such "vital information necessary to the success of its work" as the message of February 15, 1941, in which Tokyo outlined the type of information concerning American and Canadian defense preparations which it wanted from certain key consulates. Colonel Kroner, head of the Intelligence Branch of G-2, could not avail himself of Magic, although it is difficult to see how he could function properly without it.[13]

Nor was supercaution about Magic confined to General Staff level. According to Captain Albert E. Hindmarsh, who served in ONI at the time of Pearl Harbor, "Purple was not shown to Knox in the early stages at Knox's own request. Knox stated that he had many newspaper friends and so did not want things to slip out or to say what Knox knew but could not say."[14]

The Government perforce had entrusted the Magic secret to "the numerous technicians, cryptographers, translators, and clerks" necessary to process and interpret the data. Why, the congressional committee asked, could not the same trust be reposed in "ranking officials of the various departments and bureaus"?[15] Were the War and Navy departments so enamored of their technological success in breaking down Japan's diplomatic codes that they did not realize that this fact meant little unless the data gathered thereby received the necessary evaluation and dissemination?

It was fairly evident that of the two Oahu commanders Kimmel was much the better informed, because Marshall wrote Short no such voluminous, frequent, and informative letters as Stark sent to Kimmel. Yet one must interpose a word or two of caution. It was highly doubtful whether a deeper knowledge of the Purple intercepts would have made any difference on the Hawaii station. As long as Kimmel and Short understood the overall situation—and any newspaper reader knew that relations between Japan and the United States were deteriorating rapidly—they had no need to be concerned with the daily ins and outs of diplomacy.

One myth has been unusually long-lived: that the breaking of Purple provided the United States with an open sesame to every secret of Japanese planning. As late as September 21, 1974, journalist David Braaten wrote, "Uncle Sam's cryptographers eventually cracked the Japanese Purple Code. This gave our leaders advance warning of the 1941 sneak attack plans, enabling them to disperse the fleet at Pearl Harbor."[16] The Japanese confided nothing about Operation Hawaii to the Purple messages. Moreover, the Fleet was not dispersed. Had it been, the Japanese might have found much slimmer pickings.

Magic "was a priceless asset but its value in bringing to our Pacific garrisons a realization of impending war can be overemphasized," Marshall stressed to the congressional committee. "Magic need not have been, and indeed was not, necessary to a true comprehension of the situation."[17]

If Marshall meant that Magic material was not needed for a complete, realistic assessment of Japan's diplomatic and military posture, he was wrong. But if he intended to convey that a knowledge of Magic was not required to realize that relations between Japan and the United States had reached the boiling point, and that the armed forces should have been alert, he was right. Miles, too, believed that the Hawaiian commanders had all the information they should have needed. He wrote a vigorous letter concerning his testimony before the Army Board to its chairman, Lieutenant General George Grunert, on August 18, 1944:

> The Army garrison was commanded by a Lieutenant General, with the Commander-in-Chief of the United States Fleet present in Hawaiian waters. I think it fair to say that these senior and responsible officers required no specific directives as to what they should or should not do under a threat of war, or, indeed, any warnings other than the knowledge of the serious situation then existing.
> . . . When one considers the Hawaiian garrison and the Fleet in that area, with but one single potential enemy in view and carefully prepared plans to meet him, the broad knowledge which they unquestionably had of the increasing tension should have been decisive. In Washington there was absolute confidence that the knowledge of the situation had been translated into full alert.[18]

But Washington should have remembered that anyone is more likely to come to grief from scarcity of facts than through an abundance. Kimmel and Short should have received all information pertinent to their missions. The real problem was that the highest service levels seemed to have misunderstood just what this entailed. The diplomatic information obtained by means of Magic, in Stark's words, "required careful evaluation, a task which could be much better performed here in Washington where the officers charged with this task had access to other sources of information, such as the State and War Departments." No one could dispute that this procedure was sensible and necessary. Stark considered that his letters and dispatches to Kimmel and Hart conveying a distillation of current Magic information sufficed "to keep them informed on the important military and political developments in the Pacific as we knew them, and that they had received adequate information and directives to be on guard."[19]

All very well for the diplomatic and strategic fronts! But of far more direct potential interest to the commanders on Oahu was the tactical intelligence concerning the Fleet in Pearl Harbor and its defenses, which Tokyo requested and which the consulate at Honolulu supplied.

The Army and Navy on Oahu knew well that members of the Japanese consulate were spying on the military and naval installations on Oahu.[20] What they did not know was that on September 24, 1941, the nature of that espionage underwent what Kimmel later correctly termed "a significant and ominous change."[21] On that date the Japanese Foreign Ministry, at the request of Naval Intelligence, by a "strictly secret" message instructed the Honolulu consulate to make its reports concerning vessels in Pearl Harbor in accordance with specific areas. Tokyo also wanted to know when two or more vessels were moored "alongside the same wharf."[22]*

Nor was this all. Follow-up messages of almost equal significance ensued. On November 15 Tokyo instructed, "As relations between Japan and the United States are most critical, make your 'ships in harbor report' irregular, but at a rate of twice a week. Although you are no doubt aware, please take extra care to maintain secrecy."[23] To the best of our knowledge, this was the only instance of Tokyo's equating the consular reports with the state of Japanese-American relations. Further, in this message Tokyo indicated continuing interest in up-to-date information about the ships in Pearl Harbor, cautioned its consulate against establishing a habit pattern, and warned it to be extra cautious. Other implementing messages followed, all fairly stuffed with food for thought.

Here was information of direct interest to the U.S. Pacific Fleet, whose ships were being targeted in harbor, and to the Hawaiian Department, responsible for the safety of those same ships. Yet almost no one, at any level in Washington, evaluated this series as any more than evidence, in Wilkinson's words, of Japan's "nicety of intelligence."[24] After the fact there still persisted a curious inability to see how the "bomb plot" series differed from espionage messages to and from other Japanese consulates. Even Edward P. Morgan, the brilliant young lawyer who wrote the draft of the congressional committee's majority report, did not believe such a difference existed to any appreciable degree.[25]

A number of writers have delved into this fascinating aspect of

---

*See Appendix 5.

the Pearl Harbor story, among them Captain T. B. Kittredge, USNR (Retired). A few of his remarks concerning the intercepted Japanese messages and other intelligence items deserve comment because they are typical of certain misapprehensions on these subjects.

"There was seldom any information of direct military interest in these voluminous exchanges of messages between Tokyo and the Japanese diplomatic and consular missions abroad," he wrote.[26] One wonders how he arrived at such a conclusion. A large volume of routine business did indeed go back and forth, but enough was of "direct military interest" to give U.S. intelligence agencies abundant material for reflection.

At the time Kittredge published his article, the congressional committee's minority report had already discounted such excuses:

> Witnesses before the Committee, . . . in extenuation of their lack of emphasis on the probability of an attack on Pearl Harbor, called attention to the fact that Japanese agents were also reporting on the military and naval installations of the United States at Panama, the Philippines, the west coast, and other points. But . . . this fact provided no excuse whatever for minimizing the probability of an attack on Pearl Harbor any more than at any other American outpost. Nor does it excuse the failure of Washington authorities to note that far greater detail was being asked for by the Japanese about Hawaii at a time when Japanese movements in the Southeastern Pacific had to contend with the strategic position of Hawaii where the real American striking force, the fleet, rested.[27]

Testifying about the intercepts submitted to the Army Board, Clausen told the congressional committee, "The most important to me in that whole batch was the one that set up Pearl Harbor, carved it into sections, and asked that the consulate at Honolulu report regarding the ships, because I didn't see anything like that regarding any of the other ports."[28]

What is more, the value of information is measured in terms of quality, not quantity. No intelligence service can expect a steady flow of revealing data. Nor can it anticipate that the potential enemy will pinpoint the targets and the exact hours of his intended strikes. Any Japanese exchange whatever in 1941 concerning Pearl Harbor, its ships, its defenses, and the military installations on Oahu should have received careful scrutiny in Washington, if only because Pearl Harbor was the home base on the U.S. Pacific Fleet, Oahu was the foundation stone of American strategy in the Pacific, and Japanese-American relations had deteriorated markedly by the autumn of 1941.

Short and Kimmel stressed Washington's failure to advise them of the "bomb plot" series. Both men realized that this was a key factor in their defense, and made the most of it. "I do not want to attempt to summarize or even to list all the information here which the War Department had but which I did not have," affirmed Short in his initial statement to the congressional committee. "I want to refrain from hindsight evaluation of this information. But I also want to call the committee's attention to some very obvious items which had they been given to me, would have necessarily changed the picture which I then had of the crisis between the United States and Japan."[29] Among these he listed the "ships in harbor" reports:

> While the War Department G-2 may not have felt bound to let me know about the routine operations of the Japanese in keeping track of our naval ships, they should certainly have let me know that the Japanese were getting reports of the exact location of the ships in Pearl Harbor, which might indicate more than just keeping track, because such details would be useful only for sabotage, or for air or submarine attack in Hawaii. As early as October 9, 1941,* G-2 in Washington knew of this Japanese espionage. This message, analyzed critically, is really a bombing plan for Pearl Harbor.[30]

Senator Alben Barkley asked Short concerning these messages, "Do you think that if you had gotten all of those, or if the admiral had gotten them, or both of you together had gotten them, you would have reached any different conclusion from that reached by everybody in Washington?" Short replied honestly and reasonably, "I think there was a possibility because Pearl Harbor meant a little more to us. We were a little closer to the situation, and I believe we would have been inclined to look at that Pearl Harbor information a little more closely."[31]

Kimmel had none of Short's inhibitions about "hindsight evaluation." Seth Richardson asked him, "And your contention . . . is that had that information come to you it would have definitely pointed to Hawaii as a possible point of attack?" Kimmel replied firmly, "I can't gather any other conclusion from these messages." He added bluntly that if his superiors in Washington "had given them to me I can say,

---

*This was the date the Army translated the "bomb plot" message.

without any reservation whatsoever, that it would have changed my
ideas completely and every one of my staff that I have talked to. . . .
We were there. We were on the ground." Kimmel further declared
in his positive fashion, "there is no reason why they [the Japanese]
would have wanted that information unless they were going to use it
on the ships while they were in the harbor."[32]

The admiral was convinced that he could have done wonders had
he been reasonably sure at any time between November 27 and
December 7, 1941, that a surprise air attack against Oahu was in the
making.

> In that event . . . I would have put to sea with the fleet and I would
> have maintained them in a position where they could be in the best
> intercepting position. . . . I would have kept my carriers in the Ha-
> waiian area. I would have abandoned the overhaul of the *Saratoga*,
> which . . . was not entirely out of commission. . . .
> I would have had her brought back to the area and joined
> up. . . . and I would have gone ahead and exhausted the patrol
> planes and thereby curtailed my chance to carry out the raid on the
> Marshalls, because I would have considered the attack force as a
> primary objective. . . .[33]

Whether receipt of the "bomb plot" series would have galvanized
Kimmel into these actions must remain an open question. Kittredge
stated that Kimmel's and Short's interpretation of the "bomb plot"
and what it meant to them was "valid only if the information thus
obtained was in fact used by the Japanese naval staff in the instructions" to Nagumo's task force. He claimed that "if such a 'bombing
plan' for Pearl Harbor ever existed . . . the Japanese naval staff and
officers knew nothing about it."

Apparently Kittredge did not understand that the term "bomb
plot" in this connection meant a grid over the target area, not a
conspiracy to bomb. Out of this misunderstanding, he informed his
readers that "Japanese Army and Navy staffs had regarded with scorn
the laborious and encyclopedic reports from consular staffs on naval
and military matters." And he made this astounding statement: "members of the Hawaiian Consulate staff were very busy trying to invent
such a bomb plot and sell it to the High Command in Tokyo."[34]

Evidently Kittredge either accepted his own surmises as fact, or
else someone on the Japanese side efficiently pulled the wool over

his eyes.* The Third Bureau (Intelligence) of the Naval General Staff had planted Takeo Yoshikawa in the Honolulu consulate to make just such reports. Far from the consulate inventing the "bomb plot" setup, the Third Bureau through the Foreign Ministry gave the Consulate the "bomb plot" and related instructions. Throughout the cruise of the task force to Hawaii, the Naval General Staff furnished Nagumo valuable data based upon Yoshikawa's reports. The smooth interweaving of Japanese intelligence with planning and operations forms a sharp contrast to American mishandling of military information in 1941.

Lt. Cmdr. Charles C. Hiles, USN (Ret.), a student of Pearl Harbor, believed that the first "bomb plot" message and the consulate's reply "setting up the grid system alone are enough to give the show away." But when taken collectively with others in the series, "there can be no remaining doubt as to the purpose to be served. Any Intelligence Officer, then and now, who could not figure this out should be taken out and hung higher than Haman."[35] A bit drastic, yet Hiles was essentially correct.

In his interesting book on intelligence, George S. Pettee agreed that certain items, including these consular messages, "implied an attack on the fleet at Pearl Harbor."[36] Even the majority members of the congressional committee, who gave Washington the benefit of every possible doubt, stated the following concerning the "bomb plot" intercepts: "Since they indicated a particular interest in the Pacific Fleet's base this intelligence should have been appreciated and supplied the Hawaiian commanders for their assistance, along with other information available to them, in making their estimate of the situation."[37]

That is the point exactly. For this reason, Kittredge's approach was irrelevant when he expressed doubt that Kimmel's or Short's experts could have made any more of "the great volume of intercepted diplomatic messages" than did Washington.[38] That could very well

---

*Lieutenant Commander Itaru Tachibana of the Third Bureau did a little wool pulling. In filling out the intelligence section of a questionnaire for MacArthur's Headquarters in Tokyo, he did not list the Japanese consulate among the "primary sources" of Japanese information about the U.S. Pacific Fleet, its defenses and habits. To the question, "What role was played by agents in HAWAII?" Tachibana replied, "None" (*PHA*, Part 13, pp. 412–413). He knew better (see *At Dawn We Slept*, Chapter 31). One must judge his answer in the context of the time. The war crimes trials loomed in the offing and the less any Japanese admitted to knowing about Pearl Harbor the better for him.

have been. But the diplomatic messages were not the principal subject at issue. What Kimmel and Short had every right and the urgent need to receive was the full text of any exchanges between Tokyo and Honolulu that referred to ships of the Fleet or military installations in the islands, or that in any fashion pointed to tactical espionage such as evidenced in the "bomb plot" series.

In his usual sensible manner, Rochefort pointed out, "the withholding of information from Admiral Kimmel and Short, was the prerogative of Washington. However, if this withheld information deprived Admiral Kimmel of intelligence which was necessary or vital to the preparation of estimates as to Japanese intentions or to the Pacific Fleet, then Washington was and is responsible for the result."[39] Washington stands on such shaky ground in this regard that one can understand why some individuals have cried "Villain!" instead of "Fool!" To Kimmel the "bomb plot" messages were "sufficient to convince any unbiased person that Washington deliberately withheld this information in order to insure the Japanese attack."[40]

Safford was exceedingly angry over Washington's handling of this series. He insisted that he evaluated the original message accurately and attempted to get the information to Kimmel: "To Safford, the bomb plot message showed that events were speeding up, that the Japs were familiar with the possibilities of a surprise attack on Pearl Harbor, and that another delay such as this might be fatal." So he held "a quick conference" with Sadtler and Lieutenant Colonel Rex W. Minckler, chief of the Signal Intelligence Service. Then he wrote a message to Rochefort, "to be sent in a special intelligence cipher." This dispatch instructed Rochefort to arrange with Powell "to be given a daily copy of the intercepts made at Fort Shafter, and to process them without delay."

According to Safford, his message died aborning. "When this message was given to Admiral Noyes for his release, he jumped on Safford with both feet. . . . 'Absolutely no! If Admiral Bloch wants to know what is going on out there let him give the orders. I am not going to tell a District Commander how to run his job!' " Frustrated, Safford attempted a circuitous approach:

All Safford could do, under the circumstances, was to give Rochefort the daily key-changes to JD-19 (when they were sent by radio to Corregidor), adding Com 14 as an information addressee, and to hope that Rochefort would take the hint. Unfortunately, Joe—for once in his life—decided to play it straight and abide strictly by his orders which were to concentrate on Japanese Navy and not bother with DIP. When Rochefort's Monthly Report for October (1941) came in, Safford made a second attempt to get Rochefort to "process" the local (Honolulu) DIP messages, getting his intercepts from the local Army unit, but again enjoyed another chewing-out from Noyes for his presumption. A third attempt was made before the end of November, when one of the lieutenants under Safford's command was ordered to Manila by air to deliver the latest revised War Plans. Safford's verbal instructions to Rochefort were not delivered, presumably through fear of Noyes' wrath if he ever learned of it.[41]

One wonders why Safford went about the matter in such a devious way. Indeed, Rochefort later posed the question: "Knowing that we in Station Hypo had materials to read the traffic, and obviously superior translators why did he not drop me a personal note to obtain copies and deliver the product to Admiral Kimmel? With all due respect to MS5, if they were being furnished copies, I could also get copies, with or without assistance from MS5."[42]

And to his superiors in Washington, why did Safford not simply say, in effect, "I think the Japanese are conducting potentially dangerous tactical espionage on Oahu, so the Pacific Fleet and the Hawaiian Department ought to receive these intercepts"? This would have forced the issue one way or another. Presented as it was, Safford's proposal may well have struck Noyes as an officious, ill-judged attempt to interfere with Bloch's prerogatives.

Safford called the failure to provide Hawaii with the "bomb plot" series "a deliberate act of treason on the part of Marshall, Stark, Gerow, Turner and Miles. Alan Kirk went down fighting.* It was finished business by the time 'Ping' Wilkinson arrived on the scene."[43] Kirk did not go very far down. On the contrary, he became a full admiral, commanded the U.S. naval task force for Operation Overlord, and later became ambassador to Taiwan.

According to Barnes, Kirk insisted that the "bomb plot" message of September 24 be sent to Kimmel. "He was blocked in this proposal by Admiral Turner, who was supported in this by Admiral Stark. Frustrated and disgusted, Kirk left his post and sought the sea duty

---

*Captain Alan G. Kirk served as director of Naval Intelligence from April 1 to October 15, 1941, when Captain Theodore S. "Ping" Wilkinson succeeded him.

he needed to become an admiral." Barnes conceded, however, "there is no proof that this was a result of any conspiracy to keep Kimmel in the dark." He blamed Turner's conceit, self-assurance, and ignorance about Pearl Harbor's lack of facilities to decode the intercepts.[44]

Unfortunately, Kirk appeared before none of the investigative bodies, so never had the opportunity to either confirm or lay to rest these rumors as to why he left his post as director of Naval Intelligence. His successor, Wilkinson, testified, "Captain Kirk went to sea before the expiration of his tour in order to obtain an opportunity for a command which was open at the time, and I did not remain similarly." Wilkinson much preferred going to sea, and thought "that is what most of us would like to do."[45] This story of Kirk's departure is all the more credible because Intelligence duty was frequently shunned, and ambitious officers escaped it as soon as possible.

Turner's sworn testimony before the congressional committee directly contradicted Barnes's thesis. Mitchell asked Turner to assume that the "bomb plot" series had been evaluated as "some kind of a bombing pattern" and that "the information should have been sent to Honolulu." In that case, "whose business would it have been under the system between ONI and the War Plans Division at that time to bring that message and its evaluation to the attention of the Chief of Naval Operations and suggest a dispatch to the fleet at Honolulu?" Turner replied:

> I conceive that to be the duty and function of the Office of Naval Intelligence. As a matter of fact, I have no recollection of ever having seen that dispatch of the 24th of September until I returned here recently and saw the dispatch in this book. I would have initiated a dispatch on that subject. However, our relations with ONI and the other divisions were close, and if I had seen that dispatch I surmise that I would have talked it over or brought it specifically to the attention of Admiral Wilkinson. I do not know why I did not see that. I believe I would have remembered it.

Mitchell further inquired, "Well, do you not think that this message of the 24th of September . . . did change the overall picture that we had up to that time, to wit, that there was no definite information of any particular animosity toward Pearl Harbor and this changed the picture—I assume it did—in that aspect, at least, does it not?" Turner answered, "I think it changed it sufficiently so that if I had seen it I would have taken it up with Admiral Wilkinson or possibly talked it over with Admiral Ingersoll, but I would not have initiated any dispatch on that subject myself."[46]

Theobald considered the failure to pass the "bomb plot" information to Oahu was part of the alleged Roosevelt conspiracy. "Why was such irrefutable evidence of the coming attack so withheld? Why did Washington contribute so completely to the surprise feature of that attack? There can be only one answer—because President Roosevelt wanted it that way!"[47]

One need not postulate a conspiracy in order to find Washington at fault for its handling of these significant messages. The top brass did not keep Hawaii's defenders informed in this respect because they did not appreciate the implications of the messages. Had Washington taken them seriously, the War and Navy departments should, and probably would, have made sure that Short and Kimmel, respectively, saw them. Even so, evaluation of just such information was a function of the Army and Navy general staffs. They had no right to deny the commanders in Hawaii the benefit of their interpretation of the data. They were also obligated to consult the Hawaiian commands concerning such facts and deductions which touched directly upon the local situation at Oahu.

In a memorandum to Stimson concerning the Army Board's report, The Judge Advocate General somewhat glossed over the ships-in-harbor series:

> The above appear to point to some specific action against Pearl Harbor. However, this inference is in the light of after-events; at that time these radios, to an unimaginative person, were consistent with routine Japanese effort to keep themselves advised as to our naval strength in the Pacific or possible sabotage attacks on ships in Pearl Harbor by native Jap fishing boats.[48]

This is difficult to accept, for Japan did not need to know the exact berthing arrangements in Pearl Harbor to determine "our naval strength in the Pacific." And the suggestion that the consulate might be passing information to local Japanese sampans by way of Tokyo is unworthy of a serious answer. In contrast, the Navy Court concluded that the Navy Department had received messages "sent to Japanese officials in Honolulu clearly indicating that Japan was most desirous of obtaining exact information as to the ships in Pearl Harbor."[49]

At least one Army officer—Bratton—thought the Japanese were showing undue interest in Pearl Harbor, but he accepted the Navy's assurance that if war started the Fleet would be at sea.[50]

The services' self-excusing attitude in regard to the consular traffic showed them in a very unfavorable light. They claimed they knew about and read this mass of information and did not consider it important. But if the inordinate interest of Japan in the home base of the U.S. Pacific Fleet in a year of war and serious tensions in the Far East was not important, what was?

No wonder the revelation of the "bomb plot" messages during the congressional investigation so inspired columnist H. I. Phillips that prose failed him. Like a bard of old, he broke into verse to chant the saga:

> They laid Pearl Harbor out in zones—
>   And named 'em one by one!
> It didn't seem suspicious though,
>   To us in Washington.
> They plotted out the areas
>   And asked about the ships there,
> But how were we to gather that
>   Foul play was in the air? . . .
>
> The Nippies tipped their hand to us
>   And almost marked it "Rush!"—
> We read the details leisurely
>   And marked them all "hush, hush";
> We thought it would not be the thing
>   To tell to Short or "Kim"
> Far out there on the battlefront
>   With life so drab and grim.[51]

Unfortunately, U.S. leaders in Washington were so engrossed with the diplomatic exchanges that they forgot a profoundly important fact: that in the Japan of that day, diplomacy danced to the military tune. So clues to Tokyo's actual policy could be expected to lie in the military and naval information to and from Japan's consulates. Such clues were not lacking. The contention that the information from Honolulu did not differ in essentials from that emanating from

Japan's other consulates is untenable. The "bomb plot" message of September 24 and the related dispatches back and forth that followed were unique. It is amazing that no one in Army or Naval Intelligence grasped the implications of this series, because on the whole those officers did a splendid job within the limitations imposed upon them.

On the various Pearl Harbor might-have-beens, this was one area where one could reasonably postulate that proper action might well have influenced the events of December 7. It is unlikely that a fuller knowledge of the Purple messages would have had any effect upon Kimmel's and Short's attitudes. Even if Marshall had telephoned his message of December 7, and if Short had interpreted it correctly— a very big *if* indeed—the warning would have come too late for more than makeshift defense measures. As for the highly ballyhooed "winds execute" message,* its receipt would have made no difference one way or the other. However, the "bomb plot" series was in another category. Perhaps these messages would have meant to Kimmel and Short all that, with hindsight, they claimed; perhaps not. But these men deserved the chance to weigh this information.

It is difficult to pinpoint who in Washington was to blame for this most unfortunate failure to communicate with Fleet Headquarters and the Hawaiian Department. Virtually everyone concerned, except Bratton and perhaps Safford, found nothing extraordinary about the "bomb plot" messages. Even Lieutenant Commander Alwin D. Kramer, a very bright and sensitive officer on loan from the Far Eastern Section of ONI to the Translation Section of the Communications Division, sent the initial message through Navy channels marked with one asterisk, signifying "interesting," rather than a double asterisk, which he reserved for "especially important or urgent" messages.[52]

As respective chiefs of Naval Intelligence and G-2, Wilkinson and Miles had the command responsibility. The latter thought the message of September 24 just one more instance of the usual Japanese interest in American ship movements.[53] As has been mentioned, Wilkinson regarded it as an example of Japanese "nicety of intelligence," and did not recommend sending it to the Fleet.[54] Wilkinson's relative indifference was surprising in a naval officer of his back-

---

*See Chapter 19.

ground. True, he had no previous intelligence experience, but he had plenty of intelligence in the civilian sense of the term. Having been stationed at Pearl Harbor earlier in the year as skipper of the battleship *Mississippi*, he should have been able to visualize the physical layout of Pearl Harbor, and to comprehend the difference between Japan's interest in ships at moorings and her routine inquiries about ship movements. Whoever was personally at fault, failure to inform the most interested parties was clearly a serious error in judgment on the part of the Army and Navy general staffs.

CHAPTER 17

"The Pitfalls of Divided Responsibility"

Criticism of Intelligence—Intelligence work held in low esteem—Navy War Plans evaluated intelligence—Turner's mistaken evaluations—Errors at staff level

The mishandling of the "bomb plot" series was not the only incident that placed the intelligence agencies on an uncomfortable spot. Columnist Drew Pearson assigned much of the blame for Pearl Harbor to Army and Navy Intelligence, which he claimed to be "under the command of drawing room experts."[1] Journalist Frank C. Waldrop declared that ever since the Panay incident the government had a duty to know at all times what the Japanese were doing. In his opinion, the Roberts report left the FBI and Naval and Army Intelligence under a cloud.[2] Some congressmen took dead aim on those agencies. Representative Coffee of Washington poured sarcasm over Wilkinson:

> The Director of our Naval Intelligence . . . is an affable, socially inclined, cultured gentleman.
> . . . They have established rigid rules for admission into Naval Intelligence. . . . One of the indispensable qualifications is that the candidate for Naval Intelligence must come from a family at least four generations old in the United States. . . .
> Intelligence service can never be effective if it is comprised of blue bloods exclusively. . . . We need . . . men who can speak the language of the enemy, understand his habits, and mingle with him. We need men who are not fearful of getting their hands dirty; of wearing old clothes. We need men who are fearless of danger, and who glory in adventure. . . .

Next, Coffee turned his sights landward and shot Miles and his colleagues in G-2 full of holes:

The director of our Army Intelligence is another gracious and affable gentleman. . . . Places in military intelligence are reserved for members of America's best families. They are as ignorant of life in Japanese slum areas and of the influence of the geisha and Yoshiwara activities upon the soul of Japan as though they were on the planet Mars.

Had our intelligence services been on the job and had our scout patrols been properly vigilant, they would have known of the impending approach of the Japanese plane carriers or heavy bombers and certainly would have had prescience of Japan declaring war upon the United States.[3]

This was an oversimplified slam at U.S. intelligence agencies. One wonders at Coffee's reasoning which pictured the ideal intelligence officer as a grimy-handed, threadbare washbuckler fresh from the Old Country, a habitué of geisha houses. Army and Navy Intelligence had an excellent reason for preferring native Americans for several generations back. These people had no close ties with the Old World, hence were not vulnerable to emotional blackmail. Such officers as Bratton, McCollum, Kramer, and many others were no less effective because they did not eat peas with a knife. And one seriously doubts that the intelligence services wanted "fearless" men who gloried in adventure. Disregard of danger often means lack of judgment and common sense, while the adventurer frequently takes risks for the fun of it. Neither quality was desirable in an intelligence agent.

The secrets of Pearl Harbor lay in the minds of Japanese officers very similar to their American counterparts. These men knew how to keep their own counsel. A U.S. agent speaking flawless Japanese could have prowled about Japanese slums for many a long day without catching a hint of Yamamoto's plan. Coffee's outburst was part of the almost hysterical search for villains prevalent at the time.

Stimson later noted that Miles had been "unjustly criticized in respect to the Pearl Harbor situation where, instead of criticism, he deserved the highest praise."[4] The respected commentator Arthur Krock had kind words for G-2 and ONI: "That these activities shine like good deeds in a naughty world is implicit in the [Army and Navy] reports, though the handsome acknowledgment that might have been expected did not reveal itself to the careful search of this correspondent." Krock especially cited "General Miles, whose duty clearly was extremely well done," and "Admiral Wilkinson . . . with another high record of performance at the time."[5]

Still, it would be unrealistic to visualize the intelligence community as a collective Cassandra, proclaiming unpleasant truths and always ignored. Sometimes the pattern had a reverse. At a conference concerning the defense of Pearl Harbor held in Marshall's office on the morning of February 6, 1941, the Chief of Staff "indicated that the Navy had insufficient nets for defense against either submarine or plane carried torpedoes. He further indicated that there was a possibility of a Japanese attack." But Miles "stated that nothing in G-2 indicated any such probability."[6]

Yet this meeting took place in the midst of a flurry of correspondence on the subject under discussion: Ambassador Grew's celebrated message of January 27 wherein he warned that he had heard from his "Peruvian Colleague" that "in the event of trouble with the United States," the Japanese planned "a surprise mass attack on Pearl Harbor";[7]* Knox's letter to Stimson of January 24 about the security of the Fleet and its Pearl Harbor base; Stimson's reply thereto dated February 7, stressing that the Army's mission in Oahu was "to protect the base and the Navy concentrations."[8]† Possibly Miles meant that G-2 had nothing in hand pointing to actual Japanese plans and preparations for such a strike, because he "did not at any time discount the possibility of a Japanese surprise attack on Hawaii."[9]

Other staff officers were just as skeptical as Miles. On December 4, 1941, one "Smith" (probably Colonel Walter Bedell Smith, secretary of the General Staff), forwarded to Marshall a report, dated November 29, which a Mr. Stanley Washburn had sent to Knox. Washburn's remarks merited serious consideration. He thought the Japanese were "much stronger than we are apt to believe. . . . They probably have the best Naval and Military Intelligence in the world." He also stressed the Japanese penchant for surprise: "The Japanese are never without a plan in Naval, Military or Diplomatic affairs, and they almost invariably do the unexpected."

He feared an attack on the Philippines, and anticipated trouble in the Hawaiian Islands, where he considered it "logical from past experience to believe if war occurs that there will be much sabotage." He was "firmly of the opinion that every Japanese over ten, male or female, is a spy at heart." Then he scored a direct hit: "If the Japanese have submarines in the Pacific, it would not surprise me to see them

---

*See Chapter 12.
†See Chapter 20.

attack our battlefleet based at Pearl Harbor, though I doubt not that you are prepared for this contingency."

Smith's covering memorandum mentioned Washburn's warning of sabotage, adding a bit disdainfully, "There is nothing new in the letter."[10]

In 1941 Naval Intelligence suffered from lack of respect and continuity. In general, naval officers disliked intelligence duty. Stark admitted to Greaves that "ONI was not a happy job." Stark's counsel, David W. Richmond, added that

> all men bucked intelligence service. . . . With new ships being commissioned and new commands available, the men were all reaching for them. That is one lesson we should learn from P.H.; there ought to be an opportunity for advancement whether or not you can run a ship. Re ONI, it was always how quick can I get out. How can you develop talent under such conditions. The urge is to get out. It is the deadliest kind of routine work.[11]

Relating to Barnes an incident of the early 1930s which illustrated then CNO William V. Pratt's low esteem for certain key officers in ONI, Safford was brutally blunt. "At that time, Naval Intelligence was the dumping ground of the Navy, and assignment to Intelligence duties was generally considered the 'kiss of death.' "[12] Some months later, Rear Admiral Dundas P. Tucker expressed to Barnes a similar opinion: "Very unfortunately, pre-War intelligence people, especially cryptanalists [sic], were generally regarded as more or less screwballs by the service at large, and their importance was very much underrated."[13]

Army Intelligence, too, suffered from a sense of being pushed aside. At the Army hearings, board member Major General Henry D. Russell asked Brigadier General Russell A. Osmun, who had been chief of G-2's Military Intelligence Service, "Do you regard it as a badly neglected agency of the War Department in the past?" Osmun replied, "From the standpoint of military intelligence which could have been secured: yes."

The Army Board apparently thought that Nagumo's task force might have sailed to Hawaii from or through the Japanese Mandates. Osmun believed that, even with adequate G-2 personnel, they could not have discovered what might be taking place in those islands in November and December 1941. He thought the problem went "a great deal deeper" than availability of personnel. "We had a national psychology to deal with. . . . Lack of belief that we were in danger; disinclination to spend the tremendous sums of money that would be involved. . . . There was a lack of really trained Army officers available, and a general lack of comprehension at that time of the need for military intelligence."[14]

Captain Ellis M. Zacharias, a long-time naval intelligence officer, informed the congressional committee that, in his opinion, failure to appreciate the importance of intelligence was "one of the greatest contributing factors" to the disaster at Pearl Harbor.[15] In his view, intelligence was a specialty, comparable to the work of the Bureau of Medicine and Surgery.[16] On the other hand, "The orthodox and conservative type of naval officer is designed by training and indoctrination not to be an intelligence officer."[17]

The congressional committee recommended that intelligence service be upgraded. In effect, they adopted Zacharias's concept of Intelligence as a professional branch of the service, such as the Medical Corps. They explained that *"the assignment of an officer having an aptitude for such work over an extended period of time should not impede his progress nor affect his promotions"* (italics in original).[18]

The committee devoted much time and thought to intelligence. The majority report stated that Pearl Harbor portrayed

> the imperative necessity (1) for selection of men for intelligence work who possess the background, capacity, and penchant for such work; (2) for maintaining them in the work over an extended period of time in order that they may become steeped in the ramifications and refinements of their field and employ this reservoir of knowledge in evaluating data received; and (3) for the centralization of responsibility for handling intelligence to avoid all the pitfalls of divided responsibility which experience has made so abundantly apparent.[19]

The committee blamed neither G-2 nor ONI for the short-circuit of intelligence between Washington and Oahu a few days before the attack when Japan ordered her diplomats to destroy codes. But in view of the "overwhelming preponderance of testimony" that in the context of the day such destruction meant war, the lawmakers stated:

> It is clear that Washington adequately discharged its responsibility in transmitting this information to Hawaii. With the failure, however,

of Admiral Kimmel to read into this intelligence what it is agreed should have been self-evident to him, it is believed that in contemplation of the future the intelligence as well as the departmental appraisal and estimate thereof should be supplied field commanders.[20]

Here again, circumstances underlined the indivisibility of collection, evaluation, and dissemination. Pearl Harbor was less a failure of Intelligence than a failure to use the excellent data available. The fact that Washington did not evaluate this information at its real worth is inexcusable. This is especially true of the Navy Department, where Turner had insisted that since his War Plans Division "had the duty of issuing operational orders it must arrogate the prerogative of evaluating intelligence."[21]

In his testimony, Zacharias was particularly emphatic in his disapproval of this arrangement, "because the evaluations were made by certain war plans officers without a background knowledge of Japan and Japanese and they could not possibly have at their disposal all the information available."[22] He felt certain that "if the Chiefs of Intelligence had been allowed to retain that function and had the responsibility, that a great many things which did occur would not occur."[23]

Turner apparently kept this function in his own hands or at least very close to himself. Hindmarsh later told Barnes that "these were Turner's own evaluations because they were frequently in his own handwriting so that they were his own and not those of his aides."[24] The Navy and Army Plans offices were familiar with the plans for the defense of Hawaii which postulated an air attack as the major danger; yet, as we have seen, both ignored Japanese espionage messages which expressly indicated an inordinate interest in the exact position of Kimmel's ships in harbor.

Turner placed himself on a particularly hot spot when he testified that he "thought the chances were about 50–50 that we would get a heavy raid in Hawaii." He insisted that he did not stand alone, that this possibility "had been the opinion all along" expressed by the War and Navy departments, in Hawaii, and "by everybody else. . . . That was merely following along the line the Navy officers and Army officers had been thinking about for 25 years or more."[25]

One might be tempted to write off Turner's assertion as a hindsight attempt to appear omniscient in the eyes of the congressional committee. However, according to Admiral Wellborn, Turner did indeed entertain such views. Wellborn testified to Hart's investigation, "Admiral Turner felt that attack on Oahu was quite probable. Other officers felt that such an attack was entirely possible but appeared to regard it as somewhat less probable than did Admiral Turner. I believe that Admiral Ingersoll and Stark were in this category."[26] Wellborn also informed Prange that he "definitely recalled that Admiral Turner did think, at the time the 'War warning' message was prepared, that an air attack on Pearl Harbor was one of the likely possibilities."[27]

Turner believed that the "war warning" of November 27 should have sufficed for Kimmel.[28] "The defensive deployment as applied to Hawaii . . . was for the defense of Hawaii and of the west coast of the United States."[29] The message told Kimmel to prepare to execute Task H of WPL 46, which was to protect "the territory of the Associated Powers in the Pacific area." That included United States territory.[30]

William D. Mitchell, general counsel of the congressional committee until January 14, 1946, asked Turner why he had not mentioned Hawaii in that dispatch along with the Philippines, Thailand, Kra, and Borneo. Turner explained that Japan's major war effort was in that area. Kimmel "had nothing to do with that except as a later task to attempt to keep as much of the Japanese Fleet in play in the Marshalls as possible. . . . So the order to him . . . is 'Execute a defensive deployment.' "[31]

In view of the documents that Turner cited, one must concede that he had a point. The Martin-Bellinger report, for example, was jointly prepared by the Hawaiian Air Force and the Naval air forces on Oahu, and was signed by Major General Frederick L. Martin, commanding the former, and Rear Admiral Patrick N. L. Bellinger, who commanded Patrol Wing Two along with holding other positions. This report had postulated that Japan might attack Oahu, "including ships and installations on Oahu," prior to a declaration of war. This document was a virtual anticipation of Japanese aims and tactics, prepared and forwarded to Washington in March 1941, at precisely the time the Japanese were formulating the Pearl Harbor concept.[32]

Turner seemed to have been the only officer who really took such estimates at face value. But that imposed upon him a serious obligation. As the congressional committee commented, assuming Turner's statement to be correct, "There can be little doubt . . . that he could have given the commander in chief of the Pacific Fleet the benefit of his conclusions had he been disposed to do so."[33]

If Turner thought a Japanese raid on Hawaii, in addition to the major drive southward, to be a 50-percent chance, it was his clear duty to say so plainly in his directive to Kimmel. The CinCUS had a good mind, but his testimony makes obvious the fact that he was not the type to read between the lines. Thus important phraseology of the "war warning" passed over his head. Explicit mention that an attack on Hawaii was at least as probable as it was improbable could have made all the difference. "If I had believed in those days preceding Pearl Harbor that there was a 50–50 chance or anything approaching that of an attack on Pearl Harbor, it would have changed my viewpoint entirely," Kimmel testified. "I didn't believe it. And in that I was of the same opinion as that of the members of my staff, my advisers, my senior advisers."[34]

Of course, Kimmel's remarks contain an element of hindsight. But a direct warning could have done no harm, and might have done inexpressible good. Not only would it have alerted Kimmel in unmistakable terms, it would have cleared the Navy Department of blame for failing to do just that.

However, Turner inserted in the "war warning," which he drafted,[35] no hint of a 50-percent chance the Japanese would attack Hawaii.

Another message which Turner drafted reflects one of the misdirections quite prevalent at the time. On October 16, following the fall of the third Konoye cabinet, he prepared, and Stark approved— after toning it down "considerably"[36]—a warning to the three fleet commanders which contained the estimate that "hostilities between Japan and Russia are a strong possibility."[37] While Turner believed Japan would not be ready to tackle the Americans, British, and Dutch "for at least a month," it might well be in a position to strike Siberia. Japan had an army in Manchuria, and "a great part of the Navy in her home waters."[38]

Ever since Germany invaded the Soviet Union in June 1941, Turner had considered that Japan's initial move might be against Siberia, perhaps an invasion of the Maritime Provinces in August 1941.[39] His testimony made it clear that by no means did he expect the Japanese to strike the Russians in lieu of the Americans, merely prior to the Americans. In his words, "it looked like the first move might have been against Russia instead of to the south, but I felt that

that would be succeeded, if successful, by war by the Japanese against the United States."[40] In the context of the time, this estimate was not as fantastic as it may appear by hindsight. In 1941 the Soviet Union was not a superpower, and it was sorely beset by the Nazi hordes.

One story told of Turner seemed to reflect unfavorably upon his judgment. The latest of several versions came from Toland:

> During Knox's daily meeting with Stark, Turner, Noyes and other leading naval officers there was a long discussion on Japanese intentions. "Gentlemen," asked Knox, "are they going to hit *us?*"
>
> "No, Mr. Secretary," said Admiral Turner, who was generally considered the spokesman for Stark. "They are going to attack the British. They are not ready for us yet."[41]

This alleged comment was so at variance with the entire body of Turner's sworn testimony that it calls for close scrutiny. It originated in 1954, in an article by retired Vice Admiral Frank E. Beatty, who had been Knox's aide in 1941, and who was present at the meeting in question, held on the morning of December 6. Beatty related that, after the usual briefing and chart study by Wilkinson, "Secretary Knox addressed the group in general: 'Gentlemen, are they going to hit us?' An officer *whom I recollect to be Admiral Turner* quickly answered, 'No, Mr. Secretary, they are not ready for us yet; they are going to hit the British (italics supplied).[42]

So there was some doubt in Beatty's mind as to just who spoke up. That it was Turner is most unlikely. He testified unequivocally that for years he had considered war between Japan and the United States inevitable, and after June or July of 1941 "imminent."[43] On December 1, he had expressed to Wilkinson the belief that in their move south the Japanese would strike the Philippines, but Wilkinson disagreed.[44] Wilkinson's view was that Japan would not attack an American target. He was not even sure that they would take on the English directly, although the latter almost certainly would fight "in support of Siam."[45] In fact, according to Turner, on December 6, Wilkinson "informed me that he felt I was mistaken, and I asked him, 'Mistaken in what,' and he said 'Mistaken that Japan would attack the United States.' "[46] Thus Turner may have been credited with a judgment which more likely came from Wilkinson.

Looking back, Forrestal thought that War Plans should have kept a daily and weekly log, both of the information secured through the 'Magic' and other sources. He believed "a survey of such a log would have given clear indication of the rapidly accelerating deterioration of the Japanese situation which would have called for far sharper outlining of that situation to Admiral Kimmel than was given him."[47] But, unwisely, Washington did not keep such logs, or prepare historical graphs of the cumulative material received through the Japanese diplomatic and consular traffic. So the United States did not have a proper perspective on the problem.

Obviously Turner was something of a bête noire to Knox and indirectly to Stimson. On March 16, 1942, Knox told Stimson "with evident great mental relief" of certain changes he was making in "the top side" of the Navy Department. He had given King "full authority to clean out the operation bureau which apparently has been clogged up with ineffective personnel. Turner is to go to sea immediately."[48] Later that year Knox confided to Stimson "his efforts to get Turner out of the commanding position" he occupied at Guadalcanal. To this information Stimson "said a hearty Amen,—from my acquaintance with Turner in the early portion of my presence here when he was the head of the Navy Planning Division."[49]

Turner was far from popular with a number of his fellow naval officers. Tucker called him "a bull in a china shop. He was a man of inflexible mental habits, a man who wanted it all simplified, nothing complicated for him; he wanted all the answers quickly and in black and white and no difficult mental process to go through, by all means no thinking, just machine-gun answers—bang! bang! bang!"[50]

Rochefort's opinion of Turner can be summarized in the classic phrase, "expletive deleted." "He was rigid, narrow, intolerant and had no use for Intelligence in 1941. But," Rochefort added with a grin, "when he got out into the Pacific and started to fight the Japs we made a Christian out of him in no time at all."[51]

Beatty believed that Turner was the real CNO in the latter part of 1941. At top conferences of State, Army, and Navy officials, Turner usually spoke for the Navy, even if Stark was present. Undoubtedly he exerted great influence over Stark and dominated his colleagues on the staff. According to Beatty, Noyes was a "weak sister" whom Turner intimidated; Wilkinson, although honest and brainy, was helpless under Turner's domination. Beatty disliked Turner as an "arrogant bully" who had little accurate information about Japanese naval plans because he ignored and rebuffed the Magic experts. Beatty thought Turner "certainly one of the most important persons responsible if not the man mainly responsible" for Pearl Harbor.[52]

Such judgments appear harsh, but they sprang from Turner's own actions. He won his battle for the dominance of War Plans over Intelligence, and had to abide by the consequences. If his estimates had enabled the United States to fend off or at least be prepared to meet the Japanese threat at Pearl Harbor, Turner would deserve the appreciation of a grateful nation. By the same token, he could not justly avoid his share of the blame for failure. In regard to his "50–50" estimate, the congressional committee gave Turner the benefit of the doubt. Oddly enough, the minority report, which included Gerow among the Washington officials listed as responsible, did not name Turner.[53] Yet he was fully as culpable as his opposite, Gerow.

Turner must have possessed an overpowering personality, because Wilkinson was no pushover. He won the Medal of Honor for action in the Veracruz campaign. In World War II, he received the Distinguished Service Medal for his performance in the Solomons, became Halsey's deputy in 1943, and in July of that year replaced Turner as commander of the South Pacific landing operations.[54] Stark did not know Wilkinson well when he appointed him director of Naval Intelligence, but knew his reputation as "a highly intelligent man." He "unquestionably" took up Wilkinson's appointment with Knox, who was "greatly interested in the Intelligence Division, and . . . none of these moves was made without his personal O.K."[55]

Although the Army Board rapped the War Department's knuckles for its mishandling of Magic, it gave G-2 a pat on the back: "Within the scope of its activities, this division performed well. It gathered much valuable and vital data. Through Colonel Bratton it insisted on the dissemination of this information to the Field Commanders."[56]

Pettee was not so pleased. As he wrote, the use of Magic

after reception was often erratic, the evaluation of it was apparently subject to change, and the reactions of the staffs was subject to blockage, misconception, and sheer inattentiveness. With all this there is an innocence and naïveté about the testimony which suggests that the persons involved did not understand how the work should have been done, and what were the serious faults involved.

Given the recognition that Japan might blitz Pearl Harbor, that possibility had not been studied carefully enough. For, Pettee noted, "no doctrine on how to identify the symptoms" had been laid down, and the services obviously lacked "any idea that intelligence should give warning of a surprise attack before a declaration of war." He also cited Washington's failure to coordinate the data received. No one "thought of lining them all up and trying to put two and two together, otherwise than by haphazard memory. . . . There was no pretence of a considered assembly of the bits and pieces of political and military intelligence. There were only able, but much too busy, top executive officials trying to do the job of intelligence 'on the cuff.' "[57]

Despite its praise of G-2, the Army Board worried over "the mandated islands, the homeland and the home waters of the Japanese empire, and the areas in which the Japanese Navy and Army were operating. In those fields, reliance was placed upon sources of information which were inadequate."[58] The board was groping at that point, because it "made its findings at a time when they did not have the magic." Clausen sketched the interrogation of Miles:

> I remember how he sat there when he was not allowed to give magic information, and we were asking him all kinds of questions about what he knew in Washington, and whether he got his information from spies, and why didn't he have spies out in the islands; and, of course, when the magic picture unfolded, it was a different story. We knew what he was getting. We got that right out of the horse's mouth.[59]

Nevertheless, the board continued to fret over the spy situation. "The disadvantage accruing from this situation could have been calamitous. The Japanese armed forces knew everything about us. We knew little about them. This was a problem of all our intelligence agencies."[60]

However, the Japanese were not omniscient. They did not know that the United States had broken their diplomatic codes, despite a warning from their ambassador in Berlin and searching questions from Nomura. They had a bad count of Oahu's airpower. And Yoshikawa in the Honolulu consulate had not been able to size up accurately United States submarine strength, dispositions, and capabilities. Nor, so far as is known, did he report on Oahu's radar capabilities. Then, too, the U.S. Navy's excellent antisubmarine performance in Hawaiian waters came as a complete surprise to the Japanese. Above all, they misinterpreted the American spirit, although Nomura had made frequent and well-expressed attempts to bring his superiors to an understanding of the American people.

It is questionable whether even the finest intelligence could have spelled out exactly where and when the Japanese planned to make their initial strike. The prospective attacker knows what he is looking for and goes about finding it. The potential victim, utilizing intelligence for self-protection, perforce works largely in the dark. He does not, cannot, know exactly what he seeks. If he finds a direct clue, it may well be by pure luck. Even then, he may not recognize it, as is painfully clear from the misinterpretation of the "bomb plot" series.

CHAPTER 18

"A Lack of Imagination"

Criticism of Gerow—Failure to follow through on warnings—Sadtler's abortive warning of December 5—People, not the system, at fault—Dusko Popov case—Japanese not dependent upon Germans

Turner's Army opposite, Gerow, received more and harsher criticism from the Army Board than did any other officer. The board severely chastised him for his failure to follow up the War Department warnings and to appreciate the total inadequacy of Short's reply of November 27:

> The War Plans Division . . . was charged with directing the preparation of and coordinating the war plans for Hawaii. It had the responsibility and duty to insure the implementing of such plans.
>
> . . . no action after November 1, 1941, appears to have been taken by way of communications or inspections, or a full report of any sort, to reveal whether General Short was doing anything, whether he was doing it correctly, what his problems were, and what help could have been given him.
>
> The War Plans Division took no action when Short put the Alert Number 1 into operation and so reported.[1]*

This error was indefensible. When Gerow received Short's reply to the message of November 27, he assumed that it answered "the G-2 message sent out by General Miles."[2] Actually, G-2 originated no less than three sabotage messages in connection with the Army's prime alert of November 27. The first was brief, from Miles to Lieutenant Colonel Kendall J. Fielder, Short's G-2, and was strictly within Intelligence channels.[3] The other two were more detailed, and sent out by The Adjutant General to Short and to Martin's Hawaiian Air

---

*Short's Alert No. 1 was against sabotage; see Chapter 21.

Force respectively.[4] Probably Gerow meant message No. 482 of November 28, signed "Adams."* In none of the three instances, however, would the reply have been dispatched to the Chief of Staff, which is one reason why the mistake should never have occurred in War Plans. For another reason, Short's reply referred to Washington's number, 472, and even the date, November 27. No. 482 had been dispatched on the 28th.

Thus, a quick check of the number and date that Short cited against the file copies of the various dispatches would have revealed that he was replying to the one signed "Marshall," which had been "intended to warn the commanding general of the Hawaiian Department of the possibility of an attack from without, not against subversive activities."[5]

One could not reasonably expect Gerow personally to root around in the War Plans files for the message to which Short referred. One of his assistants should have performed this routine task before Gerow saw the incoming dispatch. The congressional committee took this into account:

> The supervision by the War Plans Division in this instance was slipshod. General Gerow, as head of the Division, must bear his share of responsibility for this serious error, a responsibility which he has unhesitatingly assumed. The primary responsibility, however, rests with the appropriate subordinates of General Gerow who had the duty and responsibility for supervision of details.[6]

But no one in War Plans took this elementary administrative action. Short's message "was not checked against the number," Gerow admitted, "which should have been done either by myself or someone in my division."[7] Thus Gerow had the character to acknowledge a mistake. "Gen. Gerow has often demonstrated his physical courage," remarked the Philadelphia *Record*. "But the moral courage he showed before the Pearl Harbor Committee was something finer and something rarer." The Washington *Post* also praised "the forthright manner in which he took it on the chin."[8]

But Gerow's courage and honesty could not excuse his division for its careless dealing with such an urgent matter, which was astonishing for reasons beyond office procedure. Gerow had specifically

---

*Major General Emory S. Adams, The Adjutant General.

asked for a report from Short because the War Department "had been unable in the past to get information of exactly what was being done from various overseas possessions," and in this instance they "wanted to know what measures he had taken."[9] Moreover, Gerow himself had deleted from the Marshall message a reference to subversion, so that there might be no misunderstanding of the War Department's intent. For this same reason, the G-2 dispatches had covered sabotage.[10]

In view of these precautions, the War Department was doubly culpable for the offhand treatment it gave Short's inadequate reply. In the pungent words of *Time*, Short's message was "like saying he had a butterfly net ready for a tiger."[11] What is more, he sent a long but scarcely more informative Secret Priority message to The Adjutant General in reply to No. 482.[12] This in itself should have served notice on the War Department that a misunderstanding existed.

If Gerow did indeed believe that Short had answered the Intelligence directive, No. 482, it followed that Short had not replied at all to the War Plans message, No. 472, although the latter was much more important, as the signature of the Chief of Staff indicated. In either case—ambiguous reply or no reply—Short's response to No. 472 called for immediate follow-up to be sure that he understood what was expected of him, and to clarify his actions. Gerow admitted to the congressional committee, "In the light of subsequent events, I feel now that it might have been desirable to send such an inquiry, and had such inquiry been sent it would probably have developed the fact that the commanding general in Hawaii was not at that time carrying out the directive in the message signed 'Marshall.' "[13] At the time, however, again in Gerow's words, "it never occurred to me that General Short would not take some reconnaissance and other defensive measures" upon receipt of No. 472.[14] So there was another of the understandable but unwarranted assumptions which contributed to the Pearl Harbor debacle.

Actually, both the War and Navy departments failed to perform a primary duty—to ensure that Short and Kimmel respectively were carrying out the intent of their warning messages. The *Daily Worker*, which stormed at practically everyone about Pearl Harbor, declared, "It is evident that the War and Navy Departments in Washington did not check up sufficiently on what was going on— or not going on—at Hawaii. It is apparent that some of the same disastrous complacency which permeated the high officers at Hawaii was also present in varying degrees in the War and Navy Department."[15]

The fact that the War Department "had nine days in which to check up on the state of defense in Hawaii, which it did not do," annoyed the Army Board.[16] One rebuttal would be Marshall's comment, "I am still in the position of feeling that when you give a command to a high officer you expect to have it executed."[17] However, humans are prone to misunderstanding and Washington would have done well to follow through.

The Army Board had another grievance against the War Plans Division: "It took no steps to stop the use of the Hawaiian Department as a training station and put it on a combat basis, such as an outpost should have been, with threatened war."[18] That was precisely what both services intended to effect by the warnings of November 27, but they should have spelled this out.

The Army Board also bore down heavily on Gerow for not directing activation of the Joint Hawaiian Coastal Frontier Defense Plan. This would have ensured "the functioning of the two services in the manner contemplated."[19] This was another example of the failure to issue unmistakable instructions. In the view of the air arm, that document had its weaknesses. According to "Hap" Arnold, that branch never adjudged as sound "the plans for the operation of the Army Air Force in Hawaii." He amplified, "We never considered any plans sound which did not give us full opportunity to use the heavy bombers and to get the most out of them; and we did not think that those plans permitted that. We figured that they were wasting the striking force on reconnaissance missions, so that when we had to use a striking force they would not be available." Arnold was also unhappy over "a conflict of authority, a conflict of command out there" in Hawaii. "In our opinion, there never was any clear-cut line there as to the duties of the Army and the Navy as far as the air was concerned, because the air overlaps both."[20]

In contrast, the Navy Department considered the Joint Hawaiian Coastal Frontier Defense Plan so excellent that they "sent it out to the other naval districts as a pattern for them to follow."[21] Whatever its faults, it would have placed Hawaii's defenders in a real alert status. For lack of a clear directive, it remained on the shelf. Yet Short and his Navy opposite, Bloch, could have activated it without orders from

Washington;* hence they were quite as much to blame as their superiors in this case.

In a memorandum for Stimson, The Judge Advocate General agreed with the Army Board's findings on Gerow. He "showed a lack of imagination in failing to realize that had the Top Secret information been sent to Short it could not have had any other than a beneficial effect." Gerow also failed "to make the proper deductions" from such intercepts as the "bomb plot" series. These "might readily have suggested to an imaginative person a possible Jap design on Pearl Harbor. Failure to appreciate the significance of such messages shows a lack of the type of skill in anticipating and preparing against eventualities which we have a right to expect in an officer at the head of the War Plans Division."[22]

Stimson concurred in this judgment. His report to the President included Turner by implication: "I believe the War Plans Division made a mistake in not transmitting to General Short more information than it did," he declared. "A keener and more imaginative appreciation on the part of some of the officers in the War and Navy Departments of the significance of some of the information might have led to a suspicion of an attack on Pearl Harbor."[23]

Marshall moved Gerow out of Washington early in 1942 as part of the reorganization of the War Department. He denied that Gerow's transfer had any connection with his performance of duty. "As to General Gerow, my difficulty with him was that he conscientiously overworked and stayed at the office late at night, and he was, I thought, exhausting himself, and that the thing couldn't go on," Marshall explained to Senator Ferguson. "Therefore, I gave him what everybody in the War Department wanted, a troop command . . . as both an opportunity and a rest."[24]

Another War Department staff office, Communications, fumbled a last-minute chance to bring Short in line with Washington's intentions. On December 5, Sadtler heard from Noyes of what might have been a "winds execute" message.† According to Sadtler, Noyes did not know the exact Japanese code word involved, but was quite sure it meant Great Britain.[25] Sadtler did nothing further to ascertain "the exact wording of the intercept or information which he had conveyed."

---

*See Chapter 24.
†See Chapter 19.

He was positive that the code did not signify war between Japan and the United States. Yet he "was alarmed by the series of Japanese diplomatic and consular intercepts . . . and the mounting tension," as well as this newest information from Noyes.[26]

So, after conferring with Miles and Bratton, Sadtler returned to his office "and personally typed a proposed warning." This he intended to "recommend be sent to the overseas commanders." In an affidavit for the Clausen investigation, Sadtler quoted this from memory: "C.G.–P.I., Hawaii-Panama. Reliable information indicates war with Japan in the very near future stop take every precaution to prevent a repetition of Port Arthur stop notify the Navy. Marshall." Unfortunately, he made no copy of this excellent dispatch, and later his office staff had "no recollection of the drafting of this proposed warning message."[27] Sadtler testified that after typing it, he conferred with Gerow, suggesting that a message be sent "to Panama, the Philippines, and Hawaii." But Gerow replied, "I think they have had plenty of notification."

Sadtler further asserted that he then talked the matter over with Colonel Smith, secretary of the General Staff. Beyond asking Sadtler what he had done, Smith "didn't want to discuss it further."[28] Sadtler did not show his draft to either of these officers, neither of whom remembered Sadtler's coming to see them. In fact, they thought it unlikely, since Sadtler was strictly a communications officer, and Smith was not on the Magic list.[29] Here was another example of contradictory testimony on a vital matter.

Sadtler had no idea of an assault on Pearl Harbor. He "personally thought that if the Japs attacked it would be the Panama Canal."[30] Thus, if his memory of his phraseology served him correctly, Sadtler used the term "Port Arthur" to signify an unexpected strike. It was most unfortunate that this message, if drafted as Sadtler recalled, did not go out. Someone on Oahu might have remembered that at Port Arthur in February 1904 the Japanese launched a surprise attack against the Russian Fleet in harbor, without a declaration of war. The closest analogy in 1941 was Pearl Harbor. Whether or not the warning would have alerted the addressees, no one can say. But another alarm could have done no harm and might have done some good. In sending Sadtler's message, the War Department would have discharged its duty and, incidentally, have cleared its skirts in this particular instance.

The best-known incident of a delayed warning has already been discussed—that which Marshall dispatched on December 7 as a result of Japan's "one o'clock" deadline. As mentioned, Marshall's message was delayed because atmospheric problems induced French, officer in charge of the War Department Signal Center, to use commercial means.* The congressional committee reproved French:

> While it is not regarded as contributing to the disaster . . . it is considered extremely regrettable that Colonel French did not advise the Chief of Staff upon his inability to employ the Army's radio, the anticipated means of communication, particularly when he realized the great importance of the message and the personal concern of the Chief of Staff for its expeditious transmittal.[31]

Suppose French had telephoned Marshall, saying in effect, "Sir, we have lost contact with Oahu and cannot send your message to General Short by the Army system." Would Marshall have replied in some such words as "Never mind, I'll phone him," or would he have said, "Well, use whatever means is available"? The answer must remain forever speculative. In any case, French was acting in accordance with his training by using his initiative in his own area, because a good staff officer gives his chief suggested answers, not problems to be solved. Yet had French contacted Marshall and acted upon whatever orders he received in consequence, French would have been definitely in the clear.

For all the errors at staff level, no hard evidence has come to light of any conspiracy to deprive the commanders at Hawaii of vital information. Belief in such a plot rests in part upon the misconception that the high level staffs of the armed forces were monolithic organisms. This was not the case. Such groups were made up of all sorts and conditions of officers with their own opinions and beliefs. For example, an FBI investigation in late 1941 disclosed "quite a few divergent political opinions in the War Plans Division. Certain officers were actually of the opinion that the United States was messing around business with which it should have nothing to do, and several officers were members of the America First organization while others were strongly sympathetic along that line."[32] One cannot logically conceive of such men aiding and abetting a conspiracy to drag the United

---

*See Chapter 14.

States into a war which they believed this country should avoid. Unfortunately, honest errors proved as damaging as a deliberate plot might have been.

Certain individuals blamed Pearl Harbor upon that nebulous entity, "the system." David Lawrence stated that the Roberts report "indicts a system. And that system involves, by implication, the officials in Washington as well as the commanders in the field at Pearl Harbor."[33] Mary Katherine Strong declared, "The fact that so many people have been shown to be responsible points to an indictment, not of the men, but of the system."[34] Pettee likewise observed, "A number of public comments have already drawn the appropriate moral, that it was not the men but the system of the time which was at fault."[35]

It is questionable that a change of methodology would have ensured against the Pearl Harbor disaster. People make the system. For example, Turner's aggressiveness was directly responsible for placing the evaluation of intelligence under War Plans. And once established, the system is not responsible for the mental processes of those concerned. The system was not to blame for the failure to see the importance of the "bomb plot" series and to give this information to Kimmel and Short; for the too-tight rein upon Magic; for the downgrading of intelligence as a function; for the mishandling of Short's "sabotage" message; for the failure to follow through on the warning dispatches to Hawaii. Nor could one nail to the American system such factors as Gerow's "lack of imagination" and Turner's aggressiveness, any more than one could charge the Japanese system with Yamamoto's powerful personality. The system did not spawn Yamamoto; he bent the system to his will. Indeed, few events in all history demonstrate as clearly as does the Pearl Harbor attack the overriding importance of the human element.

The man who best exemplified the dominance of the individual over the system was J. Edgar Hoover. As director of the Federal Bureau of Investigation, which was under the attorney general, he operated at a level comparable with the War and Navy Department staffs. For millions of his countrymen, Hoover was the very embodiment of the law's protection, the courageous champion of Everyman, fighting off the lawless hordes always lurking at the gates of civilization. Others saw Hoover as preeminently a master of public relations, building his reputation upon spectacular but relatively minor cases which could enhance his personal image, while organized crime, unnoted or ignored, dug itself in.

From the autumn of 1940 until the spring of 1941, Hoover was feuding with Miles, to Stimson's intense irritation. "General Miles came to me with reports of trouble with Edgar Hoover, who seems to be a good deal of a prima donna and has taken offense at some very innocent actions of Miles," the secretary of war confided to his diary on October 14, 1940. February 1941 found Stimson "much troubled" because Hoover, instead of coming to Stimson, went directly to the White House "and poisons the mind of the President." Stimson promised himself, "I am going to have a showdown to it if I know the reason why."[36]

The situation boiled to a head the next day. Late that morning, Marshall came to Stimson "in great perturbation." The Chief of Staff had received a message "from the White House through General Watson for information as to who General Miles's successor would be." Stimson instructed Marshall to tell Watson that he, Stimson, had taken the matter out of Marshall's hands and would handle it himself. Marshall also brought Stimson a letter which Hoover had written to Miles and which had reached the White House—"a very childish, petulant statement which seemed more like [that of] a spoiled child than [of] a responsible officer."

Stimson and Knox conferred with Attorney General Robert H. Jackson, who had jurisdiction over the FBI. Jackson conceded that he "had found Hoover a most difficult person to deal with." These three cabinet members agreed that they must try to work out their troubles.[37] Evidently they did, but not until May, when Stimson recorded that everything had been smoothed out between Hoover and Miles and that he had decided to keep Miles in place.[38] Apparently Hoover lost that round, but the fact that he, heading a division at staff level, could go directly to the White House and almost force the reassignment of the head of G-2, indicates both the depth of his ego and the potency of his influence.

The story of his connection with Pearl Harbor is quite complicated. In brief, it began when Dusko Popov, a counterspy known to British Military Intelligence as "Tricycle," came to the United States in August 1941, ostensibly to set up a new German spy system. He carried with him a questionnaire which, according to Sir J. C. Masterman, "contained a sombre but unregarded warning of the subsequent attack upon Pearl Harbour." About a third of this document covered "specialized and detailed" questions about Hawaii. Popov "was to operate in the United States generally, and would presumably be for some length of time in the eastern states," Masterman wrote.

"It is therefore surely a fair deduction that the questionnaire indicated very clearly that in the event of the United States being at war, Pearl Harbour would be the first point to be attacked, and that plans for this attack had reached an advanced state by August 1941."[39]

Popov later wrote that, recalling the Japanese interest in the British attack on Taranto,* he likewise promptly decided that this questionnaire indicated Japanese designs against Pearl Harbor. But, according to Popov, when he reached New York the chief of the FBI in that city thought the document "too precise, too complete, to be believed." To him it looked like a trap. But Popov assured him, "You can expect an attack on Pearl Harbor before the end of this year unless the negotiations with the Japanese produce a definite result."[40]

A few weeks later, Hoover "encountered" Popov at the New York office of the FBI. The agent wrote wryly, "I use the word advisedly. . . . There was Hoover sitting behind the desk looking like a sledgehammer in search of an anvil."[41] Popov told Hoover he had brought "a serious warning indicating exactly where, when, how and by whom your country is going to be attacked." Instead of falling on his neck in gratitude, as Popov rather ingenuously appeared to expect, Hoover informed him in no uncertain terms that he could catch spies without help from Popov or anyone else. Evidently distrustful of Popov as a double agent, and resenting encroachment on his particular domain of spycatcher, Hoover virtually tossed Popov out.[42] The counterspy suspected that his report never went beyond Hoover, and that this "irrational, ranting man . . . was the person responsible for the disaster of Pearl Harbor."[43]

Such stories are long-lived and lost nothing in the retelling. "Then in June 1941, the Abwehr,† pleased with Tricycle's performance in Britain, instructed him to go to America on an espionage mission to investigate in detail, among other targets, the air, military, and naval installations at Pearl Harbor, which the Japanese had asked the Ab-

---

*On November 12, 1940, British naval aircraft struck ⸝alian ships at anchor at Taranto in southern Italy, knocking out about half the Italian batt¹ ⸝leet for some six months.
†German Military Intelligence.

wehr to reconnoiter because of the difficulties that ethnic Japanese agents in Hawaii were encountering," wrote Anthony Cave Brown. He related the Popov-Hoover incident, then added, "Popov's questionnaire concerning Pearl Harbor was not, apparently, interpreted correctly."[44]

Far from encountering "difficulties," a Japanese in Hawaii was about as conspicuous as a Swede in Minnesota. In fact, a native of an Axis-occupied European country, such as Popov's native Yugoslavia, would be much more noticeable. Dr. Otto Kuehn, Japan's "sleeper" spy on Oahu, promptly made the FBI's list of suspects; Yoshikawa and his associates at the consulate experienced almost no trouble in obtaining whatever information they needed, and went about their business unhindered.

John Toland carried the Popov legend another step forward when he wrote, "That fall he [Popov] had personally passed on to the F.B.I. a detailed plan of the Japanese air raid which he had obtained from the Germans."[45] Whatever the document might be, by no stretch of the imagination was it a "detailed plan of the Japanese air raid."*

The questions concerning Hawaii and its installations, including Pearl Harbor, did not comprise the total or even the major part of the document. It contained a number of errors which, while minor in themselves, demonstrate that the Germans knew much less about the area than did the Japanese they were supposed to be aiding. Pearl Harbor is located on Oahu, not "Kushua"; "Wicham Field" is Hickam Field; and "Lukefield" had long been Ford Island Naval Air Station.

The most interesting aspect of the Hawaiian portion of the document is the fact that it dealt entirely with installations—hangars, depots, workshops, and so forth. It asked not one question about the items of major interest to the Japanese in planning their attack— number and types of aircraft, air scouting patterns, antiaircraft positions, ship types and movements, or mooring details such as requested in the "bomb plot" series. Only one item in the entire document, "Reports about torpedo protection nets," would have been of real help to the Japanese. And that was not included in the Hawaiian portion; it was a generalized "special task" covering the British as well as the U.S. Navy.

---

*So that the reader may form an independent judgment, the "Tricycle" paper is reproduced in full as Appendix 7.

Japan already had a most efficient spy system operating out of the Honolulu consulate which was feeding Naval Intelligence in Tokyo the information it needed to plan for an attack of the type the Japanese made. Tokyo did not need the likes of Popov to clutter up the picture with extraneous details.

One finds here the old notion that the Japanese needed German guidance through every stage of Operation Hawaii. This idea—that the Germans masterminded Japanese foreign policy, strategy, and tactics, and even contributed pilots to the Pearl Harbor striking force— arose almost immediately after the event and persisted for years. This concept was absolutely false. The Japanese were not German stooges. They planned and carried out the attack entirely on their own, and conducted their own intelligence-gathering to prepare for the strike.

To determine the opinion of knowledgeable Japanese about the Popov allegations, Prange contacted his associate Masataka Chihaya. In reply, Chihaya wrote, "Since the Japanese Navy's Pearl Harbor attack plan was top secret, it was absolutely out of question that it asked Germany to help collect information on Pearl Harbor. As a matter of fact, Japan did not inform the latter of her plan of attacking Pearl Harbor at all." In view of these facts, Chihaya rated the story as "nothing but a fake one."[46]

Otojiro Okuda dealt even more severely with the Popov legend, and he was in a position to know the facts. As assistant consul general at Honolulu during 1941, he had been in charge of the espionage centered in the consulate. "My observation concerning the alleged Popov's mission at Pearl Harbor is as follows:" wrote Okuda. "1. As far as I am concerned I have never heard of anything like that. 2. Such things could not have existed from the circumstances of that time." Asserting that any writer of historical fact should be responsible for checking out his data, Okuda added as his third point, "The author of the book is supposed to have failed to do so." Okuda concluded, "4. . . . The description is a ridiculous story fabricated by some one."[47]

Recent evidence has come to light that at least there was such a document as Popov presented. Hoover forwarded to "Pa" Watson to pass to Roosevelt photographs demonstrating the new German system of transmitting messages through microdots which Popov had shown him. Hoover also passed along an edited version of the questionnaire, omitting all the Hawaiian material.[48]

John F. Bratzel and Leslie B. Rout, Jr., the authors of the article containing the above information, asserted that

> the director's failure to transmit the entire Popov questionnaire to the White House and to military and naval intelligence agencies shows both a poverty of judgment on his part and the crippling consequences of rivalry among those governmental agencies charged with gathering and evaluating information essential to the defense of the United States.[49]

Hoover was partially vindicated in 1982 when declassified FBI documents were released showing that the FBI, acting on Popov's information, "worked with the Office of Naval Intelligence to concoct lies, filtered back through the German agent, designed to convince Japan that Pearl Harbor was better defended than it was."[50] In his book, Popov made no mention of any such filtering. On the contrary, he charged that Hoover was primarily responsible for Pearl Harbor because he had repulsed Popov and his information.

Oddly, no one who has written on the subject seems to have questioned the logic of the situation or the nature of Popov's document. German espionage in the United States was unbelievably clumsy, and the FBI had long since broken up its structure. In fact, Popov claimed that he had come to the United States to establish a new system. At that stage, the Germans were more likely to require Japanese help in spying on Oahu than the reverse.

Furthermore, quite aside from the fact that the Japanese never consulted the Germans about any aspect of Operation Hawaii, the Germans were not likely to be going out of their way to do the Japanese any favors in the summer of 1941. Berlin was most unhappy with Tokyo for not joining in the Russo-German war, and in August 1941 was still egging on the Japanese to do so.[51]

Hitler's Germany was not altruistic. If engaging in elaborate espionage anywhere, it was on behalf of one nation—Nazi Germany. And indeed a close look at the Hawaiian section of the Popov paper reveals a natural interest on the part of the Germans in the major base of what might soon become an enemy fleet. More than anything else, however, it strikes the reader as a request for information about future possible targets for sabotage, a Nazi specialty.

Had the document fallen into Short's hands, almost certainly it would have reinforced his preoccupation with sabotage. What it would have meant to Kimmel must be forever speculative. As for Washington, unhappily, the American authorities consistently ignored the really significant evidence of Japanese interest in the Navy's ships in Pearl Harbor and the installations on Oahu, evidence straight from the horse's mouth.

CHAPTER 19

"East Wind Rain"

"Winds" code established—Attempt to monitor—False "north wind" intercepts—Action of December 5—Safford's testimony—Conflicting evidence—Kramer's testimony—Briggs's statement—Safford's coded letter to Kramer—Genuine "winds execute" concerning England received December 7—No evidence of a "winds execute" for the United States

The most controversial and misinterpreted problem handled at staff level in Washington was the "winds" affair. It began with two messages from Tokyo to its Washington embassy dated November 19, 1941. The first, Circular No. 2353, read as follows:

Regarding the broadcast of a special message in an emergency.

In case of emergency (danger of cutting off our diplomatic relations), and the cutting off of international communications, the following warning will be added in the middle of the daily Japanese language short wave news broadcast.

(1) In case of a Japan-U.S. relations in danger: HIGASHI NO KAZEAME.*

(2) Japan-U.S.S.R. relations: KITANOKAZE KUMORI.†

(3) Japan-British relations: NISHI NO KAZE HARE.**

This signal will be given in the middle and at the end as a weather forecast and each sentence will be repeated twice. When this is heard please destroy all code papers, etc. This is as yet to be a completely secret arrangement.

Forward as urgent intelligence.[1]

The second circular, No. 2354, followed. It amplified and clarified the original Circular No. 2353:

---

*East wind rain.
†North wind cloudy.
**West wind clear.

When our diplomatic relations are becoming dangerous, we will add the following at the beginning and end of our general intelligence broadcasts:

(1) If it is Japan-U.S. relations, "HIGASHI".

(2) Japan-Russia relations, "KITA".

(3) Japan-British relations (including Thai, Malaya and N.E.I.); "NISHI".

The above will be repeated five times and included at beginning and end.

Relay to Rio de Janeiro, Buenos Aires, Mexico City, San Francisco.[2]

This message ensured that Japan's diplomats would have a second means of receiving the word, that is, by "general intelligence broadcasts" as well as by the "daily Japanese language short wave news broadcasts." It included Thailand, Malaya, and the Netherlands East Indies in the code word for Japanese-British relations, *Nishi.* By this addition, Tokyo strongly implied that trouble with either of those countries would involve trouble with Great Britain. Also, by the strategic placement and repetition of the key words *Higashi, Kita,* and *Nishi,* it assured that the broadcast containing the message would not slip past the listeners.

The "winds" arrangement arose because Tokyo needed to alert its diplomats in certain key cities, such as Washington, should normal communications be denied them. The signal had to come precisely in the manner and in the wording arranged, otherwise the way would be opened for a whole grab bag of misunderstandings. For one thing, the wind often does blow from the east, and may well bring rain with it. In fact, by one of those ironic coincidences that dotted the Pearl Harbor story, on December 5 Japan time (December 4 local time) the Third Battleship Division, on course for Hawaii, encountered an east wind, with cloudy conditions,[3] and the destroyer *Akigumo* ran into "occasional rain" that day.[4] So the code had to be exact to guard against the possibility of a genuine weather report confusing the diplomats. Normal communications being cut, they would have no means of requesting clarification of any obscurity. Therefore, an authentic "winds execute," as the prospective implementing message came to be called, must come in exactly by the means and in the wording and format prearranged.

Singapore intercepted the original "winds" message and passed it to the U.S. Asiatic Fleet headquarters. Admiral Hart advised OPNAV on November 28, with information copies to Kimmel, the Fourteenth and the Sixteenth naval districts.[5] On December 4 (Java time) Consul General Walter Foote at Batavia relayed the information to the State Department. The intercepts upon which he based his message used the word "war" rather than "relations in danger." But in his last sentence Foote dampened the warning: "I attach little or no importance to it and view it with some suspicion. Such have been common since 1936."[6]

On December 3 the senior United States Army representative at Java gave Miles much the same warning, but added no comment of his own.[7] However, his message bore the routing designation "deferred," the lowest priority for handling, which implied no great urgency on the part of the sender. As a result of this "deferred" priority, it was not decoded until 0145 on December 5.[8]

It may well be that the Foreign Ministry had alerted its Far Eastern stations to imminent war while using less inflammatory words to Nomura, who was not in the ministry's full confidence.

If the "winds" messages had been decoded and translated promptly, as was the case with Purple dispatches, and if an implementing message had come in within a day or two, they would have provided valuable indications of Japanese intentions. But Tokyo transmitted the establishing circulars in the J-19 diplomatic code rather than the top-level Purple, and the U.S. Navy translated No. 2353 on November 28 and No. 2354 on November 26. By that time, it was no news to anyone in authority in Washington that U.S.-Japanese relations were "becoming dangerous." Nevertheless, the War and Navy departments took the "winds" code very seriously, and put into effect prompt measures to intercept any "winds execute" message.

Colonel Robert E. Schukraft, who was in charge of radio intercepts for the Signal Intelligence Service (SIS), Colonel Minckler, and Colonel Sadtler decided to coordinate their search with the Navy. Of their own intercept facilities, they agreed to use Station 2 in San Francisco and Station 7 at Fort Hunt, Virginia. The intercept stations having no Japanese linguists, they monitored only code broadcasts.[9]

For voice coverage, the Army turned to the Federal Communications Commission, which regularly monitored Japanese weather broadcasts from Tokyo. If they intercepted an execute, they were to phone Col. Rufus S. Bratton, Chief of G-2's Far Eastern Section, day or night. Bratton kept in daily touch with the chief of the FCC's National Defense Operations or with his assistant.[10]

Miles recalled that the Army also had the SIS "check with the British to see that we did not miss that implementation, but it was a broadcast in plain Japanese that we were waiting for . . . and we undoubtedly were just as capable of picking that out of the air, or rather more so, than the British or the Dutch."[11]

On the Navy side, at the recommendation of Bratton's opposite, Commander McCollum, Wilkinson asked Noyes "to set up everything he possibly could to intercept the execute."[12] Commander Safford hastened to make the necessary arrangements, not only because of the mission's importance but because "it would be a feather in our cap if the Navy got it and our sister service didn't." He thought that the Navy's "best bet" was the station at Cheltenham, Maryland, which had been listening to broadcasts from Tokyo to Japanese merchant vessels. However, the Navy directed all its intercept stations in the continental United States "to forward all Tokyo plain-language broadcasts by teletype."[13]

The resultant workload, in Kramer's words, "was simply tremendous, swamping." From staff admirals to young watch officers, everyone was on the lookout. Kramer prepared cards with the Japanese code phrases on them for distribution to "certain senior officers of the Navy Department." These were to be taken home, in case they received a call at night.[14]

At Hawaii, Rochefort put four of his "very best language officers" on a twenty-four-hour watch on the frequencies Washington gave him, and on others which his own unit had uncovered. These added up to "all the known voice broadcasts from the Japanese Empire." He did not cover Morse frequencies. Although Rochefort did not attach much importance to the "winds execute," he did his job thoroughly.[15]

The intense monitoring turned up "a number of false alarms." Bratton "was waked up at all hours of the night on several occasions by the FCC who repeated what they had picked up, believing it to be a part of the implementing message."[16]

The FCC intercepted one such "false alarm" at about 2200 GMT on December 4 (1700 EST December 4) from Tokyo station JVW3:

Tokyo today north wind slightly stronger may become cloudy tonight. Tomorrow slightly cloudy and fine weather.

Kanagawa Prefecture today north wind cloudy from afternoon more clouds.

Chiba Prefecture today north wind clear may become slightly cloudy. Ocean surface calm.[17]

Unable to reach Bratton's office, the FCC phoned the Op-20-G watch officer, Lieutenant Francis M. Brotherhood. He was dubious about the value of the message, because "it was an expression that just didn't quite fit the code." But he was not expected "to evaluate or pass on the worth of the contents of this dispatch." Accordingly he phoned it to Noyes, who said something to the effect that "the wind was blowing from a funny direction."[18] It had been arranged that Noyes would use this or a similar phrase if he "didn't agree over the telephone that the message was authentic." Brotherhood called Safford also, but did not recall exactly what was said.[19]

This exchange caused considerable confusion. It convinced Safford that Brotherhood had received a genuine "execute" message, and Safford assured the Hart inquiry that Brotherhood could "recall having seen and having read the Winds Message." Not until Brotherhood returned in 1944 from a tour of duty in Honolulu did they straighten out the misunderstanding."[20]

By December 4, when this false message arrived, Bratton for one was convinced that the "winds execute" was no longer important. For on December 3, "we intercepted a direct order given to the Japanese Ambassador to start burning his codes. That was the purpose of the whole thing. That was it. Any winds execute message we received after that would simply just be another straw in the wind confirming what we already knew."[21]

Nevertheless, efforts to monitor for a "winds execute" continued. At 1945 on December 5, the FCC's Portland station picked up another false "north wind" message. There is little room for doubt that one of these intercepts was responsible for Turner's confusion. On December 5, Noyes had advised that a "weather message" of "north wind clear" had come in. "Well, there is something wrong about that," replied Turner, and Noyes agreed. Yet Turner thought this was a genuine execute message, and "that they had merely made a mistake about that 'North Wind' so-and-so." Not until about two months before he testified to the congressional committee, which was in December 1945, did he learn "that that was a false broadcast picked out of the ordinary news."[22]

A flurry of excitement occurred on December 5, 1941. According to Sadtler, Noyes called him on December 5 at about 0930 and said in effect, "Sadtler, the message is in!" He was not sure which one, but "thought it was the one that meant war between Japan and Great Britain." Sadtler asked Noyes for the Japanese word, but he did not know it. And Noyes asked Sadtler to inform G-2.

Sadtler went to Miles's office and told him "that the word was in." Miles sent for Bratton, who asked that the code word be verified. Thereupon Sadtler returned to his office and called Noyes on their private phone, asking him for verification, but he could not obtain it immediately, being due at a meeting in Stark's office. Sadtler went back to Miles with the information that Noyes could not verify the Japanese word, "but he was positive that it was the word meaning Japan and Great Britain, and it was the implementation of that 'Winds' message." Sadtler added to the Army Board that he was certain the message did not refer to the United States. This intercept made a great impression on him. "In fact, I think it is the most important message I ever received."[23]*

Bratton in essence substantiated Sadtler's testimony, but did not consider the message in question as world-shaking, because relations between Japan and Great Britain obviously had been on the point of rupture for several days.[24]

The most hotly debated "winds" testimony came from Safford, who from his first appearance before Hart through his last before the congressional committee, proclaimed that a "winds execute" for the United States had been received.

Safford's character and expertise in his field were above reproach.[25] "But like most geniuses he gets a bug on certain things," Admiral Tucker conceded, "and once he is smitten with an idea he never lets go. It is then that you have to watch his ultimate judgment."[26]

The force of this comment, coming from a man who deeply admired Safford, became evident as Safford's testimony developed. Much of what he told the various investigative bodies was hearsay, opinion,

---

*It was at this point that Sadtler visited Gerow and Smith in an attempt to send a warning to the overseas commanders. See Chapter 18.

and generalization. As the congressional committee's report stated rather mildly, "it appears that Safford's position before the committee was assumed after a process of elimination of possibilities and reconstruction of a situation concerning which he had only a partially independent recollection."[27]

He first testified to the Hart inquiry, laying the foundation for his "winds" position which, although it varied in details, never altered in its basic contention:

> The "Winds Message" was actually broadcast during the evening of December 3, 1941 (Washington time), which was December 4 by Greenwich time and Tokyo time. The combination of frequency, time of day, and radio propagation was such that the "Winds Message" was heard only on the East Coast of the United States, and even then by only one or two of the Navy stations that were listening for it. . . . The "Winds Message" was received in the Navy Department during the evening of December 3, 1941, while Lieutenant (jg) Francis M. Brotherhood, U.S.N.R. was on watch. . . . Brotherhood called in Lieutenant Commander Kramer, who came down that evening and identified that message as the "Winds Message" we had been looking for. The significant part of the "Winds Message" read: "HIGASHI NO KAZE AME. NISHI NO KAZE HARE. The negative form of KITA NO KAZE KUMORI". . . . The meaning of this message . . . was: "War with the United States. War with Britain, including the N.E.I. etc. Peace with Russia." I first saw the "Winds Message" about 8:00 A.M. on Thursday, December 4, 1941. Lieutenant A. A. Murray, U.S.N.R., came into my office with a big smile on his face and a piece of paper in his hand and said, "Here it is!" as he handed me the "Winds Message." As I remember, it was the original yellow teletype sheet with the significant "Winds" underscored and the meaning in Kramer's handwriting at the bottom.[28]

He added that as "a direct result of the 'Winds Message' " McCollum drafted a "long warning message" to the Asiatic and Pacific fleets, "summarizing significant events up to that date, quoting the 'Winds Message,' and ending with the positive warning that war was imminent."

Safford followed with a list of officers who, he stated, had either seen the message, "knew by hearsay" that the "winds execute" had been intercepted, or "should have some recollection of it." He claimed that he last saw the message in question "about December 14, 1941, when the papers which had been distributed in early December were assembled by Kramer, checked by myself and then turned over to the Director of Naval Communications for use as evidence before the Roberts Commission, according to my understanding at the time."[29]

Those whom Safford asserted had seen the "winds execute" were, besides himself, watch officers Brotherhood, Murray, and Lieutenant (jg) Frederick L. Freeman. None of them upheld Safford's story.[30] Of the eighteen officers who he believed knew about the "winds execute" indirectly, five did not appear before any investigation, hence their recollections are not available. Of the remaining thirteen, Lieutenant Colonel Frank B. Rowlett, who in late 1941 had been a civilian technician in SIS's Crypto-Analytical Unit, remembered only "comment to the effect" that a "winds execute" had been intercepted "shortly before 7 December 1941."[31] Seven officers denied any knowledge of a "winds execute" for the United States having come in.[32]

Sadtler's experience had been with the intercept of December 5. Even that one he knew of only by his phone conversation with Noyes. He never saw the message in question, which was unusual, because interchange between the services was normal procedure. To the best of his knowledge, the War Department never received an execute message.[33]

One of those who denied any knowledge of a "winds execute" having been received before December 7 was Lieutenant Commander George W. Linn, in December 1941 a Communications Intelligence watch officer. His testimony was particularly interesting, because he was a longtime protégé of Safford's and admired him wholeheartedly. They had been in touch via correspondence since the late 1920s, and after Linn received his commission he was called to active duty in December 1940, reporting to Safford in January 1941. That was their first meeting.[34]

An officer who seemingly confirmed Safford was Colonel Moses W. Pettigrew, executive officer, Intelligence Branch, G-2. His affidavit to the Clausen investigation read in part as follows:

That someone whom affiant does not now recall, showed affiant on or about 5 December 1941, an implementation intercept which had been received from the Navy and which indicated that Japanese-

U.S. relations were in danger; that in view of the prior intercepts which had been read by affiant he took the implementation message to mean that anything could happen and, consequently, he had prepared for dispatch to the Assistant Chief of Staff, Headquarters G-2, Hawaiian Department, Honolulu, at the request of someone whom he does not now recall, a secret cablegram, a copy of which is attached.[35]

However, the "secret cablegram" proved to be one that Bratton had drafted, which went out on December 5: "Contact Commander Rochefort immediately thru Commandant Fourteen Naval District regarding broadcasts from Tokyo reference weather."[36] This Bratton had prepared, not because a "winds execute" had come in, but because "everybody was making such a hullaballoo about this winds business" that he decided to alert the Hawaiian Department G-2 so that they could work together with Rochefort on the problem.[37]

McCollum lent no support to Safford's claim. He well remembered the Russian "false alarm" but knew of no message "which indicated that diplomatic relations with the United States would be ruptured." He flatly denied that the message he had prepared on December 4 had anything to do with a "winds execute."[38]

Kramer did not appear before Hart's inquiry, but to the Navy Court his testimony apparently confirmed Safford's account. He said that on the third or fourth of December the watch officer showed him such a message, and "walked with him to Captain Safford's office, and from that point Captain Safford took the ball." He was quite sure the words in the dispatch were *Higashi no kazeame* ("East wind rain"). He thought it was typewritten on teletype paper. He did not see the communication after that, and had no direct knowledge of its disposition.

Later in his testimony he stressed that "all that Op-20-G organization were very much on the qui vive looking for that." He thought he used the words "Here it is" when he accompanied the watch officer to Safford's office. Kramer meant "that finally a message in this plain language code had come through." To his mind, however, it did not necessarily mean war.[39]

Schukraft remembered that about two or three days before the attack Minckler had shown him a piece of yellow teletype paper "which contained what appeared to be a winds execute message." Kramer had seen it, and the Navy thought it was the real thing. It was very brief, not more than one or two lines. This did not square with the Safford message, which he described to the Army Board as "of 200 words or so."

Schukraft "concluded very positively that it was not a true winds execute message. . . . It did not follow the pattern specified by the Japanese in setting up the winds execute message." For one thing, "it was transmitted by a Morse station, and the message was in the voice form, which was impossible." And the identifying phrases "appeared in the middle of the broadcast, which, again, is not correct for the Morse broadcast." It was of the "East wind rain" type, but those were not the words of this intercept. He pointed out to Minckler the discrepancies which revealed that it "very positively was not" an authentic "winds execute."[40]

Noyes explained rather more clearly the technical aspects to which Schukraft alluded. The message had to appear in a certain way. An implementation of Circular No. 2353 had to be transmitted by voice, for No. 2354 by Morse. He did not see how such a short-wave news broadcast could have been sent from Tokyo in Morse. "You can only have a broadcast when people know when it is coming. . . . Now, if you say that you are going to put something in a news broadcast on a certain schedule and then you send it at some other time, then you certainly cannot depend on anybody hearing it who is familiar with the schedule." He added that the Japanese were "most meticulous in carrying out their own instructions."[41]

Asked if he had ever seen such a message as Safford described, Noyes replied:

> I don't believe that his description is good enough for me to answer that question. I will say, however, that the message which he describes is not an authentic execute of a winds message. . . . In the first place, . . . it was not transmitted as the Japanese said it would be, which he passes over. . . . It was sent in Morse code and not by voice. Not on the schedule and not in the broadcast which they had said they would send it. . . . But actually this one has nothing to do with "including the Netherlands East Indies," the circular that was set up—the one he says did—east wind rain. [No. 2353] had no reference to the Netherlands East Indies. . . . That would have been in the Morse one, which merely said north, east and south.

What is more, the Japanese had made no provision for any negative expression such as Safford claimed had been transmitted about Russia.[42]

Rochefort, who, with the possible exception of Safford, was the

Navy's finest communications intelligence expert, fully expected the execute to come by voice. He did not even cover Morse frequencies, because "the very setting up of the winds execute, the term itself implies, in my mind, voice."[43]

One officer whom Safford did not list gave him at least oblique support. Admiral Ingersoll recalled having seen, on or about December 4, a message "indicating that the Japanese were about to attack both Britain and the United States."[44] Later, he was not sure whether he saw this before or after December 7.[45] In any case, he placed a very low value on this information, because "if it was a genuine message, it simply confirmed what we had already sent out regarding the destruction of codes, which was absolutely positive."[46]

Ingersoll might have confused the "winds" code with the "hidden word" code which the Japanese established by Circular No. 2409 on November 27. It listed a number of code words for various countries and to cover several eventualities. The only ones that concern the problem at hand were *Minami* (the United States), *Koyanagi* (England), and *Hattori* ("Relations between Japan and . . . are not in accordance with expectations"). Any message using this code was to end with the English word *stop* "as an indicator."[47]

The message implementing this code did come in on the morning of December 7.[48] It certainly confused Kramer for some time. He did not remember the "hidden word" message until he looked over the Hewitt exhibits the day before he testified. "I had been under the impression since the hearings of last summer that it was a 'winds' message."[49]

Only one man stated unequivocally that a "winds execute" message for the United States was intercepted. However, he did not speak out until almost thirty-three years after the close of the congressional hearings. Ralph T. Briggs, the man in question, was a Navy radio intercept operator, the chief watch supervisor at the Naval Communications Station, Cheltenham, Maryland, from September 1941 to August 1942. Briefly, his story was this: During his watch on the evening of December 4, he picked up a Japanese weather broadcast; he did not recall on which frequency. They had been anticipating the phrase for a break between Japan and Great Britain, but he discovered that he had copied *Higashi no kazeame*. Briggs was convinced that his intercept was the "single and only intercept of the true winds execute message signifying a break between the United States and Japan prior to the attack on Pearl Harbor."

He claimed that, acting on instructions, he immediately put it on the circuit to downtown Washington, the 20-G terminal. Along with the original message, he made two carbon copies of the entire weather broadcast, and also made a log sheet. He stated that this was the last time he saw either message or log sheet until 1960, when he was OIC of the unit containing "all our World War II communications intelligence and crypto archives." On December 5, 1960, in searching through these archives, he located the log sheet, and added a notation: "I, RALPH T. BRIGGS, now on duty at a NAVSECGAUDET as OinC, duly note that all transmissions intercepted by me between 0500 thru 1300 on the above date are missing from these files & that these intercepts contained the Winds message warning code. My operation sign was RT."[50]

Instead of totally vindicating Safford, Briggs's statement added more convolutions to an already complicated story. Briggs claimed to have intercepted the execute on the evening of December 4. Safford originally said it was broadcast on the evening of December 3, Washington time. Then he told the Army Board that it "was received in the morning of Thursday, December 4, 1941 . . . about 8 o'clock at one of our East Coast intercept stations."[51] And he informed the Hewitt inquiry that it came in early in the morning of December 4, Washington time, rather than late the night before as he had previously testified.[52] Yet Briggs's log is dated December 2, which contradicts both Briggs's own statement and Safford's sworn testimony.[53] Briggs's own times do not agree, for the body of his statement reflects that he received the "winds execute" on the evening of December 4, whereas the times given in his notation are "0500 thru 1300"—in civilian terms, 5:00 A.M. to 1:00 P.M.

Briggs also averred that Cheltenham had anticipated receiving word of trouble between Japan and Great Britain, but received instead the code words relating to Japan and the United States. Yet Safford insisted throughout the various investigations that the "winds execute" included both Great Britain and the United States, plus "peace with Russia." This is a major discrepancy, for it is scarcely likely that Briggs would have overlooked the very phrase he expected to see.

Briggs stated that somehow Safford found that "RT" had intercepted and recorded the execute and looked him up. Briggs became convinced of Safford's accuracy, and agreed to be a witness in his behalf. This was during the congressional hearings. But a few days later Briggs's commanding officer ordered him not to confer with Safford again, and not to appear as a witness.[54]

A summons to appear before a joint committee of the Congress is not a social invitation, to be accepted or declined at will. Safford may well have hesitated to plunge Briggs into hot water, but considering the magnitude of the issues Safford honestly thought were at stake, he could not afford such delicacy. If, as he claimed, a genuine execute came in, was ignored, then removed from the files, this meant that all levels of the War and Navy departments had been involved in a cover-up, and that there had been wholesale perjury. If Safford knew of any witness who could support him, and did not insist that such a witness be summoned, he too joined the ranks of the alleged hushers-up.

It was equally interesting, although perhaps coincidental, that not until the congressional committee did Safford state flatly that Cheltenham was the station receiving the message. And he gave that committee much more technical detail as to the alleged reception than he did to any other investigation.[55]

Another of Safford's original statements demands a brief examination—his assertion that he last saw the execute in a file prepared for submission to the Roberts Commission. When Representative John W. Murphy of Pennsylvania asked if such a paper had been given his commission, Roberts replied laconically, "Was not."[56] Kramer had indeed prepared "a fairly bulky file of the traffic of the previous few weeks" for Forrestal, who was acting secretary of the navy while Knox was in Hawaii the week after the attack. This file included the "hidden word" message of December 7.[57] It is possible that Safford had seen the Forrestal rather than the Roberts file, and had confused the "hidden word" with the "winds."

Safford told the Army Board essentially the same story he had told Hart. He conceded:

> This message as received was not the way we expected it, because they had mixed up their voice procedure with the Morse code message. . . . And to further confuse it they gave a negative form of "North wind cloudy." . . . there was some confusion as to what they meant by it; but we knew from other sources that they were definitely not going to attack Russia at that particular time. . . .[58]

Thus Safford brushed aside the very factors which Noyes had testified would have convinced him the message was not authentic.

At the Hewitt inquiry, Safford continued to insist upon a "winds execute." He knew about the Russian "false alarm" of December 4, but said that this had come in "twelve hours or more after what I referred to as the true 'winds' execute had been intercepted and received."[59] This raises the question: If the true "winds execute" had come in twelve hours before, why were the services still monitoring for it?

At the completion of his testimony to Hewitt, Safford somewhat brashly asked him off the record if there was still any doubt in his mind "as to the 'Winds Message' having been sent by Japan and disseminated in the War and Navy Departments." According to Safford, Hewitt looked startled, and John F. Sonnett, the counsel for the inquiry, interposed, "Of course, I am not conducting the case and I do not know what Admiral Hewitt has decided, but to me it is very doubtful that the so-called 'Winds Execute' Message was ever sent."

After pondering a minute or two, Hewitt said to Safford, "You are not entitled to my opinion, but I will answer your question. There is no evidence of a 'Winds Execute' Message beyond your unsupported testimony. I do not doubt your sincerity, but I believe that you have confused one of the other messages containing the name of a wind with the message you were expecting to receive." Safford did not question Hewitt's integrity, but he believed that Sonnett had "succeeded in pulling the wool over his eyes."[60]

The Hewitt inquiry found Kramer retreating somewhat from his earlier position. He remembered a message coming in "some days" before the attack which might have referred to the United States, as he had testified to the Navy Court. But time had modified his memory:

> The reason for revision of my view of that is the fact that in thinking it over, I have a rather sharp recollection in the latter part of that week of feeling there was still no overt mention or specific mention of the United States in any of this traffic, which I was seeing all of and which also was the only source in general of my information. . . .
>
> For that reason, I am now at least under the impression that the message referred to England and possibly the Dutch rather than the United States, although it may have referred to the United States, too.[61]

Between the end of the service inquiries and the beginning of the congressional investigation, the Republicans selected for the latter found in the "winds execute" message a ready-made issue. Evidently referring to the Clausen and Hewitt follow-up investigations, Gearhart declared, "a tremendous effort has been made in the United States to break down the testimony of those who knew about it. . . . No stone has been left unturned in the effort to break them down."

Keefe added a note of melodrama: Kramer had been "badgered and beset by a subsequent effort to break down the testimony which he had given under oath."[62] A few days later Keefe continued, "I sincerely hope that when Captain Kramer appears as a sworn witness before the Pearl Harbor committee, he may firmly adhere to the clear-cut statement which he made when he testified before the naval court of inquiry."[63] This sounded very much like Keefe was indirectly telling a witness how to testify.

Before hearing a word of testimony, the minority members had drawn the line: Safford was the heroic defender of truth, Kramer the weakling who buckled under pressure. The minority held to this position and bequeathed it to future revisionists.[64]

The committee had Safford on the grill for about four days. Captain Robert A. Lavender, Kimmel's counsel, had carefully coached him to this effect:

> They are going to attack your testimony and yourself. You are going to have a hard time making your testimony stick. Don't argue with them. Don't add anything to what you have already said, except in answer to a direct question. Adhere to what you have said previously and try not to let them confuse you.

Safford had his own counsel while he was on the stand—Colonel Nelson B. Gaskill of the Army's JAG Corps. He "went through a postmortem" with Safford "after every session, at lunch and after closing time."[65]

Moreover, Safford "was in contact with Republican members of the committee who, no doubt, encouraged him." He had asked Linn "to attend the sessions with him to manage his papers." Linn declined for logical reasons and in sincere friendship. Ever since the investigation had been announced, Safford enthusiastically had been checking station logs hoping for a clue. He worked out times, frequencies, and possible stations; Linn then checked the microfilmed station logs.

"Time after time he would think he had it worked out," wrote Linn, "and I would have to tell him the logs did not support his theories. On several occasions I found negative information, indicating his theories were not likely or possible." So Linn feared that if he came before the committee with Safford, he might be sworn is as a witness. "The fact that we did not agree in all matters would become known and it would damage him."[66]

Safford ended his description of the receipt of the alleged "execute" in dramatic style:

> "This is *it!*" said Kramer as he handed me the Winds Message. This was the broadcast we had strained every nerve to intercept. This was the feather in our cap. This was the tip-off which would prevent the U.S. Pacific Fleet from being surprised at Pearl Harbor the way the Russians had been surprised at Port Arthur. This was what the Navy Communication Intelligence had been preparing for since its establishment in 1924—*War with Japan!*[67]

He had an explanation for the puzzling question of why Tokyo should have sent Washington a "winds execute" when normal channels remained open. According to Safford, the broadcast was aimed at London, where the Japanese ambassador "had destroyed his secret codes three days previously." Yet the London embassy did have available two nonsecret diplomatic codes, known as PA-K2 and LA, which Tokyo could have used in a pinch.[68]

Safford had convinced himself that there was "an appearance" of conspiracy in the War and Navy departments to destroy all copies of the "winds execute."[69] In this connection, perhaps the most interesting aspect of his appearance before the committee was the introduction into evidence of a long, indiscreet letter which he had written Kramer on January 22, 1944, couched in a code of Safford's devising.[70] Murphy took Safford through this epistle line by line. A statement therein that no one in Naval Operations could be trusted aroused Murphy: "I don't want any sweeping statements. We are going to get down to details. Who could not be trusted?

"Names, please.

"I am still waiting. Waiting."

But Safford had laid back his ears and gave Murphy no names.[71]

Murphy bore down even harder on Safford's charge in the letter that Kimmel and Short had been "framed." Murphy considered framing "one of the meanest and lowest crimes," and again demanded names. Safford said that he "was referring to the War and Navy Departments in general, but not to any specific individual that I can identify." His letter also stated that he had "overwhelming proof" of the guilt of Naval Operations and the General Staff. But when Murphy asked for his evidence of this "overwhelming proof," Safford answered only, "I was referring to the winds execute which had been received and no action taken on it."[72]

Senator Lucas also asked an embarrassing question about that letter: "Well, of course, you knew, Captain, that you were doing something that was wrong, and were violating naval regulations; did you not?" Redfaced, Safford paused in silence before replying, "Yes, sir."[73]

In his questioning, Keefe took pains to emphasize Safford's most appealing quality, his moral courage. Safford had made "some rather strong charges" that "may well militate against your career as a naval officer. Did you realize that when you came here to testify?"

"I realized that every time I have testified," answered Safford, nervously licking his lips and wiping them off with a handkerchief. Spectators applauded, as they did several times during his testimony.[74]

Kramer followed Safford on the stand. Since refreshing his memory by looking over the exhibit pertaining to the "winds" question, he now placed the incident of the alleged execute as about 0830 on Friday December 5. The watch officer was on his way to Safford's office when he saw Kramer in his office and called him to the door "to check his interpretation of the phraseology."

The message he saw covered no more than three lines of teletype, which would hold nowhere near 200 words. He thought the watch officer had already written the interpretation on it. Kramer had no recollection of writing on the message; if he had, "most positively" he would not have used the word *war*. Nothing in the "winds" setup justified that interpretation. He and the watch officer went to Safford's office; Kramer may or may not have said, "Here it is." He saw the document only once and for not more than fifteen or twenty seconds.[75]

Regarding the phrase for Russia, which Safford had said appeared thereon, Kramer testified: "I can categorically state that if any of that phraseology had appeared in the negative form in my mind it would have thrown the whole thing out, because there was no provision whatsoever for a negative form of any of those phrases."[76]

He now believed that the message he saw on the morning of Friday December 5, 1941, was "also a false alarm of this winds system. It was, nevertheless, definitely my conception at the time that it was an authentic broadcast of that nature." He still believed that it used the wording, but that it concerned only one country, England. He thought that the reason he had said "United States" when first asked by the Navy Court was "because of the fact we were at war with Japan, so of course, it must have been the United States."[77]

Kramer had moved far afield from Safford's position, but he had moved very close to the almost equally controversial position of Sadtler and Bratton.

One might be tempted to conclude that a "winds execute" did come in before the attack, but for England, not the United States. Yet that brings up another problem, for the Japanese did send a genuine *Nishi no kaze hare* ("West wind clear") on December 7 Washington time. This is one of the few points of general agreement in the "winds" story.[78] So why should Tokyo have sent two executes about England?

Japanese sources interrogated after the war produced no evidence of a "winds execute" for the United States. Mr. Shinroku Tanomogi, who had been head of the Overseas Department of Japan Radio Broadcasting Corporation in December 1941, did not remember *Higashi no kazeame* or any similar phrase being broadcast before December 8. He was quite sure that he would have known had this been the case.[79]

Toland repeated a story from Takeo Yoshikawa, Japan's spy on Oahu, about hearing of the attack on December 7. He related that Consul General Nagao Kita came out of the consulate and "excitedly" said, "I just heard 'East wind rain' on the short wave! There's no mistake." Toland's note stated, "This message was never intercepted by station MS-5 at Fort Shafter."[80] Nor, we dare say, by anyone else. During and after the Pearl Harbor attack, *Higashi no kazeame* would have been redundant, to put it mildly.

In summation, we cannot improve upon the conclusion which the congressional committee reached in a special appendix to its report:

> it is concluded that no genuine message, in execution of the code and applying to the United States, was received in the War or Navy Department prior to December 7, 1941. . . . In view of the preponderate weight of evidence to the contrary, it is believed that

Captain Safford is honestly mistaken when he insists that an execute message was received prior to December 7, 1941. Considering the period of time that has elapsed, this mistaken impression is understandable.

Granting for purposes of discussion that a genuine execute message applying to the winds code was intercepted before December 7, it is concluded that such fact would have added nothing to what was already known concerning the critical character of our relations with the Empire of Japan.[81]

Few sights are sadder than that of a man as gifted, dedicated, and honest as Safford wasting time, talent, and strength pursuing such mechanical rabbits as the "winds execute." Had it been intercepted and the import promptly sent to Kimmel and Short, it would not have mattered in the least, for no twist of interpretation could have transformed *Higashi no kazeame* into a warning that the Japanese were going to strike Pearl Harbor.

PART III

FIELD COMMANDERS AND OPERATORS

CHAPTER 20

"A Sentinel on Duty"

Nature of command responsibility—Short's background—Appointment to Hawaii and briefings—
Opinions of fellow officers—His staff—Methods of operating—His chief of staff—Short's failure to understand his mission—Dependence upon Navy—The
Hawaiian Department well equipped

The commanders on Oahu made their share of blun-
ders which contributed to the debacle. By the nature of their respective positions as Commander in Chief, U.S. Pacific Fleet, and
Commanding General, Hawaiian Department, Kimmel and Short
would have received the credit had their organizations discovered
and defeated the Japanese task force, or at least made it pay dearly
for victory. By the same token, they could not avoid blame for the
surprise and defeat of December 7, 1941. The armed forces hold the
officer at the top ultimately answerable for everything that happens
in his command.*

This concept presupposes that officers selected for command positions, especially at high levels, will be individuals of sufficient intelligence, experience, and initiative to run their commands within
broad guidelines and without unnecessary kibitzing from the next
higher echelon. In Stimson's words,

> we pick the best men we can for theater commanders and assign
> their mission. The manner of accomplishing the mission is their
> responsibility and we back them up. We consider it unsound to
> attempt to meddle with or make meticulous supervision of theater
> commanders in the performance of their mission, which they in the
> field are better able to judge from firsthand contact.[1]

Admiral Ingersoll spoke in a similar vein for the Navy Department:

---

*See page xxviii for simplified chart of Hawaiian Department.

A commander in chief is considered by the Navy as almost a viceroy out in his own field. They tell him in broad terms what he is supposed to do and they do not bother him with asking him how he is going to do it, or keep bothering him with whether he has done it. . . .

When you put a commander in chief out there you want to leave him, as far as possible, free to do his job, and you trust that he is going to do it, and you help him in such ways as you can, where there are things of which he has no knowledge himself.[2]

In the crisis-starred autumn of 1941, the War and Navy departments could have kept closer tabs on their "viceroys" in Hawaii and been more generous with information. Yet one cannot blink away the fact that in the ultimate test Kimmel and Short did not reveal themselves as the strong, imaginative leaders Washington expected them to be.

Short had received a direct commission in 1902, the same year he graduated from the University of Illinois, his native state. He pursued the usual course of a regular infantry officer of the early twentieth century in a variety of locations and jobs, many in the area of training. He performed well with troops in World War I, and after the Armistice was one of the hard-core group that remained overseas until July 1919. Upon his return, he resumed his upwardly mobile career. He became a brigadier general in 1937, and after two stateside command assignments, the Army called him to Hawaii.[3]

Marshall and Short had known one another since 1906. During World War I they had served together in the First Division. Short's war record, with his subsequent command experience, had impressed Marshall. Then, too, as Forrest C. Pogue pointed out, "Perhaps most important, he [Short] had done an outstanding job as assistant commandant at Fort Benning, the job Marshall once held."[4]

The Chief of Staff considered Short a "very superior officer,"[5] selected for his job because he had "demonstrated his fitness for command. . . . The officers under whom he had served since 1937 had recommended him for a division command in time of war."[6]

Marshall personally chose Short for the Hawaiian post, and summoned him to Washington to confer with him and to receive from him "special written instructions." Short also met with the General Staff sections, particularly the War Plans Division. "The purpose of this visit and these conferences was to equip him with the latest and most up-to-date information and instructions as to the responsibilities of his new command."[7]

Just how comprehensive were these briefings, by whom they were given, and how much attention Short paid to them was never determined during any of the Pearl Harbor investigations. In a series of comments concerning the Army Board of Inquiry's published report, Brigadier General Thomas North, chief, Current Group, Operations Division, made this intriguing remark: "Gen. Carl Russell, who had the Pacific desk at the time told me that Short waved aside an attempt on Russell's part to brief him. It may be inferred that Short was unfamiliar with what the War Dept knew, and did not know about Hawaii." What is more, North's comments indicate that Short was rather egotistical, insisting on corresponding with Marshall when he should have done so with War Plans.[8]

Short also somewhat "waved aside" a special report which his predecessor, Lieutenant General Charles D. Herron, had prepared for him. Herron wanted to acquaint him as fully as possible with his own experience and knowledge of the Hawaiian Department. Since Short was to arrive on the *Matsonia* and Herron to sail on the return voyage of the same ship, they would have only about two and a half days for personal conferences. So Herron sent to Short at San Francisco "certain papers and material relating to the command, for his preliminary review on the ship's journey of five days."

When he met Short on Oahu, he asked whether he had received the material and had read these papers. Short replied that he had received them at San Francisco "but that he had not given them much time while en route." In the limited time available, Herron did his best to give Short a comprehensive briefing, including his opinions on the officers and men, "of the G-2 work being done," defense plans, his all-out alert of the previous summer, the Japanese situation, and the relations existing with the Navy and with civilian agencies and the local population. He escorted Short around Oahu, showing him the installations and imparting his ideas "of possible attack and defense of that Island." Obviously Short believed that he had the whole situation well in hand, for after their talk he never asked Herron for his opinions or for information, nor did he correspond with his predecessor on "command and related problems."[9]

The seeming indifference that Short thus demonstrated in both Washington and Oahu augured ill. But once in position he fell to work with obvious determination to perform well. "He was extremely active and energetic," declared Major General Robert J. Fleming, Jr. "He covered Oahu and he covered those other islands like a tent."

In 1941 Fleming, then a major, was Short's assistant G-4 (Supply) and unofficially his troubleshooter, so he had plenty of opportunities to observe the general in action.[10]

"The members of Short's staff thought highly of him," said Colonel Robert H. Dunlop, Short's adjutant general. "I never heard one of his staff officers say anything bad about him. Of course, he was not the dashing personality of a General Patton, but everyone on Oahu thought he was doing a fine job."[11] Added Colonel Russell C. Throckmorton, the Hawaiian Department G-1 (Personnel) in December 1941, "Short was an extremely energetic officer. He made every effort to get supplies and men to Hawaii. His files bulged with requests to Washington."[12]

Short maintained friendly relations with the Navy. Kimmel "found General Short a very likable gentleman, and subsequently a very able Army officer." Thus he "had confidence" in him.[13] "Short was a very fine officer," he said later. "There was no doubt about that. I liked Short."[14] So did Admiral Arthur C. Davis, Kimmel's fleet aviation officer in 1941. He termed Short "a very tried and true general, both reasonable and sensible."[15] Vice Admiral William Ward "Poco" Smith, Kimmel's chief of staff in 1941, described the general as "very honest and dedicated," although "not the bear for work Kimmel was."[16]

Short's active concern for Hawaii's defense won him the respect of the Territory, and after the attack a number of his civilian colleagues rushed to his defense. Mayor Lester Petrie of Honolulu and a group of prominent citizens wrote to Roosevelt, assuring him of their "high esteem" and "full confidence in the character and ability" of Short "as a citizen and as an officer."[17] Hawaii's Governor Joseph B. Poindexter also sent Short a long letter of appreciation, closing graciously:

> The fact that the Japanese Government has seen fit to inflict a treacherous attack has not in any way diminished the faith of this community in your demonstrated abilities. I wish to state that the magnificent way in which the Territory of Hawaii met its problem in its crucial hour was in a large measure due to your foresight. I am deeply grateful for your efforts on behalf of the Territory.[18]

In that facet of his duties Short had been at home and fully qualified. But his background included no experience in the theory and use of airpower. Major General Brooke E. Allen, who as a captain had been an acting squadron commander of B-17s at Hickam Field in 1941, believed that "General Short had no imagination at all. He was a man of narrow vision."[19]

Apparently, too, Short suffered from an unsureness of touch at his level of command. With his focus on training and ground tactics, he could have done an outstanding job as head of a major training installation or in command of an infantry regiment. But he seemed to have been out of his depth at department level. "Short was never quite able to get beyond the regimental commander's mentality," said Brigadier General James A. Mollison.[20] In 1941 Mollison was a lieutenant colonel, and Chief of Staff of the Hawaiian Air Force.

Though a capable officer, Short lacked the intuitive feel for high command, and he did not get the best out of his official family. "He delegated to his staff little more than routine duties. His direct relationship with his G-2 [Intelligence] seemed particularly inadequate in view of the then existing tense situation," remarked the Army Board. "Although he frequently visited and consulted with his principal subordinate commanders, he held no periodic conferences, and his second in command, General Burgin,* was not taken into his confidence as to existing conditions nor was his advice sought."[21]

There seems little doubt that Short's staff in general did not match Kimmel's in its level of expertise. Nor did Short demonstrate any large degree of judgment in its selection and utilization. He juggled positions continually and not until late autumn of 1941 did his key officers jell into a fairly solid organization. Fleming thought that, on the whole, the staff was competent. He added, "I don't know if any staff ever could have kept up with as dynamic a character as General Short. He was just all over the place and frankly he made a lot of work for those guys sometimes."[22]

Contrasting Short with his predecessor, Fleming emphasized, "Herron did not bother subordinates, and let them do their jobs or at least until they proved they couldn't. And if that was the case Herron took action but in a way that left few if any scars." He made it clear that Short operated quite differently. "Short, however, got to know more about his subordinate commanders than they knew about themselves. This applied to their commands as well. Short was

---

*Major General Henry T. Burgin was commanding general of the Hawaiian Department's artillery and second in seniority to Short.

very impatient," Fleming stressed. "It was probably his main weakness. Short could bluster on occasion and as a result of his impatience and bluster some members of his staff were afraid of him."

Fleming also recalled the general as a strict perfectionist. "Short would go through the roof for the slightest deviation of what he considered perfection." Fleming added tolerantly, "I don't think Short realized this. I don't think Short ever stopped to think that he was scaring hell out of people."[23]

A commander cannot function well without the respect of his subordinates, but if he inspires fear his staff may hesitate to disagree with him or offer independent opinions. The testimony of several of Short's officers hint that such may have been the case in his command. Seldom does their testimony convey the impression that these subordinates were able to stand up to the Old Man, or even truly capable in their own fields. A case in point was Colonel William E. Donegan, who became Short's G-3 [Operations] in November 1941. Attempting to understand the functioning of this man, General Grunert, chairman of the Army's board of inquiry, asked of Colonel William S. Lawton, "What did Donegan do? His assistants seemed to do everything." Lawton, who had been Donegan's assistant, replied somewhat lamely, "He supervised the work of the other members of the section."[24] Fleming recalled that Donegan did not appreciate "some of the things Short was trying to do which would affect operations." Fleming thought that Donegan "had sort of tunnel vision . . . a very narrow viewpoint of his job."[25]

One of Short's strangest personnel actions came in the realm of G-2. Herron had brought back to active duty a reserve officer, Lieutenant Colonel George W. Bicknell; he told Short that Bicknell "was an experienced and qualified, efficient man for that position, and that it had been my intention to make him my G-2." But Short did not take the hint.[26] Nor did he retain Lieutenant Colonel Morrill W. Marston, the current G-2, "a slow-spoken, soft-speaking man from Iowa, solid rather than volatile and about as far from the 'cloak·and dagger' idea of an intelligence agent [as] you could get." Instead, Short brought in Lieutenant Colonel Kendall J. "Wooch" Fielder, his good friend and a delightful person, but with no intelligence background. Marston left Fielder "an excellent shop to move into" and Fielder took hold very well. Fleming believed the transfer from G-2 to G-4 deeply hurt Marston, whom Fleming considered to be "a great man." But Marston swallowed his feelings and "did an absolutely superb job" as G-4.[27]

Short had inherited from Herron an extremely capable chief of staff, popular and respected although "a strong hombre, strict as hell."[28] But Colonel Philip Hayes was due for rotation and Short requested as his replacement Lieutenant Colonel Walter C. "Tige" Phillips, whom he considered "a far more competent man" than Hayes on field work and training.[29] Marshall approved the selection and asked Phillips to try to "bring the Hawaiian garrison as to training" up to the standard of the best in the Army.[30]

Phillips made no major decisions without referring to Short; he did reach decisions on minor staff matters such as "Ordinary personnel matters, transferring small units from this station to that station." As Major General Walter H. Frank of the Army Board suggested, these were matters normally handled by an adjutant.[31] A chief of staff who makes no independent major decisions and offers few if any alternative views is of dubious value. But whether Phillips was ineffectual due to his own limitations or to Short's tight rein remains debatable.

"Short's selection of Phillips appears to have been a mistake," the Army Board's report observed. "An examination of Phillips' testimony as to his conception of his duty and what he did and failed to do in aiding Short to competent decisions in critical situations, is sufficient evidence of the matter."[32]

Some of Short's former associates believed that Phillips was the general's Achilles heel. Fleming "thought that he was indecisive" and "never appeared particularly interested in the special jobs" Fleming did for Short. "Phillips had been riding Short's coattails for a long time," said Fleming, "and where Short would rise so would Phillips." He added, "Phillips was often loud and presumptuous and tried to throw Short's weight around. People resented this."[33] Burgin testified frankly to the Army Board, "Normally he [Phillips] was looked upon as one of General Short's fair-haired boys, and he carried things with a pretty high hand."[34] Colonel Russell C. Throckmorton, Short's G-1 stated:

I never at any time . . . felt that Colonel Phillips was qualified to perform those important duties. I felt that he neither had the temperament nor the sense of judgment nor, perhaps, the basic knowledge; and I am frank to say that I never had a great deal of respect for him in his capacity as chief of staff, as compared with Colonel Hayes and others of my acquaintance.[35]

But to Dunlop's kindly eye, Phillips, while "a little arrogant," seemed "somewhat insecure. This no doubt was partly because he followed such a strong man as Hayes."[36] Less tolerant, Kimmel admitted, "Phillips was no good. It revealed one of Short's weaknesses that he appointed him."[37] Mollison bluntly characterized Short as "narrow, hidebound and a damn poor judge of people and staff."[38] Thus it appears that, instead of complementing each other, Short and Phillips reinforced each other's weaknesses.

For if Phillips was an ineffectual chief of staff, Short misused him in the latter part of 1941. Earlier in the year, Short had taken Hayes with him when he conferred with his naval colleagues. But in November, when Phillips, following a series of preparatory staff assignments, became chief of staff, Fleming instead of Phillips accompanied Short to these conferences with the Navy. Short explained to the congressional committee that Hayes had been in Hawaii three or four years, "knew all the Navy people and had been present at all these conferences. I took him because I thought he had considerable background of what had gone on before." Fleming "had been carrying on a great deal of liaison work with the Navy and I thought he had more of a background than my new chief of staff." For that reason, plus the fact that Fleming "was an unusually keen able officer, with a remarkable memory," Short "thought he would know a great deal about the things that Colonel Hayes had participated in."

No wonder Representative John W. Murphy of Pennsylvania asked, "How was your chief of staff ever to learn or ever to understand if you were taking the engineer to the conferences instead of your chief of staff?" Short answered, "I explained to the chief of staff anything of importance."[39]

This procedure was not a satisfactory substitute for permitting—nay, insisting upon—Phillips's presence at these meetings. It gave the chief of staff no opportunity to form his own judgments as to what was or was not important, to become acquainted with his Navy associates, and to learn the background of their mutual problems.

For that matter, Short denied himself firsthand knowledge of what went on in his department staff meetings. As a rule, he did not attend them.[40] This was poor administration and worse psychology. Inevitably his absence hinted that he did not respect his officers enough to bother hearing their reports and oral views. The value of a military staff meeting was in direct proportion to the interest and capability of the commander concerned. It was up to him whether such a conference became a productive forum for the exchange of information and ideas, or degenerated into a mere presentation of reports.

Thus Short missed the priceless opportunity to guide, encourage, and inspire his staff, watch it in action as a team, evaluate each man in comparison with his colleagues, and pinpoint areas of possible friction or weakness. Moreover, by absenting himself Short had to depend upon secondhand, necessarily watered-down, abbreviated reports of what his staff knew or thought about the week's activities and the prevailing state of affairs.

This may help account for a situation which Clausen pointed out to the congressional committee. He reminded its members that Short had told the Army Board "that he got no information from Washington." One of Clausen's investigative tasks in Hawaii was to see just what Short *had* received. He told the committee, "The files of the G-2, Hawaiian Department, and the other files over there showed that he had a great deal more information . . . than he testified before the Board regarding this general subject."[41] Clausen's testimony hinted at a serious breakdown in communications between the Hawaiian Department's staff and its commanding general. Perhaps Short's chief of staff filtered out more than he should have. In fact, Bicknell stated that Phillips told Short little "because he knew so little himself."[42]

It is unlikely that Short's selection and handling of officers had any direct effect upon the events of December 7, 1941. Kimmel operated in precisely the opposite manner. He gathered together and conferred almost daily with an unusually strong staff of highly qualified, tough-minded professionals who never hesitated to speak their minds. Yet the Japanese caught him, too, by surprise. But Short's actions in this regard are indicative of certain mindsets that would become increasingly important as 1941 sped by.

Of far more direct significance was the obvious fact that Short did not really understand his prime mission. He and many other officers on Oahu seem to have overlooked the simple fact that they would not have been there had no danger from Japan existed. Washington had placed on Oahu the heaviest concentration of military forces at any one spot under the American flag. They were in Hawaii for one purpose: to defend the Fleet and the Territory against a Japanese onslaught.

The U.S. government had spent, in Marshall's words, "hundreds of millions of dollars to make of Oahu . . . an impregnable fortress, to be used as the keystone to the defense of the United States." Moreover, "the defense of our west coast, Panama, Alaska, and other parts of the Pacific were so tied to Hawaii in the various plans adopted over the years, and the defenses installed, as a specific defense against Japan."[43] The Army and Navy had long devised their war plans predicated upon possible conflict with Japan. Both services held maneuvers in the Hawaiian area which had been virtual dress rehearsals for the attack.* On top of this, the history of American-Japanese relations since 1931 had been one of steady if gradual deterioration and was rapidly moving toward a climax.

Marshall had sent Short to this most important of all stations as what Stimson called an "outpost commander," with all the specialized duties and responsibilities of that position:

> The outpost commander is like a sentinel on duty in the face of the enemy. His fundamental duties are clear and precise. He must assume that the enemy will attack at his particular post; and that the enemy will attack at the time and in the manner in which it will be most difficult to defeat him. It is not the duty of the outpost commander to speculate or rely on the possibilities of the enemy attacking at some other outpost instead of his own. It is his duty to meet him at his post at any time and to make the best possible fight that can be made against him with the weapons with which he has been supplied.[44]

To proceed from the general to the particular, "The fundamental fact to bear in mind and from which there can be no escape is that Short was the sole responsible Army commander charged with the mission of defending Pearl Harbor," wrote Brigadier General Myron C. Cramer, The Judge Advocate General, in his comments on the Army Board's report.[45] Marshall had made this unmistakably clear when he wrote to Short on February 7, 1941, "The fullest protection for the Fleet is *the* rather than *a* major consideration for us, there can be little question about that" (Marshall's italics). Later in his letter he emphasized, "our first concern is to protect the Fleet." In his last

---

*A particularly striking example of such an exercise occurred on January 29-31, 1933.

paragraph Marshall slugged the point home once again: "Please keep clearly in mind in all of your negotiations that our mission is to protect the base and the Naval concentration, and that purpose should be made clearly apparent to Admiral Kimmel."[46] So Short had the word in plenty of time—almost ten months to the day before the skies fell in.

The Army Board hammered on the theme of Short's chief responsibility:

> The Army's mission was primarily that of protecting Hawaii, because it was the sea and air base for the fleet; and, when the fleet was in the harbor, it was there to render such protection as it could to the fleet. The protection of the Islands, other than for these purposes, was secondary and only necessary to the extent of making it possible for the Army to execute its primary mission.

The Board added that the Fleet's being in harbor increased the Army's responsibilities, because under such conditions the ships "were temporarily immobilized and particularly vulnerable to air attack."[47]

Yet Short never convinced himself that the shoe was not on the other foot. He believed that the Fleet's presence constituted a protection to the Territory. "I had the feeling, and I know it was on my part and Admiral Kimmel's that as long as he had as much of his exercises of the fleet here in Hawaiian waters, that they [the Japanese] would not try to take a chance with a carrier attack," he testified to the Roberts Commission. "If the fleet had been ordered away from the Hawaiian waters I would have been extremely apprehensive."[48] Later he told the congressional committee, "I would have been much more worried if there had been no fleet in Hawaiian waters."[49]

This notion permeated much of the Hawaiian Department. In a report dated December 22, 1941, summarizing the situation on Oahu as of 0730 on the seventh, Fielder wrote, "With the large part of the American Navy based in the Hawaiian waters the probability of an attack by the Japanese carriers was believed to be negligible."[50]

Evidence that this was not hindsight self-excusing came from Alfred R. Castle, a prominent Honolulu attorney who had long been active in the Red Cross. As a result of having been "rather closely associated" with the Japanese military in 1918, Castle felt sure that "at some time Japan would attack us." So he campaigned hard to ensure that the

Red Cross first-aid stations should be kept in service and that the Fort Shafter hospital be adequately supplied in the event of an attack. An unnamed general, a director of the local Red Cross, assured Castle that "there was absolutely no need for the service stations as long as the American Navy was in the Pacific as the Japanese would not attack." And in a conference with Short and the head of the Fort Shafter hospital Castle received "the usual statement that there would be no attack with the American Navy in the Pacific." Eventually Castle got his supplies—four days before the attack.[51]

This failure to understand his prime mission was Short's original sin. His reasoning that the Japanese might strike Hawaii if the Fleet were absent was illogical, because Kimmel's ships, not the islands, posed the only menace to Japan that the United States had in the Pacific.

One of the few of Short's officers who had a glimmering of this fact was Bicknell. Because of the deterrent effect which the American naval air forces in Hawaii might have upon Japan's war plans, he thought "that Hawaii could be placed very near the top of a list of possible attacks by the enemy." Yet even he had "no definite idea" that the Japanese would strike Hawaii.[52]

Not only did the Hawaiian Department depend upon the Navy's presence to keep Japan at bay but, rather incongruously, the Army on Oahu relied on the Navy for advance warning if the Japanese did attempt to approach the islands. A question from General Russell of the Army Board elicited this reply from Short:

> I figured as long as the Navy was there in such force that they [the Japanese] could not bring the carriers into position from which they could attack the Island without the Navy either knowing where they were or getting enough information to know that they were somewhere in the vicinity; and with the Navy away, why, I realized that they could run carriers in, without any question, and make an attack.

General Frank wanted to know upon what Short based his assumption. "Did you believe that the presence of the fleet in being at Pearl Harbor constituted a security?" Short answered, "It did, because they constantly had task forces out, and they had carriers with those task forces, and they spread their planes out from the task forces, and it seemed to me that there was every reasonable chance that they would discover enemy carriers or get enough information to know that they were dangerous."[53]

Burgin doubted that an enemy carrier could sail close enough to Oahu to launch its planes. While the Army had no means of obtaining information of such an approach, in Burgin's mind and, he was sure, in Short's as well, "was the idea that the Navy was doing the scouting, and that from the Navy we would get our information, should the enemy approach."[54]

Just how completely the Hawaiian Department and the Hawaiian Air Force leaned on the Navy is revealed in this exchange: Frank asked Mollison, "Then, just on the assurance of the Navy you were blindly confident that they were 'delivering the goods'?" Mollison replied, "That is what it amounts to. We were all so sold on the idea that the Navy had this picture, and that with the fleet in Pearl Harbor they would not dare to attack." He had no doubt that the Fleet's presence "contributed to an erroneous feeling of safety on the part of the Army."[55]

A few expressed dissenting opinions. "I have never had confidence in the Navy!" snapped Colonel William E. Farthing, who took over command of Hickam Field on November 27, 1941.[56] Brigadier General Jacob H. Rudolph, commanding the Eighteenth Bombardment Wing at Hickam, had little faith in the Navy's ability to warn of an enemy approach—"Not with those old slow-going boats [PBY's] they had. . . ."[57] But these views were aberrations from the general attitude of almost mystical faith in the Navy.

For centuries military thinkers have recognized the dangers of such complacency. "Skepticism is the mother of security," Frederick the Great instructed his generals in 1747. "Often, through an hour's neglect, an unfortunate delay loses a reputation that has been acquired with a great deal of labor. Always presume that the enemy has dangerous designs and always be forehanded with the remedy." Napoleon had laid down the maxim: "Everything which the enemy least suspects will succeed the best."[58]

The testimony of Short and his subordinates revealed that he had come to lean on the Fleet, at least psychologically, to the point that he lost sight of his own responsibilities in relation to the Fleet. Even Kimmel, ever reluctant to criticize his former colleague, who, like himself, had suffered so much, declared, "I do not want to hurt Short, but his job was to protect Pearl Harbor." Kimmel added, however,

"He did the best he could with what he had but he did not have enough material to do the job."[59]

This was a favorite rallying cry for those who wished to exculpate the Oahu commanders from all blame for Pearl Harbor. But the argument was not valid. True, Short did not have all the men and matériel he asked for, but he was far from operating on a shoestring. His own loyal and dedicated G-4, Colonel Marston, told the Army Board:

> Compared to other such organizations in the American Army, they were very well equipped. Compared to modern standards, they were not well equipped. . . . However, as an illustration of the relative importance placed on antiaircraft defense in this Department, at the time I came over in 1939 there were more active antiaircraft guns in this department in the hands of the 64th Coast Artillery Regiment, I believe, than there were in the entire continental United States.

Grunert pressed Marston: "Relatively speaking, they were relatively well equipped at that time with what was available?" Marston replied, "They were, and that equipment was being brought up just as fast as the War Department, at the instigation of the Department Commander, could bring it."[60]

Marshall testified to the congressional committee, "The military forces on Hawaii were in numbers and in equipment more nearly up to the desired standards than any other installation in the Army. My own impression was that the garrison was sufficiently established and equipped and organized to prevent a landing and to successfully resist an air attack and to defend the naval base."[61]

Marshall explained to the Navy Court of Inquiry that to supply the Hawaiian Air Force with P-36s early in 1941, Washington "reduced most of our fighter squadrons, if not all of them, down to two or three planes . . . and to that extent almost stopped training." He insisted:

> . . . Hawaii was far and away the most heavily provided installation of ours in or out of the country, for defense. It had had first priority in the Army for years, and as to the number of troops and as to equipment, it was far beyond anything else we had. . . . When we put additional aircraft into Hawaii, we denied ourselves a very large training base for the tremendous expansion . . . that we were confronted with.[62]

The unhappy crux of the manpower and matériel situation on Oahu was that the amounts available to Short had little effect upon the issue. Major General Frank B. McCoy of the Roberts Commission asked him, "If you had been furnished with all of the things you felt necessary, would that have made any difference in this particular action?" Short admitted, "I do not believe it would."[63]

Certainly it made no real difference so long as he was not mentally ready to use it. On the contrary, as more than one newspaper and congressman pointed out after the event, "had more equipment been available in Hawaii our losses might well have thereby only been proportionately greater."[64]

CHAPTER 21

"Alerted to Prevent Sabotage"

Short's preoccupation with sabotage—A widespread concept—Triple alert system—Short's installation of antisabotage alert on November 27, 1941—Opinions pro and con—Preoccupation with training—Avoided provoking Japan or alarming civilians—Analysis of results

Since Short obviously believed that he could depend upon the Navy to ward off an attack force or advise him of its approach in plenty of time to prepare his department, perhaps it was predictable that he should have turned his attention inward. He became preoccupied with the possibility of sabotage on the part of Hawaii's Japanese population, then totaling about 170,000, of whom some 37,500 were foreign-born.[1] This fixation persisted although not a single case of Japanese sabotage occurred while he commanded the Hawaiian Department. "There appears to be no substantial basis for this fear other than speculation as to what a large body of citizens and aliens of Japanese ancestry might do in case of stress," remarked the Army Board.[2]

One should try to look through Short's eyes, with the sorry record of Europe fresh before him. The fifth column had been a potent weapon in Hitler's hands. Others shared Short's suspicions. Marshall "fully anticipated a terrific effort to cripple everything out there by sabotage."[3] So did General Arnold, who realized that aircraft were especially vulnerable to that form of attack.[4]

Nor did the civil authorities in Washington ignore the unpleasant subject. When Hawaii's Governor Poindexter visited Ickes in the summer of 1941 to protest the transfer of some of the Pacific Fleet to the Atlantic, Ickes's "idea was that our concern out here was with sabotage, that we should guard against the possibility of sabotage." Then and ever after Poindexter felt "very keenly that this attitude was very largely responsible for conditions" in Hawaii. He discussed

348

the matter with Short, who informed him that "his orders stressed . . . warning against sabotage. . . . General Short was very much concerned with this sabotage business."[5]

"Sabotage permeated right on down from the War Department in Washington," said Fielder. "It was perfectly reasonable to expect sabotage from so many Japanese living in Hawaii in 1941."[6] Fielder "couldn't . . . conceive of that many people of a different race not engaging in some subversive activity in the event of hostilities."[7]

By checking with a few of Honolulu's leading citizens, Short would have received a more balanced impression. Mayor Petrie, who had lived and grown up with Hawaii's Japanese, did not consider them a menace.[8] Major General Bryant H. Wells, who had worked for the Hawaiian Sugar Planters Association since his retirement from the Army in 1935, believed that the great majority of Japanese in the Islands would be loyal. "There would be skunks, the same as there are in many other sections . . . but there wasn't anything that the great United States couldn't handle."[9]

Walter F. Dillingham, president of the Oahu Railroad and Land Company, respected Short, but he pooh-poohed any fear of trouble with the local Japanese. Many of them worked on his railroad where they had plenty of opportunity for sabotage had they been so inclined. They had "picked up and moved away from the docks in Honolulu enough dynamite and high explosives to flatten the whole city of Honolulu." He did not know of a single case of sabotage in that city.[10]

Short's predecessor, Herron, had taken a realistic attitude. He had based his war plan upon the premise that Hawaii's Japanese would be loyal. According to his estimate, "at least 5 percent were committed to the American cause. . . . Another 5 percent . . . would be irreconcilable. . . . The other 90 percent, like anybody else, would sit on the fence until they saw which way the cat was going to jump."[11]

During the post-attack investigations, Short worked hard to justify his sabotage fixation. He stressed to the Army Board, "It looked to me like with 37 percent of the population Japanese or American-Japanese . . . that in case of war with Japan, if we were not alert to the extreme, we might have very serious things happen in our air and harbor defense, particularly, and if it got out of hand there was even a possibility of an uprising."[12]

During the congressional hearings, Senator Lucas's line of questioning threw this preoccupation into sharp focus. "We can't tell what would have happened if we hadn't held a tight rein over them," the general said. "I think the feeling was . . . that if there had been any real success to the Japanese plans, that most anything might have happened." Lucas asked the natural question: "What do you call a success if December 7, 1941, wasn't a pretty fair test of success?" Back came Short's confident answer: "A landing on the island of Oahu. They immediately would have had perhaps an army of thousands, a fifth column of thousands, ready to support them." Lucas finally pried out of the general an admission that, regardless of what might or might not have happened, in actual fact there had been no acts of sabotage on December 7 "or immediately thereafter."[13]

According to Marine Brigadier General Samuel R. Shaw, a captain at the time, "The Army's intelligence estimate was that a sizeable number of local males of Japanese origin were organized and prepared to attack objectives on the island, especially the Navy Yard installations. Further, if this attack occurred, it would be coordinated with other efforts such as shelling from submarines, air efforts by flying boats from the Marshalls, or perhaps some powerful effort of a raid nature."[14]

Nevertheless Short acted as if boring from within necessarily excluded attack from without. This despite the fact that, as the respected journalist Dorothy Thompson had written, "there hasn't been a case during the whole war when an internal rising had not coincided with external aggression."[15]

Short's concentration upon sabotage combined with other circumstances to be disastrous when he reached the moment of truth in his professional life. One of those circumstances was the installation of a three-step alert system. "That was a refinement that the training men put over on General Short when he came out," explained Herron. Short's predecessor disapproved, believing firmly, "There was only one kind of alert, and that was a total alert. . . . But the training men liked refinements, and they recommended three kinds because the Navy had three kinds."[16]

Under the Short system, Alert No. 1 was "a defense against sabotage, espionage and subversive activities without any threat from the outside"; No. 2 encompassed No. 1 plus defense against air, surface, and submarine attack; No. 3 was "a defense against an all-out attack."[17]

Short's fifth column obsession, plus the fact that he had a choice of alerts, were prime factors in his decision to place the Hawaiian Department on Alert No. 1 upon receipt of the famous War Department warning of November 27. That message referred to possible "hostile action" and "hostilities," yet so imbued was Short with the concept of danger from within that he took defense measures only against sabotage. His testimony to the Army Board revealed how tragically his preoccupation had affected his judgment. "I will say frankly that I did not want to go into alert No. 2. . . . My judgment at the time was that while hostilities might take place, the hostilities, in our case, would be in all probability sabotage, or possibly uprisings."[18]

Frank pointed out that military schooling and practice indoctrinated a commander to prepare for the worst possible enemy action. Why had Short not done so? Short's reason: "Everything indicated to me that the War Department did not believe that there was going to be anything more than sabotage."[19]

Sure of himself, and not in the habit of consulting with his field commanders, Short did not seek their interpretation of the warning and their proposals for appropriate action. To Major General Durward S. Wilson, who commanded the Twenty-fourth Infantry Division at Schofield Barracks, he sent a staff officer "to explain exactly what was in the message." He did not confer personally with Wilson because, as he told the congressional committee, "General Wilson had the north sector, which was much less populated than the south sector and where we feared much less subversive measures or sabotage."[20]

Yet the testimony of those same subordinates makes questionable whether they would have seriously challenged his judgment if he had asked their opinion. Wilson thought Alert No. 1 sufficient because they could have moved higher in a few hours. He stressed that "plans were complete for the all-out attack by the Japanese. Of course we were weak in strength, but complete plans had been perfected." Grunert rang the bell: "Well, plans, of course, are good if you implement them; if you don't they are not worth a damn."[21]

Farthing drew a dismal picture of how the No. 1 alert hamstrung his field, which at best was not too well prepared to withstand attack. Hickam had no antiaircraft guns and its few machine guns "were on the ground, and they were not sighted as for air defense. We were defending against sabotage and not air attack." The post guard were armed with pistols. "The guard—everything—our whole idea there was, we thought it was going to be sabotage, and we expected the natives to uprise and come in." No ditches or slit trenches had been dug before the attack because they had not expected one.[22]

Farthing's comments are particularly astounding in view of the fact that in August 1941 he and two of his staff officers had prepared a plan for the air defense of Oahu which postulated a strike on the island from six Japanese carriers.[23]

No one informed Rudolph of the warnings of November 27, and he felt no cause for alarm when placed on the alert. "We thought it was just another one. We had had so many of them . . . and we didn't know the underlying reason for all the alerts because no one pointed out to me personally that the conditions were very critical."[24] So here was a case of crying not "Wolf! Wolf!" but "Rabbit! Rabbit!" And if an officer of Rudolph's experience could not figure out the "underlying reason" for an alert in the late autumn of 1941 without a personal briefing, he just was not paying attention.

Attempting to solve the riddle of why the best-armed and best-manned of all American installations had ignored its reason for existence, Frank asked Phillips, ". . . why in the world did you not prepare for an attack? . . . You had those 8-inch guns and the British 75s, and all your infantry mortars, and the AWS system, and the bombers, and the fighter planes, and your antiaircraft shore defense batteries—and you think that was all put there against sabotage, do you?" Either misunderstanding the thrust of the question or deliberately avoiding it, Phillips answered, "No, sir. That was for Alert 3, sir."[25]

One of the very few of Short's subordinates who disagreed with the wisdom of his action was Brigadier General Edgar King, at the time the surgeon of the Hawaiian Department. By the end of November he was "absolutely certain" that in a very short time the United States would tangle with Japan. Having "a little knowledge" of Orientals, King "reasoned that we would not be given any warning whatever." He was "extraordinarily disappointed" that the command went to Alert No. 1 instead of a more drastic alert. He had stressed "the danger of air attack over surface" because he thought it "the keenest, most dangerous element" based upon the experience of air warfare in Europe. Still, he believed it was not in his province to protest Alert No. 1 to Short because he and others on his staff "had more information than I did."[26]

Possibly the most surprising of Short's supporters in respect to the antisabotage alert was Major General Frederick L. Martin, commanding general of the Hawaiian Air Force. This experienced air officer, with his naval counterpart, Rear Admiral Patrick N. L. Bellinger, had collaborated on a plan for joint action in the event of an attack on Oahu or on United States ships in Hawaiian waters. This study became famous as the Martin-Bellinger Report. It was almost uncanny in its accurate estimate of possible Japanese action.[27]

Grunert questioned Martin as to why they had decided "that defense against sabotage was sufficient" to protect Oahu following the warnings. "Here you make an estimate and you almost dope out just exactly what the Japs did, but when the time comes, and you get a warning, you apparently forget your estimate and go to sabotage. I cannot understand what went on in the topside here." Martin stated that Short "was governed largely by the information he had from the War Department as to what he might expect. There was no indication whatever on the part of anyone that he could expect an attack from the surface of the sea or the air on the Hawaiian Islands." This drew the bolt of Grunert's lightning. "That is what he was out there for, was it not?"[28]

Martin seriously doubted the possibility of a Japanese aerial strike against Oahu "because if it failed, it meant such a reduction in their striking power that they would be confined to their home islands from then on." So why prepare for an air attack when the probable danger lay with "the Japanese population of the islands?"[29]

Martin's chief of staff, Mollison, also supported the antisabotage alert, although he admitted that the dispatch of November 27 "could not be construed as anything else but a war-warning message, there is no question about that." Nevertheless, the information reaching the Hawaiian Air Force's A-2 (Intelligence) from its naval counterpart indicated that the Navy was "pretty well convinced" that they knew "the location of every Japanese ship." Therefore Mollison was confident that "if anything was coming near Hawaii," the Hawaiian Air Force "would be duly informed."[30]

He stated that under the sabotage alert, they could disperse the planes "inside of an hour," but "it would take two or three hours to arm the planes and have them on their way." He did not think that the Hawaiian Air Force would have been substantially better off under any other alert. He explained that, although "safer from air attack" if dispersed, the planes would have required "perhaps five times the number of guards to properly safeguard them from sabotage."[31] Mollison added a little later:

> I think that every man weighs these things in the balance. If he felt that there was an air attack coming, certainly the planes would have been dispersed . . . we felt that if war was declared or started by the other side, the first things that would be done would be acts of sabotage by the nationals that were living in Oahu.[32]

According to Burgin, Short might have planned to escalate his alert status. Burgin discussed the situation with Phillips at the time. The chief of staff told him, "We will go into No. 1; then we will slide immediately to Alert No. 2, and then to No. 3." It struck Burgin that the department was "a little backwards"; they should have gone on full alert immediately. In Short's place, Burgin would have done so, because he believed "in doing the maximum rather than in doing it by dribbles."[33]

But far from escalating, Short apparently pushed his local problems into the background of his attention. Of five conferences with the Navy which the Army held between November 27 and December 4, not one pertained to their mutual alert status. The first four were concerned with the relief and reinforcement of the Marine garrisons at Wake and Midway islands. Short did not even attend the fifth, a talk between Fleming and the fleet Marine officer about the use of Marine 5-inch guns at Canton Island.[34]

Sincerely convinced that he had done the wise thing, Short advised the War Department, "Report department alerted to prevent sabotage. Liaison with Navy reurad four seven two twenty-seventh."[35] In his ex post facto self-defense, Short stressed that Washington never informed him that his actions did not fill the bill. "The War Department had 9 days in which to tell me that my action was not what they wanted," he told the congressional committee. "I accepted their silence as a full agreement with the action taken."[36]

There can be no question that this was a serious mistake on the part of the War Department. But Washington's failure to catch and correct Short's error cannot explain away the poor judgment that he displayed. In this respect, the congressional committee was less than sympathetic when Short protested that "he received other messages emphasizing measures against sabotage and subversive activities, which to his mind confirmed the accuracy of his judgment in instituting an alert against sabotage only." But, as the committee's majority report observed, these messages arrived after Short had already replied to the War Department warning of November 27, hence did not influence his original decision. Moreover, the committee believed that these later messages, far from confirming Short in his decision, should have made him question it:

> Inasmuch as General Marshall's message contained no reference to sabotage whatever, it would seem fair to suggest that upon receiving subsequent dispatches from subordinate War Department officials warning of this danger there should have been aroused in the Commanding General's mind the thought that perhaps he had misjudged the purpose of the original message.[37]

In his draft report Morgan noted another inconsistency. "The very premise on which General Short seeks to insist that the dispatches warning against sabotage and subversion confirmed his instituting an alert against sabotage only . . . is belied by his own admissions." Morgan referred to Short's assumption that the Navy was conducting reconnaissance and would warn him of any approach of danger from without.[38]

What is more, the War Department's warning message had instructed Short to undertake reconnaissance. Such an instruction could not possibly relate to anticipated sabotage on the part of the locals.

Even before the warning of November 27, Short's concentration upon sabotage had hampered the Hawaiian Air Force. Both officers and enlisted men built machine-gun emplacements, filled and stacked sandbags, and performed other chores as part of the ground defense plan. Trained pilots anticipated that in an emergency they would be expected to function as infantrymen.[39] Short seemed not to have appreciated how vital it was to keep his aircraft mobile. Certainly Arnold never foresaw that the A-2 antisabotage warning of November 28 would hamstring the Hawaiian Department's air arm. As soon as he could after the attack, Arnold phoned Martin

> to find out exactly why his airplanes had been so concentrated that they were all destroyed or damaged at once, with no chance for any to get off the ground. . . . The planes had been treated like artillery or tanks or any other war equipment, their value as a highly mobile striking weapon seemed to have been lost.[40]

Several factors other than sabotage entered into Short's decision to initiate Alert No. 1. One of these was a deep-rooted reluctance to interfere with training. Here again, one should attempt to understand Short's position. A large element in his rise to the eminence of a department commander had been his expertise in that field. One of the principal day-to-day activities of a peacetime army is training. As the years of peace roll by, a paradox may develop. The officer who excels in and genuinely enjoys a training situation will prosper. As his devotion to his textbooks, exercises, state of equipment, and such basically academic considerations continues to bring promotions and choice assignments, he would be a truly extraordinary individual if he did not become conditioned to regard a high state of training as an end in itself.

On this score commentator Royce Howes, writing in connection with the Roberts report, remarked shrewdly, "In Hawaii . . . training and the events for which training is being conducted apparently were as widely divorced in the command's mind as were the operational programs of Army and Navy." And he asked, "What better background for training than a condition of constant alarm could be provided is hard to imagine."[41]

Whatever his previous attitudes and programs, Short's concentration upon training should not have survived receipt of the warning dispatch of November 27. The congressional committee believed that message gave "ample notice to a general in the field that his training was now secondary—that his primary mission had become execution of the orders contained in the dispatch and the effecting of maximum defensive security."[42]

But Short did not see it that way. He rationalized placing Alert No. 1 into effect on the grounds that this "permitted the units to go ahead with their routine training." If that had ceased, crews would not be ready to carry out one of the Hawaiian Department's secondary missions—that of readying crews to ferry B-17s from Oahu to the Philippines.[43]

To the Army Board Short was somewhat more explicit. "Alert No. 3 would take every man, practically, so it would eliminate any training." Even Alert No. 2 would "practically put every man of the harbor defense, the antiaircraft, and the air on duties that would prohibit training." He and Martin "talked over the situation and we felt that we should do nothing that would interfere with the training or the ferrying group."[44]

Phillips echoed Short, explaining his position to the congressional committee:

Alert 2 or 3, if adopted, might help to disorganize an air raid, but an air raid was only a bare possibility. On the basis of intelligence from Washington, on the basis of what the Navy thought, and in reliance on the effectiveness of the most complete reconnaissance the Navy could furnish, we felt that preparation to defend against a bare possibility should be weighed against the urgent need to continue training.[45]

Yet that "bare possibility" constituted the primary reason for the existence of the Hawaiian Department, and for Washington's seriously shortchanging the mainland's stock of fighter aircraft to supply the Hawaiian Air Force.

In contrast, Burgin did not believe going on total alert would have handicapped training. On the contrary, it would have helped, for he could have trained "right into position."[46]

Two other elements influenced Short on that November 27. For one, to him the War Department warning indicated that Washington's paramount idea was "that they must avoid war if possible with Japan and that no intentional incident must take place in Hawaii that would provoke the Japanese or give them an excuse. Uppermost in their minds was that they did not want to be responsible for starting a war." Yet Lucas hit home when he asked Short, "And you were not going to do anything to start a war even if you had not heard anything from them, were you?" To this Short answered somewhat lamely, "Not intentionally."[47]

When Representative Murphy wanted to know why Short did not institute Alert No. 2, Short answered that the Hawaiian Department did not do so because part of the Coast Artillery was "right in the middle of the town" and the bombers, except the B-17s, would have to be sent to the outlying islands. "So there would have been a considerable amount of activity. Again perhaps the average citizens wouldn't have understood it fully but if there was a Japanese agent, who knew what he was looking for, he would have known perfectly."[48] Apparently Short had not taken into consideration the fact that the United States had every right to take whatever defensive measures it deemed necessary in its own territory, a situation which no one appreciated better than the military-oriented Japanese Government.

Thus this purely precautionary aspect of the message outweighed in Short's mind its explicit direction that this policy "should not . . . be construed as restricting you to a course of action that might jeopardize your defense."

The second factor was the message's instruction that he should not "alarm civil population." This phrase was ill-judged on the part of Washington. Of course the War Department did not want Short to start a panic in Hawaii, but the wording watered down a warning which Short was all too inclined to misinterpret. In weighing readiness to meet any possible attack against scaring some of the local populace, there should have been no contest. Burgin was absolutely right when he testified that "we should have gone into Alert No. 3, gone all-out, in spite of the fact that it would turn the whole town upside down if we had."[49]

Actually, neither Burgin nor Short, who took the War Department's charge in this regard very seriously, had any real cause to believe Oahu would quake in its collective boots at the onset of a military alert. Herron recalled that his alert of 1940 had occasioned a flurry because "the issue of ball ammunition and of ammunition to the Coast Artillery started everyone's imagination, and many people thought the Japanese Fleet was just off the coast." But none of his subsequent exercises aroused any alarm.[50]

Some of Herron's staff remembered even less reaction to the initial alert. Dunlop testified, "So far as I observed, this alert and the action of the Army in pursuance thereof did not materially alarm the civilian population."[52] Robert L. Shivers, who as head of the Honolulu branch of the FBI was even closer to the local people than Herron and his staff, testified that the populace "considered it routine Army maneuvers and was not alarmed in any way."[53]

General Wells doubted that Short's going on full alert would have disturbed anyone. "I think there might have been some people in the public that were so much interested in it that they would have liked to have gone out and seen what was happening. But the people of this island have seen alerts and have seen the command turned out to their war positions so many times that it is an old story."[54]

The Army Board declared that Short's reasoning in this instance lacked "both substance and credibility," because "the civilian population was accustomed to the continued movements of the Army and Navy in their frequent maneuvers and practice operations. . . . Then, too, the newspapers ofttimes contained much more exciting news, threats and disturbing events, than anything that an alert could stir up."[55]

The congressional committee also dismissed Short's argument as invalid: "The civil population was inured to Army and Navy maneuvers which were going on continuously. . . . In this respect the November 27 dispatch from the War Department interjected no deterrent to full and adequate defensive measures."[56]

Like all important command decisions, Short's represented the sum of various parts. Carefully, conscientiously, he analyzed the warning of November 27. But he did so in the light of his preconceptions, and took into consideration everything but his own assigned mission. Short's job was not to placate the Japanese, not to soothe the civilians of Hawaii, not to maintain his training program intact. It was not even to defend the Islands against invasion. As the Army Board stressed, that was "secondary and only necessary to the extent of making it possible for the Army to execute its primary mission." That was to protect the warships in harbor.[57]

That meant against all possible forms of dangers—not merely such perils as Short believed probable. He had no valid excuse for his total concentration upon antisabotage precautions. Alert No. 2 included everything in No. 1, as well as defense against attack from the air, the surface, and under the sea. By instituting that measure, Short could have covered, or at least watched, all danger areas. Instead, he narrowed his vision to the point where the whole military power at his command stuck its collective finger in the hole in the dyke, ignoring the sea about to pour over the top.

Following publication of the Roberts report and Short's subsequent retirement, the Army explored the possibility of courtmartialing him, later deciding against this action. At that time, however, Colonel F. Granville Munson, of the Judge Advocate General Department, thought the Army could make a good case on the grounds of neglect of duty. He indicated that Short's defense undoubtedly would be "the duty of the War Department to warn him more specifically if it had thought hostilities imminent." Munson declared that "the obvious answer" to this posture was

> that he had been warned, not once but repeatedly, both by the War Department and Navy Department messages of the imminent dangers, well before December 7, 1941; that he had been placed in a

position that every school-boy knows was one of exposure to sudden attack; that his own battle plans referred to it as "frontier"; that what the War Department may or may not have thought of the possibility of a sudden attack could not relieve him of his responsibility; that his failure to take effective and vigorous measures of defense against outside attack can not be condoned as mere errors of judgment.[58]

Marshall was sorely disappointed in Short and considered that Short had let him down in the crisis of November 27. After Short took over in Hawaii, Marshall "had reason to believe that he was performing his duties in an energetic and efficient manner." He regarded his services as "entirely satisfactory."[59] So he had no cause to fear that Short would not stand up to any military problem the Fates might toss in his direction.

In February 1942, when horseback riding with his goddaughter, Marshall let the mask slip in speaking about Pearl Harbor:

He paused, reined in his horse, and looked directly at me, his eyes boring a hole through my head while I sat in my saddle, rigid and motionless before that mesmeric glare. When he spoke again, his voice was even and controlled, and by the unemotional coldness of his tone, I knew that he was very angry. "Nevertheless, it is inconceivable to me how the attack could have been such a complete, such a total surprise. Previous alerts had been sent. They did not follow orders. They were careless and overconfident—a fatal mistake."

Marshall named no names, and his companion wondered if by "they" the general meant both the Army and Navy in Hawaii or only Short and his staff. But she did not dare to interrupt to ask.[60]

Marshall believed that the War Department had furnished Short "with sufficient information . . . on which he could reasonably and intelligently base a probable eventuality."[61] In his opinion, Short had only to obey orders. "I feel that General Short was given a command instruction to put his command on the alert against a possible hostile attack by the Japanese," he explained. "The command was not so alerted."[62] Marshall had a point. Short did not have to evaluate the message of November 27; he should have obeyed a directive which other field commanders understood and complied with.

For example, in contrast to Short's exceedingly brief reply to this warning, Lieutenant General John DeWitt of the Western Defense

Command dispatched to Marshall a detailed account of his measures to prepare his forces for action. He concluded his message, "Should hostilities occur this command now ready to carry out tasks assigned to Rainbow Five so far as they pertain to Japan. . . ." Then, too, Lieutenant General F. M. Andrews of the Caribbean Defense Command sent the War Department a long air-mail letter describing by category the numerous steps he had taken to protect the Panama Canal and other areas under his jurisdiction.[63]

The congressional committee cited a significant feature of the warning of November 27. It "was the first and only dispatch General Short had received signed by General Marshall, the Chief of Staff, since becoming commanding general of the Hawaiian Department. It was a *command directive* which should have received the closest scrutiny and consideration by the Hawaiian general" (italics in original).[64]

Stimson's official report to Roosevelt following the Army Board hearings summed up Short's part in the debacle with remarkable fairness, considering the chagrin, disappointment, anger, and grief Stimson felt at the time. He conceded that Short's superiors in Washington shared the general's "confidence that Japan would not then attack Pearl Harbor"; that the "prevailing psychology" underestimated Japan's military capability, especially in the air; that the War Department had warned Short against sabotage and alarming the local populace. But, Stimson continued:

> these matters, although they may make his action more understandable, do not serve to exonerate him for his failure to be fully alert and prepared against an air attack. He well knew that an air attack on Pearl Harbor, even if improbable, was possible. Yet he ordered an alert which he himself had prepared for use only in case of "no threat from without." Protection against the possibility of such an attack was his own definite responsibility.
>
> To sum up the situation tersely, General Short . . . chose to concentrate himself so entirely upon a defense against sabotage as to leave himself more completely exposed to an attack from without than if there had been no alert at all.[65]

That is unfortunately true. Thanks to Alert No. 1, Short's aircraft were unarmed and bunched together for easier protection against sabotage, but were sitting ducks for air attack. Ammunition was locked up in magazines, where it would be safe from tampering by unfriendly hands. If it should be needed, Short had explained to Burgin, "we would get our ammunition in plenty of time, that we would have warning before any attack ever struck."[66]

Burgin had insisted upon having some ammunition near his fixed batteries, but it was in boxes. Ammunition for the mobile guns and batteries was several miles away at Aliamanu Crater. Nor were the mobile batteries in field position.[67]

Short was a conscientious, patriotic officer who would have yielded up his life before he would knowingly have given "aid and comfort" to any potential enemy of the United States. But ironically, tragically, he had helped pave the way for the Japanese victory of December 7. He had grounded the Hawaiian Air Force; he had silenced Oahu's guns.

CHAPTER 22

"The Failure to Comprehend"

Short's failure to undertake reconnaissance—Relied upon Navy—Mishandling of radar function—Attempts by junior officers to organize radar system—Resistance at higher levels—Mistook cooperation for coordination—Disinclination to keep subordinates informed

Adding considerably to Hawaii's state of unreadiness and to Short's culpability was the fact that he ignored the War Department's instruction that he "undertake reconnaissance." Far from taking this as an order to guard against danger from without, Short assumed that Marshall had not written the message, because the Chief of Staff knew that the Hawaiian Department had turned long-range aerial reconnaissance over to the Fourteenth Naval District.[1] And the War Department must have meant the instruction about reconnaissance primarily for MacArthur, the Philippines having no such agreement.[2]

Had the Navy cared to stand upon technicalities, they could have claimed that this function was still the Army's. The Joint Coastal Frontier Defense Plan (JCD-42) was not in effect on November 27. Associate General Counsel Samuel H. Kaufman of the congressional committee noted and attempted to resolve this area of inconsistency. "Now," he asked Phillips, "will you explain to the committee, if the plan had been invoked, how you could have expected the Navy to make that long range reconnaissance?" Phillips answered vaguely, "The plan, as I recall, could have been invoked at any time. I am not extremely clear on that one point," he admitted. Yet he persisted that "long distance reconnaissance was the Navy's problem." And Representative Jere Cooper of Tennessee, the vice chairman, who was in charge at that particular session, interpolated, "Well, . . . I don't think there is any doubt about that under this record, sir."[3]

There the consensus rests, although the discrepancy has never been cleared up beyond all doubt.

Two Army officers shed light on the genesis of JCD-42. Throckmorton, Short's G-1, spoke of the Army's difficulty in persuading the Navy to reduce the joint agreement to writing. Finally, the Army wrote the agreement and Bloch signed it with minor changes.[4]

Herron explained to the Army Board how the Navy wound up with the long distance aerial scouting:

> the Navy was getting very jealous of the Army flying over the water, and of course we had to fly over the water out there in order to go up and down the Islands. . . . Well, now, in order to avoid coming to grips with the Navy definitely, we worded it that they would be responsible for distant reconnaissance, which of course is logical, as they had the only planes that could go out and stay out; and in order to assure that we could fly over the water we put ourselves down for close-in reconnaissance, without defining that, but actually it amounted to trying to train our people to spot hostile submarines which came in close to shore.[5]

This portion of Herron's testimony hints that in working out the responsibility for aerial reconnaissance both parties had been less motivated by concern for the safety of the Islands than in defining their own operational territory.

In any case, one reason for Short's instituting Alert No. 1 was his assurance, on the basis of "repeated conversations with the Navy . . . that the Japanese naval vessels were supposed to be either in their home ports or proceeding to the south."

Moreover, "a large part of the United States Fleet" was at Honolulu. The carrier task forces normally sent planes "to scour the ocean 300 miles to each side. In other words, any carrier force had a real reconnaissance for a width of 600 miles. For the two you would have 1,200 miles of the ocean in the vicinity of those two forces well covered." In addition, the Navy conducted some reconnaissance from Midway, Wake, Palmyra, and Johnston islands. "I knew these things, and it made me feel that the chance of an attack by air was very slight, or that it was highly improbable."[6]

But what about local aerial scouting? General Russell of the Army Board asked Short, "Is this an accurate statement, then, that you did not know whether or not any distant reconnaissance was being conducted from Oahu?" Short answered, "I would say that I knew that there was very little if any, because it was not an economical way to conduct it." He thought that would be "a big waste of planes."[7]

So he assumed that "operations of the task forces rendered an air attack highly improbable." Further, he "was convinced that the Navy either knew the location of the Japanese carriers or had enough information so that they were not uneasy." He also assumed that the Navy "could handle the situation."[8] He "thought they were doing everything they were capable of doing. They found nothing to alarm them. They had transmitted nothing to me. And I accepted it on that basis." Short was woefully ignorant concerning the operations of naval scouting upon which he relied so heavily. He did not know "specifically what hours they were sending out planes and things of that kind."

Lucas asked him, "You don't think it was incumbent upon you to find out when they were making reconnaissance and definitely what they were doing?" Short's reply spoke more for his sense of protocol than for his sense of mission: "It was Admiral Kimmel's definite responsibility. I thought he was an officer of sufficient experience. He knew more about reconnaissance with surface ships and submarines than I did. I felt that he could be counted on to do his job." Lucas persisted, "You just assumed that was being done?" Short answered, "Yes, sir; as far as he could do it."[9] Observed the congressional committee:

> a simple inquiry by General Short would have revealed that the task forces effected no coverage of the dangerous northern approaches to Oahu; that the Navy was not conducting distant reconnaissance; and that the Navy did not know where the Japanese carrier strength was for over a week prior to December 7. We can understand General Short's dependence on the Navy, but we cannot overlook the fact that he made these assumptions with no attempt to verify their correctness.[10]

The committee decided that while Short had advised the War Department of "liaison with Navy" following the message of November 27, "the evidence is unmistakably clear . . . that he did not establish liaison with the Navy concerning the action to be taken pursuant to the Department's warning message."[11] Indeed, the utter failure to understand the extent and nature of the Navy's reconnaissance demonstrated the lack of any real substance to the Army-Navy liaison of which Short and Kimmel were so proud.

Far from agreeing that the War Department might have meant the reconnaissance instruction only for the Philippines, Marshall outlined what action, in his opinion, Short should have taken:

> he should have been in full contact with the Navy; the arrangements should have been made so far as he could manage them through the Navy for the conduct of over water reconnaissance, of which the Navy would have the direction; his own planes, his fighter and interceptor planes in particular, should have been ready for action. . . . Pilots sufficient for the first flight should have been ready; the radar station should have run 24 hours a day as they did in Panama.[12]

There was no ambiguity about the responsibility for the last function: It belonged to the Hawaiian Department. Early in his correspondence with Marshall, Short had displayed a commendable zeal for this function as "vital to the defense of these islands."[13] Yet he mishandled it, and attempted to blame Washington for its ineptness. He told the congressional committee, "The radar system in New York City and in Seattle and in San Francisco had been completely installed some time before we received any equipment." He understood that to expedite the work New York City "hired experts" from RCA "who were familiar with this type of equipment, to assist in the installation." Short continued:

> Now, when it came to Hawaii, it was just a question of the officers digging out the thing as best they could from the pamphlets they had on the subject and instructing the men the best they could, which undoubtedly took more time. It looked like the War Department was more interested in developing radar on the mainland than in Hawaii.[14]

Just how receipt of all that equipment would have altered the situation on Oahu was debatable. Rear Admiral Joseph M. Reeves of the Roberts Commission asked Short, ". . . if you had had material and fully equipped radar stations, would you have operated them throughout the day or would you have operated them as you did on the morning of the 7th?" Short replied, "I probably would have operated them just as I did."[15]

The evidence was all too clear that the Aircraft Warning Service

(AWS) suffered from inertia and misunderstanding at high command levels on Oahu. Yet at the lower echelons existed an enthusiasm which, if properly supported, could have made the Hawaiian Department's AWS a model for the service. Colonel Kenneth P. Bergquist, who in 1941 had been operations officer of the Hawaiian Interceptor Command, was very knowledgeable in that area. Himself an airman, Bergquist thought an air attack probable, which is why he had been trying to get the AWS "operating on a 24-hour basis" if he could.[16] Not the type to stand around waiting for someone to tell him what to do, in the spring of 1941 he commenced organizing a small information center in the basement of the headquarters at Wheeler Field. "I wanted to get something started so that we would have some kind of an information center going in case of attack. . . . It was not really authorized. We had an awful time trying to get equipment for it; but by the usual methods of chiseling here and there I got the stuff."[17]

Frank asked Bergquist, "How much cooperation did you get from the Department headquarters?" Bergquist countered cautiously, "You want my opinion on that, sir?" Receiving Frank's "Yes," he continued bluntly, "Very little." He considered "that perhaps the main reason for lack of cooperation from mostly the higher headquarters was a lack of education as to what air defense was and what it could do and what the setup could do." One of his problems had been "getting the proper interest by the various agencies that had to cooperate with us on setting up and making this go."[18]

The same troubles plagued Lieutenant Commander William E. Taylor. Those few in the Navy's Bureau of Aeronautics who took fighter direction seriously considered Taylor an expert. He had had valuable experience with the British in the use of radar, and returned to the United States in the summer of 1941 to be commissioned in the Naval Reserve. That autumn he came to Pearl Harbor and Kimmel loaned him to the Hawaiian Department,[19] where he encountered the sort of situation best calculated to drive an enthusiast in a new field straight up the wall. He thought that no one, except possibly Bergquist and Short's chief signal officer, Lieutenant Colonel Carroll A. Powell, "realized exactly how important" the AWS was.[20] One problem was that various organizations were willing to send only their "excess officers" to the Information Center, whereas Taylor and the others concerned wanted good men.[21] He and his colleagues could not drum up "much interest out of the people we dealt with. . . . We saw every Chief of Staff, but we found that somebody else was always responsible."[22]

During the first week of November, Taylor inspected the installations and plans for the AWS, which was then under Powell. At the Hart investigation, Taylor unburdened himself concerning his discoveries:

> This Command appeared to have little conception of the vast function of the air warning system and exhibited very little interest in its installation. At no time before December 7, 1941, did this Command furnish either the authority or impetus badly needed to get the work or organization properly started.[23]

In contrast, the Interceptor Command, which would have to act upon the information received through radar, thoroughly understood its importance. "Although the officers concerned were not fully informed of its complicated functions, they were willing and eager to take advice and lend all assistance in their power to complete its installations." Taylor added, "They seemed relatively impotent, however, in getting assistance needed from the Commanding General's Staff."[24]

Taylor found the radar equipment inferior to any he had previously seen, although the deficiency "was due to crude mechanical construction rather than to any electronic fault. . . . The equipment had a reliable range of eighty to one hundred miles. A 'dead' area existed through a fifteen mile radius from the equipment. It was, therefore, impossible to pick up aircraft plots within the first fifteen miles off shore."

Communications equipment, mostly field phones, had been installed in the Information Center, "but liaison command lines had not been installed." The primary reason for this was "because the activities at which the liaison command lines were to terminate were uninformed as to the purpose concerning the air warning system and because the Commanding General had not taken the steps to coordinate these activities with the air warning system."[25] Furthermore, no liaison had been established between the antiaircraft command and the Information Center.

Neither had any attempt been made to disperse fighter squadrons at Wheeler Field. "No automatic aircraft recognition system was installed which would identify all types of aircraft. . . . No aircraft approach lane system had been planned. . . . No system for identifying aircraft approaching Oahu by reports from parent aviation activities had been organized." Taylor reported these appalling facts to Short, among others.[26] But obviously the general did little or nothing about these crucial problems.

To have established approach lanes and a reporting system to account for planes aloft would have cost nothing in either funds or equipment. What it did require was an understanding of the value of such data. The Battle of Britain had already demonstrated that beyond doubt.

Fleet Headquarters instructed Taylor to confer with Bellinger's Patrol Wing Two "in order to establish an aircraft identification system and aircraft approach lanes to Oahu." Accordingly, at a conference held in late November at the Information Center, "officers from all flying activities were present to discuss these matters. It was decided by the aviation activities concerned that these systems would not be put into effect until war was declared, because it was felt that activating these systems prior to that time would complicate crowded flying conditions and hinder flying training."[27]

Here again two prime misconceptions threw sand into the machinery: The idea that if war came, it would be declared with plenty of time to effect emergency measures, although the Axis nations were notorious for commencing hostilities with no such formality; and that operations had to mark time while training continued uninterrupted. Actually, instituting aircraft identification measures would have been excellent training in itself, and proper flight paths would have helped to deal with congestion in the air.

The Army offered another objection: "movements of aircraft from the United States to the Southwest Pacific were secret, and it was, therefore, not desirable to report those movements at that time." Security consciousness is essential in the military, but when a service refuses to report the movements of its own aircraft to its own headquarters, caution has degenerated from the admirable to the absurd.

As Taylor added, "It should be noted that without an aircraft movement reporting system to the Information Center, it was impossible for the Information Center to determine whether radar reports were [of] friendly or of hostile aircraft."[28] Which effectively negated the entire purpose of the AWS. On this occasion, the fleet operations officer stated that the Fleet was prepared to report its aircraft movements when so requested.

In a related and important area, Interceptor Command had to improvise. "As no controllers seemed to be forthcoming from the Hawaiian Department, Interceptor Command decided to use Squadron Commanders as controllers at the Information Center. These officers were heavily occupied with training their squadrons and were seldom available for controller training."[29]

So one of the most dynamic developments in aviation history floundered in a morass of indifference, misunderstanding, and conventional thinking in the Hawaiian Department. Likewise, Short kept the AWS under the ground forces for a considerable time after it was ready for Air Force control. Here again, Short's preoccupation with training interfered with the logical progression of Hawaii's defenses. The Army Board was particularly severe with Short in this regard. "The difficulty of putting the AWS into full operation as a practical matter," it remarked, "was the insistence of General Short that he retain control for training purposes whereas the best training would have been to put the system into practical operation."[30]

Another hitch was the Signal Corps' unwillingness to release this function. Bergquist explained:

> One of the big arguments was: we wanted to take over the radar stations and get them set up and operating. The Signal Corps said no, that was their job; they wanted to set them up and get them operating and then turn them over to us for operational control. The Department headquarters decided in favor of the Signal Corps.[31]

Obviously exasperated, the Army Board observed, "Despite the efforts of General Martin with Department Headquarters, very few results were secured in making the *Signal Corps let go their technical operation and allow the practical people who were going to operate it go to work*" (the board's italics).[32]

No valid reason existed to prevent Short from releasing the AWS to the Hawaiian Air Force. The radar operation was not ideal but it was functional. One need not charge Short and his ground forces with being deliberately obstructive; the problem appeared to have been, as Bergquist remarked, "a lack of education."[33] Colonel Lorry N. Tindall, who as a major had been one of the controllers at the Information Center on December 7, also believed that there was a "lack of push, a lack of interest, and a realization of what the thing would do" in relation to radar. It was "sort of a 'new toy.' "[34]

What practical difference Air Force control would have made on December 7, 1941, is an open question. For Short's Alert No. 1 canceled out the fighter planes necessary to act upon any information gleaned through radar. And, of course, he had overall control of the AWS.

> [He] had six mobile radar units which were available for reconnaissance use. He ordered their operation from 4 A.M. to 7 A.M. in addition to the normal training operation of radar during the day, but failed to provide the necessary officers handling the equipment with the knowledge that war was at hand in order that they would intelligently attach significance to information which the radar might develop.

Short kept his stations open from 0400 to 0700, because he considered those hours the most dangerous for an air attack.* The congressional committee added this important thought: "The very fact that radar was ordered operated at all was in recognition of the danger of a threat from without; indeed it was only in contemplation of such a threat that General Short would have been supplied radar at all."[35] This being true, Short was inconsistent in using his radar, for if, as this implied, he admitted the possibility of an air attack, why did he institute Alert No. 1? Perhaps Short answered this with his words about the radar operation: He was "doing it for training more than any idea that it would be real."[36]

In truth, an aura of unreality clung to the radar setup which Short established upon receipt of the warning of November 27. "The maximum distance radar could pick up approaching planes was approximately 130 miles out." But he kept his aircraft on four-hour notice. A little figuring should have shown the uselessness of having planes on four-hour alert to respond to a radar signal picked up 130 miles out. Thus, "a warning from the radar information center would have been of little avail."[37]

By operating this radar with neither qualified personnel to evaluate its findings nor planes to scramble at a minute's notice, Short indulged in an exercise in futility. In fact, the Interceptor Command

---

*Had the Japanese retained their originally scheduled attack time of 0630, Short would have been correct. In late October, the Japanese moved the time up to 0800.

did not officially come into being until some time after December 7, although it had been practicing as such under Brigadier General Howard C. Davidson, who commanded the Fourteenth Pursuit Wing.[38] It was only thanks to Bergquist's initiative that an officer was present at the Information Center in late November and early December. When he learned that the stations were to run from 0400 to 0700, he "could see no reason why they should just operate the station and not do anything with the information they got." So he ensured that an officer would be on duty to receive the information.[39]

An effective radar screen on December 7 required three essentials in addition to the mobile stations operating: (1) alert and experienced personnel manning the control center; (2) equally qualified pilots standing by; (3) aircraft fueled, armed, and ready. Unfortunately, because of the antisabotage alert, the very opposite existed. Short's helpless planes stood in rows, difficult to launch and perfect targets for air attack.

In a statement prepared for the congressional committee, Stimson declared that the War Department expected Short to utilize his radar fully when it directed him to take reconnaissance measures. He considered Hawaii's radar "as a most effective means of reconnaissance against air attack" and he knew that tests made in Hawaii had "indicated very satisfactory results in detecting approaching airplanes." Therefore, when he approved the warning of November 27, Stimson "assumed that all means of reconnaissance available to both the Army and Navy would be employed." That included radar.[40]

Stimson did not know personally "what the different methods of reconnaissance between the Army and the Navy would be." He anticipated that "the Navy would play a large part in the reconnaissance of Hawaii, because . . . they were the ships that were being protected, and . . . they had the mobility to make outer reconnaissance." But he had in mind "no limitation" on the type of search Short should use.[41]

Over the years, a convenient target for blame was Kermit Tyler, who as a lieutenant was on duty at the Information Center in the early hours of December 7. When Privates Joseph Lockard and George E. Elliott reported a large radar blip moving toward Oahu, Tyler believed they had picked up an incoming flight of B-17s. So he told Lockard, who had phoned in the sighting, "Well, don't worry about it."[42]

Taking into consideration Tyler's inexperience and the absence of any device whereby to distinguish between friendly or enemy planes, Short did not consider disciplinary action against him justified.[43] However, he believed that Tyler should have phoned the Pursuit Command at Wheeler Field "and they would have made the check then whether they had planes in that vicinity, before they sent anyone up to fire upon" the incoming aircraft. He claimed that Tyler was in error when he testified to the Army Board, "we had nothing on the alert. We had no planes." Short asserted that he had checked out that statement with Davidson, who "said there would be no question, that if he had received a message from Tyler to alert the command he would have turned out everything."[44] Just what "everything" could have amounted to is problematical. Frank asked Davidson, "In this No. 1 Alert was there any percentage or any number of those planes that were on an immediate alert?" Davidson replied, "I don't think so, sir. I don't know of any."[45]

The Army Board called Tyler's position "indefensible" because "he was merely there for training and had no knowledge upon which to base any action; yet he assumed to give directions instead of seeking someone competent to make a decision."[46] Technically this may be true. But with all the pussyfooting lest the Japanese be annoyed, the population be agitated, or service opposites be offended, it was refreshing to encounter a young man who acted promptly upon the information available to him and did not pass the buck. He erred because his facts did not match his initiative.

The congressional committee probed into the implications of this incident and concluded that Tyler's "fatal estimate" was less his fault than that of the Hawaiian Department. "If the Army command at Hawaii had been adequately alerted, Lieutenant Tyler's position would be indefensible," observed the majority report. "The fact that Lieutenant Tyler took the step he did, merely tends to demonstrate how thoroughly unprepared and how completely lacking in readiness the Army command really was on the morning of December 7."

The committee also noted that Lockard and Elliott debated whether or not to call the Information Center. But it had no doubt that their sighting "provided immediate and compelling reason for advising the Information Center had the necessary alert been ordered after the November 27 warning and the proper alertness pervaded the Army command." The report continued:

While it was not possible from the then state of radar development to distinguish friendly planes from hostile planes, this fact is of no application to the situation in Hawaii; for in a command adequately alerted to war any presumptions of the friendly or enemy character of approaching forces must be that they are enemy forces. . . .

The real reason, however, that the information developed by the radar was of no avail was the failure of the commanding general to order an alert commensurate with the warning he had been given by the War Department that hostilities were possible at any moment.[47]

Yet Tyler believed that had he received a strong briefing on impending war before going on duty it would have made little practical difference:

Even if I had suspected that those were enemy aircraft and I had taken immediate action, I am positive that it would not have materially changed the effects of the attack. . . . Under the general conditions existing on Oahu that morning I am not sure that I could have convinced the Navy that a flight of Japanese carrier planes was flying toward the island with the objective of attacking the fleet in Pearl Harbor. Who would have believed me? Most probably the Operations people at Hickam would not have been alarmed because they were at that moment anticipating the arrival of their own B-17 aircraft from the States which were flying toward Oahu from a northerly direction the same as the Japanese.[48]

Of course, such speculation is profitless. If Tyler's instructions had been geared to the possibility of war in the immediate future, so would those of everyone else in the armed forces on Oahu. In that case, presumably the entire attitude on the part of the Army and Navy toward such a radar sighting would have been different. As it was, had Tyler alerted the Pursuit Command, and had all concerned believed him and acted promptly, it still would have been too late, granted Short's peculiar four-hour state of readiness.

Let us imagine that everything in the AWS had been perfect that morning—that the screen caught the Japanese at the maximum range of 130 miles, that Tyler alerted ready interceptors who scrambled immediately and headed out to meet the enemy. Could these measures have made a difference? Mollison thought that with "ample warning"* the airmen "could have done a lot of damage" to the dive bombers, and "could have kept almost all of those slow-moving torpedo bombers out. Those things were just like shooting fish." He doubted that the Hawaiian Air Force "could have done a thing against them offensively as far as their carriers are concerned. . . . But we could certainly have raised cain with their formations that came in if we had 50 fighters in the air."[49]

Based upon his experience in England, Taylor believed "there were sufficient numbers of fighters at Oahu to repel the number of aircraft that actually attacked Pearl Harbor." The P-40 could not match the Zero, but he thought its performance good enough "to break up, to a large extent, a raid of the sort that came in on December 7."[50]

If Short had utilized the AWS properly, it could have given the Hawaiian Air Force time to send up all available interceptors and to disperse the remaining planes. In that event, although this action would have been too late to turn back the attack or cancel its entire effectiveness, at least Davidson's fighters would not have been destroyed on the ground and some of them, in Frank's words, "would have made it most expensive for the Japs."[51]

Still, no one can say that had the Americans taken this or that specific action, the attack would have failed or been a Pyrrhic victory for Japan. By the same token, one must avoid the defeatist attitude that no matter what the Americans did or did not do once the Japanese came within striking range, in all essentials the story would have been the same. Even if this thesis were demonstrably true—which it is not—it did not excuse Hawaii's defenders for their failure to take every means at their disposal to accomplish their mission.

If anything, Sunday should have found them particularly alert. On April 1, 1941, Stark's office had reminded all naval district commandants of the Axis pattern of attacking on weekends and national holidays.[52] It was not clear from the evidence whether the Fourteenth Naval District passed this warning to the Hawaiian Department.† If not, Bloch's command deserves censure. If it did, Short rates another minus because such notice sailed over his head.

During the Roberts inquiry, General McCoy asked Short, "Were you conscious that these Axis movements almost without exception

---

*Elsewhere Mollison estimated this as thirty minutes to two hours (*PHA*, Part 27, p. 427).
†Bloch did not pass this information to Kimmel. See Chapter 24.

took place on Sunday?" Short answered, "I don't remember that I had noted that particular thing." Then McCoy posed this query: "At any time, as far as you remember, had you thought of the fact that Sunday was the most dangerous day?" Short replied, "I had not given that particular thought."[53] Quite aside from Washington's warning, Short should have noted an Axis tactic obvious to any student of history or military affairs, or for that matter any intelligent citizen who read the newspapers or listened to the newscasts.

In the ten days between receipt of the war warning on November 27 and the attack on December 7, much could have been accomplished, and many misconceptions cleared away, if the Army and Navy on Oahu had worked together closely toward mutual understanding and joint actions. That this did not happen was not due to interservice antagonisms. On the contrary, Short worked so earnestly to keep on cordial terms with the Navy that he overshot the mark. As the Army Board observed, he was

> trying to do the job himself, which resulted in that he neither got the information completely, accurately, nor consistently, instead of delegating it to his trained staff officers dealing with equally trained staff officers of the Navy so a professional, systematic job could be done. He relied on confidence and natural trust rather than certainty of information.[54]

Short was proud of that mutual cooperation. "We had no friction at all," he insisted to the Army Board. "Admiral Kimmel and Admiral Bloch and I were on extremely friendly terms."[55]

Although not a good golfer, Short "made a special effort to play with Kimmel so they could get to know one another better," Fielder stated.[56] The admiral played for physical therapy rather than pleasure,[57] and one of his caddies recalled him as "the first cross-handed golfer I ever seen." Short "was usually tired between holes and rested on the benches."[58] So these sessions represented a sacrifice of inclination in the cause of unity.

Nor did their association end there. Many an evening Kimmel's chief of staff, "Poco" Smith, told his wife Betty, "We didn't get a thing done today. Short was in Kimmel's office all day."[59] Kimmel was very happy about their relationship. "Thank God that General Short and I are good friends officially and personally," he told Dunlop.[60] Later the admiral said, "I did not always agree with Short, but we got along. The rumor that Short and I did not get along bothered me more perhaps than anything else."[61]

Both Short and Kimmel mistook friendly cooperation for professional coordination. "Apparently Short was afraid that if he went much beyond social contacts and really got down to business with the Navy to get what he had a right to know in order to do his job," said the Army Board, "he would give offense to the Navy and lose the good will of the Navy which he was charged with securing."[62] Short's hesitancy in these areas was all the more regrettable because Kimmel much preferred plain speech and almost certainly would not have taken offense.

Short conceded to the Roberts Commission that he had not asked his Navy colleagues if they considered Alert No. 1 sufficient; he "was sure from all of our talk that everybody understood just what was being done."[63] Smith, erroneously believing that the Hawaiian Department had only one type of alert, told Kimmel that a full Army alert was in effect.[64] Bloch, too, thought that the Army was under "a complete alert" and did not find out that it had been exclusively for sabotage until Short so informed him after the attack.[65] Mistaken assumptions on both sides precluded the informed coordination so essential in this crisis.

This aspect of the problem troubled the congressional committee exceedingly. Lucas thought it "radically wrong" that the Army and Navy should not know each other's actions in such serious circumstances. "I am not censuring you at all, sir," he said to Kimmel's fleet intelligence officer, Commander Layton, "but nobody in the Navy has testified here, not even Kimmel himself, that he absolutely knew that the Army was not on full alert." Layton replied:

> I can only offer this, Senator, and this is another Army and Navy custom of long standing.
>
> If you pry into what another man is doing, he naturally resents it. He thinks he is capable of doing his job. . . .
>
> I think that is the only reason that someone did not go to the Army and ask what kind of alert they were on, and it is just the reason that the Army did not come to the Navy and ask what kind of alert we had on the ships in Pearl Harbor.

"I can appreciate that," conceded Lucas courteously. But he added some stern words:

This fleet was the most precious possession that we had in the Pacific, and under that joint agreement it was the duty of the Army to defend the fleet when it was in Pearl Harbor from a landing attack or an air raid. To me, it is inexcusable, unbelievable, that Short and Kimmel would not have a definite understanding with respect to what the other was doing.

I have never been able to understand why Kimmel and all his chiefs of staff and other subordinates would not have known that Short was on a sabotage alert, alert No. 1, in view of the crisis pending.[66]

Unfortunately, this particular example of failure to communicate was not an isolated episode. Neither Kimmel nor Bloch advised the Army of the true state of the Navy's aerial scouting following the Navy's "war warning." For that matter, Short did not ask. When he received the message of November 27 directing him to institute reconnaissance, he presumed that whoever prepared the directive "was familiar with the fact that the Navy was responsible for distant reconnaissance." But he did not request "clarification from the War Department in the event he felt the latter did not mean what it had unequivocally said." This failure the congressional committee found "inconceivable." The majority report added, "Certainly the least that General Short could have done was to advise Admiral Kimmel or Admiral Bloch and consult with them at once concerning the fact that he had been directed to undertake reconnaissance if he presumed the Navy was to perform this function."[67] In Morgan's opinion, a commanding general could not "blindly assume," without further evidence, "that the Navy is discharging a responsibility upon which he is completely dependent for his own security."[68]

The Navy did not inform Short that the Japanese had ordered destruction of their codes. As we have seen, top-ranking officers in both services who knew of this fact considered it absolute proof that Japan was planning war. Kimmel and Bloch stood alone in missing the point, and neither one passed the message to Short. Kimmel assumed that the general had received a similar one from the War Department[69]—another of those ubiquitous assumptions.

Even after the attack began, this failure to communicate persisted. The AWS did not forward to the Navy the information about the incoming Japanese flight that Lockard and Elliott logged at Opana Station, although events certainly had demonstrated its importance. Kimmel told the Roberts Commission what this meant to him:

. . . it is incomprehensible that immediately following the first attack the officer directing the Army radar reception should have failed to appreciate the importance of the information to the Navy. It should have been realized that, while this information was too late to prevent surprise, the Navy still had vital interest in the future movements of the Japanese planes as the Navy surface units were proceeding to sea in the hope of intercepting and destroying Japanese forces. . . .

The Army was responsible for . . . communicating radar information to the Navy . . . and this should have been recognized as a matter of paramount importance. With the Navy fully alerted by five minutes past eight . . . several channels of communication . . . were open for this purpose. The Navy's lack of this knowledge of the retirement courses of the Japanese destroyed the last possibility that existed on the forenoon of December 7, 1941, that the attacking Japanese forces could be brought to decisive action.[70]

Just what results a fuller exchange of information would have had is debatable. In his indorsement to the Hewitt report, Navy Judge Advocate T. L. Gatch somewhat cynically expressed doubt that more cooperation between Kimmel and Short would have had much effect, "for it is abundantly shown that they each entertained the same fallacious views, and closer understanding would most likely merely have strengthened those views."[71]

Short also played much too close a hand in dealing with his own command. "The three principal Major Generals who were commanders under Short have testified that they received substantially nothing by way of information as to the international situation except what they read in the newspapers," remarked the Army Board.[72]

Short protested to the congressional committee, "We were restricted by direct order from Marshall, from transmitting the November 27 warning to any other than the minimum essential officers."[73] But who constituted those "minimum essential officers" was up to Short to decide. One result of his overly narrow interpretation was that many of his subordinates lacked a sense of urgency appropriate to the situation. For example, the Army Board suggested that "had the personnel operating the Air Warning Service on the morning of December 7 known of the imminence of war they doubtless would have interpreted the information obtained from the radar station much differently."[74]

Short's judgment was not so flawless that he could afford this kind of isolated operation. He did not move the alert into high gear even on December 5, when the Army Air Corps dispatched a B-24 mission to Hawaii en route to scout the Japanese Mandates. This action indicated that finally Washington recognized that aerial reconnaissance of those islands overrode concern lest such action irritate the Japanese. At that late date Short still did not grasp the full meaning of events.[75] He seemed quite sure that he had everything under control when Maxim Litvinov stopped in Honolulu on his way to Washington to take up his duties as Soviet ambassador.* Litvinov told Morgenthau that

> on his route here he had talked with American army officials at various points and warned them they must be prepared for war even though negotiations for peace were going on. He mentioned that when he passed through Honolulu a few days ago . . . he talked with the General in charge there and repeated the warning he had volunteered to the other army men. The General had replied, as other army officers had, that they were prepared and ready.[76]

Short's line of defense was that Washington did not give him adequate warning of danger. One example of his rationale: "We were not alerted for an antiaircraft defense because we had not received any information indicating a probable air attack."[77] Such reasoning brought down upon Short a storm of criticism from the press. In a representative comment, the Milwaukee *Journal* conceded that Washington had overall responsibility to prepare for hostilities, and clearly had not considered Pearl Harbor "a probable target." On the other hand, "General Short was only responsible to see that Pearl Harbor, and such forces and weapons as he had, were in readiness. It has never been considered an adequate defense for any field commander that, in a period of obvious danger, he did not expect an attack."[78]

The tension with Japan was neither a recent nor a little-known manifestation. A daily glance at the front pages of the Honolulu press during that critical period should have convinced even a superficial reader that the slightest misstep could plunge the United States and Japan into war.

Short did not have to depend exclusively upon Washington or the Honolulu newspapers. His own intelligence establishment was fur-

---

*Litvinov reached Washington on December 7, 1941.

nishing him with significant information from the Far East. Bicknell, Shivers, and Captain Mayfield, head of the Navy's District Intelligence Office, were receiving copies of reports from Colonel G. H. Wilkinson, British representative of Theodore H. Davies and Co. of Honolulu. Wilkinson "was secretly working for the British Government as a secret agent in Manila." He reported by cable through the British vice consul at Honolulu, Mr. Harry L. Dawson, who was also an employee of the Davies firm. These reports made "an impressive showing of growing tension in the Far East." Bicknell incorporated much of these data into his estimates of the situation which he furnished Short.

Probably the most important of these reports reached Honolulu the night of December 3. It read in part, "Our considered opinion concludes that Japan invisages [*sic*] early hostilities with Britain and U.S. Japan does not repeat not intend to attack Russia at present but will act in South." One immediately notices the close resemblance this statement bears to the alleged "winds execute."* However, in view of the absence of direct evidence that the Japanese ever implemented the "winds" code, it is more likely that the British estimate represented, exactly as stated, their "considered opinion," based upon what the message termed "considerable intelligence confirming . . . developments in Indo-China."[79]

Bicknell asserted, "The information which was thus received from Gerald Wilkinson . . . I gave to General Short, promptly, in one form or another." He specifically cited Wilkinson's report of December 3.[80]

Wilkinson may have been, as Major General Charles A. Willoughby, MacArthur's G-2, considered, "a completely untrained civilian,"[81] but in this case Wilkinson's estimate was accurate. Had it stood alone, it might have had little significance, but coming on top of the warnings of November 27, and in the midst of continual newspaper stories concerning the mounting climax in Japanese-American relations, it added one more detail to the increasingly ominous picture.

This incident makes one wonder whether Short paid more than cursory attention to the intelligence which his G-2 personnel collected and prepared for his information so painstakingly. Perhaps part of the

---

*See Chapter 19.

problem was that Bicknell was not a regular. Bicknell believed that Short "did not have much confidence in a Reserve officer."[82]

After the attack, some of Short's own people were disgusted with him and his top generals. CWO Alton B. Freeman, who had been assistant sergeant major at Eighteenth Bombardment Wing Headquarters in 1941, remembered taking notes at a meeting following the debacle. When Short and Martin entered with Rudolph, "not a soul rose in respect to them."[83] This incident was particularly stinging because regular military personnel almost instinctively accord public respect to a superior, regardless of their personal opinions on the subject.

There can be little doubt that at the root of Short's difficulties lay that fundamental disbelief that Japan would open hostilities where, when, and in the manner that it did. Colonel W. A. Capron, Short's ordnance officer and commander of the Hawaiian Ordnance Depot in 1941, testified to the anticipation that if and when war came, "we would have plenty of advance notice. . . . We had always counted on a period between the announcement of war and the actual meeting of the enemy."[84]

So, unfortunately and tragically, Short acted upon his own estimate of the situation, an estimate he was not called upon to make. And he followed his interpretation of orders, selecting what portions thereof he would carry out, instead of obeying those orders in toto. The net result was disastrous both for Short and for the United States. No one summed up the situation better than did Stimson:

> I find that he failed in the light of the information which he had received adequately to alert his command to the degree of preparedness which the situation demanded; and that this failure contributed measurably to the extent of the disaster. . . . I find that he failed to use fully the means at hand for reconnaissance, especially the radar air warning service, which was of prime necessity; that he failed to ascertain from the Navy the extent of its reconnaissance or to collaborate with it to the end that more adequate reconnaissance should be secured. I find that he failed to have his antiaircraft defenses sufficiently manned or supplied with ready ammunition as the situation demanded.
>
> This failure resulted not from indolence or indifference or willful disobedience of orders but from a vital error of judgment, viz: the failure to comprehend the necessities of the situation in the light of

the warnings and information which he had received. . . . He entirely lost sight of the fact that the defense of his command and station against Japan was his paramount duty.[85]

One may sympathize with Short, understand his motives, and agree that Washington did not give him all the facts in its possession. But these things cannot mitigate the fact that Short failed in the event for which his whole professional life had been a preparation. He was a good man and a competent general who meant all his actions for the best. However, according to the adage, the path to hell is paved with good intentions. And the private hell in which Short spent the rest of his life had at least some paving stones of his own quarrying.

CHAPTER 23

"An Important Man in an Important Post"

Bloch's background and personality—Assignment as commandant, Fourteenth Naval District—Duties of that position—On level with Hawaiian Department—Faulty liaison with Army—Did not support AWS—Confusion about alerts and control of air operations over Oahu

The position of the Navy in Hawaii is more difficult to assess in relation to Pearl Harbor than is that of the Army. The Hawaiian Department had a clear-cut organization and chain of command. The Navy's was much more complicated, for two organizations existed on Oahu—Fleet Headquarters and the Fourteenth Naval District. Each of these had at its helm a prestigious admiral—Kimmel as CinCPAC and Bloch as commandant.*

Kimmel had no mission to protect his ships in harbor except in the context of his ultimate, inescapable responsibility for their welfare under any and all conditions. Safeguarding the Fleet at moorings in Pearl Harbor was the Army's job. Bloch was directly in charge of the Navy's share of protective measures to be taken in case of emergency. To that end, the Hawaiian Department planned and worked with the Fourteenth Naval District. Bloch's position was on a level with Short's.

On paper, Bloch appeared eminently qualified for whatever post the Navy Department might assign him. He was no stranger to the Pacific and its problems, having served in the Philippines, China, Alaska, the West Coast, Hawaii, and Samoa. Primarily a battleship and ordnance expert, he had held important posts ashore, such as commandant of the Washington Navy Yard, budget officer, and Adjutant General of the Navy Department. In 1936, he left Washington

---

*See page xxix for simplified chart of Fourteenth Naval District.

to command Battleship Division Two, and in January 1937 moved up to head the Battle Force.[1]

Bloch not only knew the Navy, he loved it—its history, customs, and traditions. "I wish to emphasize to the officers and men of the fleet that our only justification for being is to be ready to fight." Thus spoke Bloch aboard the flagship *Pennsylvania* when in late January 1938 he assumed his duties as Commander in Chief of the United States Fleet.[2]

In that capacity, Bloch had his own ideas about strategy in the Pacific, some sound, some on the unrealistic side. "Now to get down to matters in the Pacific," he wrote to Stark on August 29, 1939:

> There should always be a precept indelibly engraved on every naval officer's mind to the effect, "always have sufficient force mobilized in the Pacific and either in close support or concentrated so that any possible enemy will be confronted by an equality or superiority of forces." This means 11 BBs, 12 CAs, 12 CLs, 4 CVs and 60 DDs. When you make allowances for the number of ships which will always be under repair, this requires the entire Fleet as presently constituted for that one purpose.[3]

So Bloch wanted two-fisted clout ready to explode to action at a moment's notice. If the United States ever had to fight Japan, it must have enormous naval strength in the Pacific. This position was understandable and laudable in a man holding Bloch's job. Yet if Stark had moved to make Bloch's vision a reality, he would have denuded the Atlantic—and war in Europe would break out in three days.

Bloch admitted that he knew little about the Japanese.[4] Like many of his colleagues, he visualized a future conflict with Japan in terms of his own criteria, ideas, and specifications. In his opinion, the best way to defeat Japan was "by economic strangulation." He knew that if the Japanese succeeded in reaching and conquering Southeast Asia, they would "obtain oil, rubber, tin and other critical supplies which they do not possess now, to say nothing of foodstuffs." Therefore he reasoned, "our Fleet and forces in sufficient numbers" should be placed "at a point and so operated to prevent ORANGE [Japan] from moving south."[5]

This was an obvious strategic line to take. To counter it was precisely why Yamamoto planned the Pearl Harbor operation.

Bloch continued, "It would appear that if we are really determined to prevent the expansion of ORANGE to the southward, even to the extent of becoming involved in war, that the best course would be to move the entire Fleet as rapidly as possible to the Philippines." He realized that such action would affect U.S. "lines of communication, supplies, et cetera."[6]

He could have added that it would have brought the Fleet 5,000 miles beyond Hawaii and over 7,000 miles from the West Coast to an area totally unable to accommodate it. What is more, it would have placed the Fleet in Far Eastern waters without supporting bases, right where Yamamoto would like to find it and with the Japanese Mandates between the Fleet and Hawaii. In marked contrast to Bloch, Marshall stated that to base the Fleet in Manila would have been suicide.[7]

When the end of Bloch's tour as CinCUS approached, the Navy decided to send him to Oahu. According to Admiral Richardson, the consensus in the Navy was that "no matter where Bloch was assigned, he and his command would do a superior job."[8] This was also the opinion of Admiral Wellborn, who knew Bloch "moderately well." Wellborn described him as "a good solid citizen who would always do a creditable job in any assignment. He was not the super-intellectual but sound, dependable and unflappable."[9]

Evidently Roosevelt took a hand in Bloch's assignment, because Stark wrote to Bloch on November 13, 1939, "I believe the President will want you in Pearl Harbor."[10] Nimitz, who as head of the Bureau of Navigation (BuNAV), had charge of personnel, informed Bloch four days later that his forthcoming position was "one of the most important if not *the* most important shore billets we now have."[11]

When Bloch turned his command over to Richardson on January 6, 1940, he declared, "This Fleet is ready to fight." Richardson did not believe it. However, he made up his mind to avoid this matter if possible in his acceptance remarks. He dodged the issue cleverly, confining himself to praising Bloch's "superior qualities of mind and character and his broad professional attainment." Later, to newsmen, Richardson remarked, "From my earliest experience in the Navy, to the present, I have learned to distrust and fear the press." As he intended, the reporters present seized upon this startling comment instead of asking if he agreed with Bloch's estimate of the Fleet's state of readiness.

When Richardson assumed command, he could say honestly that Bloch had brought the Fleet "to a high state of efficiency." But he knew that it still had quite a way to go to be "ready to fight," a state which, to Richardson, obviously meant ready to win.[12]

On April 10, 1940, at the age of sixty-two, Bloch arrived in Hawaii to command the Fourteenth Naval District. Festooned with leis, he told reporters that he considered the post "tremendously important" and was "glad to have been assigned to this command." The two principal Honolulu newspapers hailed the occasion in enthusiastic editorials. The *Star Bulletin* noted that Bloch brought "a distinguished record" to his new position. "It is fitting that at a time when America relies for her safety on the strength of her arms, her most important outpost should be in such capable hands."[13] Observed the *Advertiser*, "Admiral Bloch has just relinquished the post of commander-in-chief of the U.S. fleet. His transfer to Pearl Harbor places an important man in an important post and emphasizes the strategic value of these waters in national defense."[14]

At 10:00 the next morning, clad in blazing whites and to "the strains of martial music and the booming of guns," Bloch took over command from Rear Admiral Orin G. Murfin, destined to head the Navy Court of Inquiry into the Pearl Harbor disaster. The clatter of construction rivaled the thirteen-gun salutes as Bloch's two-star flag* slid up the masthead. The new commandant praised his predecessor "and asked his staff for the same loyalty and cooperation they had given the retiring admiral."

Coincidentally, Secretary of the Navy Charles A. Edison was in Hawaii observing naval maneuvers. He announced that the Hawaiian Detachment would be stationed permanently in the Islands. He spoke at a Chamber of Commerce luncheon that day, and the gathering also honored Bloch. The admiral told the assemblage that he was happy to "come to command of the strategic point in the western frontier of the defense of the United States."[15]

This attractive picture of a big man in a big job had another side. Captain Paul B. Ryan, USN, remarked to Short's troubleshooter, Fleming, that the post of commandant of the Fourteenth Naval District "was a retirement job . . . nice quarters, not too much work. . . . We certainly had a lot of old admirals laid up in Pearl Harbor retiring in their golden years in the navy."[16]

In his draft report for the congressional committee, Morgan re-

---

*The position of CinCUS carried with it the rank of full admiral (four stars). At the end of his tour of duty, the incumbent reverted to rear admiral (two stars).

marked, "It is believed that Admiral Bloch . . . was relegated to a role of minor importance with too great a proclivity to regard his position as a sinecure." Morgan did not specify whether in his opinion Richardson and later Kimmel had pushed Bloch into a corner, or whether Bloch himself considered his job a plush preretirement post.[17] Indications are not lacking that the latter may have been the case.

From the strictly personal viewpoint, Bloch had no particular reason to knock himself out in his new position. Having already served as CinCUS, and being on his last assignment before mandatory retirement, he could expect no solid reward for even the most outstanding performance. By the same token, he could anticipate no appreciable difficulties with his superior unless he did so poorly that the Navy could not overlook it. So he was under no great pressure one way or the other.

Tall, dignified, sensitive, Bloch carried the look of authority which he enjoyed, and he exuded unruffled confidence. This "tough old bird," as Mollison called him,[18] generally kept a step or two ahead of a problem. He was scrupulously correct in naval procedure, and woe be to him who did not go through proper channels. Admiral Shoemaker called him "an old style battleship admiral who demanded respect and discipline and got it. He was also an admiral who thought that the Navy should be run by the Bureau of Ordnance and that naval aviation was but an auxiliary to the battle fleet."[19] According to Vice Admiral Maurice E. "Germany" Curts, who as a commander had been Kimmel's communications officer, Bloch did not take kindly to the "Johnnies-come-lately" who assumed control following his term as CinCUS, and he "kept a rather jealous eye on the situation in the Pacific Fleet."[20]

Few people ever outmaneuvered Bloch. He could tack for advantage in almost any sea, and he could trim his sails quickly at the least hint of rough weather. Rear Admiral Logan C. Ramsey, Bellinger's operations officer in 1941 when he was a lieutenant commander, sized Bloch up as "a smart man who always looked out for No. 1."[21] Said Admiral Furlong, "Bloch was a very thorough and practical man with a lot of brains. He had a lawyer's point of view, because many lawyers worked for him when he was in the Navy Department." At one time Bloch had been the Navy's judge advocate general.[22] "Poco" Smith remembered Bloch as "a good sea dog who wanted his ship taut. He had a good heart but he was strict."[23] Rear Admiral Milo F. Draemel, commanding Destroyers, Battle Fleet in 1941, considered

Bloch "exceptionally capable, highly intelligent and a fine officer in every respect." He added that Bloch was "well liked."[24] Indeed, he could be very charming, and Captain Walter East, who had been on his staff as a junior officer, remembered him as "a sweet old gentleman."[25]

Bloch also inspired the trust of his superiors. Knox wrote to him after visiting Hawaii in the autumn of 1940, "so long as the U.S. Navy is in the hands of men like you, I shall feel satisfied and secure."[26]

By that time, Bloch had become convinced "that the Army's means of defense, insofar as it related to aircraft, anti-aircraft guns, was insufficient. . . ." He discussed these matters with Richardson who in turn took them up with General Herron. After the relief of these two officers in February 1941, Bloch considered the problem with the new CinCPAC.[27]

He found Kimmel quite concerned "with the security of the ships in Pearl Harbor from an air attack." Bloch meant "any air attack which might develop in the course of a war"—not a surprise raid that would initiate hostilities.[28] "My relations with Admiral Kimmel were extremely good, extremely cordial," said Bloch. He "talked everything over quite fully with Admiral Kimmel,"[29] found him cooperative and saw him practically every day.[30] Bloch's relations with Short were also friendly, and they saw one another very frequently. "I felt there was a definite agreement between the General and myself as to our responsibilities," Bloch remarked.[31]

He took care of his health to such good purpose that in his eighties he still attended all the Naval Academy's football games. Said he with obvious pride, "I don't have a varicose vein in either leg."[32] But in 1941 he had passed his prime. "Seems funny that I am as old as I am," he wrote Stark two weeks after he had turned sixty-three, "for I still feel young and full of zip—except when I get sleepy!"[33]

This problem seemed to have persisted through the year. On November 14, 1941, Assistant Attorney General Norman M. Littell wrote to Marvin O. McIntyre, Roosevelt's secretary, "certain impressions" which he had gathered on an official trip to Honolulu in August. Littell had "gained impressions of weakness on all sides." He cited Bloch as "a fine and widely experienced old gentleman past sixty, who, in command of one of the most exciting naval posts under the American flag, goes to bed at 9:30 P.M., because, as he told me, he 'could not stay awake after that.' "[34]

Yet Bloch's post involved duties demanding a high degree of physical and mental alertness. Under Navy regulations, he was "in charge of the naval shore establishments and naval local defense forces." Under existing war plans, he and Short commanded "the Hawaiian coastal frontier which included Oahu and all of the land and sea areas required for the defense of Oahu." In addition, Kimmel placed Bloch in command of Task Force Four. "Its mission was to organize, train, and develop the island bases, Midway, Wake, Johnston, and Palmyra, in order to insure their own defense and provide efficient service to the fleet units engaged in advanced operations."[35]

Kimmel also designated Bloch the naval base defense officer. When Kimmel asked him to take on this job, Bloch objected that he "already had a multiplicity of duties," but would "willingly do anything that was possible."[36] In that capacity, his responsibilities included sharing with the Army "joint supervisory control over the defense against air attack"; working with the Army "to have their anti-aircraft guns emplaced"; exercising "supervisory control over Naval shore-based aircraft, arranging through Commander Patrol Wing Two [Bellinger] for coordination of the joint air effort between the Army and Navy." Then, too, Bloch was charged with control of ship movements within Pearl Harbor, maintaining necessary patrols within the harbor, operating the torpedo defense net, and controlling the destroyer patrol outside the harbor entrance.[37]

Bloch's command suffered from shortages, and the admiral frequently prodded Washington to remedy these deficiencies; however, neither aircraft nor other matériel were forthcoming. His defense forces were woefully insufficient: "4 old destroyers . . . ; 4 small minesweepers . . . ; 3 Coast Guard cutters . . . ; and the old [gunboat] SACRAMENTO. . . ."[38]

But Bloch failed to make the best possible use of what was available. Certainly he had a telephone and a staff car—all he needed to perform one of his major tasks: close coordination with the Army on all matters even remotely dealing with the defense of Oahu and the Fleet in harbor. In a prepared statement for the Navy Court, Bloch remarked, "cooperation between Army and Navy should be genuine and complete. This it was."[39] Genuine, perhaps, but far from complete.

Liaison with Short was Bloch's responsibility rather than Kimmel's. According to "Poco" Smith, however, Kimmel "felt that he was General Short's opposite" and that when in port he "should deal with the Army and with everything else."[40] Here Kimmel erred in assuming a function which should have remained strictly with Bloch. No doubt Kimmel's wish to establish cordial relations with the Army motivated him, because he and Short were the highest-ranking representatives of their respective services on Oahu. Actually, at that time the U.S. Army had no position comparable to Kimmel's, whether he wore his hat as CinCPAC or CinCUS. However well-intentioned, Kimmel's attitude blurred what should have been a clear-cut channel of communication. But that does not excuse Bloch from failing to perform his functions.

Bloch's actions indicate that he did not understand the importance of his responsibilities to cooperate with the Army. For one thing, he designated Lieutenant Harold S. Burr as liaison with Short. Bloch described Burr to the Roberts Commission as "the best available material I had. . . . He was sent to General Short's office, and he was placed to deal with me and the General and transmit information. . . . He was a bright fellow, very loyal, very willing, but not a very experienced officer."[41] To Hart's inquiry, Bloch stated that Burr "didn't know of dispatches that had been received because I didn't consider it was proper to tell him. He was quite inexperienced."[42]

Actually Burr was located, not in Short's office, but in that of then Major William S. Lawton, the Army G-3 officer charged with liaison with the Navy since August 1941. Lawton told the Army Board that Burr's duties "were not important." He was just "a messenger going back and forth . . . to get certain information, or to bring certain specific information to the Navy." Grunert asked Lawton bluntly, "Were you any better than he was for the Navy?" Lawton answered modestly, "I think I was in a position to give them better information." Burr was an intelligence officer, but when Grunert asked him, "Were you a sort of leg man for the District?" Burr replied, "Yes, sir, I would say that."[43]

One dictionary defines the military and naval usage of the word "liaison" as "the contact maintained between units in order to ensure concerted action."[44] Yet Bloch sent the Hawaiian Department as liaison officer a young lieutenant who, however bright, loyal, and willing, lacked the experience and authority necessary to represent the Navy effectively. And Bloch compounded that inexperience by deliberately keeping from Burr full knowledge of what was going on in his own organization. This at a time when thousands of lives, many capital ships, and untold sums in property values depended upon mutual understanding and fully coordinated actions between the Army and Navy.

Short's testimony to the congressional committee gave some idea of the crosscurrents set in motion by Bloch's confusing the duties of a liaison officer with those of a messenger boy. Kaufman wanted to know how Short accounted for Kimmel's testimony that he did not know the Hawaiian Department had gone on an exclusively anti-sabotage alert following receipt of the warning messages of November 27, and in fact did not know that the Army "had anything else but an all-out alert." Short answered:

> The only way I can account for that would be poor staff work on the part of the staff of the Fourteenth Naval District. . . . their liaison officer must have known exactly. We had furnished them with 10 copies of our staff operating procedure, which somebody in that naval staff certainly must have dug into and known what it meant.[45]

Somewhat later, Congressman J. Bayard Clark of North Carolina likewise reminded Short of Kimmel's testimony on that point. Once more Short shot back, "I still think it was faulty staff work on the part of the Fourteenth Naval District if he did not know."[46]

Kaufman asked Short to explain why Kimmel testified "that he understood the interceptor command was working fully and completely." This inquiry elicited another poke at Bloch's organization. "I will say again, if he understood that, it must have been due to poor staff work on the part of the Fourteenth Naval District, because their liaison officer, Lieutenant Burr, sitting in G-3, must have known exactly what we were doing."[47]

All of which was very hard on the hapless Burr, whom Bloch had tossed on the hot spot. None of the investigators of the Pearl Harbor case questioned him about his function except in connection with delivery of the "war warning" message, so no evidence exists as to just how much he did or did not know about the alert system or the interceptor command.

No aspect of the interweaving of the Hawaiian Department and the Fourteenth Naval District was more important than the AWS. Yet consideration of Bloch's position relative to that function leaves the impression that he was willing to cooperate with the Army as long as the Navy controlled the situation. Despite what the proper use and development of radar could mean to him as naval base defense officer, he knew little about the AWS. He "made no formal requests for information," but occasionally Short would tell him "something about it." Frequently some of his own subordinates would contact the Army and let him "know the situation."

Some time in the early autumn of 1941, Short came to Bloch with a request. He "wanted to begin to train his operators." But no one in the Army knew how to do so. Could Bloch do anything to help him? Bloch replied that he had no means himself, but the Fleet had both operators and installations. Bloch asked Kimmel to permit Short to send some of his men to sea to gain experience, which he did.[48] This was an excellent example of practical interservice cooperation.

But it was a different story when on November 15 the Fleet staff instructed its AWS expert, Commander Taylor, "to request control of anti-aircraft guns of ships in harbor from Com 14." Even though Taylor's request came from Fleet Headquarters, Bloch refused "on the grounds that 'No Army organization would control guns on any naval vessel. If anything comes over, we will shoot it down.' However," Taylor continued, with a hint of dryness in his words, "this control was voluntarily turned over to the Information Center on December 9, after ships' guns had shot down U.S.S. ENTERPRISE aircraft."*

Fleet Headquarters also instructed Taylor to ask Bloch for naval liaison officers for the Information Center. Bloch's chief of staff, Captain John B. Earle, informed Taylor "that these liaison officers should come from the Fleet." In other words, Bloch told Kimmel in effect, "Provide these men yourself." Next, Taylor tried Bellinger's Patrol Wing Two, but it had no men available. Finally Fleet Operations agreed to find some liaison officers; however, they did not report to the Information Center until December 8.[49] By then, of course, the enemy aircraft had come and gone.

Hart asked Taylor if he had any other instances of "lack of cooperation" from the district. His reply was a paralyzing indictment: "I can not remember receiving any active cooperation from the Fourteenth Naval District, at any time, prior to December 7."[50]

Bloch testified he knew in November "that they were training the operators and that they were having difficulties." As of December 1,

---

*This unfortunate and tragic incident took place during the confusion of December 7, 1941.

he thought "that the net was still in the condition where all the kinks were not out of it and they were still training operators and could not be depended upon." But he "had no knowledge as to whether or not they were standing regular watches on it." Nor did he "make any inquiries about it."[51] Thus Bloch, the naval base defense officer, demonstrated his disinterest in a major means of alerting Hawaii's defenders to the approach of an enemy force.

Bloch's testimony suggests that Short was dragging his feet in the matter of antiaircraft gun emplacement and Bloch was trying to hurry him. On February 20, 1941, Bloch met with Short "and emphasized the necessity of emplacing the mobile anti-aircraft in the field." Between February and October Bloch "personally examined the plans for the location of all Army anti-aircraft weapons that were to be emplaced, particularly those that were to be sited on naval reservations." Bloch's subordinates "were in constant touch with Army representatives, endeavoring to have the guns emplaced."

Some time between October 15 and November 1, Short and Kimmel talked over the matter. "General Short advised that he could not emplace these guns for several reasons, namely, the sites were not on Government land, their communications would have to be out in the open—usually in cane fields and irrigation ditches—and subject to deterioration, and that it would be extremely difficult for the personnel comprising the gun crews to be quartered and subsisted." At the time of the attack, "the Navy was making plans to mess and quarter Army gun crews on naval reservations so that Army objections would be removed."[52]

In contrast to this picture of an eager Bloch and a nitpicking Short, Fleming had at least one "somewhat shocking" contact with Bloch in a related field. Short had directed Fleming and the department surgeon "to set up an air raid precautions outfit to control air raid damage and everything like that and build static shelters." But "something we were doing on this air raids precautions business, annoyed the Navy." Short sent Fleming to Pearl Harbor to attend a meeting, where it became evident that "the Navy was not at all in favor of some of these plans that we were doing, some of the execution of those plans because we were actually having drills and everything like that. So there was a Navy officer"—here Fleming gave a reminiscent chuckle—"in this conference from the Pacific Fleet, and Admiral Bloch turned to him and asked him what his assessment was of the possibility of ever having a raid on Oahu which would require this kind of protection. . . . This guy looked very, very superior and said, 'Admiral, I don't think there's the slightest possibility of that attack.' "

Fleming formed the distinct impression that Bloch "was *unenthusiastic* . . ."—Fleming's voice underlined the adjective—"about any plans or drills that we were having trying to get ready for something in Oahu." Evidently Short did not appreciate this attitude, for Fleming added, "when I came back and reported this conversation to Short he about went through the roof."[53]

Following receipt of the "war warning" message of November 27, Bloch took for granted that the Army had gone to full alert. Actually, he did not learn otherwise until he talked with Short a day or so after the attack.[54] He thought he might have been confused because in Navy terminology Alert No. 1 was the highest degree of readiness, whereas Short's No. 1 covered antisabotage only.[55] In justice to Bloch, it was natural for him to believe that Short had instituted a more stringent alert, because in the Fourteenth Naval District "full antisabotage measures had been in effect for several months."[56]

But Bloch made no attempt to verify his assumptions. Grunert evidently found this difficult to understand. "Certainly the Commander-in-Chief of the Pacific Fleet and you, as Commandant of the Fourteenth Naval District, had an interest in the measures taken by the Army to protect Pearl Harbor," he remarked to Bloch, "and I thought possibly that might have been discussed in conference, as to whether General Short's actions in taking Alert No. 1, which was just for sabotage, was enough to protect your Navy and the fleet, or what variations of it there might be in Pearl Harbor."

Bloch did not return a forthright answer to Grunert's statement. Instead, he gave the general and his two colleagues on the Army Board an object lesson on how to drive three earnest investigators slightly mad. "I think that the Commander-in-Chief's reactions on this should be obtained from him, sir." Grunert tried to penetrate the fog with which Bloch surrounded himself: "But your reactions?" Bloch replied, "I have no recollection of any discussion on that."[57]

Bloch or anyone else in his position should have remembered any action he took prior to Pearl Harbor which redounded to his credit. So it was a fairly safe bet that Bloch did not confer with Short about

the state of the Army's alert. In fact, Bloch never claimed that he did
so confer.

Bloch also seemed to have been out of touch with the Army on
the question of technical control of air operations over Hawaii. "Did
the Navy ever check to see whether such control was being fully and
satisfactorily exercised by the Army?" asked Grunert. Bloch answered
evasively, "I don't know; I don't know. Is that part of the agreement,
General? I am quite 'at sea' as to what you want to know." Grunert's
question was perfectly clear, but he patiently amplified by quoting
the appropriate paragraph from the Army-Navy agreement: "Defensive air operation over and in the immediate vicinity of Oahu will be
executed under the tactical command of the Army. The naval base-
defense officer will determine the navy fighter strength to participate
in these missions." In view of this, he asked Bloch pointedly, "Now,
whose business was it, on the part of the Navy, to check to see whether
the Army was prepared to meet their responsibilities under that
agreement?"

From the paragraph Grunert had just read, obviously it was Bloch's
"business" or that of a designated subordinate. But Bloch slid over
the shoals smoothly. "I didn't think Navy undertook any check of the
Army for their responsibilities. This was turned over to the tactical
control of the Army." Grunert wanted to know more: "Wasn't the
Navy command concerned about whether or not the Army could fulfill
its part of the agreement?" Bloch answered, "I didn't think the Navy
lacked confidence in the Army's ability to take the tactical control of
the fighters."

A little later he tried to score a point. "I think it might clarify the
situation to say that this Joint Air Agreement, and the naval base
defense air force, was for the purpose of breaking up an air raid which
had happened, was happening, or which was imminent of happening,
when the air-raid alarm sounded."[58] Of course that would have been
much too late to make possible any reasoned and timely pooling of
resources.

In brief, the situation between Bloch and Short was similar to that
between Kimmel and the general. All concerned sincerely believed
that their cordial relations constituted all the cooperation necessary.
Unfortunately, this was not so. As the congressional committee's majority report suggested, this friendly relationship, hedged in by a
disinclination to encroach upon each other's territory, exercised a
baneful influence:

While such concern for the sensibilities of another may have social propriety, it is completely out of place when designed to control the relationship of two outpost commanders whose very existence is dependent upon full exchange of information and coordination of effort. It defeats the purpose of command by mutual cooperation and is worse than no liaison at all. At least, without the pretense of liaison, each commander would not be blindly relying on what the other was doing.

It can fairly be concluded that there was a complete failure in Hawaii of effective Army-Navy liaison during the critical period November 27 to December 7. There was but little coordination and no integration of Army and Navy facilities and efforts for defense. Neither of the responsible commanders really knew what the other was doing with respect to essential military activities.[59]

CHAPTER 24

"Peculiar, Complicated and Tense"

Fleet schedules—Drills—Lack of security consciousness—Skeptical about aerial torpedo attack—Not close
enough coordination with Fleet Headquarters—Complicated command structure—Responsibilities not
clear-cut—Receipt of "war warning"—Did not recommend long-distance air patrol—Avoided blame—
Not summoned to testify before joint congressional
committee.

Not only did Bloch display poor judgment in dealing
with the Army; in strictly naval matters he showed a comparable lack
of straight thinking. He was at least partially responsible for the Fleet's
being placed on such a rigid operating schedule that its movements
could be predicted readily. When the Fleet first permanently stationed at Pearl Harbor, Richardson kept half the ships in port, half
at sea. "He had them going in and out all the time, and that stopped
the dredging." Bloch wanted those ship movements "on certain days."
So, largely at Bloch's request, Richardson fixed the schedule. "The
reason being that I desired to economize on the tug hire," Bloch
explained. ". . . I desired to have as little interruption with the dredging operations in the channel as possible."[1]* Thus Bloch sacrificed an
important security principle—avoidance of a habit pattern—in favor
of routine business.

Later, he and Short demonstrated this same questionable sense
of priority in regard to precautions against an attack. Air raid and
blackout drills had been taking place once a week. Then, as Bloch
told the Roberts Commission:

. . . some fleet commander wrote a letter to the Commander-in-
Chief and said that some of the drills we were having were interfering
with certain other exercises he had laid out . . . and that he felt this

*See Chapter 25.

thing [surprise drills]should be laid out ahead of time. . . . I received
a directive to do it in advance and to consult everybody. . . ."

So Bloch and Short "got together" and arranged that such drills
be held on two days each in October, November, and December.
Accordingly, Bloch testified to Hart, "We definitely prefaced every
air raid drill by broadcasts on a frequency that all ships at sea were
guarding and all ships in port and all stations, telling that this was a
drill so there would be no mistake between the real thing and a drill.
We always let them know, ahead of time, when we would have a
drill."[2]

In this somewhat ludicrous situation, the fault lies equally with
the unnamed commander who complained about surprise drills, with
Kimmel who accepted his complaint and directed Bloch to comply,
and with Bloch and Short who followed through without protest. One
or the other should have pointed out that while this procedure could
teach techniques, it offered no experience in coping with the element
of surprise.

Part of the problem was Bloch's attitude toward the need for such
precautions. He wrote to a friend that he thought Hawaii "about the
most important place in the hemisphere."[3] He considered it "very
peculiar, complicated and tense," a spot "where everyone is suspect,
Japanese, Chinese, and nearly every blood in the universe is here
and how much loyalty or disloyalty exists is an unknown quantity."[4]

Yet whenever security consciousness conflicted with business as
usual, the latter prevailed hands down. In fact, according to Zacharias,
Bloch was rather antagonistic toward Intelligence and skeptical about
the need for security. Zacharias thought a contributing factor to the
Japanese success at Pearl Harbor was Kimmel's reluctance to tell
Bloch to shape up or he would find someone who would.[5]

One of those who spoke frankly to Admiral Hart about the problems encountered on Oahu in 1941 was Lieutenant William B. Ste-
phenson, USNR. In December of that year he headed the Japanese
Counter-Espionage Section of the District Intelligence Office. He
testified that Bloch was "most liberal in allowing free flow of information between the DIO and Fleet Intelligence." But

there was a general feeling in the District Intelligence organization . . . that the Commandant, namely, Rear Admiral Claude C.
Bloch, was not security conscious, nor was he too mindful of the

enemy espionage potential there. . . . On many occasions before the war, this apparent attitude of the Commandant was the cause of minor depression amongst officers in the District Intelligence organization. That was particularly apparent with regard to the Commandant's attitude toward physical security measures that the Security Section of the District Intelligence thought were necessary to the safeguarding of both the physical plant and information available in the Navy Yard at Pearl Harbor. I can, however, cite no causel [sic] connection between the Commandant's apparent attitude and the success of the Japanese attack here.[6]

Causal, no. But it was symptomatic of the complacency at high level in Hawaii as to the immunity from danger. Then, too, one must question the judgment of a commander who would permit even one of his subordinates to feel that his work was neither important nor appreciated.

Bloch told the Army Board that sometimes he gave Short some information. "On occasions he would come to my office and ask specific questions, and if I had any intelligence on the subject I would give it to him." But he did not know what Kimmel or Layton gave Short.

Indeed, an exchange between Grunert and Bloch leads one to wonder if Bloch truly understood the function of his own Combat Intelligence unit. Grunert wanted to know the source of "some information apparently about the Japanese being in home waters." Bloch told him, "It came from Washington."[7] Intentionally or not, Bloch misled Grunert. A major source of such estimates of the location of Japanese ships was Combat Intelligence on Oahu, which monitored the call signals of Japanese naval vessels.

Bloch was equally hazy about other important matters. Hart asked for his reaction to the information that the Japanese were burning their codes. "Well, I'm not sure that I remember exactly what my reaction was," replied Bloch, "except that they might be doing it and they might not be doing it, and I didn't know, I had no way of knowing what they were destroying and what they were burning and whether it was something that was really filled with meaning, or not. It might be and it might not be."[8] Bloch was one of the very few senior officers who received that bit of information without hoisting mental alarm flags.

He shared the Navy Department's opinion that no standard submarine could enter Pearl Harbor without showing her periscope, hence would be detected promptly. So they believed that an anti-torpedo net at the entrance to the harbor channel was sufficient protection rather than nets around the ships themselves.[9] Nor did Bloch visualize an attack by torpedo planes. The Navy on Oahu had received "a definite statement from the Navy Department to the effect that torpedoes could not be dropped effectively in less than 70 feet of water, and we did not have that much water here, so we did not think it was a problem." He told the Roberts Commission that he could not recall ever having seen the dispatch from the Navy Department that this depth limitation could not be considered as still applicable.[10]

Bloch referred to the memorandum from Admiral Ingersoll of June 13, 1941, to the commandants of all naval districts, warning that in view of recent developments the minimum depth of 75 feet hitherto considered necessary for successful aerial torpedo strikes no longer could be taken for granted.[11] To the Hart inquiry, Bloch flatly declared, "I never saw the modifying letter and I'm unfamiliar with it."[12] This document was so potentially applicable to Bloch's own installation that it is most difficult to believe that no one brought it to his attention or that it slipped through his memory. Certainly, the information it contained should have triggered serious rethinking of the defense measures in Pearl Harbor. Yet Bloch claimed he forgot it or never saw it, and Kimmel, who received an information copy, continued to disbelieve "that aerial torpedoes would run in Pearl Harbor. We did not give this a great deal of consideration, for that reason."[13]*

Bloch held the same attitude. He "considered a surprise air attack on Pearl Harbor prior to the declaration of war as a remote possibility." But because "it appeared impossible to successfully launch torpedoes from aircraft in Pearl Harbor, I was of the opinion that a bombing raid by aircraft would not be sufficiently profitable to cause an enemy to undertake it."[14] Moreover, while he knew that bombs were "extremely destructive," Bloch "did not have very much apprehension that battleships could be bombed enough to penetrate decks and to get into the machinery parts." The battleships were "very heavily protected against that form of attack."[15]

Then, too, Bloch's coordination with the Fleet left something to

---

*See Chapter 25 for further discussion.

be desired. "I can not say that I gave any very deep study as to what the Fleet was going to do, how they were going to do it, when they were going, or how we could preserve the security of the place after they were gone because I had so many things to do that I could only do so many," he testified to Hart.[16]

Apparently Bloch or someone on his staff was too busy to direct Fleet Headquarters' attention to the Navy Department's message of April 1, 1941, to all naval districts reminding them of the Axis tendency to attack on Saturdays, Sundays, and national holidays.[17] Kimmel informed the congressional committee that he never saw it until some time after the attack when he was in Washington. What effect a nudge from Bloch would have had upon Kimmel is problematical, for he continued his testimony, "However, I was familiar with, in general, with the activities of the Axis Powers; but I didn't then consider that Saturday and Sunday were particularly a time when the Axis would choose for such a surprise attack, and I am not convinced even today that such a thing was any more than coincidence."[18]

Kimmel's testimony does not make his meaning entirely clear. If he meant that Japan had attacked his fleet on a Sunday without reference to the pattern that Germany had established in Europe, he was correct. Nevertheless, the Japanese did not strike on Sunday by random choice. They did so because they could expect to find the most capital ships in harbor on that day. Inasmuch as the United States generally relaxed on weekends, the Navy Department had been well advised to bring the Axis habit to the attention of its district commandants. Bloch had no excuse for not passing to his Commander in Chief information which should have been kept in mind at Fleet level as well as within the Fourteenth Naval District.

Bloch's testimony to the Roberts Commission indicates that he did not know what, if any, condition of readiness prevailed aboard the ships in Pearl Harbor on the night of December 6, 1941.[19] When a member of the Navy Court asked him whether the senior officer embarked that night had been advised as to the condition of readiness, Bloch replied in the negative. But he added loftily, "It should be borne in mind that the normal condition on board ships in Pearl Harbor, with their guns ready and ammunition at the guns, a large percentage of the officers and men on board, was equal to and probably higher than the Army Alert No. 2."[20]

Relations between the district and the naval air arm were complicated to the point of fantasy, as exemplified by the Joint Air Agreement of March 21, 1941, and its implementing operating plans:

> Under this agreement Admiral Bloch, not an air officer, was acting on behalf of the Commander-in-Chief in signing the document, and there operated under him Admiral Bellinger, who had the command of the planes, so far as the Navy could implement the Agreement, as Commander of the Air Base Force. Bellinger, however, was under the command of Admiral Kimmel, and Bloch, who was charged with the responsibility for the operation orders and plans of operation for the base defense air force, had no air force with which to implement the Agreement. Bellinger had the job to do and such means as existed to do it with was Fleet aviation. Bloch had supervisory control over Bellinger, but the Commander-in-Chief, Admiral Kimmel, had to approve the Agreement.
>
> Bloch was called upon to designate the condition of readiness of the aircraft, but did not have control of the aircraft, the readiness of which he was to determine.[21]

All of which added to the welter of crossed wires that was such a vital part of the Pearl Harbor problem. Bloch compared the Base Defense Air Force to a "volunteer fire department." The aircraft had other tasks assigned them, "but when we sounded an air-raid alarm, they all got together . . ." and became the Base Defense Air Force. All fighters, Army or Navy, went to Martin; all bombers to the Navy. Oahu's defenders "had drill after drill . . . in order that the acts and operations of this Air Force would be automatic and it would not be necessary to take valuable time to give orders in case of emergency."

But here was the catch: This arrangement did not go into effect until M-Day had been declared.[22] And while the plan called for "air search for enemy ships," this was "only in the event of an attack." No plan existed for a situation short of war.[23] No wonder Grunert appeared to lose patience when questioning Lawton on this point: "That is a poor time to implement anything, after you have been hit!"[24] As Forrestal noted, the joint defense plan for Hawaii was "in writing but not in operation," and he had so reported to Knox after visiting Hawaii in August 1941.[25]

Grunert attempted to pin down Bloch. "Then, as far as you know, there were no instructions concerning a probable attack, in case of strained relations, or in anticipation of a probable attack?" To this Bloch replied, "Not so far as I know." General Frank interposed,

"Whose responsibility was it to provide that reconnaissance? It must have been somebody's." Bloch answered evasively, "I suggest that you ask the Commander-in-Chief."[26]

Grunert wanted to know who was "Bellinger's next superior" in his capacity as commander of the Air Base Force. Bloch made this extraordinary reply: "He didn't have any superior. I think that the order said that I had supervisory control to coordinate operations for the Army through him."[27]

The command situation was so confusing that General Frank asked, "Who would the Commander-in-Chief of the Pacific Fleet hold responsible in case something went wrong? Would he hold you or Bellinger?" And Bloch admitted, "I do not know."[28]

Who could blame the Army Board if it sounded somewhat desperate? "Under such circumstances the Army had a difficult time in determining under which of the three shells (Kimmel, Bloch or Bellinger) rested the pea of performance and responsibility."[29]

Bloch did not exactly clarify this confusion when testifying before the various investigations, especially concerning the responsibility for long-range aerial reconnaissance. He told the Navy Court:

> My sole connection with long-range reconnaissance was that as Commandant of the 14th Naval District I had a joint agreement with the Commanding General, Hawaiian Department which would be placed in execution on M-day, or by order of the War and Navy Departments, or upon the mutual agreement of the two local commanders of the Army and Navy, after which time it would then become a responsibility of the Navy to provide distant reconnaissance aircraft for this purpose.

He emphasized that the Navy Department had allocated such aircraft but "their delivery was indefinite."[30]

The Navy Court tried hard to lay the facts on the line. Suppose, the judge advocate asked, upon receipt of the "war warning" Bloch had felt it his duty as naval base defense officer to "send out a long-range reconnaissance." Could he have told Bellinger, "I want all the planes you've got to conduct this reconnaissance?" Bloch countered, "My duties as Naval Base Defense officer are clearly described in the Order. Nowhere in the order does it say that I shall make long distant reconnaissance." He insisted that this was up to Bellinger subject to orders of the Commander in Chief.[31]

That was not the way others understood it. "Who was charged with distant reconnaissance in that plan?" Grunert asked Lawton, the G-3 liaison officer. Lawton replied, "The Navy, sir." Grunert wanted amplification: "When you say 'the Navy,' what do you mean—the fleet, or the district, or both?" Lawton answered, ". . . The Commandant of the Fourteenth Naval District was charged with that, sir."[32]

Bellinger, too, "would have looked to him [Bloch] or to the Commander-in-Chief of the Pacific Fleet for a directive to put into effect and start operations in connection with reconnaissance."[33] Certainly there was nothing equivocal about the Joint Coastal Frontier Defense Plan (JCD-42); it specified that the commandant of the Fourteenth Naval District would provide "distant reconnaissance."[34]

Bloch finally conceded to the Army Board, "I will say that I accepted the responsibility in that agreement for distant reconnaissance for the Navy, and I did my utmost to implement my responsibility by demanding patrol planes for that purpose, but I never had any; I never had one." He stressed that his "obligation for distant reconnaissance would not become binding until that plan was operative."[35]

Bloch's testimony did not clarify just how extensively he and Short coordinated on this problem. Nor was it clear to what extent each understood the other's ability to carry out his responsibilities under JCD-42. The Army Board made every effort to clarify the position. But Bloch did not enlighten them. Either he genuinely did not comprehend what they were talking about, or he chose to dodge the question.

For example, Frank inquired, "You signed this agreement . . . with General Short, and you did not have the facilities with which to carry out your part of the agreement. Did you ever tell that to General Short?" Replied Bloch, "I think General Short knew it perfectly well." Frank wanted a straight answer. "But did you ever tell him that you did not have the equipment with which to do it?" Once more Bloch demonstrated his talent for broken-field running: "I cannot say that I have never told him and I cannot say that I did tell him."[36] However, if Bloch had laid the facts on the line to Short, no doubt he would have so testified in plain English, for that would have been to his benefit.

Bloch tried to place upon Washington the blame for failing to activate JCD-42. He argued that the Navy Department was in possession of "all available political and military information and intelligence." But it did not "follow the established and well understood procedures for meeting conditions of strained relations between the United States and Japan, for designating M-day, and for placing all concerned on a full war footing." Therefore he considered it unreasonable to imply that "those in Pearl Harbor should have done those things which better informed higher authority did not find expedient to do."[37]

This argument will not hold water. The congressional committee made this clear when it pointed out

> that the joint security measures for the protection of the fleet and the Pearl Harbor base were designed in order to coordinate joint defensive measures for defense against hostile raids or air attacks delivered *prior to a declaration of war and before a general mobilization for war*. The plan against air attack was prepared in Hawaii; it was designed to meet the peculiar problems existing in Hawaii; its invocation, implementation, and execution was essentially a responsibility resting in Hawaii. [Italics in original.][38]

In brief, the Hawaiian command did not have to wait upon Washington's declaration of M-day to put JCD-42 into effect.

On November 27, 1941, the U.S. Pacific Fleet received a "war warning" which all involved in its preparation and dispatch expected to put Hawaii "on a full war footing." The fact that it was couched in unorthodox form in no way discounted its importance and meaning. Washington officials did not expect more of Hawaii than they did of themselves; they expected—and had a right to expect—that those in Hawaii would pay attention to instructions.

As Bloch was visiting a patient in the hospital on the afternoon of November 27, he did not see this message until the next morning.[39] But, after reading it, he made no recommendation that Kimmel institute long-range aerial reconnaissance.[40] Nor did he see any reason "for reaching any independent decision" on that occasion. Frank remarked, "Well, you certainly had some professional reaction, having been in the Navy for 35 years." To this Bloch replied only, "Longer than that, sir."[41] Thus once more Bloch slipped through importunate fingers.

One or two days after reading the message of November 27, Bloch instructed the Coast Guard "to put vessels outside to run up and down and listen for submarines." The inshore destroyer captain used Bloch's office to give his skippers a pep talk about the antisubmarine alert. Despite the mounting crisis in the Pacific, Bloch took no further action.[42]

The Navy Court brought out the fact that the status of Bellinger's patrol aircraft between November 27 and the attack was Condition B-5—50 percent of both matériel and personnel on four hours' notice. This status, which Bloch had directed, was, according to Bellinger, "the normal readiness prescribed for normal conditions." He amplified, "the condition of readiness that was set was to permit the required operations from day to day in the schedule to continue without having them tied up by standing by."[43] Again, this time in the face of a clear warning, alert measures bowed to routine.

Bloch argued that Kimmel "or somebody delegated by him would be the officer who designated what reconnaissance was to be made." Kimmel's Pacific Fleet Confidential Letter 2 CL-14 (Revised) of October 14, 1941, placed "dispatch of essential planes" under the district commandant "in a supervisory way." Actually, this was done by Bellinger, who wore both hats as commander of Patrol Squadrons of the Fleet, and commander of the Naval Base Defense Air Force. To Bloch it seemed "obvious that the Commandant of the District couldn't use the patrol planes without permission of the Fleet because the planes were employed by the Fleet on other missions."[44]

But Bloch could have asked for that permission. Had he evaluated the "war warning" at its true meaning, and out of his vast experience had recommended instituting at least partial air reconnaissance, Kimmel might well have given him the green light. That is precisely what happened when, in the summer of 1941, Bloch had suggested to Kimmel that air patrols be dispatched on an arc pointing toward Jaluit. Kimmel agreed, and for several mornings flights went out in that direction to a 500-mile limit. After a few days this patrol was discontinued.[45] Bloch was rather vague as to the exact development that occasioned this search. Whatever the situation, it was much less tense than that of November 27. Thus Bloch could, and did, recommend appropriate action, as was his duty, when he thought the circumstances called for it.

None of the warning messages from Washington prior to December 7 aroused in Bloch any belief that Hawaii was in danger. He explained his thoughts on these warnings thus:

In the first place, there was nothing in these messages which so much as implied an air attack on Pearl Harbor, for the very good reason that even the originators of the dispatches had no such suspicion. In the second place, although other specific geographic objectives are mentioned, never in any dispatch is the Hawaii area so designated. Nor do the dispatches designate M-day, nor do they direct total or partial execution of the Rainbow plan. . . . None of the dispatches to Pearl Harbor gave sufficient information upon which evaluations could be made and all evaluations sent by the Navy Department related to either general possibilities, or specified the scene of probable Japanese activities in the Far East.[46]

Furthermore, resumption of the Washington discussions after the warning of November 27 "had a very definite effect" on Bloch's mind. This development left him uncertain "as to whether anything was likely to happen immediately." And "so far as the Hawaiian area was concerned," Bloch "had no feeling of impending hostilities around the 7th of December."[47] He explained to Hart, "In some way, I had gotten a date fixed in my mind that any move on the part of Japan would be April or May [1942]. How I got this information or from what source I don't know." However, Bloch was "not conscious of any lessening" of alertness in late November. "If such was the case, it must have been unconscious because I'm fully convinced that everyone out there was trying his utmost to be on his toes all the time."[48]

Bloch later absolved himself of blame in connection with the Navy's failure to institute distant air patrols on two scores: He was "a direct subordinate of the Commander-in-Chief, Pacific Fleet," and before December 7 "there never was an attack, nor did there exist positive information of the immediate imminence of an attack on Pearl Harbor."

Hence JCD-42 had not been activated. " 'Distant reconnaissance' was set forth *only* in JCD-42 as a measure to be undertaken *if, as* and *when* JCD-42 became operational" (Bloch's italics). As neither the War nor the Navy Department ordered JCD-42 activated, it was "obvious that no responsible person in Hawaii would have reason then and there to place JCD-42 in execution. And when we go down the chain of command as far as Rear Admiral Bloch . . . any implication that he ought to have, or could have, put JCD-42 in execution is not reasonable." Bloch claimed, "Having no information over and above or differing from that of the Commander-in-Chief, Pacific Fleet, he had no basis for dissenting from the decisions of the Commander-in-Chief in regard to distant reconnaissance."[49]

Bloch was a most persuasive self-advocate. But to accept his thesis in toto is to postulate that the entire chain of command existed merely as a sort of bucket brigade relaying instructions from Washington until eventually they reached the action level of the combat units. If that were true, any intelligent petty officer could have run the Fourteenth Naval District. Instead, the Navy Department considered this post worthy of such a distinguished admiral as Bloch. Moreover, Stark and his advisers held the field commanders on a loose rein, expecting them to use their heads.*

Nor was Bloch all that far "down the chain of command." Under the Navy Department, his only superior was Kimmel. Bloch was on the same level as Short. JCD-42 stated: "Such parts of this plan as are believed necessary will be put into effect prior to M-day as ordered by the War and Navy Department or as mutually agreed upon by the local commanders."[50] The congressional committee considered this provision worthy of italics:

> The Joint Coastal Frontier Defense Plan, the very document wherein the Navy assumed responsibility for distant reconnaissance, contained in an annex thereto provision for joint operations *when the Commanding General of the Hawaiian Department and the Naval Base Defense Officer agree that a threat of a hostile raid or attack is sufficiently imminent.*[51]

Thus, irrespective of Kimmel or Washington, Bloch and Short could have activated JCD-42 had the seriousness of the situation sufficiently impressed itself upon them. Yet Bloch apparently expected Washington to assume all responsibility for such action, hence his stand that his obligation for long-distance reconnaissance "would not become binding until that plan was operative."[52]

This concept was so firmly rooted in Bloch's mind that he did not appear to understand Grunert when the latter tried to fix responsibility for preattack defense. He asked, "Whose responsibility was it to initiate and coordinate efforts against a hostile attack? Was it the Army's or the Navy's?" These were straight enough questions, but Bloch answered, "I do not quite understand you." Grunert tried again:

---

*See Chapter 13.

"In case there was a hostile attack, as there was on December 7th, whose responsibility was it to initiate the offensive side of the defensive? In other words, as to aircraft, was it under the Navy, under the Army, or under both?" Bloch appeared bewildered. "I cannot answer that question. It is hypothetical, and I do not understand it."[53]

One of the strangest features of the Pearl Harbor story was this: Hawaii was the only area that totally misinterpreted the warnings of November 27.* Nor did reiteration help. On November 28, a CNO dispatch to certain Pacific subordinate commands with information to CinCPAC repeated, with specific instructions, the Army's warning of the day before.[54] Bloch saw this message. "The only items in the dispatch which made a real impression on me were those parts concerning the desire of the United States to have Japan make the first hostile act, and the other was concerning not to alarm the public," he remarked. "By implication it was my belief that it was obligatory upon the Navy to consider these same restrictions . . . it contained certain wording concerning hostile attack and alarming the public that was in the Navy dispatch of the same date. I believe that these restrictions applied to the Navy."[55]

If these were the items which impressed themselves upon Bloch, he had a peculiar sense of priorities. For one thing, contrary to his statement, the Navy's "war warning" had contained no mention of "alarming the public" or any suggestion that Washington wanted Japan to commit the first overt act. For another, both points could have been omitted from the Army's message without weakening its impact; in fact, such omission might well have sharpened its cutting edge. The armed forces naturally preferred to conduct their alerts without frightening the population. And the fact that the United States neither wished nor intended to commit the first hostile act was so obvious that it needed no underlining.

In any case, Bloch should not have permitted an information message to influence him to the point of modifying his interpretation of the Navy's instructions. Admiral Turner, chief of War Plans, explained to the congressional committee the reasons why the Navy Department had passed along the Army message. Primarily, this was "to make sure that those commanders knew what the Army was doing in their districts." The War Department's warning of November 27 had in-

*See Appendix 3.

structed its recipients to limit dissemination to the minimum number of officers, so Turner "felt it might easily be that the Army commanders would construe that so that the Navy commanders would not know what they were doing." However, he presumed that Short already had shown Kimmel the War Department warning. The second reason for relaying the dispatch to Kimmel was to let him know that the Navy Department was "sending this information to . . . the three frontier commanders, so he would not have to send something himself."[56] In brief, the Navy Department made CinCPAC an information addressee to keep Fleet Headquarters posted, and as a courtesy to save Kimmel trouble. Obviously Turner's War Plans office had no idea of watering down their own more positive instructions.

What is more, the Army Board reminded Bloch that Washington's job was not to prod an outlying installation into wakefulness. Declared Grunert, "Well, in the Army we are taught that in case you have no information, you ought to be prepared for the worst, and in an outpost like Hawaii they are always supposed to be awake and prepared for anything—that is why it is an outpost, so that people on the mainland can go to sleep." Somewhat mildly, Bloch rejoined, "Well, mind you, I am not defending anything that took place, there. I am telling you what I recollect about this thing as fully and truthfully as I can, and the people to decide are someone else." Grunert next asked, "The gist of these messages did not create a particular war consciousness on your part?" Bloch replied, "Not to me." When Frank queried, "Was the attack a complete surprise to you?" Bloch answered, "Yes, sir."[57]

Admiral Smith, Kimmel's chief of staff, tried to explain to the congressional committee the respective duties of Kimmel and Bloch in regard to the crucial question of long-range aerial patrols. "Admiral Bloch had the responsibility of conducting this search. To do so, he had to call upon the commander in chief for planes, and the commander in chief could say 'yes' or 'no,' of course.

"On the other hand," Smith emphasized, "if the commander in chief thought a long-distance reconnaissance necessary, he would have commanded Admiral Bloch . . . to carry on the search. So that after you analyze it, the responsibility comes back to the commander in chief."[58]

Bloch was not averse to sliding his responsibility in Kimmel's direction, as some of his former colleagues acknowledged. Ramsey gained the impression that Bloch "was ready to let the chips of guilt fall on Admiral Kimmel's shoulders."[59] Bloch wrote to Richardson on March 3, 1942, "I think both you and I are very lucky because the same fate might have happened to either or both of us."[60] Thus subtly did Bloch disassociate himself from Kimmel's responsibility and tragedy.

Bloch had a good opinion of himself which he did not want tarnished. "When I was Commander-in-Chief of the Fleet they [the Japanese] would not have found any of our ships here," he told the Roberts Commission. "They would have always been somewhere else." This was not a very bright remark, because his ships could not stay at sea forever. As he conceded, "sooner or later they would come in here on detachment."[61] And when they did, neither he nor anyone else could guarantee that the Japanese would not find them in Pearl Harbor.

Bloch had an image to maintain as the wise elder statesman of the Navy. Smith recognized that when he wrote Kimmel on June 10, 1944: "There is only one officer # who has stated to me that you have nothing to gain by insisting upon a public trial. You, of course, know who that officer is, and I feel that his reason is that he is protecting his own interests." Someone, probably Smith after the letter was typed, added the # alongside "officer" and neatly printed at the bottom of the letter "# Bloch."[62]

Writing to Commander Hiles on June 15, 1962, Greaves adjudged, "Actually the Navy responsibility at P.H. was legally more on the shoulders of Bloch than Kimmel, although Kimmel has never seemed to admit this much less plead it."[63]

While Kimmel had no compunction about tossing blame upward, he was not the man to insist upon the culpability of a subordinate. Ironically, when he did point out the facts to the congressional committee, it availed him nothing, for the majority report took Bloch off the hook:

> Admiral Kimmel has suggested that under the Joint Coastal Frontier Defense Plan Admiral Bloch was responsible for distant reconnaissance and had the latter desired planes he could have called upon the commander in chief of the Pacific Fleet. This suggestion, apart from being incompatible with Admiral Kimmel's stating he made the decision not to conduct distant reconnaissance, is not tenable. Admiral Bloch had no planes with which to conduct distant patrols and Admiral Kimmel knew it. While he was on the ground, it was the

responsibility of the commander in chief of the Pacific Fleet to take all necessary steps in line with a defensive deployment and in recognition of the realities at Hawaii to protect the fleet.[64]

To be sure, in the final showdown, responsibility for everything that happened in his organization devolved upon the Commander in Chief. Nevertheless, the committee's judgment reflected the luck that blessed Bloch throughout the various inquiries.

Before the Roberts Commission, he appeared at first a little unsure of himself. He was not nearly so au courant of his command as were Kimmel and Short. He brought with him his war plans officer, Commander C. B. Momsen, and frequently appealed to him for answers to questions. This body considered Bloch "a sly old fox" but did not think they could hold him responsible, because Turner "had persuaded them that the Commander-in-Chief had authority over Bloch as to his defense functions."[65] So once again Turner's hand wrote a marginal note on the pages of history.

Bloch was the first witness to appear before Hart, which may or may not reflect Hart's opinion of Bloch's proper place in the Pearl Harbor picture. But Hart was not charged with making any judgments, so there is no way of knowing what he thought of Bloch's performance.

Before the Navy Court, Bloch was on his mettle. There he faced a jury of his peers, who adjudged him an "interested party." He claimed that this surprised him. He was "much concerned because of the baneful implications and presumptions which may be attached to the term." If the commandant of the Fourteenth Naval District was not an "interested party," it was difficult to imagine who did qualify for that title. Yet Bloch bleated with an air of wide-eyed innocence, "I have had no reason to suppose that it was incumbent upon me to preserve evidence or to keep unimpaired my recollection of the details and circumstances surrounding and prior to December 7th."[66]

Perhaps Bloch lacked the imagination and sense of fitness to keep records of one of the most stunning events in American history, one which took place while he commanded the stricken installation. But surely the instinct for survival would dictate that he "preserve evidence" and promptly record his memory of the event so that he might "keep unimpaired" his recollections of that tragic day. Yet if one judges by the Navy Court's report, Bloch was in no real danger from his fellow admirals. They appear to have had no intention of blaming any naval officer for anything substantial.[67]

The Army Board was a different proposition. Here Bloch could expect no consideration beyond the courtesies usual between officers and gentlemen. He entered the fray suspiciously. After giving his name and other identifying data, he continued, "I understand my rights, and do I understand that this evidence can be used in judicial proceedings against me, in the Navy?" Colonel Charles W. West, the board's recorder, answered, "That would be for the Navy Department to determine." Bloch shot back, "You told me it was. You just told me it was. I would like to know if that is correct." West explained, "As a general proposition, any voluntary admissions are admissible before courts and boards. Now, I am not prepared to say whether some statutory provisions or regulations of the Navy Department might exclude this." Evidently satisfied, Bloch replied, "All right."[68]

Of all the testimony before the Pearl Harbor investigations, that of Bloch before the Army Board is one of the most difficult to sort out. Either he was intellectually and psychologically incapable of giving a straight answer to a straight question, or else he was deliberately throwing up a verbal smokescreen. If the latter, he certainly succeeded. Making sense of his testimony leaves one with a frustrated feeling of trying to sew together squares of gelatin. Here, as with the Navy Court, one of Bloch's objects was to convince his questioners that he had been, in his words, "really quite a small element in the whole big thing."[69] How far he succeeded with the Army Board is impossible to assess. By implication, that body cast a shadow upon him, particularly in connection with long-distance reconnaissance,[70] but it had no authority to censure anyone in the sea service.

The Army and Navy each had another opportunity to clarify Bloch's position and pin him down to specifics when they appointed, respectively, Lieutenant Colonel Henry C. Clausen and Vice Admiral H. Kent Hewitt to conduct follow-through investigations. But neither officer obtained Bloch's testimony.

The congressional committee did not summon Bloch, although they had expected to do so.[71] Probably Bloch slipped through their meshes because of the pressure of time, as did several other members of Kimmel's command. But such a consideration cannot excuse what was a major error of judgment on the part of the committee. Having been designated an "interested party" before the Navy Court, Bloch deserved the same opportunity for a public presentation as did the other two "interested parties," Stark and Kimmel. His position as Short's opposite alone should have commanded his appearance. Considering the fact that the transcript of Short's testimony covered no less than 310 pages, one can only regret that Bloch did not receive similar attention. Certainly Short's charge of "faulty staff work" between Bloch's command and the Hawaiian Department called for the closest examination. This was a much more relevant issue than the everlasting "winds execute" problem which had consumed entire days of testimony and which had only a tangential relation, if any, to why the Japanese had caught Oahu's defenders napping.

In addition to being exceedingly fortunate, Bloch had the acumen to maintain a low profile. He emulated the prudent possum, making himself as inconspicuous as possible until the prospective danger went away. He claimed to be too far down the chain of command to be blamed or even to be a major party to the drama. However untenable, that was Bloch's position and he got away with it.

But consideration of Bloch's part in the tragedy of Pearl Harbor is essential to understanding the complex, widespread nature of the problem. Basically, he shared the fundamental American error in relation to Pearl Harbor—disbelief in the reality of peril. That is why the simple instinct for survival did not enter the picture on Oahu, despite various warnings and indications of danger. Bloch did not react even when peril thrust itself under his nose, as in his failure to advise Short on the morning of December 7 of the destroyer *Ward's* encounter with a Japanese minisub at 0645.[72]

The Navy kept Bloch in position at Pearl Harbor. Later Knox brought him to the mainland where after his retirement in August 1942 he immediately returned to active duty as a member of the General Board. The Navy Department might have erred in sending Bloch to Pearl Harbor, to a job that obviously called for a vigorous man, which Bloch was not, as well as for an experienced man, which he was. Nevertheless, as commandant of the Fourteenth Naval District, responsible for assisting in the defense of Pearl Harbor and for advising the Commander in Chief, Bloch must be adjudged partially to blame for what happened on December 7, 1941.

CHAPTER 25

"Always Striving for Perfection"

Kimmel's background, character, and methods of
working—Opinions pro and con—Disbelief that aerial
torpedoes would run in Pearl Harbor—Doubts
concerning air attack—Training-minded and offensive-minded—Fleet's mission defensive for first six
months of a Pacific war

Had the U.S. Navy conducted a poll in the late au-
tumn of 1941 to determine which of its admirals seemed least likely
to go down in history identified with failure, the name of Husband
E. Kimmel would have stood near the top of the list of candidates.
This was a man to inspire confidence—experienced, forceful, dedicated, and disciplined, a perfectionist with a keen sense of mission.
In addition to these professional attributes, he embodied most of the
virtues that Americans admired: honesty, self-sacrifice, industry,
courage, devotion to family and country. At the peak of his career as
CinCPAC and CinCUS, he looked like the right man at the right
place at the right time.*

Yet in the first round of war, the Japanese hit Kimmel in the solar
plexus and he went down for the count. How did this catastrophe
happen to such a splendid officer? To what extent did he help plow
the ground for his own defeat? These are not easy questions to answer, for one must deal not only with the circumstances of the time
but with the life's work, character, and psyche of a complex individual.

Kimmel's background seemed to destine him for the army. His
father, Major Marius Manning Kimmel, had been the last link in a
chain of army officers dating back to the American Revolution. Kimmel tried for an appointment to the U.S. Military Academy, and only
when turned down for West Point did he successfully seek appointment to the U.S. Naval Academy, entering Annapolis in the class of
1904.[1]

---

*See page xxx for simplified chart of U.S. Pacific Fleet.

He graduated thirteenth in his class—a very respectable if somewhat symbolically ominous figure. Already a rigid self-image had begun to manifest itself. The Naval Academy yearbook, the *Lucky Bag*, headed each character sketch with a quotation. The midshipman who wrote up Kimmel, perhaps with a flick of malice, used a snippet from Turgenev: "He had the air of his own statue erected by national subscription."[2]

In the years between his graduation from Annapolis and the entry of the United States into World War I, Kimmel's experience was almost entirely aboard battleships and in the Navy Department. Then a lieutenant commander, he saw action abroad, and his wartime superiors rated him highly: "A splendid, all round officer with unbounded zeal and natural ability."

In September 1920 he returned stateside as assistant to the chief of the Naval Gun Factory. In December 1923 he went to sea for about eighteen months as a destroyer division commander. This tour ended in May 1925 when the Navy selected him to attend the senior course at the Naval War College—proof that his superiors had tagged him as a man to watch.

Soon after graduation came the coveted promotion to captain, and with it assignment to the Policy and Liaison Division of the Office of the Chief of Naval Operations. A man of superb presence with a gift for impressing those he met and worked with, Kimmel starred in this assignment: "A superior officer in all respects . . . "

Then in August 1928 he went back to sea as commander of Destroyer Squadron Twelve, stationed at San Diego. Admiral Smedberg recalled the exceedingly strict regimen Kimmel imposed. "The Navy can never be ready for war, in peacetime, but Kimmel was determined that ships under his command would be as ready as he could make them. We respected our Commodore, understood his rationale, but thought he was an S.O.B. of the first order," wrote Smedberg.

> After all, in 1929 the war to end all wars had been fought and won . . . , our appropriations were so pathetically small that we were not allowed more than 12 knots between ports, . . . and our pay of $185 per month didn't seem large enough to justify those 16-hour days, too many unnecessary—we thought—nights on board ship when we were in port.
>
> But that was Kimmel. His force had to be as ready as he could make it. We had to admire him for that, though sometimes we

wondered if it was his own reputation that he was working for, as well.[3]

Whether Kimmel had an eye to the main chance or toiled solely for the good of the service, the net results no doubt would be the same—a good officer steadily improving his position. After two years, the Navy Department called him back for a three-year hitch as director of ship movements, where he gained the enviable mark, "Flag Officer material." Admiral W. V. Pratt appraised him as "a humdinger. . . . I like him because he says what he thinks, never fools you and his judgment is excellent. . . . I expect to see him get to the very top some day."

In his next position, a year's tour as skipper of the battleship *New York*, he was an exacting taskmaster, yet he could unbend. His senior aviator, Logan C. Ramsey, recalled that once, returning from a routine observation flight, his engine conked out and he could not edge alongside to be hoisted aboard. Looking up at the bridge, he met Kimmel's amused eye, and shrugged helplessly. The towering battleship would have to accommodate itself to the tiny stranded plane. Grinning broadly, Kimmel snapped to attention, saluted with mock deference, and made the traditional request: "Shall I come alongside you, sir?"[4] Shortly thereafter, Kimmel joined the Battle Force as chief of staff to the commander of Battleships.

In due course Washington gave Kimmel a real look behind the scenes as the Navy Department's budget officer, and while in that position he became a rear admiral. One year later he stepped aboard the light cruiser *Honolulu* as commander of Cruisers, Battle Force, where he remained until unexpectedly tabbed as the new CinCPAC and CinCUS.

"I would have given my eye teeth to have seen your expression and to have heard your exclamation when it happened, but instead I was just sitting behind the scenes congratulating you and the Navy," Stark wrote gleefully to "Dear Mustapha" on January 13, 1941.

> I confess it came sooner than I had anticipated but that it should come, I have long had in the back of my head and while rejoicing with you I realize fully the enormous responsibilities placed on your shoulders in one of the most critical periods in our history, and where the Navy more than any other branch of the Government is likely to have to bear the brunt. . . .

. . . Of course, I do not want to become involved in the Pacific,
if it is possible to avoid it. I have fought this out time and again in
the highest tribunals but I also fully realize that we may become
involved in the Pacific and in the Atlantic at the same time; and to
put it mildly, it will be one *H---* of a job. . . .[5]

Thus, even before Kimmel formally became CinCPAC, Stark had
warned him that the United States might become involved in a two-
ocean war and that his would be, as Stark delicately put it, "one
H--- of a job."

So far, the picture is that of a winner on a steadily upward path
of alternating sea and shore duty, always in responsible posts. Even
Kimmel's marriage, although an undoubted love match, might have
been tailored to specifications. In 1912 he married Dorothy Kinkaid,
daughter of one admiral, destined to be the sister of another. The
record shows no false steps and only one disappointment at the very
beginning. And his failure to enter West Point may have been a bonus,
for it is easy to picture this proud man gritting his teeth and vowing
to show the U.S. Army that it, not he, was the loser.

Here then was a man so accustomed to success that the idea that
he might make a mistake, might fall on his face through any fault of
his own, was totally alien to him. No facet of Kimmel's character is
more obvious from his postattack testimony than this: He could not
endure criticism. Over and over he revealed his almost total inability
to admit an error, even one of judgment. "Kimmel just could not
believe he had been wrong," declared Admiral (then Commander)
Arthur C. Davis, Kimmel's fleet aviation officer. "He was inelastic in
his thinking. In a way he was the victim of his own mental system."[6]

This is not the attitude of a truly self-confident man, who can
admit his mistakes candidly and go on from there. A tip-off to Kimmel's basic insecurity is the fact that he did not bring his wife to
Hawaii. When his chief of staff, Captain Smith, asked him why, he
replied, "Well, to tell you the truth, Smith, I feel that I could not
do my job with my family present."[7] No man who is genuinely self-
assured doubts his ability to function simultaneously as husband and
worker. The decision robbed him of the refuge and psychological lift
of a good home, which he sorely missed on Oahu.[8] Born and bred in
the Navy, Dorothy Kimmel was not the woman to make unreasonable
demands on her husband. With this intelligent and understanding
wife at his side, Kimmel might have come up for air occasionally

instead of becoming virtually a gyroscope humming about the axis of his own entity.

For Kimmel was preeminently what a later generation would term a workaholic. No one could fault him on the score of neglecting his job. And he proved himself an excellent judge of men. The Navy Department selected his task force commanders, but he chose his staff. "I know of none that are better," he declared. "There may have been others just as good." When Congressman Keefe questioned him about these men, Kimmel with great pride reeled off names, ranks, decorations, and principal wartime positions.[9] Many major staff officers who served on his staff in 1941 finished their service careers as either full admirals or vice admirals.

When Kimmel formally took over command on February 1, 1941, he had promised "to maintain the fleet at the highest level of efficiency and preparedness."[10] And indeed during 1941 Kimmel did "wonders to improve the Fleet," as Davis said.[11] He worked his officers and men to the point of exhaustion. Rear Admiral Harold F. Pullen, who commanded the destroyer *Reid* on Pearl Harbor day, termed 1941 "one of the most concentrated periods of training I had ever been in. . . . We practically never went ashore."[12] Vice Admiral Ralph W. Christie, who had commanded a submarine division in 1941, recalled, "He had a reputation of being pretty hard-nosed, but everyone respected him for it. . . . We felt that he had stepped up the training and the discipline a considerable amount."[13] Rear Admiral Willard A. Kitts III, Kimmel's fleet gunnery officer in 1941, believed that "the general efficiency of ships and gunnery" was, on December 7, 1941, in "the highest state that it had ever reached in times of peace in the history of the Fleet."[14]

In the midst of the confusion and terror of December 7, Kimmel's men truly reflected great credit upon him and his subordinate commanders. Rear Admiral William L. Calhoun, who as commander, Base Force, had been on the spot, testified, "the way the personnel conducted themselves that day speaks volumes for the training and the fighting heart that had been instilled in those men by their responsible commanders."[15]

At the close of the Roberts investigation, Admiral William H. Standley told Knox that under the circumstances Kimmel and Short had to be relieved. "Yet I can't help regretting that Admiral Kimmel had to go. I have never seen the fleet in a higher state of efficiency than was evidenced by my observations during the course of our investigations at Pearl Harbor."[16]

Nevertheless one wonders whether Kimmel, who had been a superb cruiser division commander, had not risen above his level of superior performance as CinCPAC and CinCUS. "Kimmel was A-1 in the days before he became CinC," said Bloch. "He was alert, active and extremely intelligent. He was always striving for perfection."[17] This implies that Kimmel was not quite A-1 after he became Commander in Chief. In Shoemaker's opinion, "Kimmel was not the admiral to take us to war in the Pacific against the Japanese. He simply did not have the touch."[18] Tucker called him "a narrow-gauge man who just did not have the stature of a CinC."[19]

Kimmel did not seem to have been sufficiently sure of himself to rise above absorption in the day's routine. Curts recalled that Kimmel tried to do too much himself and did not delegate authority.[20] Davis, too, said, "He tended to worry about little things as much as he did about the big things. There did not seem to be too much of a differentiation in his mind on them at times."[21] Smith testified that Kimmel "even went to the extent of personally auditing the records of the number of rounds of ammunition of all sorts" on each of the outlying islands. Once he found Kimmel in his office comparing lists of ammunition with similar records Bloch had brought from the district. Smith remarked "that the Commander-in-Chief should not be counting bullets, that he had a Staff to do that." Both admirals laughed and agreed.[22] But Kimmel did not mend his ways.

Very occasionally he felt the need for a complete break. Then he would call his old friend Admiral Furlong, commander of Minecraft, Battle Force, and invite him for a Sunday drive around Oahu. Sometimes they chatted or reminisced, but generally they rode in in companionable silence, absorbing the healing peace and beauty of the island. Even on these rare jaunts, however, Kimmel could not let himself relax completely, for he always took the wheel.[23]

He was overly concerned with appearances. Although the colorful, comfortable aloha shirts were standard island garb, he forbade them to his officers. In addition, he insisted that they wear neckties and hats when ashore. The officers especially resented the hats, which they dubbed "Kimmels."[24] But the admiral had his ideas of what was proper. He even disliked the khaki working uniform, convinced that it lessened "the dignity and military point of view of the wearer" and tended "to let down the efficiency of personnel."[25]

Charles A. Russell, a chief petty officer aboard the submarine *Argonaut* in December 1941, remarked bitterly, "We spent more for bright-work polish than the Japanese spent on fuel oil."[26] While exaggerated to make the point, this was all too true in spirit. Shoemaker related that on one occasion Kimmel, discovering *Enterprise*'s side cleaners wearing dungarees, ordered the carrier's captain, "Keep your side cleaners in white uniforms."[27]*

Many agreed that Kimmel carried his devotion to duty to extremes. "The general consensus was that Admiral Kimmel was too dedicated to his job as CinC," said Captain Walter S. DeLany, the fleet operations officer and possibly the nearest to Kimmel personally of all his staff.[28] Indeed, the admiral seemed to feel guilty if he were not on the job every hour of the day. His mind and heart called so insistently for efficiency and perfection that these concepts became not only strengths but weaknesses. He was obsessed with the physical aspects of his task. One reason for his compulsive devotion to his desk may have been the fact that he was somewhat deaf, an affliction which tends to drive its victims within themselves.[29] There in the sanctuary of his headquarters Kimmel could immerse himself in details he understood without tiresome explanations, could surround himself with his staff officers who understood him almost without the need for spoken communication.

Whatever the reason, Kimmel succumbed so completely to the tyranny of his work that he left himself little time to think, to analyze the relationship of events, to grasp broad meanings. In this he resembled a man wandering through an art gallery, so intent upon studying the brushwork and texture of the paint that he misses the beauty and significance of the masterpieces. Kimmel left little room in his scheme of things for the intangibles of command—intuition and flair—which separate the great leader from the merely competent one.

Inevitably a man of such forceful personality and such exacting standards inspired strong feelings pro and con. Kimmel's superiors in Washington thought exceedingly well of him. "Kimmel was my candidate for that job when he was appointed," Ingersoll told the

---

*Side cleaners are the sailors detailed to scrub the ship's side from the main deck to the water line.

congressional committee. "I mean by that when my opinion was asked I suggested Kimmel."[30] Stark was just as definite. "There was universal regard for the right caliber of Admiral Kimmel. I think he would have been on anybody's list. He was on mine."[31]

Other admirals, such as his classmate William F. Halsey, Raymond A. Spruance, Harold C. Train, and Furlong, considered Kimmel tops.[32] Some even believed him to be "the ablest officer that the United States Navy had produced in a quarter of a century, and that one of the most serious losses we incurred at Pearl Harbor was the loss of his services."[33]

Those who entertained opposing views included Admiral Tucker, who had served "on Richardson's staff when Kimmel relieved him and chose not to stay on when asked." Tucker wrote to Barnes that Kimmel "was not generally liked because he was a bit of a martinet and detail man."[34] Vice Admiral Charles A. Lockwood had the impression that Kimmel was "arrogant, conceited, and not well informed." Davis was not too happy with his duty under Kimmel because the admiral never seemed to understand his aviators. He called them "fly-boys," which rubbed Davis and his airmen the wrong way.[35]

For about a month after assuming command, Kimmel kept Richardson's operating schedule of half the Fleet at sea, half in port. Then he split the Fleet into three task forces, keeping one, sometimes two, at sea.[36] While this was a sensible move, unfortunately the schedule was not sufficiently varied for real security. Over a period, the predictable movements of fleet units enabled Japanese agents to report to Tokyo that major vessels were invariably in port over the weekends. The almost 100-percent chance of these ships being in Pearl Harbor on a Sunday was a foundation stone of Japanese planning. In this case, Kimmel and Bloch violated a cardinal intelligence tenet: Never establish a habit pattern.

Another problem which Kimmel inherited was that of antitorpedo nets. Richardson had decided that nets around the ships were undesirable.[37] Kimmel neither rescinded nor modified this command decision.

"Most significant fact which the Pearl Harbor probers glossed over, however, was torpedo nets," wrote Drew Pearson. "Had this very elementary precaution been taken, hundreds of lives would have been saved and the backbone of the Pacific Fleet would not have been left lying on the muddy bottom at Pearl Harbor."[38]

Ideal nets were never available to Kimmel. The Navy Department had been endeavoring to develop such baffles, but as of December 7 it had not succeeded.[39] Yet if Kimmel had taken the possibility of aerial torpedo strikes on his ships as seriously as the Japanese took the possibility of antitorpedo nets being around the American vessels, the story might have been different. Thinking in terms of missiles launched from submarines, Kimmel believed the net in the channel entrance to be sufficient protection. No doubt it would have been, if he had had to contend only with conventional Japanese submarines.

But torpedoes dropping from planes were another proposition. Kimmel assumed that Pearl Harbor's shallow waters provided sufficient protection against such an attack. In February Stark had agreed;[40] then in June the Navy warned its commands that the depth of water no longer necessarily precluded aerial torpedo attacks.[41] To Kimmel and Bloch such a danger seemed remote.[42]

Kimmel had solid staff backing in his opinion. DeLany "felt the depth of water in Pearl Harbor was such that torpedoes could not be successfully launched from aircraft against ships moored in Pearl Harbor." He based this assessment upon "information available in letters" from Stark; he had no recollection of the CNO's views being modified.[43] Davis, too, ruled out the possibility, and for the same reason.[44] Indeed, it is most strange how clearly Stark's discounting letter of February 15 was remembered; how thoroughly Ingersoll's warning of June 13 was ignored or forgotten.

Even Kimmel did not handle this with his usual candor. After quoting in detail from Stark's letter of February 15, he added:

> On June 13, 1941, the Chief of Naval Operations sent another letter on the same subject to the commandants of the various naval districts, including the Commandant of the 14th Naval District a copy of which was sent to me. After reading this letter, my staff and I, as well as the Commandant of the 14th Naval District, believed that the danger of a successful airplane torpedo attack on Pearl Harbor was negligible.[45]

No mention here that the letter of June 13 had considerably modified that of February 15. Anyone who did not know the facts would gain the impression that the second letter merely followed up the first.

Captain Charles H. "Soc" McMorris, Kimmel's war plans officer, was among those who rated the possibility of an aerial torpedo strike as "very remote."[46] In the scales against such a supposedly far-off contingency the Navy on Oahu had to balance the difficulties that protective nets around the ships would impose.

"When you place these nets in the harbor off the shipside 200 feet, or 66 yards, you are encroaching very much on the seaplane takeoff," Bloch explained.[47] Then, too, "the question of getting ships in and out quickly was affected by whether or not they had nets around them." Neither Kimmel nor Bloch "wanted to hamper their mobility . . . unless it was absolutely necessary."[48] When on December 7, 1941, torpedoes dropped from the sky, those same cruisers and destroyers proved on the spot that sortie was not quite the slow proposition everyone had believed it to be under normal conditions. Yet Kimmel had good reason for skepticism about aerial torpedo strikes in harbor. Only the most imperative motivation had pushed this Japanese technique through to success.

Kimmel and his advisers not only disbelieved in danger from aerial torpedoes, they doubted the chance of an air attack of any type. "The possibility of an air attack in the Hawaiian area by Japanese forces had been given consideration," said McMorris, "and the probability of it was greatly discounted because of the distance involved and the logistic problems that would have to be met."[49] And what about the Martin-Bellinger report, ostensibly devised to counter just such an attack? Bellinger explained somewhat lamely that the plan was not an "estimate of where the Japanese would strike in the event of war"; it was an attempt "to work out a plan for the defense of Pearl Harbor." Bellinger "did not expect, as a probability, that an attack would be made on Oahu as the opening event of a Japanese-United States war."[50]

Nevertheless, Kimmel positioned his vessels with such a strike in mind. "He had all of his ships moored in such a way that there would be a 360° fire angle in case of an air attack," explained Rear Admiral Harold C. Train, who as a captain in 1941 had been chief of staff to Vice Admiral William S. Pye, commander of the Battle Force. "Had this not existed on Pearl Harbor day the situation would have been far worse."[51]

Kimmel also took special precautions when one of his flattops moored in Pearl Harbor. "A carrier in port is just nothing," he declared. He recognized that the carrier-borne planes would be both useless and vulnerable under such circumstances. Therefore, "the minute it came into port," each flattop flew its aircraft off to the naval bases, which had "ammunition, bombs, and whatnot to arm the planes of the carriers, so that in the event of being caught in port those planes could be useful."[52]

What the Navy at Hawaii really took seriously was the submarine menace. Numerous undersea contacts had occurred throughout 1941, convincing Kimmel that Japanese submarines lurked in Hawaiian waters. His orders from Washington not to bomb them made the doughty admiral "most unhappy."[53] McMorris thought sabotage or submarine attacks, especially the latter, were distinct possibilities.[54] DeLany, too, thought that any Japanese attack in the Pearl Harbor area would come from beneath the sea.[55] "We were very submarine conscious," said Smith.[56] Pye recalled that the Navy considered possible a submarine attack "as an act in advance of the declaration of war." He explained somewhat vaguely, "The basis for that argument was that destruction by torpedo from a submarine, if the submarine is not sighted or captured, can be mistaken for an internal explosion and no one can prove to the contrary. . . . There is also the possibility that the Germans might man Japanese submarines and might even move their submarines into the Pacific and attack the Fleet to cause us to go into the war with Japan."[57]

That Japan was embarked upon a course of aggression was obvious. Yet no one in high position in the Pacific Fleet seems to have entertained any real expectation that Japan would deliberately bring about war with the United States. "We knew our own potential; we thought the Japanese knew it too," stated Vice Admiral Charles F. Coe, who had been Bellinger's operations and plans officer in 1941, "and therefore we could not conceive of their attacking us under the circumstances."[58]

Nonetheless, the fact that the United States' position was becoming increasingly delicate should have been obvious to any adult who read the newspapers, and Kimmel had a better view than most, thanks to a stream of informative letters from Stark.[59] In view of those letters, one has to sympathize with the Philadelphia *Record*, which remarked during the congressional hearings that Kimmel and Short "were caught asleep at the switch—despite the fact that batteries of alarm clocks had been ringing for months." Citing eleven "specific warnings of possible hostile Jap action" from Washington to Kimmel, the newspaper asked irascibly, *"What more did Kimmel need? An engraved card from Tokyo informing him of Jap intentions?"* (italics in original).[60]

Stark had commented in one of his earliest letters to Kimmel, "It always sort of hits me with a thud when people are planning ahead and looking for something in advance rather than giving all they have to the job in hand."[61] To a certain extent that was one of Kimmel's problems—he was looking too far ahead.

Although in many ways very different from Short, Kimmel was almost equally training-minded and, like Short, he misunderstood the nature of his mission. During the congressional investigation, Morgan, who had come to admire Kimmel very much, noted that the admiral appeared consumed with the idea of honing the Fleet for action, possibly of becoming himself "the American Nelson."[62]

Kimmel's own testimony left little doubt that such was the case. He told the congressional committee, "I considered my primary responsibility out there offensive action which we expected and hoped to undertake . . ." under the Navy basic war plan, Rainbow Five (WPL-46).[63]

Yet the tasks assigned the Pacific Fleet under WPL-46 were relatively limited and envisioned neither self-defense in harbor nor a major sea battle during the early days of the Pacific war. So some of Kimmel's demands upon Washington seemed to have been based upon a rather grandiose concept of his mission. Both he and Bloch visualized the U.S. and Japanese navies maneuvering in the Pacific so as to force each other out in battle array where they could settle the question of supremacy in that ocean.[64] One single statistic should have told Kimmel that his attitude was, to put it mildly, premature: The entire Pacific Fleet possessed only eleven tankers, and of these a mere four were "suitable for fueling other ships at sea."* Kimmel conceded that to keep "the entire fleet at sea for long periods would have required not 11 tankers but approximately 75, with at least one third of them equipped for underway delivery."[65]

Thinking in terms of aggressive sea warfare, Kimmel wrote to Stark on November 15, 1941:

> We should have sufficient strength in this fleet for such effective operations as to permit cruising at will in the Japanese Mandated Island area, and even on occasions to Japanese home waters. We

---

*Seven tankers accompanied the Nagumo task force to Pearl Harbor.

should have the strength to make any enemy operations against Wake a highly hazardous undertaking. To do these things substantial increase in the strength of this Fleet is mandatory.[66]

Stark's reply, dated ten days later, was almost sharp in comparison to his usual style. He reminded Kimmel of one of the unhappy facts of life: "It was on the basis of inadequate forces that ABC-1* and Rainbow 5 were predicated and which were accepted by all concerned as about the best compromise we could get out of the situation actually confronting us." Stark agreed that "to cruise in Japanese home waters you should have substantial increase in the strength of your fleet." But he reined in Kimmel with the dampening statement that "neither ABC-1 or Rainbow 5 contemplate this as a general policy."[67]

To a point Turner agreed that the Pacific Fleet had an offensive function. "So far as Admiral Kimmel was concerned, his part in the plan was not defensive," he testified to Hart. "It required a limited offensive through the Central Pacific islands."[68] But not at once. Kimmel's initial wartime mission consisted of "defensive tasks, with the exception of a diversion toward the Marshalls and Carolines to relieve pressure on the Malay Barrier. There were other offensive tasks against Japanese communications and shipping, but those were largely tasks for submarines."

That was why the detachment of a portion of Kimmel's strength to the Atlantic in the spring of 1941 still left the Pacific Fleet "a number of capital ships equal to those in the Japanese Navy. The reason was that the center of gravity of the initial naval effort of the United States in WPL-46 was to be in the Atlantic and not in the Pacific where the role was primarily defensive."[69]

Ingersoll considered Phase I of the Pacific Fleet's own war plan† in effect at the time of the "war warning" of November 27. This meant that Japan had not yet become a combatant. One of the tasks in Phase I was: "Maintain Fleet security at bases and anchorages and at sea." This was one of the reasons why Ingersoll expected that Kimmel would

---

*ABC-1 was the short title of a report covering discussions held January 29–March 27, 1941, between representatives of the U.S. Army and Navy and the United Kingdom's Chiefs of Staff. This report outlined strategy should the United States be drawn into the war. Roosevelt did not approve it, but later in the year Rainbow Five was amended to include this strategy (PHA, Part 15, pp. 1485–1540).
†WPPac-46, July 21, 1941.

have his patrol planes out. Another reason was Task M: "Guard against surprise attack by Japan."

Ingersoll explained that offensive movement in the Marshalls was not to take place until D plus 180. For the first six months, the Pacific Fleet would operate largely on the defensive, because the United States "did not have the auxiliaries or the transports sufficient for the fleet to make an offensive movement."[70] Yet Kimmel, so full of fight, thought and reacted as if the Pacific Fleet were to steam out immediately and hit the Japanese. Moreover, he planned to go to sea personally when hostilities commenced.[71] This speaks well for his courage but is not in line with the good sense he had shown in establishing his headquarters ashore soon after becoming CinC.

To the congressional committee Kimmel held forth at length concerning the Pacific Fleet's shortages of matériel and personnel.[72] Yet from the standpoint of his actual mission, he was not in bad shape. In fact, on August 21, 1941, Stark wrote him that, "after complying with Bunav's [the Bureau of Navigation's] despatches," the Pacific Fleet would be overmanned in several key categories. And he further insisted that Washington was making greater personnel demands on the Atlantic than on the Pacific Fleet.[73] If Kimmel had spent all his energies working within the framework of his mission as it existed, instead of concentrating on his Fleet's capacity to perform hypothetical tasks in the future, he might have been more inclined to take the prompt emergency measures Washington expected of him upon receipt of the "war warning."

There was another aspect to this matter of resources which Kimmel should have considered. During the congressional hearings, the Washington *Post* pointed out that the very fact that the U.S. Pacific Fleet "was undermanned, inadequately supplied and generally unprepared for a slugging contest with the Japanese Navy . . . intensified the necessity for taking every precaution against the sort of attack which the Japanese launched." The editorial further remarked, "The great mystery is why, with so much knowledge of what the Japs were doing, was there so little action. . . ."[74]

Kimmel had taken a great deal of action all year. He almost knocked out himself as well as his subordinates in his efforts to whip the Fleet into fighting trim. But his orientation was toward the offensive, and the Japanese caught him with his defenses down. To his dying day Kimmel could not understand this bitter irony.

CHAPTER 26

"His Most Grievous Failure"

Misinterpretation of "war warning" message—Assumed danger was in Southeast Asia—Did not interpret in context of the time—Continued training program—Decided against distant air reconnaissance—Authorized depth bombing of submarine contacts

Kimmel and Short were different personalities, yet upon receipt of the warning messages of November 27, they reacted like Siamese twins. Both acted negatively, deciding that it was more important to continue to prepare for future action which might or might not develop rather than to meet the challenge of the moment.

Kimmel's position was even more difficult to understand than Short's, for the Navy Department's message contained no mention of wanting Japan to commit the first overt act and of not alarming the civilian population which, in Short's mind, blunted the thrust of the War Department's warning. Seldom if ever has a military document been so parsed and analyzed, unraveled and rewoven, discussed virtually word for word. And seldom has there been a clearer demonstration of how fatally easy it is for one group of intelligent men to misunderstand instructions which had been quite lucid to another group of equally intelligent men.

Take for example the opening sentence, "This despatch is to be considered a war warning." Turner, who prepared the message, saw nothing equivocal about this wording. Asked what he meant by it, he replied, "I meant just exactly what it said, it is to be considered a warning of approaching war."[1]

One recipient read that message loud and clear. Admiral Hart, Commander in Chief of the Asiatic Fleet, went straight to the core, almost contemptuously shucking away the layers of verbiage. "Insofar as I was concerned," he told the congressional committee, "the despatch might have ended right there, 'This despatch is to be considered a war warning.' "[2] Later Hart amplified that statement. "There were ten important words—only ten—'This . . . is . . . a war warning. . . . Execute an appropriate defense deployment,' "he told Donald G. Brownlow. "An order in five words. An order that transcended all the yakity-yak that went back and forth, and, unfortunately, added to that was some more yakity-yak. Those ten words were the whole thing."[3]

Regrettably, Hawaii's defenders were not so clear-sighted, and paid more attention to the "yakity-yak" than to the key ten words. The expression "war warning" slid over Kimmel's consciousness. Although he conceded to the congressional committee that he had never seen this expression used in all his naval experience, he "did not consider it an extraordinary term." He and those he consulted who "communicated their feelings" to him believed "that this term . . . added little, if anything, to the message of November 27."[4] He "regarded that phrase as a characterization of specific intelligence which the message contained."[5]

An equal failure of minds to meet occurred in relation to the almost equally important order: "Execute an appropriate defensive deployment." Here again, Turner considered the directive to be "perfectly specific and entirely clear." He declared that Kimmel had not complied with that order. Turner's amplifying remarks emphasized that he believed a "defensive deployment" should have included air reconnaissance.[6]

But to Kimmel the term "did not necessarily mean" any such thing:

> I might say that the "appropriate defensive deployment" and "defensive deployment" used in that . . . dispatch, was a strategic matter, not a tactical matter. It was a strategic defensive deployment— I mean our understanding was—and that was primarily to make sure that when we deployed our fleet, or put them in any position that they would not take on an offensive character or anything that the Japanese would consider as offensive.[7]

In short, Washington used the term "defensive deployment" in a positive sense, anticipating Kimmel would take active measures to defend his Fleet and the Hawaiian sea frontier against any possible threat of attack, however remote. But Kimmel's interpretation was negative, more concerned with what not to do than with taking any

local defensive posture. And obviously his view was highly colored
with the idea of not provoking the Japanese, although the Navy Department's "war warning" contained no such restriction.

Another part of the message which caused misunderstanding was
the assessment that Japan would probably initiate an amphibious
expedition against either the Philippines, Thailand, the Kra peninsula, or possibly Borneo. Turner had intended that part of the message
primarily for Hart's attention, the areas in question being within his
Asiatic Fleet's territory.[8]

Unfortunately, no one at Kimmel's headquarters said, in effect,
"So much for Tommy Hart's bailiwick. What about our own?" Instead,
a problem of misdirection arose. Rear Admiral Walter S. Anderson,
a former director of Naval Intelligence and commander, Battleships,
at the time of the attack, considered the message of November 27 "a
very serious matter." Nevertheless he "noted with specific interest
and some relief, as far as Pearl Harbor was concerned, that this
warning did not anticipate any attack on United States territory farther
East than the Philippines." He "expected something further by way
of a warning from the Department if the locations of the Japanese
task forces moved in any way to indicate a threat farther East than
the Philippines."[9]

The Navy Court of Inquiry, which seemed inclined to be as le-
nient as possible with the Navy's representatives on Oahu, thought
that

> there were good grounds for the belief . . . that hostilities would
> begin in the Far East rather than elsewhere, and that the same
> considerations which influenced the sentiment of the authorities in
> Washington in this respect, support the interpretation which Admiral
> Kimmel placed upon the "war warning message" of 27 November,
> to the effect that this message directed attention away from Pearl
> Harbor rather than toward it.[10]

This rationale is difficult to accept. When a field commander re-
ceives an "action" message warning him of imminent war, his job is
not to speculate where the blow may fall but to prepare his own
command for action. As McCollum stated, "I think that a commander
to whom such a message as that is addressed must assume that war
is going to break out over his forces and take the steps necessary to
cover it."[11]

Kimmel did not see the matter in that light. One of his sharpest complaints against the Navy Department was this:

The so-called "War warning" dispatch of November 27 did not warn the Pacific Fleet of an attack in the Hawaiian area. It did not state expressly or by implication that an attack in the Hawaiian area was imminent or probable. It did not repeal or modify the advice previously given me by the Navy Department that no move against Pearl Harbor was imminent or planned by Japan. The phrase "war warning" cannot be made a catch-all for all the contingencies hindsight may suggest.[12]

Ironically, both the Navy and War departments were "averse in being too specific as to what they believed might happen" because "that might lead the Commanders-in-Chief not to guard other matters under their cognizance."[13] This, of course, is exactly what happened at Hawaii.

Kimmel's after-the-fact attitude toward Washington's dispatch of November 27 contrasted sharply to the "war warning" he himself gave Admiral Halsey that very day. When Halsey was about to sail for Wake Island with a squadron of Marine F4Fs, a voyage of potential danger, he asked Kimmel, "How far do you want me to go?" Kimmel replied, "Goddammit, use your common sense!" For Halsey that was enough and plenty.[14*]

Just what did the Navy Department intend that Kimmel do? To the Navy Court Stark stressed his expectation that, upon receipt of the "war warning," Kimmel would institute "readiness measures ashore and afloat, distant reconnaissance and anti-submarine measures. I assumed that all measures with the Army, particularly those which had been previously agreed upon for emergency, would be implemented." But he had requested no report of action from Kimmel. "He was on the spot and had detail beyond what was available to me. I had every confidence in him, and I left the matter entirely to him, after giving him a war warning, and informing him that an aggressive move by Japan was expected within the next few days."[15]

To the congressional committee Stark was more specific. A defense against air or submarine attack—the most likely form in the Hawaiian area—was aerial reconnaissance.

---

*The *Enterprise* task force departed Pearl Harbor for Wake Island on the morning of November 28, 1941.

Therefore, I would have assumed that he would have scouted with his planes to the best of his ability with what he had. I would have assumed that he would have used his submarines to assist him in that scouting and I would have assumed he would have weighed the rest of the force he had, what he had at sea, what he had in port, as to whether he had the best balance possible to assist in that scouting.[16]

But Kimmel did none of these things. No more than Short did he comprehend that the "war warning" was a demarcation line, that the months of preparation had ended, the days of action had come. Nor did he relate it to preceding events. One of the strangest aspects of the "war warning" affair was Kimmel's, Bloch's, and Short's treatment of it as an isolated incident. If such had been the case, there would be some excuse for their failure to go all-out in response to the warnings from their respective superiors. Yet the messages of November 27 neither stood alone nor did they indicate an abrupt change in policy.

Only three days previously, on November 24, Stark had warned Kimmel and Hart that the chances of a "favorable outcome of negotiations with Japan" were "very doubtful," and that the Japanese might move "in any direction including attack on Philippines or Guam."[17] Stark believed that "if I had received a message that the Japs might make a surprise aggressive movement in any direction, I would say, well, we better look out and be ready for it."[18] Instead, Captain Smith, Kimmel's Chief of Staff, protested, "the words 'In any direction including an attack on the Philippines or Guam' implies that they are not coming any farther east than the Philippines or Guam."[19] This was very specious reasoning, and the suggestion that "any direction" did not include the east is astounding in a man of Smith's intelligence.

Stark termed the warning of November 27 "much more positive" than that of the 24th, ". . . because on the 24th we stated that favorable outcome of negotiations with Japan very doubtful; there was left a loophole. . . . We closed that loophole in the message of the 27th."[20]

What is more, the commanders on Oahu should have evaluated those dispatches in the light of the entire background of the situation. The Martin-Bellinger and Farthing reports, the Knox-Stimson letters of February 1941, the years of exercises in Hawaiian waters, the existing war plans—all these should have come sharply into focus upon receipt of the warning messages of November 27. Significant naval preparations had been under way, as Ingersoll related:

We had, for two months or more, taken steps to get our merchant vessels out of the Far East and out of the other areas in the Pacific where they could be captured by the Japanese. We began routing them far to the southard [*sic*] around Australia. The last vessels that went to the Philippines were convoyed; also we had initiated convoys in the Pacific for important cargoes going to Australia, including pilots for the Chinese air force and similar things.[21]

Then, too, as McCollum observed, "the fact that the Japanese intended to go to war carried with it the possibility of an attack on the fleet wherever it might be."[22]

The additional fact that relations between the United States and Japan had been bad for years and had deteriorated steadily throughout 1941 was no news to any intelligent American. As Stimson wrote with understandable exasperation in a statement for the congressional committee:

From some of the comments quoted in the public press, one would get the impression that the imminent threat of war in October and November 1941 was a deep secret, known only to the authorities in Washington who kept it mysteriously to themselves. Nothing could be further from the truth. . . . Aside from the war warnings which were sent to our military and naval commanders in the various theaters of danger, the imminence of war with Japan was a matter of public knowledge and the people were being warned time and time again of the danger which was approaching. One need only read the headlines of the newspapers during this period.[23]

Just a few days before receipt of the "war warning," Kimmel spoke to Colonel and Mrs. Dunlop about "the perilous lives" those in Hawaii were living. He said in effect, "We have to all be on the ball."[24]

But the dispatch of November 27 and other warning messages from Washington since the fall of the Konoye Cabinet in October 1941 did not have the impact in Hawaii that the War and Navy departments expected. Stark and his advisers had reckoned without the strength and motive force of Kimmel's vision of future great sea battles far from Hawaii. Therefore, as Smith stressed to the Navy Court, he and his staff were not thinking in terms of defending Pearl Harbor; they "were thinking about the fleet and the readiness of the fleet."[25]

Kimmel did not really credit the possibility of an attack such as the Japanese delivered on December 7. He "felt the most probable form of attack in the Hawaiian area was by submarine," with aerial bombing "a remote possibility"; the danger of a torpedo plane attack was "nil" because of the shallow water in Pearl Harbor. What is more, he shared Short's dangerous illusion that "it was much more probable that the Japs would attempt a raid on Pearl Harbor if the Fleet were away than if it were there."[26]

So he continued to place his primary emphasis upon preparations for future combat. "If we had stopped training the first time we received these alarming messages," he explained to the Navy Court, "I feel certain that by the time war was declared our ships would have been in a dangerously ineffective condition."[27] Therefore, he would not interfere with his training program unless he received "precise and accurate knowledge of the appropriate time" to do so.[28] This was asking a great deal: more "precise and accurate knowledge" than that conveyed by the admittedly unprecedented words, "This despatch is to be considered a war warning."

Yet Washington meant that significant message to send a clear signal to cease "business as usual." Ingersoll expected a change in orientation to result, that thenceforth "the training and material preparations were of secondary importance to security and deployment for war."[29] He amplified to the congressional committee,

> Up until the time that the war warning dispatch was sent the primary tasks of the fleet out in the Pacific . . . was to prepare itself for war by training and getting itself in the best material condition that it could get. . . . But once the war warning went out it seems to me. . . . that thereafter training was not the primary task and had to go along as operations would permit.[30]

Later Kimmel would not concede that a training basis precluded an alert status. "I didn't let the training program stand in the way of the alert that I considered necessary at that time. The fleet was on the alert." He added belligerently, "It was on the alert and any man who says the fleet wasn't on the alert, when the whole outfit were firing in the times that have been testified to here, well, I don't know what he means by alert."[31]

Kimmel missed the point. The fact that crews and individuals reacted promptly is a tribute to their state of readiness. If their Commander in Chief had been equally alert to the meaning of his instructions he would have deployed the Fleet as directed and instituted long-range reconnaissance.

In sending Kimmel the "war warning," the Navy Department had fully expected "that reconnaissance would be started and kept up . . . from the 27th in any case." Persistent questioning by Senator Alben W. Barkley, chairman of the congressional committee, finally pried out of Stark the admission that the Hawaiian commands "did not obey instructions."[32] Although the attack surprised Stark, he "also was surprised that . . . certain steps had not been taken to intercept it and be on the lookout for it."[33]

Senator Lucas asked Ingersoll, "Now, Admiral, if we were not going to start a real offensive until 180 days after Japan struck us, can you think of any reason whatsoever that Admiral Kimmel . . . should not have had long-range reconnaissance operating from November 27 on through . . . with whatever planes we had if it were only three?" Ingersoll answered, "I had every reason to expect that he would do that, and I was surprised that he had not done it. . . . It never occurred to me that it was not being done."[34]

Kimmel's failure to institute long-range air patrols illustrates certain aspects of his character and methods of operation. He reached his decision without consulting those subordinates whom one might logically consider to be those most concerned. As previously pointed out, Bloch, who was technically responsible for distant reconnaissance, did not receive a copy of the "war warning" until the next day.

Nor did Kimmel seek the professional judgment of his excellent fleet intelligence officer, Commander Layton. He called him in, but only to have Layton paraphrase the dispatch from Washington, then take it to Short. Layton was in Kimmel's office to show him the paraphrase he had worked out when Captain John B. Earle, Bloch's chief of staff, brought in the War Department's warning. But Layton did not take part in the ensuing discussion. No one asked his opinion and he did not offer one. In fact, in this instance he considered himself "an intruder."[35] Something is seriously wrong with any headquarters where its competent, experienced intelligence officer feels himself "an intruder" at a conference dealing with the probable onset of war.

At least Layton knew there had been such a thing as a "war warning." Bellinger, who commanded the patrol planes, was not even that well informed. He saw neither the warning of November 24 nor that of November 27 until after the attack.[36] Kimmel did not consult Bellinger and saw no reason why he should. Bellinger "was there directly under my orders, and I felt capable of giving him any orders that he required."[37] Apparently it never crossed Kimmel's mind that Bellinger could have given him authoritative facts and figures upon which to base his decision.

Representative Keefe seemed almost incredulous in discussing this situation with Bellinger:

> here is a task force commander in command of patrol planes who isn't given any information at all as to what is going on in the international situation and in relations with Japan except what you got from the newspapers, perhaps, while you were lying sick in bed 4 or 5 days before the 7th of December;* that no long-distance reconnaissance is ordered at all, some people claiming that that could not be effected because of lack of personnel and lack of planes, but you are of the opinion that if there had been a utilization of the patrol planes that were available it could have been carried on for at least a week.[38]

Bellinger was reluctant to declare openly that had he known of the "war warning" history might have been changed. "Assuming that you had been the commander out there and that you knew war was imminent, and you received a war warning message, would that have made any difference in respect to using these planes for reconnaissance work?" Senator Lucas asked. "Perhaps," Bellinger replied. ". . . God only knows what I would have done. But I can say this, that I was very much surprised when I heard that there had been a message."[39]

One cannot say definitely what the result would have been had Kimmel sought Bellinger's opinion. But Bellinger was in a position to have told Kimmel that he was "in agreement with Admiral Davis that the greatest possibility of a successful air attack lay in an attack coming in from the sector of the north because of the prevailing wind conditions" and that he had enough aircraft available to have covered that sector for a minimum of a week.[40]

Kimmel did not consult Davis either, although he was his own air staff officer, not a subordinate commander like Bellinger. He may have believed that he already knew all Davis could tell him, for Davis had attended many staff discussions throughout the year and delivered his opinion: that a surprise air attack was possible and "could only be

---

*Bellinger had been bedridden with flu from December 2 through 6, 1941 (*PHA*, Part 8, p. 3488).

prevented by the most extensive searches and efforts to intercept at sea by air and surface vessels." He also believed "Comprehensive and extensive air searches were practicable" but "would very definitely interfere with progress in general in aviation training in the Fleet." Had he been asked on November 27 what the chances were of a patrol discovering a Japanese attack force the day before an attack, his estimate would have been "fairly good, perhaps two out of three."[41]

Kimmel seemed to realize that his failure to institute long-distance reconnaissance was a serious weakness in his defense. He argued:

> For a period of ten days, as from 27 November until 7 December, approximately 30 planes were available for a 700 mile daily search— not an 800 mile search. This could at best cover about one-third of the 360 degrees of the circumference. Such a search would be in-effective. Having covered the operating areas by air patrols, it was not prudent in my judgment and that of my staff, to fritter away our slim resources in patrol planes in token searches and thus seriously impair their required availability to carry out their functions with the Fleet under approved War Plans.[42]

Bellinger testified, "For a commander to be reasonably sure that no hostile carrier could reach a spot 250 miles away and launch an attack without prior detection, would have required an effective daily search through 360° to a distance of at least 800 miles."[43] Bellinger's operations officer, Commander Ramsey—the same officer Kimmel's battleship *New York* had fished aboard so long before—believed that an aerial reconnaissance of less than 800 miles "would not protect against surprise air raid," while the range of the currently available PBYs was limited to 700 miles, covering a 144° arc.[44]

So far, Kimmel stood in firm ground. But in arbitrarily deciding that a search confined to one-third of a full circumference would be ineffective, he exercised poor judgment. Ramsey testified that, granted a supply of critical spare parts, the Patrol Wing could have operated eighteen planes on a daily search to 700 miles, covering a 144° arc. In such a sector, "we felt that, except in the single case of a widespread and pronounced front, we stood an excellent chance of detecting any sizable group of surface vessels on any given day."[45] A little later, he said, "The means at our disposal would have provided a certain degree of security, but the means were inadequate for absolute security."[46]

Contrary to Kimmel's statement, he did not face a clear-cut "either-

or" choice between a 360° search or "token searches." The alternative before him was whether or not to use his patrol planes defensively in light of the "war warning," or to hoard them for future combat.

Some believed that Kimmel acted wisely. Halsey declared that "any admiral worth his stars would have made the same choice."[47] As a natural corollary to its position concerning the "war warning," the Navy Court gave Kimmel its blessing and approval:

> Where planes are not available to cover all sectors, the selection of sectors to be omitted is left purely to chance and under such circumstances the advisability of the diversion of all planes from other duties is questionable unless there be information as to the fact of a hostile approach and of the direction, within reasonable limits, from which the approach is expected.
>
> . . . The Commander-in-Chief, Pacific Fleet, for definite and sound reasons and after making provision for such reconnaissance in case of emergency, specifically ordered that no routine long-range reconnaissance be undertaken and assumed full responsibility for this action. The omission of this reconnaissance was not due to oversight or neglect. It was the result of a military decision, reached after much deliberation and consultation with experienced officers, and after weighing the information at hand and all the factors involved. . . .
>
> It is a fact that the use of Fleet patrol planes for daily long-range, all-around reconnaissance was not justified in the absence of information indicating that an attack was to be expected within narrow limits of time. It is a further fact that, even if justified, this was not possible with the inadequate number of Fleet planes available.[48]

This was a bit much for Admiral King to swallow. In his second endorsement to the court's proceedings, he expressed his belief that Kimmel "was not on entirely sound ground in making no attempt at long range reconnaissance." Certain sectors "more dangerous than others . . . could have been covered to some extent. And it would appear that such partial cover would have been logical in the circumstances."[49] Forrestal's endorsement to the Navy and Hewitt reports was even stronger. "The evidence indicates clearly, however, that his [Kimmel's] most grievous failure was his failure to conduct long-range air reconnaissance in the more dangerous sectors from Oahu during the week preceding the attack."[50]

The point was well taken. Kimmel's lack of sufficient aircraft for

360° coverage was not a valid reason for not using his available planes. Bloch testified that the Pacific Fleet had seventy-two aircraft suitable for patrol. Of these, twenty-four were at Midway, and twelve were being overhauled. He pointed out that if the remaining thirty-six "could have maintained a 360-degree patrol as far as their radius of action would permit them to do so, it would have been very thin on the outer circumference."[51]

But thirty-six planes, while not enough for total coverage, are thirty-six more than none. And a 360° search was not needed. Carefully reasoned estimates, such as the Martin-Bellinger and Farthing reports, existed postulating that the most dangerous sectors were the north and northwest. These could have been covered adequately if not ideally. As Zacharias testified to the congressional committee, the aircraft on hand, "although limited in forces available for that work . . . nevertheless could be used and restricted to the most probable area or sector." That area he judged to be the north, because "the prevailing wind in Hawaii is from the northward sector."[52] Ramsey agreed that "in view of the prevailing wind conditions . . . and other factors, we decided the northwest sector was the most likely line of approach, and in our drills the squadron in the highest degree of readiness was always ordered to take up that sector."[53]

Not only Navy but Army aircraft could and should have been used on the basis of such estimates. The Hawaiian Air Force had available twenty-one B-18s in commission.[54] The Navy could have requested use of these medium bombers. They were obsolescent but, according to Marshall, the type was "a sturdy, reliable plane."[55] Although not perfectly suited for reconnaissance,[56] the B-18 was better than no aircraft at all. Thus Kimmel had enough resources on hand to have covered at least a portion of the critical sector of "the vacant sea" to the north and northwest. The situation called for a command decision both difficult and risky. But making just such testing, even cruel, decisions is one of a commander's main duties.

During the congressional hearings, Kimmel made a tremendous impression upon Morgan, who considered that the admiral towered above Short. "Kimmel was an extraordinarily brilliant man," he reflected, "the type of brilliance that would take a gamble. He took that gamble and he lost."[57]

No one can be sure that any reconnaissance aircraft covering the northward sea area on or before December 7, 1941, would have sighted the Japanese task force. If a sharp-eyed observer had done so, the ships in harbor could have been alert and ready, Short's fighter planes armed and in the air, the ground defenses manned and waiting. By deciding against long-range air patrols, Kimmel canceled any chance whatsoever of such a warning, left his ships vulnerable to the Japanese air attack, and himself to every investigating body that probed the disaster.

This was one area of agreement between the majority and minority reports of the congressional inquiry. "In making the decision not to conduct distant reconnaissance, Admiral Kimmel erred," declared the majority report. ". . . . He was ordered to effect an appropriate defensive deployment. This was a general directive consistent with his specific suggestion that the commander in chief of the Pacific Fleet be guided by broad policy and objectives rather than by categorical instructions."[58] This was a most telling point. Kimmel had used those very words in a formal letter to Stark on May 26, 1941,[59] and this recommendation considerably weakened his after-the-fact complaints that Washington was not sufficiently specific with him. The majority report continued relentlessly:

> He knew that one of the tasks before the outbreak of war was guarding against a possible surprise attack by Japan. He knew that the only effective means of detecting a surprise raiding force in adequate time to combat it was by distant reconnaissance. He knew the Japanese reputation for deceit and treachery. He knew the greatest danger to the Fleet at Pearl Harbor was the possibility of an air raid. He knew that the maintenance and protection of the Fleet while in its base constituted a fundamental element in making military dispositions at Pearl Harbor. He had been categorically warned of war. He knew or must have known that the necessity of Japan's striking the first blow required of him greater vigilance consistent with his fundamental duty as commander in chief to prepare for the worst contingency. He had adequate facilities to patrol the most dangerous approaches to Pearl Harbor. The decision was not a simple one, but, failing to resolve his dilemma by seeking advice from the Navy Department, Admiral Kimmel displayed poor judgment in failing to employ every instrumentality at his command to defend his fleet.[60]

The legislators who signed the majority report were just as unhappy with Kimmel's related actions and lack of actions:

the fact that there was an agreement with the Army at Hawaii whereby the Navy was to perform distant reconnaissance placed upon Admiral Kimmel the obligation of advising General Short that he had decided not to conduct such reconnaissance. . . . Admiral Kimmel's clear duty, therefore, in the absence of Navy reconnaissance was to confer with General Short to insure that Army radar, antiaircraft, and planes were fully utilized and alerted. None of these things were done. And there appears to be no substantial reason for failing to call upon the Army, consistent with the joint plans, for the six long-range bombers which were admittedly available to the Navy at Hawaii for the asking.[61]

The minority report was much more succinct, but its criticism carries a special force. Senators Brewster and Ferguson had entered the lists cocked and primed to place the entire blame for Pearl Harbor upon President Roosevelt. Yet despite their political bias they wrote:

We think in making such a decision Admiral Kimmel was unjustified in concluding, first, that there was no danger of attack at Pearl Harbor, and, second, that such a decision did not violate the fundamental proposition that no disposition should be taken which unnecessarily increased fleet peril. The absence of distant reconnaissance immediately imperiled fleet safety. We therefore think the abandonment of distant reconnaissance was unjustified.[62]

Stark had expected that upon receipt of the "war warning" Kimmel "would take dispositions to avoid surprise, so far as he could with what he had." This would include "some air patrol." In fact, when Brigadier General Joseph T. McNarney of the Roberts Commission asked Stark if he had anticipated some use to be made of Patrol Wing 2, he replied, "Decidedly, yes."[63] What is more, Ingersoll indicated that Kimmel need not confine scouting to the air. "He had lots of destroyers and submarines." Ingersoll did not want to say just what action Kimmel should have taken, but "he could have done something when the war warning dispatch went out to improve the security of his fleet."[64]

It was not only Kimmel's superiors in Washington who expected him to undertake aerial reconnaissance. In a postwar article, Vice Admiral Shigeru Fukudome, former chief of the First Bureau, Japanese Naval General Staff, listed as one of the objections to Yamamoto's risky venture: *"High probability that the task force would be spotted by enemy patrol planes at the point from which the attacking planes were to be launched, with consequent enemy interdiction"* (Fukudome's italics).[65]

Kimmel was not the type of man who would accept the fact that he had made an honest, well-reasoned judgment that in the circumstances happened to be wrong. He could not possibly be at fault, ergo, the message which triggered the action had to be the villain. In later years Kimmel dismissed the "war warning" as a "blanket notification without specifications or instructions which in time I have come to believe was intended simply to cover Washington on the events that followed."[66]

This was a long way from the truth. He had used the message as the basis for one positive, dynamic action: he ordered the bombing of any unidentified submarine discovered in the operating area of Hawaiian waters, an action he had been itching to take for months, but from which Stark had restrained him. "I felt that any submarine operating submerged in the Pearl Harbor operating area should be bombed. I had felt it a long time, and I decided on 27 November to bomb them anyhow."[67] The message of November 27 had at least that much effect upon him, so his later complaints that it was not really a warning will not stand up. Just as Short, upon receipt of the War Department warning, had acted to counter the danger in which he believed, sabotage, so Kimmel took measures against the danger which seemed real to him, submarines.

Taking the somewhat illogical attitude that if Roosevelt were to blame for Pearl Harbor, the commanders on the spot must be wholly blameless, certain revisionists worked hard to undercut the warnings of November 27. For example, Greaves advanced a truly novel theory. Writing to Barnes on July 5, 1967, he pointed out that CinCAF (Hart) preceded CinCPAC (Kimmel) among the addressees. He reached the conclusion "by the prior listing of the lower ranked Hart that it was he that the drafters had primarily in mind. HEK [Kimmel] knew this order of address and would normally take it as adding strength to the idea that Washington felt the real danger was in the Far East."

That same day, Commander Hiles wrote to Barnes with a logic which should have buried this idea forever: "Percy is all wet; the message was one of *action* to both Hart and Kimmel . . ." and both men "were bound to obey it."[68] But Barnes was almost hysterically intent upon acquitting Kimmel of all blame. Ignoring Hiles's sensible comments, he published Greaves's suggestion almost word for word:

It would, of course, be quibbling to contend that Kimmel did not know that the message was designed for him as well as Hart. But it is also a fact that, as shown by the prior listing of the lower ranked Hart, that it was the latter whom the drafters had primarily in mind. . . . It is equally true that Kimmel noted this order of address and naturally interpreted it as deliberately intended to emphasize that Washington believed that the real danger from Japan lay in the Far East. . . .[69]

Placing Hart's headquarters before Kimmel's had nothing to do with either relative rank or degree of danger. It represented merely the War and Navy departments' usual although not invariable custom of listing multiple addressees alphabetically or numerically, as the case might be. Wherever an organization appeared among a message's addressees, "action" meant just that. Stark explained, "We would not have sent this to Admiral Kimmel for action unless we had been thinking of him and the possibility of an attack in his direction, and for that reason he was put down 'for action.' "[70]

Regardless of after-the-fact rationalizations, Kimmel knew very well that the Navy Department intended him to act, and act he did. However, in making his assessment that, although the Pacific Fleet had been warned of imminent war, its training must continue uninterrupted and its patrol planes must be saved for future combat, he established the wrong priorities. Of course, the Pacific Fleet should have been properly trained and ready to take the offensive when the time came. But that time had not yet come, as WPL-46 made clear.

In the expressive French phrase, Kimmel suffered from the defects of his virtues. The very qualities—physical courage, aggressiveness, and offensive-mindedness—which should have made him a great fighting admiral worked against him in a situation calling for a dynamic defensive posture.

CHAPTER 27

"The Last Critical Stages"

Believed emergency had lessened—Did not check on
AWS or AA—Confusion over type of alerts—Midway
and Wake Island operations—Conditions of readiness—Japanese carriers unaccounted for—Significance of Japanese orders to destroy codes and coding
machines—Admiral Newton not briefed—Decision to
keep fleet in harbor—Probabilities vs. capabilities—
Hawaii not prepared

When a strong-minded, self-confident, and some-
what inflexible individual makes an estimate of the situation and acts
thereon, subsequent events are more likely to reinforce than to modify
it. Appearing before the congressional committee, Kimmel said, "all
indications of the movements of Japanese military and naval forces
which came to my attention confirmed the information in the dispatch
of 27 November—that the Japanese were on the move against Thailand or the Kra Peninsula in Southeast Asia." These indications included information copies of Navy Department messages to Hart,
reports from Hart, "from the China coast, and other sources," the
CNO's Summary of Current National Situations, and radio traffic
analyses.[1]

Furthermore, "The public press and radio news broadcasts contained accounts that negotiations were continuing after November
27. . . . In the absence of more authoritative information, I took account of this public information as to diplomatic developments. This
suggested a lessening of the emergency which prompted the so-called
'war warning' dispatch." Kimmel complained angrily, "I was not informed that the Japanese were continuing the negotiations after November 26 only as a device to cover up their plans. The Navy
Department knew this to be the fact."[2] He did not mention that as
Washington had neither rescinded nor amended the instructions of
November 27, he was duty-bound to consider them still in effect.

It was little short of absurd that a man in his position based his actions upon the media rather than upon official directions. Moreover, he was highly selective in his choice of press coverage. The Honolulu newspapers the week before the attack were far from reassuring.[3] The Honolulu *Advertiser* featured such headlines as JAPANESE MAY STRIKE OVER WEEKEND;[4] HUGE PINCER ATTACK ON U.S. BY JAPAN, FRANCE PREDICTED;[5*] PACIFIC ZERO HOUR NEAR.[6] This newspaper struck the only remotely optimistic note on December 2: JAPAN CALLED STILL HOPEFUL OF MAKING PEACE WITH U.S. But this same issue printed an excerpt from the Japanese newspaper *Asahi* which considerably darkened any bright prospects: "We are deeply impressed that the negotiations are heading toward a finale without any hope of success."[7] The Honolulu *Star-Bulletin* featured headlines equally disquieting.

Kimmel conferred with Short on November 28 about their respective warnings of the previous day. "We considered, as we did frequently before and did later, the probabilities and possibilities of an air attack on Pearl Harbor." He knew the Army had gone on alert, but he did not recall whether Short specifically mentioned the details.[8]

Short had used the instructions against alarming the civil population as one reason why he did not institute a No. 2 or No. 3 alert, yet his antisabotage preparations were so highly visible that Smith, driving home on the evening of November 27, had "great difficulty in getting to Honolulu because of the caravans of trucks and troops."[9] In the mistaken belief that Short had only one type of alert, Smith informed Kimmel that the Army had gone on full alert.[10] Kimmel never saw Short's reply to Marshall on the subject, "and was never informed of it."[11]

He kne that the aircraft warning system was being manned but, again, he "did not inquire into the details."[12] Considering the fact that he had decided against distant air patrol, it was surprising that he did not check with the Hawaiian Department concerning the mechanical means of reconnaissance available—radar. Nor did he visit the Information Center. He had never had anything to do with such an installation. "That was purely and entirely an Army function," he told the congressional committee. "I presumed that the steps necessary to make the information center or the radar informa-

---

*i.e., by Japanese and Vichy French forces in Southeast Asia.

tion . . . effective had been taken."[13] Yet one might have expected that, in view of the Hawaiian Department's principal mission to protect his ships in harbor, Kimmel would have felt enough interest in the means of doing so to ask for a briefing, or at least to look over the center.

That thought occurred to Senator Lucas, who asked him, "wasn't it almost your duty to find out definitely whether or not the radar was working in line with the warning that was given in that war message?" Kimmel answered, "I thought I knew. You must trust somebody. I couldn't do everything." A little later he testified that he did not talk with Short about radar "not only because it was an Army matter but because I had confidence in General Short."[14]

Retrospectively, Kimmel laid much stress on the aerial reconnaissance being conducted from the task forces en route to Wake and Midway respectively. In his opening statement to the congressional committee, he declared, "It was a more intensive search in the areas covered than could have been made by patrol planes based on Oahu." And, as the task forces "approached the outlying islands, these searches were conducted at a much greater distance from Oahu than any patrol plane based on Oahu could travel."[15]

All well and good, but this reconnaissance was part and parcel of the movement of the task forces and had nothing whatsoever to do with the "war warning." Moreover, a glance at a map of the Pacific will show that the searches centered upon the task forces could have availed nothing in the Hawaiian area, for they did not cover the north—the very direction whence many defenders of Oahu had agreed theoretically that a Japanese attack force would come.

By December 6 the only search in the Hawaiian area was limited to a segment with a 150-mile radius from *Enterprise*, headed home from Wake almost directly west of Oahu. And in the hours before the attack on December 7, aerial reconnaissance from Oahu consisted of a very short flight due south of Pearl Harbor—180° off the sensitive area.[16] No doubt this was the patrol which Kimmel told Seth Richardson "was covering only local areas for training purposes" and also covering "the operating area to search out the submarines."[17]

Oddly enough, Kimmel made a strong pitch to the congressional committee that "a misconception" existed about the north being the most likely direction for an attack. He admitted that he had "testified before the Roberts Commission as to the north being a dangerous sector," giving his reason. But he had "scarcely touched upon the disadvantages of the northern route"—the distance from the Japanese homeland, rough winter seas, and necessity for refueling. Therefore, he insisted that "no arc, no sector, could be ruled out."[18] This may well represent Kimmel's personal opinion, but the evaluation of the north as being indeed the most dangerous sector was too well documented for serious questioning.

In his self-defense, Kimmel laid great stress upon the Wake and Midway projects. The messages setting up those operations reached Kimmel early on November 27. These involved not only sending the carriers, "the fleet's main striking defense against an air attack," out of Hawaiian waters, but, if carried out as authorized, would have meant the loss of about half the Hawaiian Air Force's pursuit planes. "In these circumstances," Kimmel argued, "no reasonable man in my position would consider that the 'war warning' was intended to suggest the likelihood of an attack in the Hawaiian area."[19]

A number of things were wrong with this reasoning. The Wake-Midway messages did not descend upon Kimmel as a total surprise. The reinforcement of these outlying islands had been under consideration for about a month.[20] Stark's message contained no mandatory date for carrying out the order, and it did contain the qualifying phrase "provided you consider this feasible and desirable."[21] The task forces were under Kimmel's control. He, not the Navy Department, decided upon the dates of sortie,[22] and he could have withheld them entirely if he had not considered the mission sound.[23] Furthermore, the Washington message was dated November 26. Kimmel received it and he and his staff, along with Short and some of his advisers, had thoroughly discussed it and had reached their decisions before receipt of the warning messages of November 27. So the latter should have influenced consideration of the earlier dispatch, not the reverse. It never crossed Stark's mind that his message "might or might not influence" Kimmel's "estimate of the imminence of the outbreak of war."[24]

Moreover, the assessment that the Wake-Midway project would not endanger the defense of Oahu came not by implication from the Navy Department but directly from Kimmel's own war plans officer, "Soc" McMorris. Mollison pointed out that sending Army fighter planes away from Oahu would lessen the Hawaiian Department's ability to carry out its mission of defending Oahu. Kimmel asked McMorris, "What do you think about the possibility of a Japanese air attack?" And McMorris replied, "None, absolutely none."[25]

Some years later, Justice Roberts informed Charles Rugg, one of Kimmel's attorneys, that this incident had weighed heavily against Kimmel during the commission's deliberations. They believed that Kimmel should have considered and discussed the possibility more thoroughly.[26]

Secure in his agreement with McMorris's assessment, Kimmel took no special measures for protection of either the ships in harbor or the naval aircraft on Oahu. In fact, testimony revealed a certain amount of confusion as to just what condition of alert was in effect aboard the ships on December 7. Kimmel told the Navy Court, "The condition of readiness No. 3, as laid down in 2CL-41,* had been prescribed for some time before by Vice Admiral Pye, and that was in effect on the day of the attack. In addition to that, the Commander of Battleships, Battle Force, had issued an order requiring two, 5-inch guns and two, 50-calibre guns on each battleship to be manned at all times."[27]

According to 2CL-41, Condition 3 called for "Anti-aircraft battery (guns which bear in assigned sector) of at least one ship in each sector manned and ready. (Minimum of four guns required for each sector). Condition of aircraft as prescribed by Naval Base Defense Officer."[28]

Admiral Pye, however, informed the Navy Court, "There was no condition of readiness set. . . . What was in effect was the result of an order previously issued by the Commander-in-Chief Pacific Fleet, directing that anti-aircraft guns on all ships be available for immediate action." He agreed with Kimmel's figures of guns manned. Pye considered that "the condition of readiness of the anti-aircraft batteries actually was in excess of that required by . . . Base Defense Condition 3, of the order referred to."[29]

This state of affairs was sometimes termed in the investigations "an augmented Navy No. 3," which seems an accurate description. This arrangement proved totally inadequate. As the congressional committee report observed in a footnote, "Inasmuch as by far the greatest damage was effected by the torpedo planes in the first wave, a higher degree of readiness would have reduced beyond question the effectiveness of this initial thrust."[30]

Vice Admiral George C. Dyer believed that Kimmel should have maintained a modified Condition 2 readiness at all times—all AA

---

*Pacific Fleet Confidential Letter No. 2CL-41 (revised), October 14, 1941, Subject: Security of Fleet at Base and in Operating Areas (PHA, Part 15, pp. 1452-1457).

batteries manned around the clock, all ammunition supply fully available, all range-finders and fire control fully operational.[31] Dyer's description ran far ahead of Condition 2 as specified in 2CL-41: "One-half of anti-aircraft battery of all ships in each sector manned and ready. . . ."[32]

Bloch pointed out that "Conditions" were never designated "in normal peace-time" except during maneuvers. "Condition 1 is where action is imminent; Condition 2 is where you know that enemy forces are in the waters and it may happen quickly, and you have half your batteries; Condition 3, you have one quarter your batteries but you are in hostile waters."[33]

But Kimmel did not recognize that for the Pacific Fleet "normal peacetime" had ceased upon receipt of the "war warning." Beginning with November 27, he should have moved into Condition 2. That he did not do so is another minus on his record.

Measures as heroic as those which Dyer listed would have been excessive, especially if in force, as he suggested, at all times. Vessels returned to port to be refueled, refurbished, and restocked, and for their crews to secure necessary rest and recreation. This would be impossible in a constant state of combat readiness. Nor should this have been expected of them, because ships in their home port rely upon the harbor defenses for protection.

Kimmel knew that the "anti-aircraft batteries of all our ships, and particularly the battleships, were woefully inadequate." It followed that he was heavily dependent upon the Army's antiaircraft batteries, yet he never made an inspection of them nor, so far as he knew, had any of his staff.[34] He considered readiness of antiaircraft batteries the Army's responsibility—which of course it was—"and when the Army said they were on an alert I thought they knew their business and I had every reason to think so because General Short is a very capable officer."[35] He had turned the defense of the naval base over to Bloch, in whom he had "the highest confidence," and working with the Army in respect to such defenses was part of Bloch's job.[36]

Apparently, as with the radar system, it did not occur to Kimmel to take a personal look at the defenses so vital to his ships. He explained to the congressional committee that in the event of war he had fully expected to be aboard his flagship "far from Pearl Harbor." So he left the Navy's share of "joint supervisory defense" to Bloch, because "if I had constantly intruded into the day-to-day coordination

of Admiral Bloch and General Short on this matter I might very well
have undone all my security order, 2CL-41, was designed to accomplish, the working out of a permanent Army-Navy local defense coordination which would have to continue in my absence and that of
the fleet."[37]

As for the Navy's patrol planes, they remained on Condition B-5,
under which 50 percent of the planes and their personnel were on
four hours' notice. This was "the normal readiness prescribed for
normal conditions."[38]

Events by no means normal continued to occur in the ten days
between the "war warning" and the attack. Remarked the congressional committee, "Perhaps the most vital intelligence available to
the commander in chief of the Pacific Fleet indicating Pearl Harbor
as a possible point of attack was that gathered from his own Radio
Intelligence Unit at Hawaii."[39] Among the most significant items was
a report based upon this source which Layton presented to Kimmel
on December 2 in his daily intelligence briefing.[40] This study omitted
Japan's Carrier Divisions One (*Akagi* and *Kaga*) and Two (*Soryu* and
Hiryu) "because neither one of those commands had appeared in
traffic for fully 15 or possibly 25 days." In fact, there was no trace of
any Japanese flattop except Carrier Division Three, and occasionally
Four.[41]* Kimmel did not take this development lightly, yet he and
his advisers did not comprehend the implications involved when Japan's major carriers dropped out of radio traffic. To be sure, Rochefort's Combat Intelligence Unit on Oahu had lost track of Yamamoto's
flattops before. Kimmel insisted, "we had no reason to suspect that
there was a lost fleet containing the six carriers." He "wanted to know
where the Japanese carriers were" but was not "extremely disturbed."
Had he been so, he might have deduced that they were heading
toward Hawaii. But he "was not disturbed to that extent, and neither
was Captain McMorris."[42]

This makes one wonder just what would have seriously "disturbed"
Kimmel and his war plans officer. With war appearing imminent, it
behooved someone in the U.S. Navy to ask why Japan's six major
carriers had suddenly vanished. They were not moving south;

---

*Carrier Division Three (*Hosho* and *Zuiho*) was with Yamamoto's Main Body in the Inland
Sea; Carrier Division Four (*Ryujo*) was with the Southern Philippine Support Force en route
to Palau.

Rochefort had a very good line on that operation. Of course, as Captain Wilkinson later mentioned, they might have been in the Marshalls or Carolines.[43] That in itself would have been a troubling indication of a change of Japan's sea-power focus.

Another development which occurred at the same time served to confuse the issue. On December 1, the Japanese Navy changed its call signs for the second time within a month, an unheard-of action. As a result, traffic analysis had to begin again virtually from scratch after barely having time to catch up to the changes made on November 1. Among the lost call signs were those of the carriers. Therefore Kimmel insisted that the disappearance of the flattops from radio traffic did not necessarily mean that they were preserving radio silence—their transmissions might well be "included within the great volume of unidentified traffic."[44] This rationale is difficult to accept in view of the fact that on December 1 the carriers had already been unlocated for some twenty days.

Kimmel further argued that even if the flattops "were not originating radio traffic, it would not follow that the carriers were engaged on a secret mission." When they were near shore stations, traffic was handled through the stations. "Consequently, even radio silence may merely mean that the ships are at anchor in some port in home waters."[45] Whether or not through this reasoning, both Hawaii and Washington assumed that Japan's main carrier strength remained in home waters.[46]

Morgan bore down heavily on Kimmel in this respect:

> This presumption was fatal and one that Admiral Kimmel, who had received a "war warning," was not privileged to make. . . . His action manifested a lack of imagination and a failure of judgment not to be expected in one of his rank. . . . Admiral Kimmel missed his golden opportunity to correct his mistake in failing to institute distance reconnaissance after the "war warning" when he failed to order such reconnaissance upon becoming completely oblivious of the whereabouts of substantial carrier units of the Japanese Fleet at a time when their "service calls" were inexplicably changed.[47]

Although not so strongly worded, the official congressional committee report was no less censorious:

> It was fully known . . . that the missing carriers of Japan were not engaged in a movement to the south since such an operation would

be open to visual observation by our forces in the Philippines as well as by friendly powers. In consequence, only two reasonable alternatives remained—either the carriers were in home waters or they were engaged in an operation under radio silence in some direction other than to the south. It was Admiral Kimmel's duty to be prepared for the alternative most dangerous to him. . . .[48]

Possibly a tendency on Kimmel's part to regard carriers as naval auxiliaries rather than as weapons of the offensive in their own right played a part in this miscalculation. Carriers are not basically weapons of defense. While the U.S. Navy might well expect Yamamoto to keep part of his Main Body in home waters to counter any possible attack on the Japanese main islands, he scarcely needed half a dozen flattops for the job. These should have been where the offensive action was going to be. If not in the south, then where? And that target would have to be exceedingly worthwhile to justify such an awesome commitment of naval air power.

In this particular instance, the primary burden of blame unquestionably rests upon Kimmel's command. Knowing nothing about Combat Intelligence, Flynn believed that the commands on Oahu had no means of collecting information about "the possible movements of Japanese naval and aircraft and army units. . . . They depended entirely on bulletins from Washington where all the intelligence material was gathered and communicated to Hawaii . . . and other places."[49]

Flynn was miles off course. Even Safford, so firmly in Kimmel's corner, testified to Hart that Washington expected Rochefort's unit to "prevent the Fleet from being surprised as the Russians had been at Port Arthur."[50] Ingersoll explained to the congressional committee, "The information regarding the location of Japanese ships was the primary responsibility of the commander of the Pacific Fleet. He was the man who was in charge of the methods of determining the location of the Japanese Fleet through radio intelligence, as it was called."[51]

In other words, it was not up to Washington to tell Kimmel where to find Yamamoto's ships; he was supposed to tell Washington. The Japanese blackout of the task force, their dummy message traffic, and American complacency effectively canceled out the possibility of locating Japan's First Air Fleet by this means. But such factors do not excuse Oahu's defenders for not closing all mouseholes when the Japanese flattops disappeared.

Kimmel made an equally important and regrettable error in his handling of Washington's notification to him on December 3 that the Japanese had ordered certain consulates and embassies, including the one in Washington, to destroy "most of their codes and ciphers at once and to burn all other important confidential and secret documents."[52] He saw nothing in this message to give him pause. To the Roberts inquiry, held close to the event and before Kimmel had set his position in concrete, he conceded, "I didn't draw the proper answer, I admit that. I admit that I was wrong."[53] But to the Navy Court he insisted that the destruction by the Japanese of "most of their codes and ciphers . . . was entirely consistent with routine diplomatic precautions by Japan against the contingency that the United States and Britain might declare war against her and take over diplomatic residences if she took aggressive action against the Kra Isthmus."[54] He spoke in much the same terms to the congressional committee, stressing that both he and his staff had noted that the diplomatic posts in question had received orders to destroy most, not all, of their codes and ciphers.[55]

Kimmel did not pass this information along to Short. "I didn't consider that of any vital interest when I received it," he testified, "and furthermore," he added pugnaciously, "if the War Department, or the Navy Department, had considered it of such vital importance as they now say they do, they should at least have taken the precaution to tell me to give this message to General Short."[56] All of which casts a shadow upon Kimmel's initiative as well as his judgment.

In contrast, several Navy Department officers testified that, to them, the burning of codes spelled imminent war. For example, Ingersoll had no doubt at all. He explained to the congressional committee:

> If you rupture diplomatic negotiations you do not necessarily have to burn your codes. The diplomats can go home and they can pack up their codes with their dolls and take them home. Also, when you rupture diplomatic negotiations you do not rupture consular relations. The consuls stay on.
>
> Now, in this particular set of dispatches they not only told their diplomats in Washington and London to burn their codes but they told their consuls in Manila, Hong Kong, Singapore, and Batavia to burn their codes and that did not mean a rupture of diplomatic negotiations, it meant war. . . .[57]

In Hawaii, McMorris believed that the message of December 3
"was the best indication which had come to our attention that we
would be involved in the war with Japan, from the very beginning."[58]
But Kimmel did not arrive at the same interpretation. Senator Lucas
could make no sense of this. In December 1945 a Milwaukee *Journal*
reporter wrote that the senator considered

> the code burning message one of the most important sent by Wash-
> ington to field commanders in the critical days before the Japanese
> attack.
>   "I can't understand why the message that the Japanese had been
> ordered to destroy their codes didn't put every military leader on a
> full alert," Lucas said. "Even a layman knows that when codes are
> ordered destroyed, war is likely to come, and come fast."[59]

Any illusion that Japan was engaged in a purely routine procedure—"codes are burned from time to time," as Kimmel said to
Justice Roberts[60]—should have perished upon receipt that same day
of an information copy of a message from the Navy Department to
Hart advising that Japan's diplomats in London, Hong Kong, Manila,
and Washington had been ordered to destroy their Purple machines.
Batavia had already sent its machine back to Tokyo.[61] The word *Purple*
used in this context being new to Kimmel, he sent Layton to seek
out the meaning. Layton determined that this referred to a diplomatic
"electrical coding machine" and so informed Kimmel.[62] Yet the admiral, who so quickly had seized upon a single unfamiliar word,
missed the true significance: Codes might indeed be burned "from
time to time," but destruction of coding machines was a most serious
step, only undertaken in extraordinary circumstances.

Fate had given Kimmel that rarest of gifts—a second chance. But
he failed to recognize this as an opportunity to reassess the situation,
and continued on the course already set. Senators Brewster and Ferguson criticized Kimmel severely in this regard. They cited the message of December 3, as well as those of December 4 which informed
Kimmel that Guam had been ordered to destroy classified material,
and the dispatch of December 6 when the CNO authorized Kimmel
to order destruction of classified documents in the outlying islands.[63]
The two senators stated that while none of these messages

> placed Hawaii in the prime center of danger, they certainly reflected
> the last critical stages in diplomatic relations. It is well known in

diplomatic and military circles that destruction of codes, code machines, and secret documents is usually the last step before breaking off relations between governments. War does not necessarily have to follow, but it may follow either simultaneously or close on the heels of the destruction of codes. Other messages and events, supplemented by daily reports of the crisis in Honolulu newspapers, should have raised the significance of the information in the hands of Admiral Kimmel. Yet he testified that he "didn't consider that of any vital importance." . . .

General Short did not receive copies of these messages sent from Washington Naval Operations to Admiral Kimmel regarding the destruction of codes. Admiral Kimmel had the express responsibility, as part of his duty to effect liaison with General Short, to communicate this vital information to General Short. He failed to do so.

Admiral Kimmel should have been aware of the meaning of code destruction and of the Japanese reputation for surprise action. He should have been vigilant. He owed this to his position as commander of the fleet which was closely related to the scene of expected hostilities.

Admiral Kimmel failed in the performance of this obligation.[64]

These would have been harsh words from any quarter, and were particularly so coming from the two Republican senators who had hoped to place the entire blame for Pearl Harbor upon Roosevelt and his administration.

In view of Kimmel's often and fiercely expressed resentment at Washington for not keeping him fully informed and for failing to give him specific instructions, it is difficult to rationalize one of his actions during the crises of late November and early December. He permitted Rear Admiral John H. Newton's *Lexington* task force to sortie bound for Midway without showing Newton the "war warning" and without ensuring that he had been briefed. Kimmel testified that Vice Admiral Wilson Brown, commander, Scouting Force, issued Newton's orders. Kimmel had a copy of the orders he gave Brown, and it contained no mention of a "war warning." He did not know exactly what instructions Newton received from Brown.[65]

Congressman Cooper took a dim view of this. "But here was an admiral going off on a mission under your orders, in command of a task force, with some of the most valuable vessels of the United States Navy in that force, and you didn't tell him, or you don't know that anybody else ever told him?" Kimmel replied, "I have every reason to believe, and I believe, that Admiral Brown gave him the information which he needed to put him in proper shape."[66] So Kimmel—exactly like his superiors whom he criticized so harshly—assumed without direct knowledge that his subordinate had all the data he needed to carry out his mission. "Regardless of where the slip may lie," commented Morgan disapprovingly, "a commander left Pearl Harbor with a task force completely oblivious of the gravely critical relations with Japan and only 2 days before Japan struck."[67]

Newton kept up antisubmarine measures on his cruise, but he made no particular preparations for war. However, like the gallant sailor he was, Newton refused to blame anyone for his lack of specific knowledge. He was aware of the increasing tension in U.S.-Japanese relations and thought he had all the information he needed.[68]

On December 6, Kimmel and his staff considered sending the rest of the capital ships to sea, but decided against it for two reasons: the Fleet lacked air cover in the absence of its carriers, and the War Department had instructed Short against alarming the civilian population.[69] Of course, disposition of the battleships had come under discussion with receipt of the "war warning." Kimmel and Pye had talked this over, and agreed that "to send them to sea without air cover for any prolonged period would have been a dangerous course."[70]

As a controversial subject, this decision ranked second only to that against long-range air reconnaissance. Flynn declared that Roosevelt and his advisers "were directly responsible for the arrangements in Pearl Harbor which made it literally impossible for Kimmel or Short to properly defend their positions." He charged, "The fleet was moored in the harbor at the orders of Roosevelt. And Kimmel was by his instructions prohibited from moving it." Flynn's momentum carried him even further: ". . . had Admiral Kimmel taken his naval force outside of Pearl Harbor, he would probably have been court-martialed for violating the orders of the government."[71] Flynn was still harping on this theme when Kimmel testified before the congressional committee. The admiral denied that he had been under any orders obligating him to have the Fleet in harbor on December 7, 1941.[72]

Instead, he had received a specific order to execute "an appropriate defensive deployment." No fleet can deploy, defensively or otherwise, while moored in harbor. In fact, Turner defined a naval deployment as "to spread out and make ready for hostilities."[73] At least some key officers in Washington were certain that Kimmel had dispatched his ships out of harbor. When Bratton inquired a few days before the attack whether the Fleet had been properly alerted, McCollum assured him that it had gone to sea.[74]

Many of the naval officers interviewed for this study, including Admiral Nimitz, considered it most fortunate that Kimmel's ships were not in a position to encounter the First Air Fleet. Lacking air power, they would have been virtually helpless, and any American ships sunk in the Pacific would have been lost beyond the possibility of salvage.[75]

Admiral Tolley cited Hiles to the effect that, with both carriers absent, Kimmel "would never have risked a pitched battle, *if* he could have avoided one . . ." (Tolley's italics). Tolley added that Hiles, whom he termed "probably the most knowledgeable individual on the Pearl Harbor attack alive today," suggested

> that the Nimitz appraisal* is subject to some imponderable factors, not the least of which is the unlikelihood that the Japanese attacking force under Nagumo, on finding the U.S. Fleet gone from Pearl Harbor, would have lingered long enough for U.S. forces to have located it and given battle. It is a certainty that the Japanese would not have gone after the U.S. Fleet: their attack was purely a hit-and-run proposition. Such were their orders.[76]

Hiles did not know enough about the Japanese background to make an accurate appraisal. Actually, the Japanese had worked out alternative attack plans which included a thorough search for Kimmel's ships had they not been in Pearl Harbor or in Lahaina Anchorage on strike day. Operation Hawaii was no "hit-and-run proposition"; the Japanese were after the Pacific Fleet regardless of its location, and indeed would have been delighted to find it in deep waters rather than in Pearl Harbor.[77]

What is more, if Kimmel had taken the "war warning" at face value, he need not have been without air cover. Congressman Clarke asked him what he would have done had he been "reasonably sure at any time between the 27th of November and the 7th of December, that a surprise air attack was going to be made there." Kimmel responded with an illuminating exposition of the options open to him

---

*Tolley referred to a letter on the subject from Nimitz to Admiral David L. McDonald, reproduced in *U.S. Naval Institute Proceedings* (December 1966), p. 126.

had he believed an emergency to be imminent. These included putting to sea with the Fleet, aerial reconnaissance, and retention of his carriers in Hawaiian waters.[78] He estimated that as late as the night of December 6 he "could have arranged a rendezvous with Halsey and gotten out pretty much in the same vicinity with him." He could have sent out the patrol planes and recalled *Lexington.* Newton "would have been in supporting distance of the fleet by daylight the next morning."[78] It is unfortunate that these vigorous measures occurred to Kimmel only in retrospect as to what he would have done if "reasonably sure" he would soon be under attack. Seldom is a commander on the defensive in the enviable position of being fairly certain of the enemy's plans.

One day during the congressional inquiry Kimmel and Morgan lunched together, and Morgan asked the question which had bothered him throughout the admiral's testimony. "Why, after you received this 'war warning' message of November 27, did you leave the Fleet in Pearl Harbor?"

As always, Kimmel gave an honest reply to an honest question. "All right, Morgan—I'll give you your answer. I never thought those little yellow sons-of-bitches could pull off such an attack, so far from Japan."[80]

That was the crux of the matter. One cannot emphasize too strongly that all of the American failures and shortcomings contributing to the Japanese victory at Pearl Harbor stemmed from the root disbelief that the Japanese would undertake such a risky venture. In the words of the Navy Court, Kimmel and his advisers "recognized the capability of Japan to deliver a long-range surprise bombing attack and that she might attack without a declaration of war. They reasoned that she would not commit the strategic blunder of delivering a surprise attack on United States territory, the one course that irrevocably would unite the American people in war against Japan."[81]

The Army Board agreed: "The thinking in the War Department and the Hawaiian Department was faulty in that it emphasized probabilities to the exclusion of capabilities." This fundamental mistake is difficult to understand because it flew in the face of traditional military teachings: "It is a familiar premise of military procedure in estimating a situation to *select the most dangerous and disastrous type of attack the enemy may make and devote your primary efforts to meeting this most serious of the attacks,*" explained the Army Board. "In the present instance, it was clearly recognized . . . *that the most serious attack to be met by the Army and Navy was an air attack by Japan"* (italics in original).[82]

It is obvious from this review of the reactions and actions on Oahu, especially in the period November 27 through early December 7, that none of the warnings, signs, and portents caused either Kimmel or Short to ask what was the worst that this could mean for his command and to act accordingly.

Both men complained that everything would have been much different had Washington supplied them with all the information at hand, particularly the "bomb plot" series. Unquestionably, failure to ensure that the Pacific Fleet and the Hawaiian Department received these intercepts was a prime error. However, Kimmel's and Short's defense rests upon the premise that they would have read into these messages all the implications that escaped the authorities in Washington. That may well be, but the point must remain speculative, and such speculations can only mitigate, they cannot remove from either Kimmel or Short the responsibilities of command. Declared the congressional committee:

> The commanders in Hawaii were clearly and unmistakably warned of war with Japan. They were given orders and possessed information that the entire Pacific area was fraught with danger. They failed to carry out these orders and to discharge their basic and ultimate responsibilities. They failed to defend the fortress they commanded—their citadel was taken by surprise. Aside from any responsibilities that may appear to rest in Washington, the ultimate and direct responsibility for failure to engage the Japanese on the morning of December 7 with every weapon at their disposal rests essentially and properly with the Army and Navy commands in Hawaii whose duty it was to meet the enemy against which they had been warned.[83]

Certainly neither Kimmel nor Short could blame Washington for the mishandling of certain events which took place very early in the morning of December 7. First came sightings of a Japanese midget submarine in the operating area, initially at 0340, again at 0630. The prompt action of Lieutenant William W. Outerbridge and his destroyer *Ward* disposed of this intruder at 0645, but no one notified the Army. Later Bloch told Short "in the presence of Secretary Knox that at the time he visualized it only as a submarine attack and was

busy with that phase of it and just failed to notify" the general; "that
he could see then, after the fact, that he had been absolutely wrong."[84]

Why the Navy authorities did not realize that the minisub heralded a larger force remains a mystery. Such a tiny craft could not
have come all the way from Japan except by mother ship. Nor was
it likely that the Japanese skipper would have set forth on such a
venture without his country's official blessing.

The presence over Lahaina and Pearl Harbor of Japanese scout
planes, catapulted at 0530 on December 7 from the cruisers *Tone*
and *Chikuma* respectively, gave Hawaii's defenders another opportunity. About the time these scouts were making their checks—roughly
0715 to 0735—the Opana Mobile Station log shows a number of radar
contacts.[85] Presumably these and similar sightings were telephoned
to the Information Center at Fort Shafter because Lieutenant Kermit
Tyler, the pursuit officer on duty, recalled several early plots on the
board.[86] Having no way of distinguishing friend from foe, neither
Opana nor Fort Shafter could tell what these blips represented.

Privates Lockard and Elliott at that same Opana Station first picked
up the radar track of the initial attack wave at 0702 at a distance of
132 miles. Elliott telephoned the sighting to the Information Center,
but Tyler, who was expecting a flight of B-17s from the mainland,
told Elliott, "Well, don't worry about it."[87]

The failures on Oahu early in the morning of December 7 occurred
because its defenders evaluated rather than acted. Those involved in
these incidents, except for the doughty Outerbridge and the two
young men at Opana, tried to rationalize the unusual instead of acting
upon it. Although preparedness was their business, the unhappy fact
remains that the commanders on Oahu were not alert on December
7, 1941—not when a Japanese task force could approach undiscovered
to within 200 miles of Oahu; not when twenty-five enemy submarines
surrounded the island; not when Japanese patrol planes could hover
unchallenged over Lahaina and Pearl Harbor; not when the antiaircraft batteries were unready; not when most of the ammunition was
locked up in magazines; not when U.S. fighters and bombers were
bunched together at Wheeler and Hickam fields like coveys of quail;
not when a U.S. destroyer could sink a Japanese submarine in the
operating area without the Hawaiian Department being notified of
the event; not when radar operators who tracked Fuchida's first flight
all the way in received the advice, "Well, don't worry about it."

Had Oahu's commanders been the type that sought a commission because the armed forces offered a socially acceptable, not too onerous way for a gentleman to make a living; had they been lazy, incompetent, or self-centered, uncaring of their men or their country, one could waste little sympathy on them. But such was not the case. These men were capable, conscientious, and dedicated public servants, scrupulously carrying out their duties according to their lights. These were protagonists worthy of respect, and their tragedy is in a class with the greater tragedy of which it is a part.

CHAPTER 28

"It Is Inexplicable"

Anticipation of war in Southeast Asia—Warning to Philippines—MacArthur's reply—Relationship with Asiatic Fleet—Skeptical of air attack on Philippines—USAFFE notified of Pearl Harbor by 0340 December 8 local time—Clark Field attacked 1220—Planes caught on ground—Did not authorize air bombing of Japanese positions on Formosa—MacArthur retained in command

As November 1941 drew toward its close, no one could justly claim that the United States government and its armed forces were not fully aware of the Japanese designs on Southeast Asia. As previously indicated, for months the War Department had been preoccupied with that area, having reversed the policy of years in an attempt to make the Philippines defensible. To that end, they formed the U.S. Army Forces Far East (USAFFE), incorporated the Filipino armed forces therein, and recalled Major General Douglas MacArthur to active duty in command.

The War Department scheduled a massive input of B-17s, troops, and ground armament for MacArthur, all with the object of warding off or countering a threat which the Japanese made no attempt to conceal. This concentration upon Southeast Asia contributed in no small measure to both Kimmel's and Short's failure to foresee a possible Japanese attack on the Pacific Fleet in Hawaiian waters or upon Oahu, its home base. If any command under the American flag should have been alert to danger, it was MacArthur's.

Yet, as if to prove that the Pearl Harbor attack was no fluke, and that Kimmel, Short, and their subordinates had no monopoly on mistakes, USAFFE experienced a surprise at the outset of the war which in some respects was less excusable than the debacle at Oahu.

On November 27, the War Department dispatched to MacArthur a message very similar to that sent to the Hawaiian Department:

Negotiations with Japan appear to be terminated to all practical purposes with only barest possibilities that Japanese Government might come back and offer to continue period Japanese future action unpredictable but hostile action possible at any moment period If hostilities cannot comma repeat cannot comma be avoided the United States desires that Japan commit the first overt act period This policy should not comma repeat not comma be construed as restricting you to a course of action that might jeopardize the successful defense of the Philippines period Prior to hostile Japanese action you are directed to take such reconnaissance and other measures as you deem necessary period Report measures taken period Should hostilities occur you will carry out the tasks assigned in revised rainbow five which was delivered to you by General Brereton* period Chief of Naval Operations concurs and request you notify Hart. Marshall.[1]

Francis B. Sayre, high commissioner of the Philippines, recalled a conference in his office with MacArthur and Hart after receipt of this warning message:

Back and forth, back and forth over my office floor paced General MacArthur, smoking a black cigar and assuring Admiral Hart and myself in optimistic terms that due to the existing alignment and movement of Japanese troops he felt convinced that there would be no Japanese attack before the spring. Admiral Hart felt otherwise.[2]

Not the least strange of all the Pearl Harbor paradoxes is this: Four commands—the Philippines, Hawaii, Caribbean, and Western Defense at San Francisco—received the appropriate version of the famous warning message dispatched in Marshall's name. Of these, the two closest to Japan—the Philippines and Hawaii—apparently paid it the least attention, whereas Panama and the Presidio effected immediate and detailed measures of readiness.[3] MacArthur replied the next day:

Pursuant to instructions contained in your radio six two four air reconnaissance has been extended and intensified in conjunction with the Navy stop Ground security measures have been taken stop Within the limitations imposed by present state of development of this theatre of operations everything is in readiness for the conduct of a successful defense stop Intimate liaison and cooperation and cordial relations exist between Army and Navy. MacArthur.[4]

---

*Major General Lewis H. Brereton, air commander in the Philippines.

This message was in true MacArthur style of confidence and flamboyance, even to the reminder that he would be struggling against odds. But his reply was too generalized to give the War Department any clear idea of what was going on.

Certainly his last sentence could have lifted eyebrows among the knowledgeable. On December 6, MacArthur told British Vice Admiral Sir Tom Phillips that he and Hart operated "in the closest coordination. We are the oldest and dearest of friends."[5] Hart might have expressed the situation somewhat differently. He had had very little contact with MacArthur between the latter's recall to active duty and September 22, 1941, when Hart asked to meet with him. The admiral briefed him on "the inside history of the over-all planning since last January." MacArthur "listened very attentively," but his opening words in reply augured ill for mutual cooperation: "The Army is glad to know of the Navy's plans but its own plans are virtually independent thereof and there seems no possibility of conflict between them." The only naval operations which seemed even remotely to interest him were the motor torpedo boats.[6]

Hart gained the impression that MacArthur was preoccupied "with the idea that the land forces . . . are to defeat any enemy that gets landed . . ." and "to build up a land (and air) defense which will hold the most valuable portions of the groups against an enemy who definitely has command of the sea." When Hart asked him the purpose of the newly-arrived B-17s, MacArthur "replied that it was primarily for bombing an enemy expeditionary force at sea; that after Philippine cities were bombed, therein lay his weapon for retaliation." Evidently MacArthur did not see eye to eye with his superiors in Washington, who hoped that the threat of the B-17s would keep Japan out of the war. As for other measures of defense, MacArthur did not even know what radar was—Hart had to explain it to him. MacArthur told Hart where he planned to be in case of hostilities, but the admiral "noted that at no time did he even ask where I intended to be myself."[7]

After the war began, Hart recorded, "as far as MacArthur and I are personally concerned there has been very little get-together." He observed with some irritation:

It was only by using some sharpness and repeatedly interrupting him in turn that I was able to tell him anything of the Navy situation at all. He asked no questions whatever, evinced no curiosity and, as has too often been the case, the interview was quite futile as far as furthering any meeting of minds between us.[8]

Evidently the war warning crash-landed on the reef of MacArthur's preconceptions and his ignorance of the Japanese. During the high-level conference in Manila on December 6, he naïvely told Admiral Phillips, "The inability of an enemy to launch his air attack on these islands is our greatest security. Most fighters are short ranged. . . . Even with the improvised forces I now have, because of the inability of the enemy to bring not only air but mechanized and motorized elements, leaves me with a sense of complete security."[9]

Considering his geographical location and mission, MacArthur should have been alert for anything. Yet in the initial attack his command suffered much the same fate as Kimmel's and Short's.[10]

Very briefly, the facts were these: When the first Japanese wave struck Pearl Harbor at 0755 local time on December 7, 1941, the time in Manila was 0225 on December 8. About thirty-five minutes later, the first known flash from Oahu had reached the Navy at Manila.[11] By 0330 most of Hart's installations in the Philippines had been alerted.[12] MacArthur later wrote that at 0340 that morning "a long-distance telephone call from Washington" told him "of the Japanese attack on Pearl Harbor, but no details were given."[13] Apparently some source provided him with additional information, because at approximately 0530 his headquarters issued an official statement that Japanese submarines and planes had "heavily attacked" Pearl Harbor and that Japan and the United States were at war.[14]

At about that time USAFFE received a message from Marshall confirming the raid on Pearl Harbor and ordering MacArthur, "Carry out tasks assigned in Rainbow Five so far as they pertain to Japan." The dispatch ended, "You have the complete confidence of the War Department and we assure you of every possible assistance and support within our power."[15] This gave MacArthur all the authority he needed for prompt action. One of his missions under Rainbow Five, the current war plan, was "air raids against Japanese forces and installations within tactical operating radius of available bases."[16]

Evidently Marshall's confidence was temporarily misplaced. The major Japanese strike, which was against Clark Field, did not materialize until about 1220, so MacArthur's command had approximately eight hours in which to prepare to meet an attack. Yet in spite of all the preattack warnings and almost a complete working day to prepare for the worst, the air attack on the Philippines succeeded just as had the earlier strike against Oahu.[17]

Nor was this the whole story. When the War Department received no reply to Marshall's message, General Gerow telephoned MacArthur. The latter said that he had received word of the Pearl Harbor attack, but the Japanese had not hit the Philippines. He further remarked that between 2330 and 2400 the previous night radar had picked up "a Japanese bombing squadron," but it had "turned back thirty miles from the coast." Moreover, "In the last half hour our radio detector service picked up planes about thirty miles off the coast. We have taken off to meet them."

Gerow asked for an immediate report of "any Japanese operation or any indications." The two men then spoke a bit about the Pearl Harbor situation. Gerow conveyed Marshall's regards, and MacArthur answered, "Tell General Marshall 'our tails are up in the air.' "[18] Tails may have been up but planes were down. The Japanese caught the Philippine command napping, and mauled aircraft on the ground just as on Oahu.

This circumstance infuriated Marshall. In February 1942, speaking in an "iron tone of voice," he said to his goddaughter,

> As for the Philippines . . . I will tell you that four hours passed from the time news of the Pearl Harbor attack reached our Philippine headquarters until the Japanese struck the Manila airfield. Four hours, and our aircraft were still on the ground in the open—perfect targets. I had sweated blood to get planes to the Philippines. It is inexplicable.[19]

General Arnold was no less incensed. "How in the hell could an experienced airman like you get caught with your planes on the ground?" he asked Brereton in an excited voice by long-distance phone on December 11. "That's what we sent you there for, to avoid just what happened."[20]

Some of MacArthur's more ardent admirers would have one believe that a surprise was not a surprise when it happened to him. Consider this assessment by Barnes:

> One of the main myths circulated by the "blackout" and "blurout" historians is that MacArthur was actually surprised by the Japanese, even six hours after he had learned of the attack on Pearl Harbor,

and that his airplanes had remained huddled helplessly on the ground and were destroyed by the Japanese bombers as Short's had been that morning at Hawaii. They had actually been in the air on reconnaissance during the morning of the 7th,* and had just returned to refuel when the Japanese attack came, quite unexpectedly at the moment. It had been doubted that the Japanese bombers could fly from Formosa to Manila and return, and weather conditions were also such that it seemed unlikely that they would even make the attempt on the 7th.[21]

Barnes's suggestion that the Philippine command was not really caught flatfooted, that the Japanese just happened to drop by "quite unexpectedly at the moment," is startling logic. True, the situation at Clark was not analogous to that at Wheeler and Hickam. Brereton's interceptors and bombers had been on patrol, the bombers minus their bombs. But by 1130 they had returned and were being loaded. The fighters were being refueled; some pilots were in briefings, the rest at lunch.[22]

These landings, briefings, loadings, and refuelings, however necessary, should have been staggered so that the mission could continue through the noon hour. At the very least, some fighters should have remained aloft to cover the grounded planes or to signal danger. The unprotected status of the planes reflected unfavorably upon Brereton as well as upon MacArthur.

All this is an oversimplified account of a complicated and controversial historical problem which has defied satisfactory solution despite much diligent research by competent analysts. Almost ten years after the event, Arnold admitted that he had never been able "to get the real story of what happened in the Philippines."[23]

Many of the same arguments presented in extenuation of Kimmel and Short could be offered—and have been—on behalf of MacArthur: the shortage of weapons and matériel, scarcity of fields for the dispersal of aircraft, the complacent conviction of American invulnerability, the fact that the Japanese struck before the United States had completed its buildup. One may even concede that under the circumstances the Japanese would have taken the Philippines eventually, regardless of what MacArthur, his officers, and his gallant troops did or might have done on that first day of conflict.[24]

---

*Of course, this was December 8 Philippine time.

Yet, on the basis of the facts available, MacArthur and his officers displayed the same singular talent for bungling at the outset of war as did their colleagues in Hawaii, and with considerably less reason. Ever since MacArthur assumed command of USAFFE, the Philippines had been the center of American attention in the Pacific. Moreover, all concerned fully expected the Japanese to attack in Southeast Asia, just as they did. The war warning MacArthur received held no qualifying phrases that might have turned his eyes elsewhere, as Short claimed his contained. Considering the geography of Southeast Asia, the Japanese were virtually certain to try to take out the Philippines to clear their path toward southern Indochina, Thailand, Malaysia, and the Netherlands East Indies.

Thus it was most difficult to rationalize MacArthur's refusal to allow Brereton to dispatch his B-17s to bomb the Japanese on Formosa early in the morning of December 8, when time still permitted, and before the enemy attacked U.S. forces in the Philippines. Brereton wrote that at approximately 0500 that morning he reported to MacArthur's headquarters to secure his permission "to carry out offensive action immediately after daylight." But MacArthur was in conference with members of his staff and others, so Brereton could not get beyond MacArthur's chief of staff, Brigadier General Richard K. Sutherland. The latter told Brereton to ready the bombers but not to launch the strike until MacArthur approved it. However, MacArthur never gave Brereton the green light to attack Formosa.[25]

This point is highly controversial. "I wish to state that General Brereton never recommended an attack on Formosa to me and I knew nothing of such a recommendation having been made," MacArthur declared in late September 1946 after publication of *The Brereton Diaries*.[26] This statement suggests that Sutherland did not convey Brereton's request to MacArthur, which seems unlikely. In his own memoirs, MacArthur scored the same point: "Brereton never at any time recommended or suggested an attack on Formosa to me."[27] In the narrow, literal sense this is true, because Brereton did not speak with MacArthur personally at the time in question.

Much generalization and conflicting testimony—MacArthur and Sutherland versus Brereton and his staff—shadow this complicated historical problem. Yet, with all due respect to MacArthur's outstanding accomplishments, recent scholarship leaves little doubt that Brereton did request and was denied permission to send his B-17s against

Formosa that morning.[28] In any case, Marshall having directed activation of Rainbow Five against Japan, MacArthur should have ordered the mission with or without Brereton's request—unless he considered it unwise. And if he did, why did he not say so?

Sayre was very bitter about the happenings in the Philippines on December 8. Someone had informed him that Brereton "was unable to secure from General MacArthur any authority to attack until about eleven o'clock" that morning. He also learned that many of the fliers who had been on reconnaissance had returned to Clark Field at noon for refueling and "had gone into the mess to get lunch" when the Japanese attacked. It seemed incredible to Sayre that this could have happened seven or eight hours after word about Pearl Harbor had reached the Philippines.

> On this first day of the war, therefore, through the tragic blunder of failure to attack we were ignominiously stripped of the planes on which our defense heavily rested, and consequently at the mercy of the Japanese. Our Far East Air Force had been eliminated as an effective fighting force. So far as our Philippine defenses were concerned it seemed as disastrous as Pearl Harbor.
>
> We supposed that an official investigation would follow. But the war was on then and minds were immersed in the immediate problems of resistance.[29]

Far from softening Sayre toward MacArthur, the dreadful experiences which they shared seemed only "to have accentuated all their differences," and he later spoke to Sumner Welles about MacArthur with "active detestation."[30]

MacArthur wrote that when he was first informed about Pearl Harbor, he thought "the Japanese might well have suffered a serious setback." He added that "their failure to close in on me supported that belief." He maintained that he continued to think so as late as 0930 Manila time, although subsequently he learned otherwise.[31]

Regardless of what MacArthur may have thought happened in Hawaii, the United States was at war with Japan. His job was to defend the Philippines and to take all possible steps to protect his command.

There had been some speculation that the Japanese might bypass the Philippines, and they had considered that possibility. But even that shadow of doubt had faded long before 0930. At about the same moment that the first attack wave hit Pearl Harbor, the Japanese bombed the radio station at Aparri in northern Luzon. And as dawn was breaking over Mindanao far to the south, enemy dive bombers sank two PBYs resting on the waters of Davao Gulf. In that same body of water, the tender *William B. Preston* dodged the bombs, and a little later managed to evade four Japanese destroyers.[32]

The precise moment when the news of these overt acts reached MacArthur, and his reactions thereto, are not clear from any of the records presently available. Communications functioned poorly on that morning, yet from dawn until 0930 or noon is a fair stretch of time. If these events did not suffice to bring MacArthur to a full recognition that the Japanese were about to close in on him, others followed quickly which should have done so.

Thus the Japanese did not catch MacArthur unawares. What is far worse, they caught him awares. He kew they were coming, knew it for about eight hours, and still the enemy's first major bombings and strafings of U.S. planes parked helplessly on the ground left MacArthur's air force badly shattered and Clark Field almost destroyed for all tactical purposes.[33]

The parallel between the Philippine and Hawaiian theaters was so close that even some of the same myths sprang up. In a talk which Major William P. Fisher, who was at Clark Field at the time, gave before some G-4 officers on March 20, 1942, a colonel asked him, "Have you seen any indication of other than Japanese personnel?"

"Yes. Germans," replied Fisher. "I have seen one body that was apparently German—tall, blond, etc. You run into quite a few white men in their crews. It's hard to tell much about the men though after death as they are usually pretty badly smashed up and also we shot down Japanese women pilots."[34]

Whatever skepticism the idea of Japanese women combat pilots may have aroused, the rumor of white men among the Japanese attackers was taken seriously at high level. Marshall telephoned "Pa" Watson at the White House on December 9 concerning a report from MacArthur, and said, "Enemy airplanes have been handled with superior efficiency and there are some indications that his dive bombers are at least partially manned by white pilots."[35]

Despite the disaster at Clark Field and Sayre's expectation of an investigation, evidently it did not occur to anyone to relieve MacArthur. And notwithstanding his losses he never dreamed that he might be removed from command. Instead, he boldly, intuitively seized the psychological offensive, telegraphing the War Department

> that the Japanese were attempting to land in Luzon and his planes had sunk one of six transports, had made direct hits on two others, and had probably damaged the remaining three. He also telegraphed that as, in his opinion, the Japanese must have extended their forces very widely, the present time offered a golden opportunity by co-operation with the Russians to attack them from the North.[36]

Moreover, MacArthur sent a message to Arnold excusing the air forces in the Philippines of any culpability, and praising their gallantry and efficiency, a gesture which Arnold appreciated as an example of MacArthur's loyalty down channels.[37]

Faced with prohibitive odds, nevertheless MacArthur requested Washington to review the accepted strategy in the Far East "lest a fatal mistake be made." He visualized the Philippines as "the locus of victory or defeat," whose fall, with that of the Indies, would ensure loss of Singapore and the Asian mainland. "If the Western Pacific is to be saved, it will have to be saved here and now," he urged Marshall.[38]

No apologies or explanations for MacArthur! He acted upon the French proverb, *Qui s'excuse s'accuse*. Armed with the unshakable conviction that wherever the MacArthur sat must be the head of the table, the general kept the reins of initiative in his own hands, speaking, writing, and acting with such cool self-assurance that prospective critics, like old soldiers, just faded away.

No doubt the message mentioned above was one of MacArthur's "two urgent telegrams calling for help" which awaited Stimson when he reached his office at noon on Sunday December 14. He informed his diary that MacArthur had been "instigated to do so by a conference he had with Admiral Hart who took the usual Navy defeatist position and had virtually told MacArthur that the Philippines were doomed, instead of doing his best to keep MacArthur's lifeline open." Stimson, Marshall, and Roosevelt were just as convinced as MacArthur that they must stand up and fight and "make every effort at whatever risk to keep MacArthur's line open and that otherwise we would paralyze the activities of everybody in the Far East."[39]

All of which goes far toward explaining why, unlike Kimmel and Short, MacArthur kept his command and never had to face an investigation of the Japanese success in the Philippines on December 8 (local time).

Kimmel had his own ideas on the score of MacArthur's retention:

> Washington could not downgrade Short and me and MacArthur too, because then people would ask, "What in hell is wrong with Washington? Why in hell are all the outpost commanders no damn good and everyone in Washington an infallible leader?" . . .
>
> The essence of the whole sticky business was that Washington had to pinpoint one place, to fix the blame where every American could see it and understand it and that one place was Hawaii. You see, the Philippines were too far away for much understanding. But there was Hawaii and its image in the American mind—the Gibraltar of the Pacific, with the U.S. Fleet, and the Army and Air Force under General Short, Waikiki, vacation land, the Paradise of the Pacific and all that. Well, the average American could drink all that in. But not the Philippines! They were too far away, too much unknown for that much understanding. . . .[40]

Kimmel's concept of Hawaii as a glorified red herring ignored the strategy of the times. Oahu was the key to the defense of the American West Coast, as well as of any offensive toward the Far East. In American eyes, Hawaii not only *could* be defended, it *must* be defended. Kimmel's and Short's failure struck at the very heart of American security—not merely the "image" but the reality.

The attempt to assess motivation without direct evidence is always a risk, but we would like to make a suggestion as to why MacArthur escaped the fate of Kimmel and Short. The United States had just suffered two staggering defeats, and the British also took an initial blow which left them, like the Americans, bewildered and astonished. Loss of the new battleship *Prince of Wales* and the old battle cruiser *Repulse* to Japanese aerial torpedoes off the coast of Malaya on December 10 struck almost as deeply into the British psyche as Pearl Harbor into the American. The Manchester *Guardian* editorialized, "the Japanese success is for us a startling and formidable event both in its practical results and in its implications."[41] Indeed it was, for it virtually destroyed British sea power in the Far East and profoundly affected both British and American naval thinking and strategy. It also made it painfully clear that Japan's major campaign against Southeast Asia in all probability would succeed.

Boxed in by defeats, angry and frustrated, the Allies—the United

States in particular—badly needed a public hero and symbol. The American people already knew MacArthur well. He had made an excellent record in World War I and had served effectively as the Army's Chief of Staff under Hoover and Roosevelt. With his star quality and flair for public relations, he had managed to keep himself in the news even in peacetime. Now, with his strong ego drive, sense of mission, and flamboyant leadership, MacArthur, at the head of his valiant officers and men, personified American resistance to the rising tide of Japanese conquest. Even if he had failed in the Philippines, he would become a rallying point for the future.

Remembering the long course of World War II in Asia and the Pacific, and its final result, few Americans would care to deny that MacArthur justified the faith in him which his superiors demonstrated in that dismal December of 1941.

Commander Minoru Genda, Air Staff Officer, First Air Fleet, architect of the plan to attack Pearl Harbor.

Commander Mitsuo Fuchida, leader of the first air attack on Pearl Harbor. He broadcast the famous words "Tora, Tora, Tora."

Aerial view of Pearl Harbor, October, 1941 (U.S. Navy).

Aerial view of Pearl Harbor.

Pearl Harbor under attack. Note the torpedo hit on the U.S.S. *West Virginia* (U.S. Navy).

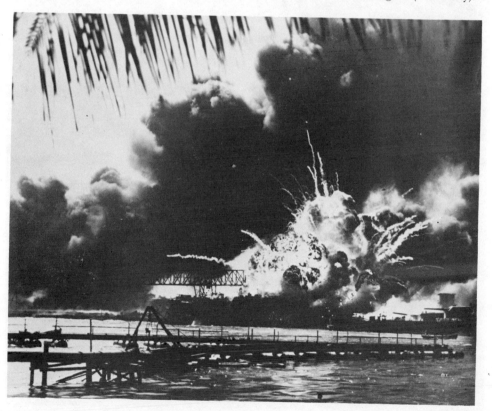

Explosion of magazine on the destroyer *Shaw* (UPI).

Spectators around a midget sub that attacked Pearl Harbor.

U.S.S. *Oklahoma* being salvaged in March, 1943 (U.S. Navy).

Pearl Harbor under siege.

The Congressional committee that investigated Pearl Harbor.

Members and staff, Army Pearl Harbor Board.

Members and staff, Navy Court of Inquiry (Slinkman Studio).

From left to right, Ensign Franklin D. Roosevelt, Jr., Winston Churchill, FDR, and Captain Elliott Roosevelt aboard the U.S. cruiser *Augusta,* prior to Pearl Harbor (UPI).

From left to right, General Douglas MacArthur, FDR, and Admiral Chester W. Nimitz.

Harry Elmer Barnes, a leading revisionist who believed that Roosevelt knew we were going to be attacked and failed to notify his commanders because he wanted to bring the United States into the war.

PART IV

THE VIEW FROM THE CROW'S NEST

CHAPTER 29

"Blessed by the War God"

Japanese made their own success—Yamamoto ultimately responsible—Naval General Staff or Navy Ministry could have forbidden Operation Hawaii—Meticulous planning and training—No "fifth column" in Hawaii but efficient espionage out of the Honolulu consulate—Initiative—Surprise—Admirals' code unbroken—Japanese controversy over "sneak attack"—Luck an important element

"**A**nd you must hand it to them," Kimmel told the Roberts Commission, "leaving aside the unspeakable treachery of it, that once they were launched on it they did a fine job."[1]

Thus with characteristic honesty Kimmel stressed to the commission, and by extension to all students of the Pearl Harbor problem, that responsibility for the attack's inception and success belongs to the Japanese. Out of the smoke arising from honest debate and sincere scholarship, as well as the miasma exuding from the swamp of buck-passing, political opportunism, and name-calling, two facts emerged: first, the Japanese planned and executed the attack entirely on their own, with no urging, tempting, or backstairs assistance from Roosevelt, Hitler, or anyone else; second, the success of the operation resulted as much from superior Japanese efforts and performance as from American miscalculations and blunders.

Here one treads on delicate ground, for it is all too easy to slip off the straight and narrow path of assessing responsibility for the Pearl Harbor attack onto the broad highway of analyzing Japanese policy which led to war with the ABCD powers. Keeping the two lines separate, one must conclude that if any single individual bears the ultimate onus—or credit—for Operation Hawaii, that person is Admiral Isoroku Yamamoto. The Pearl Harbor plan would never have sprung to life had he not planted the seed; would not have flourished except in the sunlight of his encouragement. An attack on Hawaii would have remained as academic a concept in Japan as it was in the United States had not Yamamoto forced some of his own commanders to accept it and then, by his threat of resignation, pushed it through the Naval General Staff.[2] Captain Toshikazu Ohmae, a member of the Navy Ministry in 1941 and a student of the Japanese Navy, has rightly observed, "If there had not been a Yamamoto, there would not have been a Pearl Harbor."[3]

Nor can Yamamoto avoid a share of the larger responsibility for Japan's war against the United States. Had he thrown his dynamic personality and incontestible prestige behind Japan's moderate faction, and worked as hard to sell his true wishes for peace with the United States as he did to put across his Pearl Harbor project, the history of the Far East might have taken a different turn. If he had been able to stiffen the Navy's backbone to the point where the Army had to listen to reason, diplomacy just might have had a fighting chance.

Genda wrote later that had Yamamoto been prime minister, navy minister, or chief of the Naval General Staff, war might never have come between Japan and the United States.[4] Of course, granted the climate of the times in Japan, it was even more possible that some extremist would have assassinated Yamamoto had he taken the road to peace. But regardless of the might-have-beens, Yamamoto forced Operation Hawaii on the Naval General Staff, and thus helped to lead his country into a terrible war of unforeseen magnitude.

A number of his friends and colleagues agreed that, had he lived, the International Military Tribunal of the Far East would have demanded his life. So when American airmen shot down Yamamoto's plane over the island of Bougainville on April 18, 1943, unwittingly they granted him the noblest boon he could have asked: a quick, clean death in combat instead of a criminal's end on the scaffold. "Yamamoto's death was a tragedy and yet a personal victory," said Admiral Katsunoshin Yamanashi. "In a way, destiny could not have decreed anything better—death for him on the battlefield. This was his fulfillment. His passing was a terrible blow at the time but actually the Fates were cruel only to be kind."[5]

War planning during peacetime was the responsibility of the Naval General Staff, so that organization was equally as culpable as Yamamoto. Its chief, Admiral Osami Nagano, could have ordered Yamamoto to confine his originality to operational plans implementing

Naval General Staff strategy, and to preparing the Combined Fleet for action. Chief of the Operations Section Rear Admiral Sadatoshi Tomioka felt so keenly his responsibility for the Naval General Staff's weak knees concerning Pearl Harbor that he was prepared to blow out his brains had the attack failed.[6]

Nagano took "full responsibility" for accepting Yamamoto's plan. On October 1, 1945, after his arrest as a "war criminal," he told the press that he gave his final word on Pearl Harbor "to settle a bitter contest" in the Navy. He courageously admitted the same to his war crimes interrogators a few months later, although he knew that such testimony from his own lips might doom him to hang.[7] But fate spared the old sailor this ignominy. He died of bronchial pneumonia on Sunday, January 5, 1947, in the 361st Station Hospital in Tokyo to which he had been transferred from Sugamo prison.[8]

Nagano did not attempt to blame Yamamoto, reproach his subordinates, or make cheap excuses about the pressures of the international situation. He had always taken a fatalistic attitude toward a Japanese-American War. While knowing the prospects of victory were slim, he believed that the war had to be fought. He said that after he became chief of the Naval General Staff he felt like a man in a canoe speeding down the rapids leading to Niagara Falls. No matter which way he paddled, he could go in only one direction—straight ahead toward the falls and ultimate destruction.[9] Nagano was not quite the dove of peace he would have one believe,[10] but to his credit, after the war ended, he valued the truth above his face or his neck.

Either of two other authorities might have called off the plan. As navy minister, the titular "boss of the Navy," Vice Admiral Shigetaro Shimada could have tried to blow the whistle. After becoming Navy Minister on October 18, 1941 (Japanese time), Shimada had many conferences with Yamamoto. But his diary merely records these occasions, with no indication of the subject matter of their conversations. Indeed, Shimada seemed to have been more oriented toward the ceremonial aspects of his office than to the substantive. If he ever discussed Pearl Harbor in depth with Yamamoto, let alone expressed opposition, nothing in his diary, or any other available source, so indicates.[11] So Shimada, too, must share the responsibility, if only by default.

And what about the highest peak of all—the Emperor? It is unlikely that Hirohito entertained moral qualms about the operation.

To expect him to look at Japanese problems in the light of Occidental standards would be unreasonable. He must have realized the horrifying risk. His brother, Prince Takamatsu, a member of the Operations Section of the Naval General Staff, conferred with him on the morning of November 30. Some believe that at that time Prince Takamatsu told the Emperor that members of the Navy entertained fears about the operation.[12] Hirohito may well have comprehended and perhaps shared these fears.

"In an unprecedented meeting with 24 foreign newsmen" on November 16, 1971, the Emperor denied "that he had played any military role during World War II." He added nevertheless that "certain things" occurred during the war for which he felt "personally sorry." But he did not elaborate.[13]

Thus far Hirohito has kept to himself his thoughts about Pearl Harbor, so one cannot know if he ever wanted to veto the project. The questions he put to Fuchida and Lieutenant Commander Shigekazu Shimazaki at a briefing in the Imperial Palace on December 26, 1941, expressed more humanitarian concern than jubilation. One can only note that the Emperor knew of the attack well in advance[14] and did not forbid it.

Operation Hawaii was exceedingly risky, and more than one thought it might fail. But once the Japanese decided to execute it, they did all possible to ensure its success. No detail was too minute for consideration in perfecting their plans, no effort was too great to ask of their pilots and bombardiers in preparation. The Japanese even modified weapons to achieve maximum damage, and detailed intelligence about the ships of the U.S. Pacific Fleet was a foundation stone of the operation. And the very audacity of the concept was an important element in its success.

Yamamoto was primarily responsible for conceiving the plan and pushing it through to acceptance, but its success depended upon the efforts of hundreds, from Nagumo and his staff to the unsung crew members. The daring and expertise of first-rate, experienced airmen contributed immeasurably to Japan's victory. Among them, Genda the original thinker and Fuchida the dynamic pragmatist took pride of place. One cannot say that without them the operation might have failed; however, without them it would not have been the same. "Japan evidently brought to bear upon the attack the best brains, the best equipment, and the finest intelligence, with the most expert planning, which it had," declared the Army Board.[15] That was absolutely true. Japan gave Operation Hawaii the cream of its naval air arm, and Genda and Fuchida were the crême de la crême.

No objective American observer could deny that the Pearl Harbor strike was an amazing coup. "The carefully planned, brilliantly executed attack . . . dispels any doubts that the Japanese have learned their lesson in air warfare and profited thereby," remarked the Newark *News*. " . . . . But the most rabid partisan of American air power will concede the brilliance, militarily, of Sunday's raid."[16]

No matter how brilliantly planned, the attack would not have been such a tactical victory without the accuracy of the bombardiers and torpedomen. Skillful, persistent research and diligent training of personnel repaid the Japanese many times over. Their modification of missiles contributed much to the success of the strike. Kimmel gave them full credit for developing the fins on their torpedoes that enabled the missiles to run in shallow water. "It was a device which all the brains in our own Navy Department, who had been seeking such a solution, had been unable to arrive at. Any solution of any problem appears simple when you get the answer, and the simpler the better it is."[17] Moreover, the Japanese had something which no amount of technology or training could instill—a consuming belief in their mission and in themselves.

Americans were less in agreement about the role Japanese espionage played in the attack. The various investigating bodies, not to mention the press and the public, did not have the facts necessary for a realistic evaluation. So they consistently confused a nonexistent fifth column with Japan's actual spy system operating out of its Honolulu consulate.

In Knox's report to Roosevelt following his visit to Oahu in December 1941, he correctly informed the President that the Japanese Navy had "excellent knowledge of all necessary details to plan the attack. This included exact charts showing customary positions of ships when in Pearl Harbor, exact location of all defenses, gun power and numerous other details." But Knox mistakenly attributed this to a fifth column.[18] His assessment was unfair to Hawaii's Japanese, and failed to put the finger where it belonged—on the "legal" espionage team in the consulate.

This confusion may explain why Morgan, in his excellently reasoned draft report for the congressional committee, consistently underrated Japanese intelligence concerning Oahu. "The intelligence available lending itself to an attack on Pearl Harbor was no more pronounced than that which would also have been available had Japan elected to attack, say Panama," he wrote.[19] The majority report agreed "that Japanese Hawaiian espionage was not particularly effective," adding that it was clear "beyond reasonable doubt that superior Japanese intelligence had nothing whatever to do with the decision to attack Pearl Harbor."[20]

Right there the report harnessed the horse to the cart's tailboard. Of course Yamamoto did not decide to attack the U.S. Pacific Fleet at Pearl Harbor because of available intelligence. But once the Japanese Navy began to take the possibility seriously, they stepped up their intelligence gathering on Oahu considerably. The availability of consistent, detailed information about Kimmel's ships and Short's military establishment was a large plus in developing the plan and was essential to its ultimate feasibility.

If the Japanese had had no dependable intelligence, or none at all, concerning Oahu, it is highly doubtful that they would have attempted to carry through the attack. No admiral in his right mind would send a fleet over 3,000 miles from home to the threshold of the enemy's most powerful base on the odd chance of finding the target in position. Yamamoto himself might have called off the project had the necessary data not been available.

What is equally to the point, Japanese espionage in Hawaii was far from ineffective. Naval Intelligence had dispatched Takeo Yoshikawa to the consulate for the express purpose of spying on the Pacific Fleet and on the military installations on Oahu. Up to the eve of the attack, he and his colleagues kept Tokyo supplied with information which the Naval General Staff sent in code to Nagumo's task force en route.

Japan's long-standing espionage establishment in its Honolulu consulate; the dispatching of Yoshikawa to Hawaii; Tokyo's instructions to Honolulu and its requests for specific data such as that contained in the "bomb plot" series; the special intelligence mission of submariner Commander Toshihide Maejima and air expert Lieutenant Commander Suguru Suzuki in November 1941 to obtain more detailed information[21]—these events attest to the importance the Japanese Navy placed on firsthand intelligence concerning Kimmel's ships and Oahu's defenses.

The congressional committee's majority report outlined the reasons for deciding that Japanese espionage on Oahu had been ineffective, first turning its attention to radar:

> Had Japanese espionage developed the fact that radar was in use at Hawaii and so advised Tokyo of that fact, it would seem unlikely that the attacking planes would have come in for the raid at high altitude but . . . would have flown a few feet above the water in order to take advantage of the radar electrical horizon. . . .[22]

As far as we know, Yoshikawa did not report on Oahu's radar system. Japan's Navy did not have radar, hence did not adequately understand its uses or the danger it posed as a detecting device. The airmen flew in at high altitude because that was the best way to coordinate their flight pattern, take advantage of cloud cover, and approach their targets.

The report next tackled the question of "oil storage tanks around Pearl Harbor . . . exposed and visible from the air." The committee suggested "it is questionable whether Japanese espionage had developed fully the extraordinary vulnerability of the oil storage to bombing and its peculiar and indispensable importance to the fleet."[23]

The Japanese knew all about those oil storage tanks. Their failure to bomb the Fleet's fuel supply reflected their preoccupation with tactical rather than logistical targets; it had nothing to do with the effectiveness of their espionage. Nagumo's mission was to destroy Kimmel's ships and the airpower on Oahu. If Yamamoto and his advisers chose the wrong targets, or insufficiently diversified ones, that mistake rests on their shoulders, not on the back of Japanese Naval Intelligence.

The report also stated that "other Japanese consulates were supplying Tokyo as much information as the Honolulu consulate."[24] As far as quantity is concerned, that was true. Yet a most important difference existed between the data from such consulates as Manila, Singapore, Seattle, Panama, and elsewhere and the information from Honolulu. Only that consulate supplied intelligence on berthing positions. Moreover, those reports were at the specific direction of the Naval General Staff through the Foreign Ministry, thus indicating Tokyo's interest in Kimmel's ships in harbor.

The report added, "It appears that it was not until a few days before December 7 that the Honolulu consul supplied his Japanese superior any significant information concerning the defenses of Oahu, and at a time when the attacking force was already on its way to Pearl Harbor."[25]

That was not the case. The consulate had long been seriously concerned with Oahu's defenses. Although Yoshikawa's primary mission was to report the movements and dispositions of ships, since early 1941 he had attempted to find out as much as he could about American ground and air bases, and he charted flight patterns painstakingly.

The report next pointed out:

> The date December 7 had been recognized as suitable for the attack in discussions prior to November 7. It is hardly credible that superior intelligence should have precipitated or otherwise conditioned the attack when the decision to strike on December 7 was made many days earlier and, manifestly, in the interim between the decision and the attack date the entire defensive situation at Hawaii could have changed.[26]

It was quite true that, as early as the war games held aboard Yamamoto's flagship *Nagato* on October 10–11, the Japanese had settled upon December 7 as attack day, although the date postulated in the September war games had been November 16.[27] However, the state of training and logistics precluded the earlier date. December 7 was roughly the last date before winter would set in over the northern Pacific. Then, too, the moon of December 6–7 would give the task force maximum light at the desired moment. Above all, the Pearl Harbor attack had to synchronize with the schedule of the numerous forces moving into Southeast Asia.[28]

The choice of a Sunday, however, was based largely upon intelligence. The committee touched upon that matter next:

> It is apparent from the evidence obtained through Japanese sources since VJ-day that the decision to attack on December 7 was made on the basis of the general assumption that units of the fleet ordinarily came into Pearl Harbor on Friday and remained over the weekend.[29]

No "general assumption" entered into the decision. The Japanese knew from Yoshikawa of the U.S. Pacific Fleet's dangerous habit pattern of bringing in major fleet units over the weekend.

The report continued, "Investigation conducted in Japan since VJ-day indicates, as a matter of fact, that espionage agents, apart from the consul and his staff, played no role whatever in the attack."[30] Obviously the committee did not understand Japan's intelligence system on Oahu. The Japanese kept their espionage within the consulate so that they could control and direct it, thus ensuring that those activities would remain "legal" and under the shelter of diplomatic immunity. As Fielder explained:

> Shivers of the FBI and the rest of us in G-2 were fully aware of the Japanese espionage setup on the island here, but we could do nothing about it. Japanese espionage on Oahu was legitimate espionage. They did not violate military property or trespass on any military establishment. . . . What Yoshikawa or anyone else did was within the legal limits of United States policy at the time. Yoshikawa did not push his way into any military installation, he merely went to public places. Any intelligent man in the world could have done it. Yoshikawa in short was a very observing tourist.[31]

And a clever one, for at the time Shivers did not know that Yoshikawa was Japan's top operative in Hawaii.[32]

"The sources of information employed, according to Japanese interviewed," continued the congressional majority report, "were naval attachés in the Japanese Embassy in Washington, public newspapers in the United States, American radio broadcasts (public), crews and passengers on ships which put in at Honolulu, and general information."[33]

This was true as far as it went. Preparations for the war crimes trials were under way in Japan at the time the congressional committee was deliberating. For obvious reasons the Japanese were eager to play down the Honolulu consulate as a center of espionage and to stress other, more generalized, sources of information. However, the best data which the Japanese Navy had about its Pacific rival came from that consulate.

The report stated further that as late as December 2 "Tokyo was solicitously asking its Honolulu consul" about observation balloons over Pearl Harbor and torpedo nets around warships. "The foregoing is hardly indicative of any superior sources or facilities for obtaining information."[34] Thus the committee persisted in the delusion that Tokyo only turned to the consulate for information for want of "superior sources."

As X-Day approached, the Japanese needed all possible last-minute data about Oahu's defenses. They had to face such immediate problems as the prospect of torpedo nets suddenly appearing around battleships, the presence of barrage balloons over targets, and other quick changes in the military status on Oahu. This indicates sound thinking and a good intelligence system, not a poor one. In fact, a prime worry of Rear Admiral Ryunosuke Kusaka, Nagumo's chief of staff, during the voyage was that this precious information might be cut off.[35] But up to the eleventh hour Consul General Kita continued to feed facts to the Foreign Office, which passed them to the Naval General Staff, which in turn sent them to the task force. That the Japanese attacked on the basis of this information proves its importance.

The report observed further that

> the Japanese ran the risk of tipping over the apple cart by sending out scouting planes a considerable period ahead of the bombers. . . .
> If Japan had possessed extraordinary intelligence concerning the state of Hawaiian defenses or lack thereof, it would seem improbable that she would invite disaster by taking such risks.[36]

Nagumo's scout planes took off about thirty minutes before Fuchida's first wave—not exactly "a considerable period of time." Of course this was a grave risk, but the Japanese accepted it because they wanted last-minute information which the Honolulu-Tokyo-Nagumo channel could not furnish in time. The situation on Oahu was not necessarily static. Intelligence that was correct at midnight might be outdated by dawn.

The Japanese "invited disaster" by going to war against the ABCD powers, so why expect them to gag over one of the subsidiary risks? The congressional majority assessment demonstrated again, even after the war, the same tendency to estimate Japanese intentions rather than capabilities which had played such a calamitous part in the pre–Pearl Harbor attitude.

Next, the report noted a lack of evidence that any of the Japanese consular agents "committed a single act of espionage, except as it may be inferred from the information sent by the Honolulu consul to Tokyo, which . . . was no more extensive than was being received from other consulates."[37]

True, Kita did not rely on the consular agents (toritsuginin) scattered throughout the Hawaiian Islands. Here again, the lawmakers regarded the consulate as Japan's court of last resort, instead of its prime source. And they did not remember that the extent of information counts less in military operations than its type, quality, timeliness, and accuracy, as well as proper interpretation, dissemination, and effective utilization. On this score the Japanese were far superior to the Americans.

The majority report remarked that the Japanese "bombed a vessel with lumber on its upper deck, apparently thinking it was a carrier." Hence the investigators concluded that, had the attackers known better, Japan "would not have indulged the Pyrrhic victory of destroying our lumbering battleships if she had not also hoped to find the fast striking units of the fleet."[38]

The persistent myth that the Japanese struck the target ship *Utah* and other vessels in mistake for carriers should be laid to rest. They knew, to their great disappointment, that they would find no carriers in Pearl Harbor on the morning of December 7, 1941. The solons forgot that before World War II the Japanese Navy, like the American, was a battleship navy and Yamamoto primarily a battleship admiral. He had placed his original top priority on those "lumbering" ships. It was upon Genda's recommendation in his draft plan of February to Rear Admiral Takijiro Onishi that carriers became the number one targets.[39]

The report next faulted the Japanese for their inaccurate figures— much too high—of the number of military aircraft on Oahu.[40] Yoshikawa's failure to obtain as precise a fix on aircraft as he did on ships is due less to his ineptitude than to tight security around such bases as Hickam.[41] If an agent errs, it is to his country's advantage that he overestimate the enemy rather than underestimate him.

The report ended its comments about espionage on Oahu with this remark:

> In the final analysis it is difficult to believe that Japanese espionage was actually able to develop satisfactorily the real strength of our Pacific Fleet. In December of 1941 the Japanese fleet was superior to our fleet in the Pacific. . . .
>
> If the Japanese really knew the weakness of the Pacific Fleet they must also have known that it did not present a formidable deterrent to anything Japan desired to do in the Far East. . . .

Such being the case, why did Japan invite the lightning by attacking Pearl Harbor to knock out a fleet that was no deterrent? In view of the committee's limited knowledge of the Japanese side of the picture, this was a reasonable query. The corollary they reached also seemed logical: "Japan had not been able to determine and, in consequence, was not cognizant of our real naval weakness in the Pacific."[42]

One might consider that, in sending a number of Kimmel's ships to the Atlantic in the spring of 1941, Washington had done Yamamoto's work for him. Nonetheless, the Japanese Navy knew with a high degree of accuracy the strength and composition of the U.S. Pacific Fleet at any given time, and it was still by far the major American force in the Pacific area. Yamamoto knew exactly what he was doing: he hoped to enable Japan to establish and consolidate its position in Southeast Asia before the United States could expand the Pacific Fleet into a really formidable foe. He may have acted unwisely, but he did so with his eyes open.

After weighing all the factors mentioned, the congressional committee majority reached this conclusion: "From the foregoing considerations it is proper to suggest that the role played by espionage in the Pearl Harbor attack may have been magnified out of all proportion to the realities of the situation."[43]

Evidently the lawmakers understood neither the nature of intelligence nor its part in operational planning, so they consistently missed the point. They concentrated upon the questions of whether or not Japanese espionage had anything to do with Japan's decision to attack and how much, if any, espionage took place outside the Honolulu consulate. The real question should have been: What part did espionage play in making the attack a success? That issue was not so easily sloughed off. Where the information came from was much less important than what it accomplished.

The picture of Japan which the majority report presented in these paragraphs was little less than ludicrous—a nation that measured out its fuel practically by the ounce sending a huge, oil-devouring task force of irreplaceable ships thousands of miles into hostile waters to attack a fleet of unknown strength on the "general assumption" that it might be in port. Captain J. V. Heimark, USN, assessed the situation far more accurately:

No wonder the Japanese were successful at Pearl Harbor. Nothing was left to chance or guesswork that could possibly be supplied as facts. This careful, painstaking attention to knowing the enemy paid off handsomely for the Japanese by giving the maximum achievement at minimum cost.

Now intelligence by itself accomplishes nothing. But combined with a well-planned operation, carried out by highly trained pilots flying good aircraft, the results are there for all the world to see. This chain of military success was well forged with each link strong enough to carry its share of the load.[44]

Without purpose behind Japan's spying on Oahu, it could have become a futile exercise in fact-gathering. But the Japanese knew precisely what information they wanted and how they intended to use it. Once they made up their minds exactly when they would go to war, they seized the initiative and thereby gained the advantages thereof. One of these was the choice of time to attack, which they calculated almost to the final second. The timing of the Pearl Harbor strike against the background of the diplomatic discussions in Washington and the massive advances into Southeast Asia was one of the most brilliant features of Operation Hawaii. As the aggressor, Japan chose the day and hour, based, among other things, upon a thorough knowledge not only of the habit patterns of the U.S. Pacific Fleet but of oceanography and meteorology.

Inseparable from the initiative was the element of surprise. To a large extent, as the Japanese knew, the achievement of surprise was out of their hands. Many necessary ingredients would remain beyond their control. But with few exceptions the Pearl Harbor planners took a positive attitude. Nevertheless, they tempered optimism with realism. They worked hard to secure complete surprise, that primary but elusive principle of war—but they did not rely upon it blindly. Knowing that the United States would be the most formidable foe Japan had ever faced, and that Kimmel had a splendid reputation, Yamamoto cautioned the airmen that they might well find the enemy prepared, hence the attackers might have to fight their way to their targets.[45]

Of enormous importance in maintaining secrecy, those who devised Japan's high-level admirals' code did such a thorough job that it defeated the best efforts of Rochefort and his skilled, dedicated assistants in Communications Intelligence on Oahu until after Pearl Harbor. In this code the Naval General Staff sent its messages to Nagumo's task force as it moved across the Pacific.[46] Had this code suffered the fate of Japan's diplomatic cipher systems, the Americans could have been ready and waiting for the First Air Fleet before it reached the Hawaiian area, as they were six months later at Midway.

The Japanese took advantage of every opening the United States gave them. In a conflict with the ABCD powers, whose war potential far exceeded theirs, they could not afford scruples that meant little or nothing to them. Thus, when the United States relaxed the ban on Japanese shipping in the autumn of 1941 to admit three exchange ships, the Japanese rushed into the breach. They sent effective spy missions on the first two—the *Tatuta Maru* and *Taiyo Maru*.[47] The carefully scheduled sailing of the third purported exchange ship, also the *Tatuta Maru*, to the United States in early December aided in lulling the Americans into believing that the Japanese would make no overt move, at least until after the liner had returned to Japan. This tactic even fooled Nomura.[48]

But in the main Japan's smokescreen was all the more impenetrable for being composed largely of the truth. As we have stressed, the Americans correctly estimated Japan's major target to be Southeast Asia and focused most of their attention upon that area. The Japanese made no secret of their move south, for this overt operation served to camouflage their covert operation. This very openness offered the United States a chance to become suspicious. In his "Additional Views," which Representative Keefe appended to the congressional committee's majority report, he made this valid point: "the intercepts showed that some Japanese plan went into effect automatically on November 29, from which Japan hoped to divert American suspicion by a pretext of continued negotiations. What was its nature?"[49]

On the diplomatic front, no chicanery could have carried such conviction as did Nomura's sterling character and sincere belief in his mission. And the dispatch of Kurusu to Washington appeared to be a bona fide endeavor to assist Nomura in keeping the talks alive. Apparently Kurusu performed honestly as far as he could.

During the congressional hearings, Dr. E. Stanley Jones, the Methodist missionary who had acted as the Japanese Embassy's unofficial emissary to the White House about Roosevelt's message to the Emperor,[50] publicly asserted, "There is no doubt in my mind that KURUSU came to the United States with special orders from his Emperor to arrive at a basis for peace if possible." Snapped the Louisville *Courier-Journal,*

Of course he came with such instructions. Any nation not made up of raving madmen would prefer to have its way without the necessity of fighting a major power to obtain it. But there was the rub. The only basis for peace which these envoys proposed was that America allow Japan all the fruits of her conquests to that date; that we abandon China to her bitter fate at Japanese hands; and that we yield, as CORDELL HULL put it, "The fundamental principles for which we stood in the Pacific and all over the World."[51]

An anonymous State Department official who sat in with Hull during the conversations believed that Nomura wanted peace. But, he stressed, "He wanted it at the price of our giving Japan everything she demanded."[52]

The lengthy fourteen-part message of December 6–7 also helped to throw U.S. leaders off the Pearl Harbor trail. It distracted U.S. Army and Naval Intelligence, as well as the State Department, from more significant last-minute signals. Yet it served legitimate purposes by restating the Japanese position and breaking off the Washington talks. Later the Japanese laid great stress on what they claimed to be their technical adherence to the requirements of the Third Hague Convention by arranging to deliver this, their final note, not later than 1300 EST on December 7. When this fine-cut timing slipped a gear, Nomura and Kurusu could not meet the deadline.

Ever since the facts came to light, some Japanese have made much of the tragicomic administrative delays that held up formal delivery of this note until after the strike had begun.[53] A number of sincere Japanese took the attitude that this circumstance "made the Pearl Harbor attack, originally intended as a strategical surprise attack, turn into the so-called sneak attack." In consequence, "The words 'RE-MEMBER PEARL HARBOR' became an oath that stirred up the fighting spirit of the American people," wrote Fuchida. "Successful though it was from the tactical point of view, the attack brought upon Japan a disgrace which did not vanish even after her defeat in the war."[54]

This seems to have been the attitude of Yamamoto himself, who "did not wish to dirty the pages of Japanese history with a sneak attack."[55] Some time after the strike, Genda heard that Yamamoto ordered Shigeru Fujii, a member of his staff, to find out whether the attack took place before delivery of the final note. Commander Akira Sasaki, who had been Yamamoto's air staff officer, told Genda that the admiral had ordered again and again that this point be investigated. Genda wrote that Yamamoto took the view that a samurai never tried to use his sword to kill a sleeping man, even though he attacked at night. At least the samurai would kick the pillow of his sleeping enemy before trying to kill him. "If we attacked before the ultimatum was delivered to the United States, the code of the Japanese Navy would be made antiquated," Yamamoto said.[56]

Apparently some Japanese believed that had the message been delivered on time—half an hour before the scheduled beginning of hostilities—this would have mitigated American wrath. But the Americans were not as devoted as the Japanese to the fine art of splitting hairs. Thirty minutes' notice, more or less, would not have weighed very heavily in the balance against the weeks and months Japan obviously had spent preparing for this operation while her diplomats talked in Washington.

One can understand why this historical theory appealed to many Japanese. It removed a portion of the blame for Japan's ultimate defeat from the shoulders of Yamamoto, who following his death had been held in high reverence. This thesis also came as a godsend to survivors of the Tojo regime. Shigenori Togo, Japan's foreign minister at the time of Pearl Harbor, pushed it hard after the war.[57] Naturally he jumped at the chance to take the monkey off the Foreign Ministry's back and put it on that of the Japanese Embassy in Washington, thus exculpating his own department and trying to discredit Nomura, a staunch moderate and exponent of Japanese-American friendship.

The fact is, this message, whether delivered on time or delayed as actually happened, did not even break off diplomatic relations, much less declare war. Not that the note was conciliatory. After Roosevelt read the first thirteen parts, he had remarked, "This means war."[58] But when the last section finally arrived, it was "much less severe than the strongly worded first 13 parts would have indicated."[59] This may explain why the President's reaction to it was milder than to the earlier portions. Upon reading the final installment, he observed to his naval aide, Captain John R. Beardall, "that it looked as though the Japs are going to sever negotiations, break off negotiations."[60] In any case, the document did not fulfill the purpose the Japanese claimed for it.

Some of the Japanese interviewed for this study genuinely regretted for honor's sake that events canceled out whatever warning the Americans might have read into the final note. Tomioka, for one, had hoped that if war came, it would begin in accordance with international law. Great was his mortification when he discovered that Operation Hawaii had been a "sneak attack."[61]

For the most part, however, those concerned with Yamamoto's plan thought in terms of military necessity and did not worry about legalisms. Commander Kyozo Ohashi, senior staff officer of the Fifth Carrier Division, stated frankly that he would do the same thing again in similar circumstances.[62] Vice Admiral Chuichi "King Kong" Hara, Ohashi's Commander in Chief, believed that the threat of the U.S. Fleet to Japan's southern flank had to be wiped out, even though in the long run the attack was a strategical failure.[63] To such airmen as Genda, Fuchida, and Captain Sadamu Sanagi, who as a commander had been a member of the Operations Section of the Naval General Staff, December 7, 1941, was Japan's finest hour.[64]

The fact that Japan had the best naval air arm in the world in 1941 was a primary consideration in planning Operation Hawaii. Without an air force capable of carrying it out, the plan never would have reached the drawing board. The Japanese Navy had leaders with the vision and drive to create the First Air Fleet from the means at hand, thus becoming the pioneers of the large carrier striking force. When they expanded this already formidable fleet to include six carriers, it represented the most powerful carrier task force ever launched to that date.

No little credit belongs to Nagumo and Kusaka, who had strenuously objected to Yamamoto's foolhardy venture. To make the adjustment from strong opposition to successful execution required a high order of flexibility and loyalty. Nagumo and his subordinate commanders also deserve a double plus for keeping such a huge task force together in proper formation over such a long distance without mishap and with no radio contact between ships, refueling on the way and meeting a schedule that required split-second timing.

Yet when all is said and done, sheer luck was an important ingredient in Japan's victory at Pearl Harbor. "The Japanese did the preposterous thing and as a result got away with it," said Davis. "In addition they had loads of luck."[65] The weather cooperated with unexpectedly smooth seas, which facilitated refueling, and with dense fog, which provided a natural screen. These circumstances were entirely beyond human power to arrange. Then, too, the fact that Nagumo moved his task force so far without detection depended in part upon the routes which foreign shipping would take at that time of the year. Though the Japanese could avoid well-traveled sea lanes, they had no control over foreign schedules, courses, or accidents that might send a stray vessel into the path of the task force.

Fortune smiled upon the Japanese in other ways as well. For instance, on the Sunday preceding Pearl Harbor, Short's antiaircraft had practiced simulated fire against a mock attack by Navy carrier-based planes. But, "by some stroke," as General Burgin said, they "did not go out on December 7."[66] This was because *Lexington* and *Enterprise* were at sea, hence not in a position to participate in their customary joint exercises. While the Japanese were sorely disappointed to miss the two flattops, their absence contributed to Oahu's somnolence on that morning.

Likewise, no amount of Japanese skill or planning could have arranged for a flight of B-17s to come into Oahu at almost the same time as Fuchida's first wave. Because Lieutenant Tyler thought the Opana Mobile Station had spotted the American aircraft, he did not realize that the radarscope had recorded an incoming enemy force. Moreover, at the exact moment to reveal the targets, the clouds over Oahu parted. In their audience with the Emperor, both Nagumo and Fuchida referred to this circumstance as obviously due to heavenly favor.[67] Harold T. Kay, an eyewitness to the attack, reported of the visibility, "As near perfect as could be hoped for from the point of view of the attacker, aided by light, fluffy clouds giving excellent screen to approaching planes when desired."[68]

And of course the Japanese had no way to arrange for the American blunders and misunderstandings which played such a tragically large part in the success of the attack. The Japanese could not and did not count on such occurrences, and were surprised and relieved almost beyond expression when everything worked out as it did.

Writing to Admiral Sankichi Takahashi on December 19, 1941, Yamamoto acknowledged the Japanese debt to fortune:

> As it turned out, however, I should say we were blessed by the war God, since a wide high pressure zone, the last one appearing in that district this year, prevailed in the area, extending as far as 2,000 miles. It was the first such phenomenon since 1938 and enabled refueling at sea.
>
> Such good luck, together with negligence on the part of the arrogant enemy, enabled us to launch a successful surprise attack.[69]

This was true enough, yet not the whole truth. Even such a bonanza of good fortune as the Japanese enjoyed would not have allowed them to succeed so devastatingly had they not possessed the skill and determination to take advantage of every lucky break. On December 7, 1941, Nagumo had his ships at the right place, at the right time, with the right equipment, the right information, and the right men in the right state of training and frame of mind. All those factors enabled the Japanese to make the Pearl Harbor attack a grand tactical success—yet in the long run a great strategical failure.

CHAPTER 30

"A Strategic Imbecility"

Japan's strategic ambivalence—Underestimated American tenacity—Differing opinions as to wisdom of Operation Hawaii—U.S. not threatening Japan—Japanese belief in their mission—Reliance upon intangibles—All-out in Southeast Asia vs. Pearl Harbor strategy—"Great All-Out Battle" concept—No contingency plan if Operation Hawaii succeeded—Plan did not include strikes on ground installations—Did not understand importance of logistics—Mishandled submarine warfare—Failure to follow through after Pearl Harbor—Did not fully learn lessons of naval air warfare—Japan ultimately gained because defeat in World War II broke up military stranglehold

O ccasionally military leaders forget that the object of all battles is to further national aims. However brilliantly executed, however tactically successful, unless the engagement advances the nation's foreign policy or protects the nation's interests, it is a failure. At Pearl Harbor the Japanese inflicted heavy losses upon the Americans at an astoundingly low cost to themselves. But what had they done to their own national policy and interests?

According to Captain Yasuji Watanabe of Yamamoto's staff, the Japanese believed that if they suffered defeat at Pearl Harbor, they would have lost the war.[1] This assessment was only partially correct. Win, lose, or draw at Pearl Harbor, by arousing the full might of the United States the Japanese lost before they had fairly started. In this respect Pearl Harbor is unique.

Considered as a separate unit, Operation Hawaii had a limited objective—to immobilize Kimmel's ships for at least six months, giving the Japanese time to secure their position in Southeast Asia. That was a clear-cut mission which proved attainable. But the Pearl Harbor project was only a part of Japan's overall strategy, which was surprisingly ambivalent. Intelligent Japanese understood that they could not win a protracted war against the United States. Over the long haul, American manpower, resources, industrial might and technology were bound to prevail. Yamamoto himself told Prince Konoye that in case of war with the United States he could run wild for the first six months or a year, but after that he had no confidence.[2] However, many Japanese had a poor opinion of American staying power. They considered the Americans, in Forrestal's words, "a great sprawling people afraid to fight, afraid to die, a people who thought of our purses rather than of our honor."[3] Therefore, the Japanese hoped that if they hung on long enough, the Americans might tire of the struggle and agree to some sort of arrangement. The cyclone of American wrath that Pearl Harbor generated spun into nothingness any chance of a compromise peace. Naval historian Samuel Eliot Morison summed up the matter crisply:

> . . . the surprise attack on Pearl Harbor, far from being a "strategic necessity," as the Japanese claimed even after the war, was a strategic imbecility. One can search military history in vain for an operation more fatal to the aggressor. On the tactical level, the Pearl Harbor attack was wrongly concentrated on ships rather than permanent installations and oil tanks. On the strategic level it was idiotic. On the high political level it was disastrous.[4]

Not everyone shared Morison's opinion. "The criticism of Pearl Harbor by Morison, who was forced to twist the history of the war for the U.S. Navy will be the laughingstock for the future," wrote Rear Admiral Sokichi Takagi in a somewhat defensive analysis. He considered that the best policy would have been to avoid war; however, with the decision made, he thought the Navy had to attack Pearl Harbor. After all, the attack put a number of American battleships out of commission.[5]

Admiral Fukudome also disagreed with Morison, and was much more specific than Takagi:

> When it is recalled that the success of this air attack upon Pearl Harbor nullified the U.S. Navy's *Rainbow No. 5* operational plan, and that it took two full years to recover its strength; further, that our forces, in the meantime, were able to complete without interruption the occupation of the Southern Resources Area, we, who are students of strategy, cannot agree with Dr. Morison's criticism which

assailed the tactics employed by the Japanese. In the event that the
Japanese Navy had not launched the Hawaii attack and had consequently encountered the U.S. Fleet advancing on the Marshall and
West Caroline Islands in pursuance of their *Rainbow No. 5* operational plan, it would have been impossible for the Japanese Navy to
have inflicted greater damage to them than they did in the Pearl
Harbor attack, however favorable an estimate may be applied to the
case [Fukudome's italics].[6]

One may question Fukudome's conclusion. The United States
salvaged all but two of the combat vessels struck at Pearl Harbor.
Any ships that Japan might have sunk in the open sea near the Marshalls or Carolines would have been out of the fight forever. More
important, Fukudome ignored the political consequence of Pearl Harbor which was Morison's main point.

Captain Safford was by no means persuaded that the Japanese had
been ill advised to attack Pearl Harbor. He had a low opinion of the
readiness and leadership of the prewar U.S. Navy, and pointed out
that Japan's navy was almost as large as that of the United States in
ships, while its personnel were more thoroughly trained. It had better
matériel in such critical areas as flashless powder, warhead explosives,
and optical equipment. Japanese "aircraft and flyers were much better
than we gave them credit for. In torpedoes, the Japanese stood at
the head of the class and the U.S. Navy at the foot. . . . In short,"
Safford summed up tartly, "the only way Japan could lose the war
was for Tokyo to make more mistakes than Washington."

He conceded, "Of course, if the war lasted long enough, America
would win through superior wealth, resources, industrial facilities
and manpower. . . ." But, he continued:

> Japan had licked two giants, (China and Russia) and could see the
> same defects in our national character, leadership, and initial de-
> ployment. Fortunately for us the Japs could not see the deficiencies
> of their own leadership and national character and particularly in
> their Army General Staff and high-ranking generals. The Jap admirals
> were tops, professionally, and were overmatched only by men like
> Halsey and Spruance. Certainly Naval Operations was no match for
> the Japanese Naval Staff of that period.

Granted the circumstances of the time, Safford believed that the
Japanese "would have been stupid if they had not struck . . . the
Pacific Fleet moored at Pearl Harbor. In fact it is one of the few basic

facts in the Japanese strategy which was *not* stupid" (Safford's italics).[7]

Many Japanese ex-naval officers agreed that the only valid way to evaluate Pearl Harbor was in terms of the assigned mission. While bitterly regretting the attack from the minute he heard of it, Nomura observed that it permitted Japan's rapid expansion southward.[8] Vice Admiral Jisaburo Ozawa, who commanded the Southern Expeditionary Force in 1941, insisted that Yamamoto's plan was sound strategy because it accomplished its purpose of facilitating Japan's Southern Operation. Even in the light of Japan's eventual defeat, he would have done the same thing with one exception—he would have carried out a second major attack had he been in Nagumo's place.[9] Admiral Soemu Toyoda, the last chief of Japan's Naval General Staff, knew that Pearl Harbor was a gamble, but so was Japan's whole war plan. At the time he thought that Operation Hawaii would reduce the overall risk.[10]

Former Navy Minister Shimada was among those who persisted in the belief that Pearl Harbor had been "a great success." He said as much to Rear Admiral Paulus P. Powell, who was visiting him in his prison cell after the war. Powell disagreed, pointing out Japan's failure to take American psychology into account. Shimada held to his view, so Powell, "a little miffed," retorted, "Admiral Shimada, let us judge by the results. Washington is undamaged, Tokyo is in ruins. The American Fleet is the greatest that has ever existed, the Japanese fleet is utterly destroyed, and if this is not enough to convince you, just ask yourself who is in jail, Powell or Shimada."[11]

In retrospect, and from a purely practical standpoint, Japan's decision for war with the United States is most difficult to understand, let alone rationalize. Actually, in terms of advantage to Japan, the ante–Pearl Harbor situation of the two major Pacific navies was about the best the Japanese could have devised. By merely existing, Yamamoto's Combined Fleet immobilized a large portion of the United States Fleet. That included its Commander in Chief and many of what Kimmel justly considered the best minds in that or any other navy.[12] Under the circumstances, Kimmel's ships and men were of no harm to Japan, of little good to the United States, and no help at all to Britain. This stalemate, too, favored Japan's German allies. It was much more to the benefit of Hitler that Japan tie up the U.S. Pacific Fleet rather than deliberately engage it, thereby opening a whole new theater of war. A continuation of the existing situation would have risked no Japanese lives and would have cost nothing in fuel and yen beyond normal peacetime expenses.

However, in this period of their history, the Japanese tended to think with their emotions rather than with their brains. Looking back, Genda considered that they themselves generated their sense of emergency in 1941.[13] For one thing, they held a persistent image of the United States as a malevolent giant lurking in wait to frustrate Japan's aims, even to destroy its existence. Yamamoto and his fellow strategists would not be the first people who ended up believing their own propaganda. That entire line was a triumph of expedient imagination over historical fact. Washington did not intervene when Japan entered Manchuria in 1931, when the Marco Polo Bridge incident of 1937 commenced the so-called China Incident, or when Japan expanded her war on the Asiatic mainland.

Quite the contrary! The United States supplied Japan with critical war materials year after year. Sympathy for China, scrap iron for Japan was a policy perhaps irritating to Japan's sense of symbolism, but eminently satisfactory from the practical viewpoint. Washington did not embargo scrap iron or steel for Japan until Tokyo signed the Tripartite Pact. Not until July 26, 1941, did Roosevelt cut off shipments of gasoline that could be upgraded to aviation use.

Yamanashi pointed out that recent history had conditioned Japan to believe that military adventures paid off. Nothing in Japanese experience during the Sino-Japanese War, the Russo-Japanese War, World War I, or the Manchurian Incident indicated the contrary. Hitler's victories had reinforced the belief of the Japanese that the way to get what they wanted was to seize it by force.[14]

What is more, Japan was going through a phase when those in power believed that to try to solve national problems by war and conquest was not only expedient but admirable, the only honorable choice. Virtually all responsible Japanese knew the prohibitive odds against them, yet their collective subconscious rang down a psychological curtain between their intellects and their actions. Indeed, there seems to be no folly of which individuals or nations are incapable once they are embarked on a course of "machismo."

Take the case of Rear Admiral Takijiro Onishi. "While many officers looked upon a war with the United States as an operation and measured it only by the yardstick of tactics or strategy, Onishi looked at the war with detached perspective and saw not only the beginning but also the probable end," recalled Genda's assistant, Lieutenant Commander Chuichi Yoshioka. "In this respect, Onishi was much more realistic than the average Japanese politician or naval officer."[15] Yet Onishi plunged enthusiastically into the initial planning for Pearl Harbor and supported the operation until circumstances changed his mind.[16] Nagano had likened himself to a man headed for Niagara Falls in a canoe; the Japanese Navy as a whole seemed more like one going over the falls in a barrel. It nailed itself into a small container and blindly gave itself over to Fate.

Nor was this attitude confined to the Navy. General Hideki Tojo told a friend, Mrs. Mitsutaro Araki, that, in speaking with Konoye during the latter's premiership, he had likened war to jumping from Kiyomizu Temple in Kyoto—a great plunge during which one shuts one's eyes and awaits the results of plummeting to earth.[17] The simile was more revealing than Tojo might have intended. He was not the type to expect angels to bear him up in his descent; therefore, what could be the end but broken bones, probably death?

A number of Japanese did believe quite sincerely that they enjoyed a heavenly mandate which placed them above such mundane considerations as resources and logistics. In a thoughtful article published in 1942, Ernest T. Nash reminded his readers that Japan's faith established the Emperor as divine. Then he delivered himself of a home truth: "And where faith directs, power is generated, whether for human weal or woe." To the Japanese Navy its ships "are not merely formidable machines, they are veritable temples enshrining spiritual properties." Nash continued his excellent analysis,

> Thus the Japanese soldier's sword . . . is subject to purifying rites before it is employed upon its murderous mission. Murderous, however, only to those who do not appreciate the sacred duty of its Japanese wielder to insure that his sword either be kissed in recognition of the spiritual sanction attaching to it and its possessor, or that it should kill the non-conformist who fails in "sincerity" to "cooperate" in insuring the success of its mission. . . .

Nash explained that a Japanese would rationalize such a defeat as Midway "by assuming that he allowed personal indiscipline to blunt the edge of his sword, or moral laxity to diminish the efficiency of his navigational skill."[18]

Onishi's fate perfectly demonstrated Nash's point. The admiral believed that if one gave one's all to a cause, one must win. He accepted no physical limitations upon the human will; therefore, he admitted no material reasons for Japan's defeat. It must have lost from lack of dedication and moral strength. So at the end of the war, in shame and despair he committed hara kiri.

Although by no means despising the spiritual as a source of strength, Genda believed that the Japanese relied entirely too much upon wishful thinking. They should have considered the international situation on a scientific basis and not have thought self-righteously that because Japan was a "God country" (Shimkoku) it could rely upon the one-sided support of heaven. Genda knew that nature plays no favorites. Hence he had excluded dependence upon Yamato Damashii (the Japanese spirit) from his tactical plan, because he believed the United States had a "Yankee Damashii" of its own.[19]

Captain Atsushi Oi, a keen student of the Pacific War, also declared that Japan would have been better off had her people been "more logical and scientific instead of nationalistic and emotional." Their sensibilities clouded their judgment, while the Americans, although sensitive in their way, mitigated their emotions with clear logic. In fact, at times they could be too analytical.[20] This was all too true. Based upon logical considerations, the Americans estimated that Japan would not attack Pearl Harbor from the air; they ignored the intangible forces of Japanese national emotions which enabled even such an otherwise coolly rational man as Tomioka to believe that it had been better to strike and be conquered than to wait until Japan collapsed from her own weakness.[21]

Aside from the folly of initiating war against such a combination as the ABCD powers, Japan's principal strategic error may have been that it tried to conduct two divergent campaigns at the same time. The Japanese have a saying, "He who chases two hares catches neither." The two alternatives are well personified by their devoted exponents, Kusaka and Genda.

Kusaka's strategy postulated total concentration on Southeast Asia. He regarded Yamamoto's venture as a questionable diversion of precious offensive power from the primary theater of operations. Let Japan move in where its main interests lay, using every weapon in the national arsenal, including the First Air Fleet. If Japan avoided striking United States territory, Washington would have no really grave self-interest at stake, so might confine its opposition to throwing more diplomatic notes at Tokyo. Even if Japan attacked the Philippines, Kusaka doubted that the U.S. Fleet would risk a deep penetration into the Pacific. But if the United States did dispatch its Pacific Fleet to challenge Japan's move, that would be fine with Kusaka. The nearer Kimmel's ships came to Japanese-dominated waters, the better the Combined Fleet's chances for a successful conclusion in a decisive naval engagement.[22]

Many Americans agreed in essence with Kusaka. They believed that had Japan ignored the U.S. Navy, putting all its power into a swift strike at Southeast Asia, the Japanese might have entrenched themselves before the slow processes of democracy set the American ships into action. "I think the attack on Pearl Harbor was the stupidest thing the Japanese ever did," said Bratton. "If they had gone about their way down through the Netherlands Indies, Malaya, Indochina, and leave [*sic*] us stewing in our own juices, the war might still be on, or we might still be arguing here as to what to do about it. We might never have declared war on Japan."[23]

The second choice was Genda's way: to make Operation Hawaii the central plan; to move across the Pacific with every ship and man Japan could float; to smash the U.S. Pacific Fleet at its moorings; to occupy and garrison the Hawaiian chain, then gobble up the American outer islands. Genda never ceased to regret that Japan did not "shoot the works" at Pearl Harbor.

"If only they had listened to me, we would have invaded Hawaii," he lamented in later years. "After the attack on Pearl Harbor and the other Oahu installations we could have taken Honolulu pretty easily." In Genda's opinion, "This would have deprived the American Navy of its best island base in the Pacific. It would have cut the lifeline to Australia, and that country might have fallen to us like a ripe plum." Nor did Genda's freewheeling imagination stop there. "I also was in favor of bombing the American aircraft factories and oil refineries on the California coast. In December 1941 we could have bombed San Diego, Long Beach, Portland and Seattle without much opposition."

With such a stunning series of victories pinned to the national belt, Japan's diplomats "could have tried to work out an advantageous peace settlement." Genda further explained, "We didn't seize Hawaiian territory because we didn't have any soldiers to occupy the territory. The army was saving its men for war against Russia."[24]

Safford argued that Japan's failure to make its objective the "capture of the Islands and the occupation of Oahu" was "the greatest mistake the Japs made in the entire war." He elaborated on this theme:

> The invasion fleet which hit the Philippines should have accompanied the P. H. Striking Force—to gain the fruits of victory. But this would have taken Jap Army concurrence—and the Army was in the driver's seat. The Philippines could have fallen into Jap hands like a ripe pear—once Pearl Harbor became a Jap Naval Base. . . . On the whole, the Japs spread themselves too thin.[25]

That Japan should covet the Hawaiian Islands was virtually a cliché of American military thinking. Six years to the month before the attack, G-2 estimated that one of Japan's plans probably would be "to attack at once with a view to the capture of Hawaii, Alaska, the Philippines and Guam." G-2 further suggested that the Japanese would assume "a generally active defensive attitude with the main fleet based on Japan and waging an active submarine war of attrition based on the Hawaiian Islands." This plan had among its advantages that of

> striking boldly at Hawaii, the most important strategic point in the central Pacific. It is equally important to either Blue [the United States] or Orange [Japan]. Its capture by Orange would hold the fleet in the eastern Pacific so long as Hawaii remained in Orange possession. This would in itself protect the Orange Mandated Islands and Orange proper against all Blue attacks.

However, such a plan had "grave disadvantages," among them distance. Above all, "Orange to capture Hawaii must be able to secure surprise." G-2 believed "that only a simultaneous attack and declaration of war could hope to succeed. Any period of strained relations would probably wholly negative [sic] surprise and success." Thus G-2 seriously overestimated the state of alertness which "strained relations" would produce in some quarters of the United States' armed forces. Despite the plan's drawbacks, G-2 cautioned that it contained "so many temptations and offers so many inducements which accord so nearly with the Orange character that it is safe to say that the plan has been considered and worked out in all its details and if opportunity beckons too hard Orange will succumb and make the attempt."[26]

Kimmel acknowledged that if Japan could have taken the Islands "it would have presented a very serious problem for us." But he could not bring himself to admit that the Japanese could have succeeded.

To his mind, "it would have been such a hazardous undertaking that they never would have tried it. . . . I do not believe they would have done it." Senator Lucas pointed out logically that the word "possibility" covered the surprise attack which likewise was "only a possibility. . . . But it happened."[27]

Both strategies, Kusaka's and Genda's, have much to commend them, and no doubt their relative merits will be debated as long as students of military history mull over past campaigns. However, the Japanese did not make a clear-cut choice between them. The Naval General Staff permitted Yamamoto to bully them into accepting his Pearl Harbor plan, but only as a tangential operation with an important yet limited objective. By no means had Yamamoto convinced the top brass of Operation Hawaii's necessity or its chances of success; they had folded under his threat of resignation. They doubted that the First Air Fleet could achieve surprise, hence must expect heavy losses, and questioned whether the results could justify the admittedly serious risks and probable cost.[28]

Two developments strongly suggest just how pessimistic were Japan's naval planners about Nagumo's prospects at Pearl Harbor. In the first place, plans for the long-awaited confrontation between the American and Japanese fleets, the so-called Great All-Out Battle, remained very much a part of Japanese strategy. Even after the Pearl Harbor project had been adopted, "the fundamental principle of encountering American fleets in the western Pacific remained intact as it had been," in Captain Ohmae's words. He continued:

> High ranking officers of the Naval General Staff at that time thought there were good possibilities of victory if such an operation could be carried out in the early stages of the war, but at the same time it seemed absolutely sure from any angle that the war would be a prolonged one. . . .
> . . . Consequently repeating this sort of tactics, the favorable strength ratio for Japan should be maintained, this impregnable position should be secured to wait for a favorable turn of the world situation, particularly in the European theater. Especially, Admiral Yamamoto . . . had a strong will to wage by all means a decisive sea battle by the end of 1942. . . .[29]

This strategy tacitly admitted that whatever results Nagumo might achieve at Oahu would not long upset the balance of power in the Pacific. Within a year, the Combined Fleet would have to fight a regenerated U.S. Pacific Fleet. What is more, Ohmae's remark about "subsequently repeating" expresses the thought that the Japanese knew that one Great All-Out Battle would not do the trick; they would have to keep playing return engagements merely to retain the status quo.

Genda, for one, had no use for the standard doctrine of the Great All-Out Battle,[30] but there was something to be said for it. The concept of luring the U.S. Pacific Fleet to the Western Pacific exhibited an understanding of the logistical problems in the Pacific war and the opportunity for Japan to exploit its geographical position. Retention of the plan acknowledged the reality that, even after Pearl Harbor, the U.S. Pacific Fleet would remain Japan's principal obstacle in its drive to dominate East Asia. The plan's weakness was its failure to consider that the U.S. Navy might not follow the Japanese pattern like a goose pecking after a trail of corn. Nimitz remarked that the U.S. Pacific Fleet had not the slightest intention of charging westward to fight on Japanese terms. They planned to move west when they were good and ready, not a minute before.[31] Ironically, when Yamamoto did lead forth his Main Body toward Midway for what he expected would be the long-awaited showdown, he never came within shooting distance of the American task forces.

Another demonstration of the Japanese planners' dim view of Operation Hawaii is the fact that they had no strategic contingency plan ready to implement in case Operation Hawaii turned out to be the success that it was.[32] Genda and Fuchida had worked out excellent tactical contingency plans, but such plans can only supplement strategic plans; they cannot substitute for them. And Genda and Fuchida were not in command of the First Air Fleet, much less the Combined Fleet or the Naval General Staff.

Had the Japanese possessed a plan to become effective should Nagumo soundly defeat the Americans, no doubt he would have taken Genda's advice to seek out the American carriers on December 7, 1941, and sink them if found.[33] Perhaps he would have remained in the area for a few days and hit Pearl Harbor again to put the rest of Kimmel's ships out of commission. But the Japanese planners were not psychologically geared to take advantage of such a glittering prospect. All they hoped for was to get this hazardous operation out of the way with as little damage as possible to the First Air Fleet, and bring its ships back where they belonged. Indeed, one of the stipulations Tomioka had made for his agreement to Yamamoto's plan was the return of the carriers as soon as feasible to take part in the Southern Operation.[34]

This goes far toward explaining why Nagumo and Kusaka decided to turn prows homeward as soon as the second attack wave's planes returned to their carriers. The two admirals had accomplished their mission with no damage to the ships and loss of only twenty-nine planes, which was all anyone had asked of them and much more.[35]

Safford ranged himself solidly among those who believe that the Nagumo force "should have stayed around and completed the job. . . . The Jap Navy never got another chance like this, the rest of the war." Many valuable and vital targets remained, such as the tank farms, ships in harbor, the dry docks, and scattered ships, all of whose personnel, if as mad as hornets, were "just as disorganized."[36]

Japan's most astounding tactical oversight in regard to Pearl Harbor, however, lay in the original concept. In view of the fact that rendering Kimmel's ships impotent for at least six months was the objective of Operation Hawaii, it is amazing that the planners did not include in Nagumo's mission a directive to smash the shore installations on Oahu. This would have denied the U.S. Pacific Fleet use of the only American base in the Pacific capable of maintaining it, and would have hamstrung the U.S. Navy far more effectively than by whittling at individual ships. This may well stand as the primary tactical flaw in the plan. As Bloch testified before the Hart inquiry, if Japan had struck the shore installations "we would have been damaged infinitely more than we were."[37]

But Genda later wrote that the question of demolishing the oil tanks only arose after the attack's amazing success. "That was an instance of being given an inch and asking for a mile." He insisted that the objective of the plan was to destroy American warships so they could not interfere with the Southern Operation; oil tanks did not enter into the original idea.[38]

As no one could charge Genda with lacking either imagination or breadth of vision, this uncharacteristic obtuseness could be due only to failure to understand the importance of logistics. Most Japanese naval planners apparently suffered from this same myopia toward the less glamorous necessities of modern warfare.

The Hawaiian Islands produced no oil; every drop had to be tanked from the mainland. Destruction of the U.S. Pacific Fleet's fuel reserves, plus the tanks in which it was stored, would have immobilized every ship based at Pearl Harbor, not just those struck on December 7. "All of the oil for the Fleet was in surface tanks at the time of Pearl Harbor," said Nimitz. "We had about 4½ million barrels of oil out there and all of it was vulnerable to .50 caliber bullets." He added, "Had the Japanese destroyed the oil, it would have prolonged the war another two years."[39]

Nagumo had a golden chance to repair this monumental error in mission assignment, but he was only too glad to save his precious carriers for future use.

The failure of the attackers to knock out Pearl Harbor's shore installations and to follow through with an attempt to take over Oahu seemed incomprehensible to many Americans. "So long as anything was left they had not completed the job," said Admiral Spruance. He thought the Japanese could have inflicted much more damage by hitting the submarine base, the tank farms, the docks and shops, the power plant, and the Honolulu telephone exchange.[40] Nimitz, too, emphasized that the attackers should have smashed the submarine base. "U.S. submarines were the first ships to go into action against the Japanese after the attack and they soon began to take a heavy toll of Japanese shipping," he recalled. "This attrition by our submarines weighed heavily in the scales of our eventual victory."[41]

In failing to include the submarine base among the targets at Pearl Harbor, the Japanese overlooked the fact that the undersea boat was the only ocean-going craft which could operate efficiently even though its nation did not enjoy command of the sea. Its very nature and purpose called for it to foray into enemy waters. Generally speaking, before the war the Japanese Navy did not think that American submarines would pose a threat to Japan. This idea persisted even after the outbreak of hostilities. They had little exact knowledge about U.S. submarines.[42] This tendency to shrug off the undersea menace may have had its genesis in the Japanese stressing the tactical offensive to the extent that they neglected to consider defense against enemy measures of this kind.

The Japanese Navy's cavalier attitude toward the U.S. undersea force also arose from misunderstanding the vital role merchant shipping played in winning a war. They credited their potential enemies with the same mentality. "Our Navy also estimated that the U.S. Navy had no intention to wage any extensive warfare against merchant marines," wrote Oi. "The Japanese Navy took for granted that the role to be played by American submarines would be quite the same as that of her own submarine forces, and slighted the role of commerce raiders."[43]

Japan's failure to take into account the need to keep its cargo shipping free of the submarine menace reflected its hopeful concept of a relatively rapid, purely strategical war, and its inability to make long-range plans, which Admiral Nishizo Tsukahara, Commander in Chief of the Eleventh Air Fleet in 1941, considered a serious weakness in Japan's prewar preparations.[44]

It was a measure of Japan's political and strategical shortsightedness that it traded the friendship of the ABCD powers, who could have provided it with oil and other supplies, for a sterile alliance with Germany and Italy and seizure of raw materials which it could not exploit fully because they were too far from the homeland.

Japan's planners never thought through the problem of how to move that precious oil from Southeast Asia to the home islands. The Japanese Navy consistently downgraded the vital area of protecting merchant ships—despite the example of the war in the Atlantic where the German Navy had nearly brought another island empire, Great Britain, to its knees, not by majestic sea battles but by steady U-boat attrition of merchant shipping.

In Oi's words, "American Navy men who are close students of Mahan may have doubts whether the Japanese strategists gave a moment's consideration to Mahan's lesson that only the nation which can both trade and fight will win a major war." Oi speculated that Japan's attitude might be "a problem of racial temperament." He explained, "Compared with the Europeans the Japanese are generally said to be more impetuous and less tenacious. They preferred colorful and offensive fighting to monotonous and defensive warfare. It was only natural that convoy-escorting and A/S [antisubmarine] warfare were not jobs welcomed by the Japanese Naval men."[45]

As the war progressed and American sea power grew to meet the challenge, Japan had to move its Navy to the oil, instead of bringing the oil to the great naval installations in the home islands.

By plunging into the Pacific war, Japan lost not only the official friendship of the ABCD nations and the benefits of their neutrality, it lost valuable connections in Central and South America, which it had been cultivating assiduously.[46] Throughout 1941 Japan's diplomats in Latin American capitals had been inquiring what their host nations would do if Japan and the United States went to war. The answers had been in effect that an attack upon one Western Hemisphere nation would be an attack upon all.[47]

Perhaps the Japanese had difficulty in believing that the Americas could set aside their many problems to present a solid front to outside aggression. But they did. As a result, Japan had to abandon a lucrative trade, another source of oil, the use of South American Pacific ports, and numerous active stations in its "legal" espionage system.

Just as the Japanese undercut their own best interests on the political and economic front, so they failed to use their magnificent Navy to its best advantage at and after Pearl Harbor. Yamamoto kept the Main Body of his Combined Fleet in the Inland Sea. At the time, it consisted of six battleships, two small aircraft carriers, and nine destroyers—not a weak force by any standard. Had Yamamoto augmented it by several cruisers and tankers, and sailed into the Marshall Islands when some of Vice Admiral Mitsumi Shimizu's Sixth Fleet submarines moved there, he would have been in a strategic position to exploit Japanese opportunities if the strike on Pearl Harbor proved a success. After refueling, the Nagumo force could have thundered down from the north for a second major attack while Yamamoto's Main Body steamed in from the south. In that case, the Japanese could have caught the balance of the U.S. Pacific Fleet in a giant pincers movement. In any case, after Operation Hawaii Yamamoto should have sent major fleet units to the Marshalls, Carolines, or other Japanese-held islands, whence they could harry the remnants of the U.S. Pacific Fleet before time permitted repair of the material and psychological damage inflicted at Pearl Harbor.

Of course, Yamamoto had a duty to protect the homeland, but in early December 1941 Japan had very little to fear from the Americans or British and nothing whatever from the French, Dutch, or Chinese. The ever-enigmatic Soviet Union, locked in life-and-death struggle with Germany, posed no immediate danger. The only possible threat that Japan could anticipate realistically was a submarine foray, and battleships are useless in antisubmarine warfare. Yamamoto's behavior in respect to the Main Body pointed up another major weakness in Japan's war plans—a tendency to compartmentalize. With their high sense of theater, in effect the Japanese wrote scenarios and brought each scene to a close at the artistically satisfying moment. They did not ask, "What happens next?"

Yamamoto had been disappointed when Nagumo did not strike Pearl Harbor a second major blow.[48] Yet Yamamoto was equally guilty of failure to pursue. "Thus the Japanese Navy has scant instance of a successful chase," wrote Masataka Chihaya. "I think fundamentally this is due to racial character." He cited sumo wrestling which "is not a game to the finish. A display of just one brilliant feat is all that is desired. Whether there still remains a surplus of fighting strength or not . . . is absolutely irrelevant."[49]

At the moment when Nagumo turned prows westward on December 7, 1941, Japan stood head and shoulders above any other nation in naval airpower. Yet in spite of this amazing achievement, only Japan's naval airmen appreciated the new, dominating role of carriers. Diehards could argue with considerable logic that for aircraft to destroy ships immobile at their docks proved nothing revolutionary. Surprise and initiative had triumphed over unpreparedness and smugness, as they had for uncounted centuries. Japan's failure to understand and exploit fully the shift in emphasis from surface to air always rankled with Fuchida. ". . . the American Navy learned much from the battle," he wrote. "Quite in contrast to this, the Japanese Navy proved itself not wise enough to realize the revolution in the nature of war after being satisfied with much more success than anticipated."[50]

Incredibly, the Japanese Navy broke up the First Air Fleet. They did not realize what a tremendous instrument of the offensive they had at hand, an instrument which they possessed virtually in spite of themselves. Instead, they took the attitude that with the one-shot Pearl Harbor operation out of the way, the carriers should set about their rightful business of supporting the Army.

To make sense of Yamamoto's acquiescence in thus disassembling a force which had proved its worth so overwhelmingly, one must remember his promise to the Naval General Staff that after Pearl Harbor the carriers would be available for use in the Southern Operation. No doubt Yamamoto believed that as an honorable man he must carry out his end of the bargain. Still, this development lends color to Toyoda's belief that Yamamoto did not truly understand the possibilities of naval air warfare, that he still thought in terms of the Great All-Out Battle.[51]

One can understand why students of military and naval lore do not include Yamamoto as one of the "great captains of history." As Commander in Chief of the Combined Fleet, he made mistakes, few if any worse than his Pearl Harbor project. But his position in Japanese tradition is secure. He belongs in a category even more select than that of the "great captains." He is one of those rare individuals remembered and honored for what they were rather than what they did. He had the supreme gift of inspirational leadership.

By the end of the Pacific war, the large red building that had housed the Navy Ministry and the Naval General Staff was a mass of charred ruins. *Nagato,* upon whose broad decks Yamamoto so often paced in company with his devoted staff officers, suffered destruction as a target for atom-bombing tests. Japan endured the pain and humiliation which are the inevitable lot of the loser in a major war.

"We once more refresh our horror at the colossal crime committed and are filled with a solemn sense of reflection and self-reproach," keened *Asahi* on December 7, 1945. "We sought by our own hand a world war which was reckless and outrageous and became a challenger with the result that we allowed our country to suffer serious bankruptcy from which it is difficult to recover. What was sown by us must be reaped by us."[52]

Yet the ultimate irony of the Pearl Harbor story is this: In the long run, Japan actually profited by the Pacific war, and in a totally unexpected way. In no other manner than by the utter crushing of its military power and prestige could Japan shake off the domination of the military. The Army had a stranglehold on the government, because by regulation the minister of war had to be a general on active duty, chosen by three generals, who could and did bring down cabinet after cabinet by refusing to name a minister, reassigning the incumbent, or removing him from active duty.[53] In later days, Nomura always referred to the dominance of the military over the civil arm as "the cancer of the Japanese system."[54]

Free at last from the self-perpetuating triumvirate, free of the psychology that glorified the warrior over the civilian, free of the expansionism that had stretched the whole economy out of shape, Japan could devote its enormous energies and the great gifts of its people to civilized pursuits.

Peaceful trade gave Japan access to the raw materials that had served as the principal rationalization for expansion. An enlightened program of control, rather than takeover of other people's territory, proved the answer to the overpopulation problem. Today Japan is an industrial and financial giant, winning in the factory and in the market the position it could not attain by force of arms. All of this came about with the cooperation of the nation which, according to Japan's militarists, had meant to destroy Japan entirely.

Over the broad sweep of history, it was Nomura's vision of his homeland that prevailed. He lived to see his beloved country well on the road to its true "manifest destiny"—not as Japan the overlord before whom Asia trembled, but as Japan the preceptor, carrier, banker, and manufacturer to the Far East and beyond.

CHAPTER 31

"A Mental Attitude"

Japan's psychological blunder—American attempts to explain Japan's victory at Pearl Harbor—Deceit—Surprise—U.S. overconfidence—Japan willing to accept the risk—U.S. assessment as possibility but not probability—Time factor—Hawaii's geographical isolation—"Cry wolf"—Hawaii theoretically aware of danger—U.S. underestimation of Japan

Japan's decision to initiate war on the United States by an attack on the U.S. Pacific Fleet might not have been the "strategic imbecility" it proved to be had the Americans been the type of people the Japanese thought they were. For Japan's fundamental error was neither political, strategical, nor tactical—it was psychological.

Retrospectively, it seemed incredible to any rational American that Japan would not anticipate the explosive reaction that would follow an attack on United States territory while Japan's diplomats in Washington were discussing a settlement. But this the Japanese did not do. They honestly thought they could strike Pearl Harbor, take over Southeast Asia, fight to a stalemate, then reach a compromise peace.

Throughout 1941, the United States tried to avoid a direct confrontation with Japan, even though it could have won the decision. The Japanese misinterpreted this attitude as moral weakness. At the level of the individual fighting man, the Japanese, dedicated to the samurai concept, apparently regarded GI Joe as "too dumb to find the right end of the pencil, and too scared to use it."[1] After the war, when circumstances had underlined this error, Chihaya lamented:

> When we first embarked on this war with the United States, we felt a very real fear of her enormous resources, nevertheless we were quite confident of our fighting spirit which we felt to be indisputably superior. . . . So we reckoned to beat America at the start. . . . After such initial victory we calculated to fight it through by sheer fighting

technique. With such a mental attitude we took the plunge. . . .

. . . We had entertained a great error in the survey of the American racial character. We had thought that we could easily tackle them and that a race steeped in material comfort, seemingly absorbed in the pursuit of pleasure, was spiritually degenerate. . . . We have discovered that bravery and self-sacrifice are not sole monopolies of the Japanese.[2]

The government-controlled Japanese press had conditioned its readers to an erroneous image of a badly divided and irresolute United States. Ambassador Grew had worried exceedingly about these Japanese pipe dreams. He testified to the Army Board:

> The Japanese people as a whole . . . discounted our intention to fight, or our ability to fight. They regarded us . . . as a "decadent nation," in which pacifism and isolationism practically ruled the policy of our Government . . . the Japanese people received what I considered to be a totally wrong impression of the spirit of the American people and the possibility that if sufficiently provoked the United States might go to war, and would be capable of waging total war, if it did.[3]

Unlike the Japan or Germany of the day, the United States had no sense of racial superiority, no mystical belief that it was destined to rule over a major portion of the globe and hence was fully justified in conquest by the sword. What most Americans did believe, most profoundly, was in their right to "life, liberty and the pursuit of happiness" in their own land without foreign interference. They also believed, almost as deeply, that no nation would be so foolish as to deliberately attack United States territory.

Thus the strike at Pearl Harbor was so unexpected, so stupefying, that from that day forward Americans have never ceased attempting to explain how the Japanese could have achieved surprise, let alone such an astounding degree of success.

The concept that Japan owed its victory on Oahu to sneak tactics found wide acceptance in the United States. The Hartford *Courant* observed indignantly, "the attack on Pearl Harbor occurred and was relatively successful primarily because of the almost unbelievable lack of scruples on the part of the government of Japan, which planned deliberate assault while talking peace."[4] Congressman John Jennings, Jr., of Tennessee, asserted, "This premeditated, deliberate, and cowardly attack upon the people of the United States by the assassins and bandits of the Pacific was deadly because it was treacherous and succeeded because it was unexpected."[5]

To claim that the Japanese owed their victory to surprise was all very well—but to what did they owe their achievement of surprise? That embarrassing question opened the floodgates of speculation, accusation, counteraccusation, explanation, and excuse.

Admiral Pratt wrote that men of the sea followed an honor code, so the U.S. Navy before Pearl Harbor "credited the Japanese Navy with the same high sense of honor that actuates us."[6] In a letter to The Judge Advocate General of the U.S. Army on March 1, 1944, Short's counsel made the same point: "The very fact that General Short had such a high standard of honor made it impossible for him to suspect the treacherous attack which the Japanese made."[7]

The American citizen of the day might well have wished that this high-mindedness had been leavened by a little realism. The attack was not treacherous by Japanese standards. For centuries, both at home and abroad, the Japanese had utilized the principle of initiating conflict by a surprise attack. Rear Admiral Chuichi Hara, who commanded the Fifth Carrier Division of the Nagumo task force, observed bluntly, "A surprise attack was in the tradition of the Japanese Navy, so the United States should have expected it."[8] Admiral Spruance, the hero of Midway, did not think much of the critics who belabored the Japanese for their "sneak attack." "That is the way they fought their wars, and we should have counted on surprise against us," he emphasized. "Surprise is one of the basic elements of war."[9]

Not only did the whole of Japan's military history point to an attack without warning, this had been the Axis pattern from Italy's invasion of Ethiopia in 1935 to Germany's attack on the Soviet Union in 1941. Surely any professional officer should have been able to look at the record and know what to expect.

With an objectivity astounding in the circumstances, the Lewiston (Maine) *Evening Journal* remarked, "Fundamentally it may have been madness for tiny Japan to attack mighty America; once set on such a course, however, the attack was carried out in the grand manner; to strike boldly, and first, at the heart of the enemy, is in the best tradition of military and naval lore."[10]

Despite the record of the Axis in seizing the initiative, no American attitude of 1941 stands out in sharper relief than the belief that the United States held the choice for peace or war, and enjoyed immunity to the forces of history beating around it. Americans seemed to be living in a dream world in which impeccable diplomats discussed problems reasonably and no country could find itself at war without at least the tacit consent of its people—certainly not without formal warning and time to prepare. Confidence that the United States was big enough, powerful enough, to give pause to any aggressor formed a part of this illusion.

Even those whose very lives were dedicated to defending the United States suffered from this myopia born of overconfidence. Major General Durward S. Wilson, who had commanded Short's Twenty-fourth Infantry Division, "did not think for a moment that Japan would attack the United States."[11] After the fact, the *Arizona Republic* acknowledged, "Every American, if honest with himself or herself, will admit that he or she hadn't the slightest idea that Japan would jump onto so powerful a country as this."[12]

In Rochefort's opinion, one significant reason why Japan caught the Americans napping on Oahu was the Americans' "fatal error" of believing that the Japanese would not start a war with the United States because they could not win it.[13]

At first glance, it seems reasonable that no nation will initiate a conflict without some expectation of ultimate victory. But it is not safe to assume that men of a totally different culture will share one's own thought processes. Ambassador Grew frequently warned Washington of the danger of gauging the Japanese by Western standards.[14]

Those in positions to estimate Japan's intentions apparently did not understand that to the Japanese, suicide, even on a national scale, might be preferable to real or supposed dishonor. Then, too, American leaders acted upon the basic premise that peace in itself was a desirable goal. The Japanese, however, worshipped the warrior virtues and considered armed conflict a part of the natural order, therefore not necessarily to be avoided. And they regarded death in combat from a much different angle than did their American opposites.

After the war, Chihaya wrote of the contrast between the Japanese and American attitudes toward the sacrifice of life: "Sometimes we die for death's sake, making the attainment of the objective something like a by-product. Americans . . . never court death for the love of it, but when the attainment of the objective calls for defiance of death, they do not fear to die."[15]

Many U.S. intelligence experts had spent years in Japan and understood this Japanese attitude quite well. Thus they should have comprehended that the Japanese, so practical in their foreign policy, so shrewd in business, so balanced in their art, were capable of going off the deep end militarily with total disregard for the terrible risks and loss of life.

Nevertheless, the high risk factors involved in the Pearl Harbor attack did worry its Japanese critics exceedingly. But the hazards at which the Tokyo brass had jibbed were tactical, not strategic. Most of those concerned were willing to accept the risk of war with the United States—as well as with the entire British Empire and the Netherlands—while still at war in everything but name with China.

Strategically, the United States was invulnerable to Japan. While not exempt from attack, it was impervious to serious, long-range national damage at Japan's hands. So the possible cost to itself which Japan had to evaluate, even if the Pearl Harbor attack should succeed, was not prompt tactical retaliation but eventual strategical retaliation. Thus one can understand why, although knowing that the Japanese Navy exceeded the combined forces of the U.S. and British navies in the Pacific, the Americans credited the Japanese with having better sense than to attack the United States and invite national disaster.

But this logical line of thought did not apply to Japan in 1941. The Japanese had what they considered an overriding incentive for striking the U.S. Pacific Fleet: to clear their eastern flank for the massive operations in the south where lay abundant raw materials and oil which, if properly exploited, would put Japan in a strong defensive position. They were willing to take that gamble even though the more responsible among them knew that the United States could crush Japan in a long war.

"Now, the hazard that they undertook . . . was something that I thought they would never take a chance on," Kimmel told the congressional committee. A little later he remarked, "I do not mind saying that one of the reasons why I felt Japan was not going to attack the United States was because it was national suicide for them to do so."[16]

Bloch believed the Japanese would move only against southeast China or Southeast Asia. "I didn't think that they would take on another adversary unless they had to. . . . I thought that the Japanese had their hands full . . . I don't think they wanted to go to war with us while they were in all this other trouble."[17]

As late as August 27, 1941, following the exceedingly touchy summer crisis, Bloch had written in part to his outlying station commanders, "Under no circumstances should anything be said or done . . . that will give the men the jitters or make them fearsome [*sic*] that something is about to happen, because I do not believe that is so."[18]

In these estimates Kimmel and Bloch had plenty of company throughout the armed services. Thus the U.S. Army and Navy made the mistake of assuming that the enemy's intentions would necessarily be predicated upon considerations that made sense from an Occidental point of view.

A well-known authority on military affairs, Major George Fielding Eliot, pointed out that high-ranking officers of the War Department General Staff had graduated from the Command and General Staff School when the "Method of Intentions" was taught. Eliot believed that "this faulty approach" undoubtedly contributed to the Pearl Harbor disaster. He wrote:

> It is a matter of establishing a mental atmosphere—the Japanese are probably going to do so-and-so, so it is more urgent that we act effectively, as far as we can, in that area. . . . The enemy's most probable intentions have been set up, have taken hold on thoughts and action.
>
> And the enemy does something else.[19]

In particular, the type of attack seemed to have been totally unexpected, to judge from some of the ex post facto testimony. Its army already bogged down for years in the endless, bottomless morass of China, yet obviously intent upon wholesale conquest in Southeast Asia, how could Japan possibly make a carrier-based air attack upon the United States' major Pacific base? One false move could mean the end of all Japan's grandiose war plans. As Marshall explained to the congressional committee:

> There was also this to be considered, which we always had in mind, and that is the great hazard the enemy undertook in sending his people so far from home. A surprise is either a triumph or a catastrophe. If it proved to be a catastrophe, the entire Japanese campaign was ruined. . . .
>
> So you have an enemy hazarding a great risk in this stroke.

Therefore you measure somewhat your means of defense against the hazard he is accepting in doing it.[20]

The offensive-minded Kimmel "knew the difficulties of an overseas expedition" such as Operation Hawaii. "I knew the short range, the steaming range of the Japanese aircraft carriers," he testified to the congressional committee. "I very much doubted their ability to plan and execute an attack such as they made."[21]

Bloch likewise recognized the immensity of the task. He thought primarily of "the long period of time required for carriers to traverse" the distance from Japan to Hawaii. The Japanese would have "to carry fuel enough presumably to come over and go back or to get fuel from tankers at sea"—a difficult operation.[22]

American Army and Navy leaders simply did not believe the Japanese would launch an air attack against Hawaii. "Now, about the possibility of an air raid, we did discuss it from time to time," Kimmel told the Roberts Commission. "I freely confess and so state that I considered an air raid on this place as a possibility, but by no means a probability."[23]

Bloch estimated that "an air attack by the Japanese in the Hawaiian area prior to a declaration of war was a remote possibility." He believed the order of probability to be: "(1) submarine attack against ships in operating areas . . . ; (2) blocking Pearl Harbor entrance channel . . . ; (3) laying magnetic or other mines off the entrance channel and in the approaches to the entrances to Pearl Harbor and Honolulu . . . ; (4) sabotage. . . ."[24]

Admiral Pye did not think that a Japanese air attack "was of sufficient danger, under the conditions, for changing our regular operating plan."[25] Captain McMorris declared, "I can recall no officer who felt there was a serious probability, and that perhaps all of us considered it a remote possibility."[26] Even Halsey, that staunch advocate of naval airpower, discounted the idea. "I did not think they could do it."[27]

The Army was no less skeptical. Short "believed that the possibility of an air attack was remote," largely because of the Navy's strength in the Hawaiian area.[28] General Frank of the Army Board asked Brigadier General Jacob H. Rudolph this question: "What was it [that] operated to build up this frame of mind that led you to the belief that 'it can't happen here'?" Rudolph answered honestly, "I guess I was like a great many others. I never thought that Japan would dare to do it."[29] A few days later, Frank inquired of Wilson, "Did you conceive of this air attack happening?" Wilson admitted, "No. No. I did not."[30] General Burgin stated to the Roberts Commission, "It never occurred to anybody's mind that the attack would be right here in Pearl Harbor."[31]

In addition to weighing the awesome risk, the problem of moving across the Pacific undetected and of refueling on the way, the U.S. Army and Navy leaders underestimated the Japanese naval air arm. A keen student of aviation, Bellinger realized that the Japanese "had a good air force because they have had so very much experience and practice in actual warfare." But he was mentally barricaded against reality. "I did not think they could pull off an attack like that as accurately and as well as they did," he admitted.[32] Neither did Kimmel. "I think that not only I, but all the Navy Department were very much surprised at the efficiency of their air force and the manner in which they conducted that attack."[33] Halsey stated, "I thought their equipment, according to the reports we had, was below what it turned out to be." He also testified later, "We underestimated their ability to operate carriers, or we did not give it enough consideration."[34]

No one in the Hawaiian command dreamed that aerial torpedoes could run successfully in Pearl Harbor's shallow water. Indeed, to quote Forrestal's Fourth Endorsement to the report of the Navy Court:

> The destructive potentiality of the air torpedo attack was not properly evaluated, although there was ample information available on this subject in the reports of action by and against the British. That this information was recognized is shown by the inclusion in war and defense plans of appropriate provisions for defense against this type of attack, but that it was not fully appreciated is shown by the fact that these selfsame provisions were not put into effect until the initial attack had been successful.[35]

The success of this Japanese tactic astounded Kimmel and his admirals. Nor had Bloch believed that bombs could penetrate the decks of battleships.[36]

Hawaii's defenders estimated that if by some chance the Japanese did attack, they would do so by submarine. Kimmel thought that what the Japanese "were going to do in case of war in the Pacific at all, . . . against the United States, was to have a mass submarine attack in the operating areas around Pearl Harbor."[37] Therefore, he "was constantly concerned with the question of submarines, and we took very effective steps, I think, to keep a submarine from getting any surface ships."[38] Bloch, too, "visualized heavy submarine attacks."[39] So did Admiral Brown, commander of Kimmel's Scouting Force. "I think we all had in mind the probability that Japan would have submarines in these waters before they made a declaration of war."[40] Halsey agreed. "I thought they would try some underhand method of attack, such as they did, but I thought it would be submarines."[41]

Yet for years U.S. forces in Hawaii had conducted maneuvers against the very type of strike launched against them on December 7, 1941. And why were antiaircraft batteries positioned on Oahu, if not in anticipation of at least the possibility of air raid? Certainly they were useless against submarines or sabotage or other forms of surface and undersea aggression. No wonder the congressional committee posed the "enigmatical and paramount question": *Why, with some of the finest intelligence available in our history, with the almost certain knowledge that war was at hand, with plans that contemplated the precise type of attack that was executed by Japan on the morning of December 7—Why was it possible for a Pearl Harbor to occur?*" (italics in original).[42]

This puzzle has intrigued everyone who ever tried to dig into the Pearl Harbor problem. Observed the Army Board:

> The contrast between the written statements of many of the responsible actors in this matter prior to Pearl Harbor and after Pearl Harbor, as to their estimate of an air attack by Japan on Oahu, is startling. . . .
> We must therefore conclude that the responsible authorities, the Secretary of the Navy and the Chief of Staff in Washington, down to the Generals and Admirals in Hawaii, *all expected an air attack before Pearl Harbor.* As a general statement, when testifying after the Pearl Harbor attack, they did not expect it. [Italics in original.][43]

This board suggested that the time factor might help explain the credibility gap:

> The military estimates of the situation . . . clearly show a reasoned and correctly stated analytical estimate of the situation. The missing

link in our search for the reason why steps were not taken to carry out the logic . . . seems to be in this belief that there was ample time to prepare Hawaii. . . .

As a consequence a policy was followed that was disastrous to the defense of Hawaii. They gambled upon having time for preparation that did not exist.[44]

For one thing, it was late in the year, and Japan was heavily committed elsewhere. So the commanders in Hawaii tended to believe that the opportunity for Japan's big move had still to come. Bloch wrote to Stark on October 23, 1941, "Things seem to be steaming up to a crisis and I believe that our most critical time in the Pacific area will be about next May, when the season will be right again for someone out here to start going north or south or some other way."[45] But the Japanese were not waiting for balmy spring weather to make their move.

The human inclination to believe what one wants to believe, to see what one wants to see, no doubt played a part in the Pearl Harbor drama. The United States wanted and needed time to prepare its forthcoming two-ocean navy, to get its army into shape, to build the aircraft necessary for a potent air force, and to send more aid to the Allies. Because Americans wanted and needed time, subconsciously they refused to consider the possibility that they might not have it.

One also wonders whether the climate and geography of Hawaii may not have affected its defenders. Author Stanley D. Porteus found "by no means fantastic" the idea that "the peace of Pearl Harbor" may have "contributed its share toward dulling suspicion and wakefulness."[46] Can one remain truly on the qui vive in such a setting of leisurely, peaceful beauty? The ideas of war and Hawaii seemed incongruous.

And if an enemy did approach, would not Hawaii's seas protect it? But developments of modern naval warfare had transformed the seas from moats into highways, and aircraft had left even the highway behind. In Bellinger's words, "Any island that is on the defensive where there are aircraft carriers available to come in . . . is in a very precarious position on the defensive."[47] Yet few realized the potential of the aircraft carrier and the "precarious position" of Hawaii in December 1941.

Quite the opposite! The illusion persisted throughout 1941 that Pearl Harbor was the "Gibraltar of the Pacific." Nevertheless, Pearl Harbor was not and never was intended to be a fortress as that word is understood. It protected nothing, and the Army on Oahu existed to protect it. Pearl Harbor was what the name implied—an anchorage—"a great big service station. Ships which come in here are supposed to be entitled to rest, freedom from watches, and sufficient time to put oil, food, and stores on board, and for hospitalization and recreation, and then to stay here a few days and then to go out," said Bloch. "They are not supposed to stay here. The place is supposed to be so defended that they do not have to do that."[48]

Pearl Harbor was theoretically impregnable in the sense of being inaccessible rather than unconquerable, which may be one reason why its defenders did not feel the urgency of the situation in 1941. This was Pearl Harbor's fatal weakness, for no fortress is stronger, no harbor more secure, than the alertness of its personnel. William D. Mitchell, counsel for the congressional committee, made this point in questioning General Gerow: "Is any fort impregnable, or safe from attack, however powerful it is, if the garrison is asleep at the switch?" Gerow made the only possible answer: "No, sir."[49]

Another intangible difficult to weigh in assessing ultimate responsibility for Pearl Harbor, but one which may have given the Japanese a featherweight of advantage, was the "cry wolf" syndrome. Under Kimmel, his predecessor Richardson, and others before them, Hawaii had held many maneuvers, exercises, blackouts, alerts, and warnings looking to a possible Japanese attack. "We have reams of paper here to show the exercises that we have conducted," said Pye.[50] ". . . . Once a week we had a blackout drill," Bloch testified.[51]

Of course, U.S. leaders on Oahu had the clear duty to train their officers and men against a possible Japanese strike. Yet constant drills, exercises, and false reports concerning the approach of a potential enemy who never comes can create attitudes not conducive to alert defenses. High-keyed, repetitive exercises can cause fatigue, induce indifference, and lessen sensitivity to danger. Crisis itself becomes routine. The War Department took this psychology into account in 1941. General Frank asked Marshall "Was any consideration ever given in the War Department to the possibility of a feeling of apathy that might ensue as a result of 'crying wolf! wolf!' too often?" Marshall replied, "Very much so."[52]

Among the Japanese who have voiced opinions on this question, Tomioka thought there was something in the "cry wolf" theory. He explained that Oriental tactics and psychology call for taking advantage of any weakness or temporary opening in the enemy's armor. No one can be on his toes twenty-four hours a day. The Oriental tactician awaits and exploits the "moment of relaxation" which must come.[53] Yet in the sense in which Tomioka used the expression, there never was a key "moment of relaxation" because the defenders were never truly keyed up to expect an air strike.

During the congressional investigation, Senator Brewster seemed intrigued by the "cry wolf" syndrome and questioned certain witnesses about it. "Now, Admiral Smith before the Hart committee said he thought there had been too much 'crying wolf,' that such warnings had been received not only during Admiral Kimmel's administration but also previously by Admiral Richardson," he remarked. Then he asked Kimmel, "Does that express to some extent your feeling as to the situation as far as apprising you of danger was concerned?" Kimmel replied, "To some extent, yes."[54]

But Admiral Wilkinson did not go along with that theory. Brewster wanted to know whether or not the various preattack warnings "had sort of the effect of hearing a cry of 'wolf, wolf' from them every 2 or 3 months or every month or so, with the result that they did not take it [the warning of November 27] as seriously as they would have taken it if they were in the position that you were at Washington, where you knew this time it meant business?"

Wilkinson thought, on the contrary, that "perhaps the Department refrained from sending an excessive number for that very reason, that they did not want to add up, to produce a wolf-wolf situation." Moreover, he did not believe "that there was an allayment or subsidence . . . of apprehension because of having received too many warnings."[55]

This "cry wolf" question has two sides. The congressional committee's majority report remarked, "It has been suggested, in explaining why additional warnings were not sent to Admiral Kimmel and General Short, that it was desired to avoid crying 'wolf' too often lest the department commanders become impervious to the significance of messages designed to alert them." However, the report pointed out:

> had Japan struck on November 28, the next day after the warnings, the same lack of readiness would substantially have prevailed as existed on the morning of December 7. There would have been no

lessening of alertness for the reason that the Hawaiian commands were at no time properly alert.[56]

Thus "cry wolf" in itself was a controversial subject. It was one of those nebulous psychological factors which one can argue pro and con. Some who have tried to exonerate Kimmel and Short completely attempt to have it both ways: on the one hand the two commanders had relaxed because of too many warnings; on the other hand they were not alert because they did not have sufficient warnings. Whatever the reason, the fact remains that Oahu was not ready on the morning of December 7, 1941. The question is this: Why?

Seth W. Richardson later wrote an interesting, popular account of the reasons for Pearl Harbor as he saw them. In this he stated that "after about August, 1941, and up to the attack on December 7, 1941, *the question of present danger to Pearl Harbor from such an attack seems to have faded from the minds of everyone!*" (Richardson's italics). He added, "after August, 1941, communications between Hawaii and Washington were practically barren of any reference to an attack on Hawaii or Pearl Harbor. Thus the fear of February had been supplanted by the complaisance of December 7th."[57]

It was true that after August 1941 correspondence between Hawaii and Washington held few references to "an attack on Hawaii or Pearl Harbor," if by that Richardson meant specific discussion of the subject. Nevertheless, Washington did warn Kimmel and Short a number of times after August, 1941, of possible Japanese military moves. Furthermore, all concerned had made their point in letters, plans, and other exchanges. These were matters of record. They had no reason to repeat themselves *ad infinitum* throughout the year. Moreover, as the congressional committee's minority report pointed out, "The whole raison d'être of the powerful naval and military installations in Hawaii, as publicly announced, was *defense against a Japanese attack*. Preparations for defense against attack necessarily implied the possibility of an attack" (italics in original).[58]

Nor had the awareness of danger "faded from the minds of everyone" on Oahu. In a speech in Honolulu on September 18, Kimmel had told his audience that they might "even be exposed to the physical hazards of war."[59] And in bringing his Pacific Fleet Confidential Letter No. 2CL-41 up to date on October 14, Kimmel postulated that "a declaration of war may be preceded by: (1) a surprise attack on ships in Pearl Harbor, (2) a surprise submarine attack on ships in operating area, (3) a combination of these two."[60]

Nor was the Army unaware of potential danger. On September 20, Martin prepared an exercise to be carried out on November 17–22. It had two objectives: to find and destroy the enemy at sea before he could attack, and to determine whether Japanese carriers could sneak up on Oahu undetected.[61]

Then, too, on November 5, Short issued a standing operating procedure (SOP) which superseded its tentative predecessor of July 14. Its twelve and a half printed pages, divided into five sections, covered every area of the Hawaiian Department. Detailed instructions to all major units spelled out virtually every conceivable contingency in case of attack, with the necessary actions to be taken in such event.[62] This document proves beyond doubt that Short's department had a theoretical "awareness of danger" well after August, 1941.

A genuine sense of imminent peril to Hawaii never existed, however, either before or after that date. What did exist was a sort of academic acceptance that a situation might arise involving a Japanese attack by air or submarine—more likely the latter—for which Hawaii must be prepared, just as any other military installation has its defense plan ready, regardless of how remote the possibility of attack may appear. As William H. Stringer of the *Christian Science Monitor* observed, "neither the American commanders in Washington, nor those in Hawaii, really, actually, seriously believed that a Japanese attack on Pearl Harbor was impending or likely."[63]

This lack of genuine, gut-level belief, as opposed to a cool, academic setting forth of theoretical possibilities, was the fundamental cause of the United States being caught flat-footed on December 7, 1941. All other sins of omission and commission were its sons and daughters.

Regardless of the lip service to alertness and of all the plans and exercises, at practical, working level the Hawaiian commands seemed to have thought and acted as though they were stateside stations. Take the matter of provision for protecting dependents. Lieutenant Colonel H. E. Brooks, commander, Battery A, Fifteenth Field Artillery Division, Twenty-fourth Division, had his family with him at Schofield Barracks. He testifed that neither air raid shelters nor slit trenches existed there. Apparently, he explained rather vaguely to the Army Board, some plan had been devised, "because they took care of that when it happened." But, as General Grunert pointed out, "the information was evidently not given to the families to know just what to do when it happened, without being told afterward."[64] This slipshod arrangement was eloquent testimony that those in authority on Oahu did not really expect danger, definitely not from the skies.

Numerous interrelated factors entered into this general failure to believe. One of these was the gross underestimation of Japan's economy, resources, financial position, industrial capacity, war-making capabilities, and the caliber of the Japanese people. This leitmotif had sounded throughout the U.S. press for years before the war. Even United States representatives in the Far East miscalculated. Hugh Grant, former U.S. Minister to Thailand, who had recently returned from Bangkok, estimated the situation in early December: "I am personally of the opinion that if the Japanese really want war now is the time to let them have it. I believe we could smash them within the period of a few months with our superior naval and air forces."[65]

The State Department was not immune to these views. Stanley Hornbeck wrote on October 31, 1941:

> With Japan as comparatively weak as she is today and with this country as comparatively strong as it is today, we need not fear unduly the military outcome—or even the immediate consequences—of such a conflict. This country is physically capable now of waging a properly conducted war with Japan and at the same time carrying on in the Atlantic all operations which it would be advantageous for us to make our business. . . .[66]

But the Americans were not, as Hornbeck erroneously indicated, in a position to wage a two-ocean war; the very opposite was true. Only a few days before Hornbeck's assessment, Admiral King had expressed his worry to a friend with paralyzing candor:

> The Navy cannot do much more than is now being done—we are still more than a year away from any marked accession of any ships of the "2-ocean Navy".
> The Army—when it gets trained—has, literally, "no place to go"—there aren't enough ships available (of the proper kind) to take it anywhere. The Air Corps is still in the throes of expansion—of organization—but it seems that they lack the planes to such a degree that they are not likely to be an effective force for many months— perhaps a year.[67]

Some people persisted in underestimating the Japanese even after the galling lesson of "Bloody Sunday." The very next day the Richmond *Times-Dispatch* wrote that "some of our experts think we can 'clean up' the Nipponese in six months."[68] Steve Vasilakos, the Greek peanut vendor near the White House, cut that estimate in half. "Just three months we finish them."[69] In Jefferson City, Missouri, the *Daily Capital News* stated, "Japan is shaking in her boots" and the United States would "soon starve Japan into submission."[70]

In November 1945, after the long, hard-fought war against Japan, Congressman Gearhart could still believe the Japanese stole their Pearl Harbor plans from the United States Fleet exercises: "The Japanese, who are notoriously without imagination, being familiar with the strategy through operation of their spy system, naturally decided to attack the islands in the manner which Americans had demonstrated in maneuvers was most likely to succeed."[71]

Anyone who reads American newspapers and magazines, and to a certain extent the documents, of the years before Pearl Harbor cannot miss the superiority complex, the arrogance and the overconfidence that afflicted many Americans. "We are victims of a familiar flaw in nationalistic psychology," stated the Dallas *Morning News*, "the conviction that we can lick our weight in wildcats on any day."[72] With this inflated self-image comes the conviction that when something goes wrong with American interests, somehow, somewhere, some American must be at fault. This helps to explain the conspiracy thesis and the numerous attacks on Roosevelt and other leaders in Washington.

Unfortunately, no calipers exist to measure such intangibles as superiority complex, pride, overconfidence, contempt for one's adversary, and the like; nonetheless, they were a part of that vast, complicated tragedy that was Pearl Harbor.

So perhaps it was not too surprising that the American military and naval leaders did not second-guess Yamamoto. Their opinions and attitudes sprang from the climate of the times and from the psychology of the people of which they were a part. Every one of them had served his country well in the past, and those who remained on active duty did so after Pearl Harbor. Every one of them paid for his errors in some coin—if not with a wrecked career like Kimmel and Short, at the very least in humiliation, self-blame, and above all in grief for comrades forever lost that Sunday morning.

CHAPTER 32

"In the Wake of the Pearl Harbor Disaster"

Immediate and long-range results—Loss of naval initiative—Respect for Japan's military power—U.S. mobile force remained—Shake-up in high command—Salvage of ships—American people united for war—Brought world crisis home to Americans—Air-power recognized—Call for unity of command—Loss of national self-assurance—Need for vigilance—"Imperialism" not dead—New respect for Chinese—Pearl Harbor not a sea battle in classic sense—American valor and resourcefulness under fire

The impact of Pearl Harbor was such that an entire generation of Americans tended to regard December 7, 1941, as the beginning of a new era in world history. Thus in honor of the silver anniversary of the disaster, *U.S. News & World Report* published an article entitled "25 Years After Pearl Harbor—An Attack That Remade the World." Under this encompassing heading, the magazine continued:

> The bombs that hit Pearl Harbor unleashed forces that produced a quarter century of the vastest changes the world has known.
>
> Since that morning, man has tamed atoms, moved into space, surged ahead in unprecedented prosperity in many parts of the world.
>
> Empires have vanished, maps changed, centers of power shifted. And a whole new set of problems has replaced problems of the past.[1]

The article then surveyed the vast political, economic, sociological, and technological changes that took place in the quarter of a century since December 7, 1941. However, Pearl Harbor was not the cause of these changes. Many, indeed most, would have occurred whether or not the Japanese had ever attacked the U.S. Pacific Fleet at Pearl Harbor.

Even to charge Operation Hawaii with responsibility for everything that arose from American participation in World War II would be to presuppose that, except for Pearl Harbor, the United States would never have become a combatant—by no means a provable or even a probable thesis. Nevertheless, many a filament of fate was spun forth from Oahu on that December day. Like all events, the attack produced two categories of results—immediate and long-range.

In the first phase of American shock, gloom reigned supreme. Military analyst Major George Fielding Eliot wrote, "This is perhaps the gravest hour in our national history."[2] Declared the Hartford *Times,* "We have suffered a loss that is both severe in terms of ships and men, and humiliating in the manner in which we permitted it to be brought about."[3]

The illusion that nothing could happen without United States permission died hard. Yet the United States had long since lost whatever political initiative it had in Asia, and loss of the naval initiative in the Pacific came with Pearl Harbor. "Hawaii was the key to all our operations," explained the *Wisconsin State Journal,* "and while Japan's prewar attack did not knock out this great base, the Japanese treachery did rob it and the fleet of the instant readiness America was supposed to have in the Pacific."[4]

Never had the balance of power been more rapidly and thoroughly reversed than in the Pacific by Operation Hawaii and the related Japanese campaigns. Air Chief Marshal Sir Robert Brooke-Popham considered the attack on the U.S. Pacific Fleet even more serious for the British than the loss of *Prince of Wales* and *Repulse.* "In appreciations of the situation we had always relied on the deterrent effect of the existence of this Fleet, even if the United States were not in the war from the start," he wrote. The ripples sped across the Pacific from Pearl Harbor to lap against Southeast Asian shores:

> An indirect result of the Pearl Harbor attack was to prevent the surface ships of the Asiatic Fleet from Manila cooperating with British and Dutch ships in the Java and South China Seas in accordance with the A.B.D. agreement. This Asiatic Fleet was, by orders from Washington, limited to operations between Sourabaya and Port Darwin.
>
> As a final result, the command of the sea acquired by the Japanese was greater than we had ever anticipated. We were, in effect, fighting

under conditions of which the British Empire had very little experience.[5]

Pearl Harbor, plus the sinking of the British men-of-war, had "determined the strategic pattern of at least the first period of the Pacific war," agreed *The New Republic*. "It is a pattern wholly different from that which has been confidently expected. . . . Until American reinforcements reach Pearl Harbor, therefore, the Hawaiian fleet presents no threat to Japan's home waters or her expeditionary forces. One whole side of the naval problem with which Japan would normally have to reckon has been screened off."[6]

The Pearl Harbor attack had indeed pared the claws of the American eagle. The day's losses weakened the Pacific Fleet and temporarily paralyzed its freedom of action. Bloch never spoke a truer word than when he testified to the Roberts Commission, "We are back on our heels."[7]

Any hope of reinforcing the Philippines or Singapore vanished in the smoke of the Hawaiian debacle. Stimson, who had worked hard to build up the Philippines, wrote in his diary on December 31, "now we have to sit helpless while our thirty years' successful experiment in laying the foundations of free government in the Philippine nation goes down in fragments under the military autocracy of Japan."

In his excellent reports of editorial opinion in the United States, Alan Barth observed a certain fluctuation. By December 19, 1941, he had begun to fear "that the current confidence prompted by the press will degenerate into a fresh complacency. . . . The traditional American contempt for the Japanese is not easily overcome."[8]

A perfect example of this mental holdover appeared in *The New Republic*'s issue of December 15, 1941:

> The Japanese have badly mauled Pearl Harbor; but they have not followed up their first success by the only decisive form of assault: seizure of the land by ground troops. To have attempted this would have meant risking Japan's whole battle fleet and a vast armada of transports 3,500 miles from their base; and this Japan cannot do. But so long as Pearl Harbor stands, the mid-Pacific remains ours: the attack accomplished much, but proved nothing. . . .
>
> Japan has used up her valuable store of initial surprise upon mere extremities. . . . What happens from now on will involve the frontal clash of metal on metal. And our metal is heavier.[9]

There was some truth in this comment. Yet the calm confidence that Japan could not take Hawaii echoed the old smug assurance that the Japanese would never risk an air strike on Pearl Harbor. Far from proving "nothing," Pearl Harbor had proved several things, one of these being the folly of making unqualified pronouncements of what Japan could or could not do. The attack likewise proved that Japan was prepared to take incredible chances to further its war aims. Indeed, less than six months after this article appeared, Japan initiated the battle of Midway, one of the objectives of which was the eventual takeover of the Hawaiian Islands.

But this lingering habit of underestimating the Japanese did not endure for long in the face of their amazing series of victories. "It was not until the middle of the past week that the newspapers began to realize that further serious reverses were almost certainly in store for the British and American Far Eastern forces," Barth noted on December 26. "Now, suddenly, the downswing has set in."[10]

The "downswing" continued well into 1942. "At Pearl Harbor we almost lost the war in a morning. We can still lose the war," military analyst Hanson W. Baldwin warned his readers.[11] February found Stimson worrying over evacuation of Japanese from the West Coast. He feared that the application of this policy would "make a tremendous hole in our Constitutional system." On the other hand, he thought it possible that should the Japanese obtain "naval dominance in the Pacific they would try an invasion of this country; and, if they did, we would have a tough job meeting them. The people of the United States made an enormous mistake in underestimating the Japanese. They are now beginning to learn their lesson."[12]

But few Americans, certainly not Stimson, truly doubted the Allies' ultimate victory. This long-range optimism was very different from the old fatuous cocksureness. The United States now built its house of confidence upon the rock of American strength, not upon the sands of supposed Japanese weakness. The Pearl Harbor attack and Japan's swift conquest of Southeast Asia jolted the American people into realization that in the Pacific no less than the Atlantic the free world faced a formidable foe. "Gone—and well gone—is the foolish boast that we could defeat Japan in 'three weeks,'" declared the Milwaukee *Sentinel*. "Gone is the false theory—and our shallow trust in it—that all we had to do to win the war was to send a few planes over Japan, drop a few bombs and thus dispose of the Japanese by burning their tinder-box cities and homes."[13]

Nomura followed with keen interest the progress of the war as well as American actions and public opinion. He noted this change of attitude in his diary on December 14: "They seem to have awakened from their dream of underestimating Japan's real power. Especially in regard to the real power of our Navy, particularly in its air wing, we come across comments which say that it was *grossly underestimated* and that our bombings have *fiendish accuracy*'" (Nomura's italics).

In their newfound respect for the Japanese, thinking Americans realized that a hard road lay ahead. On January 17 Stimson met with some labor leaders at the request of Secretary of Labor Frances Perkins. To this gathering Stimson laid it on the line:

> I told them that our people had grossly under-estimated the fighting capacity of the Japanese; that Japan was situated in one of the stormiest oceans of the globe and its people were among the best natural seamen in the world; that I had seen their fishing fleets when I was in the Philippines and knew how they visited all portions of the Pacific, risking every kind of weather and storm with great skill and courage. I told them that thus far the Japanese had made no mistake of strategy or tactics in the war except the one big mistake of tackling the United States, which it was up to us to prove was a mistake.[14]

Many members of Congress drew long faces, among them the ever-quotable Adolph J. Sabath of Illinois. He painted a portrait in gray of the ordeal to be faced before the gong sounded for the last round. "We will not win this war until we can show that we have fighting power that is superior to that of the enemy, both in ships and men, and that means blood and death and plenty of it."[15]

Following the unpleasant revelations in the Roberts report, Congressman Charles A. Plumley of Vermont asserted that the American people "should be given to know that this is going to be a grim, long, brutal, bloody war, not easily to be won."[16]

The press echoed this sense of realism. ". . . Although no sane person in this country doubts our ultimate success, it will be after bitter disappointments and heart-breaking delays," the *Salt Lake Tribune* cautioned its readers. "Americans will lose 'blood and sweat and tears' before the conflict is finished and undue elation now will only generate deeper gloom in the future."[17]

Knox could see both the rocky path and the shining goal at its end. He wrote to Bloch on January 19, 1942, "we are fighting with barbarians, who among other traits have also the quality of barbarian courage. They are not going to be an easy foe to crush, but in the long run there can be but one end to that road—complete victory for us."[18]

As emotions cooled to the point where a logical appraisal was possible, Americans began to realize that, in the words of the Chicago *Daily News,* "Out of our profound national humiliation . . . it is still possible to extract some grains of comfort."[19] Bloch came to believe that in a way the Japanese had done the Americans a favor, by destroying "a lot of old hardware."[20] As Professor Thomas C. Hone has written, "The American battleships were all old; several were nearly overage; most were overweight. None of the battleships in Pearl Harbor was a first-line warship in a material sense; all had recognized deficiencies."[21]

To a certain degree this was cold comfort. Obsolescent those capital ships might have been, but they were all the Pacific Fleet had. What remained, however, were cruisers, destroyers, submarines, the unglamorous but vital support ships, and, above all, the carriers *Enterprise* and *Lexington,* which had been at sea when the Japanese struck. In effect, Yamamoto had unintentionally presented the United States with a modern, carrier-oriented Pacific Fleet. And the men were there to meet the challenge. Soon the Pacific rang with new names—Halsey, Spruance, Marc A. "Pete" Mitscher, and many more, masters of naval air warfare.

Of course, at the time of Pearl Harbor the officers and men on Oahu were in no condition to indulge in such objective analyses. When Nimitz assumed command of the U.S. Pacific Fleet, he found that he had inherited officers excellent, experienced, but badly shaken. "Now all of these staffs were in a state of shell shock," Nimitz explained, "and my biggest problem at the moment was morale. These officers simply had to be salvaged." He succeeded in lifting spirits from below the decks, but it took him about six months.[22]

Nimitz owed his new command to Pearl Harbor, for one immediate result of the Hawaiian disaster was the shake-up in the Navy's high command. While such shifts are almost inevitable in war, one may assume that had the United States entered the conflict in a less humiliating fashion, Stark and Kimmel would have remained in position. To speculate whether or not this team could have led the Navy

as well as or better than did King and Nimitz is profitless. The change
did take place, and the new commanders did succeed brilliantly.

Logistically speaking, matters at Pearl Harbor were less serious
than appeared in the first shock. As previously stressed, the Japanese
had left the tank farms and machine shops intact, hence Pearl Harbor
remained, as before, the U.S. Navy's prime, indispensable base of
operations in the Pacific. And thanks to Pearl Harbor's shallow waters,
most of the damaged ships proved salvageable. The full impact of
what this would mean to the Navy only struck home to the general
public with the passage of time. But almost as soon as Nomura had
a moment to reflect upon the meaning of Pearl Harbor, he realized
that the United States would soon refloat the majority of the damaged
ships. This he considered the major tactical weakness of the operation.[23]

The story of how those vessels were restored to active duty is in
itself an inspiring record of skill and determination.[24] Eventually the
magnificent "Navy behind the Navy" salvaged all but three. Of these,
one was the old battleship *Utah,* long out of consideration for combat.
Her guns removed, she had remained on active duty only as a target
ship. She was not worth the time and expense of restoration, so she
still rests on the bottom of Pearl Harbor, the tomb of some fifty-eight
men.

Too severely smashed to be of further use, *Oklahoma* had to be
moved to clear her berth. Eventually she was refloated and dry-
docked. In December 1946, the Navy sold her for scrap. But on her
way to the mainland under tow, *Oklahoma* ran into a storm and sank
on May 17, 1947. "Everyone I knew cheered the fact," said Edgar
B. Beck, who served aboard her on December 7, 1941, "because we
never wanted the ship to become scrap."[25]

After investigation, the Navy decided to remove *Arizona*'s topside
and leave her in position, a fitting resting place for her dead. Today
a beautiful memorial covers the sunken hull, a shrine of pilgrimage
for many visitors and a silent protest against smugness and unpreparedness.

As early as December 20, 1941, *Pennsylvania* sailed under her
own steam to the West Coast for overhaul. That same day *Maryland*
and *Tennessee* were ready for action. To the great glee of all concerned, the destroyer *Shaw* left for Mare Island in California on her
own power on February 9, 1942. She fought to the end of the war,
winning eleven battle stars.[26]

At first, the only object in working on the destroyers *Cassin* and *Downes* was to clear the drydock. Upon examination, however, their machinery and hull fittings proved in better shape than expected. Eventually these parts reached Mare Island, where they became the motive power for new hulls. The reincarnated *Downes* and *Cassin* put to sea in November 1943 and February 1944, respectively. Subsequently both racked up excellent war records. [27]

Although no pessimist, Nimitz doubted that *Nevada* would ever sail again. But, incredibly, the Pearl Harbor Repair and Salvage Unit had her in drydock by February 18, 1942, and en route to Bremerton on April 22. She took part in the Aleutian campaign and the Normandy invasion, sailed back to the Pacific and all the way to Japan. [28]

California presented yet knottier problems, but she left Pearl Harbor for Puget Sound Navy Yard on October 10, 1942. Modernized and refitted there, a virtually new *California* joined the Fleet less than a year later, winning seven battle stars in the Pacific. [29]

In worst shape of all capital ships not actually lost was *West Virginia*. Her restoration surprised even the incorrigibly positive thinkers at Pearl Harbor. In a real triumph of technical skill, she was raised, sailed to Puget Sound, and celebrated the Fourth of July 1944 by heading out for combat. She was in time for the landings at Leyte Gulf and was the first old battleship to anchor in Tokyo Bay. [30]

Even the decrepit minelayer *Oglala*, a survivor of the "Old Fall River Line" passenger service and of World War I, was surfaced. She reached Mare Island and in February 1944 returned to duty in the South Pacific. [31]

But the salvage and reclamation of the ships feared lost, however important and inspirational, could not compare in importance with the welding job the Japanese had done on the American people. Yamamoto could not have devised a method more surely calculated to unite the nation and instill it with the will to win. "Isolationism and America Firstism are deader than a bombed soldier at Hickam Field," wrote *Time*'s Fillmore Calhoun from Chicago. And in Boston a sailor expressed the aggressive national will: "It's me or them—and I'll make damn sure it's not me." [32]

After Japan's surrender, an American correspondent asked Admiral Hara whether he had received any medals from the Emperor for participating in Operation Hawaii. "On the contrary," he replied, "I should have received medals from the American side rather than from the Emperor." Thus "King Kong" conveyed his conviction that, "but for the Pearl Harbor attack, the United States would not have been united as one people for war."[33]

"At Pearl Harbor was sounded the death knell of leadership of false prophets, who under delusions of keeping us out of war, would have stopped preparations for defense, and who chorused with Lindbergh that we should make friends wih Germany, the probable winner of the conflict," declared Congressman James O. Scrugham of Nevada. "Gone or quiescent are the influences that feared to offend Japan and encouraged their vast imports of war materials from the United States. A costly and tragic lesson in foreign relations has been given us."[34]

Some individuals expressed a sense of moral relief that the United States had to come out of the bushes and in effect put its money where its mouth was. "It is our gain that these attacks have unified the American people as nothing else could possibly have done and put an end to the essentially dishonest policy of taking part in war without declaring it," stated Donald W. Mitchell in *The Nation*.[35]

However, one can easily misunderstand and exaggerate the nature and extent of this unity. Those who had disliked Roosevelt's style and policies did not suddenly convert into true believers; isolationists did not change retrospectively into interventionists. What the Japanese did was harness the national energies for a clearly defined purpose.

As we have emphasized, no major cleavage had existed in goals, only in ways and means of attaining them. A mere scattering of fanatics had hoped for an Axis victory. Thus, what Pearl Harbor accomplished was not a marriage of opposite American objectives but an elimination of choices. In fact, as *The New York Times* stated in a searching analysis, a division of sentiment had often existed in the same person:

> The history of America's attitude toward the war is not the history of one fixed group of persons against another fixed group. It is the history of individual indecision, vacillation and heart-searching. . . . Many an American found himself in a state of Hamlet-like irresolution; he was an "isolationist" one day, when he thought of the fearful costs of war, . . . and an "interventionist" the next day, when some new Nazi or Japanese crime made his blood boil, or when Britain seemed in greater peril and time seemed running short. . . .
>
> That is why the treacherous attack by Japan, and the declarations of war by Germany and Italy, instantly united us and at last brought to many Americans, more than anything else, a sense of relief. Their spirit was no longer troubled; their soul was no longer divided; they knew at last what they must do.[36]

Allied to this clearing of the path was the realization that the United States had truly become a part of the world community. By the same token, the Japanese had personalized the conflict for the individual American. No longer could he or she regard the world conflict as essentially outside his or her orbit. The underhand nature of the attack gave the American people a sense of unbeatable moral ascendency, while the devastating losses in manpower and material convinced them that they faced a foe worthy of the United States' best efforts.

Indeed, the Japanese attack stimulated the realization that the true enemy of free men everywhere was the totalitarian philosophy. Many thinking Americans, in government and out, had understood the Axis aims and had tried most earnestly to warn their fellow countrymen. They organized meetings and spoke over the radio. They wrote books and articles.[37] But the most persuasive of speakers, the most logical of writers, cannot succeed unless heard and read. To a large extent, those who listened to the speeches and read the words of such modern Paul Reveres had at least a partial understanding of the danger. For one who did not comprehend, or who did not want his placid little pond ruffled, it was all too easy to tune out, literally or figuratively, anyone he did not want to hear.

There was something insidiously disarming about the very openness of the Axis aims. Before World War II, Germany and Japan flaunted their objectives and the means by which they intended to attain them. Hitler had published his blueprint for conquest in *Mein Kampf*, and his followers sang "Today Germany, tomorrow the world." In Japan the press expounded explicitly the theme of Japan's right and intention to dominate Asia and to expand to the south. Axis propagandists knew that the surest way to inspire disbelief was to tell an unpalatable truth loudly enough and often enough.

But Japanese torpedoes and bombs spoke a language everyone had to understand. Dead and crippled Americans, sunken American ships, and incinerated American planes conveyed a message that the most obtuse could not fail to read: The Axis did indeed cherish lethal intentions toward the United States; no compromise could be reached with this evil; the good life would be impossible in the Americas if they should be squeezed like lemons between a Nazi Europe and a Japanese Asia. Here was an enemy worth the cost of battle and a cause worth the best every American adult could bring to it—even life itself.

Thus, another casualty of Pearl Harbor was the United States' false sense of security. The Washington *Post* conceded that the Japanese bombs "did a lot of damage we could ill afford." Still, these same bombs "did most damage to our illusions, and in this respect the damage was a blessing. They shattered the remaining sense of aloofness and of security which the span of two great oceans had provided."[38]

With the realization that the seas no longer represented security, the Americans understood that Pearl Harbor had given the cause of aviation a high lift. But it was really the loss of *Prince of Wales* and *Repulse* that clinched the conviction that naval airpower had come to stay. The Denver *Post* remarked that Pearl Harbor "showed us how to win the war." That attack, plus the sinking of *Prince of Wales*, "taught the leaders of American armed forces a lesson which not only cost the Japs the war but hastened their downfall."[39]

Many a legislator climbed aboard the winged bandwagon. Senator Joseph C. O'Mahoney of Wyoming told his colleagues that the sinkings of the British ships demonstrated to his satisfaction

> that the fault at Pearl Harbor lay not with the personnel upon any of our naval vessels but to the fact that the new weapon of warfare, the air force, which is capable of executing tremendous destruction, has not been sufficiently developed by this nation. . . . The British battleship *Prince of Wales* and the British cruiser *Repulse* were not taken unawares. Yet they suffered exactly the same fate that was visited upon some of our vessels in Pearl Harbor.[40]

In the House of Representatives, Jed Johnson of Oklahoma called the two disasters "a costly but valuable lesson. . . . No battleship, irrespective of its size or cost, can stand the gaff against the modern air bombers, especially those equipped with torpedoes."[41]

The star of the battleship sank as that of the aircraft carrier rose. But the big-ship advocates went down fighting. "The battleship is still the core of the fleet," insisted Admiral Pratt almost three months after Pearl Harbor. He added, "Our larger aircraft carriers could be more efficient in a shuttle service for fighter planes than they would be if used to form a fleet nucleus or engage in extraneous operations."[42]

Yet as the war progressed it became more and more clear that the advocates of air power were carrying the day. The conviction that air power had come of age brought with it recognition that a separate air force was highly desirable. "Supremacy in the air for the United States is an indispensable essential to the continued existence of this democracy," asserted Senator Pat McCarran of Nevada. And he called for "the establishment of a trinity of defense for our country"—an army, a navy, and "a separate, unified air force."[43]

This question, with the closely related one of unity of command, came bobbing up throughout the war, and surfaced with each Pearl Harbor investigation. Representative George H. Bender of Ohio called vigorously for unified command: "It would seem obvious after Pearl Harbor that the division of authority prevalent there was a large contributing factor in the losses sustained by our fleet." Declared Bender sweepingly, "These are days when the sacred cows of military usage must be thrown out of the window."[44]

Throughout the summer and early autumn of 1945, a congressionally authorized investigation was under way concerning possible unification of the armed forces. This investigative body summed up its conclusions concerning "Pearl Harbor and the Issue of Unification" thus:

> It seems manifest, therefore, that the Pearl Harbor disaster did not expose a system that failed, but rather the failure of key individuals to discharge with imagination and foresight the military-naval defensive responsibilities which rested upon them. It cannot be validly contended that the parallel failures of two key individuals prove that there would have been no failure if only one key individual had been involved. . . .
>
> The Pearl Harbor experience serves mainly to emphasize the fact that no organizational form can take the place of eternal vigilance.[45]

There is considerable wisdom in this conclusion, but some question as to its objectivity. Senator David I. Walsh of the Senate Naval Affairs Committee recommended this unification study, and Ferdinand Eberstadt conducted the inquiry at Forrestal's request. The resulting report was for the use of Walsh's Committee on Naval Affairs. The Navy opposed unification fore, aft, and amidships, so a favorable report might have sent its writer to walking a figurative plank. This attitude was why the Milwaukee *Journal* remarked nastily, "What happened out there [at Pearl Harbor] as a result of our disjointed way of handling defense overshadows any theoretical advantages of separate establishments that the navy continues to cook up."[46]

The Pearl Harbor congressional committee's majority report concluded that command by cooperation was unsound by its very nature. Yet Washington had assumed that it "was working within its limitations. . . . It was only in the wake of the Pearl Harbor disaster that the inherent and intolerable weaknesses of command by mutual cooperation were exposed."[47]

For all the clamor, a Department of Defense did not come about until well after the war. And unification, in the sense that it had been urged, did not occur. The U.S. Air Force was formed essentially from the Army Air Corps. The Navy retained its own air arm, and the Army too had support planes under its aegis.

Not all the tragedy of Pearl Harbor could be measured in terms of lost men, ships, and aircraft, nor all its glory in terms of courage, unity, and the seizing of a new day. With the events of December 7, 1941, something happened to the American spirit. The flames of Pearl Harbor burned away a certain national innocence.

As a general rule, the average American of the day did not expect or fear evil at the hands of his neighbors. One trusted one's associates. Any other attitude was faintly disreputable. Much better to be deceived, which was human, than to be suspicious, which was ignoble. A part of this innocence was a creed of conduct, and one of its tenets was this: Gentlemen do not land sneak punches on each other.

But Japan hit Uncle Sam below the belt. Now a champion may be out for the count of ten and still remain a fighter of championship caliber. He may well be a better man for the experience. He may even regain his title in short order and by a decisive margin. But some element of careless self-assurance will be missing. In Robert Browning's poignant words, "Never glad, confident morning again."[48]

Pearl Harbor drove the idea of surprise attack so deeply into the national psyche that "Pearl Harbor" became almost a generic term for any sneak strike. The United States became extremely surprise-attack conscious—and rightly so. After World War II, it was generally agreed that any future attack almost certainly would be in the nature of a surprise. Therefore, the nation must be alert. "There is no defense against treachery except eternal vigilance; such vigilance as is confined not to a few officials in Washington or in isolated spots; but vigilance which includes all the people, and vigilance in which patriotism far transcends greed," warned the St. Louis *South Side Journal*. "Pearl Harbor is the price we paid for unpreparedness."[49]

With such ideas in mind, Senator Alexander Wiley of Wisconsin cautioned, "We must forevermore heed the lesson of Pearl Harbor, a lesson of vigilance, preparedness, adequacy for every future military contingency," especially in the context of the atomic age.[50] The advent of the atomic bomb and the tremendous international tensions thereby generated made it extremely unlikely that a formal declaration of war would ever again precede the fact. No aggressor could afford to tip off his intentions toward his victim. The more deadly the weapons developed, the more likely it became that a future war would begin, and to all intents and purposes end, with a surprise attack. The atomic powers have the ability to destroy a nation's industrial and population centers within minutes. Hence, wrote J. David Singer, "the vicious psychological circle" of the concept of preemptive attack.[51] The editors of *The New Republic* went even further:

> We can see now that if a long-range, nuclear strike is to have a real chance not only of "destroying" the enemy but also of eliminating the weapons with which he might almost simultaneously "destroy" us, the strike must be a genuine "first" strike—made with our full force, not with what is left after an enemy as had a chance to blunt our attack force with a first strike of his own. And this would appear to dictate that our only *convincing* threat is the threat that *we might launch a surprise attack.* [Italics in original.][52]

In other words, the concept of a retaliatory strike may be obsolete. The aggressor who hits fast enough, hard enough, and at sufficient key points, may well leave the victim nothing with which to retaliate. If this be true, the old "balance of terror" loses its terror. For at least that concept rested upon a healthy regard for what the enemy might be able to do in response to an initial attack.

More than one source pointed out that democracies are particularly vulnerable. Jonathan Daniels wrote of Pearl Harbor, "Perhaps in all history no event had ever served so well to show both the difficulties and the durability of democracy, and the ease with which those contemptuous of democracy can move to both violence and folly." He had no illusions that Pearl Harbor might be a freak of history. "The whole procession to Pearl Harbor, indeed, is a process which could be repeated again."[53]

Certainly the attack made the American people gun-shy, and taught them that peaceful intentions toward one's neighbors do not guarantee that such sentiments will be reciprocated. Fortunately, the United

States was able to ride out the Japanese strike at Pearl Harbor, as well as their conquest of Wake, Guam, the Philippines, and all of Southeast Asia. In the long run, American strength was bound to prevail, as long as the will to win existed. This the Japanese had assured by hitting Pearl Harbor. But there is no automatic guarantee of any such "happy ending" to the story for the United States if history should repeat itself.

In the days, weeks, months, and even years historically close to December 7, 1941, some experts in their fields made exaggerated claims for Pearl Harbor. "Few systems have experienced such a swift and uncompromising judgment as imperialism suffered during the ten weeks between the attack on Pearl Harbor and the fall of Singapore," wrote William Henry Chamberlin. ". . . . With dizzying, bewildering speed four great bastions of white supremacy and white prestige in the yellow and brown world of the Far East, Shanghai, Hong Kong, Manila, Singapore, fell before the Japanese onrush."[54]

Obviously, Chamberlin made the not uncommon error of equating "white supremacy" in Asia with imperialism as such. Pearl Harbor and the related Japanese campaigns did not sound the death knell of the latter. True, Japan's military exploits marked the beginning of the end of the Western brand of imperialism in the Far East. But Pearl Harbor itself resulted from Japan's determination to establish its own Asiatic empire. Germany's blatantly militaristic imperialism still dominated Europe, while the Soviet Union's more subtle ideological variety continued after the war without missing a beat.

What happened after Pearl Harbor was less a death than a birth— emergence of a new respect for the Japanese. Heretofore Japan's conquests had been at the expense of her fellow Asians. On December 7, 1941, the men of *Dai Nippon* deliberately engaged and tactically defeated the most powerful of the Western nations. For this, Americans of the day hated the individual and collective Japanese gizzard, but they had to accord the attackers a solid measure of respect, however grudging. On that day, the Western world fully accepted Japan as a potent international force. What centuries of culture had not accomplished, less than an hour of combat brought about.

With Pearl Harbor, a new element entered the American attitude toward China. Past sympathy, although very real, had sometimes contained a hint of patronage and impatience. Why did China not patch up her internal squabbles and crush the invading Japanese like an elephant stepping on a column of ants? After Pearl Harbor, however, the average American could agree with Stark's comment of the preceding summer: "I take my hat off to the Chinks."[55] It was now obvious that the Chinese had not allowed themselves to be intimidated by a house cat with delusions of grandeur; they had contained a tiger.

Noted commentator and analyst of naval affairs Fletcher Pratt reached other overdrawn conclusions from the Japanese attack:

> They had upset a strategic pattern that had ruled the Pacific since the first Roosevelt sent his fleet there in 1907, and destroyed a tactical pattern that had dominated sea warfare since the days of Queen Elizabeth. The first was that the American battleline controlled the ocean to the distance it could cruise from a friendly port without refueling; the second (and much more important) was that ultimate decision on the sea rested with the fleet able to put into its battleline the greatest number of heavy guns.
>
> By their computation, having struck our fleet from the balance sheet of the war, they were free to achieve their long-desired empire of the Indies. . . . [56]

This statement sounds authoritative at first reading, but deserves a second look. Pratt's initial premise, about "the American battleline," may be theoretically correct, but by 1941 it held little practical meaning. The ability to refuel depended not only upon the distance to "a friendly port" but upon the supply of oil. The shortage of this vital commodity bothered Kimmel almost as much as it did the Japanese. It tethered his battleships to a relatively small radius, so much so that Admiral Pye doubted the extent of their usefulness to the United States in case of war in the Pacific.[57] It also prevented Kimmel from keeping all his ships at sea and, with his shortage of tankers, materially helped formulate the pattern of comings and goings in and out of Pearl Harbor.[58]

Then too, the strike upon Oahu did not in itself alter the pattern of sea warfare, as Pratt suggested. Pearl Harbor was not a sea battle in a way that would have made sense to a Drake, a Nelson, or a Mahan. Ship did not meet ship in open waters. In terms of actual firepower on board, Kimmel far outclassed Nagumo, but situated as his battlewagons were, moored in a harbor landlocked except for a narrow channel, Kimmel could not bring his big guns into play. Ship-against-ship gunfire had no part in the Battle of Oahu which, if one views its actual course, shapes up as an air engagement, not a sea fight. It was plane against moored ship, airborne plane against unarmed, grounded plane; and in a few cases, dogfight of plane against plane.

In the latter instances, Americans gave a good account of themselves. Indeed, Pearl Harbor bestowed upon the United States one gift of pure gold immediately negotiable—proof under the worst possible conditions of the valor and resourcefulness of its junior officers and enlisted men. This, one of the first results of the battle to be recognized, may well be one of the last to lose its validity: At all levels, Americans could and would fight not only bravely but intelligently, given an urgent need and a sense of mission.

"Remember Pearl Harbor!"

Lessons of Pearl Harbor: need for alertness, adequate armed forces, and effective intelligence system—Morgan report—Dangers of assumptions and inadequate communications—Need for unity of command—Futility of war as solution to international problems—Need for mutual understanding

Most military engagements are mulled over by the soldiers and sailors of their own and later generations to learn what they may teach of tactics, strategy, and logistics. But Pearl Harbor strikes much deeper. It speaks to every thinking man and woman. "Pearl Harbor never dies," one of Kimmel's attorneys wrote to him with a touch of brooding poetry, "and no living person has seen the end of it."[1]

Americans of the day hoped that their country would take the attack to heart. "Hundreds of years from now, will this disaster be cited as a flagrant example of inattention, carelessness and failure?" asked Representative Stephen M. Young of Ohio. "If our Republic exists for thousands of years, may young Americans of the future profit by this bitter experience!"[2]

With the publication of each investigation report, certain of the nation's lawmakers stressed the urgent necessity of being on the qui vive at all times. "Remember Pearl Harbor!" Senator Alexander Wiley of Wisconsin urged his countrymen. "Let us say that we pledge this Nation to remember Pearl Harbor to the end of time, not necessarily in a spirit of revenge but so that from now on this Nation shall be constantly on the alert."[3]

Admiral Hara remarked tartly that the United States should indeed remember Pearl Harbor as a horrible example of American spiritual and psychological unpreparedness. In his opinion, on the morning of December 7, 1941, Japan presented the United States with the opportunity to destroy Japan's scoring punch. Instead, the

Americans failed miserably and suffered an ignominious defeat. They should resolve to learn the bitter lessons of that debacle. Otherwise, a Pearl Harbor in the jet-atomic age might be the last battle as well as the first.[4]

By the fourth anniversary of the attack, the phrase "Remember Pearl Harbor!" had taken on a new meaning. It had ceased to be a battle cry and had become an exhortation to self-examination and reappraisal. The *Oregonian* reminded its readers that it had been the first in the nation to use those words. Now it cautioned, "We must remember Pearl Harbor not only for the reason that Japan was treacherous, but also for the reason that we were stupid. . . . In a sense, Pearl Harbor should be our 'Wailing Wall.' "[5]

No mainland newspaper had such good reason to remember Pearl Harbor as did the Honolulu *Star-Bulletin,* and on December 7, 1945, it urged its readers to do so, "as a day of terrible warning, never to be forgotten, ever at hand, to keep us alert that it must not happen again."

Of all the newsmen who covered the congressional investigation, few if any probed more deeply than did William H. Stringer. In the *Christian Science Monitor* he asked:

> Shall we remember only the outraged national honor, the 3,000 servicemen lost, the eight battleships in Oahu mud, fishes swimming through jagged holes, and the flaming call for vengeance?
>
> Must we not also . . . look beyond the black smoke over Pearl Harbor to see where the nation erred in 1941—to find what was lacking in our national character and conduct which permitted world aggression so narrowly to miss becoming world conquest? . . .
>
> The whole pre-Pearl Harbor decade teaches, first and foremost, that diplomatic protest cannot carry far without power to back it up. . . .

Stringer also reminded his readers that the U.S. Navy had not believed "until too late" that aerial torpedoes could run in Pearl Harbor.[6]

This same thought occurred to the St. Paul *Pioneer Press,* which cited as one of the lessons of Pearl Harbor the fact that "the United States relies only at its grave peril on the weapons of victory in one war for defense against attack in the next war." Therefore, ". . . this country cannot afford to pinch pennies in voting future funds for scientific research for the military branches." The Pearl Harbor and other official reports had revealed that the United States had lagged behind the British in developing radar and behind the Germans in "the development of robot bombs and jet propulsion generally."[7]

If one had to pinpoint the single lesson of Pearl Harbor which most forcefully struck the press in the latter half of 1945 and throughout the congressional investigation, the choice would fall upon the misuse of intelligence. According to the Houston *Post,* the inquiry demonstrated "the perpetual need for a far-flung, highly-trained, skillful intelligence service, unrestricted by interdepartmental politics."[8]

The St. Paul *Pioneer Press* remarked that Japan had come to Pearl Harbor "armed with accurate information," while the United States forces "knew nothing definite about Japan's preparations . . . for a sneak attack." This must not happen again. "For safety, the United States in the future must be at least as well informed about potential enemy countries' military preparations as such countries are about ours."[9]

"The weakest branch of the American armed services . . . has undoubtedly been the intelligence branch," announced the Des Moines *Register.* Individual technicians had been competent—"witness the cracking of the Japanese code." In "most cases" the United States had the information. "But we didn't always know how to use it. . . . Knowledge wasn't related, pooled, integrated, passed on." The *Register* called for a "complete overhauling" of the intelligence community and transfusion into it of "new attitudes, prestige and talent. . . . But first must come reorganization at the top."[10]

No newspaper was more waspish about this subject than the Honolulu *Star-Bulletin:*

> The average regular naval officer looked down his nose—and still does—at the intelligence branch. Its members don't fight with guns so they can't be worth much. . . .
>
> Already . . . the navy is dismantling its intelligence by sending its best men to sea as part of the ritual which requires that a naval officer's insignia must be tarnished with salt air from time to time.

The *Star-Bulletin* called for adequate maintenance of the intelligence service and urged "explicit arrangements so that officers who specialized in intelligence . . . would not be retarded or penalized in promotion because of it."[11]

This emphasis upon intelligence figured largely in the congressional majority report. Assistant Counsel Morgan presented in his draft report twenty-five "supervisory, administrative and organizational deficiences" apparent in the Army and Navy. These the majority accepted. High-level schools of both services studied them at the direction of Nimitz and Eisenhower, then respectively CNO and Chief of Staff. Moreover, at J. Edgar Hoover's direction, Morgan lectured to the FBI about these principles.[12]

The final report explained that the committee posed these points "not for their novelty or profundity but for the reason that, by their very self-evident simplicity, it is difficult to believe they were ignored." Morgan confined himself strictly to factors illustrated by the attack, producing chapter and verse to back them up. The applicability of these points far transcends Pearl Harbor, so they deserve serious review:

"1. *Operational and intelligence work requires centralization of authority and clear-cut allocation of responsibility.*"

Morgan emphasized the lack of "the proper demarcation of responsibility" between Naval Intelligence and War Plans. "It is clear that this intradepartmental misunderstanding and near conflict was not resolved before December 7 and beyond question it prejudiced the effectiveness of Naval Intelligence."

Morgan scored Bloch's admission that he did not know whom Kimmel would hold responsible for shortcomings in regard to aircraft readiness. He also criticized Bellinger's "wholly anomalous" position whereby he was "responsible to everyone and to no one." Morgan warned, "The pyramiding of superstructures of organization cannot be inducive to efficiency and endangers the very function of our military and naval services."[13] (Or of any other organization, for that matter.)

"2. *Supervisory officials cannot safely take anything for granted in the alerting of subordinates.*"

Morgan dealt briefly here with assumptions—those slippery paving stones on the road to Pearl Harbor. "The testimony of many crucial witnesses contains an identical note: 'I thought he was alerted'; 'I took for granted he would understand'; 'I thought he would be doing that.' " With such words Morgan's analysis soared far beyond the lessons taught by a military operation, however significant, and entered into a fundamental region of the human condition. How often similar phrases signal tragedies in every area of life!

Indeed, Morgan might well have confined his lesson to his first eight words: "Supervisory officials cannot safely take anything for granted. . . ." But not just officials. Out of an abysmal ignorance of Japan and the Japanese, in 1941 the United States floated on a sea of assumptions concerning its Pacific rival.

Morgan ended his short discussion on a familiar but urgent theme: "With Pearl Harbor as a sad experience, crucial intelligence should in the future be supplied commanders accompanied by the best estimate of its significance."[14] Unhappily, supplying such "crucial intelligence" as the "bomb plot" messages accompanied by Washington's estimate of their meaning might well have muddied the waters. For if one accepts their sworn testimony, those involved with that series mistook the significance of the messages.

"3. *Any doubt as to whether outposts should be given information should always be resolved in favor of supplying the information.*"

The prime example in support of this declaration was Stark's hesitancy to send out the Japanese "one o'clock" deadline on December 7, 1941, lest he confuse the Pacific commands with too many alerts. As Morgan remarked, Stark "was properly entitled to believe that naval establishments were adequately alert, but the fact is that one— Hawaii—was not in a state of readiness." To Morgan, this one incident proved the principle.[15]

But he could have cited others. Kimmel and Short should have been informed concerning the consular intercepts in regard to Pearl Harbor and the other military installations on Oahu. How much this grievous mistake contributed to the final disaster one cannot know. But the lesson is all too clear. If the United States conducts its high-level intelligence policy the same way in the nuclear age, it will not only court its own calamity but deserve its fate.

"4. *The delegation of authority or the issuance of orders entails the duty of inspection to determine that the official mandate is properly exercised.*"

Both Washington and Hawaii came under Morgan's lash in this respect. He cited in particular the Navy Department's failure to ensure that Kimmel took a defensive deployment upon receipt of the "war warning" of November 27. He considered the administration of Kimmel's and Short's respective commands "in the critical days before December 7 . . . the epitome of worthy plans and purposes which were never implemented." He added sternly, "The job of an administrator is only half completed upon the issuance of an order; it is discharged when he determines the order has been executed."[16] His next principle was closely related:

"*5. The implementation of official orders must be followed with closest supervision.*"

Under this heading Morgan administered a brief but stinging slap to the War Department for not following through on Short's reply to the warning of November 27. Any worker on any level can profit by pondering this example. The lowliest of file clerks in War Plans could have earned himself or herself an honorable niche in American history by pulling message No. 472 from the file and clipping it to Short's reply. Then those receiving the documents would have known exactly to what Short referred. The message in Morgan's points 4 and 5 rings out loud and clear: Follow up to see if orders have been executed, and ride herd on the recipient if he has not done so.

"*6. The maintenance of alertness to responsibility must be insured through repetition.*"

Morgan cited the "cry wolf" argument, which he considered invalid. He observed that repetition could not have relaxed the Hawaiian commands because they were never truly alert to begin with.[17] Thus Morgan disagreed with the school of thought which holds that repeated warnings can blunt alertness by making the warnings commonplace. Morgan appeared to have the more cogent argument. Far better to send the fire engines on nine goose chases than hesitate the tenth time and allow a major conflagration to burn out of control.

"*7. Complacency and procrastination are out of place where sudden and decisive actions are of the essence.*"

Morgan observed that Army and Navy officials in both Washington and Hawaii "were beset by a lassitude born of 20 years of peace." This complacency was understandable but not excusable, because "the Army and the Navy are the watchdogs of the Nation's security and they must be on the alert at all times, no matter how many the years of peace."[18]

Here Morgan touched upon the most difficult psychological burden of the armed services in peacetime—how to remain mentally and emotionally keen in the midst of a population generally indifferent, even hostile, to such efforts. The task was easier in societies where a separate military caste flourished, like the German Junker and the Japanese samurai. Such men were armed with the invincible conviction of their superiority to any civilian. But the American soldier, sailor, and airman is very much a part of his people. In maintaining his alertness to anything or nothing, he has to fight his own instincts. Yet that is his job.

"8. *The coordination and proper evaluation of intelligence in times of stress must be insured by continuity of service and centralization of responsibility in competent officials.*"

Morgan expressed the logical opinion that no system could "compensate for lack of alertness and imagination. Nevertheless," he added, "there is substantial basis . . . to conclude that the system of handling intelligence was seriously at fault and that the security of the Nation can be insured only through continuity of service and centralization of responsibility in those charged with handling intelligence." Thus Morgan and later the majority of the committee accepted the concept so urgently pressed by Zacharias and others—that intelligence must not be regarded "as just another tour of duty," but as a profession.[19]

This most agreed-upon of Pearl Harbor lessons—the need for a centralized pool of intelligence—has taken a beating in the course of time. The Central Intelligence Agency as revealed unto us over the past few years is not precisely what those who suffered at and from Pearl Harbor had in mind.

As of September 1975, Representative Otis Pike of New York, chairman of the House Intelligence Committee, doubted that the United States would know of an attack about to be launched. The country has thousands of dedicated intelligence gatherers but, "above the gathering level, it just bogs down every single time. It is not absorbed, it is not delivered."[20] In other words, if Pike was correct, not quite thirty-four years after Pearl Harbor the United States was back where it started in regard to intelligence—data available but lacking proper evaluation and dissemination. This gives one a depressing look at the nation's capacity to learn from experience—witness, for example, the outbreak of the Korean War in June 1950, and the airport massacre and subsequent attack on the United States Embassy in Beirut in 1984.

In the past, the United States has been able to overcome the baneful effects of such relaxation of vigilance and failure to learn. The days of relatively slow-moving military operations gave the nation the time needed to recover its balance. But in the nuclear age, the United States needs an intelligence system so keenly honed and finely attuned that it can anticipate an attack in terms of time, method, and strength.

"9. *The unapproachable or superior attitude of officials is fatal;*

there should never be any hesitancy in asking for clarification of instructions or in seeking advice on matters that are in doubt."

One fact especially struck Morgan: In all the records of "various interpretations as to what War and Navy Department dispatches meant, in not one instance does it appear that a subordinate requested a clarification." The subordinate might avoid such a consultation to "demonstrate his self-reliance." But the investigation had revealed such a "persistent failure" in this regard that Morgan considered the lesson obvious: ". . . the military and naval forces failed to instill in their personnel the wholesome disposition to consult freely with their superiors for the mutual good and success of both superior and subordinate."[21]

"10. *There is no substitute for imagination and resourcefulness on the part of supervisory and intelligence officials.*"

Morgan believed that with a better appreciation and application of intelligence, plus a little imagination, "someone should have concluded that Pearl Harbor was a likely point of Japanese attack." The failure to do so he accorded, "at least in part," to the downgrading of the intelligence function.[22]

One might suggest that this attitude was part of the American *Zeitgeist*. Science was king, and his subjects were suspicious of anything that could not be observed under a microscope or demonstrated in repeated laboratory tests. The imaginative interpretation of intelligence is much more an art than a science. So the American intelligence community as scientists triumphed in technology and cold logic—Magic and cryptanalysis—while as artists it failed in interpretation of the facts thus gathered.

Some members of the scientific community have likewise noted that the American viewpoint "often seems . . . averse to prolonged analysis." Funds to support "the collection of data are much more readily available than funds for their analysis. . . . Pragmatism finds data more appealing than speculation about its [*sic*] meaning.

"The net result is a national information system that knows more about the trees than the forest; a national perspective which is often well-informed about the specifics but lacks a comprehensive, systematic overview."[23]

Morgan's excellent comments continued,

"11. *Communications must be characterized by clarity, forthrightness and appropriateness.*"

Morgan pointed out that the evidence reflected "an unusual number of instances where military officers in high positions of responsibility interpreted orders, intelligence, and other information and
arrived at opposite conclusions." He cited in particular the warning
messages of November 27 where Washington and Hawaii had worked
at cross purposes. "Dispatches must be unmistakably clear, forthright,
and devoid of any conceivable ambiguity." He also considered that
in these instances "brevity of messages was carried to the point of
being a fetish rather than a virtue." Dispatches must be of "sufficient
amplitude to be meaningful not only to the sender but, beyond reasonable doubt, to the addressee as well."[24]

This finding was somewhat ironic, because the usual trouble with
government communications is not fleshing out bare bones but peel-
ing off layer after layer of verbosity. As we have seen, Hart considered
that the Navy's "war warning" suffered from excessive "yakity-yak."
The problem, then, was not one of brevity but of clarity.

"12. *There is great danger in careless paraphrase of information
received and every effort should be made to insure that the paraphrased material reflects the true meaning and significance of the
original.*"

Morgan referred to Short's message of November 27, 1941, which
had been paraphrased in the War Department to read "Department
alerted to prevent sabotage. Liaison with Navy re your 472." Morgan
found it conceivable that the War Department might have interpreted
this paraphrase as meaning that Short had established liaison with
the Navy to conduct long-range reconnaissance.[25] This example might
be a little farfetched but the principle is sound. One of the most
expressive of all languages, English is also one of the trickiest. So one
must take care in rearranging it to maintain the original meaning.

"13. *Procedures must be sufficiently flexible to meet the exigencies
of unusual situations.*"

According to Morgan, the Pearl Harbor evidence showed that in
both the Army and Navy everything "seems perforce to have followed
a grooved pattern regardless of the demands for distinctive action."
He objected in particular to excessive devotion to "channels." Without
some sort of "channels," any large organization would soon be
reduced to chaos. But Morgan was correct in pointing out that procedures should be sufficiently flexible to bend in emergencies.[26]

"14. *Restriction of highly confidential information to a minimum number of officials, while often necessary, should not be carried to the point of prejudicing the work of the organization."*

Under this heading Morgan dealt with the unfortunate overprotectiveness toward Magic. This emphasized the absolute necessity of walking a figurative tightrope between preservation of secrecy and proper utilization of the information.[27]

Indeed, those in control of Magic were so obsessively concerned with security that they failed to realize the meaning of the contents of the intercepts. They resembled a certain type of collector who buys a book for its binding. He relishes the feel of the soft leather, the glow of the golden lettering, but as for reading the book—that is not in his scheme of things. Those in charge of Magic made no provision to analyze and chart the data, which would have given them day-to-day linkage from which to forge a chain of reasoning and deduction. As stressed throughout this study, cumulative intelligence is basic, but to be useful it must be interpreted and disseminated.

"15. *There is great danger of being blinded by the self-evident.*"

Virtually every witness before the congressional committee testified that "he was surprised at the Japanese attack on Pearl Harbor." Morgan thought this was "essentially the result of the fact that just about everybody was blinded or rendered myopic" by Japan's "self-evident purpose" of striking Southeast Asia. Then he added, "So completely did everything point to the south that it appears everyone was blinded to significant, albeit somewhat disguised, handwriting on the wall suggesting an attack on us elsewhere."[28]

There is another way in which the "self-evident" had been even more blinding in 1941. For years the U.S. Army and Navy had conducted war games against a Japanese air attack on Pearl Harbor. But apparently this idea had been for so long a cliché of training exercises that the reality, when it came, surprised all concerned as much as if the idea had never crossed their minds.

"16. *Officials should at all times give subordinates the benefit of significant information.*"

Morgan cited Turner's testimony "that he regarded an attack on Pearl Harbor as a 50–50 possibility. Assuming this to be correct," Morgan continued, "there can be little doubt . . . that he could have given the commander in chief of the Pacific Fleet the benefit of his conclusions had he been disposed to do so."[29] The problem went considerably beyond Turner. It harks back to Morgan's principle No. 3,

that any existing doubt should be resolved in favor of giving information to subordinates.

"*17. An official who neglects to familiarize himself in detail with
his organization should forfeit his responsibility.*"

Morgan did not spare Kimmel and Short for their lack of coordination, but he was especially incensed at Stark's and Turner's assuming without direct knowledge that Kimmel was receiving Magic.[30]
This incident underlines another lesson of Pearl Harbor: Always go
to the source; do not depend upon secondhand information when
"best evidence" is available.

Morgan had touched upon a problem inescapable in large organizations—how to achieve adequate familiarity with details without
becoming overly absorbed in those same details; how to delegate
authority while holding the reins; how to distinguish professional
coordination from personal cooperation.

"*18. Failure can be avoided in the long run only by preparation
for any eventuality.*"

On this score, Morgan wrote:

> The record tends to indicate that appraisal of likely enemy move-
> ments was divided into *probabilities* and *possibilities*. Everyone has
> admitted that an attack by Japan on Pearl Harbor was regarded as
> at least a possibility. It was felt, however, that a Japanese movement
> toward the south was a probability. The over-all result was to look
> for the probable move and to take little or no effective precautions
> to guard against the contingency of the possible action.[31]

Here was the old problem of enemy intentions versus capabilities.
U.S. military leaders in 1941 were far too concerned with what Japan
might do, not with what it was able to do. Yet history has shown that
if an enemy can launch a certain kind of attack, in all probability he
will do exactly that. His intentions cannot hurt his opponent; his
capabilities can, if properly utilized.

Thus, while the United States would infinitely prefer peace with
the Soviet Union, if the Russians and their Warsaw Pact allies are
able to overrun Western Europe in a conventional war, the United
States and its NATO allies must assume that they will do so under
the right set of circumstances. Furthermore, if the Soviets have the
capability of knocking out the United States in one huge preemptive
nuclear strike, American leaders must assume that that is what they

will do if conditions are propitious. Any other attitude on the part of
the United States would be irresponsible.

The ultimate lesson which Pearl Harbor should teach American
political and military leaders, as well as every person in the United
States, is this: Always be prepared for the worst contingency.

"19. *Officials, on a personal basis, should never countermand an
official instruction.*"

This was a slap at Stark.* As Morgan wrote, ". . . it is regarded
as an extremely dangerous practice for the Chief of Naval Operations
to express an opinion on a personal basis to an outpost commander
which has the inevitable effect of tempering the import of an official
dispatch."[32] Of course, Morgan was perfectly right.

"20. *Personal or official jealousy will wreck any organization.*"
Morgan cited the obvious instance of the squabble between ONI and
War Plans regarding evaluation of intelligence. He also referred to
"the near dispute" between Kimmel and Short as to command at
Wake and Midway. He remarked caustically:

> It is proper to suggest that, had both the commanding officers in
> Hawaii been less concerned between November 27 and December
> 7 about preserving their individual prerogatives with respect to Wake
> and Midway and more concerned about working together to defend
> the Hawaiian Coastal Frontier in the light of the warnings they had
> received, the defensive situation confronting the Japanese on the
> morning of December 7 might well have been entirely different.[33]

Morgan's next principle was a natural corollary of the preceding
one:

"21. *Personal friendship . . . should never be accepted in lieu of
liaison or confused therewith where the latter is necessary to the
proper functioning of two or more agencies.*"

This, of course, referred to the relationship between Kimmel and
Short, their rather simplistic confusion of their cordial personal in-
terchanges with the close-knit coordination of professional activities
which should have existed but did not.[34]

"22. *No consideration should be permitted as excuse for failure
to perform a fundamental task.*"

Here Morgan struck at one of the foundation stones of Kimmel's

---

*See Chapter 13.

and Short's self-defense—"the fact that they had countless and manifold duties in their respective positions." In Morgan's opinion, this assertion did not hold water.

> The most fundamental responsibility that both commanders had under the circumstances, however, was to make certain beyond any reasonable doubt that there was an integrated and coordinated employment of defense facilities consistent with the principle of command by mutual cooperation. No excuse or explanation can justify or temper the failure to discharge this responsibility which superseded and surpassed all others.[35]

What seemed to be involved here was a faulty sense of priorities. Granted that Kimmel and Short were exceedingly busy men—what commander on or near their level was not in that buildup year of 1941? But both suffered from overconcern with the routine aspects of their jobs at the expense of the truly important ones.

"23. *Superiors must at all times keep their subordinates adequately informed and, conversely, subordinates should keep their superiors informed.*"

This was closely related to Morgan's principles No. 3 and No. 16 concerning dissemination of information. In this particular instance, he had in mind the failure of subordinates to get to Marshall and Stark the first thirteen parts of the final Japanese message, and Kimmel's failure to clue in Bellinger about the "war warning." Morgan also reminded his readers of Short's failure "to inform the essential and necessary officers of his command of the acute situation" upon receipt of the "war warning."[36]

"24. *The administrative organization of any establishment must be designed to locate failures and to assess responsibility.*"

Morgan pointed out "that there was no way in which it could be determined definitely that any individual saw a particular message among the Magic materials. It does not appear that any record was established for initialing the messages or otherwise fixing responsibility." This lack of control left the subordinate who disseminated the messages "at the complete mercy of superior officers" in case a question arose as to whether or not the superior had seen the document.[37]

"25. *In a well-balanced organization there is close correlation of responsibility and authority.*"

Morgan mentioned that witnesses had testified as to their responsibilities. But in Washington as well as Hawaii no one, "except the highest ranking officers, possessed any real authority to act in order decisively to discharge their responsibilities." He urged that in the future, "There should be a close correlation between responsibility and authority; to vest a man with responsibility and no corresponding authority is an unfair, ineffective, and unsatisfactory arrangement."[38]

Careful consideration of Morgan's points reveals that many of them are separate facets of a single problem—the failure to communicate. This aspect of the matter may well stand as one of the basic causes of the Pearl Harbor tragedy, second only to the failure to believe in its possibility. One by one these failures pass in sorry review: failure to ensure understanding; failure of seniors to supply all available relevant information to juniors; failure to supervise and follow through; failure of juniors to be sure they understood their seniors; lack of clarity of expression.

The failure in 1941 to apply such principles as Morgan's cost the United States dearly at Pearl Harbor; hence they must be considered as lessons to be learned from the debacle. Any country, any organization, indeed any individual, can profit by pondering these points.

Pearl Harbor taught other lessons of broad application. One of the first and most obvious was, in Stringer's words, "Need for the United States to be adequately armed."[39] In the current state of technology, "adequate" does not mean what it did in the years immediately before Pearl Harbor—a small cadre that would be expanded when world events sounded the alarm. The nation then assumed that, granted American resources, time would permit such expansion to the degree necessary. As Secretary Henry A. Kissinger has written, "In the era of what we now call conventional weapons, the force-in-being was not nearly so significant as the industrial potential and the mobilization base." But in the nuclear age "physical conditions have basically altered. . . . The forces-in-being are almost surely decisive."[40] The United States armed services must in fact as well as in name be "forces-in-being"—mainsprings coiled for instant action, alert to exploit any advantage, powerful enough to follow through to final victory.

Traditionally the need for strong armed forces appears to be the first lesson learned and the one most vociferously expounded following initial military setbacks. It is also the first to be jettisoned as soon as the crisis has passed. Scarcely had the last shot of World War II been fired than the United States raced to demobilize and "bring the boys home." As a result, five years after the last world conflict the United States had to scrape the bottom of the barrel to put an effective fighting force in Korea.

The need for a potent, instantly effective force-in-being is particularly applicable to the United States or to any other nation which adopts a national policy of never striking first. This is the only morally justifiable attitude under most social ethics, but in the context of nuclear and missile warfare it will be infinitely more difficult to maintain than it was before World War II.

No wonder the St. Paul *Pioneer Press* listed as its first lesson of Pearl Harbor "that never again will any nation escape so lightly . . . from the consequences of a successful surprise attack. . . . If the United States again permits itself to be surprised, its whole defense system might be prostrated, its cities wiped out, millions of its people killed and the survivors made the panic stricken and helpless captives of an invasion force."

This newspaper urged international cooperation for peace. "The new weapons make surprise easy and its results tragic. For safety's sake, the United States must maintain its military power, and it must also use that power to back up world-wide efforts of nations to prevent another war."[41]

Yet the very weaponry which seems to make arms control absolutely necessary presents the nations with an almost irresistible temptation to cheat. Kissinger put a ponderous but acute finger on the problem:

> If the number of permissible long-range missiles is set at zero—if, in other words, both sides agree to destroy all I.C.B.M.'s and nuclear weapons—even a small evasion, say ten hidden missiles, will confer a decisive advantage. And such an evasion is almost impossible to discover. If the number is set very low, say at ten, an additional 15 may make a surprise attack possible. In such circumstances, there would be a dual incentive for evasion: fear of the opponent's evasion and the temptation to deal with the security problem once and for all by launching a surprise attack.[42]

Some time in the future, the human race may reach the point in moral evolution when the wars and arms races of the twentieth cen-

tury seem no more than half-forgotten nightmares of mankind's savage
past. Certainly we do not defend war per se as a reasonable institution.
Indeed, like all battles, Pearl Harbor underlined the complete futility
of trying to settle international disputes by taking to the fists. Intelligent individuals learn early in life that one can shut up an opponent
by a left to the jaw, but that such tactics can never change his con-
victions or alter the basic conditions that produced the argument.
Nations can be singularly obtuse in this matter. Perhaps this is due
to the nature of a nation, as the Durants have suggested:

> The causes of war are the same as the causes of competition among
> individuals. . . . The state has our instincts without our restraints.
> The individual submits to restraints laid upon him by morals and
> laws, and agrees to replace combat with conference, because the
> state guarantees him basic protection of his life, property, and legal
> rights. The state itself acknowledges no substantial restraints.[43]

Once a nation decides to embark upon a war of aggression, especially against a country potentially much more powerful than itself,
reason becomes the first casualty of the war. Therefore the nonag-
gressor must act upon the realization that the enemy is impervious
to logic. The United States placed its Pacific Fleet at Pearl Harbor
in the hope that it might deter Japan from further expanding its
already extensive theater of operations. Washington forgot that there
always exists a militant mentality willing to take the calculated risk.
And Japan was ready, willing, and able to do just that against the
United States.

American leaders should have been alert to such a contingency.
Hitler's career had been one calculated risk after another. Britain and
France could have halted him at the outset when he occupied the
Rhineland in March of 1936, but he weighed his chances, acted, and
won. In case American memories had faded in five years, Hitler gave
them another object lesson in June of 1941 when he attacked the
Soviet Union, although Germany was Russia's ally, was at war with
Britain, and had its forces spread over most of Europe.

With the examples of Nazi Germany and imperialist Japan in
mind, the United States should ask itself: Will the Soviet Union and
its Warsaw Pact allies take the calculated risk of challenging the United
States and its NATO partners in Europe? More than that, will the
Kremlin chance a preemptive nuclear strike against the United States?

Washington would be disastrously unwise to answer these questions in the negative on the basis of such reasoning as prevailed in 1941— that they would never dare, that they are too intelligent to take such a risk.

Pearl Harbor proved that "deterrence" is an elusive doctrine that works only against those willing to be deterred. Thus Japan, at that stage of its history convinced of its right to take what it wanted, not only failed to be deterred, it accepted the Pacific Fleet's presence at Pearl Harbor as an opportunity to rid itself of a potential threat.

Among other lessons, Pearl Harbor emphasized the absolute necessity of knowing everything possible about one's fellow passengers on the spaceship Earth. Before the Pacific conflict the United States was woefully ignorant of Japan. Experts on the Mikado's empire, his people, their history, culture, and language were as scarce as Egyptologists. Today the United States urgently needs a battery of experts on every country on earth. It is not necessary to use this knowledge against other nations; mutual understanding can make for increased mutual respect and helpfulness.

As stressed in this study, a basic factor which contributed heavily to the tragedy of Pearl Harbor was the mutual misunderstanding, resulting in mutual underestimation, that existed between Japan and the United States before December 7, 1941. Even an elementary knowledge of each other's histories would have brushed away many illusions and allowed the two peoples to see each other more clearly. This lesson need not be confined to the international scene. If anyone finds himself assessing the probable actions or reactions of another human being on the basis of stereotypes, let him pull up short and "remember Pearl Harbor."

By corollary, Pearl Harbor underscored another lesson that had long been obvious to any student of history but was evidently lost sight of during the years immediately preceding American entry into World War II. This is the folly of underestimating the will and ability of a "have-not" nation.

The decades just past have shown us more than one example. In Vietnam the United States took a beating at the hands of a nation which on paper should have folded in a month. But the United States had no real will to win and suffered appalling casualties with nothing to show for them. More recently, the Soviet Union has not been able fully to impose its will on the Afghans—most unlikely opponents for a superpower. And what American can forget the hostage crisis in Iran, where a handful of hysterical fanatics kept the United States dangling in humiliation for over a year?

Therefore, if any statesman should be tempted to base his policies on the assumption that a possible opponent is too weak in resources and economic structure to pose a formidable danger—let him "remember Pearl Harbor."

By the same token, Pearl Harbor helps to emphasize that strength and courage are not enough. In terms of matériel available on Oahu and the number and caliber of personnel, the United States was prepared to counter the strike on Pearl Harbor and inflict serious damage upon Nagumo's task force. But the Americans did not do so, because they were not alert to the possibility of such an attack. The lesson is clear: Preparedness is not alertness.

The day the Roberts report saw the light, commentator Max Lerner cited what he termed "our elephantine confidence in our industrial superiority and in the fighting heart of our people." Both were real, but something more was needed, because "to try to win the war without organizing both in an exacting economy means to waste and exploit both. That is what we have done for almost a century, whether in peace or war."[44]

As the recent surge of interest in ecology indicates, the world is at last ready to acknowledge that it can no longer afford the sort of wasteful irresponsibility in which the "have" nations indulged in the past. What is needed can be boiled down to a word that is in somewhat ill repute today—*discipline*. The armed forces used to stress: "Discipline is that which makes punishment unnecessary"—a profound truth. For without discipline punishment is certain. The United States had all the requirements for victory before Pearl Harbor, but failed to harness them.

On the twenty-fifth anniversary of Pearl Harbor, *The New York Times* declared that the day "must live in memory not only of things past and men long dead, but as a perpetual reminder to future generations that ambition must be tempered with restraint and courage with wisdom."[45]

Today, on the forty-fourth anniversary, that comment is still relevant. Application of that principle could halt many an ill-considered action in its tracks. It implies an attitude of mutual understanding and respect which has become more and more essential. As early as

December 8, 1945, the *Saturday Review of Literature* warned, "Unless the December 7, 1941, episode is placed in its long-range historical perspective, the real lesson of Pearl Harbor will have been overlooked. That lesson, fundamentally, is that American security is inseparable from world security."

Substitute the name of any other nationality for "American" and this statement remains valid. Humanity cannot afford to forget the lessons of Pearl Harbor. The world is much too small; the risk is much too great; the time is much too late.

CHAPTER 1

"WE WERE ALL OUT THERE"

1. Lynchburg *News*, December 10, 1941.
2. *New York Times*, August 30, 1945.
3. Emporia *Gazette*, December 16, 1941.
4. October 27, 1941.
5. January 27, 1942.
6. "The Day of Wrath," *Life* (December 22, 1941), p. 11.
7. "On the Record," New York *Post*, December 17, 1941. See also St. Louis *Post-Dispatch*, December 18, 1941.
8. New York *Herald Tribune*, December 18, 1941.
9. December 21, 1941.
10. December 14, 1941.
11. See for example H. C. Engelbrecht and F. C. Hanigher, *Merchants of Death* (Garden City, N.Y, 1937); Richard Lewisohn, *Basil Zaharoff, Munitions King* (Philadelphia, 1934); P. J. Noel-Baker, *Hawkers of Death* (London, 1934) and *Private Manufacturers of Armaments* (London, 1936).
12. *Report of the Special Committee on Investigation of the Munitions Industry, United States Senate: Munitions Industry,* Seventy-fourth Congress, First Session, Report No. 944, Part 3 (Government Printing Office, Washington, D.C., 1936), p. 8.
13. Ibid., Preliminary Report, p. 256. For an interesting study of Nye, see Wayne S. Cole, *Senator Gerald P. Nye and American Foreign Relations* (Minneapolis, 1962).
14. Merze Tate, *The United States and Armament* (New York, 1948), pp. 134, 140 (hereafter cited as *United States and Armament*).

15. Samuel E. Morison, *The Rising Sun in the Pacific* (Boston, 1950), p. 30. Hereafter cited as *Rising Sun in the Pacific;* Stephen E. Pelz, *Race to Pearl Harbor: The Failure of the Second London Naval Conference and the Onset of World War II* (Cambridge, Mass., 1974), pp. 197–203.

16. *United States and Armament,* pp. 76–77.

17. Forrest C. Pogue, *George C. Marshall: Ordeal and Hope* (New York, 1966), pp. 1, 6–7 (hereafter cited as *Ordeal and Hope*).

18. Harry A. Toulmin, Jr., "General Mitchell Was Right," *Scribner's Commentator* (April 1941), p. 29. Later Toulmin served as executive officer of the Army Pearl Harbor Board.

19. *Congressional Record,* Vol. 90, Part 6, September 7, 1944, p. 7593.

20. Ibid., Vol. 83, Part 9, Appendix, January 31, 1938, pp. 381–82.

21. Ibid., March 21, 1938, pp. 1139–40.

22. Ibid., January 18, 1938, p. 239.

23. Ibid., February 14, 1938, p. 239.

24. Ibid., Vol. 90, Part 6, September 7, 1944, p. 7594; *Rising Sun in the Pacific,* p. 31.

25. "Books in Review," *New Republic* (January 5, 1942), p. 25.

26. Washington *Post,* January 5, 1943.

27. Leonard Baker, *Roosevelt and Pearl Harbor* (New York, 1970), p. 43 (hereafter cited as *Roosevelt and Pearl Harbor*).

28. Wayne S. Cole, *America First: The Battle Against Interventionism, 1940–1941* (Madison, Wis., 1953), p. 6 (hereafter cited as *America First*).

29. *Roosevelt and Pearl Harbor,* pp. 255, 250.

30. Morgenthau Presidential Diary, May 20, 1940, Papers of Henry Morgenthau, Jr., Franklin D. Roosevelt Library, Hyde Park, N.Y. (hereafter cited as Morgenthau Presidential Diary).

31. Wayne S. Cole, *Charles A. Lindbergh and the Battle Against American Intervention in World War II* (New York, 1974), pp. 209, 89, 90. See also *The Wartime Journals of Charles A. Lindbergh* (New York, 1970).

32. Emporia *Gazette,* December 16, 1941.

33. January 27, 1942.

34. "On the Record," Washington *Star,* January 28, 1942.

35. *Hearings before the Joint Committee on the Investigation of the Pearl Harbor Attack, Congress of the United States,* Seventy-ninth Congress, Part 39 (Washington, D.C., 1946), p. 343 (hereafter cited as *PHA*).

36. August 31, 1945.

37. December 7, 1945.

38. December 7, 1945.

39. This editorial appeared in the current *United States News.* Quoted in *Congressional Record,* Vol. 88, Part 8, Appendix, February 10, 1942, p. A479.

40. January 25, 1942.

CHAPTER 2

"SLOW IN WAKING UP"

1. *Congressional Record,* Vol. 87, Part 9, December 15, 1941, p. 9827.

2. Ibid., December 12, 1941, p. 9721.

3. Washington *Star,* January 27, 1942.

4. *Congressional Record,* Vol. 88, Part 1, February 3, 1942, p. 952.

5. September 24, 1945.

6. *New York Times,* April 21, 1938.

7. Washington *Post,* January 28, 1942.

8. December 8, 1941.

9. December 23, 1941.

10. January 27, 1942.

11. January 28, 1942.

12. Honolulu *Advertiser,* December 7, 1966.

13. For detailed statistics, see *PHA,* Report, p. 550.

14. For detailed statistics, see *PHA,* Report, pp. 551–52.

15. Honolulu *Advertiser,* December 3, 1941. For an account of this conference, see Gordon W. Prange, *At Dawn We Slept* (New York, 1981), Chapter 66 (hereafter cited as *At Dawn We Slept*).

16. Honolulu *Advertiser,* December 5, 1941.

17. Atlanta *Constitution,* December 18, 1941.

18. *Conressional Record,* Vol. 87, Part 9, December 8, 1941, p. 9534.

19. Ibid., Vol. 88, Part 1, January 27, 1942, p. 747.

20. Ibid., Vol. 87, Part 9, p. 9449.

21. *Roosevelt and Pearl Harbor,* pp. 270–71.

22. *Newsweek* (August 28, 1944), p. 43.

23. *Congressional Record,* Vol. 90, Part 6, p. 7596.

24. *Newsweek* (August 28, 1944), p. 43.

25. *Congressional Record,* Vol. 84, Part 2, p. 1705.

26. *Newsweek* (August 28, 1944), p. 43.

27. *Congressional Record,* Vol. 84, Part 2, February 21, 1939, p. 1706–08. The debate on Guam appears on pp. 1705–22, 1744–82, 1832–42.

28. Ibid. (February 23, 1939) pp. 1838–40.

29. "Washington Memo," New York *Post*, August 26, 1944.

30. Diary of Admiral William D. Leahy, Leahy Papers, Library of Congress, Box 9 (hereafter cited as Leahy Diary).

31. *Newsweek* (August 28, 1944), p. 43.

32. "Washington Memo," New York *Post*, August 26, 1944.

33. January 26, 1942.

34. *Congressional Record*, Vol. 88, Part 1, February 3, 1942, p. 948.

35. Ibid.

36. Ibid. pp. 949–50.

37. For a discussion of these matters, see *At Dawn We Slept*, Chapters 44, 54.

38. *Congressional Record*, Vol. 90, Part 6, September 5, 1944, p. 7520.

39. Ibid., Vol. 87, Part 10, Appendix, March 13, 1941, p. A1156.

40. Ibid., Part 11, Apendix, April 4, 1941, p. A1637.

41. Ibid., Part 4, May 9, 1941, p. 3862.

42. Ibid., Part 6, September 19, 1944, p. 7916.

43. December 19, 1945.

44. *Congressional Record*, Vol. 87, Part 4, pp. 3613–18.

45. Ibid., Vol. 90, Part 11, Appendix, September 6, 1944, p. A4015.

46. *Roosevelt and Pearl Harbor*, p. 195.

47. *Congressional Record*, Vol. 87, Part 6, July 16, 1941, pp. 6100–13.

48. *Ordeal and Hope*, pp. 153–54.

49. *Congressional Record*, Vol. 87, Part 6, July 10, 1941, p. 5963.

50. Ibid., Part 13, Appendix, August 1, 1941, p. A3717.

51. Ibid., Part 6, August 1, 1941, p. 6571.

52. Ibid., August 4, 1941, p. 6682.

53. Ibid., August 6, 1941, p. 6821.

54. Ibid., August 7, 1941, p. 6851.

55. Ibid., Part 13, Appendix, August 15, 1941, p. A4000.

56. Ibid., Part 6, August 12, 1941, p. 6998.

57. Ibid., Part 7, August 12, 1941, p. 7007.

58. Ibid., Part 6, August 6, 1941, p. 6821.

59. Ibid., August 8, 1941, p. 6921.

60. Ibid., Part 7, August 12, 1941, p. 7021.

61. Ibid., August 12, 1941, p. 7036.

62. Ibid., p. 7066.
63. Ibid., p. 7074; *Ordeal and Hope*, p. 154.

CHAPTER 3

"TOO DEEPLY TO BURY THEIR HATE"

1. Letter, Taussig to Prange, January 8, 1963.
2. London *Times* and Chicago *Tribune*, June 21, 1944.
3. Chicago *Tribune*, June 21, 1944.
4. See for example John T. Flynn's pamphlet, *The Truth About Pearl Harbor* (privately printed in New York City, 1944), p. 15 (hereafter cited as *Truth About Pearl Harbor*); George Morgenstern, "The Actual Road to Pearl Harbor," p. 385 (hereafter cited as "Actual Road"; this is one of a series of essays contained in Harry E. Barnes, ed., *Perpetual War for Perpetual Peace* [Caldwell, Ida., 1953; hereafter cited as *Perpetual War*]); William Henry Chamberlin, *America's Second Crusade* (Chicago, 1950), p. 177 (hereafter cited as *Second Crusade*). Charles C. Tansill used Lyttelton's remark as one of three with which he preceded his essay, "Japanese-American Relations, 1921–1941: The Pacific Back Road to War," in *Perpetual War*, p. 269 (hereafter cited as "Japanese-American Relations").
5. In addition to the works cited above, some major revisionist books include Charles A. Beard, *President Roosevelt and the Coming of the War 1941* (New Haven, 1948; hereafter cited as *Roosevelt and the Coming*); George Morgenstern, *Pearl Harbor: The Story of the Secret War* (New York, 1947; hereafter cited as *Pearl Harbor*); RADM. Robert A. Theobald, *The Final Secret of Pearl Harbor* (New York, 1954; hereafter cited as *Final Secret*); Husband E. Kimmel, *Admiral Kimmel's Story* (Chicago, 1955; hereafter cited as *Admiral Kimmel's Story*); John Toland, *Infamy: Pearl Harbor and Its Aftermath* (New York, 1982; hereafter cited as *Infamy*).
6. See for example William S. Neumann, "How American Policy Toward Japan Contributed to War in the Pacific," in *Perpetual War; Second Crusade*.
7. See *Roosevelt and the Coming*. For a witty, urbane examination and refutation of Beard's position, see Samuel Eliot Morison, "History Through a Beard," in Samuel Eliot Morison, *By Land and By Sea* (New York, 1954).
8. Harry E. Barnes, "What Happened at Pearl Harbor?" *Peace News* (London), December 7, 1962, hereafter "What Happened"; Harry E. Barnes, "Whose 'Day of Infamy'? Pearl Harbor After Twenty Years," unpublished article, courtesy Dr. Barnes, pp. 20–25. Prange knew Barnes fairly well, talked with him at length about Pearl Harbor, and had considerable correspondence with him. Barnes offered to try to obtain financial help for Prange in his forthcoming Pearl Harbor study, contingent upon his writing it from the revisionist standpoint. Prange explained that he could not proceed on the basis of preconceived ideas,

consciously selecting data to fit a predesignated frame of reference. If the facts he unearthed fitted the revisionist thesis, he would use them accordingly; but he could not and would not commit himself in advance to any school of thought. Unfortunately, Barnes appeared honestly incapable of understanding that attitude. Letter, Barnes to Prange, February 28, 1964, Prange files; interview with Barnes, August 28, 1944.

9. Curtis B. Dall, *F.D.R., My Exploited Father-in-Law* (Tulsa, Okla., 1967), p. 133. Hereafter *F.D.R.* An indication of the identity of the "Advisors" is contained in a letter from Percy L. Greaves, Jr., to Barnes, May 31, 1962:

". . . He [Dall] believes in the Khazar conspiracy idea of history with emphasis on the Rothschild family intrigue to manage the finances of all the world powers, including the United States.

"He had some interesting inside information on Baruch and Frankfurter and felt that FDR was not a free man when it came to policies that led to war. The funds that supported him were, in his opinion, responsible for his policies that took us into war to the great financial profit of certain interests. . . . In his opinion we went to war because the Zionists wanted it and so did the international bankers." (Papers of RADM. Husband E. Kimmel, University of Wyoming, Laramie, Wyo., Box 11; hereafter cited as Kimmel Papers.)

In an interview in *Spotlight*, December 5, 1977, Dall named "international financiers and Zionist leaders" including Bernard Baruch and Felix Frankfurter as being behind Roosevelt's policy.

10. Interview with Crawford, August 8, 1964. Interviewed at the same time, CPO Harry Rafsky, who had been enlisted aide to RADM. William L. Calhoun, commander, Base Force in 1941, agreed with Crawford.

11. Interview with Smart, August 21, 1964.

12. Interview with Forrow, August 16, 1964.

13. *Roosevelt and Pearl Harbor*, p. 312.

14. Papers of Charles C. Hiles, University of Wyoming, Laramie, Wyo., Box 15 (hereafter cited as Hiles Papers).

15. RADM. Kemp Tolley, *Cruise of the Lanikai: Incitement to War* (Annapolis, 1973), pp. 61, 64 (hereafter cited as *Cruise of the Lanikai*).

16. *Infamy*, p. 274.

17. Ibid., p. 90.

18. *F.D.R.*, p. 162.

19. Kimmel, Adm. Husband E., Memorandum, "Interview With the President, 1425–1550, Monday June 9, 1941," Navy Dept. OP-120-2-McC, Classified Operational Archives Branch, Naval History Division, Washington Navy Yard, D.C. See *At Dawn We Slept*, pp. 139–40, for a brief account of the Roosevelt-Kimmel meeting.

20. Harry E. Barnes, "Summary and Conclusions," in *Perpetual War*, p. 642 (hereafter cited as "Summary and Conclusions").

21. "Dane-Geld," quoted in *The Oxford Dictionary of Quotations* (London, 1955), p. 295.

22. Seijiro Otaka, *Kishu-ka Boryaku-ka (Surprise Attack or Treachery)*, (Tokyo, 1954), p. 6.

23. Capt. (later Lt. Gen.) Minoru Genda, who developed the tactical plan for the Pearl Harbor attack, considered this the summit of his career in the Imperial Japanese Navy. Interview with Genda, August 31, 1955.

24. *Infamy*, p. 318.

25. See *At Dawn We Slept*, p. 344.

26. Interviews with Genda, April 6, June 6, and June 10, 1947; VADM. Ryunosuke Kusaka, August 24, 1947, and March 7, 1949 (hereafter Kusaka).

27. Interview with Mikawa, January 12, 1949.

28. Interview with Fukudome, May 4, 1950.

29. Interview with Yoshioka, September 23, 1949.

30. Interview with Fuchida, April 9, 1949.

31. *Truth About Pearl harbor*, pp. 3, 13, 28.

32. John T. Flynn, "The Final Secret of Pearl Harbor," p. 15 (hereafter cited as "Final Secret"). This article first appeared in the Chicago *Tribune*, September 2, 1945, and later was published in pamphlet form.

33. Letter, Edward F. Hanify to Kimmel, August 30, 1953, Kimmel Papers, Box 7.

34. Letter, Greaves to Barnes, May 31, 1962, Kimmel Papers, Box 11.

35. *Infamy*, p. 319.

36. September 24, 1945.

37. William F. Friedman, "Certain Aspects of 'Magic' in the Cryptological Background of the Various Official Investigations into the pearl Harbor Attack," NA, RG 457, SRH 125, Box 9.

38. Papers of Harry Elmer Barnes, University of Wyoming, Laramie, Wyo., Box 61 (hereafter cited as Barnes Papers).

39. For some additional views of Prange's on revisionism, see *At Dawn We Slept*, pp. 839–50.

CHAPTER 4

"BAIT FOR A JAPANESE ATTACK"

1. Frederic R. Sanborn, "Roosevelt is Frustrated in Europe," in *Perpetual War*, p. 221 (hereafter cited as "Roosevelt is Frustrated").

2. Harry E. Barnes, "Pearl Harbor After a Quarter of a Century," *Left and Right:*

A Journal of Libertarian Thought, Vol. IV, 1968, p. 109. Hereafter "PH After ¼ Century."

3. John Costello, *The Pacific War, 1941–45* (New York, 1982), pp. 641–43. Costello's footnotes covering this incident cite no primary source, only *Cruise of the Lanikai.*

4. *PHA,* Part 5, pp. 2190–91.

5. Ibid., Part 14, p. 1407.

6. Ibid., Part 5, p. 2191.

7. "Actual Road," p. 360.

8. *PHA,* Part 4, p. 2044; Part 26, pp. 437, 440.

9. Ibid., Part 9, pp. 4252–54.

10. Ibid., Part 4, pp. 2044–46, corrected by Part 5, p. 2238.

11. Ibid., Part 9, p. 4253.

12. Ibid., Part 3, p. 1248.

13. Ibid., Part 2, pp. 955–59.

14. Ibid., Part 4, p. 1618.

15. Ibid., Part 5, pp. 2416–18.

16. Ibid., Part 10, p. 4807. According to Tolley, the third ship was to have been the schooner *Molly Moore.* See *Cruise of the Lanikai,* p. 272.

17. "PH After ¼ Century," p. 110.

18. *Cruise of the Lanikai,* p. 264.

19. Log of *Isabel,* NA, RGN, Records of the Bureau of Naval Personnel, report of John Walker Payne, Jr., U.S. Naval Archives, Washington Navy Yard, Washington, D.C. Quoted in *Cruise of the Lanikai,* p. 269.

20. "PH After ¼ Century," p. 110.

21. Letter, with attached chronicle of U.S.S. Lanikai from commissioning on December 5, 1941, to April 27, 1942, Tolley to Chief, BuNAV, April 28, 1942, Subject: "Ship's Log," NA, RG 24, Record of the Bureau of Naval Personnel, National Archives, Washington, D.C. As Tolley was the only officer assigned and had neither clerical assistance, standard forms nor Navy Department publications aboard, he kept an informal "chronicle" in lieu of a log.

22. Chronicle log of *Lanikai,* National Archives, Washington, D.C.

23. *Cruise of the Lanikai,* p. 270.

24. Ibid., p. 279.

25. Letter, Hart to RADM. Reginald R. Belknap, June 20, 1954. Papers of RADM. Reginald R. Belknap, National Historical Foundation, Washington, D.C.

26. Letter, Tolley to Hiles, November 6, 1970, Hiles Papers, Box 18.

27. *PHA,* Part 10, pp. 4807–08.

28. RADM. Julius Augustus Furer, *Administration of the Navy Department in*

World War II (Washington, D.C., 1959), p. 47 (hereafter cited as *Administration of the Navy Department*).

29. Letter, Greaves to Barnes, December 21, 1962, Barnes Papers, Box 62.

30. *PHA*, Part 2, p. 956.

31. Ibid., Part 6, pp. 2872–73.

32. Ibid., Report, pp. 266-P, 528.

33. *Infamy*, pp. 279–80, 285, 317N. The Haan story begins on p. 260, the Clear story on p. 261. Frequently Toland's documentation is disappointing, and in a number of cases he cited messages and letters supposedly sent which could not be found.

34. Copy of this study is in the Prange files. It was probably written in August 1942.

35. Mitsuo Fuchida, *Shinjuwan Sakusen No Shinso; Watakushi Wa Shinjuwan Joku Ni Ita* (Nara, Japan, 1949), pp. 128–29 (hereafter cited as *Shinjuwan Sakusen No Shinso*).

36. Minoru Genda, *Shinjuwan Sakusen Kaikoroku* (Tokyo, 1962), p. 263 (hereafter cited as *Shinjuwan Sakusen Kaikoroku*).

37. Ryunosuke Kusaka, *Rengo Kantai* (Tokyo, 1952), pp. 22–24 (hereafter cited as *Rengo Kantai*).

38. Letter, Chihaya to Dillon, March 30, 1982.

39. Interview with Lt. Cmdr. Susumu Ishiguro, April 6, 1948.

40. Honolulu *Star-Bulletin*, December 7, 1966. The reporter was interested in the document in connection with quite another subject. The Department of Defense advised the newspaper "that the log was destroyed after being transferred to the Federal Communications Commission."

41. *Infamy*, p. 318.

42. Ibid., pp. 280–81.

43. Ibid., p. 286.

44. Ibid., p. 299.

45. Ibid., pp. 316–17. In preparing his interesting and incisive article, "Day of Infamy, Decades of Doubt" (*New York Times Magazine*, April 29, 1984), Telford Taylor attempted to determine what if any degree of friendship existed between Roosevelt and McCollough. He found that neither James MacGregor Burns, Joseph P. Lash, nor Arthur Schlesinger, Jr., all well-known historians of the Roosevelt era, nor Grace Tully, Roosevelt's private secretary, were familiar with his name. Nor did research at the Roosevelt Library reveal any mention of him. Taylor concluded that while the two men might have been acquaintances or even friends, he doubted that the relationship "was of such intimacy and trust that Captain McCollough could command the President's ear, either directly or through Mr. Hopkins."

46. *PHA*, Part 17, p. 2636.

47. Ibid., pp. 2638–39.

48. Ibid., Part 15, p. 1896.

49. Letter, Chihaya to Dillon, March 30, 1982.

50. Oral History Interview with Mr. Robert D. Ogg, NA, RG 457, Records of the National Security Agency, SRH 255, pp. 2, 10.

51. Ibid., pp. 52, 27.

52. Ibid., pp. 14, 20–21.

53. Ibid., pp. 35–36.

54. Ibid., pp. 53–54.

55. Ibid., pp. 58, 68–69.

56. Ibid., p. 43.

57. See for example Diary of RADM. Sadao Chigusa, November 27 through December 6, 1941 (hereafter cited as Chigusa Diary).

58. *Infamy*, Berkley edition, pp. 344–45.

59. Interview with Imaizumi, June 29, 1950.

60. *Infamy*, Berkley edition, p. 341.

61. *Infamy*, pp. 282–83.

62. Ibid., p. 286.

63. *PHA*, Part 17, pp. 2636, 2638.

64. Log of *Enterprise*, December 3, 1941, reproduced in *PHA*, Part 16, pp. 2054–57.

65. *Infamy*, p. 298.

66. Washington *Post*, September 12, 1945.

67. Letter, Barnes to Prange, November 1, 1963.

68. Elting E. Morison, *Turmoil and Tradition: A Study of the Life and Times of Henry L. Stimson* (Boston, 1960), pp. 519–20 (hereafter cited as *Turmoil and Tradition*).

69. Jonathan Daniels, *White House Witness, 1942–1945*, (New York, 1973), p. 50. For an excellent discussion of Roosevelt in relation to the Navy, see Lt. Col. George V. Fagan, USAF, "F. D. R. and Naval Limitations," *United States Naval Institute Proceedings* (April, 1955), pp. 411-18.

70. *Ordeal and Hope*, p. 22.

71. *Turmoil and Tradition*, p. 527.

CHAPTER 5

"TO AVOID WAR WITH JAPAN"

1. For an excellent discussion of these and related matters, see Sir Llewellyn Woodward, *British Foreign Policy in the Second World War*, Vol. II (London, 1971) (hereafter cited as *British Foreign Policy*).

2. Papers of Franklin D. Roosevelt, Franklin D. Roosevelt Library, Hyde Park, N.Y., Map Room File, Box 1 (hereafter cited as Roosevelt Papers).

3. Ibid.

4. David Dilks, ed., *The Diaries of Sir Alexander Cadogan, 1938–1945* (New York, 1972), pp. 299, 309 (hereafter cited as *Cadogan Diaries*).

5. Ibid., pp. 311, 375.

6. Telegram, Churchill to Roosevelt, October 4, 1940, Roosevelt Papers, Map Room File, Box 1.

7. Telegram, Churchill to Roosevelt, December 7, 1940, Roosevelt Papers, Map Room File, Box 1.

8. Roosevelt Papers, Presidential Secretary's File, Box 59 (hereafter cited as PSF).

9. Winston S. Churchill, *The Grand Alliance* (Boston, 1950), pp. 587–88 (hereafter cited as *Grand Alliance*).

10. *Truth about Pearl Harbor*, p. 5.

11. See for example *Roosevelt and Pearl Harbor*, p. 71.

12. Roosevelt Papers, PSF, Box 63.

13. Percy L. Greaves, Jr., "The Pearl Harbor Investigations," in *Perpetual War*, p. 410 (hereafter cited as "PH Investigations").

14. The text of ABC-1 is reproduced in *PHA*, Part 15, pp. 1485–1550.

15. *PHA*, Part 15, p. 1564. See pp. 1551–84 for full text of ADB.

16. Ibid., pp. 1678–79. For an excellent account of these prewar discussions and plans, see Mark S. Watson, *Chief of Staff: Prewar Plans and Preparations* (Washington, 1950), pp. 367–410. This volume is one of the series, *United States Army in World War II*, subseries *The War Department*.

17. Herbert Feis, "War Came at Pearl Harbor: Suspicions Considered," *Yale Review* (Spring 1956), pp. 381–82 (hereafter cited as "War Came").

18. *PHA*, Part 9, p. 4277.

19. Ibid., Part 5, pp. 2332–33, corrected by Part 6, p. 2673.

20. Ibid., Part 5, p. 2390.

21. Ibid., Part 3, pp. 993–94.

22. Ibid., Part 5, p. 2392.

23. *Cadogan Diaries*, p. 353.

24. Anthony Eden, *The Memoirs of Anthony Eden, Earl of Avon: The Reckoning* (Boston, 1965), p. 358 (hereafter cited as *Reckoning*).

25. *British Foreign Policy*, p. 122.

26. *PHA,*, Part 19, pp. 3447–49.

27. Ibid., pp. 3450–51.

28. Roosevelt Papers, PSF, Box 41. A paraphrase appears in *PHA*, Part 19, pp. 3452–53.

29. *Truth about Pearl Harbor,* p. 5. For an account of the ship transfers in question, see *At Dawn We Slept,* Chapters 15–16.

30. Diary of Henry L. Stimson, Yale University Library, New Haven, Conn., April 24, 1941 (hereafter cited as Stimson Diary).

31. *Cadogan Diaries,* pp. 393–94.

32. *British Foreign Policy,* pp. 138, 140.

33. *Cruise of the Lanikai,* p. 42.

34. *Final Secret,* p. 4.

35. "PH After ¼ Century," p. 19.

36. *Second Crusade,* p. 142.

37. *Cadogan Diaries,* p. 398.

38. *PHA,* Part 14, pp. 1273–74. The entire State Department Memorandum of Conversation, August 10, 1941, appears on pp. 1269–74.

39. State Department Memorandum of Conversation, August 17, 1941, Papers of Cordell Hull, Library of Congress, Washington, D.C., Box 60 (hereafter cited as Hull Papers).

40. The Earl of Birkenhead, *Halifax* (Boston, 1966), p. 525 (hereafter cited as *Halifax*).

41. *Grand Alliance,* pp. 539, 547.

42. Ibid., p. 595.

43. *Cruise of the Lanikai,* p. 20.

44. Dispatch to British Chiefs of Staff by Air Chief Marshal Sir Robert Brooke-Popham covering his tenure as Commander in Chief, Far East, October 17, 1940 to December 27, 1941. Supplement to the London *Gazette,* January 20, 1948, pp. 535, 554 (hereafter cited as Brooke-Popham Dispatch).

45. Ibid., p. 545.

46. Ibid., p. 554.

47. *British Foreign Policy,* pp. 164, 169.

48. Ibid., pp. 170–71.

49. *Grand Alliance,* pp. 600–01.

50. *British Foreign Policy,* p. 173; *Halifax,* p. 529. See also *At Dawn We Slept,* pp. 451–52; 467–68.

51. *Cadogan Diaries,* p. 415.

52. *Reckoning,* p. 365.

53. Stimson Diary, December 1, 1941.

54. *PHA,,* Part 11, p. 5215; Part 15, pp. 1770–71.

55. Ibid., Part 11, pp. 5215–16; Part 15, pp. 1772–73.

56. Ibid., Part 11, p. 5216; Part 15, p. 1773.

57. Ibid., Part 11, p. 5219.

58. Ibid., Part 2, p. 494; Part 14, p.1247; Hull Papers, Box 60.

59. *PHA*, Part 2, p. 494; Hull Papers, Box 60.

60. *PHA*, Part 2, p. 493; Part 14, p. 1246. Ferguson erroneously referred to this message as dated December 2. Actually it was dated December 6.

61. Ibid., Part 11, p. 5472.

62. *Cruise of the Lanikai*, p. 65.

63. Cordell Hull, *The Memoirs of Cordell Hull*, Vol. II (New York, 1948), p. 1092 (hereafter cited as *Hull Memoirs*).

64. *PHA*, Part 10, pp. 5082–83.

65. Ibid., p. 5081.

66. Ibid., p. 5084.

67. Ibid., pp. 5086–87.

68. Ibid., Part 11, pp. 5514–15.

69. Ibid., Part 10, p. 4803.

70. Ibid., Part 14, p. 1412.

71. *Grand Alliance*, p. 601.

72. S. Woodburn Kirby, *The War Against Japan*, Vol. I (London, 1957), p. 177. The story of "Matador" appears on pp. 76–78, 173–74.

73. Brooke-Popham Dispatch, pp. 546, 555.

74. "PH After ¼ Century," p. 36.

75. *PHA*, Part 34, p. 60.

76. Ibid., p. 61; Part 29, p. 2301.

77. Ibid., Part 34, p. 172.

78. Ibid., Part 29, p. 2303.

79. Ibid., Part 34, p. 63.

80. Ibid., p. 172.

81. "PH After ¼ Century," p. 112. See *Pearl Harbor*, pp. 306–07; "PH Investigations," pp. 430–31; Ladislas Farago, *The Broken Seal* (New York, 1967), pp. 347–48 (hereafter cited as *Broken Seal*).

82. *PHA*, Part 34, p. 172.

83. "PH After ¼ Century," pp. 106, 114.

84. *PHA*, Part 12, p. 252.

85. *Final Secret*, p. 117.

86. *PHA*, Part 33, p. 756.

87. See for example Washington *Post*, December 6, 1941.

CHAPTER 6

"HE HAD SUPREME RESPONSIBILITY"

1. *Congressional Record,* Vol. 88, Part 8, Appendix, p. A295.
2. "National Whirligig," Houston *Post,* January 30, 1942.
3. January 26, 1942.
4. *PHA,* Part 6, pp. 2714–15.
5. Robert E. Sherwood, *Roosevelt and Hopkins: An Intimate History* (New York, 1948), p. 191 (hereafter cited as *Roosevelt and Hopkins*).
6. Joseph P. Lash, *Roosevelt and Churchill 1939–1941: The Partnership That Saved the West* (New York, 1976), pp. 177, 237 (hereafter cited as *Roosevelt and Churchill*).
7. Letter, Alfred M. Landon to Raymond Clapper, February 21, 1942. Papers of Raymond Clapper, Library of Congress, Box 50 (hereafter cited as Clapper Papers).
8. *Roosevelt and Pearl Harbor,* p. 187.
9. Letter, G. H. Corse, Jr., to Raymond Clapper, December 31, 1941, Clapper Papers, Box 50.
10. Emporia *Gazette,* December 16, 1941.
11. Dexter Perkins, "Was Roosevelt Wrong?" *Virginia Quarterly Review* (Summer 1954), pp. 360–62, (hereafter cited as "Was Roosevelt Wrong?").
12. Ibid., pp. 363, 365.
13. *Halifax,* p. 520.
14. Letter, E. C. Evans to Harold Young, Assistant to Vice President Wallace, November 17, 1941. Papers of Henry A. Wallace, Library of Congress, Box 13 (hereafter cited as Wallace Papers).
15. Letter, E. C. Evans to Harold Young, October 15, 1941, Wallace Papers, Box 13.
16. Drafts and correspondence concerning the modus vivendi are reproduced in *PHA,* Part 14, pp. 1084–1177.
17. This letter is undated, but from its position in the diary was obviously written in late November 1941. Morgenthau Presidential Diary, pp. 1034–35.
18. Houston *Post.*
19. Interview with Furlong, November 16, 1962.
20. For a discussion of these subjects, see *At Dawn We Slept,* pp. 149–53, 255–57.
21. January 27, 1942.
22. See for example Gordon W. Prange, *Target Tokyo* (New York, 1984).
23. John Morton Blum, *From the Morgenthau Diaries: Years of Urgency, 1938–1941* (Boston, 1965), pp. 348, 351 (hereafter cited as *Years of Urgency*).

24.   Stimson Diary, October 1 and 2, 1940.

25.   Washington *Post.*

26.   *Infamy,* pp. 275–76.

27.   Press Conference, Havana, Cuba, July 27, 1940, Hull Papers, Box 12.

28.   *PHA,* Part 2, p. 507.

29.   Memorandum, Ralph Ingersoll to Col. William J. Donovan, October 21, 1941, Papers of Harry Hopkins, Franklin D. Roosevelt Library, Hyde Park, N.Y., Box 308 (hereafter cited as Hopkins Papers).

30.   VADM. George C. Dyer, *On the Treadmill to Pearl Harbor: The Memoirs of Admiral James O. Richardson, USN (Retired),* (Washington, 1973), p. 125 (hereafter cited as *On the Treadmill*).

31.   *Rising Sun in the Pacific,* p. 31.

32.   *Congressional Record,* Vol. 90, Part 11, Appendix, August 28, 1944, p. A3964.

33.   Ibid., Part 6, September 18, 1944, p. 7877.

34.   *PHA,* Part 16, p. 2148.

35.   Morgenthau Presidential Diary, p. 1047.

36.   This plan is reproduced in *PHA,* Part 15, pp. 1429–34.

37.   *PHA,* Part 28, p. 919.

38.   Ibid., Part 29, p. 2312.

39.   Ibid., Report, p. 543.

40.   Ibid., Part 3, p. 1173.

41.   Washington *Evening Star,* January 16, 1941.

42.   *Nation* (February 21, 1942), p. 211.

43.   *Hull Memoirs,* Vol. II, p. 1104.

44.   June 30, 1944.

45.   Houston *Post,* November 29, 1941.

CHAPTER 7

"ON LINES OF NATIONAL POLICY"

1.   For a discussion of these moves, see *At Dawn We Slept,* Chapters 15–16.

2.   Memorandum, Hornbeck to Welles, September 21, 1940, Papers of Stanley K. Hornbeck, Hoover Institution on War, Revolution and Peace, Stanford, Calif., Box 309 (hereafter cited as Hornbeck Papers).

3.   *PHA,* Part 2, p. 548.

4.   "Washington Scene," Milwaukee *Sentinel,* November 29, 1945.

5.   November 7, 1945.

6. Unpublished autobiography of Stanley K. Hornbeck (hereafter cited as Hornbeck autobiography), Hornbeck Papers, Box 497.

7. *PHA*, Part 22, p. 522.

8. January 7, 1946.

9. *PHA*, Part 4, p. 1995.

10. Ibid., Part 5, p. 2190.

11. Ibid., Part 9, p. 4260.

12. Ibid., Report, p. 266C.

13. Stimson Diary, May 5, 1941.

14. Ibid., April 25, 1941.

15. New York *Herald Tribune*, May 17, 1941.

16. Ibid.

17. *PHA*, Part 5, p. 2413.

18. Ibid., p. 2290.

19. Ibid., pp. 2217–18.

20. Ibid., p. 2189.

21. Ibid., Part 6, p. 2824.

22. Ibid., p. 2566.

23. Ibid., p. 2847.

24. Ibid., Part 9, p. 4260.

25. Ibid., pp. 4257–58.

26. Leahy Diary.

27. Interview with Oikawa, April 10, 1949.

28. Interview with Watanabe, March 18, 1949.

29. VADM. Shigeru Fukudome, Former IJN, "Hawaii Operation," *United States Naval Institute Proceedings* (December 1955), p. 1317 (hereafter cited as "Hawaii Operation.").

30. *PHA*, Part 2, p. 658.

31. Ibid., Part 5, pp. 2269–70.

32. Ibid., Part 1, pp. 262–63.

33. Ibid., Part 32, pp. 625, 627.

34. Ibid., Part 22, p. 431.

35. Ibid., Part 6, p. 2831.

36. Ibid., Part 32, p. 282.

37. Ibid., Part 3, p. 1262.

38. Ibid., Part 5, p. 2105.

39. Ibid., Part 28, p. 906.

40. Ibid., Report, p. 266B.

41. Ibid., Part 27, p. 129.

42. Ibid., Part 6, p. 2827.

43. Ibid., p. 7, pp. 3332–33.

44. For an account, see *At Dawn We Slept*, pp. 533–34, 538.

45. *PHA*, Part 26, pp. 88–9.

46. Washington *Evening Star*, January 17, 1941.

47. Ibid., June 8, 1941.

48. *PHA*, Part 29, pp. 1642–43.

49. Ibid., Report, p. 546.

50. Interview with Spruance, September 5, 1964.

51. "Why the Fleet Could Not Retreat to the West Coast," *Newsweek* (December 3, 1945), p. 36.

52. Interview with Furlong, December 1, 1962.

53. *PHA*, Part 10, p. 4821.

54. Letter, Greaves to Barnes, December 21, 1962, Barnes Papers, Box 62. Some of the former U.S. naval officers who assisted Prange in this study made the same point.

55. *PHA*, Part 1, p. 265.

56. *Truth About Pearl Harbor*, p. 31.

57. Chicago *Tribune*, September 2, 1945, quoted in *Congressional Record*, Vol. 91, Part 12, Appendix, September 12, 1945, p. A3853. Flynn expressed the same judgment, in slightly different words, in "Final Secret," p. 14.

58. For a full account, see *At Dawn We Slept*, Chapters 3, pp. 11 and 12.

59. January 7, 1946.

60. Edward P. Morgan, "An Approach to the Question of Responsibility for the Pearl Harbor Disaster," p. 164 (hereafter cited as Morgan Report). Morgan prepared this as a draft report for the Congressional Committee.

CHAPTER 8

"LOOKING IN THE WRONG DIRECTION"

1. Letter, Greaves to Barnes, December 21, 1962, Barnes Papers, Box 62.

2. Stimson Diary, June 23, 1941.

3. Ibid., July 1, 1941.

4. *PHA*, Part 16, p. 2175.

5. *Ordeal and Hope*, p. 72.

6. *Hull Memoirs,* Vol. II, p. 969.

7. *Ickes Secret Diary,* p. 549.

8. Joseph C. Grew, *Ten Years in Japan* (New York, 1944), p. 395 (hereafter cited as *Ten Years in Japan*).

9. State Department Memorandum of Conversation, July 25, 1941, Hull Papers, Box 60.

10. Military Attaché Report No. 10,505, August 21, 1941, Hopkins Papers, Box 193.

11. State Department Memorandum of Conversation, July 18, 1941, Hull Papers, Box 60.

12. Military Attaché Report No. 2, August 6, 1941, Hopkins Papers, Box 193.

13. Military Attaché Report No. 60, September 18, 1941, Hopkins Papers, Box 193.

14. Hopkins Papers, Box 193.

15. *PHA,* Part 16, p. 2171.

16. Ibid., Part 14, p. 1341.

17. State Department Memorandum of Conversation, July 18, 1941, Hull Papers, Box 60.

18. Letter, Roosevelt to Churchill, October 15, 1941, Roosevelt Papers, PSF, Box 35.

19. *PHA,* Part 5, p. 2328.

20. "Military aspects of the situation that would result from the retention by the United States of a military (including naval) commitment in the Philippine Islands," Hopkins Papers, Box 308. For an interesting discussion of the United States' Philippine strategy and the Orange Plans, see Louis Morton, *United States Army in World War II: The War in the Pacific: Strategy and Command: The First Two Years* (Washington, 1962), pp. 21–44 (hereafter cited as *Strategy and Command*).

21. Stimson Diary, August 19, 1940.

22. *PHA,* Part 18, p. 2894.

23. Memorandum for the Secretary of War, October 8, 1941, Subject: Strategic Concept of the Philippine Islands, NA, RG 107, Box 11.

24. Louis Morton, *United States Army in World War II, The War in the Pacific, The Fall of the Philippines,* (Washington, D.C., 1953), pp. 9–30 (hereafter cited as *Fall of the Philippines*).

25. Henry L. Stimson and McGeorge Bundy, *On Active Service in Peace and War* (New York, 1947), p. 388 (hereafter cited as *On Active Service*). See also *Fall of the Philippines,* pp. 11–12.

26. *PHA,* Part 16, p. 2176.

27. *Strategy and Command,* pp. 98–100.

28. Memorandum for the Secretary of War, October 8, 1941.

29. Stimson Diary, September 12, 1941.

30. Ibid., September 25, 1941.

31. Ibid., September 30, 1941.

32. A copy of this letter is attached to Stimson's diary entry of October 21, 1941. A copy is also in NA, RG 107, Box 15.

33. Memorandum for the Secretary of War, October 18, 1941.

34. Perhaps he did raise this question, but Prange found no hint of it in his years of research, nor have we in our recent research.

35. Stimson Diary, October, 9, 1941.

36. *PHA*, Part 15, p. 1635. See *At Dawn We Slept*, Chapter 14.

37. Ibid., Part 7, p. 3203.

38. Ibid., Part 6, p. 2569.

39. Stimson Diary, October 28, 1941.

40. Ibid., November 27, 1941.

41. *PHA*, Part 14, p. 1329.

42. Ibid., pp. 1056–57.

43. Ibid., p. 1403.

44. Ibid., Part 12, p. 105.

45. Ibid., p. 137.

46. Ibid., p. 155.

47. Ibid., p. 154.

48. Ibid., Part 35, p. 74.

49. See for example State Department Memoranda of Conversations, October 28, November 7, 18, 19, and 22, 1941, Hull Papers, Box 60.

50. Attachment to State Department Memorandum of Conversation, November 20, 1941, Hull Papers, Box 60.

51. Stimson Diary, November 26, 1941.

52. Memorandum for the President, November 26, 1941, Subject: Japanese Convoy Movement towards Indo-China, NA, RG 107, Stimson "Safe File," White House Correspondence, Box 15.

53. *Pacific War*, pp. 628 ff.

54. Stimson Diary, November 28, 1941.

55. *PHA*, Part 12, p. 189.

56. Ibid., Part 8, p. 3829.

57. Interview with Layton, July 22, 1964.

CHAPTER 9

"WITH KNIVES AND HATCHETS"

1. *Current Biography* (New York, 1940), p. 412.
2. Freda Kirchwey, "The Fruits of Appeasement," *Nation* (December 13, 1941), p. 599.
3. Freda Kirchwey, "Partners in Guilt," *Nation* (December 27, 1941), p. 656.
4. January 27, 1942.
5. Robert Bendiner, *The Riddle of the State Department* (New York, 1942) pp. 6–7 (hereafter cited as *Riddle*).
6. Ibid., p. 11.
7. Morgenthau Diaries, Book 469.
8. March 9, 1942.
9. December 20, 1941.
10. *PHA*, Part 3, p. 1148.
11. Washington *Post*, August 27, 1944.
12. Washington *Star*, August 26, 1944.
13. Washington *Post*, August 27, 1944.
14. Milwaukee *Sentinel*, November 5, 1945.
15. "Japanese-American Relations," p. 307.
16. Memorandum of telephone conversation between Hull and Willkie, May 15, 1941, Hull Papers, Box 49.
17. Letter, Hull to Judge R. B. C. Howell, Nashville, Tenn., June 5, 1941, Hull Papers, Box 49.
18. Diaries of Adolf A. Berle, Jr., Franklin D. Roosevelt Library, Hyde Park, N.Y., entry of November 7, 1940, Box 212 (hereafter cited as Berle Diaries).
19. Ibid., October 25, 1940, Box 212.
20. Ibid., December 1, 1941, Box 213.
21. "Washington Merry-Go-Round," Honolulu *Star-Bulletin*, January 5, 1946.
22. Interviews with Senator Guy M. Gillette, February 19, 1955, and Representative Martin Dies, March 1, 1955. See *At Dawn We Slept*, Chapter 31.
23. Interview with RADM. Dundas P. Tucker, August 22, 1964 (hereafter Tucker). See *At Dawn We Slept*, Chapter 18.
24. For a consideration of Kuehn's role, see *At Dawn We Slept*, Chapter 38.
25. File RG 457 at the National Archives is replete with evidence of widespread Japanese intelligence activities.
26. *PHA*, Part 2, p. 612.
27. Ibid., Part 5, pp. 2410–11.

28. State Department Memorandum of Conversation, Roosevelt and Nomura, July 24, 1941, Hull Papers, Box 60.

29. *Years of Urgency,* p. 351.

30. Stimson Diary, October 1 and 2, 1940.

31. Ibid., October 11 and 19, 1940.

32. Harold L. Ickes, *The Secret Diary of Harold L. Ickes,* Vol. III, *The Lowering Clouds 1939–1941* (New York, 1954), p. 330 (hereafter cited as *Ickes Secret Diary*).

33. Ibid., p. 583.

34. Ibid., pp. 591–92.

35. Takushiro Hattori, *Daitoa Senso Zen-shi (The Complete History of the Greater East Asia War),* (Tokyo, 1953), p. 166 (hereafter cited as *Complete History*).

36. See for example *Asahi,* August 4, 1941, and *Japan Times and Advertiser,* August 5, 1941.

37. Far East Military Tribunal, interrogation of Maj. Gen. Akira Muto, August 15, 1946.

38. Memorandum for the files of telephone conversation between Hull and Welles, August 2, 1941, Hull Papers, Box 72–73.

39. Unsigned, undated statement, "The freezing of Japanese assets on July 26, 1941, and discontinuance of trade with Japan," Hull Papers, Box 72–73.

40. Berle Diaries, July 19, 1941, Box 213.

41. Ibid., July 23, 1941, Box 213.

42. *Years of Urgency,* p. 380.

43. *Riddle,* pp. 17–18.

44. Ibid., pp. 21–22.

45. Memorandum for the files of telephone conversation between Hull and Welles, July 23, 1941, Hull Papers, Box 72–73.

46. Interview with Onoda, Septemer 8, 1949.

47. Interview with Tomioka, September 8, 1947.

48. Sir George Sansom, "Japan's Fatal Blunder," *International Affairs,* (October 1948), p. 547.

49. For some representative views, see such revisionist studies as *Roosevelt and the Coming; Back Door; Pearl Harbor; Second Crusade; Perpetual War.*

50. State Department Memorandum of Conversation, Welles and Nomura, July 23, 1941, Hull Papers, Box 60.

51. State Department Memorandum of Conversation, Hull and Nomura, August 6, 1941, Hull Papers, Box 60.

52. Interview with Tomioka, July 16, 1947.

53. For a full account, see *At Dawn We Slept,* Chapter 37.

54. Hornbeck Autobiography, Hornbeck Papers, Box 497.

55. For an excellent account of this incident, see R. J. C. Butow, *The John Doe Associates: Backdoor Diplomacy for Peace, 1941* (Stanford, Calif., 1974, hereafter cited as *John Doe Associates*). For another interesting discussion, see John H. Boyle, "The Walsh-Drought Mission to Japan," *Pacific Historical Review* (May 1965).

56. *Hull Memoirs*, Vol. II, p. 985; *John Doe Associates*, p. 135; Herbert Feis, *The Road to Pearl Harbor: The Coming of the War Between the United States and Japan* (Princteon, N.J., 1950), p. 175 (hereafter cited as *Road to Pearl Harbor*).

57. *John Doe Associates*, pp. 61, 64.

58. Ibid., pp. 50–51, 55–60.

59. Ibid., p. 314.

60. Ibid., p. 41.

61. Ibid., p. 108.

62. Ibid., pp. 44–45.

CHAPTER 10

"UNSURMOUNTABLE OBSTACLES"

1. Admiral Kichisaburo Nomura, "Stepping-Stones to War," *United States Naval Institute Proceedings* (Septcmber 1951), p. 930 (hereafter cited as "Stepping Stones").

2. *PHA*, Part 5, p. 2206.

3. "Was Roosevelt Wrong?" pp. 369–70.

4. *PHA*, Part 14, pp. 1356–58.

5. Ibid., Part 2, p. 413.

6. Roosevelt Papers, PSF, Box 63.

7. State Department Memorandum of Conversation, March 8, 1941, between Hull and Nomura, Hull Papers, Box 60.

8. Ibid., October 9, 1941, between Hull, Nomura, Ballantine, and Shigeyoshi Ohata, Hull Papers, Box 60.

9. "Actual Road," p. 318.

10. Berle Diaries, December 11, 1939, Box 211.

11. *Truth About Pearl Harbor*, p. 7.

12. *Congressional Record*, Vol. 87, Part 14, Appendix, December 9, 1941, pp. A5492–93.

13. Interview with Admiral Kichisaburo Nomura, May 7, 1949 (hereafter cited as Nomura).

14. "Stepping-Stones," p. 928.

15. Ibid., pp. 928–29.

16. Toshikazu Kase, *Journey to the "Missouri"* (New Haven, 1951), p. 42 (hereafter cited as *Journey to the "Missouri"*).

17. "Actual Road," p. 323.

18. Berle Diaries, October 6, 1940, Box 212.

19. September 19, 1940.

20. October 1, 1940. Quoted in *The Japan Advertiser*, October 2, 1940.

21. September 28, 1940.

22. Ibid.

23. Schroeder, Paul W., *The Axis Alliance and Japanese-American Relations, 1941* (Ithaca, 1958).

24. State Department Memorandum of Conversation, March 14, 1941, Hull Papers, Box 60.

25. Ibid., November 27, 1941, Hull Papers, Box 60.

26. Ibid., October 28, 1941, Hull Papers, Box 60.

27. Ibid., November 19, 1941, Hull Papers, Box 60.

28. *PHA*, Part 20, p. 4532.

29. "Summation of Situation, Malaya, as of June 1, 1941," Brink to G-2, Philippine Department, Hopkins Papers, Box 193.

30. Chihiro Hosoya, "Miscalculations in Deterrent Policy: Japanese-U.S. Relations, 1938–1941," *Journal of Peace Research* (1968, No. 2) pp. 104, 108.

31. "Stepping-Stones," p. 930.

32. "Was Roosevelt Wrong?" p. 366.

33. State Department Memorandum of Conversation, November 19, 1941, Hull Papers, Box 60.

34. See for example *Pearl Harbor,* pp. 138–41.

35. "Japanese-American Relations," p. 306.

36. *Second Crusade,* p. 163.

37. "Was Roosevelt Wrong?" pp. 368–69.

38. Hornbeck Autobiography, Hornbeck Papers, Box 397. See also R. J. C. Butow, "Backdoor Diplomacy in the Pacific: The Proposal for a Konoye-Roosevelt Meeting, 1941," *The Journal of American History* (June 1972), p. 62 (hereafter cited as "Backdoor Diplomacy").

39. *PHA*, Part 2, p. 715.

40. Ibid., pp. 665–66.

41. See *At Dawn We Slept*, pp. 212–13.

42. *PHA*, Part 2, p. 663, corrected by part 5, p. 2482.

43. Letter, Grew to Kimmel, February 27, 1955, Kimmel Papers, Box 8.

44. *John Doe Associates*, pp. 255–56.

45. December 27, 1945.

46. State Department Memorandum of Conversation, August 17, 1941, Hull Papers, Box 60; Diary of Admiral Kichisaburo Nomura, August 28, 1941, Prange files (courtesy Admiral Nomura; hereafter cited as Nomura Diary).

47. *PHA*, Part 2, p. 425.

48. Ibid., pp. 425–26.

49. Military Attaché Report No. 10,578, October 20, 1941, Hopkins Papers, Box 193.

50. Interview with Nomura, May 7, 1949.

51. Joseph C. Grew, *Turbulent Era: A Diplomatic Record of Forty Years, 1904–1944, Part II* (Boston, 1952), p. 1329 (hereafter cited as *Turbulent Era*).

52. *Complete History*, p. 182.

53. *Ten Years in Japan*, p. 427; *At Dawn We Slept*, p. 184.

54. *At Dawn We Slept*, pp. 111, 177.

55. In a statement of August 31, 1951, prepared for Prange, Col. Takushiro Hattori asserted that the vice war minister knew about Pearl Harbor, but he erroneously named him as Lt. Gen. Hyotaro Kimura.

56. *Complete History*, p. 169. In his statement to Prange of August 31, 1951, Hattori listed the chief of the military affairs bureau as among the select group of Army officers in the Pearl Harbor secret, but gave his name as Kenryo Kimura.

57. R. J. C. Butow, *Tojo and the Coming of the War* (Princeton, 1961), pp. 170–71; 243–44 (hereafter cited as *Tojo*). For an excellent account of the liaison conference's composition and function, see pp. 149–50.

58. *Complete History*, p. 169.

59. Curt Reiss, *Total Espionage* (New York, 1941), pp. 219–20. See also *Tojo*, pp. 34–35, 78, 115; and Ellis M. Zacharias, *Secret Missions* (New York,, 1946), p. 18 (hereafter cited as *Secret Missions*).

60. *PHA*, Part 2, p. 426.

CHAPTER 11

"CRIMINATION AND RECRIMINATION"

1. *PHA*, Part 12, p. 154. In his unpublished diary, Nomura dated this visit on November 18; however his report states November 17, and it is obvious from the sequence of events that the latter is correct.

2. State Department Memorandum of Conversation, November 18, 1941, Hull Papers, Box 60; Nomura Diary, November 18, 1941. See also *PHA*, Part 12, pp. 146–152; Department of Defense, *The "Magic" Background of Pearl Har-*

bor (Washington, 1977), Vol. IV, Appendix, pp. A75–81 (hereafter cited as *"Magic" Background*); *Hull Memoirs*, Vol. II, pp. 1064–67.

3. *PHA*, Part 20, p. 4538.

4. Ibid., Part 12, p. 155.

5. Hull Papers, Box 72–73. For a further discussion of Nomura's suggested pull-back, and Japan's Proposal B, see *At Dawn We Slept*, Chapter 44.

6. *Pearl Harbor*, pp. 150–51.

7. "Actual Road," pp. 340–41.

8. Morgan Report, p. 41; *PHA*, Report, p. 41.

9. *"Genesis and Character of the American Government Communication to Japan's Spokesmen of November 26, 1941,"* December 4, 1942. Hornbeck Papers, Box 335 (hereafter cited as "Genesis and Character"). Hull used this study of Hornbeck's in written replies to some queries propounded him by Ferguson following Hull's oral testimony to the Congressional Committee. See *PHA*, Part 11, pp. 5370–71.

10. *British Foreign Policy*, p. 161.

11. *PHA*, Part 2, pp. 558–59, corrected by Part 11, p. 5308.

12. November 24, 1945.

13. *PHA*, Part 2, p. 497.

14. "Genesis and Character."

15. *PHA*, Part 12, pp. 155–56.

16. Ibid., Part 4, p. 1874.

17. Norman Hill, "Was there an Ultimatum Before Pearl Harbor?" *American Journal of International Law* (April, 1948), p. 366 (hereafter cited as "Was There an Ultimatum?").

18. "Genesis and Character."

19. *PHA*, Part 2, p. 554.

20. *Hull Memoirs*, Vol. II, p. 1073.

21. *PHA*, Part 14, pp. 1103–06.

22. *Hull Memoirs*, Vol. II, p. 1081.

23. For correspondence on this subject see *PHA*, Part 14, pp. 1160–61, 1300.

24. *PHA*, Part 5, p. 3237. For further discussion of the modus vivendi, see *At Dawn We Slept*, Chapter 45.

25. *Hull Memoirs*, Vol. II, p. 1081.

26. Hull Papers, Box 49.

27. Ibid.

28. Ibid.

29. *PHA*, Part 2, pp. 434, 451.

30. Hull Papers, Box 49. For more about Hull's note, see *At Dawn We Slept,*, Chapter 49.

31. *PHA,* Part 2, p. 437.

32. Attachment to State Department Memorandum of Conversation, November 26, 1941, Hull Papers, Box 60.

33. Roosevelt Papers, PSF, Box 83. For representative press comments see the New York *Herald Tribune* and Baltimore *Sun,* November 26, 1941; New York *Sun* and New York *World Telegram,* November 27, 1941; Honolulu *Star-Bulletin,* November 27 and 28, 1941.

34. Editorial, May 15, 1954, p. 10.

35. Chicago *Tribune,* December 7, 1966.

36. Congressional Record, Vol. 91, Part 8, p. 10446.

37. *At Dawn We Slept,* Chapters 77–78.

38. December 1, 1945.

39. Washington *Post,* November 2, 1945. See also Milwaukee *Sentinel,* November 1, 1945, and San Francisco *Chronicle,* November 2, 1945.

40. *Final Secret,* pp. 4, 21–22.

41. *PHA,* Part 2, p. 555.

42. *Second Crusade,* pp. 167–68.

43. Berle Diaries, December 7, 1941, Box 213.

44. "Genesis and Character."

45. See *At Dawn We Slept,* Chapter 74.

46. *Ten Years in Japan,* p. 483.

47. *PHA,* Part 2, pp. 685, 569, 772.

48. See *At Dawn We Slept,* Chapter 75.

49. *PHA,* Part 35, p. 19.

50. September 1, 1945.

51. Diary of Breckenridge Long, pp. 519–20, Papers of Breckenridge Long, Library of Congress, Box 4 (hereafter cited as Long Diary).

52. "War Came," pp. 488–89.

53. "Was There an Ultimatum?" pp. 363–65.

54. November 27, 1945.

55. November 24, 1945.

56. "Was There an Ultimatum?" pp. 365–67.

57. See *At Dawn We Slept,* Chapter 49.

58. Masuo Kato, *The Lost War* (New York, 1946), p. 76 (hereafter cited as *The Lost War*).

59. San Francisco *Chronicle,* July 21, 1946.

60. *The Lost War*, p. 75.

61. *Oregonian*, November 19, 1945.

62. "The Fateful 17th October," translated by J. Weiller.

63. *Final Secret*, p. v.

64. *PHA*, Part 6, p. 2524.

65. State Department Memorandum of Conversation, December 1, 1941, Hull Papers, Box 60; *Hull Memoirs*, Vol. II, p. 1090.

66. *Hull Memoirs*, Vol. II, pp. 1101, 1105.

67. Berle Diaries, December 8, 1941, Box 213.

68. *Hull Memoirs*, Vol. II, pp. 1109–10, 1714–19.

69. Drew Pearson, "Washington Merry-Go-Round," Bismarck *Tribune*, January 17, 1946.

CHAPTER 12

"TO HELP AND SERVE"

1. For representative stories see Chicago *Tribune*, December 22, 1941; San Antonio *Express*, January 25, and *Salt Lake Tribune*, January 26, 1942.

2. St. Louis *Post-Dispatch*, December 9, 1941.

3. December 13, 1941.

4. St. Louis *Post-Dispatch*, December 12, 1941.

5. December 11, 1941. The *Tribune* expressed similar sentiments on December 19, 1941.

6. December 19, 1941.

7. December 22, 1941.

8. Ibid.

9. Chicago *Tribune*, January 25, 1942.

10. *PHA*, Part 24, pp. 1363–64. See *At Dawn We Slept*, Chapter 5.

11. *PHA*, Part 14, pp. 1003–04. See *At Dawn We Slept*,, Chapter 7.

12. Indianapolis *Star*, January 25, 1942.

13. Chicago *Tribune*, January 26, 1942.

14. Ibid.

15. January 27, 1942.

16. March 9, 1942, p. 321.

17. Interview with Furlong, December 1, 1962.

18. Letter, Knox to E. P. Bell, August 30, 1940, Papers of Frank Knox, Library of Congress (hereafter cited as Knox Papers).

19. *PHA*, Part 14, p. 954; Honolulu *Advertiser*, September 7 and 14, 1940; Honolulu *Star-Bulletin*, September 9 and 14, 1940.

20. *PHA*, Part 14, p. 952.

21. Letter, October 1, 1940, Bloch to Stark, papers of Claude C. Bloch, Library of Congress, Box 4 (hereafter cited as Bloch Papers).

22. Honolulu *Advertiser*, September 14, 1940.

23. Stimson Diary, April 15 and October 21, 1941.

24. Ibid., October 23, 1941.

25. Ibid., November 7, 1940.

26. Admiral William H. Standley and RADM Arthur A. Ageton, *Admiral Ambassador to Russia* (Chicago, 1955), p. 29 (hereafter cited as *Admiral Ambassador*).

27. William L. Langer and S. Everett Gleason, *The Challenge to Isolation* (New York, 1952), p. 509 (hereafter cited as *Challenge to Isolation*).

28. Morgenthau Presidential Diary, April 18, 1940, p. 466.

29. This letter is undated, but an attached note indicates that it refers to Roosevelt's "Unlimited National Emergency" speech of May 27, 1941. Roosevelt Papers, PSF, Box 66.

30. For a full account, see *At Dawn We Slept*, Chapter 69.

31. Interview with Martin, September 14, 1971.

32. December 15, 1941.

33. December 17, 1941.

34. The original Knox report is in the Roosevelt Papers, PSF, Box 64. It is reproduced in *PHA*, Part 5, pp. 2338–45, and Part 24, pp. 1749–56.

35. Interview with Kimmel, November 30, 1963.

36. *New York Times*, April 29, 1944.

37. Stimson Diary, June 3, 1941.

38. Ibid., November 24, 1942.

39. Ibid., February 21, 1942.

40. New York *Herald Tribune*, May 16, 1941.

41. *New York Times*, April 29, 1944.

42. January 26, 1942.

43. March 9, 1942, p. 321.

44. *Turmoil and Tradition*, p. 489.

45. Stimson Diary, March 28, 1943.

46. Ibid., December 18, 1940.

47. Ibid., February 28, 1945.

48. Berle Diaries, October 21, 1940, and November 8, 1940, Box 212.

49. *Turmoil and Tradition,* pp. 493, 489.

50. Other typical comments appear in Stimson's diary on December 13, 16, and 19, 1940.

51. Letter, Morgenstern to Barnes, November 26, 1961, Barnes Papers, Box 59.

52. For a discussion of this meeting, see *At Dawn We Slept,* Chapter 45.

53. *Pearl Harbor,* p. 329.

54. *Road to Pearl Harbor,* pp. 314–15.

55. Richard N. Current, "How Stimson Meant to 'Maneuver' the Japanese," *The Mississippi Valley Historical Review* (June 1953), p. 70, fn. 10.

56. Stimson Diary, October 16, 1941.

57. Ibid., November 6, 1941.

58. *Hull Memoirs,* Vol. II, p. 1080.

59. Roosevelt Papers, PSF, Box 83.

60. Stimson Diary, December 19, 1940.

61. Ibid., September 23, 1941.

62. *PHA,* Part 11, p. 5197.

63. Richard N. Current, *Secretary Stimson: A Study in Statecraft* (New Brunswick, N.J., 1954), pp. 175, 188 (hereafter cited as *Secretary Stimson*).

64. See *At Dawn We Slept,* Chapters 71, 75.

65. *PHA,* Part 14, p. 1330.

66. Ibid., Part 11, pp. 5429–30.

67. Ibid., Part 29, p. 2075.

68. See *At Dawn We Slept,* Chapter 16.

69. *PHA,* Part 5, p. 2175. See *At Dawn We Slept,* pp. 251–52.

70. VADM. Frank E. Beatty, "Another Version of What Started War with Japan," *U.S. News & World Report* (May 28, 1954), p. 50 (hereafter cited as "Another Version").

CHAPTER 13

"FAULTS OF OMISSION"

1. *On the Treadmill,* p. 450.

2. September 1, 1945.

3. *PHA,* Part 5, p. 2143.

4. Ibid., Part 32, p. 67.

5. Stimson Diary, May 7, 8, and November 27, 30, 1941.

6. Ibid., November 17, 1944.

7. Barnes Papers, Box 62.

8. Letter, Greaves to Barnes, December 21, 1962, Barnes Papers, Box 62.

9. *PHA*, Report, p. 180. See *At Dawn We Slept*, Chapter 31.

10. Letter, Greaves to Barnes, December 21, 1962.

11. *PHA*, Part 5, p. 2177.

12. Ibid., Report, p. 263.

13. Ibid., Part 9, p. 4439.

14. *On the Treadmill*, p. 450.

15. *PHA*, Part 6, p. 2834.

16. Ibid., Part 39, pp. 318, 339–40.

17. Ibid., pp. 339–40.

18. Donald G. Brownlow, *The Accused: The Ordeal of Rear Admiral Husband E. Kimmel, U.S.N.* (New York, 1968), pp. 121–22, 149, 109 (hereafter cited as *The Accused*).

19. Washington *Daily News*, December 6, 1956.

20. *PHA*, Part 5, p. 2176.

21. Letter, Greaves to Barnes, December 21, 1962.

22. *PHA*, Part 5, p. 2174. For more on this subject, see *At Dawn We Slept*, Chapter 31.

23. For further discussion of this power struggle, see *At Dawn We Slept*, Chapter 9.

24. *PHA*, Part 39, p. 365.

25. Ibid., Part 24, pp. 1363–64; Part 14, p. 1044. See *At Dawn We Slept*, Chapters 4–5.

26. *PHA*, Report, p. 78.

27. Ibid., Part 14, p. 1327; Part 16, p. 2214.

28. Ibid., Part 16, p. 2225.

29. Ibid., Part 26, p. 159.

30. Ibid., Report, p. 265.

31. Ibid., Part 39, p. 353.

32. Ibid., Part 5, p. 2136.

33. Ibid., p. 2213.

34. Ibid., p. 2246.

35. *On the Treadmill*, p. 450.

36. A number of Rochefort's Combat Intelligence Summaries are reproduced in *PHA*, Part 17.

37. *PHA*, Part 5, p. 2132.

38. Washington *Star*, January 27, 1942.

39. *PHA*, Part 33, pp. 713, 715.

40. Ibid., Part 32, p. 546.

41. Ibid., p. 55.

42. Ibid., p. 546.

43. Letter, Hiles to Barnes, October 9, 1966, Barnes Papers, Box 73.

44. *PHA*, Part 8, pp. 3434, 3393. See *At Dawn We Slept*, Chapter 59.

45. *PHA*, Part 36, p. 27.

46. Ibid., Part 8, pp. 3433–34.

47. Ibid., pp. 3388–90, 3412; Part 4, p. 1970.

48. Ibid., Part 9, p. 4518; Part 15, p. 1633; Part 5, pp. 2132–33.

49. Ibid., Part 14, p. 1411.

50. Interview with Dyer, October 20, 1969.

51. *PHA*, Part 32, p. 99.

52. Diaries of James V. Forrestal, Princeton University Library, Princeton, N.J., November 27, 1944 (hereafter cited as Forrestal Diaries).

53. *PHA*, Part 39, p. 381.

54. *On the Treadmill*, pp. 450–51.

55. For an account of the circumstances of Richardson's dismissal, see *At Dawn We Slept*, Chapter 5.

56. *PHA*, Part 36, p. 576.

57. *On the Treadmill*, pp. 353, 359–61.

58. Ibid., p. 361.

59. Interview with Shoemaker, January 31, 1963.

60. Interview with East, August 7, 1964.

61. Notes on this study which Safford prepared for Prange (hereafter cited as Safford Notes).

62. Comments of VADM. Charles Wellborn, Jr., to Prange, August 10, 1977 (hereafter cited as Wellborn Comments).

63. *New York Times*, April 23, 1940.

64. Comments of VADM. W. R. Smedberg III to Prange, July 27, 1977 (hereafter cited as Smedberg Comments).

65. Fleet Admiral Ernest J. King and Cmdr. Walter M. Whitehead, *Fleet Admiral King: A Naval Record* (New York, 1952), pp. 354–55 (hereafter cited as *Fleet Admiral King*).

66. *PHA*, Part 39, pp. 344–45.

67. Ibid., p. 383.

68. *Fleet Admiral King*, p. 632.

69. Stimson Diary, November 23, 1944.

70. Letter, Greaves to Barnes, December 21, 1962.

71. Courtesy of Admiral Kimmel. See also *Fleet Admiral King*, pp. 633–34.

72. January 19, 1942, pp. 59–60.

73. *Roosevelt and Hopkins*, p. 164.

74. *Strategy and Command*, p. 81.

75. *PHA*, Part 26, p. 420.

CHAPTER 14

"OUT OF EFFECTIVE CONTACT"

1. Katherine T. Marshall, *Together: Annals of an Army Wife* (New York, 1946), p. 109 (hereafter cited as *Together*).

2. Leonard Mosley, *Marshall: Hero for Our Times* (New York, 1982), p. 199 (hereafter cited as *Marshall*).

3. *Together*, p. 110.

4. *PHA*, Part 27, p. 16.

5. Albert Wedemeyer, *Wedemeyer Reports!* (New York, 1958), p. 122 (hereafter cited as *Wedemeyer Reports!*).

6. Dean Acheson, *Present at the Creation: My Years in the State Department* (New York, 1969), p. 215. A number of letters from various correspondents addressed to "Dear George" appear in the Papers of General of the Army George C. Marshall, George C. Marshall Research Foundation, Lexington, Va. (hereafter cited as Marshall Papers).

7. Interview with Rochefort, August 26, 1964.

8. *PHA*, Part 3, pp. 1406–07.

9. Ibid., Part 32, p. 557.

10. *Wedemeyer Reports!*, pp. 382, 121–22.

11. *PHA*, Part 9, p. 4519.

12. Ibid., Part 34, p. 33; Part 27, p. 109; Part 23, 1103.

13. Ibid., Part 27, p. 114.

14. Ibid., Part 35, pp. 211–12.

15. Ibid., Part 3, p. 1532, corrected by Part 5, p. 2485.

16. Ibid., Part 23, p. 1081.

17. Ibid., Part 29, p. 2313.

18. Ibid., Part 3, p. 1289.

19. Ibid., p. 1213.

20. Ibid., p. 1289.

21. *Infamy*, p. 320.

22. See *At Dawn We Slept*, pp. 118–20.

23. *F.D.R.*, p. 133.

24. *Final Secret*, p. 116.

25. Interview with Dunlop, October 23, 1963.

26. *PHA*, Part 10, p. 4814.

27. Ibid., Part 23, p. 977.

28. Ibid., Part 7, p. 3010.

29. Ibid., Part 3, p. 1103, corrected by Part 5, p. 2483.

30. Ibid., Report, p. 266-H.

31. Ibid., Part 3, pp. 1429–30.

32. Ibid., Part 9, p. 4515.

33. Ibid., Part 29, pp. 2409, 2411.

34. Ibid., Part 3, p. 1427.

35. Ibid., Part 2, p. 513.

36. Ibid., Part 9, p. 4472.

37. Undated letter, Barnes to Safford, Hiles Papers, Box 16.

38. Safford Comments.

39. December 7, 1941.

40. *PHA*, Part 3, p. 1110.

41. Ibid., Part 11, pp. 5193–94.

42. Ibid., Part 3, pp. 1113, 1115.

43. Rose Page Wilson, *General Marshall Remembered* (Englewood Cliffs, N.J., 1968), p. 245 (hereafter cited as *General Marshall Remembered*).

44. *PHA*, Part 29, pp. 2410, 2420.

45. Ibid., Part 3, p. 1108.

46. Ibid., Part 9, p. 4517.

47. Charles Hurd, *Washington Cavalcade* (New York, 1948), p. 264; *Together*, pp. 124–26; *Ordeal and Hope*, pp. 190, 433.

48. See *At Dawn We Slept*, Chapter 80.

49. *PHA*, Part 5, pp. 2335, 2210.

50. Ibid., Part 29, pp. 2409–10.

51. Ibid., Part 39, pp. 144–45.

52. *Ordeal and Hope*, p. 228.

53. Maj. Gen. H. D. Russell, "More Light on Pearl Harbor," *U. S. News & World Report* (May 7, 1954), p. 32.

54. Harry E. Barnes, "A Historian Investigates a Tough Question: Where Was the General?" Chicago *Tribune,* December 7, 1966, Special Supplement, pp. 8–9.

55. *Final Secret,* p. 119.

56. Ibid., pp. 121–22.

57. Letter, Safford to Hiles, May 25, 1962, Barnes Papers, Box 64.

58. *PHA,* Part 27, p. 14.

59. Stimson Diary, February 16, 1943.

60. Forrest C. Pogue, *George C. Marshall: Education of a General* (New York, 1963), pp. 280, 325–26 (hereafter cited as *Education of a General*).

61. *Marshall,* p. 122.

62. Dean Acheson, *Morning and Noon* (Boston, 1965), p. 165.

63. James McGregor Burns, *Roosevelt, The Soldier of Freedom* (New York, 1970), p. 85 (hereafter cited as *Soldier of Freedom*).

64. *Education of a General,* p. 324.

65. A number of examples are contained in the Roosevelt Papers, PSF, Boxes 3 and 63.

CHAPTER 15

"A FINGER OF BLAME"

1. *Ordeal and Hope,* p. 429.

2. Interview between Henry C. Clausen and Harry E. Barnes, January 3, 1964, courtesy of Barnes (hereafter cited as Clausen-Barnes interview).

3. *PHA,* Part 39, p. 145.

4. Stimson Diary, November 14, 1944.

5. Ibid., September 16, 1943.

6. Ibid., September 15, 1943.

7. *New York Times,* August 30, 1945.

8. *On Active Service,* p. 391.

9. August 30, 1945.

10. *Marshall,* p. 183.

11. *PHA,* Part 3, p. 1422.

12. Ibid., Part 39, p. 265.

13. Ibid., p. 256.

14. Ibid., pp. 261–62.

15. Ibid., Part 29, pp. 2328–29.

16. Ibid., Part 3, pp. 1119–20.

17. Ibid., p. 1145.

18. Ibid., p. 1150.

19. Ibid., p. 1145.

20. Ibid., Part 39, p. 264.

21. Ibid.

22. Ibid., Part 3, p. 1425.

23. Ibid., Part 14, p. 1330.

24. Ibid., Part 39, p. 263.

25. Ibid., Part 3, p. 1036.

26. Ibid., Part 33, p. 828.

27. Ibid., Part 3, pp. 1420–21.

28. Ibid., Part 23, p. 1079.

29. Ibid., Part 3, p. 1421.

30. Ibid., p. 1151.

31. Ibid., p. 1218.

32. *Ordeal and Hope*, p. 212.

33. *PHA*, Report, p. 256.

34. Ibid., Part 3, p. 1050.

35. Ibid., Part 15, p. 1635. See *At Dawn We Slept*, Chapter 14.

36. *PHA*, Part 29, p. 2320.

37. Ibid., Part 15, p. 1627.

38. Ibid., Part 3, p. 1171.

39. Ibid., Part 32, p. 562.

40. *Time* Office Memorandum, Robert Sherrod to David Hulburd, November 15, 1941, Hanson W. Baldwin Collection, Marshall Papers.

41. Ibid.

42. Ibid.

43. Hanson W. Baldwin Collection, Marshall Papers.

44. *Ordeal and Hope*, pp. 202–03.

45. *PHA*, Part 33, p. 824.

46. Ibid., Part 35, p. 104.

47. Ibid., Part 3, p. 1211, corrected by Part 5, p. 2484.

48. Ibid., Part 35, pp. 23–24.

49. Ibid., Part 23, pp. 646–47, 653.

50. Ibid., Part 35, p. 82; Part 36, p. 227.

51. Ibid., Part 3, p. 1181, corrected by Part 5, p. 2484.

52. Ibid., p. 1514.

53. Ibid., p. 1512.

54. Ibid., pp. 1514–1516.

55. Ibid., Part 35, p. 19.

56. *Infamy*, p. 321.

57. Letter, Greaves to Barnes, March 25, 1963, Barnes Papers, Box 63.

58. Letter, Hoehling to Barnes, April 12, 1963, Barnes Papers, Box 64.

59. *PHA*, Part 34, pp. 90–91.

60. Ibid., pp. 91–92.

61. Ibid., pp. 92–93.

62. Ibid., pp. 101–02.

63. Ibid., p. 86.

64. Ibid., p. 79.

65. Ibid., pp. 78–79.

66. Ibid., p. 80.

67. Ibid., p. 81.

68. Ibid., Part 3, p. 1335.

69. Ibid., p. 1162.

70. Ibid., Part 34, p. 86, 88.

71. Ibid., Part 36, p. 306.

72. Ibid., p. 70.

CHAPTER 16

"PRIMARILY A FAILURE OF MEN"

1. General Hugh S. Johnson, "The General Staff and Its New Chief," *Life* (August 21, 1939), p. 62.

2. *Congressional Record*, Vol. 91, Part 12, Appendix, September 18, 1945, p. A3919. This extract is from an article by Senator Wiley which he inserted into the *Congressional Record*. The article was scheduled to appear in the October issue of *Washington News Digest*.

3. *PHA*, Report, p. 572.

4. Ibid., p. 505.

5. Ibid., p. 266C.

6. Honolulu *Star-Bulletin*, September 1, 1945.

7. "Today and Tomorrow," *Washington Post*, December 20, 1945.

8. December 9, 1941.

9. *PHA*, Part 2, pp. 876–77, corrected by Part 5, p. 2488.

10. Interview with Layton, July 22, 1964.

11. *PHA*, Part 3, p. 1515. Anyone who has gone through the Magic messages on file in the National Archives can testify that, if anything, Marshall understated the case.

12. Ibid., Part 6, pp. 2834–35.

13. Ibid., Report, pp. 261–62. The message of February 15, 1941, appears in Part 12, p. 311. See also *"Magic" Background*, Vol. I, p. A82.

14. Memorandum of interview, Barnes and Hindmarsh, January 9, 1964, Hiles Papers, Box 29.

15. *PHA*, Report, p. 262.

16. Washington *Star-News*.

17. *PHA*, Part 3, p. 1362.

18. Ibid., Part 30, pp. 2977–78.

19. Ibid., Part 5, p. 2133.

20. Interviews with Lt. Gen. Charles D. Herron, June 10, 1955 (hereafter cited as Herron) and Col. George Bicknell, September 8, 1967 (hereafter cited as Bicknell).

21. *PHA*, Part 6, p. 2542.

22. Ibid., Part 12, p. 261; *"Magic" Background*, Vol. III, Appendix, pp. A189–90.

23. *PHA*, Part 12, p. 262; *"Magic" Background*, Vol. IV, Appendix, p. A147.

24. *PHA*, Part 4, p. 1840.

25. Interview with Morgan, October 27, 1976. This represents perhaps the main area of difference between Morgan's draft and the final report. "Bomb plot" material in the final congressional report (*PHA*, Report, pp. 187–90, 233–34) does not appear in Morgan's draft.

26. "Muddle before Pearl Harbor," *U.S. News & World Report* (December 3, 1954), p. 120 (hereafter cited as "Muddle before Pearl Harbor").

27. *PHA*, Report, p. 524.

28. Ibid., Part 9, p. 4423.

29. Ibid., Part 7, p. 2954.

30. Ibid., pp. 2956–57.

31. Ibid., p. 3012.

32. Ibid., Part 6, p. 2610.

33. Ibid., p. 2707.

34. "Muddle before Pearl Harbor," p. 132.
35. Letter, Hiles to Barnes, August 3, 1966, Barnes Papers, Box 72.
36. George S. Pettee, *The Future of American Secret Intelligence* (Washington, 1946), p. 4 (hereafter cited as *Future of American Secret Intelligence*).
37. *PHA*, Report, p. 252.
38. "Muddle before Pearl Harbor," p. 137.
39. Letter, Rochefort to Barnes, November 7, 1966, Hiles Papers, Box 13.
40. This notation appears in Kimmel's handwriting on the cover sheet of a chapter entitled "The Bomb Plot" of an unpublished book manuscript by Hiles. Hiles Papers, Box 30.
41. Safford Notes. In these notes, Safford referred to himself in the third person.
42. Letter, Rochefort to Barnes, November 7, 1966.
43. Safford Notes.
44. "PH After ¼ Century," pp. 28–29. A number of interesting letters and memoranda on this subject may be found in the Unversity of Wyoming collection, especially Hiles Papers, Boxes 8, 13, and 15; Barnes Papers, Box 134; and Kimmel Papers, Box 13. Toland accepted this story of why Kirk left ONI. (*Infamy*, pp. 58–60).
45. *PHA*, Part 4, p. 1807.
46. Ibid., p. 1922.
47. *Final Secret*, pp. 46–47.
48. *PHA*, Part 39, p. 252.
49. Ibid., p. 325.
50. Ibid., Part 9, p. 4534. See *At Dawn We Slept*, Chapter 31.
51. "The Once Over," Mobile *Register*, December 7, 1945.
52. *PHA*, Part 9, pp. 4195–96.
53. Ibid., Part 2, p. 886.
54. Ibid., Part 4, pp. 1748–49.

CHAPTER 17

"THE PITFALLS OF DIVIDED RESPONSIBILITY"

1. "Washington Merry-Go-Round," *Oregon Journal* (Portland), December 11, 1941.
2. "It's Still Question Time," Washington *Times-Herald*, January 26, 1942.
3. *Congressional Record*, Vol. 87, Part 14, Appendix, December 8, 1941, pp. A5552–53. Yoshiwara was Tokyo's red light district.
4. Stimson Diary, February 3, 1942.

5. *New York Times*, September 4, 1945.

6. Memorandum of conference, Marshall Papers, Research File.

7. *PHA*, Part 14, p. 1042. See *At Dawn We Slept*, Chapter 4.

8. Ibid., Part 3, pp. 1064–65.

9. Ibid., Part 2, p. 819.

10. Marshall Papers, Research File.

11. Letter, Greaves to Barnes, December 21, 1962, Barnes Papers, Box 62.

12. Letter, Safford to Barnes, November 7, 1962, Barnes Papers, Box 62.

13. Letter, Tucker to Barnes, August 12, 1963, Barnes Papers, Box 65.

14. *PHA*, Part 27, pp. 78–79.

15. Ibid., Part 7, p. 3317.

16. Ibid., p. 3343.

17. Ibid., p. 3319.

18. Ibid., Report, p. 257.

19. Ibid., p. 258.

20. Ibid., p. 206.

21. Ibid., p. 254.

22. Ibid., Part 7, p. 3342.

23. Ibid., p. 3319.

24. Memorandum of interview, Barnes and Hindmarsh, January 9, 1964, Hiles Papers, Box 29.

25. *PHA*, Part 4, pp. 1962–63.

26. Ibid., Part 26, p. 424.

27. Wellborn Comments, August 10, 1977.

28. *PHA*, Part 4, p. 1963.

29. Ibid., p. 1950.

30. Ibid., p. 1958.

31. Ibid., p. 1964.

32. The entire Martin-Bellinger report appears in *PHA*, Part 22, pp. 349–54. For a discussion of this important document, see *At Dawn We Slept*, Chapter 10.

33. *PHA*, Report, p. 262.

34. Ibid., Part 6, p. 2608.

35. Ibid., Part 4, p. 1916.

36. Ibid., p. 1944; Part 16, p. 2214.

37. Ibid., Part 14, p. 1327.

38. Ibid., Part 4, pp. 1945–46. See *At Dawn We Slept*, Chapter 36.

39. *PHA*, p. 2008; Part 16, p. 2176.

40. Ibid., Part 4, p. 2008.

41. *Infamy*, p. 297. Toland cited as his source an article by Beatty in *National Review*, December 13, 1966, p. 1261.

42. "Another Version," p. 49.

43. *PHA*, Part 4, p. 2017. See also p. 1984.

44. Ibid., Part 26, p. 303; Part 36, p. 233.

45. Ibid., Part 4, p. 1877. See also pp. 1757, 1776.

46. Ibid., p. 1984.

47. Forrestal Diaries, November 27, 1944.

48. Stimson Diary, March 16, 1942.

49. Ibid., October 30, 1942.

50. Interview with Tucker, August 29, 1964.

51. Interview with Rochefort, August 26, 1954.

52. Inteview between VADM. Frank E. Beatty and Dr. Harry Elmer Barnes, June 29, 1962 (courtesy Dr. Barnes; hereafter cited as Beatty-Barnes Interview).

53. *PHA*, Report, p. 573.

54. Washington *Post*, December 18, 1945; Washington *Star*, February 21, 1946.

55. *PHA*, Part 5, p. 2358.

56. Ibid., Part 39, pp. 221, 141.

57. *Future of American Secret Intelligence*, pp. 6–7.

58. *PHA*, Part 39, p. 141.

59. Ibid., Part 9, p. 4479.

60. Ibid., Part 39, p. 141.

CHAPTER 18

"A LACK OF IMAGINATION"

1. *PHA*, Part 39, p. 142.

2. Ibid., Part 4, p. 1638.

3. Ibid., Part 14, p. 1329.

4. Ibid., p. 1330. For a discussion of this message, see *At Dawn We Slept*, Chapter 51.

5. Ibid., Part 3, p. 1024.

6. Ibid., Report, p. 204.

7. Ibid., Part 23, p. 1106.

8. Both dated December 7, 1945.

9. *PHA*, Part 23, p. 1111.

10. Ibid., Part 3, pp. 1023–24.

11. December 17, 1945, p. 21.

12. *PHA*, Part 18, p. 3009.

13. Ibid., Part 3, p. 1031.

14. Ibid., p. 1033.

15. January 27, 1942.

16. *PHA*, Part 39, p. 114.

17. Ibid., Part 3, p. 1514.

18. Ibid., Part 39, p. 142.

19. Ibid., p. 176.

20. Ibid., Part 27, pp. 92–93.

21. Ibid., Part 9, p. 4298.

22. Ibid., Part 39, p. 265.

23. Ibid., Part 35, p. 18.

24. Ibid., Part 3, pp. 1190–91.

25. Ibid., Part 29, pp. 2430–31; Part 10, pp. 4629, 4634.

26. Ibid., Part 35, p. 98.

27. Ibid., p. 99.

28. Ibid., Part 29, pp. 2430–31.

29. Ibid., Part 35, p. 99.

30. Ibid., Part 10, p. 4659.

31. Ibid., Report, p. 226.

32. Quoted in *Wedemeyer Reports!*, p. 25.

33. Washington *Star*, January 26, 1942.

34. Mary Katherine Strong, "Washington at Pearl Harbor," *Current History*, February 1946, p. 132 (hereafter cited as "Washington at Pearl Harbor").

35. *Future of American Secret Intelligence*, pp. 5–6.

36. Stimson Diary, February 12, 1941.

37. Ibid., February 13, 1941.

38. Ibid., May 12, 1941.

39. J. C. Masterman, *The Double Cross System in the War of 1939 to 1945* (New Haven, 1972), pp. 79–80 (hereafter cited as *Double Cross*).

40. Dusko Popov, *Spy Counter-Spy* (New York, 1974), pp. 158–159 (hereafter cited as *Spy Counter-Spy*).

41. Ibid., p. 168.

42. Ibid., pp. 169–80.

43. Ibid., pp. 119, 203.
44. Anthony Cave Brown, *Bodyguard of Lies* (New York, 1975), pp. 60–61.
45. *Infamy*, p. 14.
46. Letter, Chihaya to Prange, February 13, 1978.
47. Statement by Otojiro Okuda to Prange, February 10, 1978.
48. John F. Bratzel and Leslie B. Rout, Jr., "Pearl Harbor, Microdots, and J. Edgar Hoover," *American Historical Review*, December 1982, pp. 1346–47.
49. Ibid., p. 1349.
50. John Estel (AP) "Hoover Shared Spy Disclosure on Pearl Harbor," Pittsburgh *Post-Gazette*, April 1, 1982.
51. *PHA*, Part 18, p. 2948.

CHAPTER 19

"EAST WIND RAIN"

1. *PHA*, Part 12, p. 154; *"Magic" Background*, Vol. V, p. 51.
2. *PHA*, Part 12, p. 155; *"Magic" Background*, Vol. V, p. 51.
3. War Diary of Third Battleship Division, December 5, 1941, Prange files.
4. Chigusa Diary, December 5, 1941.
5. *PHA*, Part 18, p. 3303; *"Magic" Background*, Vol. V, p. 52.
6. *PHA*, Part 18, pp. 3303–04.
7. Ibid., p. 3304; *"Magic" Background*, Vol. V, p. 53.
8. *PHA*, Part 9, p. 4214.
9. Ibid., Part 10, pp. 4914–15.
10. Ibid., p. 4915; Part 18, p. 3305; Part 29, pp. 2336, 2429; Part 34, p. 17.
11. Ibid., Part 2, p. 981.
12. Ibid., Part 8, p. 3385.
13. Ibid., pp. 3580–81; Part 26, p. 393.
14. Ibid., Part 36, pp. 81–82; Part 33, p. 853; Part 10, p. 4787.
15. Ibid., Part 10, pp. 4700, 4705–06. See also Part 36, p. 36.
16. Ibid., Part 9, p. 4520.
17. Ibid., Part 18, p. 3306.
18. Ibid., p. 3305; Part 36, p. 88; Part 33, p. 843.
19. Ibid., Part 10, p. 4732; Part 36, p. 89.
20. Ibid., Part 26, pp. 394–95; Part 29, p. 2379.
21. Ibid., Part 9, p. 4522. Among those who agreed with Bratton's assessment were

Ingersoll (Part 33, pp. 469, 807; Part 9, p. 4225); Schukraft (Part 10, pp. 4920, 4929); Noyes (Part 10, pp. 4729, 4753); Turner (Part 26, p. 283).

22. Ibid., Part 18, p. 3306; Part 4, pp. 1968, 2035.

23. Ibid., Part 10, p. 4630; Part 29, p. 2430. See also Part 34, p. 68. Noyes did not recall this telephone conversation (Part 10, p. 4733), and Miles did not remember this meeting (Part 35, p. 102).

24. Ibid., Part 29, p. 2337. See also Part 35, p. 97; Part 34, pp. 21–22, and Part 9, p. 4521.

25. Ibid., Part 9, pp. 3555–56; letter, Tucker to Barnes, April 18, 1962, Barnes Papers, Box 60.

26. Interview with Tucker, August 22, 1964. Originally Safford had been "very bitter" against Kimmel, believing that he had received a warning based on the "winds" code. When he found no such message went out, he became a firm supporter of Kimmel and very suspicious of certain top brass in Washington. He took the position that a "winds execute" had come in, had been suppressed, and later destroyed (PHA, Part 8, pp. 3858–59, 3655).

27. PHA, Report, p. 481.

28. Ibid., Part 26, pp. 393–94.

29. Ibid., pp. 393–95.

30. Ibid., Part 33, pp. 839–40; Part 36, pp. 258–59, 91.

31. Ibid., Part 35, p. 34.

32. Ibid., pp. 90, 97, 103, 106; Part 34, p. 17; Part 29, pp. 2338–39; Part 9, p. 4528; Part 4, p. 1760; Part 36, p. 90; Part 33, p. 804.

33. Ibid., Part 34, p. 86; Part 10, p. 4631.

34. Ibid., Part 36, p. 87; Information from Captain George W. Linn, USNR (Ret.), SRH 081, RG 27, NSA/CSS, MacArthur Archives, Norfolk, Va. (hereafter cited as Linn statement).

35. PHA, Part 35, p. 23.

36. Ibid., p. 24. Lt. Col. C. C. Dusenbury, Bratton's assistant, made the same mistaken interpretations (Part 35, p. 25).

37. Ibid., Part 9, pp. 4347, 4541, 4543, 4595–96. See also Part 29, p. 2339. For further discussion, see At Dawn We Slept, p. 459.

38. Ibid., Part 36, p. 24; Part 8, pp. 3387–88. For a brief discussion of the abortive McCollum message, see At Dawn We Slept, p. 455.

39. Ibid., Part 33, pp. 853–54, 871, 876.

40. Ibid., Part 10, pp. 4916–18; Part 29, p. 2371.

41. Ibid., Part 10, pp. 4726–27.

42. Ibid., p. 4732. McCollum also stressed that the value of the code was "wholly dependent upon the use of particular and precise Japanese words, used in a precise position within a broadcast" (Part 8, p. 3386).

43. Ibid., Part 10, p. 4705–06.

44. Ibid., Part 26, p. 469.

45. Ibid., Part 33, p. 807.

46. Ibid., Part 9, pp. 4225–26.

47. Ibid., Part 12, p. 186.

48. Ibid., Part 8, p. 3920; Part 9, pp. 3970–71.

49. Ibid., Part 36, pp. 80, 82.

50. NSA interview with Mr. Ralph T. Briggs, January 13, 1977, MacArthur Archives, NA, RG 457, Record of National Security Agency SRH051; also NSA/CSS Cryptologic Document, (hereafter cited as Briggs interview). The log cited is reproduced in *Infamy* among the illustrations opp. p. 176.

51. *PHA*, Part 29, p. 2371.

52. Ibid., Part 36, p. 73.

53. Briggs interview.

54. Ibid.

55. *PHA*, Part 8, p. 3579.

56. Ibid., Part 7, p. 3268.

57. Ibid., Part 8, p. 3920.

58. Ibid., Part 29, pp. 2371–72.

59. Ibid., Part 36, p. 75.

60. Ibid., Part 18, p. 3346.

61. Ibid., Part 36, p. 81.

62. *Congressional Record*, Vol. 91, Part 8, November 6, 1945, p. 10446.

63. Ibid., November 14, 1945, p. 10685.

64. See for example *Infamy*, of which Safford is the hero.

65. Letter, Safford to Hiles, April 4, 1967, Hiles Papers, Box 14.

66. Linn statement.

67. *PHA*, Part 8, p. 3586.

68. Ibid., pp. 3585, 3625–26.

69. Ibid., p. 3652.

70. Ibid., pp. 3700–04. Costello featured parts of this letter, duly decoded, on pp. 646–47 of *The Pacific War*. He cited the National Archives file holding this letter. It has been available for years as part of the congressional committee testimony and Prange was thoroughly familiar with it, as well as with Safford's testimony concerning it.

71. Ibid., p. 3722.

72. Ibid., pp. 3723–25.

73. Ibid., p. 3858; Milwaukee *Journal*, February 6, 1946. Kramer was, "to put it mildly, flabbergasted" at Safford's letter. He read only the first few paragraphs, then put it away with his other papers (Part 9, p. 4082).

74. *PHA*, Part 8, p. 3808; Washington *Post*, February 5, 1946. Far from suffering at the hands of a vengeful Establishment, Safford received the Legion of Merit in ceremonies at the Navy Department on February 11, 1946. And in 1958 Congress awarded him a tax-free $100,000 in well-deserved appreciation for his brilliant work in naval communications—"some 20 cryptographic inventions he developed between 1936 and his retirement in 1953. Congress noted in passing the bill that Capt. Safford had been unable to apply for patents on his inventions due to secrecy requirements, and that his contributions to the nation had thus gone unrewarded." (*PHA*, Part 9, p. 4661; Washington *Star-News*, May 18, 1973).

75. *PHA*, Part 8, pp. 3914, 3917. That helped explain a minor but nagging puzzle— why had Kramer been involved at all? His section handled translations, and the operative code words would be in Japanese, as established. Their English meaning was irrelevant.

76. Ibid., Part 9, p. 3932.

77. Ibid., p. 3936.

78. Among those who remembered this message were Safford (*PHA*, Part 8, p. 3629); Bratton (Part 9, p. 4522); Linn (Part 36, p. 87); McCollum (Part 36, p. 24; Part 8, p. 3387); Wilkinson (Part 36, p. 235; Part 4, p. 1760). Evidence of such a message also came from Japanese sources that MacArthur's headquarters in Tokyo interrogated at the War Department's request. (Part 18, pp. 3306–09).

79. *PHA*, Part 18, p. 3310.

80. *Infamy*, p. 308. We suspect this message was received only by Yoshikawa's imagination. From the fairly straightforward testimony he gave Prange in 1950 and 1955, his statements have grown more and more lurid with each passing year.

81. *PHA*, Report, p. 486.

CHAPTER 20

"A SENTINEL ON DUTY"

1. *PHA*, Part 29, p. 2086.

2. Ibid., Part 9, pp. 4241–45.

3. Based upon Short's career brief. See *At Dawn We Slept*, pp. 53–54.

4. *Ordeal and Hope*, p. 171.

5. *PHA*, Part 32, p. 553.

6. Ibid., Part 29, p. 2401.

7. Ibid., Part 39, pp. 55–56.

8. Marshall Papers, Research File.

9. *PHA*, Part 35, p. 100. For an account of the Herron alert, see *At Dawn We Slept*, pp. 37–38.

10. Taped reminiscences of Maj. Gen. Robert J. Fleming, Jr., March 7 and 31, 1975, Hoover Institution on War, Revolution and Peace, Stanford, Calif. (hereafter cited as Fleming tape). This extract is from the tape of March 31, 1975.

11. Interview with Dunlop, October 23, 1963.

12. Interview with Throckmorton, September 11, 1967.

13. *PHA*, Part 6, pp. 2574, 2607.

14. Interview with Kimmel, December 2, 1963.

15. Interview with Davis, January 18, 1963.

16. Interview with Smith, November 29, 1962.

17. *PHA*, Part 24, pp. 1794–95.

18. Ibid., pp. 1795–96.

19. Interview with Allen, June 8, 1962.

20. Interview with Mollison, November 8, 1963.

21. *PHA*, Part 39, p. 60.

22. Fleming tape, March 31, 1975.

23. Interview with Fleming, June 24, 1977.

24. *PHA*, Part 28, p. 1397.

25. Fleming tape, March 31, 1975.

26. Interview with Bicknell, September 7, 1967; *PHA*, Part 35, p. 60.

27. Fleming tape, March 31, 1975; reply by Fleming, January 11, 1977, to questionnaire submitted to him by Prange (hereafter cited as Fleming questionnaire). Fielder owed his nickname to a typographical error. He was a football star at Georgia Tech, and a sportswriter urged spectators to "Watch Fielder." In print it came out "Wooch Fielder," and the name stuck. Interview with Fielder, September 11, 1967.

28. Interview with Dunlop, October 23, 1963.

29. *PHA*, Part 7, p. 3098.

30. Ibid., Part 10, pp. 4933–34.

31. Ibid., Part 27, p. 591.

32. Ibid., Part 39, p. 60.

33. Fleming tape, March 31, 1975; interview with Fleming, June 24, 1977.

34. *PHA*, Part 28, p. 1368.

35. Ibid., Part 27, p. 733.

36. Interview with Dunlop, October 38, 1963.

37. Interview with Kimmel, November 30, 1963.
38. Interview with Mollison, November 8, 1963.
39. *PHA*, Part 7, pp. 3097–98.
40. Interview with Bicknell, September 7, 1967.
41. *PHA*, Part 9, p. 4411.
42. Interview with Bicknell, September 7, 1967.
43. *PHA*, Part 3, pp. 1795–96.
44. Ibid., Part 11, p. 5428.
45. Ibid., Part 39, p. 253.
46. Ibid., Part 27, pp. 17–18.
47. Ibid., Part 39, p. 52.
48. Ibid., Part 22, p. 85.
49. Ibid., Part 7, p. 3077.
50. Ibid., Part 22, p. 25.
51. Letter, Alfred R. Castle to Kimmel, February 3, 1965, Kimmel Papers, Box 12.
52. *PHA*, Part 10, pp. 5117–18.
53. Ibid., Part 27, pp. 191–92.
54. Ibid., Part 28, p. 1356.
55. Ibid., p. 422.
56. Ibid., Part 27, pp. 432, 437.
57. Ibid., p. 639.
58. Maj. Thomas R. Phillips, *Roots of Strategy: A Collection of Military Classics*, (Harrisburg, 1940), p. 364.
59. Interview with Kimmel, November 30, 1963.
60. *PHA*, Part 29, p. 1628.
61. Ibid., Part 3, p. 1081. For similar statements by Marshall, see Ibid., p. 1277; Part 29, pp. 2317–19.
62. Ibid., Part 32, pp. 554–55.
63. Ibid., Part 23, p. 987.
64. Morgan Report, p. 109. For representative comments on this point see *People's Daily World* (San Francisco), January 28, 1942; *Congressional Record*, Vol. 88, Part 1, January 27, 1942, pp. 743, 752.

CHAPTER 21

"ALERTED TO PREVENT SABOTAGE"

1. *PHA*, Part 23, p. 1081.
2. Ibid., Part 39, p. 63.

3. Ibid., Part 23, p. 1081.

4. Ibid., Part 2, pp. 834–35.

5. Ibid., Part 29, pp. 1643–44.

6. Interview with Fielder, September 12, 1967.

7. *PHA*, Part 28, p. 1540.

8. Ibid., pp. 1411–13.

9. Ibid., pp. 1417, 1422.

10. Ibid., pp. 1428–29, 1441.

11. Ibid., Part 27, p. 124.

12. Ibid., p. 208.

13. Ibid., Part 7, pp. 3067–68.

14. Brig. Gen. Samuel R. Shaw, "Marine Barracks, Navy Yard Pearl Harbor, December 1941," *Shipmate* (December 1973), pp. 16–17 (hereafter cited as "Marine Barracks"). Shaw commanded A Company and was senior watch officer.

15. "On the Record," Washington *Star*, January 28, 1942.

16. *PHA*, Part 27, p. 125.

17. Ibid., p. 156.

18. Ibid., p. 222.

19. Ibid., p. 232.

20. Ibid., Part 7, p. 3101.

21. Ibid., Part 27, p. 709.

22. Ibid., pp. 433, 435.

23. Ibid., Part 14, pp. 1021–31. See *At Dawn We Slept*, pp. 186–88.

24. Ibid., Part 27, p. 635.

25. Ibid., p. 596.

26. Ibid., Part 28, p. 1406.

27. This report appears in its entirety in *PHA*, Part 22, pp. 349–54. See *At Dawn We Slept*, pp. 93–95.

28. *PHA*, Part 28, p. 958.

29. Ibid., p. 962.

30. Ibid., Part 27, pp. 413–14.

31. Ibid., pp. 414–15.

32. Ibid., p. 421.

33. Ibid., Part 28, pp. 1364, 1367.

34. Ibid., Part 24, p. 1779.

35. Ibid., Part 14, p. 1330.

36.   Ibid., Part 7, p. 2922. For similar statements see Part 27, p. 158, and Part 32, p. 188.

37.   Ibid., Report, pp. 121–22.

38.   Morgan Report, p. 123.

39.   Interview with Allen, July 17, 1962.

40.   General of the Air Force H. H. Arnold, *Global Mission* (New York, 1949) pp. 271–72 (hereafter cited as *Global Mission*). See *At Dawn We Slept*, pp. 420–21.

41.   Detroit *Free Press*, January 26, 1942.

42.   *PHA*, Report, p. 126.

43.   Ibid., Part 32, p. 185.

44.   Ibid., Part 27, pp. 157–58. Short expressed himself in a similar vein to the congressional committee. See Part 7, pp. 2942–43.

45.   Ibid., Part 10, p. 4938.

46.   Ibid., Part 28, p. 1367.

47.   Ibid., Part 7, p. 3032.

48.   Ibid., p. 2985.

49.   Ibid., Part 28, p. 1364.

50.   Ibid., Part 27, p. 125.

51.   Ibid., Part 35, p. 33.

52.   Ibid., p. 47.

53.   Ibid., p. 44.

54.   Ibid., Part 28, p. 1420.

55.   Ibid., Part 39, p. 63.

56.   Ibid., Report, p. 124.

57.   Ibid., Part 39, p. 52.

58.   Ibid., Part 10, p. 3212.

59.   Ibid., Part 29, p. 2401.

60.   *General Marshall Remembered*, p. 246.

61.   *PHA*, Part 29, p. 2313.

62.   Ibid., Part 3, p. 1434.

63.   Ibid., Part 14, pp. 1331–33. The reader interested in comparing Short's actions with those of DeWitt and Andrews is referred to Ibid., pp. 1330–33. MacArthur's reactions in the Philippines left something to be desired. See Chapter 28.

64.   Ibid., Report, p. 127.

65.   Unpublished long form of report of Stimson's conclusions concerning the Army Board's report. His memorandum attached thereto is dated January 3, 1945.

NA, RG 107, Entry 74A, Box 2, folder "Army Pearl Harbor Board," Stimson "Safe File" (hereafter cited as Stimson Conclusions).

66. *PHA*, Part 28, pp. 1359–60.
67. Ibid., Part 22, p. 168.

CHAPTER 22

"THE FAILURE TO COMPREHEND"

1. *PHA*, Part 7, p. 3048.
2. Ibid., p. 3016.
3. Ibid., Part 10, p. 4945.
4. Ibid., Part 27, p. 734.
5. Ibid., pp. 118–19.
6. Ibid., p. 157.
7. Ibid., pp. 205–06.
8. Ibid., p. 166.
9. Ibid., Part 7, pp. 3038–39.
10. Ibid., Report, p. 125.
11. Ibid., p. 129.
12. Ibid., Part 3, p. 1425.
13. Ibid., p. 1069. See *At Dawn We Slept*, p. 62.
14. *PHA*, Part 7, p. 3039.
15. Ibid., Part 23, pp. 989–90.
16. Ibid., Part 27, p. 624.
17. Ibid., p. 627.
18. Ibid., pp. 618–19.
19. Ibid., Part 26, pp. 375–79.
20. Ibid., Part 27, p. 561.
21. Ibid., p. 558.
22. Ibid., p. 563.
23. Ibid., Part 26, p. 379.
24. Ibid., p. 380.
25. Ibid.
26. Ibid., pp. 380–81.
27. Ibid., pp. 381–82.
28. Ibid., p. 382.

29. Ibid.

30. Ibid., Part 39, p. 102.

31. Ibid., Part 27, p. 620.

32. Ibid., Part 39, p. 108.

33. Ibid., Part 27, p. 619.

34. Ibid., Part 22, p. 233; Part 29, p. 2295.

35. Ibid., Report, p. 127. See *At Dawn We Slept,* p. 322.

36. *PHA,* Part 22, p. 35.

37. Ibid., Report, p. 129.

38. Ibid., Part 28, p. 1357.

39. Ibid., Part 27, p. 621.

40. Ibid., Part 11, p. 5425.

41. Ibid., Part 29, p. 2079.

42. Interview with Tyler, August 21, 1964; *PHA,* Part 27, p. 569; Part 22, p. 223. See *At Dawn We Slept,* p. 501.

43. *PHA,* Part 7, p. 3035.

44. Ibid., pp. 3111–12.

45. Ibid., Part 29, p. 2112.

46. Ibid., Part 39, p. 97.

47. Ibid., Report, pp. 141–42.

48. Interview with Tyler, August 21, 1964.

49. *PHA,* Part 27, p. 431.

50. Ibid., Part 26, p. 385.

51. Ibid., Part 28, p. 991.

52. Ibid., Part 14, pp. 1395–96.

53. Ibid., Part 22, p. 97.

54. Ibid., Part 39, p. 130.

55. Ibid., Part 27, p. 209. See also Part 7, pp. 3038–39.

56. Interview with Fielder, September 11, 1967.

57. Interviews with VADM. Walter S. DeLany, November 2, 1962 (hereafter cited as DeLany); Smith, November 14, 1962.

58. Letter, Herman Lau to Kimmel, December 7, 1964, Kimmel Papers, Box 12.

59. Interview with Smith, June 14, 1964.

60. Interview with Dunlop, October 10, 1963.

61. Interview with Kimmel, November 30, 1963.

62. *PHA,* Part 39, p. 127.

63. Ibid., Part 22, p. 103.

64. Ibid., Part 7, pp. 3371–72.

65. Ibid., Part 22, p. 474.

66. Ibid., Part 10, p. 4872.

67. Ibid., Report, pp. 126–27.

68. Morgan Report, p. 126.

69. *PHA*, Part 27, p. 789; Part 6, pp. 2596–97, 2764. See *At Dawn We Slept*, pp. 447–50.

70. *PHA*, Part 23, p. 1162.

71. Ibid., Part 39, p. 388.

72. Ibid., p. 88.

73. Ibid., Part 7, p. 3192.

74. Ibid., Part 39, p. 90.

75. Ibid., Part 24, p. 1780. See *At Dawn We Slept*, pp. 461–63.

76. Memorandum for Secretary's Files, December 11, 1941, Morgenthau Diaries, Book 471.

77. *PHA*, Part 7, p. 3192.

78. January 25, 1946.

79. *PHA*, Part 35, pp. 147–48, 135.

80. Ibid., p. 32.

81. Ibid., pp. 86–87.

82. Ibid., Part 10, p. 5119.

83. Interview with CWO Alton B. Freeman, August 19, 1964.

84. *PHA*, Part 28, p. 1055.

85. Stimson Conclusions.

CHAPTER 23

"AN IMPORTANT MAN IN AN IMPORTANT POST"

1. *PHA*, Part 22, pp. 459–60.

2. *New York Times*, January 30, 1938.

3. Bloch Papers, Box 4.

4. Interview with Bloch, November 28, 1962.

5. Bloch Papers, Box 4.

6. Ibid.

7. *PHA*, Part 11, p. 5186.

8. *On the Treadmill*, p. 467.

9. Wellborn Comments.

10. Bloch Papers, Box 4.

11. Ibid., Box 3.

12. *On the Treadmill*, pp. 168–71, 467, 4.

13. Honolulu *Star-Bulletin*, April 10, 1940.

14. April 10, 1940.

15. Honolulu *Star-Bulletin*, April 11, 1940; Honolulu *Advertiser*, April 12, 1940.

16. Fleming Tape, March 31, 1975. Ryan interviewed Fleming for this tape.

17. Morgan Report, p. 264.

18. Interview with Mollison, November 8, 1963.

19. Interview with Shoemaker, January 31, 1963.

20. Interview with Curts, November 16, 1962.

21. Interview with Ramsey, December 6, 1962.

22. Interview with Furlong, November 16, 1962; *New York Times*, November 10, 1937.

23. Interview with Smith, November 29, 1962.

24. Interview with Draemel, January 17, 1963.

25. Interview with East, August 7, 1964.

26. Letter, Knox to Bloch, September 25, 1940, Bloch Papers, Box 2.

27. *PHA*, Part 26, p. 12.

28. Ibid., p. 13.

29. Ibid., p. 16.

30. Ibid., pp. 18, 23.

31. Ibid., p. 27.

32. Interview with Bloch, November 28, 1962.

33. Letter, Bloch to Stark, July 15, 1941, Bloch Papers, Box 4.

34. *PHA*, Part 20, p. 4482. See *At Dawn We Slept*, p. 354.

35. *PHA*, Part 6, p. 2894.

36. Ibid., p. 2894; Part 22, pp. 461–62.

37. Ibid., Part 6, pp. 2894–95.

38. Ibid., Part 33, pp. 714–15.

39. Ibid., p. 717.

40. Ibid., Part 26, p. 45.

41. Ibid., Part 22, p. 468.

42. Ibid., Part 26, p. 28.

43. Ibid., Part 28, pp. 1389–90, 1596.
44. *Random House Dictionary of the English Language* (New York, 1971).
45. *PHA*, Part 7, p. 2984.
46. Ibid., pp. 3057–58.
47. Ibid., p. 2994.
48. Ibid., Part 26, p. 20.
49. Ibid., p. 381.
50. Ibid., p. 384.
51. Ibid., pp. 20–21.
52. Ibid., Part 33, pp. 722–23.
53. Fleming Tape, March 31, 1975.
54. *PHA*, Part 22, p. 474; Part 32, p. 303.
55. Ibid., Part 26, p. 25.
56. Ibid., Part 32, p. 303.
57. Ibid., Part 27, pp. 787–88.
58. Ibid., pp. 771–72.
59. Ibid., Report, p. 153.

CHAPTER 24

"PECULIAR, COMPLICATED AND TENSE"

1. *PHA*, Part 22, pp. 490–91.
2. Ibid., p. 473; Part 26, p. 19.
3. Letter, Bloch to RADM. A. S. Carpenter, March 19, 1941, Bloch Papers, Box 1.
4. Letter, Bloch to Maj. Gen. Thomas Holcomb, USMC, June 1, 1941, Bloch Papers, Box 2.
5. *PHA*, Part 18, p. 3296.
6. Ibid., Part 26, pp. 361–62.
7. Ibid., Part 27, p. 782.
8. Ibid., Part 26, p. 27.
9. Ibid., Part 22, p. 472.
10. Ibid., p. 492.
11. Ibid., Part 33, p. 1318. See *At Dawn We Slept*, p. 159.
12. *PHA*, Part 26, p. 36.
13. Ibid., Part 32, p. 255.

14. Ibid., p. 302.
15. Ibid., Part 22, p. 495.
16. Ibid., Part 26, p. 33.
17. Ibid., Part 14, p. 1395. See *At Dawn We Slept*, p. 96.
18. *PHA*, Part 6, p. 2620.
19. Ibid., Part 22, p. 471.
20. Ibid., Part 32, p. 300.
21. Ibid., Part 39, p. 68.
22. Ibid., Part 27, pp. 769–70.
23. Ibid., p. 774.
24. Ibid., Part 28, p. 1393.
25. Forrestal Diaries, November 27, 1944.
26. *PHA*, Part 27, p. 774.
27. Ibid., p. 769.
28. Ibid., p. 793.
29. Ibid., Part 39, p. 69.
30. Ibid., Part 32, p. 305.
31. Ibid., p. 307.
32. Ibid., Part 28, p. 1389.
33. Ibid., Part 32, p. 515.
34. Ibid., Part 15, p. 1432.
35. Ibid., Part 27, pp. 774–75.
36. Ibid., p. 776.
37. Ibid., Part 33, p. 715.
38. Ibid., Report, pp. 86–87.
39. Ibid., Part 22, p. 464.
40. Ibid., Part 32, p. 307.
41. Ibid., Part 27, pp. 784–85.
42. Ibid., Part 22, pp. 464–65.
43. Ibid., Part 32, p. 504.
44. Ibid., Part 26, p. 18.
45. Ibid., Part 22, p. 464; Part 26, p. 23.
46. Ibid., Part 33, pp. 725–26.
47. Ibid., Part 26, pp. 24–25.
48. Ibid., pp. 100–01.
49. Ibid., Part 33, pp. 716–19.

50. Ibid., p. 1155.

51. Ibid., Report, p. 127.

52. Ibid., Part 27, p. 775.

53. Ibid., p. 778.

54. Ibid., Part 33, pp. 1177–78.

55. Ibid., Part 32, p. 304.

56. Ibid., Part 4, pp. 1954–55.

57. Ibid., Part 27, p. 791.

58. Ibid., Part 8, pp. 3544–45.

59. Interview with Ramsey, December 6, 1962.

60. Bloch Papers, Box 43. Bloch expressed the same view to Prange in an interview of November 27, 1962.

61. *PHA*, Part 22, p. 480.

62. Kimmel Papers, Box 4.

63. Hiles Papers, Box 9.

64. *PHA*, Report, p. 114.

65. Memorandum of conversation between Charles Rugg and Associate Justice Roberts, November 14–15, 1944 (courtesy Dr. Barnes; hereafter cited as Rugg-Roberts conversation).

66. *PHA*, Part 32, p. 13.

67. See *At Dawn We Slept*, Chapter 75.

68. *PHA*, Part 27, p. 765.

69. Ibid., p. 798.

70. Ibid., Part 39, pp. 64–69.

71. Ibid., Part 6, p. 2528.

72. See *At Dawn We Slept*, Chapter 60.

CHAPTER 25

"ALWAYS STRIVING FOR PERFECTION"

1. The sketch of Kimmel's career given in this chapter is based upon his service record and "Officer's Record of Fitness" (courtesy Kimmel). A very brief account is also given in his statement to the congressional committee, *PHA*, Part 6, p. 2498.

2. *Lucky Bag*, Class of 1904, p. 42.

3. Smedberg comments, July 27, 1977.

4. Interview with Ramsey, December 6, 1962.

5. *PHA*, Part 16, pp. 2144–45.

6. Interview with Davis, January 30, 1963.

7. Interview with Smith, November 14, 1962

8. *The Accused*, p. 91.

9. *PHA*, Part 6, pp. 2896–99. Kimmel expressed similar sentiments in an interview of November 30, 1963.

10. Honolulu *Advertiser*, February 2, 1941.

11. Interview with Davis, January 30, 1963.

12. Interview with Pullen, September 17, 1964.

13. Honolulu *Star-Bulletin*, May 15, 1968.

14. *PHA*, Part 32, p. 388.

15. Ibid., p. 596.

16. *Admiral Ambassador*, p. 88.

17. Interview with Bloch, November 28, 1962.

18. Interview with Shoemaker, January 31, 1963.

19. Interview with Tucker, August 22, 1965.

20. Interview with Curts, November 16, 1962.

21. Interview with Davis, January 30, 1963.

22. *PHA*, Part 26, pp. 73–74.

23. Interview with Furlong, November 16, 1962.

24. Interview with Capt. Wilfred J. Holmes, September 15, 1967.

25. *PHA*, Part 26, p. 2234.

26. Interview with Russell, August 6, 1964.

27. Interview with Shoemaker and Coe, January 31, 1963.

28. Interview with DeLany, November 2, 1962. Among those expressing similar views were Draemel (interview of January 17, 1963) and Smith (interview of November 14, 1962).

29. A number of Kimmel's former staff officers were reluctant for Prange to mention Kimmel's handicap, and Prange had no difficulty in communicating with him. But the problem is obvious from the many times during the investigation when Kimmel had to ask his questioners to repeat themselves. On one such occasion he told Congressman Clark, "I am deaf." (*PHA*, Part 6, p. 2704.)

30. *PHA*, Part 9, p. 4229.

31. Ibid., Part 5, p. 2474.

32. Fleet Admiral William F. Halsey and Lt. Cmdr. J. Bryan III, *Admiral Halsey's Story* (New York, 1947), p. 70 (hereafter cited as *Admiral Halsey's Story*); interviews with Spruance, September 5, 1964; Train, November 26, 1962; Furlong, November 16, 1962.

33. *The Accused,* p. 175.

34. Letter, Tucker to Barnes, April 18, 1962, Barnes Papers, Box 60.

35. *The Accused,* p. 175.

36. *PHA,* Part 23, p. 1220.

37. Ibid., Part 14, p. 975.

38. "Washington Merry-Go-Round," Dallas *Morning News,* February 15, 1946.

39. *PHA,* Part 5, p. 2350; Part 23, p. 1092.

40. Ibid., Part 23, p. 1137.

41. Ibid., Part 33, p. 1318.

42. Ibid., Part 6, p. 2509.

43. Ibid., Part 32. pp. 378–79.

44. Ibid., Part 26, p. 108.

45. Ibid., Part 6, pp. 2508–09.

46. Ibid., Part 32, p. 568.

47. Ibid., Part 22, p. 493.

48. Ibid., Part 26, p. 36.

49. Ibid., Part 32, pp. 568–69.

50. Ibid., p. 518.

51. Interview with Train, November 27, 1962. Vice Admiral Smith made the same point in an interview of November 14, 1962. See also his testimony to the Hart inquiry, Part 26, p. 46.

52. *PHA,* Part 22, p. 430.

53. Ibid., Part 32, pp. 232–33.

54. Ibid., p. 368.

55. Ibid., p. 378.

56. Ibid., Part 26, p. 51.

57. Ibid., Part 32, p. 334.

58. Interview with Coe, January 3, 1963.

59. A large selection of the correspondence between Stark and Kimmel appears in *PHA,* Part 16.

60. January 5, 1946.

61. *PHA,* Part 16, p. 2146. This letter is undated, but from the content obviously it was written early in 1941.

62. Interview with Morgan, October 26, 1976.

63. *PHA,* Part 6, p. 2838.

64. Interview with Shoemaker, January 31, 1963.

65. *PHA,* Part 6, p. 2504.

66. Ibid., Part 16, p. 2253.

67. Ibid., p. 2223. Rainbow Five (WPL-46) is reproduced in Part 18, pp. 2877–2941. The portion pertaining to the Pacific Fleet appears on pp. 2889–94.

68. Ibid., Part 26, p. 265.

69. Ibid., pp. 459–60.

70. Ibid., Part 9, pp. 4279–80, 4242–43. WPPac-46, July 21, 1941, is reproduced in full in Part 17, pp. 2568–2600.

71. Ibid., Part 26, p. 16.

72. Ibid., Part 6, pp. 2497–2511.

73. Ibid., Part 16, p. 2178.

74. November 25, 1945.

CHAPTER 26

"HIS MOST GRIEVOUS FAILURE"

1. *PHA*, Part 33, pp. 876–77.

2. Ibid., Part 10, p. 4825.

3. *The Accused,* p. 110.

4. *PHA,* Part 6, p. 2630.

5. Ibid., Part 32, p. 234.

6. Ibid., Part 4, pp. 1991, 1996.

7. Ibid., Part 6, p. 2730.

8. Ibid., Part 4, p. 1991.

9. Ibid., Part 26, p. 430.

10. Ibid., Part 39, p. 321.

11. Ibid., Part 8, pp. 3445–46.

12. Ibid., Part 6, p. 2518.

13. Ibid., Part 33, p. 878.

14. *Admiral Halsey's Story,* pp. 73–74.

15. *PHA,* Part 33, p. 56.

16. Ibid., Part 5, pp. 2450–51.

17. Ibid., Part 14, p. 1405.

18. Ibid., Part 5, p. 2200.

19. Ibid., Part 36, p. 209.

20. Ibid., Part 5, p. 2200.

21. Ibid., Part 26, p. 470.

22. Ibid., Part 8, p. 3437.

23. Ibid., Part 11, p. 5418.

24. Interview with Dunlop, October 10, 1963.

25. *PHA*, 22, p. 415.

26. Ibid., Part 32, pp. 221–22.

27. Ibid., p. 220.

28. Ibid., Part 33, p. 696.

29. Ibid., Part 32, p. 543.

30. Ibid., Part 9, p. 4295.

31. Ibid., Part 6, p. 2609.

32. Ibid., Part 5, p. 2203.

33. Ibid., p. 2222.

34. Ibid., Part 9, p. 4280.

35. Ibid., Part 10, pp. 4856, 4863.

36. Ibid., Part 8, p. 3504.

37. Ibid., Part 6, p. 2756.

38. Ibid., Part 8, pp. 3505–06.

39. Ibid., p. 3486.

40. Ibid., p. 3504.

41. Ibid., Part 26, pp. 104–05, 109.

42. Ibid., Part 33, p. 709.

43. Ibid., Part 8, p. 3454.

44. Ibid., Part 32, p. 441.

45. Ibid., p. 447.

46. Ibid., p. 450.

47. *Admiral Halsey's Story*, p. 71.

48. *PHA*, Part 39, pp. 308–09.

49. Ibid., p. 338.

50. Ibid., p. 368. Forrestal's original Fourth Endorsement, quoted here, was not made public because it contained references to Magic. In the version deleting those references, dated August 13, 1945, which Truman released on August 29, 1945, "most grievous failure" was altered to "most serious omission." Ibid., p. 382.

51. Ibid., Part 22, p. 487.

52. Ibid., Part 7, p. 3326.

53. Ibid., Part 32, p. 452.

54. Ibid., Part 12, p. 323.

55. Ibid., Part 3, p. 1085.

56. Ibid., Part 27, p. 423.

57. Interview with Morgan, October 26, 1976.

58. *PHA*, Report, p. 116.

59. Ibid., Part 16, p. 2238.

60. Ibid., Report, pp. 116–17.

61. Ibid., p. 117.

62. Ibid., p. 548.

63. Ibid., Part 23, pp. 1086–87.

64. Ibid., Part 9, pp. 3294–95.

65. "Hawaii Operation," p. 1319.

66. Washington *Star*, April 4, 1954.

67. *PHA*, Part 32, pp. 232–33.

68. Barnes Papers, Box 75.

69. "PH After ¼ Century," pp. 57–58.

70. *PHA*, Part 5, p. 2259.

CHAPTER 27

"THE LAST CRITICAL STAGES"

1. *PHA*, Part 6, pp. 2521–22.

2. Ibid., p. 2524.

3. A selection of these headlines appears in *PHA*, Part 30, pp. 2974–76.

4. November 30, 1941.

5. December 3, 1941.

6. December 5, 1941.

7. *PHA*, Part 6, p. 2974.

8. Ibid., Part 6, p. 2582.

9. Ibid., Part 8, p. 3528.

10. Ibid., Part 7, pp. 3371–72.

11. Ibid., Part 6, p. 2584.

12. Ibid., Part 32, p. 256.

13. Ibid., Part 6, p. 2586.

14. Ibid., pp. 2742, 2744.

15. Ibid., p. 2532.

16. Ibid., Part 21, Exhibit 16 following p. 4780.

17. Ibid., Part 6, p. 2605.

18. Ibid., pp. 2601–02.

19. Ibid., p. 2520.

20. Ibid., Part 5, p. 2154.

21. Ibid., Part 17, p. 2479.

22. Ibid., Part 5, p. 2154.

23. Ibid., Part 6, p. 2612.

24. Ibid., Part 32, p. 57.

25. Interview with Mollison, April 11, 1961. See also *PHA*, Part 27, p. 412 and Part 28, p. 1497.

26. Rugg-Roberts conversation.

27. *PHA*, Part 32, p. 215.

28. Ibid., Part 15, p. 1456.

29. Ibid., Part 32, p. 323.

30. Ibid., Report, p. 118.

31. Interview with Dyer, October 20, 1969.

32. *PHA*, Part 15, p. 1455.

33. Ibid., Part 22, p. 471.

34. Ibid., Part 6, p. 2580.

35. Ibid., p. 2584.

36. Ibid., p. 2581.

37. Ibid., pp. 2582–83.

38. Ibid., Part 32, p. 508.

39. Ibid., Report, p. 133.

40. Ibid., Part 10, pp. 4837–38. See *At Dawn We Slept*, Chapter 54.

41. *PHA*, pp. 4838–39.

42. Ibid., Part 6, pp. 2523–24.

43. Ibid., Part 4, p. 1878.

44. Ibid., Part 6, pp. 2522–23.

45. Ibid., p. 2523.

46. Ibid., Part 10, pp. 4839–40; Part 15, pp. 1895–96.

47. Morgan Report, pp. 137–38.

48. *PHA*, Report, p. 136.

49. *Truth about Pearl Harbor*, p. 19.

50. *PHA*, Part 26, p. 388.

51. Ibid., Part 9, p. 4241.

52. Ibid., Part 14, p. 1407.

53. Ibid., Part 22, p. 379.

54. Ibid., Part 33, pp. 704–05.

55. Ibid., Part 6, p. 2521.

56. Ibid., p. 2764.

57. Ibid., Part 9, p. 4226. See *At Dawn We Slept*, Chapter 55.

58. *PHA*, Part 26, p. 260.

59. December 3, 1945.

60. *PHA*, Part 22, p. 379.

61. Ibid., Part 14, p. 1408.

62. Ibid., Part 10, p. 4842; Part 33, p. 833.

63. Ibid., Part 14, p. 1408.

64. Ibid., Report, p. 554.

65. Ibid., Part 6, pp. 2654–56.

66. Ibid., p. 2657.

67. Morgan Report, p. 106.

68. *PHA*, Part 26, pp. 342–48.

69. Interview with Smith, November 29, 1962.

70. *PHA*, Part 6, p. 2536.

71. *Truth about Pearl Harbor*, pp. 23, 32, 26–27; Chicago *Tribune*, September 2, 1945, quoted in *Congressional Record*, Vol. 91, Part 12, Appendix, September 12, 1945, p. A3855.

72. *PHA*, Part 6, p. 2906.

73. Ibid., Part 4, p. 1950.

74. Ibid., Part 9, p. 4580.

75. Interviews with Fleet Admiral Chester W. Nimitz, September 4, 1964 (hereafter Nimitz); Holmes, March 15, 1971; Shoemaker and Coe, January 31, 1963.

76. *Cruise of the Lanikai*, pp. 90–91.

77. Interview with Fuchida, February 29, 1948.

78. *PHA*, Part 6, p. 2707.

79. Ibid., p. 2612.

80. Interview with Morgan, October 26, 1976.

81. *PHA*, Part 39, p. 314.

82. Ibid., p. 75.

83. Ibid., Report, p. 238.

84. Ibid., Part 27, p. 170. For a full account of these early actions of December 7, 1941, see *At Dawn We Slept*, pp. 484–85, 495–98.

85. *PHA*, Part 10, Record of Readings opposite p. 5058.

86. Ibid., Part 18, p. 3015.

87. Ibid., Part 10, pp. 5029–46. See also Record of Readings opposite p. 5058; Part 27, p. 569; Part 22, p. 223; interview with Tyler, August 21, 1964. For further discussion, see *At Dawn We Slept*, pp. 499–501.

CHAPTER 28

"IT IS INEXPLICABLE"

1. *PHA*, Part 14, p. 1329.

2. Francis B. Sayre, *Glad Adventure* (New York, 1957), p. 221 (hereafter cited as *Glad Adventure*). This quotation appears on p. 354 of the manuscript of Sayre's book located in his papers in the Library of Congress, Box 24 (hereafter cited as Sayre Papers).

3. *PHA*, Part 14, pp. 1328–33.

4. Ibid., p. 1329.

5. Report of Conference, December 6, 1941, Papers of Admiral Thomas C. Hart, Operational Archives, Navy Historical Center, Washington Navy Yard, Washington, D.C. (hereafter cited as Hart Papers).

6. Memorandum of Conversation between Admiral Hart and General MacArthur, Hart Papers.

7. Ibid.

8. Memorandum, December 23, 1941, Subject: Last Two Interviews with General MacArthur to Date, Hart Papers.

9. Report of Conference, December 6, 1941, Hart Papers.

10. For an excellent account of the initial day's activities, see Robert F. Futrell, "Air Hostilities in the Philippines, 8 December 1941," *Air University Review* (January–February 1965), pp. 33–45 (hereafter cited as "Air Hostilities").

11. Walter D. Edmonds, "What Happened at Clark Field," *Atlantic* (July 1951), p. 19 (hereafter cited as "What Happened").

12. Walter D. Edmonds, *They Fought with What They Had* (Boston, 1951), p. 75 (hereafter cited as *They Fought with What They Had*).

13. General of the Army Douglas MacArthur, *Reminiscences* (New York, 1964), p. 117 (hereafter cited as *Reminiscences*).

14. *They Fought with What They Had*, p. 75.

15. NA, RG 165, Box 1962.

16. *Fall of the Philippines*, p. 82.

17. "What Happened," p. 19; *Fall of the Philippines*, p. 86.

18. John Jacob Beck, *MacArthur and Wainwright: Sacrifice of the Philippines*

(Albuquerque, 1974), p. 13 (hereafter cited as *MacArthur and Wainwright.* See also *Strategy and Command*, p. 140.

19. *General Marshall Remembered*, p. 246.

20. Lt. Gen. Lewis H. Brereton, *The Brereton Diaries: The War in the Air in the Pacific, Middle East and Europe* (New York, 1946), p. 50 (hereafter cited as *Brereton Diaries*).

21. "PH After ¼ Century," p. 68.

22. *Fall of the Philippines*, pp. 81–82; *MacArthur and Wainwright*, p. 14.

23. *Global Mission*, p. 272.

24. See for example *They Fought with What They Had*, pp. ix–xi, xiv; "What Happened," p. 33.

25. *Brereton Diaries*, pp. 38–39.

26. *New York Times*, September 28, 1946. Quoted in "Air Hostilities," p. 40.

27. *Reminiscences*, p. 120.

28. "Air Hostilities," p. 44.

29. *Glad Adventure*, p. 223. The printed version of this quotation differs slightly from the phraseology on p. 357 of the manuscript, Sayre Papers, Box 24.

30. Letter, Welles to Roosevelt, April 14, 1942, Roosevelt Papers, PSF, Box 79.

31. *Reminiscences*, p. 117.

32. *They Fought with What They Had*, p. 76.

33. "What Happened," p. 31.

34. Roosevelt Papers, PSF, Safe File, Box 6.

35. Memorandum, Watson to Roosevelt, December 9, 1941, Roosevelt Papers, PSF, Box 49.

36. Stimson Diary, December 10, 1941. MacArthur's message appears on p. 17, *MacArthur and Wainwright*.

37. *Global Mission*, p. 272.

38. Message, MacArthur to Marshall, December 13, 1941, quoted in *Strategy and Command*, p. 150.

39. December 14, 1941.

40. Interview with Kimmel, November 29, 1963.

41. December 11, 1941.

CHAPTER 29

"BLESSED BY THE WAR GOD"

1. *PHA*, Part 22, p. 427.

2. Interviews with Fukudome, May 4, 1950, and RADM. Kameto Kuroshima, May 12, 1948 (hereafter Kuroshima). See *At Dawn We Slept*, Chapter 37.

3. Interview with Ohmae, January 22, 1947.

4. *Shinjuwan Sakusen Kaikoroku,* p. 138.

5. Interview with Admiral Katsunoshin Yamanashi, June 21, 1951 (hereafter Yamanashi).

6. Tomioka stressed this determination to Prange several times in the course of approximately forty interviews held during 1947–1965. See *At Dawn We Slept,* Chapter 53.

7. Interrogation of Nagano, March 26, 1946, at Sugamo Prison, Tokyo, Far East Mil. Trib., File No. 19, pp. 11–12; Bismarck *Tribune,* November 19, 1945.

8. *Nippon Times,* January 7, 1947; *Stars and Stripes,* Far East edition, same date.

9. Interviews with Oikawa, April 1, 1949, and VADM. Mitsumi Shimizu, November 20, 1948 (hereafter Shimizu).

10. Nagano's had been a rather belligerent voice in Japan's liaison conferences for 1941. See Nobutake Ike, ed., *Japan's Decision for War: Record of the 1941 Policy Conferences* (Stanford, Calif., 1967).

11. "Extracts from the Diary of VADM. Shigetaro Shimada," *Bungei Shunju* (December 1976), pp. 363–68.

12. Ibid., p. 367; Diary of Marquis Koichi Kido, November 30, 1941; interview with Watanabe, May 29, 1948.

13. Washington *Post,* November 17, 1971. Hirohito did not mention David Bergamini's book, *Japan's Imperial Conspiracy* (New York, 1971), but the press report noted that this work "evidently spurred" the question submitted before the meeting which elicited the Emperor's denial.

14. Interviews with Fuchida, July 29, 1947, and Tomioka, August 12, 1947. See *At Dawn We Slept,* Chapter 68.

15. *PHA,* Part 39, p. 122.

16. December 10, 1941.

17. *PHA,* Part 6, p. 2618.

18. Ibid., Part 5, pp. 2342–43.

19. Morgan Report, p. 151.

20. *PHA,* Report, p. 146.

21. See *At Dawn We Slept,* Chapter 39.

22. *PHA,* Report, p. 146.

23. Ibid.

24. Ibid.

25. Ibid., pp. 146–47.

26. Ibid., p. 147.

27. *Hawaii Sakusen,* pp. 102, 112; Diary of RADM. Giichi Nakahara, October 11, 1941.

28. Interview with Tomioka, August 12, 1947.

29. *PHA*, Report, p. 147.

30. Ibid.

31. Interview with Fielder, September 12, 1967.

32. *PHA*, Part 35, p. 336. In a memorandum to ONI dated January 4, 1942, Shivers wrote that during an interview with Richard Kotoshirodo "it was developed that TADASI MORIMURA . . . is without doubt the person charged by the Japanese Government with the collection of military information in the Territory of Hawaii. This is substantiated by the statements of other members of the clerical staff of the Consulate and by MORIMURA's apparent activity." "Tadashi Morimura" was Yoshikawa's alias. See also *PHA*, Part 24, p. 1309.

33. Ibid., Report, p. 147.

34. Ibid., p. 148.

35. *Rengo Kantai*, p. 28.

36. *PHA*, Report, p. 148.

37. Ibid.

38. Ibid., p. 149.

39. Interviews with Genda, March 25, 1947; March 15, 1948; November 4, 1950; Report which Genda prepared for Prange on the subject of Pearl Harbor, May 1947 (hereafter cited as Genda's Analysis).

40. *PHA*, Report, p. 149.

41. Interview with Takeo Yoshikawa, September 10, 1955.

42. *PHA*, Report, p. 149.

43. Ibid., p. 150.

44. Capt. J. V. Heimark, "Know Thine Enemy," *United States Naval Institute Proceedings* (August 1959), p. 67.

45. *At Dawn We Slept*, p. 344.

46. *PHA*, Part 36, pp. 61–62.

47. See *At Dawn We Slept*, Chapter 39.

48. *PHA*, Part 12, p. 227; *"Magic" Background*, Vol. IV, Appendix, p. A218. This message from Nomura to Tokyo asking that Hidenari Terasaki remain as a member of the embassy in Washington until "the sailing of the 19th" of December reveals that Nomura regarded the *Tatuta Maru* mission as a valid one. See *At Dawn We Slept*, p. 44.

49. *PHA*, Report, p. 266-F. Keefe referred to Tokyo's message to Nomura and Kurusu of November 22, 1941, which established a deadline for the discussions of November 29, after which "things are automatically going to happen." Ibid., Part 12, p. 165; *"Magic" Background*, Vol. IV, Appendix, p. A89.

50. Gwen Terasaki, *Bridge to the Sun* (Chapel Hill, N.C., 1957), pp. 66–69. See *At Dawn We Slept*, pp. 451–52.

51. December 7, 1945.

52. Des Moines *Register,* December 26, 1945. The official was probably Joseph W. Ballantine, who frequently attended the Hull-Nomura meetings.

53. See *At Dawn We Slept,* pp. 466, 489–90, 502.

54. *Shinjuwan Sakusen No Shinso,* p. 209.

55. Interview with Kuroshima, May 17, 1948.

56. *Shinjuwan Sakusen Kaikoroku,* p. 171.

57. Shigenori Togo, *The Cause of Japan* (New York, 1956), pp. 210–13.

58. *PHA,* Part 10, p. 4662.

59. Ibid., Report, p. 221.

60. Ibid., Part 11, p. 5274.

61. Interview with Tomioka, January 4, 1948.

62. Interview with Ohashi, November 25, 1949.

63. Interview with Hara, September 2, 1955.

64. Interview with Sanagi, August 29, 1949.

65. Interview with Davis, January 30, 1963.

66. *PHA,* Part 28, p. 1357.

67. Interview with Fuchida, July 29, 1947.

68. Summary of Verbal Report Submitted to Colonel Bicknell and Lieutenant Dyson, USA, by Harold T. Kay, NA, RG 107, Record of the Office of the Secretary of War, Army Pearl Harbor Board Material, Box 8, p. 1.

69. Courtesy of RADM. Teikichi Hori.

CHAPTER 30

"A STRATEGIC IMBECILITY"

1. Interview with Watanabe, February 21, 1949.

2. *Reports of General MacArthur: Japanese Operations in the Southwest Pacific Area, Vol. II, Part I* (Washington, D.C., 1966), p. 33, n. 1.

3. Address by Forrestal at a special convocation of Princeton University, June 21, 1944. Reproduced in *Congressional Record,* Vol. 90, Part 10, Apprendix, June 22, 1944, p. A3287.

4. Samuel Eliot Morison, "The Lessons of Pearl Harbor," *Saturday Evening Post* (October 26, 1961), p. 27.

5. Sokichi Takagi, "Shinjuwan Kogeki: No Hyoketsu Kudara (Making the Decision To Attack Pearl Harbor)," *Bungei Shunju* (December 1956) pp. 256–60.

6. "Hawaii Operation," p. 1328.

7. Replies by Safford to an undated questionnaire, Barnes Papers, Box 81.

8. Interview with Nomura, May 7, 1949.

9. Interview with Ozawa, December 22, 1948.

10. Interview with Toyoda, June 16, 1950.

11. Letter, Powell to Kimmel, February 22, 1955, Hiles Papers, Box 9. Powell had a long career in naval intelligence and cryptography.

12. *PHA,* Part 6, p. 2905.

13. *Shinjuwan Sakusen Kaikoroku,* p. 154.

14. Interview with Yamanashi, June 21, 1951.

15. Interview with Yoshioka, September 22, 1949.

16. See *At Dawn We Slept,* Chapters 3, 32.

17. Interview with Ms. Araki, January 6, 1965. She was a friend and confidante to many in high places during those exciting days. See also *Tojo,* p. 267.

18. Ernest T. Nash, "Understanding the Japanese," New York *Herald Tribune,* June 18, 1942.

19. *Shinjuwan Sakusen Kaikoroku,* pp. 14, 155.

20. Interview with Oi, September 26, 1955.

21. Interview with Tomioka, April 16, 1949.

22. Interview with VADM. Ryunosuke Kusaka, December 27, 1947; *Rengo Kantai,* pp. 2–3.

23. *PHA,* Part 9, p. 4564.

24. Interview with Genda by Lloyd Shearer and Jess Gordon, "Parade," Washington *Post,* December 2, 1956. Genda expressed similar ideas in numerous interviews with Prange.

25. Safford replies to undated questionnaire, Barnes Papers.

26. Memorandum, AC/S G-2 for the AC/S WDP, "Current Estimate of the Situation—Orange Plan," December 24, 1935, NA, RG 165, Entry 65, Box 212D, WDGS-MID 1917–1941 (242–12), p. 25.

27. *PHA,* Part 6, p. 2905.

28. *Hawai Sakusen,* pp. 97–99, lists the objections which Tomioka presented. See also *At Dawn We Slept,* Chapter 22. Tomioka as well as Fukodome and others spoke in much the same terms to Prange in numerous interviews.

29. Extract from one of a series of studies which Ohmae prepared for Prange. In Prange files.

30. Interview with Genda, March 22, 1947; Genda's Analysis.

31. Interview with Nimitz, September 4, 1964.

32. Interview with Oikawa, April 11, 1949.

33. Interview with Genda, June 4, 1947.

34. Interviews with Cmdr. Tatsukichi Miyo, May 30, 1949, and Tomoika, August 5, 1947.

35. For a full discussion of this decision, see *At Dawn We Slept*, Chapter 65.

36. Safford replies to undated questionnaire, Barnes Papers.

37. *PHA*, Part 26, p. 101.

38. *Shinjuwan Sakusen Kaikoroku*, p. 188.

39. Interview with Nimitz, September 4, 1964.

40. Interview with Spruance, September 5, 1964.

41. Interview with Nimitz, September 4, 1964.

42. Interview with Masataka Chihaya, February 5, 1947.

43. Atsushi Oi, "Why Japan's Anti-Submarine Warfare Failed," *United States Naval Institute Proceedings* (June 1952), p. 588.

44. Interview with Tsukahara, May 14, 1949.

45. Oi, Atsushi, "Why Japan's Anti-Submarine Warfare Failed," pp. 587–601.

46. The files of Magic messages in the National Archives, especially RG 457, show voluminous traffic between Tokyo and various locations in Central and South America.

47. *PHA*, Part 15, pp. 1316–25.

48. Interview with Tomioka, December 8, 1947.

49. Unpublished manuscript by Masataka Chihaya on the war in the Pacific, in Prange files, pp. 68–69 (hereafter cited as Chihaya MS).

50. *Shinjuwan Sakusen No Shinso*, p. 212.

51. Interview with Toyoda, June 9, 1950.

52. Quoted in *Newsweek* (December 17, 1945), p. 52.

53. For an interesting discussion of this system, see Hugh Byas, *Government by Assassination* (New York, 1942), pp. 134–36.

54. Interview with Nomura, May 7, 1949.

CHAPTER 31

"A MENTAL ATTITUDE"

1. San Francisco *Chronicle*, January 2, 1946.

2. Chihaya MS, pp. 109–11.

3. *PHA*, Part 29, p. 2145.

4. December 16, 1941.

5. *Congressional Record*, Vol. 87, Part 9, December 8, 1941, p. 9534.

6. *Newsweek* (December 14, 1942), p. 42.

7. *PHA*, Part 19, p. 3849.

8. Interview with Hara, September 22, 1955.

9.   Interview with Spruance, September 22, 1965.

10. December 8, 1941.

11. *PHA*, Part 27, p. 709.

12. December 11, 1941.

13. Interview with Rochefort, August 26, 1964.

14. See especially Grew's evaluation of November 3, 1941, which appears in *PHA*, Part 14, pp. 1051–57.

15. Chihaya MS, pp. 115–19.

16. *PHA*, Part 6, pp. 2596, 2637.

17. Ibid., Part 22, p. 505. See also p. 484.

18. Bloch Papers, Box 1.

19. New York *Herald Tribune*, December 5, 1945.

20. *PHA*, Part 3, p. 1083.

21. Ibid., Part 6, p. 2596.

22. Ibid., Part 22, p 485.

23. Ibid., p. 387.

24. Ibid., Part 33, p. 726.

25. Ibid., Part 22, p. 535.

26. Ibid., p. 527.

27. Ibid., Part 23, p. 614.

28. Ibid., Part 27, p. 208.

29. Ibid., p. 639.

30. Ibid., p. 706.

31. Ibid., Part 22, p. 170.

32. Ibid., p. 587.

33. Ibid., Part 6, p. 2596.

34. Ibid., Part 23, p. 614; Part 26, p. 325.

35. Ibid., Part 39, p. 380.

36. Ibid., Part 22. See pp. 333, 495, 535, 583 for the testimony respectively of Kimmel, Bloch, Pye, and Bellinger on these points.

37. Ibid., Part 6, p. 2705.

38. Ibid., Part 22, p. 432.

39. Ibid., pp. 470–71.

40. Ibid., Part 23, p. 760.

41. Ibid., p. 614.

42. Ibid., Report, p. 253.

43. Ibid., Part 39, pp. 76–77.

44. Ibid., p. 125.

45. Bloch Papers, Box 4.

46. Stanley D. Porteus, *And Blow Not the Trumpet: A Prelude to Peril* (Palo Alto, Calif., 1947), p. 2.

47. *PHA*, Part 22, p. 570.

48. Ibid., p. 489.

49. Ibid., Part 4, p. 1670.

50. Ibid., Part 22, p. 540.

51. Ibid., p. 492.

52. Ibid., Part 27, p. 33.

53. Interview with Tomioka, May 4, 1951.

54. *PHA*, Part 6, p. 2833.

55. Ibid., Part 4, p. 1908.

56. Ibid., Report, p. 256.

57. Seth W. Richardson, "Why Were We Caught Napping at Pearl Harbor?" *Saturday Evening Post* (May 24, 1947), p. 21.

58. *PHA*, Report, p. 523.

59. Honolulu *Star-Bulletin*, September 18, 1941.

60. *PHA*, Part 22, p. 341.

61. Ibid., Part 24, pp. 2010–11.

62. Ibid., pp. 2107–20.

63. December 21, 1945.

64. *PHA*, Part 27, p. 509.

65. Quoted in article by Wilfred Fleischer in the New York *Herald Tribune*, December 2, 1941.

66. Hull Papers, Box 72–73.

67. Letter, King to Mr. L. F. V. Drake, October 24, 1941. Papers of Fleet Admiral Ernest J. King, Library of Congress, Washington, D.C., Box 8.

68. December 8, 1941.

69. Quoted in article by Thomas R. Henry in the Washington *Evening Star*, December 8, 1941.

70. December 20, 1941.

71. *Congressional Record*, Vol. 91, Part 8, November 6, 1945, p. 10449.

72. December 10, 1941.

CHAPTER 32

"IN THE WAKE OF THE PEARL HARBOR DISASTER"

1. December 12, 1966, p. 47.

2. Washington *Evening Star,* December 10, 1941.

3. December 16, 1941.

4. December 26, 1941.

5. Brooke-Popham Dispatch, p. 558.

6. December 22, 1941, p. 851.

7. *PHA*, Part 22, p. 479.

8. Roosevelt Papers, PSF Box 83. Barth was assigned to the Treasury Department, reporting to Ferdinand Kuhn, Jr., the assistant to the secretary, until the latter part of December 1941 when he transferred to the Office of Facts and Figures. Beginning with January 2, 1942, he reported to Archibald MacLeish.

9. William Harlan Hale, "After Pearl Harbor," p. 816.

10. Roosevelt Papers, PSF Box 83.

11. *New York Times,* January 29, 1942.

12. Stimson Diary, February 18, 1942.

13. December 13, 1941.

14. Stimson Diary, January 17, 1942.

15. *Congressional Record,* Vol. 88, Part 1, January 20, 1942, p. 505.

16. Ibid., January 17, 1942, p. 737.

17. December 11, 1941.

18. Bloch Papers, Box 2.

19. December 12, 1941.

20. Interview with Bloch, November 28, 1962.

21. Thomas C. Hone, "The Destruction of the Battle Line at Pearl Harbor," *U.S. Naval Institute Proceedings* (December 1977), p. 58.

22. Interview with Nimitz, September 4, 1964.

23. Interview with Nomura, May 7, 1949.

24. Anyone interested in pursuing this subject further is referred to VADM. Homer N. Wallin, *Pearl Harbor: Why, How, Fleet Salvage and Final Appraisal* (Washington, D.C., 1968).

25. Ibid., pp. 254–61; interview with Beck, August 6, 1964.

26. Wallin, op. cit., pp. 189–205.

27. Ibid., pp. 206–211. See also Cmdr. John D. Alden, "Up From Ashes—The Sage of *Cassin* and *Downes,*" *U.S. Naval Institute Proceedings* (January 1961), pp. 33–41.

28. Wallin, op. cit., pp. 211–22.

29. Ibid., pp. 222–33.

30. Ibid., pp. 233–42.

31. Ibid., pp. 243–51.

32. The correspondents of *Time, Life,* and *Fortune, December 7: The First Thirty Hours* (New York, 1942), pp. 46, 65.

33. Interview with Hara, September 2, 1955.

34. *Congressional Record,* Vol. 88, Part 1, January 27, 1942, p. 732.

35. Donald W. Mitchell, "What the Navy Can Do," *Nation* (December 20, 1941), p. 633.

36. December 21, 1941.

37. For a brief, readable example of this literature, see Hendrik Willem van Loon, *Our Battle* (New York, 1938).

38. December 23, 1941.

39. "That's That," January 13, 1946.

40. *Congressional Record,* Vol. 87, Part 9, December 12, 1941, p. 9721.

41. Ibid., December 15, 1941, p. 9826.

42. Adm. William V. Pratt, "We Must Take the Offensive," *Newsweek* (March 2, 1942), p. 23.

43. *Congressional Record,* Vol. 88, Part 1, January 12, 1942, pp. 251–52.

44. Ibid., February 16, 1942, p. 1299.

45. *Report to Hon. James Forrestal, Secretary of the Navy, on Unification of the War and Navy Departments and Postwar Organization for National Security,* Seventy-ninth Congress, 1st Session, October 22, 1945, p. 183.

46. December 3, 1945.

47. *PHA,* Report, p. 245.

48. "The Lost Leader."

49. December 19, 1945.

50. *Congressional Record,* Vol. 91, Part 6, September 6, 1945, p. 8352.

51. J. David Singer, "Surprise Attack," *Nation* (January 30, 1960), p. 92.

52. "Surprise Attack," *New Republic* (February 29, 1960), pp. 3–5.

53. "Pearl Harbor Sunday," p. 477.

54. William Henry Chamberlin, "The Clay Feet of Imperialism," *Asia* (May 1942), p. 279.

55. *PHA,* Part 16, p. 2177.

56. Fletcher Pratt, *The Navy's War* (New York, 1944), p. 38.

57. *PHA,* Part 36, p. 401.

58. Ibid., Part 6, p. 2504.

CHAPTER 33

"REMEMBER PEARL HARBOR"

1. Letter, Hanify to Kimmel, August 30, 1953, Kimmel Papers, Box 7.
2. *Congressional Record,* Vol. 87, Part 14, Appendix, December 9, 1941, p. A5500.
3. Ibid. Vol.. 88, Part 1, February 5, 1942, p. 1047.
4. Interview with Hara, September 6, 1955.
5. December 7, 1945.
6. December 7, 1945.
7. August 31, 1945.
8. December 10, 1945.
9. August 31, 1945.
10. January 25, 1946.
11. January 9, 1946.
12. *New York Times,* November 28 and December 3, 1946; interview with Morgan, October 26, 1976.
13. *PHA,* Report, pp. 253–54. All italics are in original.
14. Ibid., pp. 254–55.
15. Ibid., p. 255.
16. Ibid., pp. 255–56.
17. Ibid., p. 256.
18. Ibid., p. 257.
19. Ibid., pp. 257–58.
20. Washington *Post,* September 29, 1975.
21. *PHA,* Report, p. 258.
22. Ibid., p. 259.
23. Amitai Etzioni, "Fact-Crazy, Theory-Shy?" *Science* (October 23, 1970), p. 321.
24. *PHA,* Report, pp. 259–60.
25. Ibid., pp. 260–61.
26. Ibid., p. 261.
27. Ibid., pp. 261–62.
28. Ibid., p. 262.
29. Ibid., pp. 262–63.
30. Ibid., p. 263.
31. Ibid.

32. Ibid., pp. 263–64.

33. Ibid., p. 264. For a discussion of this dispute, see *At Dawn We Slept*, pp. 400–01.

34. *PHA*, Report, pp. 264–65.

35. Ibid., p. 265.

36. Ibid.

37. Ibid., pp. 265–66.

38. Ibid., p. 266.

39. *Christian Science Monitor*, February 9, 1946.

40. Henry A. Kissinger, "Arms Control, Inspection and Surprise Attack," *Foreign Affairs* (July 1960), p. 557.

41. August 31, 1945.

42. Kissinger, op. cit., p. 561.

43. Will and Ariel Durant, *The Lessons of History* (New York, 1968), p. 81.

44. Max Lerner, "The Margin of Waste," *New Republic* (January 26, 1942), p. 109.

45. December 7, 1966.

APPENDICES

The Pearl Harbor Investigations

ROBERTS COMMISSION

December 22, 1941–January 23, 1942

Associate Justice Owen J. Roberts, U. S. Supreme Court, chairman
Admiral William H. Standley, USN (Ret.), member
RADM. Joseph M. Reeves, USN (Ret.), member
Maj. Gen. Frank B. McCoy, USA (Ret.), member
Brig. Gen. Joseph T. McNarney, USA, member
Walter Bruce Howe, recorder
Lt. Col. Lee Brown, USMC, legal adviser
Albert J. Schneider, secretary

HART INQUIRY

February 22–June 15, 1944

Admiral Thomas C. Hart, USN (Ret.)
Capt. Jesse R. Wallace, USN, counsel*
Lt. William M. Whittington, Jr., USNR, assistant counsel

ARMY PEARL HARBOR BOARD

July 20–October 20, 1944

Lt. Gen. George Grunert, president
Maj. Gen. Henry D. Russell, member
Maj. Gen. Walter H. Frank, member

---

*Relieved on May 9, 1944, when Whittington became counsel

647

Col. Charles W. West, recorder
Maj. Henry C. Clausen, asst. recorder
Col. Harry A. Toulmin, Jr., executive officer

NAVY COURT OF INQUIRY

July 24–October 19, 1944

Admiral Orin G. Murfin, USN (Ret.), president
Admiral Edward C. Kalbfus, USN (Ret.), member
VADM. Adolphus Andrews, USN, member
Cmdr. Harold Biesemeier, USN, judge advocate

HEWITT INVESTIGATION

May 15–July 11, 1945

VADM. H. Kent Hewitt
Mr. John F. Sonnett, counsel
Lt. Cmdr. Benjamin H. Griswold, USNR, aide to Admiral Hewitt
Lt. John Ford Baecher, USNR, assistant to Mr. Sonnett

CLAUSEN INVESTIGATION

November 23, 1944–September 12, 1945

Lt. Col. Henry C. Clausen, JAGD

CLARKE INVESTIGATION

September 14–16, 1944
July 13–August 4, 1945

Col. Carter W. Clarke, USA
Lt. Col. Ernest W. Gibson, USA

JOINT CONGRESSIONAL COMMITTEE

November 15, 1945–July 15, 1946

Alben W. Barkley, senator from Kentucky, chairman
Jere Cooper, representative from Tennessee, vice chairman
Walter F. George, senator from Georgia
Scott W. Lucas, senator from Illinois

Owen Brewster, senator from Maine
Homer Ferguson, senator from Michigan
J. Bayard Clark, representative from North Carolina
John W. Murphy, representative from Pennsylvania
Bertrand W. Gearhart, representative from California
Frank B. Keefe, representative from Wisconsin

COUNSEL (THROUGH JANUARY 14, 1946)

William D. Mitchell, general counsel
Gerhard A. Gesell, chief assistant counsel
Jule M. Hannaford, assistant counsel
John E. Masten, assistant counsel

(AFTER JANUARY 14, 1946)

Seth W. Richardson, general counsel
Samuel H. Kaufman, associate general counsel
John E. Masten, assistant counsel
Edward F. Morgan, assistant counsel
Logan J. Lane, assistant counsel

Japanese Proposals of November 20, 1941

1. Both the Governments of Japan and the United States undertake not to make any armed advancement into any of the regions in the South-eastern Asia and the Southern Pacific area excepting the part of French Indo-China where the Japanese troops are stationed at present.

2. The Japanese Government undertakes to withdraw its troops now stationed in French Indo-China upon either the restoration of peace between Japan and China or the establishment of an equitable peace in the Pacific area.

In the meantime the Government of Japan declares that it is prepared to remove its troops now stationed in the southern part of French Indo-China to the northern part of the said territory upon the conclusion of the present arrangement which shall later be embodied in the final agreement.

3. The Government of Japan and the United States shall cooperate with a view to securing the acquisition of those goods and commodities which the two countries need in Netherlands East Indies.

4. The Governments of Japan and the United States mutually undertake to restore their commercial relations to those prevailing prior to the freezing of the assets.

The Government of the United States shall supply Japan a required quantity of oil.

5. The Government of the United States undertakes to refrain from such measures and actions as will be prejudicial to the endeavors for the restoration of general peace between Japan and China.

(Hull Papers, Box 72–73.)

"War Warning" Messages of November 27, 1941

PRIORITY MESSAGE NO. 472 TO COMMANDING GENERAL, HAWAIIAN DEPARTMENT:

Negotiations with Japan appear to be terminated to all practical purposes with only the barest possibilities that the Japanese Government might come back and offer to continue Period Japanese future action unpredictable but hostile action possible at any moment Period If hostilities cannot comma repeat cannot comma be avoided the United States desires that Japan commit the first overt act Period This policy should not comma repeat not comma be construed as restricting you to a course of action that might jeopardize your defense Period Prior to hostile Japanese action you are directed to undertake such reconnaissance and other measures as you deem necessary but these measures should be carried out so as not comma repeat not comma to alarm civil population or disclose intent Period Report measures taken Period Should hostilities occur you will carry out the tasks assigned in rainbow five so far as they pertain to Japan Period Limit dissemination of this highly secret information to minimum essential officers

MARSHALL

(*PHA,* Part 14, p. 1328)

TOP SECRET NAVY MESSAGE:

November 27, 1941
From: Chief of Naval Operations
Action: CINCAF, CINCPAC
Info: CINCLANT, SPENAVO
272337

This dispatch is to be considered a war warning X Negotiations with Japan looking toward stabilization of conditions in the Pacific have ceased and an aggressive move by Japan is expected within the next few days X The number and equipment of Japanese troops and the organization of naval task forces indicates an amphibious expedition against either the Philippines Thai or Kra peninsula or possibly Borneo X Execute an appropriate defensive deployment preparatory to carrying out the tasks assigned in WPL46 X Inform district and army authorities X A similar warning is being sent by War Department X Spenavo inform British X Continental districts Guam Samoa directed take appropriate measures against sabotage.

(*PHA*, Part 14, p. 1406.)

Proposed Modus Vivendi

November 25, 1941

The representatives of the Government of the United States and of the Government of Japan have been carrying on during the past several months informal and exploratory conversations for the purpose of arriving at a settlement if possible of questions relating to the entire Pacific area based upon the principles of peace, law and order and fair dealing among nations. These principles include the principle of inviolability of territorial integrity and sovereignty of each and all nations; the principle of non-interference in the internal affairs of other countries; the principle of equality, including equality of commercial opportunity and treatment; and the principle of reliance upon international cooperation and conciliation for the prevention and pacific settlement of controversies and for improvement of international conditions by peaceful methods and processes.

It is believed that in our discussions some progress has been made in reference to the general principles which constitute the basis of a peaceful settlement covering the entire Pacific area. Recently the Japanese Ambassador has stated that the Japanese Government is desirous of continuing the conversations directed toward a comprehensive and peaceful settlement in the Pacific area; that it would be helpful toward creating an atmosphere favorable to the successful outcome of the conversations if a temporary *modus vivendi* could be agreed upon to be in effect while the conversations looking to a peaceful settlement in the Pacific were continuing; and that it would be desirable that such *modus vivendi* include as one of its provisions some initial and temporary steps of a reciprocal character in the resumption of trade and normal intercourse between Japan and the United States.

On November 20 the Japanese Ambassador communicated to the Secretary of State proposals in regard to temporary measures to be taken respectively by the Govenment of Japan and by the Government of the United States, which measures are understood to have been designed to accomplish the purposes above indicated.

653

These proposals contain features which, in the opinion of this Government, conflict with the fundamental principles which form a part of the general settlement under consideration and to which each Government has declared that it is committed.

The Government of the United States is earnestly desirous to contribute to the promotion and maintenance of peace in the Pacific area and to afford every opportunity for the continuance of discussions with the Japanese Government directed toward working out a broad-gauge program of peace throughout the Pacific area. With these ends in view, the Government of the United States offers for the consideration of the Japanese Government an alternative suggestion for temporary *modus vivendi*, as follows:

MODUS VIVENDI

1. The Government of the United States and the Government of Japan, both being solicitous for the peace of the Pacific, affirm that their national policies are directed toward lasting and extensive peace throughout the Pacific area and that they have no territorial designs therein.

2. They undertake reciprocally not to make from regions in which they have military establishments any advance by force or threat of force into any areas in Southeastern or Northeastern Asia or in the southern or the northern Pacific area.

3. The Japanese Government undertakes forthwith to withdraw its armed forces now stationed in southern French Indochina and not to replace those forces; to reduce the total of its forces in French Indochina to the number there on July 26, 1941; and not to send additional naval, land or air forces to Indochina for replacements or otherwise.

The provisions of the foregoing paragraph are without prejudice to the position of the Government of the United States with regard to the presence of foreign troops in that area.

4. The Government of the United States undertakes forthwith to modify the application of its existing freezing and export restrictions to the extent necessary to permit the following resumption of trade between the United States and Japan in articles for the use and needs of their peoples:

(a) Imports from Japan to be freely permitted and the proceeds of the sale thereof to be paid into a clearing account to be used for the purchase of the exports from the United States listed below, and at Japan's option for the payment of interest and principal of Japanese obligations within the United States, provided that at least two-thirds in value of such imports per month consist of raw silk. It is understood that all American-owned goods now in Japan the movement of which in transit to the United States has been interrupted following the adoption of freezing measures shall be forwarded forthwith to the United States.

(b) Exports from the United States to Japan to be permitted as follows:

(i) Bunkers and supplies for vessels engaged in the trade here provided for and for such other vessels engaged in other trades as the two Governments may agree.

(ii) Food and food products from the United States subject to such limitations as the appropriate authorities may prescribe in respect of commodities in short supply in the United States.

(iii) Raw cotton from the United States to the extent of $600,000 in value per month.

(iv) Medical and pharmaceutical supplies subject to such limitations as the appropriate authorities may prescribe in respect of commodities in short supply in the United States.

(v) Petroleum. The United States will permit the export to Japan of petroleum, within the categories permitted general export, upon a monthly basis for civilian needs. The proportionate amount of petroleum to be exported from the United States for such needs will be determined after consultation with the British and the Dutch Governments. It is understood that by civilian needs in Japan is meant such purposes as the operation of the fishing industry, the transport system, lighting, heating, industrial and agricultural uses, and other civilian uses.

(vi) The above stated amounts of exports may be increased and additional commodities added by agreement between the two governments as it may appear to them that the operation of this agreement is furthering the peaceful and equitable solution of outstanding problems in the Pacific area.

5. The Government of Japan undertakes forthwith to modify the application of its existing freezing and export restrictions to the extent necessary to permit the resumption of trade between Japan and the United States as provided for in paragraph four above.

6. The Government of the United States undertakes forthwith to approach the Australian, British and Dutch Governments with a view to those Governments' taking measures similar to those provided for in paragraph four above.

7. With reference to the current hostilities between Japan and China, the fundamental interest of the Government of the United States in reference to any discussions which may be entered into between the Japanese and the Chinese Governments is simply that these discussions and any settlement reached as a result thereof be based upon and exemplify the fundamental principles of peace, law, order and justice, which constitute the central spirit of the current conversations between the Government of Japan and the Government of the United States and which are applicable uniformly throughout the Pacific area.

8. This *modus vivendi* shall remain in force for a period of three months with the understanding that the two parties shall confer at the instance of either to ascertain whether the prospects of reaching a peaceful settlement covering the entire Pacific area justify an extension of the *modus vivendi* for a further period.

There is attached in tentative form a plan of a comprehensive peaceful settlement covering the entire Pacific area as one practical exemplification of the kind of program which this Government has in mind to be worked out during the further conversations between the Government of Japan and the Government of the United States while this *modus vivendi* would be in effect.

(Hull Papers, Box 72–73.)

Japan's "Bomb Plot" Message

From: Tokyo (Toyoda)
To: Honolulu
September 24, 1941
J-19
#83
Strictly secret

Henceforth, we would like to have you make reports concerning vessels along the following lines insofar as possible:

1. The waters (of Pearl Harbor) are to be divided roughly into five sub-areas. (We have no objection to your abbreviating as much as you like.)

Area A. Waters between Ford Island and the Arsenal.

Area B. Waters adjacent to the Island south and west of Ford Island. (This area is on the opposite side of the Island from Area A.)

Area C. East Loch.

Area D. Middle Loch.

Area E. West Loch and the communicating water routes.

2. With regard to warships and aircraft carriers, we would like to have you report on those at anchor, (these are not so important) tied up at wharves, buoys and in docks. (Designate types and classes briefly. If possible we would like to have you make mention of the fact when there are two or more vessels along side the same wharf.)

Trans. 10/9/41

(*PHA*, Part 12, p. 261; *"Magic" Background*, pp. A189–90.)

656

The Hull Note of November 26, 1941

Copy of document handed
by the Secretary of State
to the Japanese Ambassador
on November 26, 1941

STRICTLY CONFIDENTIAL,
TENTATIVE AND WITHOUT
COMMITMENT

November 26, 1941

OUTLINE OF PROPOSED BASIS FOR AGREEMENT BETWEEN THE UNITED STATES AND JAPAN

Section I

Draft Mutual Declaration of Policy

The Government of the United States and the Government of Japan both being solicitous for the peace of the Pacific affirm that their national policies are directed toward lasting and extensive peace throughout the Pacific area, that they have no territorial designs in that area, that they have no intention of threatening other countries or of using military force aggressively against any neighboring nation, and that, accordingly, in their national policies they will actively support and give practical application to the following fundamental principles upon which their relations with each other and with all other governments are based:

(1) The principle of inviolability of territorial integrity and sovereignty of each and all nations.

(2) The principle of non-interference in the internal affairs of other countries.

(3) The principle of equality, including equality of commercial opportunity and treatment.

(4) The principle of reliance upon international cooperation and conciliation for the prevention and pacific settlement of controversies and for improvement of international conditions by peaceful methods and processes.

The Government of Japan and the Government of the United States have agreed that toward eliminating chronic political instability, preventing recurrent economic collapse, and providing a basis for peace, they will actively support and practically apply the following principles in their economic relations with each other and with other nations and peoples:

(1) The principle of non-discrimination in international commercial relations.

(2) The principle of international economic cooperation and abolition of extreme nationalism as expressed in excessive trade restrictions.

(3) The principle of non-discriminatory access by all nations to raw material supplies.

(4) The principle of full protection of the interests of consuming countries and populations as regards the operation of international commodity agreements.

(5) The principle of establishment of such institutions and arrangements of international finance as may lend aid to the essential enterprises and the continuous development of all countries and may permit payments through processes of trade consonant with the welfare of all countries.

Section II

Steps to be Taken by the Government of the United States and by the Government of Japan

The Government of the United States and the Government of Japan propose to take steps as follows:

1. The Government of the United States and the Government of Japan will endeavor to conclude a multilateral non-aggression pact among the British Empire, China, Japan, the Netherlands, the Soviet Union, Thailand and the United States.

2. Both Governments will endeavor to conclude among the American, British, Chinese, Japanese, the Netherland and Thai Governments an agreement whereunder each of the Governments would pledge itself to respect the territorial integrity of French Indochina and, in the event that there should develop a threat to the territorial integrity of Indochina, to enter into immediate consultation with a view to taking such measures as may be deemed necessary and advisable to meet the threat in question. Such agreement would provide also that each of the Governments party to the agreement would not seek or accept preferential treatment in its trade or economic relations with Indochina and would use its influence to obtain for each of the signatories equality of treatment in trade and commerce with French Indochina.

3. The Government of Japan will withdraw all military, naval, air and police forces from China and from Indochina.

4. The Government of the United States and the Government of Japan will not

support—militarily, politically, economically—any government or regime in China other than the National Government of the Republic of China with capital temporarily at Chungking.

5. Both Governments will give up all extraterritorial rights in China, including rights and interests in and with regard to international settlements and concessions, and rights under the Boxer Protocol of 1901.

Both Governments will endeavor to obtain the agreement of the British and other governments to give up extraterritorial rights in China, including rights in international settlements and in concessions and under the Boxer Protocol of 1901.

6. The Government of the United States and the Government of Japan will enter into negotiations for the conclusion between the United States and Japan of a trade agreement, based upon reciprocal most-favored-nation treatment and reduction of trade barriers by both countries, including an undertaking by the United States to bind raw silk on the free list.

7. The Government of the United States and the Government of Japan will, respectively, remove the freezing restrictions on Japanese funds in the United States and on American funds in Japan.

8. Both Governments will agree upon a plan for the stabilization of the dollar–yen rate, with the allocation of funds adequate for this purpose, half to be supplied by Japan and half by the United States.

9. Both Governments will agree that no agreement which either has concluded with any third power or powers shall be interpreted by it in such a way as to conflict with the fundamental purpose of this agreement, the establishment and preservation of peace throughout the Pacific area.

10. Both Governments will use their influence to cause other governments to adhere to and to give practical application to the basic political and economic principles set forth in this agreement.

(Attachment to State Department Memorandum of Conversation, November 26, 1941, Hull Papers, Box 60.)

Popov Questionnaire

**BRITISH SECRET SERVICE TRANSLATION
OF THE GERMAN QUESTIONNAIRE WHICH
TRICYCLE TOOK TO AMERICA**

Naval Information.—Reports on enemy shipments (material foodstuffs—combination of convoys, if possible with names of ships and speeds).

Assembly of troops for oversea transport in U.S.A. and Canada. Strength—number of ships—ports of assembly—reports on ship building (naval and merchant ships—wharves (dockyards)—state and private owned wharves—new works—list of ships being built or resp. having been ordered—times of building.

Reports regarding U.S.A. strong points of all descriptions especially in Florida—organisation of strong points for fast boats (E-boats) and their depot ships—coastal defence—organisation districts.

Hawaii.—Ammunition dumps and mine depots.

1. Details about naval ammunition and mine depot on the Isle of Kushua [sic] (Pearl Harbour). If possible sketch.

2. Naval ammunition depot Lualuelei. Exact position? Is there a railway line (junction)?

3. The total ammunition reserve of the army is supposed to be in the rock of the Crater Aliamanu. Position?

4. Is the Crater Punchbowl (Honolulu) being used as ammunition dump? If not, are there other military works?

Aerodromes.

1. *Aerodrome Lukefield.*—Details (sketch if possible) regarding the situation of the hangars (number?), workshops, bomb depots, and petrol depots. Are there underground petrol installations?—Exact position of the seaplane station? Occupation?

2. *Naval air arm strong point Kaneche.*—Exact report regarding position, number of hangars, depots, and workshops (sketch). Occupation?

3. *Army aerodromes Wicham Field and Wheeler Field.*—Exact position? Reports regarding number of hangars, depots and workshops. Underground installations? (Sketch.)
4. *Rodger's Airport.*—In case of war, will this place be taken over by the army or the navy? What preparations have been made? Number of hangars? Are there landing possibilities for seaplanes?
5. *Airport of the Panamerican Airways.*—Exact position? (If possible sketch.) Is this airport possibly identical with Rodger's Airport or a part thereof? (A wireless station of the Panamerican Airways is on the Peninsula Mohapuu.)

Naval Strong Point Pearl Harbour.
1. Exact details and sketch about the situation of the state wharf, of the pier installations, workshops, petrol installations, situations of dry dock No. 1 and of the new dry dock which is being built.
2. Details about the submarine station (plan of situation). What land installations are in existence?
3. Where is the station for mine search formations [Minensuchverbaende]? How far has the dredger work progressed at the entrance and in the east and southeast lock? Depths of water?
4. Number of anchorages [Liegeplaetze]?
5. Is there a floating dock in Pearl Harbour or is the transfer of such a dock to this place intended?

Special tasks.—Reports about torpedo protection nets newly introduced in the British and U.S.A. navy. How far are they already in existence in the merchant and naval fleet? Use during voyage? Average speed reduction when in use. Details of construction and others.
1. Urgently required are exact details about the armoured strengths of American armoured cars, especially of the types which have lately been delivered from the U.S.A. to the Middle East. Also all other reports on armoured cars and the composition of armoured (tank) formations are of greatest interest.
2. Required are the Tables of Organisation (TO) of the American infantry divisions and their individual units (infantry regiments, artillery "Abteilung" and so forth) as well as of the American armoured divisions and their individual units (armoured tank regiments, reconnaissance section, and so forth). These TO are lists showing strength, which are published by the American War Department and are of a confidential nature.
3. How is the new light armoured car (tank)? Which type is going to be finally introduced? Weight? Armament? Armour?

1. Position of British participations and credits in U.S.A. in June 1940. What are England's payment obligations from orders since the coming into force of the Lend Lease Bill? What payments has England made to U.S.A. since the outbreak of war for goods supplied, for establishment of works, for the production of war material, and for the building of new or for the enlargement of existing wharves?

2. Amount of state expenditure in the budget years 1939/40, 1940/41, 1941/42, 1942/43 altogether and in particular for the army and the rearmament.

3. Financing of the armament programme of the U.S.A. through taxes, loans and tax credit coupons. Participation of the Refico and the companies founded by it (Metal Reserve Corp., Rubber Reserve Corp., Defence Plant Corp., Defence Supplies Corp., Defence Housing Corp.) in the financing of the rearmament.

4. Increase of state debt and possibilities to cover this debt.

All reports on American air rearmament are of greatest importance. The answers to the following questions are of special urgency:

   I. How large is—
      (a) the total monthly production of aeroplanes?
      (b) the monthly production of bombers [Kampfflugzeuge]?
      (c) "   "   "   " fighter planes?
      (d) "   "   "   " training planes
         [Schulflugzeuge]?
      (e) "   "   "   " civil aeroplanes
         [Zivilflugzeuge]?

   II. How many and which of these aeroplanes were supplied to the British Empire, that is to say—
      (a) to Great Britain?
      (b) to Canada?
      (c) to Africa?
      (d) to the Near East?
      (e) to the Far East and Australia?

  III. How many U.S.A. pilots finish their training monthly?

  IV. How many U.S.A. pilots are entering the R.A.F.?

Reports on Canadian Air Force are of great value.

All information about number and type (pattern) of front aeroplanes [Frontflugzeuge]. Quality, numbers and position of the echelons [Staffein] are of great interest. Of special importance is to get details about the current air training plan in Canada, that is to say: place and capacity of individual schools and if possible also their numbers. According to reports received every type of school (beginners'—advanced—and observer school) is numbered, beginning with 1.

(*Spy Counter Spy*, opp. p. 148.)

SELECTED BIBLIOGRAPHY

UNPUBLISHED SOURCES

Barnes, Harry E. "Whose 'Day of Infamy'? Pearl Harbor After Twenty Years." Unpublished article, Prange files, courtesy Dr. Barnes.

———. Letters to Prange, November 1, 1963, and February 28, 1964. Prange files.

———. Interview with VADM. Frank E. Beatty, USN (Ret.), June 29, 1962. Prange files, courtesy Dr. Barnes.

———. Interview with Lt. Col. Henry C. Clausen, January 3, 1964. Prange files, courtesy Dr. Barnes.

Chihaya, Masataka, letter to Prange, February 13, 1978. Prange files.

———. Letter to Dillon, March 30, 1982. Prange files.

———. Unpublished manuscript on the war in the Pacific. Prange files.

Far East Military Tribunal, Interrogation of Maj. Gen. Akira Muto, August 15, 1946. Prange files.

———. Interrogation of Admiral Osami Nagano, March 26, 1946. Prange files.

Fleming, Maj. Gen. Robert J., Jr., Reply, January 11, 1977, to questionnaire submitted by Prange. Prange files.

———. Taped reminiscences, March 7 and 31, 1975, Hoover Institution on War, Revolution and Peace, Stanford, Calif.

Friedman, William F. "Certain Aspects of 'Magic' in the Cryptological Background of the Various Official Investigations into the Pearl Harbor Attack." Record Group 457, SRH 125, Box 9, National Archives, Washington, D.C.

Genda, Miroru. Report on Pearl Harbor prepared for Prange, May 1947.

Hattori, Col. Takushiro. Statement prepared for Prange, August 31, 1951. Prange files.

Summary of Verbal Report Submitted to Colonel Bicknell and Lieutenant Dyson,

U.S. Army, by Harold T. Kay. Record Group 107, Record of the Office of the Secretary of War, Army Pearl Harbor Board Material, Box 8, National Archives, Washington, D.C.

Kimmel, Adm. Husband E. Memorandum, "Interview with the President, 1425–1550, Monday, June 9, 1941," Navy Dept. OP-12D-2-Mc. Originally secret, since declassified. Naval History Division, Washington Navy Yard, D.C.

———. Service record and Officer's Records of Fitness. Prange files, courtesy Admiral Kimmel.

Information from Captain George W. Linn, USNR (Ret.), SRH 081, Record Group 27, NSA/CSS, Archives of General of the Army Douglas MacArthur, Norfolk, Va.

Log of *Isabel*, Record Group 24, Records of the Bureau of Naval Personnel, National Archives, Washington, D.C.

Memorandum, AC/S G-2 for the AC/S WDP, "Current Estimate of the Situation—Orange Plan," December 24, 1935. Record Group 165, Box 212D, WDGS-MID 1917–1941 (242–12), National Archives, Washington, D.C.

Morgan, Edward P. "An Approach to the Question of Responsibility for the Pearl Harbor Disaster." This is the draft report which became the basis for the majority report of the joint congressional committee. Prange files, courtesy Mr. Morgan.

National Security Agency. Interview with Mr. Ralph T. Briggs, January 13, 1977. Record Group 457, Records of the National Security Agency, SRH 051, National Archives, Washington, D.C.

Ogg, Robert D. Oral History Interview. Record Group 457, Records of the National Security Agency, SRH 255, National Archives, Washington, D.C.

Ohmae, Capt. Toshikazu. Series of studies which he prepared for Prange. Prange files.

Okuda, Otojiro. Statement prepared for Prange, February 10, 1978. Prange files.

Rugg, Charles. Memorandum, November 16, 1944, of conversation between Rugg and Justice Roberts held November 14 and 15, 1944. Prange files, courtesy Dr. Barnes.

Safford, Capt. Laurence F. Notes concerning Pearl Harbor prepared for Prange. Prange files.

Smedberg, VADM. W. R. III. Comments to Prange, July 27, 1977. Prange files.

Stimson, Henry L. Unpublished long form of report on Stimson's conclusions concerning the Army Board's report, with attached memorandum, January 3, 1945. Record Group 107, Entry 74A, Box 2, folder "Army Pearl Harbor Board," Stimson "Safe File." National Archives, Washington, D.C.

Tolley, Kemp. Letter to Chief, BuNav, April 28, 1942, Subject: "Ship's Log," with attachment. Record Group 24, Records of the Bureau of Naval Personnel, National Archives, Washington, D.C.

Wellborn, VADM. Charles, Jr. Comments to Prange, August 10, 1977. Prange files.

Yamamoto, Adm. Isoroku. Letter to Adm. Sankichi Takahashi, December 10, 1941. Prange files, courtesy of RADM. Teikichi Hori.

Yokosuka Naval Air Corps, Air Branch Committee, Battle-lessons Investigation Committee, "Lessons (air operations) of the Sea Battle Off Hawaii." Prange files.

DIARIES

(Some of these diaries have been published in whole or in part; however, Prange used the unpublished versions exclusively.)

Adolph A. Berle, Jr., Franklin D. Roosevelt Library, Hyde Park, N.Y.

RADM. Sadao Chigusa (courtesy of Admiral Chigusa), Prange files.

James V. Forrestal, Princeton University Library, Princeton, N.J.

Marquis Koichi Kido, Extracts in Prange files.

Adm. William D. Leahy, Library of Congress, Washington, D.C.

Breckenridge Long, Library of Congress, Washington, D.C.

Henry Morgenthau, Jr., Franklin D. Roosevelt Library, Hyde Park, N.Y.

RADM. Giichi Nakahara (courtesy of Admiral Nakahara), Prange files.

Adm. Kichisaburo Nomura (courtesy of Admiral Nomura), Prange files.

Henry L. Stimson, Yale University Library, New Haven, Conn.

War Diary of First Destroyer Division, Prange files.

War Diary of Third Battleship Division, Prange files.

COLLECTED PAPERS

Harry Elmer Barnes, University of Wyoming Library, Laramie, Wyo.

RADM. Reginald R. Belknap, National Historical Foundation, Washington, D.C.

RADM. Claude C. Bloch, Library of Congress, Washington, D.C.

Raymond Clapper, Library of Congress, Washington, D.C.

James V. Forrestal, Princeton University Library, Princeton, N.J.

Adm. Thomas C. Hart, Operational Archives, U.S. Naval Historical Division, Washington Navy Yard, D.C.

Cmdr. Charles C. Hiles, University of Wyoming Library, Laramie, Wyo.

Harry Hopkins, Franklin D. Roosevelt Library, Hyde Park, N.Y.

Stanley K. Hornbeck, Hoover Institution on War, Revolution and Peace, Stanford, Calif.

Cordell Hull, Library of Congress, Washington, D.C.

RADM. Husband E. Kimmel, University of Wyoming Library, Laramie, Wyo.

Fleet Admiral Ernest J. King, Library of Congress, Washington, D.C.

Frank Knox, Library of Congress, Washington, D.C.

Adm. William D. Leahy, Library of Congress, Washington, D.C.

General of the Army Douglas MacArthur, Douglas MacArthur Memorial, Norfolk, Va.

General of the Army George C. Marshall, George C. Marshall Research Foundation, Lexington, Va.

Military History Division, National Archives, Washington, D.C.

Naval History Division (in particular its voluminous records of "Magic" intercepts), National Archives, Washington, D.C.

Records of the Bureau of Naval Personnel, National Archives, Washington, D.C.

Franklin D. Roosevelt, Franklin D. Roosevelt Library, Hyde Park, N.Y.

Francis B. Sayre, Library of Congress, Washington, D.C.

Henry A. Wallace, Library of Congress, Washington, D.C.

OFFICIAL PRIMARY SOURCES

Congressional Record, Volumes 83–91, Government Printing Office, Washington, D.C., 1938–45.

Hearings Before the Joint Committee on the Investigation of the Pearl Harbor Attack, Congress of the United States. Seventy-ninth Congress, Government Printing Office, Washington, D.C., 1946.

Investigation of Un-American Propaganda Activities in the United States, Hearings Before a Special Committee on Un-American Activities, House of Representatives. Seventy-seventh Congress, First Session, on H. Res. 282, Appendix VI, Report on Japanese Activities, Government Printing Office, Washington, D.C., 1942.

Report of the Special Committee on Investigation of the Munitions Industry, United States Senate: Munitions Industry. Seventy-fourth Congress, First Session, Report No. 944, Part 3. Government Printing Office, Washington, D.C., 1936.

Report to Hon. James Forrestal, Secretary of the Navy, on Unification of the War and Navy Departments and Postwar Organization for National Security. Seventy-ninth Congress, First Session. October 22, 1945. Government Printing Office, Washington, D.C., 1945.

INTERVIEWS

Maj. Gen. Brooke E. Allen
Ms. Mitsutaro Araki
Dr. Harry Elmer Barnes
CWO-4 Edgar B. Beck
Col. George Bicknell
RADM. Claude C. Bloch

Masataka Chihaya
VADM. Charles F. Coe
John Crawford
VADM. Maurice E. Curts
Adm. Arthur C. Davis
VADM. Walter S. DeLany

Rep. Martin Dies
RADM. Milo F. Draemel
Brig. Gen. Robert H. Dunlop
VADM. George C. Dyer
Capt. Walter J. East
Brig. Gen. Kendall J. Fielder
Maj. Gen. Robert J. Fleming, Jr.
CPO Thomas E. Forrow
CWO Alton B. Freeman
Capt. Mitsuo Fuchida
RADM. Shigeru Fukudome
RADM. William R. Furlong
Capt. Minoru Genda
Sen. Guy M. Gillette
VADM. Chuichi Hara
Lt. Gen. Charles D. Herron
Capt. Wilfred J. Holmes
Capt. Kijiro Imaizumi
Lt. Cmdr. Susumu Ishiguro
RADM. Husband E. Kimmel
RADM. Kameto Kuroshima
VADM. Ryunosuke Kusaka
RADM. Edwin T. Layton
Adm. Harold M. Martin
VADM. Gunichi Mikawa
Cmdr. Tatsukichi Miyo
Brig. Gen. James E. Mollison
Edward P. Morgan
Fleet Admiral Chester W. Nimitz

Adm. Kichisaburo Nomura
Cmdr. Kyozo Ohashi
Capt. Toshikazu Ohmae
Capt. Atsushi Oi
Adm. Koshiro Oikawa
Capt. Sutegiro Onoda
VADM. Jisaburo Ozawa
RADM. Harold F. Pullen
CPO Harry Rafsky
RADM. Logan C. Ramsey
Capt. Joseph J. Rochefort
Charles A. Russell
Cmdr. Sadamu Sanagi
VADM. Mitsumi Shimizu
RADM. James Shoemaker
Lt. Cmdr. Harley F. Smart
VADM. William Ward Smith
Adm. Raymond A. Spruance
Col. Russell C. Throckmorton
RADM. Sadatoshi Tomioka
Adm. Soemu Toyoda
Adm. Harold C. Train
Adm. Nishizo Tsukahara
RADM. Dundas P. Tucker
Lt. Col. Kermit Tyler
Capt. Yasuji Watanabe
Adm. Katsunoshin Yamanashi
Takeo Yoshikawa
Cmdr. Chuichi Yoshioka

PUBLISHED SOURCES

ARTICLES

Alden, Cmdr. John D. "Up From Ashes: The Saga of *Cassin* and *Downes*." *United States Naval Institute Proceedings* (January 1961).

Barnes, Harry E. "A Historian Investigates a Tough Question: Where Was the General?" Chicago *Tribune* (December 7, 1966).

―――. "Pearl Harbor After a Quarter of a Century." *Left and Right: A Journal of Libertarian Thought,* Vol. IV. (1968).

―――. "Summary and Conclusions." In *Perpetual War for Perpetual Peace,* Harry E. Barnes, ed. Caldwell, Ida.: Caxton Printers Ltd., 1953.

―――. "What Happened at Pearl Harbor?" *Peace News* (London; December 7, 1962).

Beatty, VADM. Frank E. "Another Version of What Started War with Japan." *U.S. News & World Report* (May 28, 1954).

Boyle, John H. "The Walsh-Drought Mission to Japan." *Pacific Historical Review* (May 1965).

Bratzel, John F., and Leslie B. Rout, Jr. "Pearl Harbor, Microdots, and J. Edgar Hoover." *American Historical Review* (December 1982).

Butow, R. J. C. "Backdoor Diplomacy in the Pacific: The Proposal for a Konoye-Roosevelt Meeting, 1941." *The Journal of American History* (June 1972).

Chamberlin, William Henry. "The Clay Feet of Imperialism." *Asia* (May 1942).

Current, Richard N. "How Stimson Meant to 'Maneuver' the Japanese." *The Mississippi Valley Historical Review* (June 1953).

Edmonds, Walter D. "What Happened at Clark Field." *Atlantic* (July 1951).

Estel, John (AP). "Hoover Shared Spy Disclosure on Pearl Harbor." Pittsburgh *Post-Gazette* (April 1, 1982).

Etzioni, Amitai. "Fact-Crazy, Theory-Shy?" *Science* (October 23, 1970).

"Extracts from the Diary of VADM. Shigetaro Shimada." *Bungei Shunju* (December 1976).

Fagan, Lt. Col. George V. "F.D.R. and Naval Limitations." *United States Naval Institute Proceedings* (April 1955).

Feis, Herbert. "War Came at Pearl Harbor: Suspicions Considered." *Yale Review* (Spring 1956).

Flynn, John T. "The Final Secret of Pearl Harbor." Chicago *Tribune* (September 2, 1945).

Fukudome, VADM. Shigeru. "Hawaii Operation." *United States Naval Institute Proceedings* (December 1955).

Futrell, Robert F. "Air Hostilities in the Philippines, 8 December 1941." *Air University Review* (January–February 1965).

Greaves, Percy L., Jr. "The Pearl Harbor Investigations." In *Perpetual War for Perpetual Peace*, Harry E. Barnes, ed. Caldwell, Ida.: Caxton Printers Ltd., 1953.

Hill, Norman. "Was There an Ultimatum before Pearl Harbor?" *American Journal of International Law* (April 1948).

Hone, Thomas C. "The Destruction of the Battle Line at Pearl Harbor." *United States Naval Institute Proceedings* (December 1977).

Hosoya, Chihiro. "Miscalculations in Deterrent Policy: Japanese–U.S. Relations, 1938–1941." *Journal of Peace Research* (November 2, 1968).

Johnson, General Hugh S. "The General Staff and Its New Chief." *Life* (August 21, 1939).

Kirchwey, Freda. "Partners in Guilt." *The Nation* (December 27, 1941).

———. "The Fruits of Appeasement." *The Nation* (December 13, 1941).

Kittredge, Capt. T. S. "The Muddle Before Pearl Harbor." *U.S. News & World Report* (December 3, 1954).

Kissinger, Henry A. "Arms Control Inspection and Surprise Attack" *Foreign Affairs* (July 1960).

Lerner, Max. "The Margin of Waste." *The New Republic* (January 26, 1942).

Mitchell, Donald W. "What the Navy Can Do." *The Nation* (December 20, 1941).

Morgenstern, George. "The Actual Road to Pearl Harbor." In *Perpetual War for Perpetual Peace*, Harry E. Barnes, ed. Caldwell, Ida.: Caxton Printers Ltd., 1953.

Morison, Samuel Eliot. "History Through a Beard," In Samuel Eliot Morison, *By Land and By Sea*. New York: Alfred A. Knopf, 1954.

———. "The Lessons of Pearl Harbor." *Saturday Evening Post* (October 26, 1961).

Nash, Ernest T. "Understanding the Japanese." New York *Herald Tribune* (June 18, 1942).

Neumann, William L. "How American Policy Toward Japan Contributed to War in the Pacific." In *Perpetual War for Perpetual Peace*, Harry E. Barnes, ed. Caldwell, Ida.: Caxton Printers Ltd., 1953.

Nomura, Admiral Kichisaburo Nomura. "Stepping-Stones to War." *United States Naval Institute Proceedings* (September 1951).

Oi, Atsushi. "Why Japan's Anti-Submarine Warfare Failed." *United States Naval Institute Proceedings* (June 1952).

Perkins, Dexter. "Was Roosevelt Wrong?" *Virginia Quarterly Review* (Summer 1954).

Pratt, Adm. William V. "We Must Take the Offensive." *Newsweek* (March 2, 1942).

Richardson, Seth W. "Why Were We Caught Napping at Pearl Harbor?" *Saturday Evening Post* (May 24, 1947).

Russell, Maj. Gen. H. D. "More Light on Pearl Harbor." *U.S. News & World Report* (May 7, 1954).

Sanborn, Frederic R. "Roosevelt Is Frustrated in Europe." In *Perpetual War for Perpetual Peace*, Harry E. Barnes, ed. Caldwell, Ida.: Caxton Printers Ltd., 1953.

Sansom, Sir George. "Japan's Fatal Blunder." *International Affairs* (October 1948).

Shaw, Brig. Gen. Samuel R. "Marine Barracks, Navy Yard Pearl Harbor, December 1941." *Shipmate* (December 1973).

Singer, J. David. "Surprise Attack." *The Nation* (January 30, 1960).

Strong, Mary Katherine. "Washington at Pearl Harbor." *Current History* (February 1946).

Takagi, Sokichi. "Shinjuwan Kogeki: No Hyoketsu Kudaru [Making the Decision to Attack Pearl Harbor]." *Bungei Shunju* (December 1956).

Tansill, Charles C. "Japanese-American Relations, 1921–1941: The Pacific Back Door to War." In *Perpetual War for Perpetual Peace*, Harry E. Barnes, ed. Caldwell, Ida.: Caxton Printers Ltd., 1953.

Taylor, Telford. "Day of Infamy, Decades of Doubt." *The New York Times* (April 29, 1984).

Toulmin, Harry A. "General Mitchell Was Right." *Scribner's Commentator* (April 1941).

Waldrop, Frank C. "It's Still Question Time." Washington *Times-Herald* (January 26, 1942).

BOOKS

Acheson, Dean. *Morning and Noon.* Boston: Houghton Mifflin Co., 1965.

——. *Present at the Creation: My Years in the State Department.* New York: W.W. Norton & Co., 1969.

Arnold, General of the Air Force H. H. *Global Mission.* New York: Harper & Brothers, 1949.

Baker, Leonard. *Roosevelt and Pearl Harbor.* New York: Macmillan Co., 1970.

Barnes, Harry E., ed. *Perpetual War for Perpetual Peace.* Caldwell, Ida.: Caxton Printers Ltd., 1953.

Beard, Charles A. *President Roosevelt and the Coming of the War, 1941.* New Haven: Yale University Press, 1948.

Beck, John Jacob. *MacArthur and Wainwright: Sacrifice of the Philippines.* Albuquerque: University of New Mexico Press, 1974.

Bendiner, Robert. *The Riddle of the State Department.* New York: Farrel & Rinehart, 1942.

Bergamini, David. *Japan's Imperial Conspiracy.* New York: William Morrow & Co., 1971.

Birkenhead, The Earl of. *Halifax.* Boston: Houghton Mifflin Co., 1966.

Blum, John Morton. *From the Morgenthau Diaries: Years of Urgency, 1938–1941.* Boston: Houghton Mifflin Co., 1965.

Brereton, Lt. Gen. Lewis H. *The Brereton Diaries: The War in the Pacific, Middle East and Europe.* New York: William Morrow & Co., 1946.

Brown, Anthony Cave. *Bodyguard of Lies.* New York: Harper & Row, 1975.

Brownlow, Donald G. *The Accused: The Ordeal of Rear Admiral Husband Edward Kimmel, U.S.N.* New York: Vantage Press, 1968.

Burns, James MacGregor. *Roosevelt, The Soldier of Freedom.* New York: Harcourt Brace Jovanovich, Inc., 1970.

Butow, Robert J. C. *The John Doe Associates: Backdoor Diplomacy for Peace, 1941.* Stanford, Calif.: Stanford University Press, 1974.

Byas, Hugh. *Government by Assassination.* New York: Alfred A. Knopf, 1942.

Chamberlin, William Henry. *America's Second Crusade.* Chicago: Henry Regnery & Co., 1950.

Churchill, Winston S. *The Grand Alliance.* Boston: Houghton Mifflin Co., 1950.

Cole, Wayne S. *America First: The Battle Against Interventionism, 1940–1941*. Madison, Wisc.: University of Wisconsin Press, 1953.

———. *Charles A. Lindbergh and the Battle Against American Intervention in World War II*. New York: Harcourt Brace Jovanovich, 1974.

———. *Senator Gerald P. Nye and American Foreign Relations*. Minneapolis: University of Minnesota Press, 1962.

The Correspondents of *Time, Life* and *Fortune*. *December 7, The First Thirty Hours*. New York: Alfred A. Knopf, 1942.

Costello, John. *The Pacific War 1941–1945*. New York: Rawson, Wade, 1981.

Current Biography. New York: The H. W. Wilson Co., 1940.

Current, Richard N. *Secretary Stimson: A Study in Statecraft*. New Brunswick, N.J.: Rutgers University Press, 1954.

Dall, Curtis B. *F.D.R., My Exploited Father-in-Law*. Tulsa, Okla.: Christian Crusade Publications, 1967.

Daniels, Jonathan. *White House Witness, 1942–1945*. Garden City, N.Y.: Doubleday, 1975.

Dilks, Davis, ed. *The Diaries of Sir Alexander Cadogan, 1938–1945*. New York: G.P. Putnam's Sons, 1972.

Durant, Will and Ariel. *The Lessons of History*. New York: Simon & Schuster, 1968.

Dyer, VADM. George C. *On the Treadmill to Pearl Harbor: The Memoirs of Admiral James O. Richardson, USN (Retired)*. Washington, D.C.: Naval Historical Division, Department of the Navy, 1973.

Eden, Anthony. *The Memoirs of Anthony Eden, Earl of Avon: The Reckoning*. Boston: Houghton Mifflin Co., 1965.

Edmonds, Walter D. *They Fought with What They Had*. Boston: Little, Brown, 1951.

Engelbrecht, H. C., and F. C. Hanighen. *Merchants of Death*. Garden City, N.Y.: The Garden City Publishing Co., 1937.

Farago, Ladislas. *The Broken Seal*. New York: Random House, 1967.

Feis, Herbert. *The Road to Pearl Harbor: The Coming of the War Between the United States and Japan*. Princeton, N.J.: Princeton University Press, 1950.

Flynn, John T. *The Truth About Pearl Harbor*. (Pamphlet privately printed in New York, 1944.)

Fuchida, Mitsuo. *Shinjuwan Sakusen no Shinso; Watakushi Wa Shinjuwan Joken Ni Ita*. Nara, Japan: Yamato Taimusu Sha, 1949.

Furer, RADM. Julius Augustus. *Administration of the Navy Department in World War II*. Washington, D.C.: Navy History Division, Department of the Navy, 1959.

Genda, Minoru. *Shinjuwan Sakusen Kaikoroku*. Tokyo: Yomiuri Shimbun, 1972.

Grew, Joseph C. *Ten Years in Japan*. New York: Simon & Schuster, 1944.

———. *Turbulent Era: A Diplomatic Record of Forty Years, 1904–1945, Part II*, Walter Johnson, ed. Boston: Houghton Mifflin Co., 1952.

Halsey, Fleet Admiral William F., and Lt. Cmdr. J. Bryan III. *Admiral Halsey's Story.* New York: McGraw-Hill Book Co., 1947.

Hattori, Takushiro. *Daitoa senso zen-shi (The Complete History of the Greater East Asia War).* Tokyo: Hara Shobo, 1953.

Hoag, C. Leonard. *Preface to Preparedness: The Washington Disarmament Conference and Public Opinion.* Washington, D.C.: American Council on Public Affairs, 1941.

Huie, William Bradford. *The Case Against the Admirals: Why We Must Have a Unified Command.* New York: E. P. Dutton & Co., 1946.

Hull, Cordell. *The Memoirs of Cordell Hull.* New York: Macmillan Co., 1948.

Hurd, Charles. *Washington Cavalcade.* New York E. P. Dutton, 1948.

Ickes, Harold L. *The Secret Diary of Harold L. Ickes,* Vol. III, *The Lowering Clouds 1939–1941.* New York: Simon & Schuster, 1954.

Ike, Nobutake, ed. *Japan's Decision for War: Records of the 1941 Policy Conferences.* Stanford, Calif.: Stanford University Press, 1967.

Kase, Toshikazu. *Journey to the "Missouri."* New Haven: Yale University Press, 1950.

Kato, Masuo. *The Lost War.* New York: Alfred A. Knopf, 1946.

Kimmel, Husband E. *Admiral Kimmel's Story.* Chicago: Henry Regnery Co., 1955.

King, Fleet Admiral Ernest J., and Walter Muir Whitehead. *Fleet Admiral King: A Naval Record.* New York: W. W. Norton & Co., 1952.

Kirby, S. Woodburn, et al. *The War Against Japan,* Vol. I. London: H. M. Stationery Office, 1957.

Kusaka, Ryunosuke. *Rengo Kantai.* Tokyo: Mainichi Shimbun, 1952.

Langer, William L., and S. Everett Gleason. *The Challenge to Isolation.* New York: Harper & Brothers, 1952.

Lash, Joseph P. *Roosevelt and Churchill 1931–1941: The Partnership That Saved the West.* New York: W. W. Norton & Co., 1976.

Lewinsohn, Richard. *Basil Zaharoff, Munitions King.* Philadelphia: J. B. Lippincott Co., 1934.

Lindbergh, Anne Morrow. *The Wave of the Future.* New York: Harcourt Brace & Co., 1940.

Lindbergh, Charles A. *The Wartime Journals of Charles A. Lindbergh.* New York: Harcourt Brace Jovanovich, 1974.

Lucky Bag, Class of 1904. Annapolis: U.S. Naval Academy, 1904.

MacArthur, General of the Army Douglas. *Reminiscences.* New York: McGraw-Hill Book Co., 1964.

The "Magic" Background of Pearl Harbor. Washington, D.C.: Department of Defense, 1977.

Marshall, Katherine T. *Together: Annals of an Army Wife.* New York: Tupper & Love, 1946.

Masterman, J. C. *The Double Cross System in the War of 1939 to 1945.* New Haven: Yale University Press, 1972.

Morgenstern, George. *Pearl Harbor: The Story of the Secret War.* New York: The Devin-Adair Co., 1947.

Morison, Elting E. *Turmoil and Tradition: A Study of the Life and Times of Henry L. Stimson.* Boston: Houghton Mifflin Co., 1960.

Morison, Samuel E. *By Land and By Sea.* New York: Alfred A. Knopf, 1953.

————. *The Rising Sun in the Pacific.* Boston: Little, Brown & Co., 1948.

Morton, Louis. *United States Army in World War II: The War in the Pacific: Strategy and Command: The First Two Years.* Washington, D.C.: Department of the Army, Office, Chief of Military History, 1962.

————. *United States Army in World War II: The War in the Pacific: The Fall of the Philippines.* Washington, D.C.: Department of the Army, Office, Chief of Military History, 1962.

Mosley, Leonard. *Marshall: Hero for Our Time.* New York: Hearst Books, 1982.

Noel-Baker, P. J. *Hawkers of Death.* London: The Labour Party, 1934.

————. *Private Manufacturers of Armaments* (2 vols). London: V. Gollancz, 1936.

Otaka, Seijiro. *Kishu-ka Boryaku-ka (Surprise Attack or Treachery).* Tokyo: Jiji Tsushin-sha, 1954.

The Oxford Dictionary of Quotations (Second Edition). London: Oxford University Press, 1955.

Pelz, Stephen E. *Race to Pearl Harbor: The Failure of the Second London Naval Conference and the Onset of World War II.* Cambridge, Mass: Harvard University Press, 1964.

Pettee, George S. *The Future of American Secret Intelligence.* Washington, D.C.: Infantry Journal Press, 1946.

Phillips, Maj. Thomas R. *Roots of Strategy: A Collection of Military Classics.* Harrisburg, Pa.: The Military Service Publishing Co., 1940.

Pogue, Forrest C. *George C. Marshall: Education of a General.* New York: Viking Press, 1963.

————. *George C. Marshall: Ordeal and Hope, 1939–1942.* New York: Viking Press, 1966.

Popov, Dusko. *Spy Counter Spy.* New York: Grosset & Dunlap, 1974.

Porteus, Stanley D. *And Blow Not the Trumpet: A Prelude to Peril.* Palo Alto, Calif.: Pacific Books, 1947.

Prange, Gordon W. *At Dawn We Slept.* New York: McGraw-Hill Book Co., 1981.

————. *Target Tokyo: The Story of the Sorge Spy Ring.* New York: McGraw-Hill Book Co., 1984.

Pratt, Fletcher. *The Navy's War.* New York: Harper & Brothers, 1944.

The Random House Dictionary of the English Language. New York: Random House, 1971.

Reiss, Curt. *Total Espionage.* New York: G. P. Putnam's Sons, 1941.

Reports of General MacArthur: Japanese Operations in the Southwest Pacific Area, Vol. II, Part I. Washiigton, D.C.: U.S. Government Printing Office, 1966.

Sayre, Francis B. *Glad Adventure.* New York: Macmillan Co., 1957.

Schroeder, Paul W. *The Axis Alliance and Japanese-American Relations 1941.* Ithaca, N.Y.: Cornell University Press, 1958.

Sherwood, Robert E. *Roosevelt and Hopkins: An Intimate History.* New York: Harper & Brothers, 1948.

Standley, Adm. William H., USN (Ret.) and RADM. Arthur A. Ageton, USN (Ret.) *Admiral Ambassador to Russia.* Chicago: Henry Regnery Co., 1955.

Stimson, Henry L. and McGeorge Bundy. *On Active Service in Peace and War.* New York: Harper & Row, 1947.

Tansill, Charles C. *Back Door to War.* Chicago: Henry Regnery Co., 1952.

Tate, Merze. *The United States and Armament.* New York: Russell & Russell, 1948.

Terasaki, Gwen. *Bridge to the Sun.* Chapel Hill, N.C.: University of North Carolina Press, 1957.

Theobald, Robert A. *The Final Secret of Pearl Harbor.* New York: Devin-Adair Co., 1954.

Togo, Shigenori. *The Cause of Japan.* New York: Simon & Schuster, 1956.

Toland, John. *Infamy: Pearl Harbor and Its Aftermath.* Garden City, N.Y.: Doubleday & Co., 1982.

Tolley, RADM. Kemp. *Cruise of the Lanikai: Incitement to War.* Annapolis, Md.: Naval Institute Press, 1973.

Tsunoda, Hitoshi, et al. *Hawai Sakusen.* Tokyo: Boeicho Boei Kenshujo Senshishitsu, 1967.

van Loon, Hendrik Willem. *Our Battle.* New York: Simon & Schuster, 1938.

Wallin, VADM. Homer N. *Pearl Harbor: Why, How, Fleet Salvage and Final Appraisal.* Washington, D.C.: Naval History Division, Department of the Navy, 1968.

Watson, Mark S. *United States Army in World War II: The War Department Chief of Staff: Prewar Plans and Preparations.* Washington, D.C.: History Division, Department of the Army, 1950.

Wedemeyer, Albert C. *Wedemeyer Reports!* New York: Henry Holt & Co., 1958.

Wilson, Rose Page. *General Marshall Remembered.* Englewood Cliffs, N.J.: Prentice-Hall, 1968.

Woodward, Sir Llewellyn. *British Foreign Policy in the Second World War,* Vol. II. London: H. M. Stationery Office, 1971.

Zacharias, Ellis M. *Secret Missions.* New York: G. P. Putnam's Sons, 1946.

NEWSPAPERS

Arizona Republic (Phoenix)
Atlanta *Constitution*
Baltimore *Sun*
Bismarck *Tribune*
Charlotte (W. Va.) *Gazette*
Chicago *Daily News*
Chicago *Sun*
Chicago *Tribune*
Christian Science Monitor
Daily Worker (New York, N.Y.)
Dallas *Morning News*
Denver *Post*
Emporia *Gazette*
Hartford *Courant*
Hartford *Times*
Honolulu *Advertiser*
Honolulu *Star-Bulletin*
Houston *Post*
Indianapolis *Star*
Japan *Advertiser*
Japan *Times and Advertiser*
Jefferson City (Mo.) *Daily Capital News*
Lewiston (Me.) *Evening Journal*
London *Gazette*
Louisville *Courier-Journal*
Lynchburg *News*
Madison (Ind.) *Courier*
Mainichi Shimbun
Meridian (Miss.) *Star*
Milwaukee *Journal*
Milwaukee *Sentinel*
Mobile *Register*
Nashville *Tennesseean*

Newark (N.J.) *News*
New York *Daily News*
New York *Herald Tribune*
New York *Post*
New York *Sun*
New York Times
New York *Tribune*
New York *World Telegram*
Nichi Nichi
Nippon Times
Oregon Journal (Portland)
People's Daily World (San Francisco)
Philadelphia *Record*
Pittsburgh *Post-Gazette*
Richmond *Times-Dispatch*
Salt Lake Tribune (Salt Lake City, Utah)
San Antonio *Express*
San Francisco *Chronicle*
Seattle *Post-Intelligencer*
South Side Journal (St. Louis, Mo.)
Springfield (Mass.) *Union*
Stars and Stripes (Far East edition)
St. Louis *Post-Dispatch*
St. Louis *Star-Times*
St. Paul *Pioneer Press*
The Times (London)
Tokyo *Asahi*
Washington *Daily News*
Washington *Evening Star*
Washington *Post*
Washington *Times-Herald*
Wisconsin State Journal (Madison)